C by Discovery

L. S. Foster

California State University
Long Beach

Titles of Related Interest:

The DOS 5 Companion
by David Moody

The DOS 5 Coursebook
by Forest Lin

The 1-2-3 Coursebook
by Forest Lin

Assembly Language for the IBM PC Family
by William Jones

The DOS Coursebook
by Forest Lin

The DOS Primer
by Dorothy Calvin

Modern Fortran 77/90
by Gary Bronson

Scott/Jones Inc., Publishers
P.O. Box 696
El Granada CA 94018

ISBN 0-9624230-2-5

Printed in the United States of America

Library of Congress Cataloging-in-Publication Data

QA76.73.C15F67 1991   91-9928
005.26′ 2--dc20   CIP

Illustrations: Janice Maupin
               2603 Sheldon Drive
               Richmond, CA 94803

Production: Fog Press
Book Manufacturing: Malloy Lithographing

Contents

Preface

There is a saying attributed to an ancient Chinese scholar which goes something like this:

> I hear, and I forget.
> I see, and I remember.
> I do, and I understand.

Most of us learn by a combination of audio, visual and kinetic activities. Each of us has a different balance of these three elements for optimal learning. Instead of trying to teach the subject by only having the student "see" and "hear," I have tried to provide a way for them to also "do and understand."

Discovering C by doing:

Programming is not a spectator sport. Much of what we try to teach about any given language only becomes meaningful when students use or "do" something with the information. In this book I have consistently tried to encourage students to roll up their sleeves and work with C, in order to appreciate not only the subtleties of the language, but also its power.

Learning Activities

As a means toward that end, "Learning Activities" are interspersed throughout this book. They provide a means of requesting a student to spend just a little more time thinking about and experimenting with a concept or an example program. An activity can be as simple as executing a program to verify the student's understanding. In many cases, an activity consists of executing a program, modifying the source, executing it again, and then undertaking the important final step of verbalizing what the experiment illustrated. The use of the text does not depend on the assignment of the Learning Activities, but I believe that learning will be much more effective when they are used.

Source code on disk

To help the students make more effective use of their time, the source code for the programs in the text are provided on floppy disk. This enables students to move immediately to actively learning, instead of having to spend time typing the programs. The shorter the link between "seeing" and "doing," the less diluted the "AHA" experience will be.

Selected Answers

Lastly, to "close the loop" on Learning Activities, I have provided selected answers to these Activities in the back of the text. Students can determine which elements of the language are giving them a difficult time, and which have been mastered. Between the answers and the computer response to the programs, the students are able to get close to 100% feedback on these activities.

Exercises and Programming Problems

The end of each chapter contains Exercises and Programming Problems, a second type of "doing." These exercises range from questions designed to review concepts from the chapter to programming projects. In general, the exercises at the end of the chapter will take the students more time than the Learning Activities and are designed to allow the students to put the concepts learned to use.

Discovering C by seeing:

Since programming is a game of both concepts and detail, ultimate understanding of code comes from closely examining the details. Through the use of **Notes** in the example programs, the student is directed immediately to the new concepts in the code and the accompanying explanation.

Asking the students to learn to program by "seeing" annotated code is similar to asking students to learn to write essays by having them analyze works of literature. Students use analytic skills when reading someone else's program. It is a part of the educational experience and cannot be ignored, but it should be accompanied with a full educational package.

A Closer Look

I wished for this text to give more than a cursory mention to some key topics. These passages are prefaced by the term **A Closer Look,** and in many cases they exceed other C texts in depth and breadth. This discussion has been isolated in these sections for several reasons: It allows inclusion or exclusion of the material as time and interest dictate. The remainder of the text does not make reference to this material. Finally, it provides explanation of concepts for the interested student without necessitating that the point be belabored in class.

A Word of Warning

Some common programming pitfalls with the C language are presented in **Word of Warning** sections. A mistake is made, and the student is asked to execute the program and suffer the consequences. In my observation, a student needs this experience to help avoid certain errors. Rather than have the error occur and create a moment of panic the night before a major project is due, it will occur during a non-threatening time. Even if the mistake is repeated during the coding of a major project, the experience of having seen this consequence before should help.

The Programmer's Handbook

It is impossible to give every example that a student needs in a text. At some point the student will want to know something beyond the classroom discussion and will dig into the text and reference material for the additional information necessary to solve a problem. By including the Programmer's Handbook, I have tried to provide a "reference within a text." In documenting the C library functions I have tried to state the type of the parameters to each function in a way which will alleviate a point of confusion.

To the Instructor:

I have not found it necessary to discuss all of the sample programs in class. I have assigned them as reading material, but have chosen for discussion those that give the final picture. As specific examples, in Chapter 3, the introductory discussion on type `int` is recapped in the program that discusses all of the integer types. While the concepts should be mentioned, the inclusion of the earlier programs is for the students benefit, and need not be included in class discussion. As another example, in Chapter 10, a very simple program that opens and closes a file is given. When I have included that as part of the class discussion, I invariably get some students who resist checking on the return value of `fopen()` even though I have stressed that it should be done. I think that students need to see this simple use as a beginning point in their learning process, but discussing it seems to leave them with the impression that it is acceptable to open files without checking for errors. By assigning it as reading, but discussing only the other versions, this problem is somewhat alleviated.

There is some flexibility in the order that the chapters can be covered. For example, Chapter 3 can come before or after Chapter 2. Also, Chapter 6 can be discussed before Chapters 4 and 5. Chapter 8 can be moved to an earlier position in the course as well.

To the Student

This book has been written for you. The programs and Learning Activities have been designed to let you learn with efficiency. It will still take some effort and dedication, but by simply executing the sample programs as you study them and following the Learning Activities, you should be able to conquer the material easily. The difference is that executing the sample programs provides the kinetic learning experience, that allows you to satisfy the audio, visual, and kinetic senses necessary to learning. When the school term gets hectic, don't let up on this course. A little time spent each day with the Learning Activities should allow your mind to process the material while you are involved in other school or work activities. Don't leave it all until the end.

Acknowledgments

This book began as an idea, but it wouldn't have turned into a book without the contributions of a lot of other people.

I received some extremely insightful feedback from the following colleagues. Some of them provided feedback about the outline for the book, and some of them gave detailed reviews of chapters. All of them were extremely helpful.

Stan Wileman
University of Nebraska

Ken Collier
Northern Arizona University

Stephen Allan
Utah State University

Charles Hall
North Carolina State University

Cay Horstman
San Jose State University

Andrew Lopez
Texas A & M University

Thomas Cheatam
Western Kentucky University

John Crenshaw
Western Kentucky University

Stan Ferrell
Virginia Tech

Gordon Hoagland
Ricks College

Kerry Hays
San Jose City College

D. Hanscom
University of Utah

Clifford Shaffer
Virginia Tech

Mladen Vouk
North Carolina State University

Peter Bahrs
University of Southwestern Louisiana

Julius Nadas
Wilbur Wright Community College

Duane Jordan
Texas Tech University

Margaret Zinky
Phoenix college

My departmental Chair, Dr. Edward Evans, and the Dean of the College of Engineering, Dr. Richard Williams, provided me with the support and encouragement that any author needs as they try to turn an idea into a reality. I am fortunate to have them at California State University Long Beach.

I have been fortunate to have colleagues in my department who generously provided me with their time and teaching instincts when I came to them with a question I was unable to resolve. I was also fortunate to have Janet Leimer help this project negotiate some last-minute logistics.

This book has distinctive illustrations provided by Janice Maupin, whose full crediting is listed on the copyright page. These illustrations are intended to remind students (and sometimes us professors as well!) that it's all right to laugh once in awhile while learning. Janice does not know C, and it's a testimony to her that she was able to read through the entire manuscript with one hand while she did research in library after library art section with the other hand—and made something quite nice happen.

My publisher Richard Jones has been a great source of solicited (and unsolicited) ideas about this project. Some of these I agreed with and included. He has also usually done what he said he would do, which may not be a common characteristic of publishers. Many publishers and authors end up as opponents, and I'm glad that we still view ourselves as being on the same side.

Sheryl Rose, who copyedited the manuscript, and the staff at Fog Press, who typeset the manuscript, have added their care and technical expertise as they transformed a manuscript into a book. Sheryl Strauss proofread the pages in addition to myself and my students, and noticed many things which would have otherwise found their way into the finished book. The efforts of these professionals added substantially to this work.

My students inspired me to write a book worthy of their efforts at trying to learn. They also discovered many typos and errors as I class-tested page proofs. Whatever errors still exist in the final product would have increased manyfold without their keen eyes, prompt questions, and attention to detail.

Finally, I could not have completed this book without the patience, love, and understanding of my partner, friend, and spouse Dusty Foster.

L. S. Foster
Long Beach, California

Getting Started

Chapter 1

1.1   What to Expect from C

A programmer who considers programming in a new language should make certain observations about that language. Most programmers would consider the level of the language, the programming environment, the portability and efficiency of the programs written in that language, and ease of maintaining and modifying the programs. Each of these considerations should be evaluated in relation to the particular programming application.

Language Level

One distinction made among languages is the level. A computer language can be classified as high, intermediate, or low level. The lowest level languages, those that the computers understand directly, are the machine languages. Higher level languages more closely resemble the way human beings think and speak. Programs

1

written in languages other than machine language must undergo some sort of translation to machine language to be executed.

Assembly languages are low-level languages because they relate directly to the underlying hardware. Operating systems, monitors, and similar programs are often written in assembly language so they can access the specifics of the hardware. Business and scientific applications are frequently programmed in higher level languages so they can be transferred (ported) from computer to computer easily.

In terms of language level, C is an intermediate- to high-level language, yet it allows the programmer to control the hardware. This facility is not always available in other high-level languages. Therefore C is used to write programs from business applications to operating systems.

Programming Environment

Another distinction among languages is the process of translation into machine language. The name of the translation process for an assembly language program is assembly. For higher level languages, two processes are common: interpretation and compilation.

When a program is compiled, a second program called a compiler reads each statement and translates it directly into machine language. The machine code is stored in a separate file. The program in its original form is the source code; the machine language translation of the program is the object code. After all statements in a program have been translated, program execution occurs by executing the object code. No further code processing is necessary.

When a program is interpreted, a second program called an interpreter processes the statements in the program sequentially. During execution, the interpreter translates each statement into machine language and executes it before processing the next statement. This continues until execution of the program terminates. Each time the program executes, the interpretation process is repeated.

Both methods have their advantages with different applications. Most high level languages have developed either as a compiled language or an interpreted language, depending on the most common usage. Traditionally, C has been a compiled language.

Most implementations of C allow the source code to be divided among different files and allow each file to be compiled separately. The object code resulting from the compilation of one source module will not execute until it is linked with the remainder of the program. A program called a linker, a link editor, or a linking loader combines the object code files for each source file into an executable form. The advantages to this modular system include ease of maintenance and the possibility of more structured code. In this way, code written in C can often be combined with code written in other languages.

Portability and Efficiency of C Code

A portable program is one that executes properly without modifications on all types of computers. Few, if any, programs have this ultimate portability, but a degree of portability is a worthwhile programming goal. The source code for a portable program does not depend on any specific parts of the computer hardware. Each compiler and operating system assigns the storage for a program's use. To be portable, source code should be written in the standards for the programming language. It should not use any of the extra features supplied in a particular compiler or interpreter. The portability of source code is an advantage that any high-level language has over assembly language.

The efficiency of the object code is an advantage that assembly language has over any higher level language. Generally, object code from a well-written assembly language program is more compact and faster than that from a high-level language program with the same functionality. However, compilers have been developed that produce object code optimized in terms of speed and compactness.

Since the publication of the ANSI standards for C and the emergence of compilers meeting those standards, programmers can write source code that will port more easily to many different computers. Because C is a higher level language, its object code may not be as small or fast as that from an assembly language program. But C object code has a reputation for being compact and fast when compared to code from programs written in other high-level languages.

Ease of Maintenance

A program's development can continue throughout its period of use. The specifics of the application may change with time, and new or previously unknown situations may uncover bugs in the original code. Either of these situations mandates that modifications be made to the original source code program. These types of changes characterize the maintenance phase of a program.

Through years of experience, programmers have developed the technique of structured programming to aid in the development of readable and easily maintained programs. This method is a desirable way of writing source code in any programming language.

Three of the goals of structured programming are to write programs that are modular in nature, readable, and easily modified. Programs with these properties usually consist of many short subprograms. Each subprogram performs one task necessary to the program. Several related subprograms might be collected in a file. The subprograms in each file can be tested, debugged, and compiled separately.

Separate compilation of source code files can be a time-saving feature because a change made to one file does not require recompiling the whole program. Also, choosing the subprograms in each file carefully makes program modification easier.

Suppose a program must be modified because of a hardware change. If all the code that is dependent on the hardware in question were in one file, then modifications could be limited to that one file. In contrast, an alternate method of programming would allow the hardware-dependent code to appear anywhere in a program. A change in the hardware would then require a time-consuming and painstakingly close inspection of the program code for possible change.

C lends itself naturally to structured modular programming. A program in C can be written as a sequence of subprograms, and where appropriate, subprograms can be written as tools. Related subprograms can be kept in separately compiled files.

While it is possible to write unreadable code in C, it is just as easy to write readable code. Judicious decisions about programming style result in readable, easily maintained source code.

To summarize, C is a popular programming language. It allows a programmer control over a computer that is not usually possible with other high-level programming languages. Yet, in contrast to most assembly languages, C programs can be ported to different computers with relative ease. C also lends itself naturally to structured modular programming. Subprograms are fundamental to C programs, and most implementations of C allow code to be kept in separately compiled files. Although performance varies from compiler to compiler, object code from C source programs can be expected to be compact and fast in comparison with object code from other high-level languages.

1.2   Fundamentals—Reserved Words, Identifiers, and the Character Set

Reserved Words

Reserved words or keywords in C and in other programming languages are the words that are part of the language itself. They are used as control statements, data types, and other elements of the language. Although we will discuss each language element later, you might gain an overview of the features of C by inspecting the list of keywords in the Programmer's Handbook.

Identifiers or Names in C

An identifier is an allowed sequence of characters that can be used for the name of a variable, a subprogram, or another element in a program. In C, the following rules establish the allowable identifiers.

1.   They can consist of letters, digits, and underscores.
2.   They must start with a letter or underscore. Note that the functions in the C library often have names that start with an underscore. The names in the library were chosen in an attempt to avoid conflict with names that a programmer might choose. Therefore, it is usually better to choose identifiers that do not start with an underscore.
3.   The C language considers upper- and lowercase letters to be different. For example, the identifiers a1 and A1 are different. Both counter and Counter are legal identifiers in C, and counter is different from Counter.
4.   The limit on the number of significant characters allowed in an identifier can vary among compilers. Compilers following the ANSI standards for C recognize 31 significant characters in an identifier. Older compilers may not recognize that many characters. Additional restrictions exist for identifiers referenced in several different files. These identifier references must be resolved by a linker before program execution.

5. An identifier must not be identical to any keyword in C. As examples, count, first_char, ByteCount, TRUE, and char1 are all valid identifiers; the words in the following list are not:

`1st_integer`	does not start with a letter or underscore
`void`	is identical with a keyword
`last-time`	contains the illegal character ' - '

The Character Set

A character set for a language defines the characters that can be used in the source code, or input and output by a program. Some characters have special meaning for a language and must be available in the character set.

A character set for C should contain both upper- and lowercase alphabetic characters, the digits, and most of the punctuation, formatting, and graphic characters. The ASCII collating sequence is used most often, but other sequences such as EBCDIC could be used.

Theoretically, any C compiler will be matched to the available character set on the underlying computer so that it is possible to deviate from the above requirements. Note that C source code that uses a character set with different characteristics may not be portable. We will assume the use of the ASCII character set for the examples in this text. A few of the algorithms in the examples rely on the use of ASCII characters and may not work with another character set. These algorithms will be noted when they arise.

Format of C Programs

C is a free-format language. That is, the programmer may format the source code in the way that makes it most readable. There are no requirements that code begin in a certain column, that statements must be contained on a single line, or that comments must be located in a special place.

The blank, line feed, backspace, horizontal tab, vertical tab, form feed, and carriage return are the whitespace characters. Whitespace characters separate identifiers or other elements (tokens) in the source code. Otherwise, the compiler ignores them. Whitespace may be used to enhance a program's readability.

The idea of a token in a programming language is important in understanding how a compiler views a program. The compiler divides a C program into groups of characters that belong together. Each group is a token. Then the compiler inspects the sequence of tokens to generate the object code. Each keyword in a language is a token; so is any identifier. Other examples of tokens include a left parenthesis, a right parenthesis, a left or right brace, and each operation symbol, like those for assignment or addition.

1.3   Subprograms or Functions in C

A subprogram is essential in writing structured modular code. A C program is a
collection of subprograms called functions. A function in C differs from those in
other languages in that a value is not always associated with the function's name.
Other languages may have both subroutines or procedures and functions. In contrast,
all subprograms in C are functions whether a value is associated with the function
name or not.

A function in ANSI C has the following general form:

```
type function_name (formal parameter declarations)
opening brace
    variable declarations
    code
closing brace
```

For an older compiler, the first line would be replaced with the two lines:

```
type function_name (formal parameters)
formal parameter declarations
```

Discussion of the components of the declaration of a function will appear later
in the text. The minimum essentials are given below. Every function must have at
least the following components:

```
function_name
pair of open and close parentheses
pair of open and close braces
```

A function with the name does_nothing is declared below. It has the minimum
components of a function, but nothing more.

```
does_nothing()
{
}
```

The function's name, `does_nothing`, is an example of an identifier in C. The opening and closing parentheses signify to the compiler that `does_nothing` is a function. (We will follow the function name with a pair of parentheses when referring to a function in this text.) The opening and closing braces would enclose the executable code and variable declarations. In this example, there is no executable code between the braces; this function will compile correctly, but true to its name, it does nothing.

There are five tokens in the function `does_nothing()`. The tokens are: the identifier, does_nothing; the opening parenthesis; the closing parenthesis; the opening brace; the closing brace. Each token has a special meaning to the compiler.

The Shortest C Program

With the fundamentals out of the way, we are ready to start writing C programs. Every program must contain certain elements. In particular, it must have a function with the name main. When a C program executes, the execution begins with the statements in the function main(). Example 1-1 illustrates the shortest C program that will compile and run on any standard C compiler. Note that main() is a function and therefore must have the same elements as the function does_nothing() that we saw earlier.

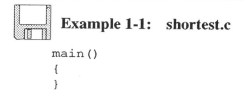 **Example 1-1:   shortest.c**

```
main()
{
}
```

Because C is a free-format language, the spacing in the program is up to the programmer. The above program could be written as

```
main(){}
```

just as well. Acceptable C programming style is discussed in Chapter 2.

Calling a Function

We will next add a line of executable code to main(). We will have it call the function does_nothing() that was illustrated in the last section. Example 1-2 demonstrates the technique of calling a function. This is a complete program that will compile and execute on any standard implementation of C.

Recall that a function named main() is mandatory. This time main() contains an executable line of code, the call to a function named sub_funct(). At execution time, control will be passed to sub_funct() for execution of any code there. In this example, sub_funct() contains no executable statements. Therefore control passes back to the function main() and execution ends.

Example 1-2:   shortsub.c

```
/* This is a comment */
/*                    shortsub.c
 *
 *    Synopsis  -  Control is passed from the function main() to the
 *                 function sub_funct() and back.
 *
 *    Objective -  Illustrates a subfunction and function call.
 *
 */

main()
{
        sub_funct();            /* Notes  1 and 2 */
}

sub_funct()                     /* Note 3 */
{
}
```

As indicated in shortsub.c, comments in C programs start with /* and terminate with */. A comment may not be contained within another comment.

In this text, comments contain reference numbers for the notes that explain the points illustrated by the program. Note 1, Note 2, and Note 3 in the program refer to the following explanations. Lines of code with these comments refer to new elements of the C language. Study them carefully.

Note 1: This line of code is our first example of an executable statement in C. It is terminated with a semicolon (;). Every statement in C must have a semicolon to terminate it.

Note 2: This statement is an example of a function call in C. A function is invoked by its name followed by a set of opening and closing parentheses. If there were actual parameters for the function call, they would appear within the parentheses. When execution reaches this line of code, execution control passes to does_nothing().

Note 3: This line starts the declaration of the function sub_funct(). Note the placement of sub_funct(). It does not need to appear before main() and must not appear inside main(). A C program is a sequence of functions. A function cannot be declared inside another function. Nesting of functions is not legal in C. Note also that the first line of the function declaration, the one containing the name of the function, does not terminate with a semicolon.

Learning Activities

2.   List all the separate tokens in the program shortsub.c.

3.   Modify shortsub.c by adding a function named funct() and have both main() and sub_funct() call funct().

1.4   An Introduction to Output in C

The two programs that we have seen will compile and run,* but they contain no productive statements. We will add executable statements to our programs gradually. The first addition we will make is to have the program produce output. In C, input and output are not part of the language, but are supplied as functions in the standard C library. The output function we will investigate first is printf(). Example 1-3 presents a simple usage of printf(). Additional uses will be discussed throughout the text. One rationale for presenting this type of program early is that once programmers know how to obtain output in a language, they can test the rest of their code.

Example 1-3:   output.c

```
/*                      output.c
 *
 *    Synopsis  -  Outputs a single line on the terminal screen.
 *
 *    Objective -  Illustrate a printf() call for output in C.
 */
#include <stdio.h>                          /* Note 1 */

main()
{
        printf ("Testing, 1, 2, 3\n");      /* Notes 2, 3, and 4 */
}
```

---

* Many C compilers require the extension .c for the names of the source code files. Therefore, the names of the files for the programs in this text all end with .c.

To get an overview of the program output.c, we first notice that it consists of the single function main(). There are no subprograms in this code. The function main() has only one statement. This one statement contains three new ideas that are described below.

Note 1: This line contains the first example of a preprocessor directive. It begins with the symbol '#'. The preprocess phase of compilation handles preprocessor directives before the code is compiled. This `#include` directive causes the external file named stdio.h to be read into the source file at this point. (The file stdio.h is a standard header file supplied with each C compiler.) The angle brackets < and > surrounding the file name signal the location of the file. Standard header files are generally kept in a special location in the directory structure of the computer system.

The contents of a header file might include constants and type definitions developed for use in the source code. The inclusion of this file for this program is not absolutely necessary, but in ANSI C compilers, the file stdio.h contains some information about the printf() function. More about the contents of this file will be discussed in Section 10.8.

On many computer systems, a separate program called the preprocessor handles the preprocessor directives. On other systems, the preprocess phase is an integral part of compilation. Other preprocessor directives are discussed in Sections 1.7, 11.7, and 11.8.

Note 2: If we read from both ends of the line toward the middle, we notice the tokens `printf`, `(`, `)`, and `;`. The semicolon terminates the statement. The parentheses suggest to the compiler (and to us) that printf() is a function. It is part of the standard C library and will print formatted output. The actual parameters to the function are inside the parentheses. The function printf() can be used in many ways which will be explored in later programs in this text.

Note 3: The actual parameter to printf() is `"Testing, 1, 2, 3\n"`. This is an example of a string in C. A string is a sequence of characters from the underlying character set. A programmer signifies to the compiler and the readers of the program that such a sequence is a string by enclosing the sequence in double quotes. During compilation, the compiler stores a string in the object code by storing the sequence of characters inside the pair of double quotes. It terminates that sequence with a null character, the first character in the ASCII collating sequence. The compiler keeps track of the location of the string in memory. When printf() outputs the string, it starts at the first character and stops when it reaches the terminating null. We will study strings in more depth in Chapter 5.

Notice the difference between strings and characters. In a C program, strings appear between pairs of double quotes (`"`) while single characters appear between pairs of single quotes (`'`). In particular, consider the string `"a"` and the single character `'a'`.

The single character `'a'` is a member of the underlying character set; it has an integer value associated with it, namely, the value it corresponds to in the collating sequence. In ASCII, the null character corresponds to the integer 0; the horizontal tab corresponds to 9; the character `'0'` corresponds to 48; `'a'` corresponds to 97, and so on. In C, the character `'a'` can often be used interchangeably with the integer 97.

In contrast, the double quotes in `"a"` signify a string to the compiler. Strings are handled differently from single characters. Specifically, they are stored in a special place in the object code and terminated with a null character. When the compiler sees `"a"` in the source code, it stores the character `'a'` followed by a null character in the object code. The compiler keeps track of the location of the string in memory.

Note 4: Looking inside the string, we see the word `Testing` and some digits separated by commas. The symbols `\n` terminate the string. The pair of characters `'\'` and `'n'` when written together as `\n` represent a newline. The backslash (\) is an escape character. It escapes or changes the usual meaning of the character following it. With `\n`, the usual meaning of n as the fourteenth letter in the lowercase alphabet is no longer valid. Instead the backslash followed by an `'n'` means the end of a line. On a UNIX system, this is the line feed character, the character associated with 10 in the ASCII collating sequence. On a microcomputer running the MS-DOS operating system, the `'\n'` in this context represents the carriage return–line feed combination. Note that the method of terminating a line may differ with different computer systems. The use of the `'\n'` to represent the end of a line is one way in which C source code is portable. The compiler and operating system take care of the specific details.

Using the backslash to escape the usual meaning of characters and impart special meanings is a common practice in C. Other examples of this escape mechanism appear below:

`\t`	the tab character
`\b`	the backspace character
`\"`	the double quote character in a string
`\'`	the single quote character
`\\`	the backslash character
`\0`	the null character

For example, the symbols `\"` would be used to write a quoted statement within a string. The sentence of dialogue

"So what?" said she.

would be written

```
"\"So what?\" said she.\n"
```

as a string in C. Here, the usual meaning of the double quote would be to terminate the string. The backslash alters this meaning; the escaped meaning is that of a double quote. Another example is using the backslash to escape the meaning of a single quote to end the designation of a character. That is, `'\''` represents the single character `'` in C.

The representation of the null character by `\0` is a special case of a more general concept in C. That is, any member of the underlying character set can be represented by a backslash followed by a leading zero and its underlying integer value expressed in octal. For example, the character `'a'` has decimal value 97 or octal value 141. It can be represented to the compiler as `'a'` or `'\0141'`. This fact is especially useful for the nonprinting characters. The BEL character can be represented by `'\007'`. (BEL is the three-character mnemonic for the character that rings the bell on the terminal.)

Learning Activities

4. *C by Discovery* Get to know your compiler. Determine the error messages from your compiler for the following deliberate syntax errors:

   a missing closing brace
   omitting the () in a function call
   a missing " in a printf() call
   a missing ; at the end of a statement
   putting a ; after the first line in a function declaration

5. Write a C program to ring the bell on your terminal.

6. Write a C program that writes three lines of text (your choice of text) to the terminal screen. Have your output double spaced.

7. What would be output by the following line of code? How would it appear on the terminal?

```
printf ("\t\"whoops\b\b\b\bew\n\"\n");
```

1.5   Input and Output with Variables

In this section, we discuss the mechanism of using variables. C is a strongly typed language and requires that a variable must be declared before it can be used. The declaration establishes the name and type of the variable.

Keywords designate each built-in type. The name must be an identifier. The first variables we will work with have the type `int`. The keyword `int` is the name for a built-in data type used to represent integers.

To declare a variable with type `int`, state the type, follow it with the variable name, and terminate it with a semicolon. The following line of code declares a variable of type `int` with the name `counter`:

```
int counter;
```

Once a variable is declared, it can be used in many ways. A value can be given to a variable with an assignment statement. The symbol for the assignment operator is a single equal sign, =. The simplest form of an assignment statement consists of a variable name followed by an equal sign, followed by a value and terminated by a semicolon (;). The statement

```
counter = 1;
```

assigns the value 1 to the variable `counter`. The program in Example 1-4 illustrates the declaration of a variable of type `int`, the assignment of a value to that variable, and the output of that value with the C library function printf().

Example 1-4:   intvar1.c

```
/*                  intvar1.c
 *
 *    Synopsis  -  Declares a variable of type int, assigns a value
 *                 to it, and outputs its value in decimal.
 *
 *    Objective -  Illustrates variable declaration, assignment, and
 *                 output of a variable with printf().
 */

main()
{
        int prime;                                          /* Note 1 */

        prime = 2;                                          /* Note 2 */
        printf ("The only even prime is %d.\n", prime);   /* Note 3 */
}
```

To get an overview of this program, notice that there is one function, the mandatory function named main(). Three C statements make up the code for main(). The first two statements are explained in Notes 1 and 2. The third statement is a call to printf(). Notice that the form of this printf() call is different from previous examples. Note 3 discusses the differences.

Note 1: This line of code declares a variable named `prime` to have type `int`. The type appears first, followed by the variable name and the terminating semicolon. During compilation, space will be allotted for storage of a variable of type `int`.

Note 2: This is an example of an assignment statement. When this statement executes, the value 2 is placed in the storage location for the variable `prime`. If referenced later, the value of `prime` will be 2. A single equal sign, =, is the symbol for assignment in C.

Note 3: The printf() function outputs the value of the variable `prime`. Here, printf() takes two actual parameters. The two parameters are inside the parentheses and separated by a comma. The second parameter is the variable `prime`. The first parameter to printf() is the string

```
"The only even prime is %d.\n".
```

It contains instructions for the output of the value of `prime`. Again, the double quotes suggest to the compiler that this is a string; ' \n' is a newline. The first parameter to the printf() function must always be a string, the control string. The only unfamiliar symbols in this first parameter are the '%' and the 'd'. This combination of characters is an embedded conversion specification. The percent sign indicates that the next character or characters will specify that a conversion must take place before output. The 'd' suggests that a value will be converted to decimal. Each conversion specification should be accompanied by an additional parameter after the control string. The value of the expression in the next parameter position is the value that is to be converted and output. Here the value of `prime` is output. Other possibilities for conversion specifications for printf() will be discussed later.

Learning Activities

8. In the printf() call in the program intvar1.c, describe the use of each of the following characters.

  a. " (double quotes)
  b. \ (backslash)
  c. , (comma)
  d. . (period)

9. a. Predict the output of intvar1.c. Write your predicted output in the boxes below. Write one character per box.

  b. Execute intvar1.c to verify that your prediction is correct.*
     Make sure that you understand the program before going on.

Variable Initialization

Variables in C can be initialized at declaration time. The line of code

```
int counter = 1;
```

declares a variable named `counter` of type `int` and sets its initial value to 1. This statement would replace the following two lines of code:

```
int counter;
counter = 1;
```

More than one variable can be declared in one declaration. Commas separate the names of the variables in the declaration. The code

```
int first, second;
```

declares two variables of type `int` with names `first` and `second`.

The program in Example 1-5 illustrates the techniques of declaring and initializing multiple variables of type `int`. The discussion of this program follows.

---

* The instruction "Execute intvar1.c" is not technically correct. What we mean when we use an expression like that in this text is that the student should compile the source code file and execute the resulting object code file.

Example 1-5:   intvar2.c

```
/*                    intvar2.c
 *
 *    Synopsis  -  Four variables of type int are declared and
 *                 initialized. Their values are output with
 *                 calls to printf().
 *
 *    Objective -  Illustrates declaration of more than one variable
 *                 in one statement, both with and without
 *                 initializers. Also illustrates the use of
 *                 printf() with multiple conversion specifications
 *                 in its control string.
 */

main()
{
        int first, second;                          /* Note 1 */
        int third = 3,
            fourth = 4;                              /* Note 2 */

        first = 1;
        second = 2;
        printf ("First is %d, second is %d, ", first, second);
                                                     /* Note 3 */
        printf ("third is %d, and fourth is %d.\n", third, fourth);
}
```

Again, there is a single function, main(). Seven lines of source code are between the braces that enclose the code for main(). The first three lines of code are variations of declarations. Two assignment statements follow, and the last two statements are variations of printf() calls. The variations are explained in the notes below.

Note 1: Two variables of the same type can be declared in the same declaration in C. This line of code declares two int variables named first and second. The names of multiple variables declared in the same declaration must be separated with commas.

Note 2: Before reading further, locate the terminating semicolon in this declaration. The declaration begins with the token int and continues onto the following line, where it terminates with a semicolon. This code also declares two variables of type int. Their names are third and fourth. An equal sign, =, and the following numerical values initialize the variables third and fourth at time of declaration. The variable third was initialized to 3 and fourth was initialized to 4. The term initializer refers to the expression that follows the equal sign. This example shows the simplest form of an initializer.

Note 3: Each printf() call is similar to the one in intvar1.c, but the control strings now contain two embedded conversion specifications. Also, two additional parameters follow the control string. Each conversion specification in the control string gets the value to be converted from a separate parameter. The parameters must appear in the same order as the corresponding conversion specifications. In each statement, the first %d in the control string converts the value in the first parameter; the second %d converts the value in the last parameter. More conversion specifications can appear in the control string, but each must be associated with an additional parameter after the control string. The function printf() takes a variable number of parameters.

Learning Activities

10. How many lines of text will be output when intvar2.c executes?

11. *C by Discovery*   Find out if it is possible to start a string on one line of source code and terminate it on another line. That is, either modify an existing program or write a short program with a string running over at least two lines. See if you get either compile or run-time errors.

12. Modify intvar2.c in the following ways:
    a. Initialize both `first` and `second` in the declaration instead of the assignment statements.

    b. Have all output done by a single call to printf(). (The statement may be too long to fit on your terminal screen. Since C is a free-format language, one statement can continue on a second line of source code. Experiment to find the positions where the statement can be legally separated into two or more lines of code.)

13. *C by Discovery*   To get to know your compiler better, determine the error messages, if any, for the following errors. If there are no compile-time error messages, try to execute the program. What happens?
    a. In a printf() call, what happens if the number of parameters after the control string is greater than the number of conversion specifications in the control string?

    b. In a printf() call, what happens if the number of additional parameters is less than the number of conversion specifications?

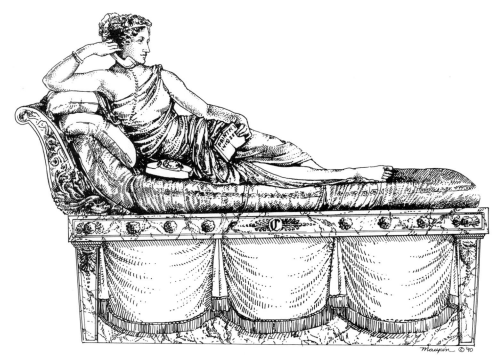

An alternate view of having all the output done by a single call to printf(). Based on *Venus Victrix (Princess Pauline Bonaparte Borghese as Venus)* **by Onotonio Canova, 1808.**

Input with `scanf()`

The function scanf(), from the C library, does formatted input. Scanf() converts input from the ASCII representation entered at the keyboard to the internal representation used by the computer. It reads a sequence of characters on the screen and converts them to a value of the requested type. More specifically, if told to read a decimal integer, scanf() looks for a sequence of digits and converts them to an integer value.

Like printf() for output, scanf() can be used to input many different things. In this section, we will use it to input values of type `int`.

Scanf() is similar to printf() in other ways. Both are functions in the standard C library. The first argument to both functions is a control string with embedded conversion specifications, and both functions take a variable number of parameters. The first parameter is always a control string, and there is one additional parameter for each conversion specification in the control string. The additional arguments to scanf() tell it where to put the value it read. For example, in the statement

```
scanf("%d", &intvar);
```

the control string is `"%d"`. It contains a single conversion specification, `%d`, which suggests that the value to be input will be in a decimal representation.

The second parameter tells scanf() where to put the value it input. Here the input value will be assigned to `intvar`. The declaration of `intvar` as a variable of type `int` must appear before its use in this line of code. The `&` is the address operator. It indicates a reference to the memory address of that variable. That is, `&intvar` tells scanf() the location in memory where it is to store the input value.

The program input1.c in Example 1-6 illustrates the use of scanf() to input a decimal value. It also introduces the hexadecimal conversion specification, `%x`, for use with printf() when it outputs the address of the variable `intvar`. The address operator, `&`, can be used in both printf() and scanf() calls.

 Example 1-6:   input1.c

```
/*              input1.c
 *
 *    Synopsis  -  A variable of type int is declared. Its address
 *                 is output. The input of an integer value is
 *                 requested. When input, it is echoed back to the
 *                 terminal.
 *
 *    Objective -  Illustrates input of an integer value with
 *                 scanf(). Shows the syntax for the address of
 *                 a variable.
 */

main()
{
        int intvar;
        printf ("The address of intvar is %x in hexadecimal.\n",
                                    &intvar);       /* Notes 1 and 2 */

        printf ("\nEnter an integer value: ");
        scanf ("%d", &intvar);                      /* Note 3 */
        printf ("The value you entered was %d.\n", intvar);
}
```

The example has only a single function, main(), with a single variable of type `int` declared. There are four other lines of code, three printf() calls with a call to scanf() between them.

Note 1: This note refers to the conversion specification in the control string to this printf() call. The `%x` suggests that the next parameter to printf() should be an integer value and that the value should be converted to hexadecimal by printf() for output. The characters used will be the hexadecimal digits ′0′ through ′9′, and ′a′, ′b′, ′c′, ′d′, ′e′, ′f′. When the uppercase characters, ′A′, ′B′, ′C′, ′D′, ′E′, ′F′, are desired, the conversion specification %X can be used.

Note 2: The second parameter to this printf() call is &intvar. This is the address of the variable intvar. During compilation, memory is allocated for each variable declared. The address is the location of the memory allocated for the variable.

Note 3: In this statement, the function scanf() reads the value entered by the user at the terminal. The first parameter to scanf() is a control string with a single conversion specification, %d. This suggests that the value entered will be interpreted as a decimal value. The second parameter, &intvar, is the location in memory where scanf() is to store the value it reads. It needs to be an address or pointer value. Here it is the address of intvar. When intvar is accessed in the next line of code, its value will be the value entered from the terminal.

A word of caution. As will be seen in Chapters 3 and 10, scanf() is a multipurpose input function. Like most multipurpose input functions, it can return unexpected values if the input does not exactly match the conversion specifications. An exercise below addresses this fact.

Learning Activities

14. Execute the program input1.c to make sure that it works as you expected.
15. *C by Discovery*

   a. Experiment with erroneous inputs to input1.c. For example, type alphabetic characters instead of digits or type digits and nondigits intermixed. Try typing a few blanks or tabs before, between, and after the digits.

   b. Describe what happens in each case in part a.

   c. Try to generalize the behavior of scanf() for each case in part a.

The hexadecimal conversion specifications, %x and %X, can be used with any integer value with both printf() and scanf(). Besides decimal and hexadecimal conversions, both printf() and scanf() will convert an integer value to or from octal. The corresponding conversion specification for octal is %o. The program input2.c in Example 1-7 illustrates the use of these three conversion specifications in both printf() and scanf(). The discussion of that program starts here.

Example 1-7:   input2.c

```
/*              input2.c
 *
 *   Synopsis    -  A variable of type int is declared. The input of
 *                  an integer value is requested and then output
 *                  three times.  The input and output is done in
 *                  decimal, hexadecimal, and octal.
 *
 *   Objective   -  Illustrates input and output of an integer
 *                  value with scanf() and printf() using the
 *                  conversion specifications %d for decimal, %x
 *                  for hexadecimal, and %o for octal.
 */

main()
{
        int intvar;

        printf ("Enter a decimal integer value: ");
        scanf ("%d", &intvar);
                                                    /* Note 1 */
        printf ("The hexadecimal equivalent of that value is %x.\n",
                         intvar);

        printf ("Enter a hexadecimal integer value: ");
        scanf ("%x", &intvar);                     /* Note 2 */
                                                    /* Note 3 */
        printf ("The value you entered was %o in octal.\n", intvar);

        printf ("Enter an octal integer value: ");
        scanf ("%o", &intvar);                     /* Note 4 */
        printf ("The value you entered was %d in decimal.\n", intvar);

}
```

The overview of the program reveals a single function, main(), with a single variable of type int declared. The next nine lines of code consist of three sequences of a printf() call, a scanf() call, and a printf() call.

Note 1: Note the conversion specification %x in the control string to printf(). This suggests that the value of intvar will be converted to hexadecimal when it is output. In the previous statement, scanf() read a decimal value and stored that value in the internal machine representation in the variable intvar. This value can be converted to any representation before output.

Note 2: In this call to scanf(), the value entered on the terminal is assumed to be in hexadecimal. Scanf() looks for characters ′0′ through ′9′ and ′a′,′b′,′c′, ′d′,′e′,′f′. It converts the value it finds to the internal representation for type int and stores the value in intvar.

Note 3: The %o in the control string requests a conversion to octal before output. Note that the internal representation of a value of type int is in binary. Scanf() and printf() perform conversions to and from this internal representation.

Note 4: The %o indicates a conversion to octal on input by this scanf() call. Scanf() looks for a sequence of the digits ′0′ through ′7′ and, if found, converts the octal value to the internal representation and stores it in intvar.

Both printf() and scanf() are useful functions for conversions and formatted input and output. Remember that scanf() can give unexpected results if the input does not match the specifications.

Learning Activities

16. Predict the output of the program input2.c for each following input sequence:

a. 243
   a45
   132

b. 255
   ff
   177

17. Execute input2.c with the above input sequences to check your predictions.

1.6 Arithmetic Operations

The arithmetic operations that are available for quantities of type int and the other arithmetic types in C are:

+	addition
−	unary minus and subtraction
*	multiplication
/	division
%	remainder

When these operations are applied to variables of type int, the result, by default, is of type int.

This is true of the division operation also. When the operation / is applied to positive integer values, / is truncating division. The fractional part is truncated. In particular, the value of 2/3 is 0, 3/2 is 1, 13/4 is 3, and so on.

If the operands of / are not positive integers, the results need some explanation. First, if the mathematical quotient of the two operands is an integer, the result is that integer. For example,

the value of −6/3 is −2
the value of 6/−3 is −2
the value of −6/−3 is 2

However, when the indicated quotient is not an integer, as in 5/−3, −5/3, or −5/−3, the result may vary from compiler to compiler. The result could be either of the two integers closest to the arithmetic quotient. For example, the value of −5/−3 is either 1 or 2, and the value of −5/3 is either −1 or −2. To ensure that a program is portable, its calculations should never depend on a quotient involving a negative integer.

If a and b are variables of type int, the expression

    a % b

represents the remainder when a is divided by b. This operator is referred to as the remainder or modulus operator; the symbol for the operator is a percent sign. For example,

    7 % 3 is 1

since 7/3 is 2 with remainder 1. By the same reasoning,

    8 % 3 is 2
    9 % 5 is 4

The modulus operator and the division operator are related by the fact that when a and b are variables of type int,

    a = (a/b)*b + (a%b)

This means that the same portability problem exists with the remainder operator applied to negative operands as with the division operator.* That is, the values of −7%−3, −7%3, and 7%−3 may vary between systems since they are dependent on the corresponding values of −7/−3, −7/3, and 7/−3. It is best to write programs that avoid the ambiguity that arises with negative divisors or dividends.

The program in Example 1-8 illustrates the arithmetic operations +, −, *, /, and % in a program with variables of type int.

Notice that four variables are declared of type int. Of these, only the variable a has been initialized. The declarations are followed by a sequence of assignment statements interspersed with calls to printf().

---

* The ANSI standards for C guarantee that the absolute value of the remainder, a%b, is less than the absolute value of the divisor, b. No other guarantees are made about the values of a/b and a%b.

Example 1-8:   arith.c

```
/*                  arith.c
 *
 *   Synopsis   -   Calculates arithmetic operations with variables
 *                  of type int and outputs the resulting values
 *                  in decimal.
 *
 *   Objective  -   Demonstrates the operations +, -, *, /, and % on
 *                  variables of type int.
 */

main()
{
        int a = 2,
            b, c, d;

        c = a + 4;                                  /* Note 1 */
        b = a - 3;                                  /* Note 2 */
        d = -a;                                     /* Note 3 */
        printf ("b is %d,\nc is %d, and\nd is %d.\n\n", b, c, d );

        c = a * 3;                                  /* Note 4 */
        b = a / 3;                                  /* Note 5 */
        d = a % 3;                                  /* Note 6 */
        printf ("Now\nb is %d,\nc is %d, and\nd is %d.\n", b, c, d);

}
```

Note 1: The addition operation is illustrated here. The variable c receives the value of a + 4.

Note 2: The subtraction operation. The variable b receives the value of a − 3.

Note 3: The unary minus operation. After execution of this statement, the value of d is the negative of the value of a.

Note 4: The multiplication operation is performed here. The value of a is multiplied by 3 to get the new value of c.

Note 5: This statement demonstrates the division of two integers. Since both dividend and divisor are positive, the operation is truncating division.

Note 6: This statement illustrates the modulus operation. Again, since both divisor and dividend are positive, there is no ambiguity about the new value of d.

Learning Activities

18. a. How many lines of output will there be from arith.c?

    b. Predict the output of arith.c. Write the output in the spaces below. Write one character per space. Indicate end of lines with the symbol '\n'.

    c. Execute this program to verify your answers to parts a and b.

19. *C by Discovery* Find out how your compiler handles integer division and the modulus operator when at least one operand is negative:

    a. Write a short program that performs integer division and the remainder operation and outputs the results of both operations.

    b. Test your program with different values of the operands.

    c. Explain what happens with your compiler for a quotient a/b when either a, b, or both are negative and when the mathematical quotient of a divided by b is not an integer value.

Precedence of Arithmetic Operations

The precedence of the arithmetic operations follows the rules of mathematics. The unary minus has the highest precedence; the multiplicative operations, *, /, and %, come next; and the additive operations , + and −, have the lowest precedence. All of the arithmetic operators have precedence over the assignment operator.

Highest precedence: unary minus −
                                 *, /, %

Lowest precedence: +, −

Within each group, the operations associate from left to right. For example, `a*b/c` is evaluated as `(a*b)/c` and `2*a + 4/b` is evaluated as `(2*a) + (4/b)`.

These precedence rules can be overruled by judicious placement of parentheses. A parenthesized expression will be evaluated first. A full precedence chart for the arithmetic operations and all other operations in C appears in the Programmer's Handbook.

The program in Example 1-9 illustrates precedence for some combinations of the arithmetic operations.

Example 1-9:   preceden.c

```
/*                  preceden.c
 *
 *   Synopsis   -   Five variables of type int are declared.
 *                  Arithmetic operations are performed and the
 *                  resulting values are output.
 *
 *   Objective  -   To illustrate the relative precedence of
 *                  arithmetic operations and to see how the meaning
 *                  can be changed by the addition of parentheses.
 */

main()
{
        int a=4, b=2, c=3, d, e;

        d = a* -b + c;                          /* Note 1 */
        e = a* -(b + c);
        printf ("d is %d, e is %d,\n", d, e);

        d = a+b * c;                            /* Note 2 */
        e = (a+b) * c;
        printf ("d is %d, e is %d,\n", d, e);

        d = b % c + a;                          /* Note 3 */
        e = b % (c + a);
        printf ("d is %d, e is %d,\n", d, e);

        d = c - b / a * a;                      /* Note 4 */
        e = (c - b) / (a * a);
        printf ("d is %d, e is %d,\n", d, e);

}
```

The program consists of the function main(). Variables a, b, c, d, and e are declared with initial values given to a, b, and c. The following code is broken into four sequences consisting of assignment to d, assignment to e, and a call to printf() to output their current values. Note that the expression assigned to d differs from the one assigned to e only in the addition of parentheses.

Note 1: The expression assigned to d is evaluated as

(a* (-b)) + c

by the natural precedence of the arithmetic operators.

Note 2: In this assignment, the natural precedence causes the expression a + b * c to be evaluated as a + (b * c).

Note 3: The expression b % c + a is evaluated as (b % c) + a.

Note 4: The natural precedence of operators and order of evaluation causes the expression c − b / a * a to be evaluated as c − ((b/a) * a)

Learning Activities

20. Predict the output of preceden.c. Execute the program to verify your prediction and correct any mistakes in your understanding.

21. a. If the variables a, b, and c have been declared as type int and have the values 4, 5, and 2 respectively, evaluate the following expressions as they would be evaluated on your system:

    i.   a % −b + 5

    ii. c − b * a

    iii. c * c + b * a / 3

    iv. a − b − c * a % b

    b. To verify your answers to part a, write a short program in C that declares and initializes a, b, and c and outputs the values of the four expressions.

The program fahrcels.c in Example 1-10 accepts input of a temperature in degrees Fahrenheit and outputs the Celsius equivalent. Since this program uses variables of type int, it will not record the fractional part of the temperature. The discussion of that program is presented below.

Example 1-10:   fahrcels.c

```
/*              fahrcels.c
 *
 *   Synopsis   -   Converts a temperature entered in degrees
 *                  Fahrenheit to Celsius. Uses variables of type int.
 *
 *   Objective  -   To illustrate a practical use of arithmetic
 *                  operators.
 */
```

```
#include <stdio.h>

main()
{
        int fahrenheit, celsius;                    /* Note 1 */

        printf("Enter a temperature in fahrenheit: ");
        scanf("%d", &fahrenheit);

        celsius = 5 * (fahrenheit - 32) / 9;     /* Note 2 */

        printf("%d in Fahrenheit is %d in Celsius.\n",
                        fahrenheit, celsius);
}
```

The function main() has two variables of type `int` declared. The variable `fahrenheit` is initialized by a call to scanf() to input its value. The Celsius temperature is calculated and output.

Note 1: The variables `fahrenheit` and `celsius` are both declared to be of type `int`. In order to record the fractional part of the temperature, a different type must be used. Chapter 3 discusses other numeric types in C.

Note 2: This line of code does the conversion from Fahrenheit to Celsius. First the parenthetical expression is evaluated, then the multiplication and truncating division by the constant factors 5 and 9 are performed.

Learning Activities

22. Compile and execute fahrcels.c. Test it with the following input values: 212, 32, 213, 35, and 40. Check the results of the program by calculating the Celsius temperature by hand.

23. a. Modify the program fahrcels.c by changing the line

```
        celsius = 5 * (fahrenheit - 32) / 9;
```
    to
```
        celsius = 5/9 * (fahrenheit - 32);
```
    b. Compile and run the modified program with the same input as for activity 1. Explain the results.

Compound Assignment

The assignment statement

```
a = a + 4;
```

can be shortened to

```
a += 4;
```

This is called compound assignment. When a single variable is being changed with any operation, it can be done with compound assignment. For any operation, the expression

```
a  op=  b  is equivalent to a = a op b
```

For example,

```
a *= 3      is equivalent to a = a * 3
a += 4      is equivalent to a = a + 4
```

Compound assignment also can be used with division and the modulus operation. Example 1-11 illustrates this.

 ### Example 1-11:   compound.c

```
/*              compound.c
 *
 *    Synopsis  -  Uses compound assignment to change the value of
 *                 an integer variable a and outputs the changed
 *                 value with printf().
 *
 *    Objective -  Illustrates compound assignment in C with
 *                 several different arithmetic operations.
 */

main()
{
        int a = 0;

        a += 4;                                        /* Note 1 */
        printf("a is %d.\n", a);

        a *= 3;                                        /* Note 2 */
        printf ("a is now %d.\n", a);

        a -= 4;                                        /* Note 3 */
        printf ("a is now %d.\n", a);

        a /= 2;                                        /* Note 4 */
        printf ("a is now %d.\n", a);
```

```
    a %= 5;                                         /* Note 5 */
    printf ("a is now %d.\n", a);
}
```

This program contains a single function named main(). An integer variable named a is declared and initialized to zero. A sequence of compound assignment statements is followed by calls to printf().

Note 1: The statement a += 4; is equivalent to a = a + 4;. A new value of the variable a is established.

Note 2: Compound assignment is used with the multiplication operation. This statement is equivalent to a = a * 3;.

Note 3: Subtraction can be done with compound assignment also.

Note 4: This is an example of compound assignment with division. Because both operands are positive, the result is unambiguous.

Note 5: The modulus operation is applied with compound assignment. Note that the result is not ambiguous in this case either.

Compound assignment can be used whenever a single variable is being changed. It also can be used with operations other than the arithmetic operations.

Learning Activities

24. Part of the output from compound.c is given below. Complete the output by writing down the value of a in the output from each of the printf() calls.
    ```
    a is _____.\n
    a is now _____.\n
    a is now _____.\n
    a is now _____.\n
    a is now _____.\n
    ```

25. What is the value of int1 after the following code sequence has been executed?
    ```
    int int1 = 5, int2 = 7;

    int2 /= int2 - int1;
    int1 *= int1 + int2;
    ```

26. Try to find a way to compare the object or assembly code generated by the statement
    ```
    a = a + 4;
    ```
    with the code generated by the equivalent statement
    ```
    a += 4;
    ```
    Based on your comparison, give some reasons for using one form over the other. Which form do you think is preferable?

The Increment and Decrement by 1 Operations

Another shortcut in source code is provided for incrementing a variable by 1. The following statements increment the variable a by 1.

```
a = a + 1;
a += 1;
a++;
```

The third statement uses the increment by 1 operator, ++. This operator can be used immediately before or after a variable anywhere in an expression. If the ++ is placed immediately after the variable, as in a++, then the value of a is incremented *after* it is accessed for use in the expression. If the ++ is placed immediately before the variable, as in ++a, then the value of a is incremented *before* a is used in the expression.

For example, compare the two expressions a++ * 4 and ++a * 4. If the value of the variable a is 3, then the expression

```
a++ * 4
```

yields the value 12. After evaluation of that expression, the value of a becomes 4. However, if the value of the variable a is 3, then the expression

```
++a * 4
```

would have the value 16 since a would be incremented before it is multiplied by 4. Again, the value of a is 4 after evaluation of the expression.

The corresponding decrement by 1 operator is --. When placed immediately after a variable in an expression, as in a--, the value of the variable is decremented by 1 after accessing the value in the expression. The operator -- can also be placed immediately before a variable, as in --a, and the value of the variable is decremented before it is accessed in the expression.

The program increment.c in Example 1-12 illustrates the increment and decrement by 1 operators.

 Example 1-12:   increment.c

```
/*                  increment.c
 *
 *    Synopsis   -  Assigns values to b using the increment and
 *                  decrement by 1 operators with a. Outputs values
 *                  of a and b.
 *
 *    Objective  -  To demonstrate the increment and decrement by
 *                  1 operators.
 */

main()
{
        int a = 3, b;
```

```
        b = a++;                                        /* Note 1 */
        printf ("b is %d, and a is %d.\n", b, a);

        b = ++a;                                        /* Note 2 */
        printf ("Now b is %d, and a is %d.\n", b, a);

        b = 5 % --a;                                    /* Note 3 */
        printf ("Now b is %d, and a is %d.\n", b, a);
        printf ("Now b is %d, and a is %d.\n", ++b, a--); /* Note 4 */
        printf ("Now b is %d, and a is %d.\n", b, a);
}
```

This program consists of the single function main(). Two variables of type int are declared, and the variable a is initialized to 3. The remainder of the program is a sequence of assignment statements and printf() calls.

Note 1: The current value of a is assigned to b, and a is incremented after the assignment. This leaves b with the value 3 and a with the value 4.

Note 2: In this statement, a is incremented before its value is assigned to b. This leaves both b and a with the value 5.

Note 3: Here a is decremented to 4 before the modulus operation is performed. Therefore, the value 1 is assigned to b.

Note 4: In this printf() call, the value of b is incremented before it is output while the value of a is decremented after it is output. The resulting values are output in the next call to printf().

Learning Activities

27. a. Predict the output of increment.c if each statement of the form
        ```
        printf ("b is %d, and a is %d.\n", b, a);
        ```
    is changed to
        ```
        printf ("b is %d, and a is %d.\n", b--, a++);
        ```
    Write the new values of a and b for each of the printf() calls.
        b is ____ and a is ____ .\n
        Now b is ____ and a is ____ .\n
        Now b is ____ and a is ____ .\n
        Now b is ____ and a is ____ .\n
        Now b is ____ and a is ____ .\n

    b. Make the changes and execute the program to verify your answers.

28. Predict the output of the following program.

```c
/*                    laincr.c
 *
 *    Synopsis  - Outputs values of int1, int2 and int3.
 *
 *    Objective - To provide practice with automatic
 *                increment and decrement.
 *
 */

#include <stdio.h>

main()
{
    int int1 = 4,
        int2 = 7,
        int3;

    int3 = ++int1 * --int2;
    printf("%d  %d  %d\n", ++int1, int2--, --int3);
    printf("%d  %d  %d\n", int1, int2, int3);
}
```

1.7   Introduction to Structured Programming in C

The goals of structured programming include writing source code that is modular in nature, easily modifiable, robust (handles errors gracefully), and readable. A modular program is composed of many independent subprograms. Each subprogram or function in C should be designed to do one task, and should not be too long to be understood easily. Another programming goal is to write subprograms that are tools and can be used with little or no modification in many programs. If a subprogram is to be a useful tool, it should not depend on any variables or constants not declared in the function.

With a few new concepts we can start to write structured, modular, modifiable C code and write functions that are tools. The new concepts are constant definitions, the syntax of parameter passing in C, and the `return` statement. The concepts we will discuss in this section include constant definitions with the preprocessor and elementary methods of having functions communicate with the rest of the program without direct dependence on program variables.

The preprocessor constants add to readability and allow a program to be more easily modified. For example, consider a situation in which a company commissions a software developer to write a payroll program. The company currently has 100 employees, and the program needs to reference a certain maximum number of employees several places in the code. The programmer, being farsighted, allows for a maximum of 150 employees, and the program works well for several years. However, the company expands beyond all expectation, and when they add their 151st employee, they experience trouble with their payroll program and call the programmer back in. If the programmer had defined the maximum number of employees as a constant identifier in one place and always referenced that value by using the identifier, it would be a simple matter to change the value of the constant identifier and recompile the program. However, if the programmer had used the value 150 throughout the code, then he or she must painstakingly search the source code for all references to the 150; determine, by context, if that value was referring to the maximum number of employees or to some other quantity; and change all of those and only those that are relevant.

In C, one way of defining constants is with the preprocessor. We discussed the preprocessor directive `#include` in Section 1.4. The `#define` directive is the second preprocessor directive that we will discuss. For the situation described above, the directive would be

```
#define MAXEMPLOYEES    150
```

It should appear in the source code file before other references to MAXEMPLOYEES. Older versions of C compilers may require that the character # appear in the first column of a line and that no whitespace appear between the # and the word `define`. These restrictions have been eased in the ANSI C standards.

During the preprocess phase of compilation, the preprocessor searches through the source code for all references to the identifier MAXEMPLOYEES and replaces each one with the expression 150. When the program is modified by replacing the value 150 with 200 or another suitable constant, it must be recompiled. The preprocessor again seeks out all occurrences of the identifier MAXEMPLOYEES and this time replaces each one with the value 200.

The methods of letting a function communicate with the rest of the program without depending directly on program variables have their beginnings in mathematical notation. For example, in mathematical functional notation,

$$y = f(x)$$

indicates that

1. f is a function
2. its value depends on the value of x, its argument
3. y takes on that particular value of f

In this context, x is called the independent variable and y is the dependent variable. In C, the terminology is somewhat different: x is called the parameter or argument to f, and y is said to store the value returned by f. However, the concept is the same.

Values can be passed to a function by the use of parameters. The declaration of a function must include the declaration of its arguments.* For example, if the function f(x) were being written in ANSI C and if x were an integer parameter, the ANSI C declaration would begin with the line

```
f(int x)
```

before the opening brace for the function. This informs the compiler that the function f takes a single parameter that will be referred to by the name x in the body of the function and that the parameter type is int. An alternate syntax is used in older compilers to convey the same information. In this example, the alternate declaration for the function f() would be

```
f(x)
int x;
```

Parameters will be discussed further in Chapter 3.

A value can be established for a function by means of the return statement. When the return statement appearing in a function is followed by an expression, two things happen when that statement is executed. First, the expression is evaluated. Second, the function stops executing and returns the value of the expression to its calling environment. In the following program, the line

```
y = f(x);
```

calls the function f(). The line

```
return 2;
```

causes the function f() to stop executing and return the value 2. This value is then assigned to y. The second call to f() is in the line

```
f(x);
```

This time, when the return statement is executed, the function terminates, the value 2 is returned to main(), and execution continues on the next line of main(). However, the return value, 2, is ignored. Neither use is an error, but ignoring a return value may elicit a warning message from some compilers.

```
main()
{
    int x, y;
    y = f(x);               /* first call to f(x)  */
    f(x);                   /* second call to f(x) */
}
f(int x)
{
    return 2;               /* return 2 to main()  */
}
```

---

* Learning to program is like learning to drive a stick shift car. There are a lot of things to see and do at one time. When you turn a corner in the car, you must watch for pedestrians and other cars, steer, put in the clutch, shift the gears, turn on the blinker and alternately put on the brake and the gas. At first these activities are overwhelming; later they become second nature.

Similarly, when writing a program in C, you must pay attention to keywords, types, braces, single quotes, double quotes, semicolons, parentheses, functions, commas, operators and so on. Therefore, we have delayed including some of the features of the C language until the reader has become accustomed to the features in the list above. In particular we will start including the return type in a function declaration in Section 3.10.

This is just an introduction to the `return` statement. We will discuss it again in Chapter 6.

The program funct1.c of Example 1-13 declares a function sqr() that takes one integer parameter and uses a `return` statement to return a value to the calling environment, main(). The function main() illustrates three different ways of calling sqr() and handling its return value. The discussion of that program follows.

Example 1-13:   funct1.c

```
/*                  funct1.c
 *
 *    Synopsis  -  Outputs the squares of the values 2, 5, and 9.
 *
 *    Objective -  To illustrate parameters to a function and one
 *                 form of the return statement.
 */

#include <stdio.h>

main()
{
        int x, y;

        y = sqr(2);                              /* Note 1 */
        printf ("2 squared is %d.\n", y);

        printf ("5 squared is %d.\n", sqr(5));   /* Note 2 */

        x = 9;
        y = sqr(x);                              /* Note 3 */
        printf ("%d squared is %d.\n", x, y);
}

/********************************* sqr()  ******************/
/*      returns the square of its argument
 */
sqr(int arg)                                     /* Note 4 */
{
        return (arg * arg);                      /* Note 5 */
}
```

As an overview, we see that funct1.c is composed of the two functions main() and sqr(). The function sqr() consists of a single `return` statement. The function main() consists of calls to the function sqr() where the result is usually assigned to the variable y and calls to printf() to output the result.

Note 1: In this call to sqr(), the value 2 is called the actual parameter. During this execution of sqr(), 2 will be substituted for the formal parameter.

Note 2: In this call to printf(), the parameter following the control string is a call to the function sqr(). The value returned by sqr() is output.

Note 3: The variable x is the actual parameter to sqr() in this call. Both constants and variables can be used as parameters to this function.

Note 4: The function definition starts with this line. The parameter is declared here and on the next line of code. The declaration gives the compiler the following information: the number of parameters to this function, the type of the parameters, and the names by which they will be referenced in the body of the function. In this case, there is one parameter of type `int` with the name `arg`.

In ANSI C compilers, these two lines of code before the opening brace for the function body can be replaced with the single ANSI C prototype,

```
sqr (int arg)
```

Note that it contains the same information as the older form of the declaration.

Note 5: The `return` statement gives the function the value of the expression in parentheses. In this case, the square of `arg` is returned. When this statement is executed, the function stops executing and the value is returned to the calling environment, main().

Learning Activities

29. Compile and execute funct1.c as it is. Then add some additional calls to the function sqr() and compile and run it again.

30. Write a function cube() that takes a single parameter of type `int` and returns the cube of its parameter. Use the function sqr() from funct1.c and your function cube() in a program that inputs a value x of type `int` and outputs the value of the polynomial $x^3 + x^2$.

The example program convert.c of Example 1-14 gives another example of a function that communicates with the main program by means of two parameters and a `return` statement. In this program, a preprocessor-defined constant has been declared so that the program can be easily modified. The program directs the user to input a value in a given base. That value is then converted to decimal by the function todecimal(). The parameters inform the function of the number to be converted, `original`, and the `base` of the number. Since C does not have a facility to input numbers in bases other than decimal, hexadecimal, and octal, the input is done as if the number were decimal. The function then isolates the individual digits so that the true value of the input can be calculated.

Note that this program has many limitations. First, the limit of 32767 is put on the input value because that is the largest integer value that can be input on many computers. Second, the program will not work correctly for a number whose base is greater than 10 because the input is limited to decimal digits. Third, no error checking is done on the input values. For a base 5 number, the digits used are 0 through 4. If the user enters a digit greater than 4, the program will accept it as correct. You will learn how to correct these limitations after studying the material presented in Chapters 2 and 3. At that time the program could be rewritten using one of the loops in C.

Example 1-14: convert.c

```
/*                  convert.c
 *
 *   Synopsis  -  Accepts input of a number in base 5 and outputs
 *                the decimal representation of that number.
 *
 *   Objective -  To illustrate the use of a preprocessor-defined
 *                constant to make a program easily modifiable, and
 *                the use of parameters and return values to make a
 *                function independent.
 */

#define BASE  5                                    /* Note 1 */
#include <stdio.h>

main()
{
        int original;

        printf ("Convert integers in another base to decimal\n");
        printf ("-----------------------------------------\n");
        printf ("Current base is %d.\n", BASE);        /* Note 2 */

        printf ("\n\nEnter an integer less than 32767 in base %d: ",
                                   BASE);
        scanf("%d", &original);
                                                       /* Note 3 */
        printf ("Thank you, the converted value is %d.\n",
                           todecimal(original, BASE));
}
```

```
/********************************  todecimal()   *************/
/*      Converts an integer from another base to decimal.
 *      The other base is the second parameter to the function,
 *      the number to be converted is the first.
 */

todecimal(int number, int base)                          /* Note 4 */
{
        int digit1, digit2, digit3, digit4, digit5, converted;

                        /*  isolate the digits in number   */
        digit1 = number % 10;                            /* Note 5 */
        number /= 10;
        digit2 = number % 10;
        number /= 10;
        digit3 = number % 10;
        number /= 10;
        digit4 = number % 10;
        number /= 10;
        digit5 = number % 10;

        converted = digit1 + digit2 * base               /* Note 6 */
                + digit3 * base * base
                + digit4 * base * base * base
                + digit5 * base * base * base * base;
        return (converted);                              /* Note 7 */
}
```

The program consists of the functions main() and todecimal(). Note that main() consists of calls to printf() and scanf(). The last printf() call contains a call to the function todecimal() as a parameter.

Note 1: The identifier BASE is defined to be the constant value 5. As it is, this program converts base 5 numbers to decimal. If a program is needed to convert base 7 numbers to decimal, this constant definition should be changed to 7 and the program recompiled. No other change is needed.

Note 2: The preprocessor finds all occurrences of the identifier BASE like the one on this line and replaces them with the value 5.

Note 3: The call to todecimal() appears as the second argument to this printf() call. The first parameter, original, is the number to be converted and the second parameter is the constant BASE, indicating to the function that the first number is to be treated as base 5.

Note 4: The formal parameters to todecimal() are number and base. Both are of type int. The compiler will not consider BASE and base as the same value because of the upper/lowercase difference. It is only because BASE is passed as the second parameter that it takes the place of base here. In general, the names of the actual parameters are unrelated to the names of the formal parameters.

Note also that todecimal() is an independent subfunction. It does not depend directly on any values declared in main(). It could be moved to another program and would perform identically.

Note 5: When the number was input by scanf(), it was input as decimal because there is no immediate facility for input in base 5. To interpret the number correctly, it is necessary to isolate each digit. This is done by taking the remainder when the number is successively divided by 10. For example, if the input is 124, number % 10 evaluates to 4 and the first digit is isolated. After dividing number by 10, the expression number % 10 evaluates to 12 % 10 or 2, and so on.

Note 6: To reconstruct the input as a base 5 number, each successive digit is multiplied by an additional factor of 5 to get the true value.

Note 7: This value is returned by todecimal(). The main program outputs it as a decimal value.

Learning Activities

31. Compile and test convert.c as it is. Test it with base 5 values for which you know or can easily calculate the decimal equivalent.

32. Find out if it is possible to stop the compilation after the preprocess phase has been completed. If so, find out how to do it and inspect this file after preprocessing. You should see the substitutions of the value 5 for the identifier BASE throughout the code as well as certain changes caused by the included file, stdio.h. What other changes do you notice?

33. If you are not yet certain how the algorithm for isolating the digits works, put some printf() calls after each statement in the form
    ```
    number /= 10;
    ```
    that outputs the value of the number and the digit that was just calculated. Hand calculate the values for the input value 124.

34. Modify the program so that it will calculate the decimal equivalent for a number entered in base 7 and test it again.

35. Will changing %d to %x in the scanf() call allow the BASE to be larger than 10? Test it by making that change, changing BASE to 12, compiling and executing it several times. Enter some base 12 numbers, using the letter a for 10 and the letter b for 11. Does the program work correctly? If it doesn't, correct it.

Language Elements Introduced in This Chapter: A Review

** Comments **
> /* This is a comment. */

** Control Statements **
> `return`   Used to impart value to a function and to return control from a function to the calling environment.

** Conversion Specifications **
> `%d`   conversion to or from decimal
> `%x`   conversion to or from hexadecimal
> `%o`   conversion to or from octal

** Escape Characters **
> ' \ ' escapes the usual meaning of the next character
> Examples:
> `\t`   the tab character
> `\c`   a carriage return
> `\b`   the backspace character
> `\"`   the double quote character in a string
> `\'`   the single quote character
> `\\`   the backslash character
> `\0`   the null character
> `\n`   the newline character

** Functions **
> Subprograms must have a name (identifier), a pair of parentheses, and a pair of braces.

** Function calls **
> Consist of the function name, a pair of parentheses, and a semicolon. Any actual parameters appear between the parentheses.

** Identifiers **
> Consist of letters, underscores, and numbers. They must not start with a number and must not conflict with any keyword.

** Library Functions **
> `printf("control string", parameters);`
> > Does formatted output. Takes one additional parameter for each conversion specification in the control string.
> `scanf ("control string", parameters);`
> > Does formatted input. Takes one additional parameter for each conversion specification in the control string.

** Operators **
> `=`   assignment
> `+`   addition
> `−`   unary minus and subtraction
> `*`   multiplication
> `/`   division
> `%`   remainder
> `+=, -=, *=,` compound assignment

```
        /=, %=
        ++                      increment by 1
        --                      decrement by 1
```
** Parameters to Functions **
      Declarations: `f(intx)`   (ANSI Prototype)
```
                                or
                                f(x)
                                int x;
```
** Preprocessor Directives **
      `#include`   includes a source file or header file at that point
                         in the code
      `#define`   used to define constants for easy readability and
                         maintainability
** Types **
      `int`
** Variable Declarations **
      Consist of the type name followed by a comma-separated list of variables and a terminating semicolon.

Things to Remember

1. Unlike most upper-level languages, C allows a programmer a measure of control over the hardware.
2. The underlying character set must have most of the characters in the ASCII collating sequence. ASCII will be used in this text.
3. C distinguishes between uppercase and lowercase alphabetics.
4. C is a free-format language.
5. All subprograms in C are called functions.
6. Every C program must have a function named main().
7. The printf() function will do output in C. It takes a variable number of arguments. The first argument is a control string that contains conversion specifications. One additional argument should appear for every conversion specification in the control string.
8. When operating with integers, the division operator, /, is related to the remainder operator by the equation
    $$a = (a/b) *b + (a\%b)$$
    When the signs of a and b differ and b does not divide a evenly, the only guarantee is that the absolute value of a%b is less than the absolute value of b.
9. The precedence of the multiplicative operators, *, /, and %, is greater than the precedence of the additive operators, + and −. The precedence of the arithmetic operators is greater than that of assignment (including compound assignment). For operators of equal precedence, the expressions are evaluated from left to right.

10. When the increment by 1 (++) and decrement by 1 (--) operators appear in an expression, the placement of the operator determines the order of evaluation. If the operator appears to the left of a variable, the operator is evaluated before the expression, but if the operator appears to the right of a variable, the expression is evaluated first.

11. The goals of structured programming include writing source code that is modular in nature, easily modifiable, robust (handles errors gracefully), and readable.

12. Each subprogram or function should be designed to do one task and should not be too long to be understood easily. When possible, tools should be written that can be used with little or no modification in many programs. Tools should not depend on any variables or constants not declared in the function.

1.8   Exercises and Programming Problems

1. Which of the following are legal identifiers in C?

```
to_dec      1more         forget-it         hex2dec
floater     horrendous    rub-a-dub-dub      Let_it_be_me
two+four     UPPER        l_o_n_g            _3angle
```

2. If x, y, and z are variables of type int with values 4, -3, and 9 respectively, what is output by the following sequence of printf() calls?

```
printf ("%d, %d, %d\n", x + 2%x, ++z % x, y++ /x);
printf ("%d, %d, %d\n", x+y+z++, 3*y/2, 3/2*y);
printf ("%d, %d, %d\n", ++y + ++z, x - 4, 2 * x % 3);
```

3. Write a C program to output a triangle of asterisks with five rows. Your output should look like the figure below.

```
        *
      *   *
    *   *   *
  *   *   *   *
*   *   *   *   *
```

4. Write a C program to output your initials in block letters. For example,

```
LLL              SSSSSSSSSSS         FFFFFFFFFFFF
LLL              SSS       SSS       FFF
LLL              SSS                 FFF
LLL              SSSSSSSSSSS         FFFFFFFFF
LLL                        SSS       FFF
LLL              SSS       SSS       FFF
LLLLLLLLLLL      SSSSSSSSSSS         FFF
```

5. Write a program to input two integer values and output their sum and their difference. A sample run of the program follows. The user input is in **boldface.**

```
Enter an integer: 45
Enter another integer: 83
45 + 83 = 128
45 - 83 = -38
```

6. Write a program that accepts input of a number of seconds and outputs the equivalent number of hours, minutes, and seconds. A sample run follows with the user input in **boldface.**

```
Enter the number of seconds: 3920
1 hour, 5 minutes, 20 seconds.
```

7. Write a program that will input an integer and output the minimum number of quarters, dimes, nickels and pennies needed to make up the input amount. Two sample runs follow with user input in **boldface.**

```
Enter the amount for which change must be created: 67
2 quarter(s), 1 dime(s), 1 nickel(s) and 2 penny(ies)
Enter the amount for which change must be created: 45
1 quarter(s), 2 dime(s), 0 nickel(s) and 0 penny(ies)
```

8. Write a program that adds two fractions. Your output need not be in lowest terms. A sample run follows with user input in **boldface.**

```
First Fraction:
Enter the numerator: 2
Enter the denominator: 3
Second Fraction:
Enter the numerator: 3
Enter the denominator: 8
2/3 + 3/8 = 25/24
```

9. Write a program that inputs the length and width in integers and outputs the area and the perimeter of a rectangle. Sample run with user input in **boldface.**

```
Rectangle Geometry
------------------
Enter the length: 5
Enter the width: 4
A rectangle with length 5 and width 4 has area 20 and
 perimeter 18.
```

10. Write a program that will input a decimal value and output the equivalent value in octal and hexadecimal. Sample run with user input in **boldface.**

```
Enter a decimal integer: 35
35 decimal is 43 octal and 23 hexadecimal.
```

Gaining Control

2.1   Expressions and Statements

In Chapter 2 we will study expressions and control statements. Expressions are sequences of tokens that can be evaluated to a numerical quantity. They range from a single number or identifier to a more complicated sequence of tokens. Expressions can contain any of the operators in C. In this section, the discussion involves expressions with either arithmetic operators or the assignment operator.

Expressions in C can be classified as *lvalues* or *rvalues*. The term *lvalue* refers to an expression that has a *location* in memory. Modifiable lvalues can be used on the *l*eft-hand side of an assignment statement. For example, the name of a variable is an lvalue. Modifiable lvalues are expressions whose values can be either changed or evaluated.

In contrast, an *rvalue* can be evaluated but cannot be changed. For example, the single character token '5' is an rvalue. If a variable named x has been previously declared, the expression 2*x + 5 is also an rvalue. An *rvalue* cannot be used on the left-hand side of an assignment statement. It may only be used on the right-hand side.

First we consider arithmetic expressions. Assume x and y have been declared as a variable of type int. The following table gives legal C expressions and their corresponding classification as rvalues or lvalues.

Expression	*Lvalue*	*Rvalue*
x	yes	yes
x + 3	no	yes
y	yes	yes
2*y − 7	no	yes
x * (−2/y + 7 % x)	no	yes

Note that some expressions are both lvalues and rvalues. Any variable is an lvalue and an rvalue.

The use of the assignment operator, =, creates a quantity known as an assignment expression. An assignment such as

```
x = 5
```

is considered to be an expression and can appear anywhere that any other expression can appear in a C program.

The assignment operator is a binary operator. It has a lower precedence than any of the arithmetic operators. An assignment expression has the form

```
expr1 = expr2
```

where expr1 must be an lvalue and expr2 is an rvalue. When this assignment expression is evaluated, expr2 is fully evaluated before the assignment is made and the assignment expression itself takes on that value. The numerical value of

```
x = 5
```

is 5. The assignment expression

```
x = 2 * 5 − 3
```

has the value 7 because that is the numerical value of the expression on the right-hand side of the assignment operator.

C programmers can use statements like

```
x = y = 2;
```

because this is equivalent to the parenthesized statement

```
x = (y = 2);
```

Here the assignment is made to y and the value of that assignment expression, 2, is assigned to x. The assignment operator associates from right to left.

In C, a statement formed by placing a semicolon at the end of a statement is known as an expression statement. Some examples of expression statements are:

```
x + 3;
2*x − 5;
x = 6;
```

If either of the first two of these expression statements appeared in a program, the value of the expression would be calculated, but no additional action would take place because none is indicated. The calculated value is discarded. Some compilers give a warning message for expression statements like these that have no effect on the program. It is important to note that an assignment statement is also a form of the expression statement.

The program express.c in Example 2-1 illustrates expression statements and the value of assignment statements. We will see more uses for expression statements when we study control statements later in this chapter.

The overview of the program reveals three declared variables of type int, a sequence of printf() calls, and some miscellaneous expression statements.

Example 2-1:   express.c

```
/*                express.c
 *
 *    Synopsis  -  Assigns and outputs values of the variables
 *                 x and y.
 *
 *    Objective -  Demonstrates expression statements and the
 *                 values of assignment statements.
 */

#include <stdio.h>

main()
{
    int x = 1, y, z;

    printf ("Value of x, %d\n", x);                     /* Note 1 */
    printf ("Value of 2*x + 5, %d\n", 2*x + 5);         /* Note 1 */

    printf ("Value of assignment to x, %d\n", x = 5);   /* Note 2 */
    printf ("Value of assignment to y, %d\n",
                        y = 2*x++ + 1);                 /* Note 3 */
    printf ("x is %d and y is %d\n", x, y);

    3*x + 5;                                            /* Note 4 */
    z = y = 4*x + 5;                                    /* Note 5 */
    printf ("y is %d and z is %d.\n", y, z);

}
```

Note 1: These two familiar types of printf() calls illustrate that the parameters after a control string are expressions and those expressions are evaluated when the program executes.

Note 2: Since an assignment is an expression, it can appear anywhere that any other expression can appear. The assignment is made and the value of the assignment expression is output by the call to printf().

Note 3: The value of this assignment expression is the value of the quantity being assigned to y. After the assignment, the value of x is incremented by 1. This incrementation has no effect on the value of the assignment statement or the value assigned to y.

Note 4: This is an example of an expression statement that has no effect on the execution of the program. It consists of an expression followed by a semicolon. When this statement executes, the expression is evaluated and the value is discarded. Although this statement is legal in C, some compilers will give warnings because it has no effect on the calculations in a program.

Note 5: In this statement, the expression 4*x + 5 is evaluated first. The value is assigned to y and becomes the value of the assignment statement. That value is then assigned to z. This one statement is equivalent to the statements

```
y = 4*x + 5;

z = y;
```

or the single parenthesized statement

```
z = (y = 4*x + 5);
```

In summary, the important points are that expressions are evaluated when a program executes and that an assignment is an expression that can appear in a C program wherever any other expression can appear. We will see how this fact allows C source code to be written in a compact manner.

Learning Activities

1. Before running express.c,
    a. Identify the expressions in each of the printf( ) calls.

    b. Predict the output of the program.

    c. Make a list of the expressions in the program above. Which are lvalues? Which are rvalues?

2. Compile and execute express.c to check your answer to part b in question 1. If your answer to part b was wrong, make sure you know why. Correct your concepts.

2.2   Blocks and Compound Statements

A *compound statement* is a sequence of statements that can be used anyplace in the syntax that a simple statement can be used. It is a common construct in most programming languages. In C, a compound statement is called a *block*. The syntax of the C language allows more than just a sequence of statements. Local variable declarations can be included with the executable statements in a block. Assuming that both x and y have been declared as variables of type int, both of the following examples are compound statements or blocks in C.

```
1.   {
         x = 4;
         y = x + 3;

     }
2.   {
         int i;

         i = 5;
         x = (i++) +3;
         y = i - 4;

     }
```

A block must begin with an opening brace and terminate with a closing brace. The contents of the block may consist of declarations, statements, both or neither. All declarations in a block must appear before the statements. A block can be placed anywhere in a program that a simple statement can be placed.

The scope of the variables declared in a block is from the point of declaration to the end of the block. These variables are local in the sense that the surrounding function does not know about variables declared inside a block. However, the statements in a block can access any variables that the surrounding function can access. We will learn more about the scope of variables in Chapter 8.

The program block.c in Example 2-2 illustrates the scope of variables within functions and blocks. In general, it is a better idea *not* to give the same name to different variables.

Example 2-2:   block.c

```
/*              block.c
 *
 *   Synopsis  -  The values of two variables named i are output
 *                in two different blocks.
 *
 *   Objective -  To illustrate block structuring of C source
```

```
 *              code.
 */

#include <stdio.h>

main ()
{
        int i = 3;

        {                                               /* Note 1 */
                int i = 5;                              /* Note 2 */
                                                        /* Note 3 */
                printf ("In the inner block, i is %d.\n", i);
        }

        printf ("In the outer block, i is %d.\n", i); /* Note 4 */
}
```

An overview of the program reveals a single function named main(). Inside main(), a variable named i of type int is declared. A block follows. It is delimited by the open and close braces. Inside the block, another variable named i is declared and initialized. Calls to printf() appear both inside and after the end of the block.

Note 1: The brace, {, signifies the beginning of an interior block in the function main(). Each block can have its own set of internal declarations and statements. A block is also known as a compound statement. Compound statements must be surrounded by braces. A compound statement can appear anywhere a statement can appear.

Note 2: This is an internal declaration. The values for this variable are unknown outside the block. Each variable declared inside a block is allocated memory that is only active while that block is executing. When there are conflicting variable names, the name in the executing block dominates.

Note 3: The printf() call outputs the value of the variable i that was declared inside the block. When a single identifier like i is used to access two different variables, the variable that was declared in the nearest block to the executing statement is chosen.

Note 4: The variable i that was defined in main() is output here. This call to printf() has no knowledge of any of the variables or statements inside the block because the memory for variables in the block was allocated temporarily and is no longer active. The value output is 3.

Learning Activities

3. Predict the output from the program block.c.

4. In the program block.c,
   a. Suppose that the line `int i = 5;` is deleted. Predict what would happen if you attempt to execute the modified program on your computer system. Choose your prediction from the choices below.

      i.   The program won't compile.
      ii. The program compiles but has a runtime error.
      iii. The program compiles and executes but the output is

      ```
      In the inner block, i is 3.
      In the outer block, i is 3.
      ```

      iv. The program compiles and executes but the output is

      ```
      In the inner block, i is 5.
      In the outer block, i is 5.
      ```

      v.   The program compiles and executes with no changes from the original program.

   b. Suppose that the line `int i = 3;` is deleted. Predict what would happen if you attempt to execute the modified program on your computer system. Choose your prediction from the choices in part a.

   c. Suppose that the line `int i = 5;` is changed to read `i = 5;`. Now predict what would happen if you attempt to compile and execute the program. Choose your prediction from the choices in part a.

Another illustration of variable hiding appears in the program block2.c in Example 2-3. This program will *not* compile because the surrounding program does not know about the declaration inside the block.

Example 2-3:   block2.c

```
/*              block2.c
 *
 *   Synopsis  -  This program will not compile.
 *
 *   Objective -  To illustrate the fact that variables declared
 *                inside a block are unknown by the rest of the
 *                program.
 */

#include <stdio.h>
```

```
main()
{
    {
            int i;                              /* Note  1  */
            scanf ("%d", &i);
    }

    printf ("i is %d.\n", i);              /* Note  2  */
}
```

The function main() in this program consists of a declaration and two executable statements; one of the statements is a compound statement or a block. The variable declaration is contained within the inner block.

Note 1: The variable i is declared of type int. This variable is local to the block delimited by the inner pair of braces.

Note 2: This line causes a compile-time error because it references the variable i. Because i was declared within a block and this statement is outside that block, the variable i is unknown in this part of the program.

A Word about Style

Valid reasons for making declarations of variables inside blocks exist, but as a general stylistic rule, a program is more readable if all the declarations for a function appear in one place. Therefore, this facility of allowing auxiliary declarations in a block should be used with discretion.

2.3   The if and if-else Statements

A conditional statement allows a program to test a condition and then choose code to execute depending on the outcome of that test. The if statement is the conditional statement in C. Its syntax is

```
if (expression)
    statement;
```

The expression must be in parentheses and the statement can be any allowable C statement.

The expression is referred to as the *control expression*. Any expression can be used in that position; its value will be interpreted as either true or false. During execution, the expression is evaluated. If the value is nonzero, the expression is interpreted as true and is executed. If the value of the expression is zero, the statement is not executed.

The program if1.c in Example 2-4 gives a simple example of an `if` statement. In this program, the conditional expression for the `if` statement is

```
sum < 20
```

or "sum is less than 20." If the value of `sum` is indeed less than 20, the value of the expression is 1; otherwise, the value is 0. Other relational expressions are discussed in Section 2.4.

Example 2-4:   if1.c

```
/*                   if1.c
 *
 *    Synopsis  -  A decimal integer is input, added with CONST, and
 *                 the sum is output. If the sum is less than 20, a
 *                 message is output.
 *
 *    Objective -  Illustrates the simplest form of the if
 *                 statement.
 */

#define CONST 5
#include <stdio.h>

main()
{
        int sum, intvar;

        printf ("Enter a decimal integer: ");
        scanf ("%d", &intvar);
        sum = add_const(intvar);
        printf ("%d + %d is %d.\n", intvar, CONST, sum);

        if (sum < 20)                              /* Notes 1 and 2 */
                printf ("The number is small.\n");
}
/*************************************    add_const()    *******/
/*  add_const() returns the sum of its argument and CONST.
 */
add_const(intvar)
int intvar;
{
        return (intvar + CONST);
}
```

An overview of this program reveals two familiar preprocessor statements and two functions. In addition to the function main(), the function add_const() appears. It returns the value of CONST plus its argument. The conditional statement appears towards the end of main().

Note 1: The conditional if statement starts on this line and terminates on the next. The parentheses enclosing the control expression are a mandatory part of the syntax.

Note 2: The control expression in this example is a relational expression. As would be expected, it is true when the value of sum is less than 20 and false otherwise. That is, it has value 1 when sum is less than 20 and 0 otherwise.

Learning Activities

5. In the program if1.c,
    a. Circle the entire conditional statement.
    b. What is the control expression?
    c. For each of the input values below, state whether the control expression is true or false and give the output for the program.

Input value	Control expression	Program output
Example: 10	true	10 + 5 is 15. The number is small.
5	_____	_____
15	_____	_____
20	_____	_____

6. Execute the program if1.c to check your answers to question 1.

A Word about Style

General stylistic guidelines suggest placing the statement to be conditionally executed in an indented position on a separate line. This placement aids readability, but is not required by the compiler.

The `if-else` Statement

The program if1.c outputs a message only if the value of sum is less than 20. If you
want the program to output a different message (or take some different actions) for
any value of the variable sum, use the `if-else` statement. Its syntax is

```
if (expression)
        statement1;
else
        statement2;
```

If expression tests true (nonzero), statement1 is executed. If expression
tests false (zero), statement2 is executed.

The program in Example 2-5 is a modification of if1.c that prints a message for
any value of sum. It uses an `if-else` statement.

Example 2-5:   if2.c

```
/*                if2.c
 *
 *    Synopsis   -  A decimal integer is input, added to CONST, and
 *                  the sum is output. If the sum is less than 20,
 *                  one message is output.  If not, another message is
 *                  output.
 *
 *    Objective  -  Illustrates a simple form of the if-else
 *                  statement.
 */

#include <stdio.h>
#define CONST 5

main()
{
        int sum, intvar;

        printf ("Enter a decimal integer: ");
        scanf ("%d", &intvar);
        sum = add_const(intvar);
        printf ("%d + %d is %d.\n", intvar, CONST, sum);

        if (sum < 20)
                printf ("The number is small.\n");
        else                                            /* Note 1*/
                printf ("Oops, too big.\n");
}
```

```
/*************************************       add_const ()      *******/
/*  add_const () returns the sum of its argument and CONST.
 */
add_const (intvar)
int intvar;
{
        return (intvar + CONST);
}
```

This program is similar to that in Example 2-4 above. The only difference is the change from an `if` statement to an `if-else` statement at the end of the function main().

Note 1: This `else` is paired with the preceding `if`. When `sum` is greater than or equal to 20 the printf() call on the next line is executed. Stylistically, the token `else` should be on a separate line from the previous statement and should be indented as least as far as the `if`.

Learning Activities

7. In the program if2.c, for each of the given input values, state whether the control expression is true or false and give the output for the program.

	Input value	Control expression	Program output
Example:	10	true	10 + 5 is 15. The number is small.
	5	_____	_____
	15	_____	_____
	−20	_____	_____

8. Execute the program if2.c to check your answers to question 1.

The program if3.c in Example 2-6 illustrates the use of a numerical expression in an `if-else` statement. A function named odd() is defined. It takes a parameter of type `int` and returns the remainder when the parameter is divided by 2. That is, it returns the value 1 when the parameter is odd and 0 when the parameter is even. This value is tested in the main program with an `if` statement; 1 is interpreted as true since it is nonzero. The value 0 is false.

Example 2-6:   if3.c

```
/*                    if3.c
 *      Synopsis  -   The program prompts for and accepts input of a
 *                    decimal integer.  It then tests to see if that
 *                    integer is even or odd.  The results of the test
 *                    are output.
 *
 *      Objective -   Illustrates an if-else statement and the use
 *                    of a function call in a control expression.
 */

#include <stdio.h>

main()
{
        int intvar;

        printf ("Enter a decimal integer: ");
        scanf ("%d", &intvar);

        if ( odd(intvar) )                              /* Note 1 */
                printf ("%d is odd.\n", intvar);
        else                                            /* Note 2 */
                printf ("%d is even.\n", intvar);
}
/***************   odd()   ***********************************/
/*   Returns 1 if argument is odd, 0 otherwise.
 */
odd(int intvar)                                         /* Note 3 */
{
        return (intvar % 2 );                           /* Note 4 */
}
```

This program consists of two functions, the mandatory function named main() and a function named odd(). Scanning the code, we see that main() has one variable declared, a call to printf() for output, a call to scanf() for input, and an if-else statement. The function odd() consists of a single return statement.

Note 1: The expression in this if-else statement is a function call. C expects the function name to have a value when it returns from the call. The value is tested; a nonzero value causes the first printf() call to be executed.

Note 2: If the value returned from odd() is zero, the second printf() call is executed.

Note 3: The function odd() is declared. It takes a single parameter of type int.

Note 4: The value returned is the remainder when the parameter is divided by 2. That is, if the parameter is 1, 3, 5, 7, . . . , the remainder is 1 and the expression odd(intvar) evaluates to 1; it would test true in the control expression for the conditional. However, if the parameter is 0, 2, 4, 6, 8, . . . , the remainder is zero, odd(intvar) is zero, and the control expression would test false. Similar results would be obtained with negative input.

Learning Activities

9. In the program if3.c predict the output for each of the following inputs.

Input	Output
35	
-22	
0	

10. Execute the program if3.c to test your answers to question 1.

Compound `if-else` Statement

The statement after the else part of an if-else statement can be another if-else statement. This construct is called a nested or compound if-else statement. The syntax for this type of statement is:

```
if (expression)
   statement;
else if (expression)
   statement;
else if (expression)
   statement;
   .
   .
   .
else
   statement;
```

The effect is to create a multiway decision statement. Exactly one of the subsidiary statements will be executed. If one of the expressions in the list tests true, the accompanying statement will be executed. If none of the statements tests true, then the statement associated with the final else will be executed.

The program if.c in Example 2-7 illustrates a nested if-else statement. It plays a guessing game with the user.

Example 2-7:   if.c

```
/*              if.c
 *
 *   Synopsis  -  Plays a one-time guessing game with the user. The
 *               user enters a number, which is compared with TARGET.
 *               The computer issues a diagnostic message and then
 *               the correct result.
 *
 *   Objective -  Illustrates the if-else statement.
 */

#include <stdio.h>
#define TARGET 17

main()
{
        int guess;

        printf ("I'm thinking of an integer.\n");
        printf ("Try to guess it now. ");

        scanf ("%d", &guess);

        if (guess < TARGET)                             /* Note 1 */
                printf ("Too low.\n");
        else if (guess > TARGET)                        /* Note 2 */
                printf ("Too high.\n");
        else                                            /* Note 3 */
                printf ("You guessed it!\n");

        printf ("The number was %d.\n", TARGET);
}
```

An overview of this program reveals a single function named main(). One variable of type int is declared. Calls to printf() for output are followed by a call to scanf() for input. A compound if-else statement follows.

Note 1: The first expression in the compound if-else statement is the relational expression (guess < TARGET). If it is true, the following printf() call is executed and the if-else statement is terminated. In this case, the next statement to be executed is the call to printf() at the end of the program. If the expression (guess < TARGET) is not true, execution continues after the first else.

Note 2: The second expression to be tested is the expression (guess > TARGET) that appears on this line. If it is true, the printf() call on the next line is executed. This terminates the execution of the compound `if-else` statement and control passes to the call to printf() at the end of the program. If the expression (`guess > TARGET`) is not true, control stays with the compound `if-else` statement.

Note the indentation for the compound `if-else` statement. This style is one of the accepted ways of formatting this statement. Other methods of formatting are also acceptable; they usually involve more indentation. The important point is that this is a compound `if-else` statement and only one of the statements will be executed.

Note 3: If neither of the above expressions tests true, then `guess` is equal to `TARGET`. In this case the statement following this `else` will be executed before the final printf() call.

Learning Activities

11. What must the input have been if the third line of output from the program if.c is

    ```
    "You guessed it!"
    ```

12. What is the maximum number of output lines from if.c? What is the minimum number of lines? Give a reason for your answer.

In the case of a statement with the syntax

```
if (expression1)
  if (expression2)
        ifstatement;
  else
        elsestatement;
```

the pairing of the `else` is with the closest `if` without a corresponding `else`. In the above case, nothing is executed when `expression1` tests false. If `expression2` tests false, `elsestatement` is executed. If a programmer wishes to have the `else` paired with the first `if`, braces must be added to create a block for the inner `if` as shown below:

```
if (expression1) {
    if (expression2)
        ifstatement;
}
else
        elsestatement;
```

In this case, when `expression1` is false, `elsestatement` is executed. The program in Example 2-8 has this type of structure. The program illustrates a simple error check on input. Code like this might be included as part of a larger program in which execution would continue once the input was validated.

Example 2-8:   errorchk.c

```c
/*                   errorchk.c
 *
 *   Synopsis  -  Prompts for and accepts input of an integer.
 *                The integer is tested to see that it meets the
 *                stated criteria.  If it doesn't, an error
 *                message is output.  If all criteria are met,
 *                execution terminates silently.
 *
 *   Objective -  Illustrates the necessary grouping of if and
 *                associated else statements.
 */
#include <stdio.h>

main()
{
        int inputint;

        printf ("Enter a positive even ");
        printf ("number that is less than 20.\n");
        scanf ("%d", &inputint);

        if (inputint < 20) {                             /* Note 1 */
                if ( odd(inputint) )
                   printf ("Sorry that number wasn't even.\n");
                else if (inputint <= 0)
                   printf ("That number wasn't positive.\n");
        }                                                /* Note 2 */
        else
                printf ("That number was too big.\n");
}

/******************************************  odd()   *********/
/*    odd() returns a 1 if intvar is odd and a 0 if not.
 */

odd (int intvar)                                         /* Note 3 */
{
        return(intvar % 2);
}
```

This program consists of two functions, main() and odd(). The function main() consists of a printf() call followed by a scanf() call. The remainder of this function is a combination `if-else` statement. The function odd() consists of a single `return` statement.

Note 1: The `if-else` structure begins on this line. The brace is necessary to create a self-contained block for the inner `if-else` statement so that there is no possibility of pairing the second `else` with the third `if`. The code could be restructured to avoid this problem entirely, but restructuring would not address the concept of matching `if`s and `else`s.

Note 2: The brace ends the block so that the `else` on the next line is paired with the first `if` in the program.

Note 3: The function odd() is identical to the function odd() in previous examples. This is an example of a tool that can be moved from program to program without change.

Learning Activity

13. Consider the program errorchk.c with the following changes. Remove the braces from the lines containing the comments /* Note 1 */ and /* Note 2 */. Which of the following statements would be true?

    a. It would no longer compile.
    b. If the input was 4, the output would be
        "That number wasn't positive."
    c. If the input was −1, the output would be
        "That number wasn't positive."
    d. If the input was 8, the output would be
        "That number was too big."

2.4   Relational Operators and Expressions

We saw some of the relational expressions in use in the last section. The relational operators are:

<=	is less than or equal to
>=	is greater than or equal to
==	is equal to
!=	is not equal to
>	is greater than
<	is less than

For example, the expression

        x == 3

could be tested to determine whether x is equal to 3. If x is 3, the value of the expression $(x == 3)$ is 1, which is nonzero and interpreted as true. If x is not 3, the value of $(x == 3)$ is zero or false. The expression

        3 == 2 + 1

would always test true while the expression

        3 != 2 + 1   or 3 is not equal to 2 + 1

would always test false.

    The actual value assigned to an expression formed with a relational operator is 1 if the relation is true and 0 if it is false. The fact that the relational expressions actually have values is illustrated in the program relation.c in Example 2-9.

Example 2-9: relation.c

```
/*                    relation.c
 *
 *    Synopsis   -   Prints out values of relational expressions.
 *
 *    Objective  -   To illustrate that relational expressions are
 *                   given the values of 1 for true and 0 for false.
 */

#include <stdio.h>

main()
{
        int x = 3;
                                                /* Note 1 */
        printf ("The value of (x == 3) is %d.\n", x == 3);
        printf ("The value of (x != 3) is %d.\n", x != 3);

        printf ("The value of (3*x - 4 <= 3) is %d.\n",
                               3*x - 4 <=3);

        printf ("The value of (x >= 3) is %d.\n", x >= 3);
        printf ("The value of (2*x %% 3 > 3) is %d.\n", /* Note 2 */
                               2*x % 3 > 3);

        printf ("The value of (25 / (2*x) < 3) is %d.\n",
                               25 /(2*x) < 3);
}
```

This program has a single variable named `x` of type `int`. The remainder of the program consists of printing out the decimal values of expressions involving `x` in conjunction with relational expressions.

Note 1: In each of the printf() calls, the expression with the relational operator is evaluated and its decimal value is output. The following points are important to understand.

1. Each expression has a value of either 1 (true) or 0 (false).
2. The expressions can involve arithmetic operators as well as the relational operators.
3. The precedence of all the arithmetic operators is higher than that of any of the relational operators, thus eliminating the need for additional parentheses.

Note 2: The `%%` in the control string to printf() is the conversion specification for the output of a single `%`.

Learning Activities

14. Predict the value of each expression output by relation.c. Run the program to verify your predictions. Make sure you resolve any differences between your predictions and the actual output.

15. Consider the final printf() call in relation.c. What would be the output if the parentheses were removed from both occurrences of `2*x` in that statement?

A Word of Warning

One common mistake made by new C programmers, especially those who have previously programmed in Pascal, is illustrated in the program mistake1.c of Example 2-10.

Example 2-10:   mistake1.c

```
/*              mistake1.c
 *
 *    Synopsis   -   Accepts input of a value of type int and outputs
 *                   messages about its value.
 *
 *    Objective  -   To further illustrate that an assignment is
 *                   an expression.
 */

#include <stdio.h>
```

```
main()
{
        int intvar;

        printf ("Enter a decimal value : ");
        scanf ("%d", &intvar);

        if ( intvar = 3)                              /* Note 1 */
                printf ("It's THREE!!\n");

        printf ("The value of intvar is %d.\n", intvar);

}
```

This program has a single variable `intvar` of type `int`. The printf() and scanf() calls establish a value for `intvar`. Then a conditional statement with an expression involving `intvar` is executed. Finally, the value of `intvar` is output by the last call to printf().

Note 1: This program outputs the line

```
        It's THREE!!
```

for any input value of `intvar`. The mistake lies in the fact that the single equal sign, =, does assignment and an assignment expression takes on the value of the quantity being assigned. In this case the value assigned to `intvar` is 3, which is nonzero and therefore tests true. The printf() call will always execute and the value of `intvar` will always be 3 after that statement. The programmer may have meant

```
        if (intvar == 3)
                printf ("It's THREE!!\n");
```

instead. This is an easy mistake to make and a hard bug to find.

Learning Activities

16. Execute the program mistake1.c with several different inputs to make sure that you understand what is happening.

17. Predict the output from the following program. How many lines will be output?

```
/*                      exrcse2.c
 *
 *      Synopsis  -   Tests relational expressions, and
 *                    produces appropriate messages.
 *
 *      Objective -   Provides practice with relational
 *                    expressions.
 */
```

```
#include <stdio.h>

main()
{
        int x = 2,
            y = 4;

        if ( x = 3 )
            printf ("it's three!\n");
        else if (x = 4)
            printf ("it's four!\n");

        printf ("The value of x is %d.\n", x);

}
```

Operator Precedence

The relational operators have lower precedence than any of the arithmetic operators, but higher precedence than assignment operators. For example, in the expression

        4 <= z + 3

the subexpression z + 3 would be evaluated first. The resulting value would then be compared with 4. However, the expression

        4 <=   x=z+3

is illegal in C. Because assignment has a lower precedence than either <= or +, the compiler interprets this expression as an attempt to assign the value z+3 to the expression 4 <= x. This is not allowed because 4 <= x does not have a storage location in memory (it is not an lvalue). This error is a compile-time error. That is, it is caught by the compiler.

Note that an assignment can be done within a relational expression with the use of added parentheses. In the expression

        4 <= (x = z +3)

the assignment of z + 3 to the variable x is done before the < = operator is considered. The comparison would be made between the value of x after the assignment and the value 4.

Another aspect to be aware of when using relational expressions is that an expression like

        3 < x < 7

is evaluated as

        ((3 < x) < 7)

For example, if the current value of x is 0, the expression 3 < x is 0. The expression 3 < x < 7 becomes 0 < 7. Because 0 is less than 7, the expression ((3 < x) < 7) or (3 < x < 7) is true when x is 0. By similar arguments, 3 < x < 7 is also true when x has the values –1, 3, 4, 7, 10, or any value of type int. In fact, the expression (3 < x < 7) is true for any value of x. Expressions like this one should be avoided in C code.

Learning Activity

18. Predict the output of the following program:

```
/*                      exrcse1.c
 *
 *      Synopsis  -     Prints out values for several expressions
 *                      involving combinations of relational
 *                      operators.
 *
 *      Objective -     To give practice with the precedence
 *                      of the relational expressions.
 */

#include <stdio.h>

main()
{
        int x = 4, y = 2;

        printf ("The value of 3<x<y is %d.\n", 3<x<y );
        printf ("The value of x<3<y is %d.\n", x<3<y );
        printf ("The value of 3<x<1 is %d.\n", 3<x<1 );
        printf ("The value of 3<x<2 is %d.\n", 3<x<2 );
        printf ("The value of 3<(x=y) is %d.\n", 3<(x=y) );
        printf ("The value of y=x<4 is %d.\n", y=x<4 );
}
```

2.5 The while Loop

Iteration is an important part of programming languages and programs. For example, in Example 2-7 where the computer played a guessing game with the user, the game would have been more interesting if the user had been able to continue playing until guessing the number.

A while loop can be used to allow this continued interchange between user and computer. The syntax of C's while loop is as follows:

```
while (expression)
      statement;
```

The parentheses around the expression are mandatory. The statement can be a compound statement, a conditional statement, another while loop, or any of the other legal C statements that we will discuss.

When the while loop is executed, the expression inside the parentheses is evaluated for the first time. If the value of expression is nonzero, statement is executed and expression is evaluated again. The statement is executed each time `expression` tests true (nonzero). The first time `expression` evaluates to false (zero), the loop terminates.

The program while.c in Example 2-11 is an extension of the guessing game introduced in Example 2-7. In this version the user continues to play until guessing the correct number.

Example 2-11:   while.c

```
/*              while.c
 *
 *    Synopsis  -  Plays a guessing game with the user.  The user
 *                 is asked to enter choices until guessing the
 *                 computer's number.
 *
 *    Objective -  Illustrates the while statement and compound
 *                 statements in  C.
 */

#include <stdio.h>
#define TARGET 17
#define TRUE 1                             /* Note 1 */
#define FALSE 0                            /* Note 1 */

main()
{
        int guess, correct;

        correct = FALSE;
        printf ("I'm thinking of a number.\n");
        while (correct == FALSE) {         /* Notes 2 and 3 */
                printf ("Try to guess it now. ");
                scanf ("%d", &guess);
                if (guess < TARGET)
                        printf ("Too low!\n");
                else if (guess > TARGET)
                        printf ("Too high!\n");
                else {
                        printf ("You guessed it!\n");
                        correct = TRUE;
                }
        }                                  /* Note 4 */
}
```

The overview of this program reveals two variables of type `int`. An assignment statement initializes the variable `correct` and a call to printf() starts the game. The major part of the code is contained within a `while` loop. The statement consists of a call to printf(), a call to scanf(), and a compound `if-else` statement. This last component is very much like the compound `if-else` statement in the program if.c in Example 2-7.

Note 1: These preprocessor statements define values for the identifiers TRUE and FALSE for the rest of the program. With these definitions, it is possible to simulate Boolean variables. An `int` variable named `correct` is declared and is used as a flag. Although the user's guess is wrong, the value of `correct` remains FALSE. When the number is guessed, the value of `correct` is changed to TRUE.

Note 2: The relational expression (`correct` == FALSE) serves as the test expression in the `while` loop. The expression is evaluated and if it is nonzero (true) the loop is entered. The expression must appear in parentheses.

Note 3: The statement for this `while` loop is a compound statement. Notice the placement of the opening brace for this block. This placement is preferred by many C programmers who have learned to look at the right end of a line of code for an indication of what is coming next. Another acceptable placement for the opening brace is on a line by itself directly under the 'w' in `while`.

Note 4: Notice the placement of the closing brace for each block. In this programming style, the closing brace is positioned in the same column as the first letter in `while`. Because the opening and closing braces for a compound statement are single characters rather than complete words, be careful where you place them. They need to be easily visible in the code.

Learning Activities

19. In while.c, what is the statement associated with the final `else` in the compound `if-else` statement? How many statements make up this compound statement?

20. Consider the following input for while.c:

           3   10   15   50   25   20   17

   a. How many times is the following statement executed?

```
        printf ("Try to guess it now. ");
```

   b. How many times is the following expression evaluated?

```
        (correct == FALSE)
```

Using `getchar()` and `putchar()` in a `while` Loop

Suppose we want to write a program that takes input from standard input (usually the keyboard) and copies that input back to standard output (usually the terminal screen). A program with this property is called a *filter*. Two utilities, getchar() and putchar(), are provided to input and output a single character from the terminal. The utility getchar() reads a character from the keyboard and returns the corresponding integer value. The utility putchar() takes an argument of type int and outputs the corresponding ASCII character on the terminal screen. The utilities getchar() and putchar() are usually implemented as macros and therefore involve less overhead than calls to scanf() and printf() to do the same thing.

The program in Example 2-12 reads input from standard input and echoes that input to standard output.* To use this program, a user must be able to signal the end of the input from the terminal. On a UNIX system, the end of the input file can be signaled by typing CONTROL-D as the first character on a new input line. On an MS-DOS system, the end of the input file is signaled by typing CONTROL-Z.

When getchar() senses the end-of-file, it returns a special value to the program. This value is usually –1. In the file stdio.h, a preprocessor statement is used to make the association between the value –1 and the identifier EOF, which is a mnemonic for end-of-file.

The program inout1.c in Example 2-12 copies its input to its output. To terminate the program, the symbol for end-of-file for the system must be signaled from the keyboard.

 Example 2-12:   inout1.c

```
/*                  inout1.c
 *
 *    Synopsis  -   Takes input from the keyboard and echoes that
 *                  input back to the terminal.
 *
 *    Objective -   Illustrates another use of the while loop and
 *                  leads into the discussion of inout2.c.
 */

#include <stdio.h>

main()          int  a ~ 27/5;
{
        int iochar;                             /* Note 1 */

        iochar = getchar();                     /* Note 2 */
        while (iochar != EOF) {                 /* Note 3 */
```

* Most filters will modify the input data before it is output.

```
        putchar(iochar);                    /* Note 4 */
        iochar = getchar();                 /* Note 5 */
    }
}
```

The executable statements for this program consist of an assignment statement followed by a while loop. The statement for the while loop is compound and has a call to putchar() and an assignment statement. The only variable is of type int.

Note 1: The variable iochar (which stands for input/output character) is declared to be of type int. It is used to receive the input characters returned by getchar(). The type int is necessary because getchar() returns a value of type int.

Note 2: Input is done with a call to getchar(). The returned value is stored in the variable iochar.

Note 3: The value of iochar is compared with EOF. When end-of-file is signaled from the keyboard, getchar() returns the value EOF (defined as −1 in stdio.h) to the executing program. When the value of iochar is not EOF, the loop is entered and the compound statement is executed. When iochar is equal to EOF, the while loop terminates.

Note 4: The macro putchar() is used to output the character stored in iochar.

Note 5: Another character is read from the keyboard. This character is compared with EOF at the top of the while loop.

A Word of Warning

It is a common error to use a type char with a call to getchar(). Because getchar() returns a value of type int, use a variable of type int in these assignment statements.

Learning Activities

21. Find out how to signal the end-of-file from the command line on your system.
22. Inspect the file stdio.h on your system. Find the line where EOF is defined.
23. *C by Discovery* Execute the program inout1.c. Is the result what you expected? Describe the keyboard interaction with the program. What character must you enter in order to get the input to echo back?*

---

* This activity deals with the buffered input that is encountered on UNIX and PC systems. The program output may not appear until after the user presses the Return key.

Note that in the previous program, the input is done in two places, before entering the `while` loop and again at the bottom of the `while` loop. Using the concept that, in C, an assignment is an expression and therefore has a value, we can combine the two input statements into one that occurs exactly at the top of the `while` loop. The expression

```
iochar = getchar()
```

permits a character to be entered from the terminal and assigns the integer value of that character to the variable `iochar`. The value of the assignment expression is the value assigned to `iochar`. This value can be immediately compared with EOF with an expression like

```
(iochar = getchar()) != EOF
```

The assignment is made and the value of `iochar` is compared to EOF. The resulting statement is a relational expression that has the value 1 when `iochar` is not the same as EOF and the value 0 when it is the same. This is the expression that drives the `while` loop in the program inout2.c in Example 2-13. The program again echoes its input to its output, but does input in only one place, in the expression at the top of the `while` loop. A `while` loop similar to the one in inout2.c is commonly used in programs that need to read through all their input one character at a time.

Example 2-13:   inout2.c

```
/*                  inout2.c
 *
 *    Synopsis   -   Takes input from the keyboard and echoes that
 *                   input back to the terminal.
 *
 *    Objective  -   Illustrates the use of an assignment statement as
 *                   part of the test expression in a while loop.
 */

#include <stdio.h>

main()
{
        int iochar;                                        /* Note 1 */

        while ( (iochar = getchar()) != EOF)               /* Note 2 */
                putchar (iochar);                          /* Note 3 */
}
```

Note that this program is shorter than the last one. The variable iochar is again declared as type int. However, now the executable code consists of a single while loop whose inner statement is a single call to putchar().

Note 1: Again, iochar must be of type int because it is used to store the int value returned by getchar().

Note 2: The relational expression compares the value EOF with the value of the assignment expression

```
iochar = getchar()
```

A character is input from the command line by getchar() and is stored in iochar by the assignment operator, =. The value given to the assignment expression is the value input by getchar(). If the end-of-file is sensed, this value will be EOF and the loop will terminate. Otherwise, the call to putchar() will be executed and another value will be input at the top of the loop.

Note 3: The call to putchar() causes the character stored in iochar to be output to the terminal. This statement is not executed when the end-of-file is sensed.

C accepts this type of concise and cryptic source code. There are different opinions about the desirability of programming in this style. Most people would find inout2.c harder to read than inout1.c the first time they see it. However, much of the existing C source code is written in this idiomatic style, so C programmers expect code like this. Some compilers are able to better optimize this code and produce shorter and more efficient object code.

Learning Activities

24. Which of the example programs in Chapter 1 and Chapter 2 are filters?

25. Assuming that the input to the program inout2.c consists of the following four characters,

```
ABC<EOF signal>
```

trace execution of the program by evaluating each expression for the given input value. The trace for the input of the 'A' is shown.

Expressions	Input Values			
	A	B	C	EOF signal
getchar()	65			
iochar = getchar()	65			
iochar	65			
iochar != EOF	1			
((iochar = getchar()) != EOF)	1			

26. Assume that `iochar` has been declared as a variable of type `int`. What are the input values, if any, that will terminate the following `while` loops? If you think any of the examples will produce errors, state the reason for the error.

```
while ( (iochar = getchar()) != '9')     _____
        putchar (iochar);
while ( (iochar = getchar()) != 9)       _____
        putchar (iochar);
while ( (iochar = getchar()) != 64 )     _____
        putchar (iochar);
while ( (iochar = getchar()) != '64')    _____
        putchar (iochar);
```

2.6 Logical Operators and Expressions

When a test must be made on two or more conditions in an `if-else` statement or in a loop, expressions can be combined by using the logical operations in C. They are listed below:

`!`	logical not
`&&`	logical and
`||`	logical or

The logical and, `&&`, is a binary operator; it is used to combine two expressions into one. The syntax for using `&&` to combine two expressions is as follows:

```
expression1 && expression2
```

where `expression1` and `expression2` can be any legal C expressions. The expression involving `&&` is true (nonzero) when both `expression1` and `expression2` are nonzero. C only evaluates as much of the expression as necessary to determine the truth value.

A truth table can be used to represent the values of an expression formed with a logical and.

expression1	expression2	(expression1 && expression2)
true	true	true
true	false	false
false	—	false

To evaluate the expression involving the logical and, `expression1` is evaluated first. If it has a nonzero (true) value, then `expression2` is evaluated. If both expressions have nonzero values, then (`expression1 && expression2`) is given a value of 1 or true; otherwise, the value of (expression1 && expression2) is 0 or false. However, if expression1 has a value of 0 (false), then the logical and expression, (expression1 && expression2), is given a value of 0 or false; expression2 is not evaluated.

Note that the truth table contains only three possible combinations for the truth values of expression1 and expression2. The cases

expression1	*expression2*
false	true
false	false

have been combined into the single case

expression1	*expression2*
false	—

This was done to emphasize the fact that the C compiler only checks the second expression when it is necessary to determine the value of the logical and expression. The logical and expression is false when expression1 is false; the value of expression2 is not checked. Some interesting consequences of this fact are presented in Example 2-14 and the exercises.

The logical or, | |, is also used to combine two expressions. Its syntax is:

```
expression1 || expression2
```

where expression1 and expression2 must be legal C expressions. No other requirement is imposed on them. A logical or expression is true if either expression1 or expression2 or both are nonzero. Again, C only evaluates as much as necessary to determine the truth value.

The truth table values of expression1, expression2 and expression1 || expression2 follow:

expression1	*expression2*	*(expression1 || expression2)*
true	—	true
false	true	true
false	false	false

To evaluate a logical or expression, expression1 is evaluated first. If it has a nonzero value, (expression1 || expression2) is given a value of 1 (true). In this case, expression2 is not evaluated. If expression1 has a 0 value, expression2 is evaluated. If it is nonzero, the logical or expression is given a value of 1 (true); if expression2 is 0, the logical or expression is given a value of 0 or false.

Again, the table contains only three of the four possible combinations of the truth values of expression1 and expression2. The C compiler only evaluates the second expression when its value is necessary to determine the value of the logical or statement.

A third logical operation is the logical not (!). It takes a single operand. Its use in an expression has the syntax

```
!expression1
```

When this expression is evaluated, the value of expression1 is computed. If expression1 has a nonzero (true) value, the value of !expression1 is 0 (false). If expression1 evaluates to 0 (false), !expression1 evaluates to 1 or true. The following truth table illustrates this:

expression1	*!expression1*
true	false
false	true

The program logic1.c in Example 2-14 outputs the values of some logical expressions and illustrates their syntax. It does not provide an example of the use of the logical operations. That will be done later.

Example 2-14:   logic1.c

```
/*              logic1.c
 *
 *   Synopsis  -  Outputs a table of values of some logical
 *                expressions and examples of the effect of
 *                evaluating the logical expressions on embedded
 *                variable operations.
 *
 *   Objective -  To illustrate syntax and evaluation of logical
 *                expressions.
 */

#include <stdio.h>

main()
{
        int  i = 3,
             j = 0;

        printf ("Examples of the logical expressions\n");
        printf ("-----------------------------------\n");

                                                    /* Note 1 */
        printf ("    i && j              %d\n",  i && j );
                                                    /* Note 2 */
        printf ("    i || j              %d\n",  i || j );   /*
```

```
                                                            /*Note 3 */
    printf ("        !i                  %d\n",       !i    );
    printf ("        !j                  %d\n",       !j    );
                                                          /* Note 4 */
    printf ("(i > 0) && (j < 7)     %d\n", (i > 0) && (j < 7) );
    printf ("(i < 0) || (j < 7)     %d\n", (i < 0) || (j < 7) );
    printf ("!(i > 5) || (j > 0)    %d\n", !(i > 5) || (j > 0));

    printf ("\nExamples of the effects on the variables\n");
    printf ("-----------------------------------------\n");
    printf ("Initially,   \t\ti   %d,\t\tj   %d\n", i, j);
    printf ("i || j++     %d,",   i || j++);       /* Note 5 */
    printf ("\t\ti   %d,\t\tj   %d\n", i, j);
    printf ("i && j++     %d,",   i && j++);       /* Note 6 */
    printf ("\t\ti   %d,\t\tj   %d\n", i, j);
}
```

This program contains two variables of type int that are initialized when they are declared. The remainder of the program consists of printf() calls. Most of the printf() calls consist of the output of the values of some examples of logical expressions involving the variables.

Note 1: The value of the simple logical and expression i && j is output in decimal. The possible values for the expression are 0 and 1. In this specific case the value of 0 would be assigned because the value of j is 0 or false.

Note 2: The value of the expression i || j is output in decimal. Because the value of i is 3 (not 0), this expression is given the value 1 without even looking at the value of j.

Note 3: This time the value of !i is output. Because i is nonzero, !i is 0.

Note 4: In the next three printf() calls, the expressions whose values are output involve both logical operators and relational operators. Parentheses are inserted to indicate which operations are evaluated first. The unary operator, !, has higher precedence than the binary operators. You are asked to predict the output of the rest of the program in the Learning Activities.

Note 5: In the next two printf() calls, the value of a logical or expression is output along with the subsequent values of the variables i and j. Notice that in the second operand of the logical or, i || j++, the increment operator is applied to j. Remember that with the logical or, if the first operand is nonzero, the second operand is not evaluated. Therefore, the increment operator has no effect since the expression j++ is not evaluated. Programmers need to be aware of this consequence of the method of evaluating logical operations.

Note 6: A similar situation exists in the next two lines of code except that the logical operator is &&. Now the second operand will only be evaluated when the first operator is nonzero. Therefore, it is only in this case that the variable j is incremented.

Learning Activities

27. a. Predict the output of the program logic1.c by filling in the blanks below:

```
Examples of the logical expressions
    i && j                       0
    i || j                       1
    !i                           0
    !j                           _____
(i > 0) && (j < 7)               _____
(i < 0) || (j < 7)               _____
!(i > 5) || (j > 0)              _____
Examples of the effects on the variables
Initially,              i  3,              j _____
i || j++ _____,         i _____,           j _____
i && j++ _____,         i _____,           j _____
```

b. Execute the program to verify your predictions. Make sure you resolve any differences between your prediction and the actual output.

28. a. Predict the output of logic1.c for the following values of i and j:

```
    i        j
    0        7
    8        2
    0        0
```

b. Modify the program logic1.c to interactively ask for and input values for i and j. Execute the program with the three inputs from part a to verify your predictions.

c. Execute your modified program with different inputs until you see the pattern and are clear about the concepts.

Precedence of the Logical Operators

Among the logical operators, the logical not has higher precedence than the logical and, which has higher precedence than the logical or. The two binary operators are both left associative. That is, an expression like

```
    i || j || k
```

is evaluated as indicated by the following insertion of parentheses:

```
    ( (i || j) || k)
```

That is, i || j is evaluated first. Then its result is combined in the second logical or operator with k.

An Example

The program tabs.c in Example 2-15 gives an example of how to combine the concepts that we have studied to write a simple but useful program in a structured way.

The problem addressed by this program is to copy a program's input to its output but to replace every tab character and every CTRL-A with five spaces. There is no new element of the language C in this program, but we will discuss the reasons for many of the statements as well as many design decisions that were made. This is another example of a filter.

Example 2-15:   tabs.c

```
/*                 tabs.c
 *
 *    Synopsis  -  A filter that processes its input by replacing
 *                 every tab character and ^A character with TABSTOP
 *                 spaces.
 *
 *    Objective -  Illustrates the use of a logical operator in a
 *                 structured program that contains a useful tool.
 */
#include <stdio.h>
#define TAB        '\t'
#define ALTTAB     1                          /*  CTRL-A in ASCII */
#define TABSTOP    5
#define SPACE      ' '                /* the ASCII space character */

main()
{
        int iochar;

        /*  The following while loop processes each input
         *  character.  If the character is one of the two
         *  designated tab characters, the function processtabs()
         *  is called. Otherwise, the character is output with
         *  putchar().
         */

        while ((iochar = getchar()) != EOF)
                if ( (iochar == TAB) || (iochar == ALTTAB) )
                        processtabs(TABSTOP, SPACE);
                else
                        putchar (iochar);
}
```

```
/********************************** processtabs () **********/
/* The function processtabs() will output tabstop
 * characters every time it is called.
 */

processtabs (tabstop, character)
int tabstop, character;
{
        int colcount = 0;

        while (colcount++ < tabstop)
                putchar (character);
}
```

The program consists of two functions, main() and processtabs(). Since there are no new C constructs in this program, the usual notes have not been included. However, several points about the use of the C language are illustrated with this program:

1. The function main() consists of a familiar `while` loop that works through all the input. The input is done only at the top of the `while` loop. The input value is assigned to `iochar` and is tested against EOF. The `while` loop executes until the end-of-file is sensed.

2. Inside the `while` loop, each character is compared to both TAB and ALTTAB. If one of the tab characters has been input, the function processtabs() is called to output the desired number of spaces. Otherwise, the input character is echoed back to the terminal by putchar().

3. The function processtabs() is a tool. It has one purpose: to produce some output. It is passed parameters indicating which characters and how many of them to output and then does its job and nothing more. It doesn't access any variables outside its own code, and has no restrictions on identifier names that must be used. It also doesn't check the input characters or guess in any other way at the programmer's intent in calling its code. It is important for its use as a tool that this function does not do any input or make any decisions itself about which or how many characters to output. The function code is complete in itself. It could be used in any program as it is.

4. Notice the constant definitions. The definitions of TAB and ALTTAB allow easy modification of the program to output the spaces for other characters instead of just the tab character and CTRL-A. The definitions of TABSTOP and SPACE also allow ease of modification. A modification of TABSTOP changes the number of spaces that are output every time the function processtabs() is called. A modification to SPACE changes the character that is output.

2.7 The for Loop

The second iterative loop in C is the for loop. Its syntax is as follows:

```
for (initialization; test; processing)
        statement;
```

where for is the keyword and initialization, test, and processing are expressions. Any or all of the three expressions may be omitted, but the opening and closing parentheses and the semicolons must be included.

The initialization expression is evaluated once as the loop is entered. It is generally used to initialize variables for the loop. The test expression is evaluated as a condition for continuing the loop. If the value of test is nonzero, statement is executed; if the value is zero, the execution of the for loop is terminated. The test expression is evaluated every time execution control reaches the top of the loop.

The expression processing does bottom-of-the-loop processing. This expression is evaluated after statement is executed each time through the loop.

The execution of the for loop can be diagrammed as follows:

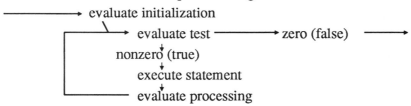

Note that a code segment equivalent to the above for loop can be written with the while loop as follows:

```
initialization;
while (test) {
        statement;
        processing;
}
```

Here, the statements initialization; and processing; are the expression statements that are formed by placing a semicolon after an expression. Executing these statements is the same as evaluating the expression.

Simple examples of the for loop appear in the program for.c in Example 2-16. The three variations of the for loop in the program illustrate some of the different ways the expressions can be used.

Example 2-16:   for.c

```
/*                      for.c
 *
 *      Synopsis  -   Three for loops. The first for loop counts by
```

```
*                       1; the second for loop counts by 2; the third
*                       for loop calculates a factorial.
*
*    Objective   - To illustrate the syntax and the flexibility of
*                  the for loop.
*/

#include <stdio.h>
#define LAST 7

main()
{

      int count,
          factorial;

      printf ("Counting.\n");
      for (count = 1; count < LAST; count++)   /* Note 1 */
              printf ("%d\n", count);

      printf ("\nCounting by two.\n");
      for (count = 0; count < 2*LAST; printf ("%d\n", count += 2))
      ;                                         /* Notes 2 and 3 */

      printf ( "\nCalculating factorials.\n");
      for ( factorial = 1, count = 1; count <= 7;
                      factorial *= count++)
      ;                                         /* Note 4 */
      printf ("%d! is %d.\n", LAST, factorial);
}
```

This program consists of the single function named main(). Two variables of type int are declared. The program consists of some printf() calls and three variations of a for loop.

Note 1: This is the simplest example of a for loop. The initialization expression consists of the assignment expression, count = 1. The assignment is made at the beginning of the loop execution.

The test expression is count < LAST. It is evaluated to determine whether the loop will execute or not. If the value is nonzero (true), the loop will execute. If it is zero, the loop terminates.

The bottom of the loop processing consists of the expression count++. It is evaluated (count is incremented) after the loop statement is executed. The printf() call serves as the statement in this for loop.

Note 2: In the second for loop, the initialization expression is again a simple assignment. The test expression,

```
count < 2*LAST
```

is somewhat more complicated than in the first loop. Any expression can be placed in this position. This expression tests false and the loop terminates when `count` is equal to `2*LAST`.

The bottom of the loop `processing` can be any expression that has a value. In this example, the fact that the printf() library function returns a value makes this a legitimate expression. The evaluation of this expression causes the printf() function to be executed. Note that `count` is incremented by 2 when this statement is evaluated so that the loop "counts by 2."

Note 3: The semicolon on this line is the null statement. The syntax of the `for` loop requires that a statement be included, but in this case, since the bottom of the loop `processing` includes a call to printf(), no additional code is needed. The semicolon serves as the statement required by the syntax for this loop.

Note 4: Look at the `initialization` expression in this `for` loop. It consists of everything from the opening parenthesis to the first semicolon. That is, the `initialization` expression consists of

```
factorial = 1, count = 1
```

This expression is an example of a *comma expression*; the comma is the *comma operator* in C. It signifies sequential execution of the expressions before and after the comma. The expression on the left is evaluated first; its value is discarded, but the assignment is done. Then the expression on the right is evaluated. The value of a comma expression is the value of the expression on the right.

In this loop, the bottom of the loop `processing` is the compound assignment statement that multiplies the variable `factorial` by the increasing value of `count`. Again, the semicolon or the null statement is the statement required in the `for` loop. The function printf() is called once, after the `for` loop terminates.

Notice how flexible the `for` loop is. A loop control variable may increase or decrease by any value. The variable can change by addition, subtraction, multiplication, division or taking the modulus. However, it is not necessary to use a loop control variable. For example, the loop

```
for (;;)
    printf ("still going.\n");
```

is an infinite loop. The `initialization`, `test`, and `processing` expressions are all optional in the `for` loop and can be omitted, as in this example. No initialization is done, no test is made for continuing, and no processing is done at the bottom of the loop. The loop just keeps on executing.

A Word about Style

The comma has syntactic uses other than that of the comma operator. It is used in declarations, initializations, and passing parameters to functions. Programmers should be careful not to use the comma operator where it might be mistaken for one of these other uses of the comma.

Learning Activities

29. Write a `for` loop that outputs the following values:

    ```
    1, 2, 4, 8, 16, 32, 64, 128, 256, 512
    ```
    a. Use a printf() call as the statement in the `for` loop.

    b. Use a null statement as the statement in the `for` loop.

30. Write two different `for` loops that output the following values:

    ```
    8, 7, 6, 5, 4, 3, 2, 1
    ```
31. Write a `for` loop that outputs the first 10 positive integers in the following format:

    ```
    1       2       3       4       5
    6       7       8       9       10
    ```

    Use two variables, one for the value to be output and one as a column counter. Initialize both variables in the initialization expression by using the `comma` operator.

2.8   Making C Readable—Programming Style

By now we have discussed enough of the language to address the issue of programming style. C uses many combinations of symbols like ++ and −− for automatic increment and decrement and &&, ||, and ! for the logical operators. Because of this and other reasons that we shall see, it is very easy to write unreadable code in C. It is only slightly more difficult to make it readable. It is important to give thought to programming style in C. Some points, like one command statement per line of source code and the use of mnemonics for identifiers, are standard guidelines for programming in any upper-level language.

C is a free-format language. The programmer is free to decide on the placement of the code elements as well as the names of the program elements. A clear programming style can be developed. Consistency is very important.

Some of the points in C programming style are discussed below.

Choice of Identifiers

A programmer chooses names for the variables and functions used in a program. Generally, those variables have meaning and should be named accordingly. Similarly, functions have a purpose and their names should convey that purpose. The identifiers chosen for the variable names and the function names should be mnemonic—they should portray the significance of that variable or function to the reader. For example, consider the following two statements:

```
z = x * y;
service_charge = number_of_checks * CHARGE_PER_CHECK;
```

In the first example, you can easily see that the result of multiplication operation is assigned to the variable z, but nothing else of meaning is apparent. However, in the second statement, the variable names indicate the intent of the statement as well as the nature of the program it might appear in. The fact that the identifier CHARGE_PER_CHECK is in uppercase indicates that it could be a preprocessor-defined constant.

Indentation

The use of indentation is very important to a C program's readability. Typically, the amount of indentation depicts the level of nesting. For example, if the statement portion of a while loop consists of a compound statement, each statement in the compound statement should be indented the same amount. Also, the statements in the compound statement should be indented more than the while statement itself. Programs in C are more readable when the indentations are larger than two or three spaces. Traditionally, a full tab stop of indentation is used for each new level of nesting.

Consider the following code segments and notice the difference that the indentation makes. To read the code, assume that rownum, colnum, and matrixelt are declared variables of type int, that NUMROWS and NUMCOLUMNS are preprocessor-defined constants, and that calculate() is a function that calculates and returns an element of a product matrix given the position. In this situation, the code segment outputs a matrix in a rectangular format. In the first code segment, the code lines are not indented at all.

```
for (rownum = 1; rownum <= NUMROWS; rownum++) {
for (colnum = 1; colnum <= NUMCOLUMNS; colnum++) {
matrixelt = calculate (rownum, colnum);
printf ("\t%d", matrixelt);
}
printf ("\n");
colnum = 1;
}
```

The next code segment differs only in its indentation. However, it should be easier to recognize the structure of the nested for loop.

```
for (rownum = 1; rownum <= NUMROWS; rownum++) {
    for (colnum = 1; colnum <= NUMCOLUMNS; colnum++) {
        matrixelt = calculate (rownum, colnum);
        printf ("\t%d", matrixelt);
    }
    printf ("\n");
    colnum = 1;
}
```

Placement of Braces

Several methods are acceptable for the placement of the braces that surround a compound statement in C. The important point is consistency. A reader should be able to see the beginning and ending of a block of code by looking in the same place each time.

In this text, the following method is used:

1. The opening brace for a function is placed in the first column; the function's closing brace appears in that column also.
2. The opening brace for a compound statement associated with an `if`, a `while`, a `do-while` (see Chapter 6), or a `for` statement is placed on the right end of the line containing the statement's keyword. As an example, consider the nested `for` loop in the code segment above. In this way, the end of a line becomes a point of tension for the reader. The closing brace appears in the same column as the first character in the control word. That is, it appears in the same column as the `i` from the `if`, the `w` from the `while`, the `d` from the `do-while`, or the `f` from the `for` loop.
3. An independent compound statement or block has its opening brace in the column that best indicates its nesting level. The closing brace appears in the same column.

"In this text...the closing brace will appear in the same column as the first character..." Based on a limestone relief of a funeral procession, 19th Dynasty, (artist unkown.)

Another acceptable style is to place both opening and closing braces on separate lines in the column that conveys the nesting level of the compound statement. Two copies of a `while` loop appear below. The first loop has its braces placed in the style suggested by points 1, 2, and 3 above. Assume `count`, `number`, and `sum` have type `int`.

```
while ( count++ < 5 ) {
        printf ("Enter a number : ");
        scanf("%d", &number);
        sum += number;
    }
```

The second loop has an alternate acceptable placement of the braces.

```
while ( count++ < 5 )
{
            printf ("Enter a number : ");
            scanf("%d", &number);
            sum += number;
}
```

Because programming style is largely a matter of personal taste, it is not important to adopt either method. However, it is necessary to choose some method of indentation and placement of braces that indicates nesting level and to use it consistently.

Block Structuring

Programs written in a top-down structured style are easier to read and maintain than those not written in that style. This means writing short blocks of code because it is much easier to read and understand 10 lines of code than 100. Each block should be designed to perform a single task. In C the block is usually packaged as a function. Once each block of code makes sense, the whole program follows more easily. Writing short code blocks that perform different tasks becomes more important as the length and complexity of the program increases.

Use of Parentheses

C has specific precedence rules so that the compiler will automatically know the meaning of any legal expression in a source code program. The use of parentheses aids the reader. For example, consider the following two lines of code. The first is a legal C expression. The compiler will have no problem interpreting the code, but a reader might have trouble interpreting it correctly.*

```
i = i + 5 % j != 3*i - 4/j %2;
```

The second expression differs from the first only in the addition of parentheses so that a reader will not have to dig for a precedence chart.

```
i = ( ( i + (5 % j)) != ( (3*i) - ((4/j) %2) ));
```

Comments

It is hard to overstate the importance of comments in a computer program. It is so much easier to see what a program does if you can get a general idea of its function before wrestling with the details in the source code. There are many styles of commenting a program, from placing comments on every line to writing paragraphs of comments for every function and major code block. Again, the method you choose largely depends on personal taste. However, it is important to spell out the significance of every variable in comments and to explain the algorithms. It is also important to make the comments as clear as possible. Comment lines that merely restate the code without giving more insight are useless.

---

* Try to interpret this assignment statement both with and without the parentheses. What possible values could be assigned to `i`?

Paragraphing

C source code can be made more readable by creating cohesive paragraphs of code surrounded by blank lines and comments. That is, a `while` loop with an embedded compound statement could be separated from the surrounding code by putting blank lines both before and after the loop. Consider the difference in the following two examples.

The actual code in both code segments is identical. The purpose is to calculate a non-negative integral power of an integer. The code prompts for and accepts input of an integer value for the base and a non-negative integer value for the power. Then a `for` loop is used for the actual calculation. In the first copy of the code, no paragraphing was done.

```
int base, power, count, result;
printf ("To calculate the power of a number, ");
printf ("enter an integer for the base: ");
scanf ("%d", &base);
printf ("Enter a non-negative integer power: ");
scanf ("%d", &power);
for (count = 0, result = 1; count < power; count++)
          result *= base;
printf ("The result is %d\n", result);
```

In the second copy, the code was paragraphed into five sections of code by including blank lines between (1) the declarations, (2) the prompt for and input of the base, (3) the prompt for and input of the power, (4) the calculation of the result, and (5) the output of the result.

```
int base, power, count, result;

printf ("To calculate the power of a number, ");
printf ("enter an integer for the base: ");
scanf ("%d", &base);

printf ("Enter a non-negative integer power: ");
scanf ("%d", &power);

for (count = 0, result = 1; count < power; count++)
     result *= base;

printf ("The result is %d\n", result);
```

Whitespace

The judicious placement of blanks, tabs, and newlines enhances the readability of C source code. Complicated expressions can be clarified for the reader and the groupings of symbols emphasized. Consider the following two versions of a familiar C source code expression. This is the control part of a `while` loop that reads terminal input until the end-of-file is sensed. In the first example, no whitespace is included.

```
while((iochar=getchar())!=EOF)
```

The second example is easier to read because most of the tokens are separated by whitespace.

```
while ( ( iochar = getchar() ) != EOF )
```

However, both examples compile and execute properly.

Each element of programming style makes a small but significant difference in the readability of C source code.*

Language Elements Introduced in This Chapter: A Review

** Blocks and Compound Statements **
- Can contain both declarations and executable code.
- Treated as a single statement.
- Delimited by a pair of braces.
- Variables declared in a block are unknown outside the block.

** Control Statements **

```
if (expression)
        statement;

if (expression)
        statement1;
else
        statement2;

while (expression)
        statement;

for (initialization; test; processing)
        statement;
```

** Macros **

getchar()   Reads a single character from standard input and returns the `int` value.

putchar()   Takes an `int` between 0 and 127 as a parameter and outputs the corresponding character on standard output.

EOF   Stands for end-of-file, usually has value –1, returned by getchar() when end-of-file is sensed.

** Operators **

Relational operators

<=	is less than or equal to
>=	is greater than or equal to
==	is equal to

---

* Often a C compiler comes with a program that formats C source code in a specific style. The most notable example is cb, the *c b*eautifier program that is part of the UNIX operating system. If such a program exists on your system, it is worth learning to use now. It makes writing programs in an acceptable style much easier, and can sometimes be used to find some elusive syntax errors.

!=	is not equal to
>	is greater than
<	is less than

Logical operators

&&	logical and
||	logical or
!	logical not

Comma operator

,	causes sequential evaluation of expressions it separates

Things to Remember

1. lvalues refer to expressions that have a location in memory.
2. rvalues can be evaluated, but cannot be changed.
3. An assignment is an expression. It has the value of the quantity being assigned.
4. An expression with a nonzero value is evaluated as true; an expression with value zero is evaluated as false.
5. Each `else` is paired with the nearest `if`.
6. Remember to use == to test equality. Don't use =.
7. The relational operators have lower precedence than any of the arithmetic operators, but higher precedence than assignment operators.
8. A filter is a program that reads from standard input and writes to standard output.
9. The macros getchar(), putchar(), and EOF are declared in stdio.h.
10. Remember to use type `int` to store the return value from getchar(), because getchar() returns an `int` value.
11. The expression ((iochar = getchar()) != EOF) is often used to drive a `while` loop that is to work through all the input in a program.
12. The value of an expression involving one of the logical operators is either 1 (true) or 0 (false).
13. The precedence of the logical operators from high to low is !, &&, and ||.
14. Get in the habit of using good programming style. C needs more whitespace than other programming languages.

2.9   Exercises and Programming Problems

1. Assume that the variables x, y, and z have been declared as follows:

    ```
    int x = 5, y = -1, z = 3;
    ```

    a. Categorize each expression below as either an lvalue or an rvalue.

    ```
    x + y        _____
    2*x + 3      _____
    z + 1        _____
    ```

```
x++              _____
y                _____
x = y + 5        _____
x <= z           _____
```

b. Evaluate each of the following C expressions. (Evaluate each expression separately. Do not assume they are in a program.)

```
2*x + 5          _____
x = y % z        _____
x >= 2           _____
x = 3219         _____
x == 3219        _____
y / z * 2        _____
!(x - 3)         _____
z || y           _____
! (y + 1)        _____
```

2. What is the output for the following program? Write each character of output in boxes like those below. Write one character per box.

```
/*               epp2.c               */

main()
{
     int i, j;

     i = 2;
     j = 1;
     while ( (i > -5) || (j-- > 0) ) {
          if ( (j % 2) && (i-- % 3) )
               printf ("%d", j);
          else
               printf ("%d\n", i);
     }
}
```

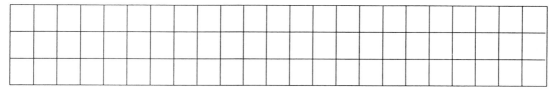

3. Will the following program compile as it appears or are there syntax errors?

```
/*               epp3.c               */

     # include <stdio.h>

main()
```

```
{
        int count, done;

        done = 0;
        for count = 0, count < 5, count++) {
                if count % 2
                        printf ("count is odd.\n, count)

}
```

a. If there are syntax errors, fix them; preserve the original intent of the program. Make your changes on the copy of the program above.

b. After the corrections have been made, give the output of the program.

---

4. Rewrite the following program with better style. Incorporate as many of the style points mentioned in Section 2.8 as possible.

```
/*                      epp4.c                      */

#include <stdio.h>
main ()
        {
int y,x = 0;
printf ("Enter your integers now.\n");
printf ("Enter one integer per line and press return.\n");
printf (">>> ");
while ((scanf ("%d",&y))!=EOF){
x=x+y; printf (">>> "); }
printf ("The sum is %d.\n", x); }
```

(Hint: If your system has a C beautifier program, start by running this source code through that program.)

5. How many times are each of the following indicated statements executed when the following code segment is executed? Fill in the number of times each statement is executed in the blank immediately to the left of the statement.

```
        int i, j;

        for (i = 1; i <= 4; i++)
                for (j = i; j >= 1; j--)
_____                printf ("%d ", j);

                        i = 0;
                        j = 3*i;
_____        while ( i != j+4 )
_____                i = i + 1;

        i = 5;

        i = 4;
```

```
        if (i <= 10)
               i++;
_____
```

6. a. Compile the program inout2.c of Example 2-13 but stop the compilation after the preprocess phase.

    b. Compare the original source code and the preprocessed code. In the latter, circle the changes that were made by the preprocessor.

    c. Get a hard copy of stdio.h from your system and compare its contents to the changes you have circled.

    d. Try to explain how the preprocessor expands macros like getchar().

7. Write a function named `positive` that takes a single argument of type `int` and returns a value that will test true if the argument is positive and false otherwise. Test your function with the program below.

```c
/*                     epp7.c                     */

#include <stdio.h>

main()
{
        int inputint;

        printf ("Enter an integer and ");
        printf ("press return after the prompt.\n");
        printf ("Signal EOF when you are done.\n");
        printf (">>> ");

        while ( scanf ("%d", &inputint) != EOF) {
                if (positive(inputint) )
                        printf ("That one was positive.\n");
                else
                        printf ("That one wasn't.\n");
                printf (">>> ");
        }
}
```

8. The purpose of the following program is to count the whitespace, the digits, the uppercase alphabetics and the lowercase alphabetics in the input. There are bugs in the program. Fix it.

```c
/*                     epp8.c                     */


#include <stdio.h>

main()
{
        int     iochar,
                numdigits = 0,
                numlower = 0,
                numupper = 0,
                numwhites = 0;
```

```
        while ( (iochar = getchar()) != EOF) {
            if ( (iochar = ' ') || (iochar = '\t')
                                || (iochar = '\n') ) {
                numwhites++;
                putchar (iochar);
            }
            else if ( ('0' <= iochar) && (iochar <= '9') ) {
                numdigits++;
                putchar (iochar);
            }
            else if ( ('a' <=  iochar) && (iochar <= 'z') ) {
                numlower++;
                putchar (iochar - 32);
            }
            else if ( ('A' <=  iochar) && (iochar <= 'Z') ) {
                numupper++;
                putchar (iochar);
            }
            else putchar (iochar);
        }

        printf ("%d white characters, %d digits, ",
                numwhites, numdigits);
        printf ("%d lowercase have been converted to ",
                numlower);
        printf ("uppercase and %d uppercase.\n", numupper);
    }
```

a. Execute the program in its present form using input for which it is easy to predict the output.

b. Analyze the program from the output obtained through the testing and tentatively make some changes.

c. Retest it after each change until you are sure that the bugs are gone.

9. The purpose of the following program is to check input. It is only supposed to accept a value between 0 and 20 and continually ask for input until the correct quantity is entered. However, there is a bug in it.

```
/*                      epp9.c                      */

#include <stdio.h>
#define TRUE  1
#define FALSE 0

main()
{
    int correct, inputint;

    inputint = -1;
    correct = FALSE;
    while (!correct) {
        if ( 0 < inputint < 20) {
            printf ("Thank you.\n");
            correct = TRUE;
        }
```

```
            else   {
                    printf ("Enter an integer between 0 and 20: ");
                    scanf ("%d", &inputint);
            }
        }
    }
```

a. Fix the bug so that the program behaves as stated above.

b. After the program is working, modify it to give diagnostic help to the person who runs the program.

10. Write a function that will take a variable of type int and output it with a dollar sign preceding the number and a decimal place before the last two digits. For example, the value 8530 should be output as $85.30. Name your function printmoney() and have it take the variable of type int as a parameter. Test it with the program below. Your output should be:

```
                $.12
                $10.00
                $253.04
                $.00
                $1.45
```

```
/*                      prob10.c
 */

#include <stdio.h>

main()
{
        printmoney(12);
        printf("\n");
        printmoney(1000);
        printf("\n");
        printmoney(25304);
        printf("\n");
        printmoney(0);
        printf("\n");
        printmoney(145);
        printf("\n");
}
```

11. Write a C program that plays a number guessing game with the user. A sample run for the game would be as follows: User input is in **boldface**.

```
Welcome to the game of Guess It!

I will choose a number between 1 and 100. You will
try to guess that number. If you guess wrong, I will
tell you if you guessed too high or too low. You
have 6 tries to get the number.

OK, I am thinking of a number. Try to guess it.

Your guess? 50
Too high!
Your guess? 12
Too low!
Your guess? 112
Illegal guess. Your guess must be between 1 and 100.
Try again. Your guess? 23
**** CORRECT****

Want to play again? y
OK, I am thinking of a number. Try to guess it.
Your guess? 23
**** CORRECT ****

Want to play again? n
Goodbye, it was fun. Play again soon.
```

12. Write a C program that will input positive decimal integer values and output the prime factorizations of the input values. A sample run is below. User input is in **boldface**.

```
So you want some numbers factored. Give them to me
one by one and I will do the factoring.

Number?  12
The prime factorization of 12 is 2*2*3.

Number?  1050
The prime factorization of 1050 is 2*3*5*5*7.

Number?  <CR>
You're welcome. The bill is in the mail.
```

13. Indicate the output of each printf() call below in the spaces to the right.

```
/*                      epp13.c                      */

#include <stdio.h>

main()
{
        int i, count = 0;

        for ( i = 8; i >= 0; i--) {
                if (!(i%4) || (i--%3)) {
```

```
                                        i--;
                                        count++;
                             }
                }


                printf ("%d\n", count);              _____

                printf ("%d\n", count && ++i);       _____

                printf ("%d\n", !count);             _____

                printf ("%d\n", i > 0);              _____

                printf ("%d\n", 0 < count < 3);      _____

        }
```

14. a. The following program does not compile. Remove all syntax errors so that
it compiles and runs properly. Preserve the original intent of the program.

```
        /*                      epp14.c                      */

        #include <stdio.h>

        main()
        {
                int i;

                i = 1;
                printf ("counting\n;
                while (i < 100) {
                        int j = 1;
                        printf ("%4d", i);
                        if !(i++ % 16)   {
                                printf ("\n");
                                j++
                        else printf (" ");
                }
                prinf ("\nThe number of lines printed was %d.\n", j);
        }
```

b. Predict the output of the program after the syntax errors have been removed.
Write the output characters in the boxes below, one character per box.

Basic Types

Chapter 3

3.1   Introduction to Scalar Types in C

Now that expressions, some operators, and the elementary control statements have been discussed, we will study variables with scalar types. Variables are used to hold data while a program is executing. In C, each variable must be declared before it is used. When a variable is declared, a type is assigned to it. During the compilation/link process, memory is reserved for each variable. The amount of memory that is reserved corresponds to the stated type.

Types in C can be divided into scalar types, aggregate types, function types and the void type. In this chapter we will discuss most of the scalar types, those that can contain only a single data value at any time. In contrast, aggregate types can store multiple data items and include arrays, structures, and unions. These will be discussed in Chapters 4, 7, and 9. Function types and the void types will be discussed in this chapter also.

Computer Memory

To understand how numbers are represented in a computer, it is necessary to understand a little bit about a computer's memory.

Every modern computer has a memory. When a program is executed, the memory is used for two things. The object code is loaded into memory, and the program data (values of variables, etc.) are kept in memory.

Portions of memory can be referenced in several ways. For example, we can talk about a bit, a byte, or a word of memory. Each bit holds 0 or 1. A byte is a sequence of several bits. For example, 8 bits = 1 byte is a popular size. Similarly, a word is a collection of one or more bytes. Two of the more common word sizes are 2 bytes and 4 bytes. Byte size and word size may vary with the computer; the sizes depend on the underlying hardware.

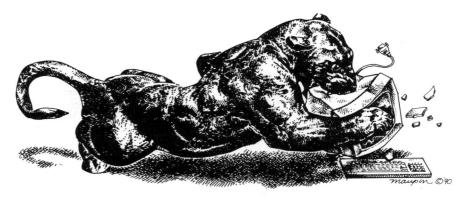

"The byte size...may vary with the computer; the size depends on the underlying hardware." From the painting *Jaguar Devouring a Crocodile* by Antoine-Louis Barye, c. 1850–1855

When a byte or word contains a number, some of the bits might be 1 and others would be 0. The resulting configuration is called a bit pattern.

For example, assume that a byte consists of 8 bits and that a word consists of two bytes. Then,

1	0	1	1	0	1	1	0

is an example of one of the possible bit patterns in a byte, and

1	0	1	1	1	1	1	1	0	0	0	1	1	0	0	1	0

is an example of one bit pattern in a word of memory. These bit patterns can be interpreted in different ways by the compiler. Thus, it is possible to have different scalar types.

The scalar types can be classified as arithmetic types, enumerated types, and pointer types. In this chapter we will discuss the arithmetic types. Pointers will be introduced in Chapter 4 and enumerated types in Chapter 7.

The arithmetic types can be further classified as integer types and floating point types. We'll discuss the integer types first.

3.2 Variables of Type `int` Revisited

One of the integer types in C is the type `int`. This scalar type was first discussed in Chapter 1 where variable declarations were introduced. Output and arithmetic operations were also discussed there. The type `int` is a type that C provides to store integer values.

In mathematics, the term *integers* refers to all the whole numbers, 0, 1, 2, 3, 4, 5, 6, ... together with their negatives, −1, −2, −3, −4, −5, ... There are an infinite number of integers. On a computer, it is not possible to represent every integer. Instead, a range of integers is represented. The range is usually

```
-m, -m+1, -m+2, . . . , -2, -1, 0, 1, 2, 3, . . . m-2, m-1
```

where m is a power of 2. The actual value of m depends on the hardware characteristics and the particular implementation of the language.

Most implementations of C let a variable of type `int` occupy a word in the specific computer. Type `int` can be handled very efficiently. Throughout the language, where a default type is provided, it is generally the `int` type. The disadvantage of associating the size of a variable of type `int` with the size of a word on the underlying hardware is that the size of a word varies with different hardware. A word might consist of 16 bits on one computer and 32 bits on another. The largest value that could be represented with a variable of type `int` would vary also. For example, if an `int` is stored in 16 bits, the largest integer that can be represented is 32767 or $2^{15} - 1$. If an `int` is stored in 32 bits, the largest integer that can be represented is 2147483647 or $2^{31} - 1$.

The `sizeof` Operator

C provides an operator named `sizeof` that gives the number of bytes associated with a specified type or a variable. The syntax of the sizeof operator is similar to that of a function. Its operand can be placed in parentheses. Therefore, in this text, we will refer to this operator as sizeof(), using the same notation as for C library functions.

The sizeof() operator takes either an expression or a type name as an argument and returns the number of bytes in that argument. The operator sizeof() does only what is necessary to determine the number of bytes in the expression. The value of a sizeof() operation can be determined at compile time. It never depends on runtime values of variables or expressions, only on the types involved.

For example, in

```
sizeof (int)
```

the operand is `int` and the number of bytes needed to store an `int` will be returned. In the example

```
sizeof (intvar + 3)
```

the operand is the expression `intvar` + 3. Since `intvar` + 3 has type `int`, the number of bytes needed to store an `int` will be returned here also.

Our first use for sizeof() is to determine how many bytes a variable of type `int` occupies. The program sizeof1.c in Example 3-1 illustrates this. Other uses for sizeof() will be discussed later.

Example 3-1: sizeof1.c

```
/*                 sizeof1.c
 *
 *   Synopsis   -   Outputs the number of bytes in type int by using
 *                  sizeof(), and outputs values of intvar1 and
 *                  intvar1 + 1.
 *
 *   Objective  -   To illustrate ways of using the sizeof()
 *                  operator and to help determine the range of a
 *                  variable of type int.
 */

#include <stdio.h>

main()
{
        int intvar1, intvar2;

        intvar2 = sizeof(intvar1);                          /* Note 1 */

                                                            /* Note 2 */
        printf ("The number of bytes in an int is %d. ",
                        sizeof(int));
                                                            /* Note 3 */
        printf ("To repeat, that's %d. Once again, %d.\n",
                sizeof(intvar2), intvar2);

        intvar1 = 32767;                                    /* Note 4 */
        printf ("intvar1 is %d. intvar1 + 1 is %d.\n",
                                intvar1, intvar1 + 1);

}
```

This program is simple in structure. Two variables of type `int` are declared. The executable code consists of assignment statements and calls to the printf() library function.

Note 1: The operator sizeof() is applied to the variable `intvar1`. The value of the expression `sizeof(intvar1)` will be the number of bytes of memory used for the variable `intvar1`. When sizeof() is applied to the name of a variable, it returns the amount of storage (in bytes) allotted for that variable; that is, it returns the amount of storage allotted for an `int`.

Note 2: In the following call to printf(), the operator sizeof() is applied to the type `int`. When sizeof() is applied to any C type, the value returned is the number of bytes of memory allotted for any variable of that type.

Note 3: The next printf() call outputs the values `sizeof(intvar2)` (or the number of bytes allotted for `intvar2`) and `intvar2`, which contains the number of bytes allotted for `intvar1` from the preceding assignment statement. Since both variables are of type `int`, these values should be the same as the value output by the first call to printf().

Note 4: The value 32767 is assigned to `intvar1`. The following printf() call outputs this value and 1 + the value. Note that when an `int` value occupies 16 bits, 32767 is theoretically the largest value that can be stored in type `int`. The purpose of this statement is to investigate how values greater than this maximum value are handled by C. The activities below address this issue.

Learning Activities

1. Run sizeof1.c and note what `sizeof(int)` is with your implementation of C. Find out the number of bits to a byte on the computer you are using.

2. If x has the value of `sizeof(int)` that was determined by executing the program sizeof1.c and y is the number of bits to the byte that you determined in completing activity 1, calculate $2^{x*y-1} - 1$. If this value differs from 32767, modify sizeof1.c by replacing the value 32767 by the value that you calculated. Execute the program again. Be sure that you understand the output. Explain your results.

3.3   Different Integer Bases

It is important to realize that the internal representation of an integer is the 0s and 1s of a specific bit pattern. An integer is stored in binary representation. For example, assuming that a byte consists of 8 bits and that a word consists of 2 bytes,

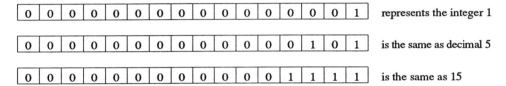

| 0 | 0 | 0 | 0 | 0 | 0 | 0 | 0 | 0 | 0 | 0 | 0 | 0 | 0 | 0 | 1 | represents the integer 1

| 0 | 0 | 0 | 0 | 0 | 0 | 0 | 0 | 0 | 0 | 0 | 0 | 0 | 1 | 0 | 1 | is the same as decimal 5

| 0 | 0 | 0 | 0 | 0 | 0 | 0 | 0 | 0 | 0 | 0 | 0 | 1 | 1 | 1 | 1 | is the same as 15

The representation of an integer in terms of a specific base is a matter of keeping track of the multiple of each of the powers of the base that makes up the number. The multiples of each power are written in a specific location. If the base is 10, as in a decimal representation, the digits needed to keep track of the multiples are 0 through 9. For a base 8 or octal number, the digits needed are 0 through 7. For a base 2 or binary number, the digits are 0 and 1. For a base 16 or hexadecimal number, the digits are 0, 1, . . . , 9, a, b, c, d, e, and f. The a represents the decimal 10; the b represents 11; c is 12; d is 13; e is 14; and f is 15.

For example, the value of decimal number 125 is

$$1 * 10^2 + 2 * 10^1 + 5 * 10^0$$

The rightmost position holds the multiples of 10^0, the next position to the left holds the multiples of 10^1, and the leftmost position of this number holds the multiples of 10^2. The value of the hexadecimal number 1b2f is

$$1 * 16^3 + b * 16^2 + 2 * 16^1 + f * 16^0$$

Replacing the b by 11 and the f by 15, we see that the number 1b2f in hexadecimal is the same as the number 6959 in decimal. The value of the binary number 10111 is

$$1 * 2^4 + 0 * 2^3 + 1 * 2^2 + 1 * 2^1 + 1 * 2^0$$

or 23 in decimal.

One method of conversion from decimal to binary is to divide the decimal number by 2 and keep the remainder as the first bit (rightmost bit) of the binary number. Then the quotient is divided by 2 again and the remainder becomes the second bit of the binary representation. This process continues until the quotient is zero. For example, the process of converting the number 11 to binary is shown in Figure 3-1.

The conversion of a binary number to decimal proceeds by multiplying the leftmost bit by 2, and adding in the next bit to the right. Then the result is multiplied by 2 and added to the next bit to the right. This process continues until the rightmost bit has been added to the result. For example, the process of converting the bit pattern 10110 to decimal is shown in Figure 3-2.

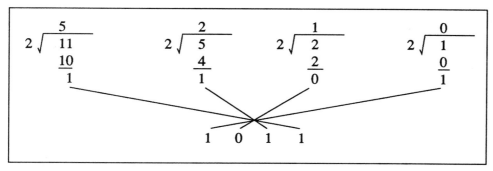

Figure 3-1

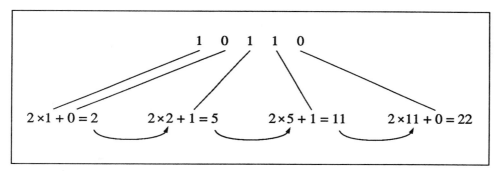

Figure 3-2

Conversions between binary and hexadecimal are easier since each four binary digits translate directly to one hex digit. The table below shows the translation.

Decimal	Hexadecimal	Binary
0	0	0000
1	1	0001
2	2	0010
3	3	0011
4	4	0100
5	5	0101
6	6	0110
7	7	0111
8	8	1000
9	9	1001
10	a	1010
11	b	1011
12	c	1100
13	d	1101
14	e	1110
15	f	1111

All that is necessary to convert a hexadecimal number to binary is to convert each hexadecimal digit to binary. For example, to convert the hexadecimal number 1f3a to binary,

1	f	3	a
0001	1111	0011	1010

and the binary representation is 0001111100111010.

Learning Activities

3.   a. Convert each of the following decimal integers to binary:

   278   1295   31   832

   b. Convert each of your binary answers from part a to hexadecimal.

4.   a. Convert each of the following hexadecimal numbers to binary:

   1000   ffff   1ab   2e

   b. Convert each of your binary answers from part a to decimal.

5.   Find a method of converting directly from hexadecimal to decimal and back again. Test the method with the numbers in problems 1 and 2.

6.   In an octal representation, each octal digit translates directly to three binary digits.

   a. Construct a chart like the one above that shows the binary representation for the octal digits 0 through 7.

   b. Use that chart to convert the following octal integers to binary:

   1735   361   14315

   c. Use the chart to convert the following binary integers to octal:

   11010110   100011001   11010

Conversions to Other Bases with printf() and scanf()

The decimal representation output when the %d conversion specification is used with printf() is obtained by converting the internal binary representation of an integer into a decimal representation and using the digits from the character set for the output. Using the %d conversion specification with scanf() for input causes a representation of an integer as a sequence of ASCII digits in the input string to be converted to the internal binary representation before storage.

Printf() and scanf() can be used for other conversions also. An integer value can be output or input in hexadecimal with printf() or scanf() by using %x or %X as the conversion specification. The %x specification expects the hexadecimal digits 0, 1,

2, 3, 4, 5, 6, 7, 8, 9, a, b, c, d, e, and f while the %X specification uses 0, 1, 2, 3, 4, 5, 6, 7, 8, 9, A, B, C, D, E, and F.

Conversion to or from octal is accomplished with the %o conversion specification. The octal digits 0, 1, 2, 3, 4, 5, 6, and 7 are used. Note that neither %x, %X, or %o will output negative values. The bit pattern is always assumed to represent a non-negative integer.

The program printhex.c in Example 3-2 illustrates these conversions. It will input a decimal integer and convert it to hexadecimal and octal.

Example 3-2: printhex.c

```
/*               printhex.c
 *
 *   Synopsis  -  Inputs a decimal integer, echoes it, and outputs
 *                the hexadecimal and octal equivalents.
 *
 *   Objective -  Illustrates the printf() conversions to
 *                hexadecimal and octal.
 */

#include <stdio.h>

main()
{
        int intvar;
        printf ("Conversions: Decimal to Hex and Octal\n");
        printf ("-------------------------------------\n");
        printf ("Enter a decimal number :   ");
        scanf ("%d", &intvar);                          /* Note 1 */

        printf ("You entered %d.\n", intvar);
                                                        /* Note 2 */
        printf ("That number is %x in hexadecimal,", intvar);

        printf (" and %o in octal.\n", intvar);         /* Note 3 */
}
```

Note that the executable code in this program consists only of calls to printf() and scanf().

Note 1: The call to scanf() contains a %d conversion specification. From the current position, the input will be searched for a string of digits, 0, 1, 2, 3, 4, 5, 6, 7, 8, and 9. The string that is found will be interpreted as decimal and converted to the corresponding integer. For example, the character '1' followed by the character '3' will be interpreted as the integer 13. The bit pattern

0	0	0	0	0	0	0	0	0	0	0	0	1	1	0	1

will be stored in the location for the variable intvar.

Note 2: The %x conversion specification is used in the printf() call. The bit pattern that is stored in intvar will be converted to a hexadecimal representation before output. Continuing the above example, if the decimal value 13 was input, the hexadecimal value d will be output. The underlying bit pattern remains unchanged.

Note 3: The %o conversion specification is used here. That same bit pattern will be converted to octal before output. If decimal 13 was input, octal 15 will be output.

Learning Activities

7. a. In the following chart, several inputs for printhex.c are given. Assuming 16 bits for an int value, predict the bit pattern and the hexadecimal and octal output for each of the input values.

Input	Bit Pattern	Hexadecimal	Octal
29	_ _ _ _ _ _ _ _ _ _ _ _ _ _ _ _	_____	_____
3	_ _ _ _ _ _ _ _ _ _ _ _ _ _ _ _	_____	_____
256	_ _ _ _ _ _ _ _ _ _ _ _ _ _ _ _	_____	_____
251	_ _ _ _ _ _ _ _ _ _ _ _ _ _ _ _	_____	_____

   b. Execute the program to verify your predictions.

8. Modify printhex.c by replacing the %x conversion specification with %X and execute the program again. Test with several different inputs so that you can see the differences.

9. Modify printhex.c to take input values in hexadecimal and output the corresponding decimal and octal values for the input.

3.4   Character Variables

Because it is sometimes desirable to represent different ranges of integers, types other than int are available. In this section, we discuss a type that will hold a member of the underlying character set. It is one of the integral types in C.

The range of integers from 0 to 127 (or 0 to $2^7 - 1$) can be represented with 8 bits (usually 1 byte) on a computer. The ASCII character set consists of 128 characters. Each element of this character set can be associated with an integer value between 0 and 127. Conversely, each integral value in this range can be translated to an ASCII character.* C provides another integer type named `char` to represent characters or integers in this range. Values of type `char` are stored in one byte of memory.

The declaration of a variable of type `char` is similar to declaration of a variable of type `int`. The simplest form of a declaration starts with the data type, followed by the variable names, and terminated by a semicolon. As with integers, a variable of type `char` may or may not be initialized at the time of declaration. The program charvar.c in Example 3-3 has a declaration of a variable of type `char`.

The program also illustrates some of the other modes of output that are available with the printf() function. For example, the value of a `char` variable can be output as a character with the conversion specification %c. A `char` variable can also be output in a numeric form. The value that is output is the integer value that corresponds to the ASCII character.

For example, in the ASCII character set, the character '0' is associated with decimal 48; the character 'B' is associated with decimal 66; and the character '{' is associated with decimal 123. These values are indicated in the ASCII character set in the Programmer's Handbook. The integer associated with the value of a character variable can be output in decimal form by a printf() call. This is done by specifying the %d conversion specification in the control string. The value 66 would be output by the printf() call

```
printf ("%d", 'B');
```

Any variable of type `char` or `int` can also be output in octal by specifying a %o in the conversion specification, or in hexadecimal with a %x conversion specification. The statements

```
printf ("B is character '%c', decimal %d,",'B','B');
printf (" octal %o, and hexadecimal %x.\n", 'B','B');
```

would output the following:

```
B is character 'B', decimal 66, octal 102, and hexadecimal 42.
```

The computer actually stores any integer (including a value of type `char`) in a binary representation consisting of 0s and 1s. When an integer is output, it can be converted to a form that is more easily read by a human being. The programmer specifies the desired form with the conversion specification in the printf() control string. The program charvar.c gives examples of this.

---

* This is also true for character sets other than ASCII. There will be a one-to-one correspondence between some subset of the integers and the elements of the character set. However, the specific subset of the integers, the number of characters, the actual characters, and the correspondence may differ. The use of an ASCII character set will be assumed in this text.

Example 3-3:   charvar.c

```
/*                charvar.c
 *
 *   Synopsis  -  Variables of type char and int are declared.  The
 *                sizeof() the char type is output.  Then a value is
 *                assigned to each variable and output with different
 *                conversion specifications.
 *
 *   Objective -  Illustrates the relationship between type char and
 *                type int and some of the different conversion
 *                specifications with printf().
 */
#include <stdio.h>

main()
{
        char    charvar;                                /* Note 1 */
        int     intvar;
                                                        /* Note 2 */
        printf ("The sizeof type char is %d byte.\n",
                        sizeof(char));
        charvar = 'c';                                  /* Note 3 */
                                                        /* Note 4 */
        printf("charvar is the character %c.\n", charvar);
        printf ("It can be output in decimal as %d, in octal as %o, ",
                        charvar, charvar);
        printf ("or in hexadecimal as %x.\n", charvar);

        intvar = 73;
        printf("Intvar is the decimal integer, %d.\n", intvar);
        printf("It can be written in hex, %x, or octal, %o, ",
                                        intvar, intvar);
                                                        /* Note 5 */
        printf("or even treated as the character %c.\n", intvar);
}
```

An overview of charvar.c reveals a single function, main(). Two variables are declared, one of type int and one of type char. After a printf() call involving the sizeof() operator, the code sequence of an assignment statement followed by printf() calls appears twice.

Note 1: A variable of type char is declared. The name of the variable is charvar. The declaration consists of the keyword char, the variable name, and the terminating semicolon.

Note 2: The sizeof() operator is applied to type `char`. The parentheses are necessary when sizeof() is used with a type. The value `sizeof(char)` will probably be 1 because most computers use one byte to store a character.

Note 3: An assignment statement can be used to establish the value of `charvar`. The single quotes indicate to the compiler that the value is from the underlying character set.

Note 4: This note refers to the following three printf() calls. The first printf() call is used to print out the value of `charvar`. The only way in which this statement differs from the printf() calls we have seen previously is that the new conversion specification, `%c`, is used to indicate that the value should be output as a character. The next two printf() calls illustrate other conversions that can be used to output `char` values. They can be output in decimal, octal, or hexadecimal. Decimal is indicated with a `%d` conversion specification, as before; the conversion specification for octal is `%o`, and hexadecimal output is indicated with `%x`. The numerical value is the number associated with the character in the underlying character set.

Note 5: In this printf() call, the character associated with a 73 in the underlying character set is output. With the ASCII character set, an uppercase 'I' would be output in the indicated place in the sentence.

Learning Activities

10. What is the underlying character set for the C compiler on the computer system you are using? Get a chart for that character set so that you can answer the following questions. A chart for the ASCII character set appears in the Programmer's Handbook at the end of this text.
    a. What is the subset of the integers associated with the character set?
    b. How many bits would be needed to store the largest integer in the subset?
    c. How many characters are in the character set?
    d. Are the uppercase alphabetics contiguous in the character set? What integer is associated with 'A'? With 'B'? With each of the uppercase alphabetic characters?
    e. Answer the questions in part d for the lowercase alphabetic characters.
    f. Are the digits '0', '1', '2', . . .'9' contiguous in the character set? What integers are associated with the digits?

11. a. Predict the values that will be output by charvar.c when the assignments to `charvar` and `intvar` are changed to assign the comma character to `charvar` and 52 to `intvar`.
    b. Check your values in part a by modifying the program and executing it.

12. Combine the declaration and initialization of `charvar` into one declaration statement with an initializer.

3.5 Types `short int` and `long int`

We mentioned that the `int` type is handled more efficiently than the other types in C. However, the way in which it is handled usually depends on the size of a word in the hardware on which it is implemented. This is not always the most efficient use of memory, and may not always produce the desired results when a program is ported to other computers. Therefore, still more integer types have been provided.

The other integer types in C include `short int` and `long int`, also referred to as `short` and `long`. The keywords `short` and `long` loosely refer to the amount of memory needed to store the values. That is, theoretically, a variable of type `short int` would be used to store values that are relatively small and would take fewer bytes of memory. A variable of type `long int` would be used for larger values, those taking more bytes of memory. In reality, the specifications for the relative sizes of `short int`, `int`, and `long int` are not precise.

Variances Among Versions of C

Prior to the creation of the ANSI standard for C, all that a programmer was guaranteed was that type `short` occupied no more bytes than type `int`, and type `long` occupied no fewer bytes than type `int`. It was possible for all three types to occupy the same amount of storage. This flexibility in implementation allows the C language to work more efficiently with the underlying hardware. The ANSI standards for C now include minimal ranges that must be represented by each of the integral types. These values are discussed with Example 3-6 in Section 3.7.

We have seen the sizeof() operator used with types `int` and `char`. It can be used with all other types also.

Input and Output of short and long Values

Values of variables of type `short int` and `long int` can be output in decimal, hexadecimal, or octal. However, the printf() and scanf() functions need to know if the quantity to be output or input is a `long int` or a `short int`. An `'l'` (lowercase `'L'`) is used with the conversion specification to indicate a `long int`. For example, in a printf() call, the conversion specification `%lx` would indicate that an expression with type `long int` should be converted to hexadecimal for output. The conversion specifications `%ld` and `%lo` indicate conversion of a `long int` to decimal and octal, respectively. Similarly, an `'h'` indicates a short value to printf() and scanf(). For example, in a scanf() statement, `%hd` would indicate the input of a `short` decimal value while `%hx` would signal a `short` hexadecimal value.

The program ints.c in Example 3-4 illustrates the declaration of variables of type `short int` and `long int` and uses the sizeof() operator to output their relative sizes, as well as those of the other integer types.

Example 3-4: ints.c

```
/*                 ints.c
 *
 *    Synopsis  -  Prints the sizeof() the different integer types
 *                 and some values for variables of each type.
 *
 *    Objective -  Demonstrates the sizeof() operator and different
 *                 integer types.
 */

#include <stdio.h>

main()
{
        short shortvar;                                  /* Note 1 */
        long  longvar;                                   /* Note 2 */
        int intvar;

        printf ("A char has %d byte.\n", sizeof (char) );
        printf ("An int has %d bytes.\n", sizeof (int) );
                                                         /* Note 3 */
        printf ("A long int has %d bytes.\n", sizeof longvar );
        printf ("A short int has %d bytes.\n", sizeof shortvar );

        shortvar = 32767;
        intvar = 32767;
        longvar = 32767;
                                                         /* Note 4 */
        printf ("shortvar is %hd. shortvar+1 is %hd.\n"
                            shortvar, shortvar+1);
        printf ("intvar is %d. intvar+1 is %d.\n", intvar, intvar+1);
                                                         /* Note 5 */
        printf ("longvar is %ld. longvar+1 is %ld.\n",
                            longvar, longvar+1);

}
```

The executable code in main() consists of calls to printf() and assignment
statements.

Note 1: A variable named short var is declared. Its type is short or short int. The
declaration could also have been

```
        short int shortvar;
```

The keyword int is optional.

Note 2: The variable `longvar` is of type `long` or `long int`. The keyword `int` is optional here also.

Note 3: The operator sizeof() is used with a variable name as an argument in the next two printf() calls. The sizeof() a `long int` and a `short int` will be output. Parentheses are not necessary in the syntax for sizeof() in this case, but they could be inserted.

Note 4: All three variables have been initialized to 32767. This integer is the largest integer that can be represented with a type associated with 16 bits of memory. In the next printf() calls, the values of each variable and the variable plus one are to be output. The second value will very probably be beyond the range your computer system handles properly for a `short int`. It may also be outside the range for an `int` type. This causes an error commonly referred to as overflow. However, the value should be within the range for a `long int`. Make sure you execute this program to see how these values are handled.

Note 5: The last printf() call uses the conversion specification `%ld` for a `long int` to be output in decimal.

Learning Activities

13. a. If the sizeof() operator is available on your system, run ints.c to determine the sizeof() each integer type on your implementation of C. Also note how the output of the value 32768 is handled with each integer type. Try to figure out the reason for the results you obtain.

b. Modify ints.c by changing the conversion specification `%ld` to `%d`. Execute the program again. Does the result change? Try to explain why or why not.

c. Now modify ints.c by changing all the `%d` specifications to `%ld` and execute it one more time. Did the result change? Try to explain why or why not.

14. a. Calculate the range of values that can be handled by types `short int`, `int`, and `long int` on your system. Use the results from question 1. (Hint: You will need to know the byte size on your computer as well as the value of the sizeof operator() on each of the integer types. Assume that a byte contains n bits and that the sizeof() operator says that m bytes are occupied by a certain type. Then 2^{mn} different integers can be represented by the type in question.)

b. The program ints.c was written assuming that a `short int` would occupy 16 bits, a `long int` would occupy 32 bits, and an `int` would occupy either 16 or 32 bits.

   i. If the memory allotment is different from that on your computer, modify the program by changing the 32767 to the largest value that can be stored in a `short int` and execute the program again. That is, force an overflow error on the `short int` variable. Try to explain the result.

   ii. Modify the program by inserting the largest value that can be stored in an `int` and execute the program again. This time an overflow error will have been forced on both the `int` and the `short int` variables. Try to explain the results. (Note: The full explanation for results obtained by executing these modifications of ints.c involves type conversions. The underlying concepts will be discussed in Section 3.11.)

3.6 Unsigned Types

The types `int`, `long`, and `short` discussed previously allow both positive and negative values. However, some applications require only non-negative values. For these, C provides the types named `unsigned int`, `unsigned long int`, and `unsigned short int`. The sizeof() each of these types is the same as the related signed type; the possible bit patterns are also the same. However, the interpretation of these bit patterns differs. The range of integers that can be represented with type unsigned is

$$0, 1, 2, 3, \ldots, 2^m-1$$

where m is the total number of bits involved in the underlying type. For example, if an `int` variable is stored in 16 bits, then the range of values that can be represented by an `unsigned int` is

$$0, 1, 2, \ldots, 2^{16}-1 \text{ or } 0, 1, 2, \ldots, 65535$$

If a variable with type `long` is stored in 32 bits, then the range of values that can be represented by an `unsigned long int` is

$$0, 1, 2, \ldots, 2^{32}-1 \text{ or } 0, 1, 2, \ldots, 4294967295$$

The results of the arithmetic operations on the unsigned types also differ because the result is always interpreted as a value in this range. For example, if an `int` occupies 16 bits, the result of the operation $4-5$ when stored in an unsigned int will be 65535 because the bit pattern for -1 in a signed type (all ones) is identical to the largest value that can be represented with an unsigned type. The program unsigned.c in Example 3-5 addresses this phenomenon.

A variable of type `unsigned int` can be declared in two ways. The declarations

```
unsigned positive;
```

and

```
        unsigned int positive;
```

both declare a variable named `positive` with type `unsigned int`. That is, the keyword `int` is optional. A variable named `bigvalue` of type `unsigned long int` can be declared as either

```
        unsigned long int bigvalue;
```

or

```
        unsigned long bigvalue;
```

Again, the keyword `int` is optional. Declarations of variables of type `unsigned short int` follow the same pattern.

The conversion specification used with printf() and scanf() for an unsigned decimal is `%u`. It tells the printf() and scanf() functions to convert the value to or from unsigned decimal. The `%x` and the `%o` conversion specifications indicate *unsigned* conversion to hexadecimal and octal, respectively. The `%u` conversion specification is used in Example 3-5.

 Example 3-5:   unsigned.c

```
/*               unsigned.c
 *
 *    Synopsis  -  Variables of types unsigned int and int are
 *                 declared. The same values are assigned to each
 *                 and the values are output with calls to printf().
 *
 *    Objective -  To illustrate some of the differences between
 *                 the types unsigned int and int.
 */

#include <stdio.h>

main()
{
        unsigned positive;                               /* Note 1 */
        int signedvar;

        positive  = 65535;                               /* Note 2 */
        signedvar = 65535;
        printf ("%u  %d\n",positive, signedvar);

        positive  *= 2;                                  /* Note 3 */
        signedvar *= 2;
        printf ("%u  %d\n", positive, signedvar);
```

```
    positive  += 3;                                    /* Note 4 */
    signedvar += 3;
    printf ("%u  %d\n", positive, signedvar);

    positive  = 40000;                                 /* Note 5 */
    signedvar = 40000;
    printf ("%u  %d\n", positive, signedvar);

    positive  = 4 - 5;                                 /* Note 6 */
    signedvar = 4 - 5;
    printf ("%u  %d\n", positive, signedvar);

}
```

In this program, two variables are declared, one of type int and one of type unsigned int. The same value is assigned to each variable and the value is output with a call to printf(), using the %u conversion specification for the unsigned int and the %d conversion specification for the int. This is repeated so that five values for each variable are output.

Note 1: The variable positive of type unsigned int is declared. The keyword int is optional. That is, the declaration could also have read
unsigned int positive;

Note 2: The value 65535 is assigned to both variables. This value is the largest value that can be represented with 16 bits and an unsigned type. Note that this program will compile on most C compilers even though the value could be out of range for the variable signedvar. The following printf() call outputs both values. The %u conversion specification is used for the unsigned int.

Note 3: The values of both variables are multiplied by 2. The arithmetic for the unsigned type is done modulo 2^m where m is the total number of bits used to store an unsigned int. If 16 bits are used to store an int value, there would be an overflow error on both variables.

Note 4: The value 3 is added to both values. Again, the arithmetic with the unsigned type is done modulo 2^m. That is, whenever an arithmetic result exceeds $2^m -1$, the counting starts at 0 again. For example, if m = 16, the following relations hold for unsigned quantities:

$$65534 + 1 = 65535 \quad \text{but} \quad 65535 + 1 = 0$$
$$65535 + 3 = 2 \quad \text{and} \quad 2 * 65535 = 65534$$

Note 5: If an int is stored in 16 bits, this value, 40000, will be beyond the largest value that an int can correctly store but in the middle of the correct range for an unsigned int.

Note 6: These assignment statements attempt to store a negative value in both variables. The value in the unsigned int will be interpreted as positive. When using unsigned int types, be aware that certain arithmetic operations with positive integers may yield negative results. Unless this is a planned outcome, these results will be incorrectly interpreted within the program.

Learning Activities

15. Calculate the maximum integer value that can be stored in an unsigned int on your computer system. This value will be $2^m - 1$ where m is the number of bits used to store an integer.

16. Modify the program unsigned.c by replacing the 65535 with the value you calculated in part 1 and replacing the 40000 with any value between $2^{m-1} - 1$ and $2^m - 1$. Note that if m = 16 for your computer system, you will not have to make any modifications.

17. Predict the output of unsigned.c with the modifications you made in problem 2.

18. Execute the modified version of unsigned.c. If the results are different from your prediction, find out why and correct your understanding.

3.7   ANSI C and Integer Types

The keyword signed is new in ANSI C. The declaration

```
signed char charvar;
```

declares a variable of type signed char with the name charvar. Since type char can be either signed or unsigned by implementation default, this use provides a method of ensuring that a char variable is signed. The keyword signed can be used in combination with short, int, and long in a declaration, but since those types are signed by default, it is unnecessary.

The ANSI standards for C specify minimal ranges that must be represented by each of the integral types. The ranges are specified below.

Integral Type	Guaranteed Range (it may be wider)
signed char	−127 to 127
unsigned char	0 to 255
signed short	−32767 to 32767
unsigned short	0 to 65535
signed int	−32767 to 32767
unsigned int	0 to 65535
signed long	−2147483647 to 2147483647
unsigned long	0 to 4294967295

However, an implementation of C may enlarge these ranges. The actual maximum and minimum values that can be represented for each of the integral types is supplied in an implementation of ANSI C by a set of preprocessor-defined constants. These constants are declared in a header file named limits.h.

The program limits.c in Example 3-6 outputs the values of some of the constants
in that file.

 Example 3-6: limits.c

```
/*                 limits.c
 *
 *   Synopsis  -   Outputs values of some constants in limits.h.
 *
 *   Objective -   To illustrate limits.h and the relative ranges of
 *                 values that can be represented with the integral
 *                 types.
 */

#include <stdio.h>
#include <limits.h>

main()
{
        printf ("Contents of limits.h\n\n");
        printf ("Constant\tValue\n");
        printf ("--------\t-----\n");
                                                /* Note 1 */
        printf ("CHAR_BIT\t%d\n", CHAR_BIT);
        printf ("CHAR_MAX\t%d\nCHAR_MIN\t%d\n", CHAR_MAX,
                        CHAR_MIN);
        printf ("SCHAR_MAX\t%d\nSCHAR_MIN\t%d\n", SCHAR_MAX,
                        SCHAR_MIN);
                                                /* Note 2 */
        printf ("INT_MAX \t%d\nINT_MIN \t%d\n", INT_MAX,
                        INT_MIN);
        printf ("LONG_MAX\t%ld\nLONG_MIN\t%ld\n", LONG_MAX,
                        LONG_MIN);
        printf ("SHRT_MAX\t%hd\nSHRT_MIN\t%hd\n", SHRT_MAX,
                        SHRT_MIN);
                                                /* Note 3 */
        printf ("UCHAR_MAX\t%u\nUINT_MAX\t%u\n", UCHAR_MAX,
                        UINT_MAX);
        printf ("ULONG_MAX\t%lu\nUSHRT_MAX\t%u\n", ULONG_MAX,
                        USHRT_MAX);

}
```

The executable code in this program consists solely of printf() calls.

Note 1: The following three printf() calls output the values of the constants relevant to char type variables. The constant CHAR_BIT is the number of bits in a char. The constants CHAR_MAX, CHAR_MIN, SCHAR_MAX, and SCHAR_MIN will be the maximum and minimum values that can be represented by types char and signed char. Notice that if the char type is signed by default on an implementation, the corresponding values will be the same.

Note 2: The next three calls to printf() output the maximum and minimum values for the types int, long int, and short int. Again, notice that type int may be identical to either long int or short int in any implementation. The results of this program should help you determine if this is true.

Note 3: The last two printf() calls output the maximum values for types unsigned char, unsigned short, unsigned long, and unsigned int. The minimum value representable for any of these types is 0; it will not vary between implementations.

Learning Activities

19. If your compiler conforms to the ANSI C standards, compile and execute the program limits.c. Inspect the output for any surprises. Reconcile the results with the results of the other programs in this section (especially with the output from ints.c).

20. If your compiler conforms to the ANSI C standards, inspect a copy of the header file limits.h to see the other values that are declared in that file.

An Example

The program factors.c in Example 3-7 contains some of the concepts we have been discussing. This program will list all prime factors of an integer greater than 2. For example, if the number input is 12, the output would be

```
Prime factors of 12 are 2 2 3.
```

Example 3-7:   factors.c

```
/*              factors.c
 *
 *   Synopsis   -   Outputs the prime factors of each integer (>2)
 *                  that is input.
 *
```

```
 *     Objective -  An example of a useful working program.
 */

#include <stdio.h>

main()
{
        unsigned number, factor;      /* number will store the
                                       * input, and factor drives
                                       * the for loop to find
                                       * the factors.
                                       */

        printf ("This program will print the prime factors ");
        printf ("of an integer that is greater than 2.\n\n");

        /* Prompt for and input the integer. */
        printf ("Enter an integer that is greater than 2 : ");
        scanf ("%u", &number);

        printf ("Prime factors of %d are ", number);
        for (factor = 2; factor <= number; factor++)

                /* if factor divides number evenly */
                if ( ! (number % factor) ) {

                  /* output factor */
                  printf("%d " , factor);

                  /* take the factor out of number */
                  number /= factor;

                  /* decrement factor so that it can test
                   * for a repeated factor.
                   */
                  factor--;
                }
        printf("\n");
}
```

This program contains a single function, main(). Calls to printf() output the purpose of the program and prompt for input. After input with scanf(), the prime factors are extracted with a for loop. Each of the integers between 2 and number are tested to see if they divide number evenly. The test (! (number % factor)) is interpreted as follows: The remainder when number is divided by factor is calculated and negated. If factor divides number evenly, the expression (number % factor) is zero, and the expression ! (number % factor) has the value 1 or true. If factor does not divide number evenly, then the test expression evaluates to 0 or false. When a factor is found, it is output, the factor is divided out of number, and factor is decremented so that the same factor will be tested again in the for loop. In this way, repeated factors are found.

Learning Activities

21. a. Test factors.c with different inputs. What happens if the input is negative?

    b. If an error occurred with the input of a negative number, try to modify the program to handle the error properly.

22. Modify factors.c so that the output has the form

    ```
    12 = 2 * 2 * 3;
    ```

23. Note that factors.c tests all integers less than the input number as possible factors. This is inefficient since not all integers tested are prime. In particular, the only even prime is 2.

    a. Modify the program so that the only even number tested is 2.

    b. How much work would a program have to do to be sure that it was only testing primes as factors? Would this be an increase or decrease in efficiency over factors.c?

3.8 Bit Operations on the Integer Types

A special set of operations, the bit operations, can be used on the integer types. They operate on the bit pattern of the stored values. The bit operations are:

~	negation
>>	shift right
<<	shift left
&	bitwise logical and
^	bitwise logical xor
|	bitwise logical or

Before looking at a program, we will discuss examples of the bit operations. For the examples, assume that the short type occupies 16 bits of storage and that the following declarations have been made:

```
short       intvar1,     intvar2;
char        charvar1,    charvar2;
```

The negation operator, ~ (a tilde), is a unary operator; it operates on the bit pattern of an integer quantity by replacing all the 0 bits by 1 and all of the 1 bits by 0. The syntax for the negation operator is

> `~expression`

where the expression must have one of the integer types. For example, if `intvar1` is a variable of type `short` and has the value 5, its bit pattern (assuming 16 bits for type `short`) is

0	0	0	0	0	0	0	0	0	0	0	0	0	1	0	1

The bitwise negation of `intvar1` is denoted `~intvar1` and has the following bit pattern:

1	1	1	1	1	1	1	1	1	1	1	1	1	0	1	0

Its value would be −6 in signed decimal format or fffa in unsigned hexadecimal format.

As another example assume that `charvar1` has the value `'F'`. In the ASCII character set, its bit pattern is

0	1	0	0	0	1	1	0

The bit pattern of `~charvar1` is

1	0	1	1	1	0	0	1

Its value is outside the ASCII range of 0 to 127.

The bitwise logical and, `&`, is a binary operator. It combines the bit patterns of two quantities of one of the integer types to form a third bit pattern. Its syntax is

> `expression1 & expression2`

The corresponding bits of each pattern are combined under the following rules: If both bits are 1, the corresponding bit in the result is 1; otherwise, the corresponding bit in the result is 0. The rules are summarized in the table below.

i^{th} bit in expression1	i^{th} bit in expression2	i^{th} bit in expression1 & expression2
1	1	1
1	0	0
0	1	0
0	0	0

For example, assume that `intvar1` has value 23 and `intvar2` has value 456. Their bit patterns are

intvar1	0	0	0	0	0	0	0	0	0	0	0	1	0	1	1	1

intvar2	0	0	0	0	0	0	0	1	1	1	0	0	1	0	0	0

The bit pattern of the expression `intvar1 & intvar2` is

intvar1 & intvar2	0	0	0	0	0	0	0	0	0	0	0	0	0	0	0	0

and its value is 0.

Suppose `charvar1` is 'a' and `charvar2` is '5'. The associated bit patterns for the ASCII character set are

charvar1	0	1	1	0	0	0	0	1

charvar2	0	0	1	1	0	1	0	1

The bit pattern for `charvar1 & charvar2` is

charvar1 & charvar2	0	0	1	0	0	0	0	1

This is the bit pattern for the character '!' in the ASCII character set.

The bitwise logical or, `|`, is also a binary operation. It operates on two bit patterns to form a third. The syntax for the bitwise logical or is

```
expression1 | expression2
```

A bit in the resultant pattern is a 1 if either of the corresponding bits in the operands is a 1; if both of the corresponding bits in the operand are 0, the bit in the result is 0. This rule is reflected in the table below.

i^{th} bit in expression1	i^{th} bit in expression2	i^{th} bit in expression1	expression2
1	1	1
1	0	1
0	1	1
0	0	0

Consider the bitwise logical or applied to the variables `intvar1` and `intvar2` with values 23 and 456 respectively. The bit patterns for `intvar1`, `intvar2` and `intvar1 | intvar2` are shown below.

intvar1	0	0	0	0	0	0	0	0	0	0	0	1	0	1	1	1

intvar2	0	0	0	0	0	0	0	1	1	1	0	0	1	0	0	0

intvar1	intvar2	0	0	0	0	0	0	0	1	1	1	0	1	1	1	1	1

The decimal value of `intvar1 | intvar2` is 479.

The next bit operation is the bitwise logical xor, `^`, a carat. An xor expression combines two other expressions and has the syntax

```
expression1 ^ expression2
```

It assigns 1 to the resultant bit if the corresponding bits in the two operands are different and 0 if they are the same. The rule is condensed in the table below.

i^{th} bit in expression1	i^{th} bit in expression2	i^{th} bit in expression1 ^ expression2
1	1	0
1	0	1
0	1	1
0	0	0

For example, consider the bitwise logical xor applied to `charvar1` and `charvar2` with the values 'a' and '5' respectively. The bit patterns for `charvar1`, `charvar2`, and `charvar1 ^ charvar2` are presented below.

`charvar1`	0	1	1	0	0	0	0	1

`charvar2`	0	0	1	1	0	1	0	1

`charvar1 ^ charvar2`	0	1	0	1	0	1	0	0

The character value of `charvar1 ^ charvar2` is 'T'.

The effect of the binary bitwise operations on any bit x is summarized in the table below.

Operation on the bit x	Result
0 | x	x
1 | x	1
0 & x	0
1 & x	x
0 ^ x	x
1 ^ x	~x (the negation of x)

The right and left shifts are also binary operations, but they work differently. The syntax for the right shift is

```
expression1 >> expression2
```

and the syntax for the left shift is

```
expression1 << expression2
```

where both `expression1` and `expression2` must have an integer type. However, the expression on the right, `expression2`, represents the number of bits that `expression1` is to be shifted; it must be non-negative. For example, assume that `intvar1` has the value 1. The bit pattern is

`intvar1`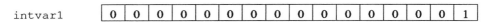

The bit patterns and values of several shifts of `intvar1` are presented below.

Shift	Bit Pattern	Value
`intvar1 << 1`	0 0 0 0 0 0 0 0 0 0 0 0 0 0 1 0	2
`intvar1 << 2`	0 0 0 0 0 0 0 0 0 0 0 0 0 1 0 0	4
`intvar1 << 3`	0 0 0 0 0 0 0 0 0 0 0 0 1 0 0 0	8
`intvar1 << 5`	0 0 0 0 0 0 0 0 0 0 1 0 0 0 0 0	32
`intvar1 << 7`	0 0 0 0 0 0 0 0 1 0 0 0 0 0 0 0	128

Inspecting the patterns and values above, we can see that each shift left by one bit multiplies the value of `intvar1` by 2. This pattern does not hold when ones are shifted off the left edge of the bit pattern or if a 1 is shifted into the leftmost bit in a signed quantity. Similarly, each right shift of `intvar1` divides its value by 2 (truncating integer division) until the value becomes zero.

As another example, suppose that `intvar2` has the value 10,549, which has the corresponding bit pattern

`intvar2`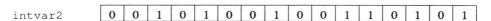

The following shifts have the illustrated results.

Shift	Bit Pattern	Value
`intvar2 >> 1`	0 0 0 1 0 1 0 0 1 0 0 1 1 0 1 0	5274
`intvar2 >> 3`	0 0 0 0 0 1 0 1 0 0 1 0 0 1 1 0	1318
`intvar2 << 1`	0 1 0 1 0 0 1 0 0 1 1 0 1 0 1 0	21098
`intvar2 << 3`	0 1 0 0 1 0 0 1 1 0 1 0 1 0 0 0	18856

Note that in a right shift, any 1s at the right end of the bit pattern are shifted off the end and discarded. The bits at the left end of the word are filled in with 0s. Similarly, in a left shift, the bits at the left end of the word are shifted out and discarded. The bits at the right end of the word become 0s. The shifting is done to the bit patterns; the interpretation of those bit patterns depends on the type of the expression. For example, if a 1 is shifted into the leftmost bit, a previously positive expression could become negative. The interpretation of right shifts of negative expressions could vary with each implementation. The meaning is not specified by the language.

The program in Example 3-8 illustrates the bit operations. It also illustrates hexadecimal initialization of variables of type `unsigned int`. To indicate an integer in hexadecimal within C source code, it is only necessary to begin the integer with the characters `0x` or `0X` (a zero followed by an `'x'` or `'X'`). The `0x` signifies to the compiler and reader that the following value is hexadecimal and will be written using the hexadecimal digits `0, 1, 2, . . . , 9, a, b, c, d, e, f`. The hexadecimal digits `0, 1, 2, . . . , 9, A, B, C, D, E, F` are used after a leading `0X`. An octal representation of an integer can be indicated by starting the number with a leading `0`. For example, in a C source program, the following are equivalent.

decimal	*hexadecimal*	*octal*
23	0x17	027

In the following program, the variables of type `unsigned int` are initialized using a hexadecimal representation. Then the results of several combinations of the bit operations are output.

Example 3-8:   bitop.c

```
/*                  bitop.c
 *
 *    Synopsis  -  Outputs the results of bit operations on
 *                 variables of type unsigned int.
 *
 *    Objective -  Illustrates operations on bits.
 */
#include <stdio.h>

main()
{
        unsigned int w1, w2, w3;                    /* Note 1 */

        w1 = 0x523;                                 /* Note 2 */
        w2 = 0x746;
        w3 = 0x13a;

        printf("w1 & w2 = %x\n", w1&w2);            /* Note 3 */
        printf("w1 | w2 = %x\n", w1|w2);            /* Note 4 */
        printf("w1 ^ w2 = %x\n", w1^w2);            /* Note 5 */
        printf("~w1 = %x\n", ~w1);                  /* Note 6 */
```

```
printf("w1 | (~w1 & w3) = %x\n", w1|(~w2&w3)); /* Note 7 */
printf ("~(~w1 | ~w3) = %x\n", ~(~w1|~w3) );

w1 ^= w2;                                       /* Note 8 */
printf ("w1 is %x, w2 is %x\n", w1, w2);

/*  Shifting bits in a word */
w1 = 0x1;
w2 = 0x422;
w1 = w1<<3;                                      /* Note 9 */
w2 <<= 1;                                        /* Note 10 */
printf ("w1 = %x\t w2 = %x\n", w1, w2);
printf ("w2 >> 2 is %x.\n", w2>>2 );            /* Note 11 */
}
```

A single function named main() contains variable declarations and initializations. The executable code consists of assignment statements and printf().

Note 1: The variables have been declared as type `unsigned int` to ensure that each of the operations is defined. This avoids confusion when the high bit is set to 1 by the bit operations.

Note 2: These three statements initialize the variables. The values are written as hexadecimal constants, signified by the `0x` before the value. Constant values can be written as octal constants by including a leading 0 (zero). For example, `523` is a decimal constant in C, `0523` is an octal constant, and `0x523` is a hexadecimal constant. In this program, hexadecimal is used since each hexadecimal digit translates to four bits. The effect of the bit operations will be easy to calculate.

Note 3: The value of the bitwise and (`&`) of `w1` and `w2` is output in hexadecimal by this call to printf().

Note 4: This statement outputs the hexadecimal of the bitwise or (`|`) for the same two values.

Note 5: The bitwise xor (`^`) with `w1` and `w2` is illustrated here.

Note 6: The bitwise negation takes a single operand. The value of the bitwise negation of `w1` is output in hexadecimal.

Note 7: The next two statements illustrate some combinations of the bit operations. Among these bitwise operators, negation has highest precedence, followed by bitwise and, xor, and or. They associate from left to right. In these statements, the parentheses help specify the order of evaluation.

Note 8: The bitwise operators `&`, `^`, and `|` can be used in compound assignment statements also. The given statement is equivalent to

```
w1 = w1 ^ w2.
```

Note 9: The value of `w1` is shifted left by three bits. Notice that a left shift of one bit multiplies an unsigned value by 2 unless overflow occurs. Shifting by two bits multiplies this value by 4, and shifting by three bits multiplies the value by 8.

Note 10: The shift operators can also be used with compound assignment. This statement shifts the bits in `w2` one position to the left.

Note 11: The `>>` operator is the right shift. Here the value of `w2` shifted to the right two bits is output. Note that each shift to the right by one bit effects truncating division by two on an unsigned value until the value reaches zero. The value of `w2 / 4` is output by this statement.

Learning Activities

24. a. Predict the values output by bitop.c.

    ```
    w1 & w2 = _____
    w1 | w2 = _____
    w1 ^ w2 = _____
    ~w1 = _____
    w1 | (~w1 &w3) = _____
    ~(~w1 | ~w3) = _____
    w1 is _____, w2 is _____
    w1 = _____  w2 = _____
    w2 >> 2 is _____.
    ```

    b. Execute bitop.c to check your predictions in part a.

25. a. In bitop.c, rewrite the statement associated with **Note 9** as a compound assignment.

    b. Write a statement using the bit operations that would multiply `w3` by 64.

26. Write a short program that tests the validity of all the examples presented in this section before bitop.c.

Precedence of Bitwise Operators

The precedence of the bitwise operators is as follows: The bitwise negation has the highest precedence. The shifts are next in precedence level, followed by the bitwise and, the bitwise xor, and finally the bitwise or. The precedence of these operators in comparison with the other C operators is illustrated in the Programmer's Handbook. However, if the expression is at all complicated, it is better to use parentheses to avoid reader confusion.

Using Masks

One common use of the bitwise operations is in working with masks. For example, the integer 8 has a bit pattern of

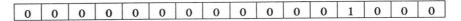

That is, the fourth bit is 1 and all the rest are 0. The expression 8 can be used to test the fourth bit of an `int` variable. For example,

```
intvar1 & 8
```

will be 0 (false) if the fourth bit of `intvar1` is 0 and nonzero (true) if the fourth bit is 1. This type of expression can be used as a conditional expression in an `if`, `while`, `do-while` or `for` statement.

The expression

```
intvar1 | 8
```

is guaranteed to have a 1 in the fourth bit. The fourth bit of `intvar1` can be set using that expression in conjunction with an assignment statement as in

```
intvar1 = intvar1 | 8;
```

or more simply with the compound assignment statement

```
intvar1 |= 8;
```

As an example of the practical use of the bitwise operations, consider a word processing package that uses the ASCII character set and stores each character in a single byte. Since there are 128 ASCII characters, ranging from 0 to 127, and the range of nonnegative integers that can be represented in an 8-bit byte is from 0 to 255, the eighth bit of each byte is used to keep track of the program's formatting options. This is done by using the bit patterns with a 1 in the eighth bit to depict the different options for formatting. For example, the value 128, with bit pattern

1	0	0	0	0	0	0	0

might be used to toggle underlining. The value 129 with bit pattern

1	0	0	0	0	0	0	1

might be used to toggle bold print. The value 141 might be used to indicate a carriage return inserted by the word processing program rather than by the author; this value differs from the usual carriage return in the ASCII character set only by the eighth bit being set. If another program, like one to list the file at the terminal, needs to access the information in this file, the other program will not understand the word processor's special use of the eighth bit. Some of these special bytes need to be removed and some of them need to have the eighth bit reset to 0.

The program listit.c in Example 3-9 is a filter that will delete any byte in its input with the eighth bit set to 1, with the exception of the values 138 (the word processor's version of the line feed character) and 141 (its version of a carriage return). For these exceptional values, the program will simply set the eighth bit to 0.

The program is written as a filter so that to work properly, it must be executed with input redirection from an input file. If input redirection is not available on your computer system, you will not be able to test the program easily. It would be necessary to have the program open a file. File handling will be discussed in Chapter 10.

Example 3-9:   listit.c

```
/*                    listit.c
 *
 *   Synopsis  -  Masks out the high bit on characters WP_LINEFEED
 *                and WP_CARRETURN and deletes other characters with
 *                the high bit set while copying input to output.
 *
 *   Objective -  Illustrates use of masks with the bit operations.
 */

#include <stdio.h>
#define HIGHBIT         128                          /* Note 1 */
#define NOHIGHBIT       127
#define WP_LINEFEED     138
#define WP_CARRETURN    141

main()
{
        int iochar;
        while ( (iochar = getchar()) != EOF) {
                if (HIGHBIT & iochar) {              /* Note 2 */
                    if ( (iochar == WP_LINEFEED) ||
                                (iochar == WP_CARRETURN) )
                            putchar (iochar & NOHIGHBIT);  /* Note 3 */
                }                                    /* Note 4 */
                else
                    putchar (iochar);
        }
}
```

Several preprocessor constants are defined. The function main() consists of a single `while` loop that will read terminal input character by character until end-of-file is sensed. The body of the `while` loop contains a single `if-else` statement. The statement associated with the `if` is another `if` statement.

Note 1: The preprocessor constant HIGHBIT has the following bit pattern:

1	0	0	0	0	0	0	0

That is, the first bit is 1 and all other bits are 0. This will be used to test a byte to see if the high bit is 1. The preprocessor constant NOHIGHBIT has a 0 in the high bit and all the other bits are 1. That is, it has the bit pattern

0	1	1	1	1	1	1	1

NOHIGHBIT will be used with & to set the high bit to 0. The next two preprocessor constants define the exceptional values discussed above.

Note 2: The expression (HIGHBIT & iochar) will have a nonzero value when iochar has its high bit set and 0 otherwise. This is an example of masking. The lower bits have been masked out.

Note 3: The high bit will be 0 in the expression NOHIGHBIT & iochar since the high bit in NOHIGHBIT is 0. However, the lower seven bits will be identical to those in iochar. In this expression, the high bit of iochar was masked out; the low bits were unchanged.

Note 4: This brace delimits the end of a block that was opened on the line marked by /* Note 2 */. There is a single if statement inside this block. Note that the braces are necessary in this case to insure correct execution of the program. Without them, the following else would be paired with the closest if.

Learning Activities

27. What would be the output (if any) when each of the bytes whose bit patterns appear below is input to listit.c?

Bit Pattern   **Output**

1	0	0	0	1	0	1	0

_____

0	1	1	0	1	0	0	0

_____

1	1	1	1	0	1	0	0

_____

1	0	0	0	1	1	0	1

_____

28. If the braces on the lines marked by /* Note 2 */ and /* Note 4 */ in listit.c were omitted, give the output of the modified program for the same four bytes.

29. If your system can do input and output redirection, create a file with the four bytes above (you might have to write a program to create the file) and run both versions of the program to check your answers.
30. Suppose that MASK is a preprocessor constant defined by

```
#define MASK 0x7c
```

and that iochar is of type int.
a. What is the bit pattern for MASK?

b. Using the value from part a, write the value of the bits that are determined in the expressions below. Put a question mark for each bit that depends on the value of iochar. The first two bits in the first expression have been done for you.

Expression	Bits
MASK | iochar	? 1 _ _ _ _ _ _
MASK & iochar	_ _ _ _ _ _ _ _

3.9 Floating Point Types

Values like 2.5, 3.14159, 2.467e+002, 4.0, and 2.718 are known as floating point values in C. These values may have a nonzero fractional part. The representations, 2.5, 3.14159, 4.0, and 2.718 are expressed in decimal notation. The representation 2.467e+002 is an exponential representation that is equivalent to 246.7. The number after the e indicates the number of places that the decimal point must be moved to represent the number in decimal notation. As other examples,

```
2.954200e+01      is the same as 29.542
3.04215e-0003     is the same as .00304215
```

Floating point numbers can be used as constants or stored in variables of the appropriate type. An example of a preprocessor directive to declare a floating point constant is

```
#define PI 3.14159
```

C provides the types float, double, and long double to store floating point values as variables. The type float is used for single-precision floating point numbers. The type double is for double-precision floating point numbers; another term for double is long float. The type long double is for extra precision. The type long double is an addition to the C language by the ANSI standards.

Note that not all of the real numbers can be represented with the floating point types. As with the integers and type int, each floating point type represents real numbers in a certain range. The actual range may vary with the implementation, but the ANSI standards guarantee that double is no less precise than float and that long double is no less precise than double.

The ANSI C compilers supply a header file named float.h that contains implementation-dependent information about the range of each type of floating point variable. The information is similar to the information in limits.h that refers to the integer types.

A declaration of a variable of type `float` minimally consists of the keyword, `float`, followed by the variable name and terminated with a semicolon. For example,

```
float floatvar;
```

declares a variable of type `float` named `floatvar`. Similarly,

```
double doublevar;
```

declares a variable of type `double` named `doublevar`.

Floating point variables can be initialized when they are declared in the same way as variables of the integer types. For example,

```
float floatvar = 2.765;
```

declares a variable named `floatvar` of type `float` with the initial value 2.765.

Some of the operations that can be used with expressions of type `float` or `double` are the arithmetic operators (+, −, *, and /), the relational operators (==, !=, <, <=, >, and >=), and the logical operators (!, &&, and ||). The result of any of the arithmetic operators when applied to values of type `double` is another value of type `double`. However, when a relational or a logical operator is applied to a value of type `float` or `double`, the result will be of type `int`. Examples appear below. Assume that each of the numeric quantities has type `double`.

Expression	Value	Type
2.5 + 5.7	8.2	double
2.5 <= 3.62	1	int
2.5 == 3.62	0	int
2.5 / 3.62	0.6906	double
2.5 && 3.62	1	int
2.5 | 3.62	not defined	error
!2.5	0	int
!0	1	int

These results are consistent with the interpretation of 0 as false and of 1 or any nonzero quantity as true. As an additional example, 2.5 && 3.2 is true because both operands are interpreted as true. Also, !2.5 is false because 2.5 is nonzero or true.

Input and Output of Floating Point Values

The functions printf() and scanf() have different conversion specifications for `float` or `double` values. The conversion specifications are %e, %f, and %g.

With the scanf() function, all of these conversion specifications work for values in a decimal or exponential format. A length specifier can be used with the conversion specification to indicate the size of the variable. The statements

```
scanf ("%f", &varname);
scanf ("%e", &varname);
```

expect to read a floating point value and expect the variable `varname` to have type `float`. The statements

```
scanf ("%lf", &varname);
scanf ("%le", &varname);
```

expect a floating point value also. However, the `'l'` (lowercase L) indicates that `varname` is expected to be of type `double`. The conversion specifications `%lE` and `%lg` tell scanf() to convert to type `double` also. The conversion specifications `%Lf`, `%Le`, `%LE`, and `%Lg` are used with both printf() and scanf() to indicate type `long double`. The `'L'` is only used in ANSI C compilers to indicate type `long double`.

Two additional conversion specifications, `%E` and `%G`, are available for use with printf(). The meanings of the conversion specifications with printf() are illustrated in the following example. The value 3456.78 can be output in the following forms:

```
3456.780000     with the statement printf ("%f\n", 3456.78);
3.456780e+003   with the statement printf ("%e\n", 3456.78);
3.456780E+003   with the statement printf ("%E\n", 3456.78);
```

The `%f` conversion specification writes the floating point number in decimal form. The `%e` conversion specification writes the number in exponential notation; the number after the `e` is the power of 10 that must be multiplied by the number before the `e`. The `%E` conversion is the same as the `%e` except that an uppercase `E` is used in the output. The `%g` conversion specification may write the floating point value in either decimal or exponential notation. Consult the *Programmer's Handbook* for details.

The field width and the precision with which a number is printed can also be controlled. In the examples above, the default field width and precision was used. The minimum field width or minimum number of spaces to be output can be specified by placing a decimal integer between the `'%'` and the conversion specification. For example:

```
printf("12345678901234567890123456789012345678 90\n");
printf("The number is %15f\n", 1.2);
```

should give the following output:

```
12345678901234567890123456789012345678 90
The number is        1.200000
```

The output of the string of digits is included only to indicate that 15 spaces are used for the output of 1.2. The 15 spaces include the decimal point and blank padding to the left of the number.

The precision is specified by a period followed by a decimal integer that indicates the number of decimal places to be displayed. For example, the statement

```
printf("12345678901234567890123456789012345678 90\n");
printf ("The number is %15.2f\n", 1.2);
```

should give the output below:

```
12345678901234567890123456789012345678 90
The number is           1.20
```

The syntax for the integer and floating point conversions is illustrated in the program floatpt.c in Example 3-10. The declaration of a variable of each built-in floating point type is also illustrated.

Example 3-10:   floatpt.c

```
/*              floatpt.c
 *
 *   Synopsis  -  The values of variables of type float, double, and
 *                long double are assigned and output in different
 *                formats by printf().  The sizeof() each type is
 *                also output.
 *
 *   Objective -  Illustrates declaration, assignment, and some of the
 *                output options with printf() of floating point
 *                variables.
 */

#include <stdio.h>

main()
{
        float    floatvar;                              /* Note 1 */
        double   doublevar;
        long double ldvar;

                                                        /* Note 2 */
        printf ("The number of bytes in a float is %d.\n",
                                sizeof(float) );
        printf ("The number of bytes in a double is %d.\n",
                                sizeof(double) );
        printf ("The number of bytes in a long double is %d.\n",
                                sizeof(long double) );


        floatvar = 65.328;                              /* Note 3 */
                                                        /* Note 4 */
        printf ("floatvar has the value %7.2f.\n", floatvar);
        printf ("It can also be written in the form %10.3e.\n",
                                floatvar);
        printf ("It can also be written in the form %10.3E.\n",
                                floatvar);
        printf ("It can also be written in the form %10.3g.\n",
                                floatvar);
```

```
    doublevar = 1.2465e-5;                          /* Note 5 */
    printf ("doublevar has the value %6.3f.\n",doublevar);
    printf ("It can also be written in the form %7.5e.\n",
                            doublevar);
    printf ("It can also be written in the form %7.5E.\n",
                            doublevar);
    printf ("It can also be written in the form %7.5g.\n",
                            doublevar);

    ldvar = 584.365E+17;                            /* Note 6 */
    printf ("ldvar has the value %7.2Lf.\n", ldvar);/* Note 7 */
    printf ("It can also be written in the form %10.3Le.\n",
                            ldvar);
    printf ("It can also be written in the form %10.3LE.\n",
                            ldvar);
    printf ("It can also be written in the form %10.3Lg.\n",
                            ldvar);
}
```

The program consists of variable declarations, assignment statements, and calls to printf().

Note 1: Variables of types `float`, `double`, and `long double` are declared.

Note 2: The number of bytes occupied by each of the floating point types is output using the sizeof() operator.

Note 3: Decimal notation can be used in assignment statements to variables of type `float`, `double`, and `long double`.

Note 4: The next three calls to printf() give examples of output using the three different conversion specifications that are available for the floating point types.

Note 5: Exponential form can also be used for a floating point constant.

Note 6: The exponent can be signified with either '`e`' or '`E`'.

Note 7: The conversion specifications in these printf() calls include '`L`' to indicate that the value is of type `long double`.

Learning Activities

31. Execute the program floatpt.c to become familiar with the notation used for floating point types.

32. If you have an ANSI C compiler,

    a. Inspect the header file float.h to see the predefined constants and their meaning.

    b. Write a program to output the values of the constants using printf() and the appropriate conversion specifications.

    c. Experiment with output and calculations with values like FLT_MAX + 1 to discover how out-of-range values are handled. Do they cause compile-time errors, runtime errors, or no errors?

An Example

The program slope.c in Example 3-11 pulls together concepts that we have already discussed to create a useful program. In this program, the user is asked to enter the x and y coordinates of two points. The program will then calculate the slope and the y-intercept of the line through the two points and output the equation of the line.

Example 3-11:   slope.c

```
/*              slope.c
 *
 *    Synopsis  -  The user enters the coordinates of two points and
 *                 the program will output the equation of the line
 *                 through those two points.
 *
 *    Objective -  To illustrate the use of floating point types in
 *                 an applied program.
 */

#include <stdio.h>

main()
{
        float x1, y1, x2, y2;         /* The points */
        float slope, y_int;
```

```
/*  Input the coordinates of the points */
printf("Enter the first point.\n");
printf("x: ");
scanf("%f", &x1);
printf("y: ");
scanf("%f", &y1);
printf("Enter the second point.\n");
printf("x: ");
scanf("%f", &x2);
printf("y: ");
scanf("%f", &y2);

/*  Check for a vertical line */
if (x1 != x2) {
    /* the line is not vertical, calculate the
     * slope and y intercept
     */

    slope = (y2 - y1) / (x2 - x1);
    y_int = y1 - slope*x1;
    if (slope == 0)             /* horizontal line */
        printf("The equation is y = %5.2f\n", y1);
    else
        printf("The equation is y = %5.2fx + %5.2f\n",
                            slope, y_int);
}
else                            /* vertical line */
printf ("The equation is x = %5.2f\n", x1);

}
```

The program consists of a single function, main(). The program uses printf() calls for prompts and for the output of results. Input is done with scanf(). Before calculating the slope, the program checks to see if the line is vertical. If this check were not done, the calculation of slope might cause an error. Note that the program uses different printf() calls to output a vertical or a horizontal line.

Learning Activities

33. In testing slope.c, find out what happens when an integer is input as a coordinate of a point. Does an error condition occur? Is the output correct?

34. *C by Discovery*
    a. When executing slope.c, what happens on your system when an alphabetic character is typed as the first character of the coordinate of a point? This should create an error condition. Is it caught at compile time, at runtime, or not at all?

    b. Think of a way to avoid this error condition. Don't implement it at this time.

35. Rewrite slope.c to omit the calculation of the slope for a horizontal line (y1 equals y2).

3.10 Function Types and Return Values

In C, functions as well as variables have types. The default type of a function is type `int`. Any other function type should be declared.

In Chapter 1 we discussed some uses of the `return` statement. When a function uses the `return` statement to return a value, the value of the expression becomes the value of the function. The type of the expression becomes the type of the function.

If the type of the returned expression is `int`, the function has type `int` also. An example of an ANSI C declaration of a simple function of type `int` is the function positive() below:

```
positive(int x)
{
        return ( x>0 );
}
```

Since the value of the expression $x>0$ is either 0 or 1, the function returns an `int` value. Therefore, the function itself has the default type `int`. Even though it is not necessary, we could include an explicit declaration of the function type in the function definition as shown below:

```
int positive(int x)
{
        return ( x>0 );
}
```

The first line of the function definition is a declaration.* It contains the function type, int, the function name, positive, and the name and type of the formal parameters, if any. (In this case there is one formal parameter with the name x of the type int.) For functions of type int, the declaration of the type is not necessary because int is the default. However, if a function returns a value of any other type, the function type must be declared. For example, the function cubit() below returns a value of type double. The function must be declared as shown.

```
double cubit(double x)
{
        return (x*x*x);
}
```

When one function calls another function, the calling function must know the type of the called function. If the type of the called function is not int, the type must be declared where the calling function can see it. This declaration is similar to the first line of a function definition. An ANSI C prototype declaration consists of the type followed by the function name and a pair of parentheses. For example, the prototype declaration of the function cubit() would be

```
double cubit(double x);**
```

This declaration could appear in the declaration section of the function block of the calling function or it could appear above the function. The program circle.c in Example 3-12 has two examples of function prototype declarations in two different locations in the program.

Some functions in C do not return values. For example, a function could be written to do output. The function might not need to return a value. These C functions would be more like subroutines or procedures in other languages. The type void is given to functions that don't return a value. Because this type differs from the default int type, it needs to be declared explicitly also. The declaration should

---

* This syntax for the declaration of the parameters is new with ANSI C. With older C compilers the parameter name appears between the parentheses but the type declaration appears on a separate line of source code above the opening brace for the function code. The declaration of the function positive() for an older compiler would be

```
int positive(x)
int x;
{
        return ( x>0 );
}
```

For a transitional period, the ANSI C compilers will accept the old-style declaration. The ANSI C prototype declarations will be used from this point on in this text. If you are not working with an ANSI C compiler, you will need to modify the function declarations in the programs before running them.

**This syntax is new with ANSI C. It is called a function prototype. The parameter names in a prototype declaration do not have to be predeclared. In fact, the parameter names can be omitted entirely, as in this alternate prototype:

```
double cubit (double);
```

These function declarations for an older compiler will not mention the parameters at all. For example, the old-style declaration of cubit() would be

```
double cubit();
```

If you do not have an ANSI compiler, the prototype declarations will need to be changed before executing the programs. The purpose of prototyping will be discussed in Chapter 8.

appear in at least two places: in the first line of the definition of the function and in a location either inside the function block for a calling function or outside and above the function blocks of all the functions that call it. The following is an example of a function of type `void`.

```
void printit(float result)
{
    if (result > 0)
        printf("The result is %5.2f\n", result);
    else
        printf("Invalid result\n");
}
```

When the function printit() is called, the prototype declaration

```
void printit(float result);
```

should be seen by the calling function.

There are two points to note. First, before this section of the text, we failed to declare the types of the subfunctions used in the example programs. The types of those functions were either `int` or `void`.

It is not necessary to declare functions of type `int` since that type is the default type. The compiler expects every function without an explicit type declaration to return a value of type `int`.

It was not proper to omit the `void` type declarations of the functions that did not return a value, but it is not essential to include it either. As mentioned before, the compiler expects the function to return a value of type `int` and it provides a location for the returned value. When the function is truly a `void` function, that location is unused, but no error occurs. However, when a function is declared to have type `void`, the overhead of preparing the location for the return value can be avoided and the program may run more efficiently.

Second, note that main() is a function and, like every function, should have a declared type. Most of the time, the type of main() is `void`. This should be declared with the definition of main(), but the declaration of main() where the calling environment can see it can be omitted.

The program circle.c illustrates the declaration of functions that do not return type `int`. In the Learning Activities that follow you will see what happens when that declaration is omitted.

Example 3-12:   circle.c

```
/*              circle.c
 *
 *    Synopsis  -  Accepts input of the radius of a circle and
 *                 outputs the area and circumference.
 *
 *    Objective -  To illustrate the declaration and use of
 *                 functions with type other than int.
 */
```

```
#include <stdio.h>
#define PI 3.1415926

double area(double r);                                      /* Note 1 */

void main()                                                 /* Note 2 */
{
        double radius;
        double circumference(double r);                     /* Note 3 */

        printf("Program to calculate area and circumference ");
        printf("of a circle.\n");
        printf("------- -- --------- ---- --- ------------- ");
        printf("-- - -------\n");

        printf("Please enter the radius : ");
        scanf ("%lf", &radius);

        printf("The area of a circle with radius %5.2lf is %5.2lf.\n",
                            radius, area(radius));
        printf("The circumference of the circle is %5.2f.\n",
                            circumference(radius));
}
/************************************   area()    ************/
/*      area()
 *      calculates the area of a circle given its radius.
 */
double area(double r)                                       /* Note 4 */
{
        return (PI*r*r);
}
/*****************************   circumference()   ********/
/*      circumference()
 *      calculates the circumference of a circle given its radius.
 */
double circumference(double r)                              /* Note 4 */
{
        return (2*PI*r);
}
```

This program consists of three functions, main(), area() and circumference(). The function main() announces the intent of the program, inputs a value for the variable `radius` and outputs the results of the calls to the other two functions.

Note 1: The function area() takes a parameter of type `double` and returns a value of type `double`. The prototype declaration must appear where the calling function, main(), can see it. The position above the start of any function in a source code file is a position that is visible to any function in the file. This declaration and others like it could also be collected in a header file. The `#include` preprocessor directive would be used to include the contents of the header file in the program. We continue the discussion of communication between different parts of a program in Chapter 8.

Note 2: Since the function main() will not return any value to its calling environment, main() has function type `void`. The program will execute and give the same results when this type is not declared, but execution can be more efficient if the type is declared.

Note 3: The function circumference() must be declared because it returns a type other than `int`. The declaration of the parameter to circumference() is part of this ANSI C prototype. In this position, the declaration is local to the function main().

Note 4: The type declaration precedes the function name in the definition of each of the functions, area() and circumference(). This declaration is not necessary when the function returns a value of type `int`. The declaration of the parameter to each of these functions will be part of the ANSI C declaration.

Learning Activities

36. Execute circle.c to make sure that it works correctly as given. (If you do not have an ANSI C compiler, the function declarations will need to be modified.)

37. *C by Discovery* Modify circle.c in each of the following ways. You will be creating error conditions. After each modification try to compile and execute the program again. Notice how your system handles each of the errors. Is an error caught at compile time, at runtime, or not caught at all? If the program executes, does it give the correct results?

    a. Remove the declaration of area() that appears above the function main().

    b. Remove the function type declaration from the definition of area().

    c. Remove both of the declarations mentioned in parts a and b.

    d. Try to generalize from these experiences about the types of functions, their declarations, and their return values.

38. Look back through the programs preceding this section and correctly fill in the types for any functions. Compile and run them again to make sure that they work correctly.

3.11 Types of Expressions and Automatic Conversions

In C, every expression has an associated type. Operators and operands within the expression combine to determine the expression's type.

Expressions whose final value is the result of a logical operator or a relational operator have type `int`. The operators involved are `!`, `&&`, `||`, `==`, `!=`, `<`, `<=`, `>`, and `>=`. The result of any of those operations can be thought of as true or false. C assigns a value of 1 to a true statement and a value of 0 to a false statement.

Some type conversions are done in calculating the final value of expressions involving the arithmetic operators. These conversions need to be understood in order to understand C's treatment of types. The rules appear below.

First, all values of type `char` or `short` (or `unsigned char` and `unsigned short`) are converted to type `int` (or `unsigned`) before any processing is done. The types `char`, `unsigned char`, `short`, and `unsigned short` are used for storage, not for calculations.

After these initial conversions, expressions involving the unary operators `-`, `--`, and `++` will have a type matching the type of the operand. For example, if `intvar` is a variable of type `int`, and `floatvar` is a variable of type `float`, then the expressions `-intvar`, `--intvar`, and `intvar++` are all of type `int`. The expressions `-floatvar`, `--floatvar`, and `floatvar++` are all of type `float`. Note also that `-charvar` is of type `int` even if `charvar` was declared to have type `char`.

In expressions involving only the binary arithmetic operators, `+`, `-`, `*`, `/`, the type of the expression depends on the operands. If all the operands are of the same type, the expression will have that type. After the declaration

```
int intvar_1, intvar_2;
```
the expressions `intvar_1 + intvar_2`, `intvar_1 - intvar_2`, `intvar_1 * intvar_2`, and `intvar_1 / intvar_2` are of type `int`. As mentioned in Chapter 1, the operator `/` produces truncated quotients when both operands are of type `int`. For example, $3/2$ is equal to 1.

The expressions resulting from combinations of operations like

```
(intvar1 * 2) / (intvar2 -24)
```
where `intvar1` and `intvar2` are still of type `int` have the `int` type also.

Similarly, after the declarations

```
float floatvar1, floatvar2;
```
the expressions `floatvar1+floatvar2`, `floatvar1-floatvar2`, and `(floatvar1-floatvar2) / (floatvar1+floatvar2)` are all of type `float`.

In general, if all the operands in an arithmetic expression have the same type, then the expression will retain that type. However, it is possible to write expressions in which the operands are of different types. When this is done, explicit rules are applied to determine the expression's type.

The actual calculation of the value of an arithmetic expression is done with the types `int`, `unsigned`, `long`, `unsigned long`, `float`, `double`, and `long double`. The general idea is that when the result of a binary operator is evaluated, both operands are converted to a single type that will accurately represent all the possible values but not waste storage space. Rules for automatic conversions on the above types are as follows. At most one of the conversions takes place for each binary operator in the expression.

1. If an expression contains an operand of type `long double`, the other operand is converted to `long double` before calculating the expression's value. The conversion is finished.

2. Otherwise, if there exists an operand of type `double`, the other operand is converted to type `double` before calculation. This concludes the conversion in this case.

3. Similarly, if one operand is of type `float`, the other operand is converted to type `float` and the conversion terminates.

If the conversion is not finished, the operands must all be of the integral types `long`, `unsigned long`, `int`, or `unsigned int`.

4. Of these, the type `unsigned long` dominates in that one operand of type `unsigned long` causes the other operand to be converted to that type.

5. Operands of types `long int` and `unsigned int` in the same expression are converted to type `long int` if the range of values representable by type `unsigned int` is a subset of the range representable by type `long`. Otherwise, both values are converted to type `unsigned long int`.

6. Otherwise, if one operand has type `long`, the other is converted to type `long`.

7. If one operand has type `unsigned`, the other operand is converted to type `unsigned`.

8. Otherwise, both operands are of type `int`.

After all automatic conversions have taken place, the arithmetic operations are applied. The type of the resulting expression matches the type of the operands after conversion.

For example, assume that the declarations

```
short s;
unsigned u;
double d;
```

have been made. In evaluating the expression

```
(s + u) * d
```

the following automatic conversions are made:

1. Before starting the evaluation, s is converted to type `int`.

2. In evaluating the result of the addition operation, s is converted from type int to type unsigned. The bit pattern remains the same, but assuming that an int occupies 16 bits of memory, the value −3 would be interpreted as 65532 (or 65535 − 3). Note that 65535 is the largest value representable with an unsigned int.

3. The addition is performed. It yields an expression of type unsigned int.

4. Since the multiplication operator combines an operand of type unsigned int with an operator of type double, the unsigned int value is converted to type double before multiplying.

5. The multiplication is performed. The type of the resulting expression is double.

Quick Reference for Conversions

With only minor exceptions, the automatic conversions in C can be viewed as finding a dominating type in an expression involving a binary operator and converting the values in that expression to that dominating type. A list of the dominating types from most to least dominating follows:

```
long double
double
float
unsigned long
long
unsigned
int
```

The exceptions arise in that for any expression involving only char, signed or unsigned char, short, or unsigned short, the dominating expression will be of type int or unsigned. Also, for expressions consisting of types long int and unsigned int, the dominating type depends on the implementation. It may be either unsigned long int or long int.

Ranges of values that can be represented by different types are implementation dependent. That is, some compilers may represent a short with 16 bits, an int with 16 bits, and a long with 32 bits while others may represent a short with 16 bits, an int with 32 bits, and a long with 32 bits. Similar size differences occur in the floating point types.

The ANSI standard for C requires that two header files be supplied with information on the ranges that are representable with the arithmetic types.

The file limits.h contains information about the range of values that can be represented by the integral types. Values from limits.h were output by the program limits.c from Example 3-6. The file float.h contains similar information for the floating point types.

Learning Activities

39. If you have an ANSI C compiler and if you didn't do this in an earlier learning activity, write a program that will output some of the constants in the header file float.h. Pattern your program after limits.c. Inspect the output and reconcile this with your understanding of the internal representation of floating point variables.

40. Consider the following declarations:

```
char c1, c2;
int i;
long l;
unsigned u;
unsigned short us;
unsigned long ul;
float f;
double d;
```

What are the types of the following expressions?

```
c1 + 3
(us + f) * i
(ul % c1) / i
us + c1
d + f + ul
u + l
3 * us
c1 + c2
```

3.12   Cast Expressions or Forced Type Conversions

After the automatic conversions, the operands of a binary operator are of the same type. By default, the resultant expression has the same type as its converted operands. However, sometimes it is necessary or preferable to compare or calculate with different types, and sometimes the default conversions do not give the desired resultant type. A *type cast* can be used in these situations.

The type of an expression can be temporarily changed with a type cast. A cast consists of a pair of parentheses enclosing a type specifier. It is a unary operator in C. For example:

```
(float)
```

is the syntax for a cast to type float. If the variable intvar has been declared of type int, the expression

```
(float) intvar;
```

will have type float in the statement in which it was used. The type of intvar is not permanently changed. Similarly, the cast (unsigned) expression

forces expression to be interpreted as an unsigned int type. The cast

        (short) expression

forces expression to be treated as a short int.

A cast can be constructed with any of the basic types in C. The data types we will study in later chapters are candidates for casts as well as the scalar types presented in this chapter.

Example 3-13 shows one use for a type cast. The purpose of the program cast.c is to calculate the average of three integers. The method used is to input the integers as type int, add them, and then divide the sum by 3. The choice of type int could be dictated by storage efficiency as well as potential other uses for these variables if the program were to be expanded. The problem is that if the three data values and their sum are of type int, when the sum is divided by 3 (another int value), the result will also be of type int; the division would be integer division. One solution is to use a cast to type float on the variable sum. That would force this value to type float, and the division would no longer truncate the fractional part.

Example 3-13:   cast.c

```
/*                      cast.c
 *     Synopsis  -  Inputs three integers and outputs their average.
 *
 *     Objective -  Illustrates one use of type casts.
 */
#include <stdio.h>

void main ()
{
        float average;                                      /* Note 1 */
        int first_num, second_num, third_num, sum;

        printf ("This program  will calculate the ");
        printf ("average of three integers.\n");
        printf ("Enter the integers now. Press Return after each one.\n");

        scanf ("%d", &first_num);
        scanf ("%d", &second_num);
        scanf ("%d", &third_num);

        sum = first_num + second_num + third_num;
        average = ( float ) sum / 3;                        /* Note 2 */
        printf ("The average of your data is %6.3f.\n", average);
}
```

The three calls to printf() output information and instructions on how to use this program. The three scanf() calls input the data values. The last statements in the program calculate the average and output it.

Note 1: Notice that average has been declared of type float. This is necessary so that fractional values can be represented.

Note 2: The variable sum is of type int. The number 3 is also an int. Normally, the expression

```
sum/3
```

would also be of type int. In order to force it to be of type float, a cast is used. The cast consists of a set of open and close parentheses enclosing a type name. The cast is a unary operator and has higher precedence than the division operator. The variable sum is interpreted as a float value; the operation performed in this statement is floating point division instead of integer division because of this cast.

Many other uses for type casts will arise later in the text. One of their main uses is in C library functions. The library functions are very serviceable, but some of them return types that are not identical to the types used in a program even though the information returned by the function is in a format that can be used. A type cast might be used with a library function to force the conversion of the returned value to match the existing types in a program.

There are no restrictions on the use of type casts. Any type in a C program can be cast to any other type. However, data might be lost. For example, if doublevar had been declared as type double, then the cast

```
(char) doublevar
```

would minimally truncate the fractional part of doublevar when evaluating the expression. If the integer part of doublevar was outside the range representable by a char, additional data would be lost.

Learning Activities

41. a. Run cast.c several times with different input to make sure that you see what is happening. Input numbers whose sum is not evenly divisible by 3.

   b. Remove the cast from the sum/3 statement and execute the program again to see what the difference is.

   c. Explain what happens in your own words.

42. Obtain and read a copy of the manual page for scanf().

43. *C by Discovery* The program cast.c instructs the user to separate the input values with carriage returns.

   a. Is this necessary for the program to work correctly?

   b. If not, can you modify the scanf() calls so that it is necessary?

3.13   A Closer Look at Storage of Scalar Data

This section provides technical insight into the storage of scalar data. It is beneficial to understand the behavior of the CPU during memory storage and recall. This knowledge can often aid in debugging a program or simply recognizing the limitations of the computer.

Recall that scalar data is stored in bundles of bits called bytes and groups of bytes called words. These groups of bits offer a binary method for representing character, integer and floating point data. In this section we take a closer look at exactly how this data is stored as well as the ramifications of these storage techniques. We will categorize all of the C data types into two groups: integral types and floating point types as follows.

Integral Types	*Floating Point Types*
char or signed char	float
unsigned char	double
int	long double
short int	
long int	
unsigned int	
unsigned short int	
unsigned long int	

Additionally, we will examine these categories in light of two very important considerations: accuracy and precision. Accuracy refers to the exactness of a number while precision refers to the number of fractional digits represented by a number. For example the integer 3 has a great deal of accuracy but very little precision while the real number 3.1415926535... (Pi) has a great deal more precision at the expense of accuracy or exactness. It is important to understand that many numbers are both accurate and precise.

Finally, it is important to point out that in any discussion on data storage we move outside the realm of ANSI C Standards and into the realm of machine dependencies and architectural specifics. Data storage on any computer is dictated by the machine architecture rather than by any one programming language that might be implemented on that machine. However, there are some standards for machine architectures that will allow the reader to generalize the information presented here.

Integral Types

We will consider the memory storage of the integral types first, as they are easier to understand and the method of storage as a binary value is relatively straight forward.

Typically, scalar types are stored in groups of bits where the "leftmost" bit is called the *sign bit*. The sign bit tells the CPU whether to treat the number as a negative number (sign bit set to one) or a positive number (sign bit set to zero).

char data types

Single character data typically occupies 8 bits or 1 byte using the ASCII value associated with the character being stored.

Example:

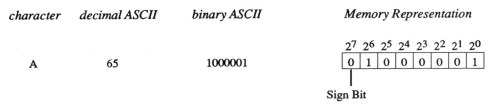

character	*decimal ASCII*	*binary ASCII*	*Memory Representation*
A	65	1000001	

Note: The exponential value above each bit in the example is the place value that it represents.

The ASCII values range from 0 to 127 and include 128 different values. Only the rightmost seven bits are necessary to represent all of these values. Because of this, the sign bit is typically ignored in the storage of character data. This generally means that the sign bit is set to zero. However, it is possible to use a variable of type char to store values between -128 and 127.

Some computers use the values in the range 127 and 255 for special characters which are not part of the standard ASCII character set. In order to use these characters, the sign bit must be treated as a digit in the binary number. The sign bit can be used as the next digit by preceding char with the modifier unsigned. Thus, the range of potential values is between 0 and 255 for a total of 256 different values.

Although typically considered bad programming style, it is sometimes useful to use char or unsigned char for variables used to hold small integers in order to save memory. The limitation of this is the drastically reduced range of integers which are representable. Consider the following program which prints out the hexadecimal values of the positive integers between 0 and 255.

```
main()
{
        unsigned char num;    /* Num stores integers in
                                 the range 0-255 */
        for (num=0; num < 256; ++num)
            printf("%d decimal = %x hexadecimal.\n",
                   num, num);
}
```

Since we know that num will never hold a value outside the range 0-255 we can save a little memory by declaring it unsigned char. The comment is important so that the program is clear to a third party reader.

Two's Complement for Negative Numbers

It is appropriate at this point to consider the previous program with a few minor modifications.

```
main()
{
        char num;    /* Num stores integers in the range
                        -128 to 127 */
        for (num = -128; num < 128; ++num)
                printf("%d decimal = %x hexadecimal.\n",
                        num, num);
}
```

In this program we have changed the declaration of num in order to use the sign bit to distinguish between negative and positive numbers. In this section we will take a more detailed look at the use of the sign bit in the storage of negative numbers.

At the outset it seems very logical to think of negative numbers in terms of their positive counterparts, with the sign bit set to one. Because of the problem discussed below, this method is not in general use.

Example:

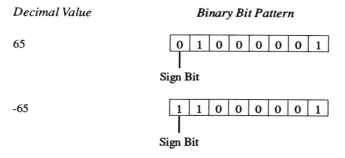

Decimal Value   *Binary Bit Pattern*

65

-65

This method of representing negative numbers is called as *Sign and Magnitude*. There is, however, a fairly major problem with this method. Consider the following bit patterns:

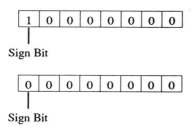

Literally interpreted, the first is equal to −0 while the second is equal to 0. To the microprocessor these two values are not equal to one another. This presents a problem which must be solved in a way that is more effective than a simple sign and magnitude representation.

One's complement is another representation method. In this method, bits are simply complemented across the entire number. That is, the 0 bits are "flipped" to 1 and the 1 bits to 0. In the following example 65 is converted to –65. Note that the role of the sign bit has not changed.

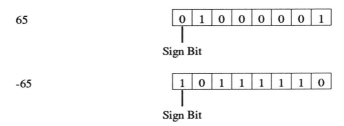

Now we must ask the question, "Does this solve the negative zero problem?" Consider the following bit patterns.

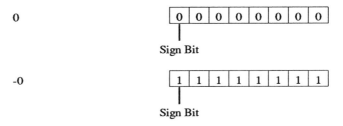

Remembering that we want 0 and –0 to be equal, it seems that one's complement is not a solution at all, if anything it causes our problem to be worse. However, if we ask what will cause the "negative zero" to have the same bit pattern as zero, we can see that adding one will accomplish this goal. Remember that since we are manipulating binary numbers, when one is added to one it is necessary to carry into the next place value. Adding one to an eight bit binary value consisting of all ones results in eight zeros and one carry bit.

$$1\ 1\ 1\ 1\ \ 1\ 1\ 1\ 1$$
$$+\ 1$$
$$\overline{\hspace{3cm}}$$
Carry Bit —> $1\ 0\ 0\ 0\ 0\ \ 0\ 0\ 0\ 0$

Since we are only manipulating 8 bit values at this point there is no room for the 9th "carry bit" so we disregard it letting it "fall off the end." The resulting 8-bit value has the same bit pattern as zero and the negative zero problem is solved. This technique of flipping bits and adding one is known as *two's complement*. It solves the "negative zero" problem. Applying two's complement to the values from our previous examples yields the following results.

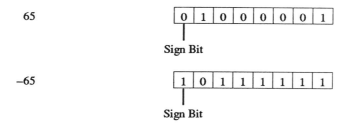

65

Sign Bit

−65

Sign Bit

The steps for converting from positive to negative using two's complement (i.e., flip all bits and add one) also hold for converting from negative to positive. Test this statement using the bit pattern for −65.

Range of `signed char`

With an understanding of how negative numbers are represented, it is appropriate to ask, "What are the maximum and minimum values that can be stored in a `signed char` variable?" Clearly the maximum value can be derived by setting the sign bit to zero and all other bits to one.

Maximum 8-bit Value? $0111\ 1111_2$ 127_{10}

The most intuitive approach to determining the minimum value is to convert the maximum value to a negative number by applying two's complement.

Minimum 8-bit Value? $1000\ 0001_2$ -127_{10}

Therefore, −127 can be represented; are there any smaller values that can be represented? Rephrasing this question we might ask, "Can anything be subtracted from −127 so that the result is legitimate (still negative)?" Considering the bit pattern for −127 we can see that 1 can be subtracted without affecting the sign bit.

$$
\begin{array}{lll}
 & 1000\ 0001 & -127 \\
 & \underline{\qquad -\ 1} & \underline{-\ 1} \\
\text{Minimum 8-bit Value?} & 1000\ 0000 & -128_{10}
\end{array}
$$

Interestingly enough, when we try to convert this to its positive counterpart by flipping bits and adding one we arrive back at the same number.

	$1000\ 0000$
Flip all bits	$0111\ 1111$
Add one	$1000\ 0000$

Also notice that when one is added to +127 the result is −128. This creates a "wrap-around" effect at each end of the range of values. This information is often very useful for debugging programs. Whenever large positive numbers are arithmetically manipulated and the result is an unexpected negative number it may be that the maximum value of that variable has been exceeded. This is called *arithmetic overflow*. Similarly, if two very small negative numbers are subtracted from one another the result may be a very large positive number. This is called *arithmetic underflow*. The solution is to declare the variable using a data type that allows a larger maximum value.

int Data Types

In the previous section we used char variables in order to store integers. As was noted earlier this is not typically considered good programming style but can sometimes be useful as a memory saving technique. It is useful in a discussion on integer storage techniques, to talk about 8-bit values, since their size and range are easily comprehensible. It is appropriate, at this juncture, to discuss the storage of other integral data types in light of the previous discussion.

Of all of the data types supported by the C language the int types are the most machine dependent in terms of their size and range. The sizeof() operator in C offers a very useful tool for answering questions about integer variables on a particular machine. Conversely, the actual method of storage of integers will be fairly consistent from machine to machine. Integers are stored as a direct binary representation of their decimal counterparts with negative numbers stored using two's complement conversion. Keeping these ideas in mind we will now look at the specifications regarding the size and range of int and its variations.

The value returned by sizeof (int) is determined by the computer's word size. Most microcomputers in use today have a word size of either 16 or 32 bits, while most time shared computers have a word size of 32 bits and some even have 64 bit word sizes. The following table shows the range of numbers representable on computers of different word sizes.

Computer Word Size	Minimum int	Maximum int
8 bits	$-2^7 = -128$	$2^7 - 1 = 127$
16 bits	$-2^{15} = -32768$	$2^{15} - 1 = 32767$
32 bits	$-2^{31} = -2{,}147{,}483{,}648$	$2^{31} - 1 = 2{,}147{,}483{,}647$

The ability to transport a program from computer to computer is often a necessity. One can imagine the possible difficulties that might arise when a program written for a computer with a 32 bit word size is executed on a 16 bit word computer. The risk of arithmetic overflow and underflow is quite high. For this reason C supports the modifiers short and long to help remedy this potential problem.

The C modifier unsigned offers a method for increasing the maximum size of an int variable at the expense of disallowing any negative values. The range of unsigned int is not any larger than int. Rather, it is scaled up so that the minimum integer is 0 and the maximum integer is dependent upon the computer word size. The following table shows the minimum and maximum values for unsigned int on various computers.

Computer Word Size	Minimum `unsigned int`	Maximum `unsigned int`
8 bits	0	$2^8-1 = 255$
16 bits	0	$2^{16}-1 = 65535$
32 bits	0	$2^{32}-1 = 4,294,967,296$

Floating Point Types

The storage of real numbers is more complicated than the storage of integers. The technique for managing real values is dependent upon the design of the microprocessor being used. Therefore, there are many different methods used. The Institute of Electrical and Electronics Engineers (IEEE) has devised a standard for the storage of real numbers. This standard has become widely implemented and will be the method presented here.

Floating point notation or exponential form offers a convenient notation for representing real numbers. A number expressed in this notation consists of three parts: a *mantissa*; an *exponent*; and a *base*. The examples below show several floating point representations for the fixed point value, 22.375.

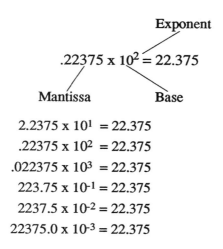

$$2.2375 \times 10^1 = 22.375$$
$$.22375 \times 10^2 = 22.375$$
$$.022375 \times 10^3 = 22.375$$
$$223.75 \times 10^{-1} = 22.375$$
$$2237.5 \times 10^{-2} = 22.375$$
$$22375.0 \times 10^{-3} = 22.375$$

Notice that there are many different ways to represent the same fixed point value. One way to reduce the number of different floating point representations involves *normalizing* the decimal point. That is, adjust the decimal point so that it is immediately left of most significant digit. The *normalized floating point* equivalent of 22.375 is .22375 x 10^2. This technique comes in handy when we store real numbers in memory.

If the base of a floating point value can be implicit then the only relevant components remaining are the mantissa and the exponent. Sometimes you may see floating point values written: .22375 E+02. In such cases it may be assumed that the base is 10. We will also take advantage of this idea when storing real numbers.

Storage of `float` types

At this point it is appropriate to ask questions about the `sizeof(float)` and the arrangement of that memory. Although the size of a float variable is somewhat machine dependent it is much more predictable than the size of an `int` and fluctuates much less from machine to machine. Most computers, both personal and time shared, typically store single precision real numbers in 32 bits. With this assertion in mind let us explore how that memory is managed. IEEE standards dictate that the thirty-first bit is the sign bit. It will play the same role as the sign bit of an integer. The next eight bits are used to store the exponent while bits 0-22 will store the mantissa. The following diagram gives a visual representation of these assignments. Notice that the normalization of the floating point number causes the position of the binary point to fall in the same place regardless of the value. This eliminates the need to explicitly represent the point.

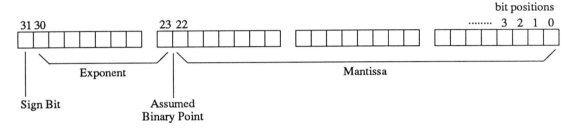

Now, if the base ten, fixed point value 22.375 is to be stored in this format, there are a number of conversions that must take place. The following is a list of steps necessary to manually convert a base ten, fixed point value into a binary floating point value using the IEEE format.

1. Convert the fixed point base ten value into a fixed point binary number.
2. Convert fixed point binary number into normalized floating point binary number with a binary exponent.
3. Determine and set sign bit.
4. Set bit pattern for mantissa.
5. Calculate and set bit pattern for exponent.

Now let us examine each step in detail.

1. *Convert fixed point base ten to fixed point binary.*

    In order to make this conversion by hand (most calculators do not handle real number conversions) it is necessary to divide the number into its two components: integral part and fractional part, convert each component and combine the results. Converting integers has already been discussed in section 3.3 but we will step through the algorithm using the integral part of our number: 22.

    a. *Convert Integral Part.*

22 % 2 = 0	int(22 / 2) = 11 /* Remember that % evaluates the remainder
11 % 2 = 1	int(11 / 2) = 5 while int (22/2) performs integer division*/
5 % 2 = 1	int(5 / 2) = 2

$2 \% 2 = 0$ $\text{int} \, (\, 2 \, / 2) = 1$ /* Because the result is 1 this becomes
                                        the final digit as well as our terminal
                                        condition */

$22_{10} = 10110_2$ /* Integral part has been converted */

b. *Convert Fractional Part.*

Converting a fractional base ten value to binary by hand is very similar to converting an integer. However, rather than dividing by two, we shall multiply by two. After each multiplication step, the value in the ones place will be used to build the binary value. First you should become comfortable with the fractional place values. These follow the pattern that is created by the integral binary place values.

$$\ldots 2^3 \; 2^2 \; 2^1 \; 2^0 \; . \; 2^{-1} \; 2^{-2} \; 2^{-3} \ldots$$
$$\ldots 8 \quad 4 \quad 2 \quad 1 \; . \; \tfrac{1}{2} \; \tfrac{1}{4} \; \tfrac{1}{8} \ldots$$

Binary Place Values

So, following the steps described above, we shall convert the fractional part of our number: .375.

$.375 * 2 = 0.750$ /* The integral part is 0 this dictates the binary 2^{-1} place */
$.750 * 2 = 1.500$ /* The integral part is 1 this dictates the binary 2^{-2} place */
$.500 * 2 = 1.000$ /* The integral part is 1 this dictates the binary 2^{-3} place
                              a zero in the fractional part indicates our terminal condition*/

$.375_{10} = .011_2$ /* The fractional part has been converted */

c. *Combine integral and fractional parts.*

$$22.375_{10} = 10110.011_2$$

2.   *Convert fixed point binary number into normalized floating point binary number with a binary exponent.*

Now that we have a fixed point binary number, converting it to a floating point value is relatively simple. First, we must normalize the binary point so that the most significant digit is in the 2^{-1} place. Next, we will calculate the exponent by determining how many places the binary point must travel to return to its place in the fixed point value. Finally, we will convert the exponent to a binary value.

1. $10110.011 = .10110011 * 2^x$ /* Remember that our base is now 2 rather
                                        than 10 */

2. $10110.011 = .10110011 * 2^5$ /* Exponent is still in base 10 */

3. $10110.011 = .10110011 * 2^{101}$

3. *Determine and set sign bit.*

Now we can begin to "plug in" some of the bits that will determine our 32 bit value. The sign bit represents the sign of the entire value. Since 22.375 is positive, the sign bit will be set to 0.

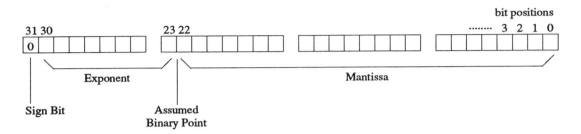

4. *Set bit pattern for mantissa.*

We can plug in the mantissa beginning with the twenty-second bit (i.e., assumed binary point) and pad trailing bits with 0.

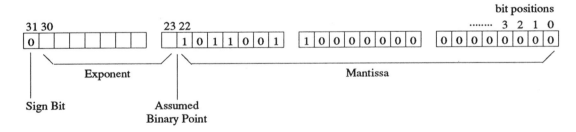

5. *Calculate and set bit pattern for exponent.*

Finally, we need to store the bit pattern for the exponent. There are a few problems that must be resolved before we merely plug in the 101 which was calculated earlier. In this example we are lucky because the exponent is a positive value. However, it is very likely that we may need to manipulate a very small value such as .00000375. As you can see, normalizing the decimal means moving it to the right, thus causing the exponent to be negative ($.375 * 10^{-5}$). Since the sign bit is already reserved for the sign of the entire value, it is necessary to address the problem of how to handle the sign of the exponent. One thought that immediately comes to mind is to reserve bit 30 to be the sign of the exponent. Although this seems like a logical solution it turns out that designing a microprocessor to handle this is not very straight forward. Instead we will use what is called a *biased exponent* to handle this problem. That is, we will add a constant to the exponent so that the sign will always be positive.

During our discussion on two's complement we manipulated an 8 bit value where one bit was reserved as the sign bit and the other seven bits determined the magnitude of the value. In that 8 bit value we were able to represent all integers between −128 and +127 inclusive. Since the exponent in our current example is an 8 bit value, we must make sure that the same range of values is possible. Note that if we bias the exponent by automatically adding 128 then our exponent will fall in the range 0 to 255 inclusive. By doing this we have eliminated the need for a sign since none of these values are negative. At the time of output 128 can be automatically subtracted, thus returning the biased exponent back to its original value. If we apply the 128 bias to the exponent in our example we have:

$$\begin{array}{ll} 0\,0\,0\,0\,0\,1\,0\,1 & 5 \\ +\,1\,0\,0\,0\,0\,0\,0\,0 & +\,128 \\ \hline 1\,0\,0\,0\,0\,1\,0\,1 & 133 \end{array}$$

and our final bit pattern is shown below.

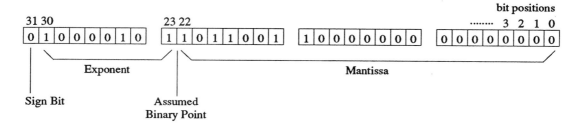

Note that the bias will only be 128 if the exponent requires 8 bits. If the exponent occupies a different number of bit positions, the bias will be altered accordingly.

Storage of double types

A brief comment must be made about the C data type double. Double precision numbers typically occupy 64 bits. Using a similar IEEE format a variable of type double has a sign bit, and 11 bit exponent (therefore the bias is 2^{10} or 1,024), and a 52 bit mantissa. It is not difficult to see that the magnitude of a number of this size more than doubles while the precision is doubled.

Range of float and double

We can see that the largest possible float will be a value which has a biased exponent of 255 (i.e., 127 unbiased) and a mantissa with all bits set to 1. A few points must be mentioned regarding larger values.

First, after converting a binary mantissa of 23 bits to its base ten equivalent the resulting value will be at most 8 digits. Therefore with an exponent of greater than 23, the value loses accuracy and becomes a close approximation. That is to say any digits after the first 7 or 8 in the original value are not likely to be correct. However, magnitude is maintained. So, although very large exponents are possible when manipulating floating point values, we must be satisfied with accuracy up to approximately 16 million.

The same argument holds for variables of type `double`, except that in this case we have exponents up to 1,023 yet the binary mantissa is at most 52 bits. This translates into an accuracy of at most 16 places. Any digits after that are not accurate.

Precision and Accuracy Revisited

At the beginning of this section the terms precision and accuracy were introduced. Upon learning about storage techniques for integral scalars and floating point scalars one might ask, "Why not use `float` to declare all of my variables? It doesn't use any more space and the values can be much larger and can be fractional if need be." There is a very good reason for *not* making this decision, having to do with precision versus accuracy.

Notice that the method of storage for the integral types guarantees exactness as long as the value being stored remains within the range representable by the particular declaration. Because the binary value being stored is a direct binary equivalent of the original value, there is no room for loss of exactness or accuracy. On the other hand, let us consider the decimal value $.1_{10}$. If we convert this value to its binary equivalent we arrive at:

$$.1 * 2 = 0.2$$
$$.2 * 2 = 0.4$$
$$.4 * 2 = 0.8$$
$$.8 * 2 = 1.6$$
$$.6 * 2 = 1.2$$
$$.2 * 2 = 0.4$$

$$.$$
$$.$$
$$.   \text{Result: } 0 \ 0 \ 0 \ 1 \ 1 \ 0 \ 0 \ 1 \ 1 \ 0 \ 0 \ . \ . \ .$$

The result is a repeating pattern similar to the base ten value $1/3$. Therefore, a seemingly harmless value like .1 loses accuracy while maintaining precision. Consider the following program:

```
main()
{
        float i;
        for (i = .1; i <= 1.0; i += .1)
                printf("%f", i);
}
```

Although it would appear that this loop will simply iterate 10 times there is no guarantee of this. On a different computer this loop might behave differently.

It is important to use the appropriate variable declaration according to the task that variable will be expected to perform. As a C programmer you may not often have the need to mentally convert values into their bit patterns. However, it is useful to have a general understanding of these ideas as an aid in debugging as well as avoiding arithmetic errors and machine dependency errors.

Language Elements Introduced in this Chapter: A Review

** Constant Expressions **

Leading 0X or 0x indicates a hexadecimal number.
Leading 0 indicates an octal number.
All other numerical constants are assumed to be decimal.

** Control Statements **

```
return expression;
```

** Conversion Specifications **

character representation
  %c for character representations
long int representation
  %ld, %lx, %lo
short int representation
  %hd, %hx, %ho
unsigned representation
  %lu, %hu, %u
float representation
  %5.2f for decimal point representation
  %5.2e, %5.2E for exponential representation
  %5.2g for minimal space floating point representation

In the above and all floating point representations,
5 is the minimum field width, and 2 is the precision.

double representation
  %lf, %le, %lE, %lg with scanf()
long double representation
  %Lf, %Le, %LE, %Lg

** Function Declarations **

Must include type returned if that type is not int.
```
double  exp(x)
double x;

double  exp(double x)   /* ANSI prototype */
```

** Operators **
  sizeof()   Takes an expression or a type as an argument and returns the
              number of bytes allocated for that type.

Bit Operators
    ~   negation
    &   bitwise logical and
    | bitwise logical or
    ^   bitwise logical xor
    >>   shift right
    <<   shift left

Cast Operator
(type)

** Types **

char	Holds a character from the underlying character set
short int	
long int	
unsigned types	Represent non-negative integers
unsigned short	
unsigned long	
unsigned char	
unsigned int	
signed	Allow signed and unsigned char (ANSI C only)
float	
double	
long double	(ANSI C only)
void	Used with functions

Things to Remember

1. Computer memory is divided into bits, bytes, or words.
2. A range of integers can be represented from
$-m, -m+1, -m+2, \ldots, -2, -1, 0, 1, 2, 3, \ldots m-2, m-1$ where m is a power of 2.
3. Bit patterns can be interpreted differently and therefore we can have different types.
4. ANSI C has specified the minimal ranges for each type. The range was not specified before these standards appeared.
5. In ANSI C, information about the integer types is in the header file limits.h.
6. The precedence of the bitwise operators from highest to lowest is ~, >> and <<, &, |, ^.
7. A common use of the bit operators is to test or set certain bits with a mask.
8. In ANSI C, information about the floating point types is kept in the header file float.h.

9. The type of a function is the type of the expression (if any) associated with the `return` statement. Functions that do not return a value have type `void`.
10. Declarations of functions not returning an `int` should appear both with the function definition and where any calling function can see it.
11. When types `char` or `short` are used in an expression or when an expression involves mixed types, C's automatic conversions occur before the expression is evaluated.
12. A cast can be used to temporarily change the type of an expression. When casting from a longer type to a shorter type, data can be lost.

3.14 Exercises and Programming Problems

1. a. Write a program that will input a sequence of 20 integers and output their average.

   b. Modify the original program so that the average is output as the integer closest to the actual average. For example, if the actual average is 67.8, the rounded value 68 should be output. If the average is 24.3, 24 should be output. The average 38.5 should be rounded to 39.

2. a. Write a program that will input a sequence of float values and output the maximum and the minimum of the input values.

   b. Repeat problem 1b for the program you wrote in 2a.

3. Write a program using bit operations that will test each input integer to see if it is divisible by 4.

4. Write a program that will update a bank balance. A sample run is below. The user's response is in **boldface**.

```
BANK ACCOUNT PROGRAM
--------------------
Enter the old balance: 1234.50
Enter the transactions now.  Enter an F for the transaction
type when you are finished.
Transaction Type (D=deposit, W=withdrawal, F=finished): D
Amount: 568.34
Transaction Type (D=deposit, W=withdrawal, F=finished): W
Amount: 25.68
Transaction Type (D=deposit, W=withdrawal, F=finished): W
Amount: 167.40
Transaction Type (D=deposit, W=withdrawal, F=finished): F
Your ending balance is  $1609.76
Program Ending
```

5. Write a program that converts an integer into another base. The input integer could be in decimal, octal, or hexadecimal. The output could be converted into either of the bases. A sample run is below. The user's response is again in **boldface**.

```
INTEGER CONVERSION PROGRAM
--------------------------
Base of input (d=decimal, h=hexadecimal, o=octal): d
Number: 178
Base of output (d=decimal, h=hexadecimal, o=octal): h
The integer 178 in decimal is equivalent to b2 in
hexadecimal.
Another number? (Y/N)   Y
Base of input (d=decimal, h=hexadecimal, o=octal): o
Number: 423
Base of output (d=decimal, h=hexadecimal, o=octal): d
The integer 423 in octal is equivalent to 282 in
decimal.
Another Number? (Y/N)   N
Goodbye!
```

6. Expand the program from exercise 5 to accept input of an integer in a binary representation and to include an option to output the binary representation of the input number.

7. Write a program to output an ASCII chart like the one below. The number to the left of the character is in hexadecimal.

00 nul	01 ^A	02 ^B	03 ^C	04 ^D	05 ^E	06 ^F	07 ^G
08 ^H	09 ^I	0a ^J	0b ^K	0c ^L	0d ^M	0e ^N	0f ^O
10 ^P	11 ^Q	12 ^R	13 ^S	14 ^T	15 ^U	16 ^V	17 ^W
18 ^X	19 ^Y	1a ^Z	1b esc	1c fs	1d gs	1e rs	1f us
20 sp	21 !	22 "	23 #	24 $	25 %	26 &	27 '
28 (	29)	2a *	2b +	2c ,	2d −	2e .	2f /
30 0	31 1	32 2	33 3	34 4	35 5	36 6	37 7
38 8	39 9	3a :	3b ;	3c <	3d =	3e >	3f ?
40 @	41 A	42 B	43 C	44 D	45 E	46 F	47 G
48 H	49 I	4a J	4b K	4c L	4d M	4e N	4f O
50 P	51 Q	52 R	53 S	54 T	55 U	56 V	57 W
58 X	59 Y	5a Z	5b [	5c \	5d]	5e ^	5f _
60 `	61 a	62 b	63 c	64 d	65 e	66 f	67 g
68 h	69 i	6a j	6b k	6c l	6d m	6e n	6f o
70 p	71 q	72 r	73 s	74 t	75 u	76 v	77 w
78 x	79 y	7a z	7b {	7c		7d }	7e ~	7f del

The characters from 0 through 1f hexadecimal are control characters. Experiment or read a manual to determine which of the control characters rings the bell on the terminal. Which is the carriage return? The line feed? The horizontal tab? The form feed?

8. Write a program that will accept an integer between 1 and 100 as input and will output its prime factors. (A prime factor of a number is a prime number that divides the number evenly. A prime number is a number that is greater than one whose only factors are itself and 1. For example, 2, 3, 5, 7, 11, 13, and 17 are prime numbers.) A sample run of the program is below. The user's input is in **boldface**.

```
Enter a number between  1 and 100:  345
TOO LARGE!  Enter a number between 1 and 100:  -15
TOO SMALL!  Enter a number between 1 and 100:  34
The prime factors of 34 are  2 and 17.
Another number?  (Y/N)  Y
Enter a number between 1 and 100:  83
The number 83 is prime.
Another number?  (Y/N)  N
Goodbye!
```

9. A bank wants to classify its customers as "Regular," "Special," or "VIP" according to their bank balance. A customer with less than $10,000 is a "Regular" customer. A customer who has between $10,000 and $50,000 is "Special." A customer with more than $50,000 is a "VIP." The home office wants a monthly report on the number of "Regular," "Special," and "VIP" customers at each branch. The office is not interested in names, addresses, or actual balance in this report. Write a program that a bank employee can run to generate a report to send to the home office. The employee will enter the current bank balance. The computer will tally the figures and create the report.

10. The Acme Real Estate Company is planning an apartment complex. The company figures that during the first year, its income will be $450 per month from each studio apartment, $550 per month from each one-bedroom apartment, and $700 per month from each two-bedroom apartment. Each studio apartment will be 200 square feet in size; each one-bedroom apartment will be 300 square feet in size, and each two-bedroom apartment will be 450 square feet in size. The building cost is $75 per square foot. To aid in planning, the company wants a program that will allow it to input the number of studios, one-bedroom, and two-bedroom apartments and will calculate the total size of the building needed to house the apartments, the total building cost, and the expected income for the first year and output those results in report form. Write this program and structure it so that Acme can enter as many sets of data as desired at one time. A sample run is below.

```
ACME REAL ESTATE PLANNING PROGRAM
---------------------------------
How many studio apartments?  5
How many one-bedroom apartments? 12
How many two-bedroom apartments? 10
Report for 5 studio apartments
12 one-bedroom apartments
10 two-bedroom apartments

                  Space          Costs          Income
       Studios:   1000           75000          27000
  One-Bedrooms:   3600          270000          79200
  Two-Bedrooms:   4500          337500          84000
       ------------          ------          ------
Totals     Space: 9100   Cost: 682500          190200

Do you want to enter another set of data (y/n)?  n
Thank you
```

Pointers and Arrays

Chapter 4

In this chapter, we will look at pointers and arrays. A pointer type is a scalar type. It holds one value at a time. The value stored in a variable of pointer type is an address of another value. An array is an aggregate type that stores multiple data values of the same type. Even though they seem to be different concepts, a special relationship exists between arrays and pointers in C. This relationship needs to be carefully examined.

4.1   Getting Started with Pointers

The concept of a pointer is an important one in many programming languages. It is doubly important in C because of the ways in which arrays, strings, and function parameters are implemented. Because this concept is so critical, we will start with the basics.

Computer Memory and Addresses

The amount of memory available for a program to use varies from computer to computer, but whatever the size, a program keeps track of the memory in use by a numbering system. A number is associated with each byte or word. That number is called the address of the byte or word. Some computers have an address assigned to each byte; these are referred to as byte-addressable computers. Other computers are word-addressable; they assign an address to each word, but not necessarily to each byte.

For illustration, let's assume the following memory configuration for a computer. A byte consists of 8 bits and each word consists of 2 bytes. Suppose that the computer has 1 megabyte or 2^{20} bytes of memory. Assume the computer is byte addressable and the addresses range from 0 through $2^{20} - 1$. We can picture the memory in the two ways shown in Figure 4-1.

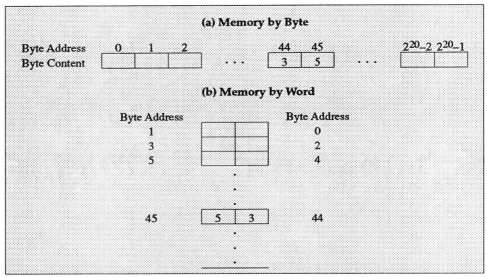

Figure 4-1

In parts a and b of the figure, the value 3 is stored in the byte with address 44, and the value 5 is stored in the byte with address 45. The interpretation of the values is up to the program, the programmer, and the operating system. Each value stored in a byte may be interpreted separately, or two or more bytes may be interpreted together.

Now consider an error-free C program with an integer variable declared. When the program is loaded into memory, the loader will decide where the current value of the variable will be stored. An appropriate number of bytes will be reserved for values of the variable. That space is referenced by the address.

C has several mechanisms that allow a programmer to access the memory address of a variable during program execution. One mechanism that we have already seen is to specify the address of a variable with the & operator. This operator, discussed previously in relation to the function scanf(), is used to show scanf() where to put a value that it reads. C allows us to print the addresses of variables during program execution. This is illustrated in the program in Example 4-1.*

---

* The programs in this chapter are designed to illustrate the underlying concepts of pointers and arrays. Only a few programs illustrate using the concepts. The use of pointers is addressed throughout the remainder of the text.

Example 4-1:   address1.c

```
/*                      address1.c
 *
 *    Synopsis  -  Prints the address of a variable.
 *
 *    Objective -  Illustrates addresses in memory and C's ability
 *                 to output them.
 */

void main()
{
        int intvar;

        printf ("Values of intvar are stored in the memory");
        printf (" location %x.\n", &intvar);              /* Note 1 */
}
```

This program has one variable of type `int`. The executable code consists of two calls to printf().

Note 1: The syntax, `&intvar`, refers to the address of the variable `intvar`. The value assigned by the computer is converted to hexadecimal and output by printf(). Addresses of memory locations are often referenced in either hexadecimal or octal. The output from this program cannot be predicted without precise knowledge of the action of the loader. *

Learning Activities

1.   How many lines of output will address1.c generate?

2.   What modifications need to be made if the address of `intvar` is to be output in octal? In decimal?

3.   To get to know your compiler, modify address1.c by adding a character variable and variables of type `float` and `double`. Have each of their addresses output by the program. Are the addresses related as you would expect? Consider the sizeof() each data type in answering this question.

*With ANSI C, the %p conversion specification could be used to output addresses. The format output with %p is implementation dependent. If you are not using an ANSI C compiler, adjustment of the output types may be necessary to get accurate results.

Pointers

Another technique to determine the address of a variable is to use a pointer variable. A pointer variable stores the address of a memory location. When we say that a pointer variable "points" to another variable we mean that it stores the address of the memory location allocated for values of the other variable.

In C, pointers are considered to be separate data types. Each of the data types `char`, `int`, `float`, and `double` has a corresponding pointer data type, pointer to `char`, pointer to `int`, pointer to `float`, and pointer to `double`. In fact, every data type has a corresponding pointer type. Note that this allows data types such as a pointer to a pointer to an `int` (double indirection), and so on.

In a pointer variable declaration, an asterisk, `*`, is placed immediately to the left of the variable name. For that variable, the notation `int *` signifies the type pointer to `int`. The notation `char *` signifies the type pointer to `char`. The `*` following any type name signifies a pointer to that type. The fact that pointers are data types implies that we can declare variables of pointer types and assign and access their values in a way similar to variables of other types.

Declaring a pointer variable is the same as declaring a variable of any other type. The type is followed by the variable name. For example, the declaration

```
int *intptr;
```

declares a variable named `intptr` that has type `int *` or pointer to `int`. Similarly, the declaration

```
char *charptr;
```

declares a variable named `charptr` that has type `char *`. Pointers to the other types are declared in the same way. The program address2.c in Example 4-2 illustrates the declaration and a very simple use of a pointer variable.

Example 4-2:   address2.c

```
/*              address2.c
 *
 *   Synopsis   -  Prints the address of a variable.
 *
 *   Objective  -  Demonstrates pointers as addresses in memory.
 *                 Gives the syntax of declaring a pointer to an
 *                 integer and one technique of initializing a
 *                 pointer.
 */
```

```
void main()
{
        int intvar;
        int *ptr_to_intvar;                             /* Note 1 */

        printf ("The value of ptr_to_intvar is %x.\n",
                ptr_to_intvar);                         /* Note 2 */

        ptr_to_intvar = &intvar;                        /* Note 3 */

        printf ("The address of intvar is %x.\n", &intvar);
        printf ("The value of ptr_to_intvar is %x.\n",
                ptr_to_intvar);                         /* Note 4 */
}
```

Variables of type int and int * are declared. The value of both variables are output before and after initialization of the pointer variable.

Note 1: A pointer to an integer is declared. The tokens int * are used to indicate the data type pointer to integer. The variable name follows the asterisk.

Note 2: The value of the pointer variable is printed. Since no initialization has been done, this value could contain garbage data from some previous use of memory or could contain the value zero. In either case the value would not refer to a legitimate memory location. Referencing an improper memory location will most likely cause a runtime error. Pointer variables, like all other variables in C, must be explicitly initialized.

Note 3: This assignment statement is used to initialize the value of the pointer variable. After the execution of this statement, the two variables intvar and ptr_to_intvar are related, as shown below. The addresses shown are fictitious.

Variable	Address	Contents
ptr_to_intvar	7802	8000
.	.	.
.	.	.
.	.	.
intvar	8000	????

Note 4: The hexadecimal value of the variable ptr_to_intvar is identical to the address of the variable intvar that was output by the previous printf() call.

Learning Activities

4. The syntax for declaring a pointer to an integer is
```
    int *variable_name;
```
Experiment with address2.c and your compiler to see if the syntax
```
    int * variable_name;
```
is allowed.

5. What would the expression &ptr_to_intvar reference?

6. Write a declaration of a variable named char_ptr of type pointer to char. Rewrite address2.c to use the variable char_ptr to output the address of a character variable.

4.2 Pointer Arithmetic

To further understand a pointer to a type as a separate data type, consider the program address3.c in Example 4-3. It is a modification of address2.c.

Example 4-3: address3.c

```
/*                    address3.c
 *
 *   Synopsis   -  Uses pointers to print the addresses of a char
 *                 variable and an int variable and the address of
 *                 the next available memory location for each
 *                 data type.
 *
 *   Objective  -  Illustrates what is meant by a pointer to int
 *                 being a separate data type. Demonstrates syntax
 *                 of declaring a pointer to a char variable,
 *                 initialization of pointer variables, and
 *                 the result of adding 1 to pointer variables
 *                 of different types.
 */
```

```
#include <stdio.h>

void main()
{
        int intvar, *int_ptr;                          /* Note 1 */
        char charvar, *char_ptr = &charvar;            /* Note 2 */

        int_ptr = &intvar;

        printf ("The address of charvar is %x.\n", char_ptr);
        printf ("The next character could be stored at %x.\n",
            char_ptr + 1);                             /* Note 3 */

        printf ("The address of intvar is %x.\n", int_ptr);
        printf ("The next integer could be stored at %x.\n",
            int_ptr + 1);                              /* Note 4 */

}
```

Variables of type int, int *, char, and char * are declared. Their values
are initialized and output with calls to printf().

Note 1: Notice the declaration of an integer variable and a pointer to an integer on the same
line. A comma is used to separate the two variable declarations.

Note 2: Here, a character variable and a variable of type pointer to char are declared on
the same line of code. Further, char_ptr has been initialized to point to
charvar. C's initialization features are available with pointer types also. Note
that int_ptr could have been initialized in this way.

Note 3: Since pointer to char is a separate data type, the expression char_ptr + 1
references the address of the next character. The + 1 adds the sizeof() one char
to the address in char_ptr.

Note 4: Again, since pointer to int is a separate data type, the expression int_ptr + 1
references the address of the next integer. That is, C's automatic conversion takes
over and converts the 1 in the above expression to 1 integer address. In this case
the + 1 adds the sizeof() one int to int_ptr. It may be necessary to execute the
program address3.c and think about the results to fully understand this concept.

Learning Activities

7. Execute the program address3.c. Are the results what you expected?

8. Use the output from address3.c to predict the output from the statements
   ```
   printf("%x\n", char_ptr + 2);
   printf("%x\n", int_ptr + 2);
   ```
   if they were added to your program. Verify your predictions by modifying and executing the programs.

9. Which of the following statements will be true for all implementations of C?
   The value of (int_ptr + 1) is 1 more than that of int_ptr.
   The value of (int_ptr + 1) is 2 more than that of int_ptr.
   The value of (int_ptr + 1) is 4 more than that of int_ptr.
   The value of (int_ptr + 1) is sizeof(int) more than that of int_ptr.

10. Predict the relationship between (&intvar + 1) and (int_ptr + 1). Check the actual relationship by making appropriate modifications to address3.c and executing it.

The previous program introduced the concept of pointer arithmetic. Certain arithmetic operations are allowed that either combine two pointers or combine a pointer and an integer.

As demonstrated in the last program, an integer value can be added to or subtracted from a pointer variable. For example, if floatptr had been declared as type float *, the expression

```
floatptr + 1
```

would also have type float *. It would evaluate to the address of the location in memory where the next float value could be located. Its value would be sizeof (float) larger than the value of floatptr. Similarly,

```
floatptr + 2
```

would be the address of the location in memory where the second consecutive float value after floatptr could be placed, and

```
floatptr - 1
```

would be the address of the location where a float value could be placed immediately before floatptr in memory. All of these values will differ by a multiple of sizeof(float).

The expression ++`floatptr` would reference the next location in memory where a `float` value could be stored. The value of `floatptr` would be incremented by `sizeof(float)`. The only instance in which this would be a legal memory reference is when that location in memory had been allocated to store a value of type `float`. Similarly, after evaluation of the expression `floatptr--`, `floatptr` would contain the previous possible address of a float value. The memory reference would only be legal when that location is designated to hold values of type `float`.

If `floatptr1` and `floatptr2` have both been declared as type `float *` and initialized with legitimate addresses of `float` values, the expression

```
floatptr1 - floatptr2
```

is defined to be the integer k such that

```
floatptr2 + k == floatptr1
```

The integer k will represent the number of `float` values that could be stored between the two addresses. The subtraction of two pointer variables is only defined when both variables are pointers to the same type. Note that the expression

```
floatptr1 + floatptr2
```

is *not* a legitimate expression in C.

Other allowable operations on pointers include comparison of two pointers with the relational operators. It is also legal to cast a pointer type to another pointer type or to an integer.

The identifier `NULL` is defined to be 0 in several of the standard header files including stdio.h. `NULL` has a special use with pointers.

The assignment

```
pointervar = NULL
```

is the programmer's way of indicating that `pointervar` does not point at an object. This condition can be included as part of a test for a loop or a conditional statement. Some examples appear below:

```
if (pointervar)
        varble = *pointervar;
```

or

```
while ((j < 5) && (!pointervar))
        do_something();
```

Other possible uses for these operations involve concepts that we have not studied yet.

Learning Activities

11. Write a short C program that declares pointer variables to each of the basic types `char`, `short`, `int`, `long`, `float`, and `double`. Have your program output the values of several of the pointer arithmetic expressions like those given previously with `floatptr`. Predict the output of your program and then compile and execute it. (Hint: You will need to know the sizeof() the basic types in order to predict properly.) Reconcile any differences between your predictions and the actual output.

12. Modify your program by adding an expression involving the sum of two pointers like `floatptr1 + floatptr2`. This should cause an error condition. Is it a compile-time error or a runtime error? Experiment to find out.

4.3   Dereferencing a Pointer Variable

We have used pointers to print the addresses of variables in an executing program with the main objective of illustrating the basics of pointers. In practice, this technique is useful for debugging programs, but is not often a permanent part of a program.

Before investigating how pointers are used in C, we need to learn another pointer syntax and technique.

If `int_ptr` is declared as a pointer to integer, we know that legal values for `int_ptr` are addresses of integers. If the syntax

        `*int_ptr`

is used in any expression other than a declaration, it refers to the contents of the current address in `int_ptr`. Using `*` in this way is known as dereferencing a pointer. Figure 4-2 demonstrates this relationship in two different ways.

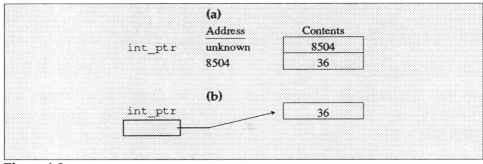

Figure 4-2

In parts a and b of the figure, `*int_ptr` has the value 36. In general, an upper-level language gives a programmer little or no control over the memory addresses that are used by a program. That is, a programmer controls what is stored in memory, but not where it is stored. However, C does allow the programmer some control over where the program data is stored. A diagram similar to Figure 4-2b is commonly used to show the relationship between a pointer and its contents. The program pointer.c in Example 4-4 illustrates the distinction between a pointer (an address) and its contents (the contents of the address).

Example 4-4: pointer.c

```
/*                      pointer.c
 *
 *    Synopsis  -  Assigns a value to a char variable twice and
 *                 prints that value and its memory address.
 *
 *    Objective -  Demonstrates how to reference the contents of a
 *                 pointer variable.
 */
#include <stdio.h>

void main()
{
        char c,
             *ptr_c = &c;                              /* Note 1 */

        c = 'Q';

        printf ("The value of c is %c.\n", c);
        printf ("ptr_c points to %c.\n", *ptr_c);      /* Note 2 */
        printf ("The character %c is stored in hex %x.\n", c, ptr_c);

        *ptr_c = 'r';                                  /* Note 3 */

        printf ("The value of c is now %c.\n", c);     /* Note 4 */
        printf ("ptr_c now points to %c.\n", *ptr_c);
        printf ("The character %c is stored in hex %x.\n", c, ptr_c);

}
```

Variables of type `char` and `char *` are declared and initialized. The remainder of the code consists of assignment statements and calls to printf().

Note 1: Again, a character variable and a variable of type pointer to character have been defined. Since C is a free-format language, the `char` declaration begun on the previous line continues until the `;` on this line. The syntax `*ptr_c` has two different meanings. If it is preceded by a data type in a declaration, it signifies the declaration of a pointer to that data type. However, in any other context, it signifies the contents of a pointer type variable.

Note 2: After initializing the value of the character variable, that value can be accessed either by referencing the character variable as in the previous printf() call, or by referencing the contents of the corresponding pointer variable as shown in this line of code.

Note 3: Assignments can be made to the contents of a properly initialized pointer variable. The contents of the address that is currently in the variable `ptr_c` are changed. Notice that the syntax `*ptr_c` can be used on the left side of an assignment statement as well as the right.

Note 4: The previous assignment statement changed the value of the variable c also. The execution of these two printf() calls will illustrate that fact.

The unary operators, `&` and `*`, in the syntax of pointers have equal precedence with each other and the unary arithmetic operators. Expressions combining them are evaluated left to right. The unary operators have higher precedence than the binary operators. For the full picture on precedence, see the chart in the Programmer's Handbook.

Learning Activities

13. Execute the program pointer.c to verify that your understanding of the output is correct.

14. Given the declaration
    ```
    char *char_ptr;
    ```
    and the following memory configuration,

Variable	Address	Contents
char_ptr	100	108
	•	
	•	
	•	
	108	'H' →
	109	'e'
	110	'l'
	111	'l'
	112	'o'
	113	'\n'

state the value that is referenced by each of the following expressions, if possible. Some of the values may be unknown.

```
*char_ptr        H
*char_ptr + 1     I
*(char_ptr + 1)   e
(*char_ptr) + 1   I
*char_ptr + 3     k
*&char_ptr        105
&char_ptr         100
&char_ptr + 2     102
```

15. Write code to change the value of the variable c in pointer.c to `'A'` in two different ways. One way must involve using the variable `ptr_c`.

16. Modify pointer.c so that it will use pointers to initialize and change the value of an integer variable.

The asterisk, `*`, appears in the declaration of a pointer variable in C and also when the pointer is dereferenced to access the contents of the address in the pointer variable. This seems to be two different uses for the symbol `*`, but another way of interpreting a declaration makes the syntax more straightforward. Consider the declaration

```
int *intptr;
```

We can interpret this declaration as saying that the expression `*intptr` is an `int`. Because `*intptr` is the symbol for a dereferenced pointer, this implies that `intptr` is a pointer to an `int`. This method of interpreting C declarations will help to demystify the declarations in later chapters.

Pointer Initialization and the Null Pointer

When a pointer is declared, the C compiler will set aside storage for the value of the pointer (an address); however, it will not initialize the pointer. A newly declared pointer will not reference a legal memory address. It is up to the programmer to properly initialize a pointer type variable. A pointer is generally initialized with an assignment statement. It is legal to assign the address of a declared variable of the proper type to a pointer type variable. It is also legal to assign the value of another pointer type to a pointer variable, as in the following statements:

```
int_ptr = &intvar;
int_ptr1 = int_ptr2;
```

It is also possible in C to make assignments like

```
int_ptr = (int *)1000;
```

to assign the address 1000 to `int_ptr`. Note that the value 1000 will be converted to the type pointer to `int` with the cast `(int *)`.

There are several cautions to be observed when trying a direct address assignment such as this. In a multiuser multitasking environment, take care to use addresses within the allotted memory space. If an ordinary user tries to read or write outside of his or her memory space, a runtime error will occur. In some implementations of C on microcomputers, these assignments are always legal, but writing into certain memory locations may erase other data needed by the operating system. However, it is partially because C has the capability to access specific memory locations that it is an appropriate language for writing operating systems.

C reserves the value NULL for a special assignment to all types of pointer variables. It signifies that a pointer does not point to a legal address in memory. It is a value that a program can test in a conditional statement. The program in Example 4-5 illustrates a simple use of the value NULL. More will be seen later in the text.

Example 4-5:   pointer2.c

```
/*              pointer2.c
 *
 *    Synopsis  -  Reads a single character entered from the
 *                 keyboard and prints the entered value unless
 *                 it was a newline.
 *    Objective -  Illustrates use of NULL and relational
 *                 expressions with pointers.
 */
#include <stdio.h>                                   /* Note 1 */

void main()
{
        int c, *input_ptr = &c;                      /* Note 2 */

        printf ("Please enter a character from the keyboard");
        printf (" or press return.\n");

        if ( (*input_ptr = getchar() ) == '\n')      /* Note 3 */
                input_ptr = NULL;                    /* Note 4 */

        if (input_ptr == NULL)                       /* Note 5 */
                printf ("Just a return was typed.\n");
        else
                printf ("The character %c was entered.\n",
                        *input_ptr);
}
```

"The program asks for input of a character and uses if and if-else statements to test the input and decide on the appropriate output." Based on *The Creation of Man* by Michelangelo, 1508.

Variables of type int and int * are defined. The program asks for input of a character and uses if and if-else statements to test the input and decide on appropriate output.

Note 1: The value NULL is defined as 0 in the include file stdio.h. The line #define NULL 0 could be used instead if there is no other need for the file stdio.h. When NULL is defined this way, it can be accessed as both a character and an integer because it causes a replacement in the source code before compilation and is not tied to any type.

Note 2: Again, the declaration of the pointer variable allots space for the pointer. The declaration of the int variable c and the initialization of input_ptr as the address of c assigns a valid memory location to the pointer.

Note 3: Input is done with getchar(). This time the value returned is stored as the contents of input_ptr and then tested to see if the first character input was a return.

Note 4: The value NULL is assigned to a pointer variable in the case where a return was the first key pressed.

Note 5: The value of input_ptr is tested. If the value of the pointer is NULL, the return key was pressed. In terms of programming style, this test could have been made directly on the contents of input_ptr (or c), but there are times when it is handy to be able to test the value of the pointer itself rather than the contents. The objective of this program was to illustrate that technique in a simple situation. The other relational tests that can be used with a pointer and NULL or with two pointer variables are equality (==), inequality (! =), is greater than (> or >=), or is less than (< or <=).

Learning Activities

17. Why has input_ptr been declared as a pointer to int and why is c declared as an integer? In this program could these variables have been declared as types char * and char instead?

18. Which of the other operators could have been used to test to see if input_ptr was NULL? Rewrite that conditional statement in two different ways.

4.4 Passing Parameters to Functions

The first use we will see for pointers is in passing parameters to functions. Examples of functions that take parameters have appeared earlier in the text. This section will explore the role of pointers in parameter passing.

The parameters as they appear in the definition of the function are called formal parameters. The parameters that appear in function calls are known as actual parameters. The names and types of the formal parameters must appear inside the parentheses that follow the name of the function in the definition.

In other languages, two basic methods of passing parameters to subprograms may be available. Parameters could be "passed by reference" or "passed by value." If a parameter is passed by reference, the address of that parameter's storage location is known to the subprogram so that operations may be done directly on the parameter. The subprogram will be able to change the value of the parameter. If a parameter is passed by value to a subprogram, a copy is made of the current value of that parameter. The function will operate on the copy of the parameter. When a parameter is passed by value, the original parameter will not be changed by the subprogram.

In C parameters are passed by value. The parameters to a C function will not be changed by the function. However, sometimes it is desirable to have a subprogram effect a change on a variable from another part of the program. In these situations, pass by reference parameters can be simulated. The method is to pass the address of the variable as an actual parameter to a function. The address itself will not be modified by the function, but the contents of that address can be changed. The corresponding formal parameter will be declared as a pointer. The program param.c of Example 4-6 demonstrates the fact that parameters in C are passed by value and illustrates the method of simulating pass by reference parameters.

Example 4-6:   param.c

```
/*                param.c
 *
 *    Synopsis  -  Outputs the values of variables and parameters
 *                 before, during, and after a function call.
 *
 *    Objective -  Illustrates passing parameters by value and
 *                 by reference.
 */

void main()
{
        int x, y, *int_pointer;
        void changit ( int x, int *int_pointer);

        x = 1;
        y = 3;
        int_pointer = &y;                                /* Note 1 */

        printf("In main before the call to changit,");
        printf(" x = %d, *int_pointer = %d, y = %d\n",
                                    x, *int_pointer, y);

        changit(x, int_pointer);                         /* Note 2 */

        printf("In main after the call to changit,");    /* Note 3 */
        printf (" x = %d, *int_pointer = %d, y = %d\n",
                                      x, *int_pointer, y);
}

/*********************************** changit() ***********/
/*   changit() - assigns values to x and *int_pointer and
 *               outputs the assigned values.
 */

void changit ( int x, int *int_pointer)                  /* Note 4 */
{
        x += 5;
        *int_pointer += 5;                               /* Note 5 */
                                                         /* Note 6 */
        printf ("In changit, x = %d, *int_pointer = %d.\n",
                                        x, *int_pointer);
}
```

The function main() declares and initializes variables and outputs their values before and after a call to the function changit(). The function changit() makes assignments to its parameters and outputs their values.

Note 1: The variable `int_pointer` has been declared as a pointer to type `int`. Here it is initialized to contain the address of the variable `y` in preparation for the call to changit(). The function changit() will be used to change the value of `y`.

Note 2: In the call to changit(), the actual parameters are `x` and `int_pointer`. Both of these parameters are passed by value. A copy will be made of their current values and changit() will work on the copies. However, by passing the address of the variable `y` as a parameter to the function, we have constructed a situation in which `y` is passed by reference to changit(). We have set up the situation so that changit() can change the value of `y`.

Note that an equivalent call to changit() can be made that does not necessitate the use of a pointer variable. That call would be

```
changit (x, &y);
```

The output of the program would be identical when this function call replaces the existing one.

Note 3: The values of the variables are output after the call to changit(). The value of `x` is unchanged by the execution of the function, but the value of `y` and `*int_pointer` have been changed.

Note 4: The first formal parameter to changit() is `x`; it corresponds to the actual parameter `x` in the function call. Any changes to the actual parameter `x` that occur during the execution of the function will be discarded when the function terminates.

The second formal parameter to changit() corresponds to the actual parameter `int_pointer`. It is of type `int *`. The parameter will be an address of an integer. Passing the parameter in this way allows the function to make a change to the variable `y` in main(). The use of a pointer is necessary when simulating pass by reference.

Note 5: In the previous statement, a change was made to the formal parameter `x`. This change affects only the copy of `x`, not `x` itself. In this statement, a change is made to the contents of the address in `int_pointer`. This will change the corresponding variable `y` in main(). The function changit() can directly access the address of the variable in the calling function and therefore it can modify its contents.

Note 6: The values of the formal parameters are output in this printf() call. They will be different from the values of the variables `x` and `*int_pointer` in main(). The function changit() can change its formal parameters; the corresponding actual parameters in the calling function may or may not be changed.

A Closer Look

The execution environment for a function is created when a function is called and destroyed when it terminates. The environment includes values for the function's local variables and parameters. Each time the function is called, the current values of the actual parameters are copied to the execution environment where the function will access them. Changes to the parameters are made to these copies. The values of the actual parameters are only touched when the address of that parameter is passed to the function.

In the program param.c, when changit() is called, both the function main() and the function changit() are active. The diagram in Figure 4-3 indicates the two separate execution environments for these functions. The values for each variable indicate the original values and trace the changes that occur.

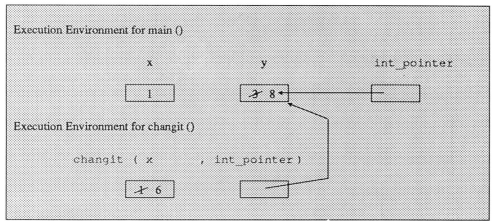

Figure 4-3

Again, the two values in the boxes illustrate the changes that take place during execution of the program. Notice that the value of x in main() was not touched. The modification was made to the copy of x that was passed to changit(). Notice also that the value of int_pointer in main() will not be touched, but the value of *int_pointer or y was changed.

Learning Activities

19. Execute the program and make sure that the output meets your expectations. Correct any misunderstandings you may have had.

20. Complete the following program so that the output is as stated. Fill in the formal parameters, the function definition, the declaration of switchxz() in or above main(), and the actual parameters.

OUTPUT:

```
1:  y is 4, x is 5, and z is 7.
2:  y is 4, x is 7, and z is 5.
```

```
                PROGRAM:
/*                          la20.c                                    */
#include <stdio.h>

void main()
{

    int x, y, z, *int_pointer;

    x = 5;
    y = 4;
    z = 7;

    int_pointer = &x;
    printf ("1:  y is %d, x is %d, and z is %d.\n", y, x, z);
    switchxz (         ,        );                    /*  fill in */
    printf ("2:  y is %d, x is %d, and z is %d.\n", y, x, z);
}

void switchxz (        ,        )                     /*  fill in */
{                                                     /*  fill in */
            /*  fill in code that will result
             *  in the values for x and z being switched.
             */
}
```

> HINT: The function switchxz() takes two parameters and must inter-
> change the values of x and z. The actual parameters should be the
> address of x and the address of z. The formal parameters should be
> declared appropriately. In the function code for switchxz(), the
> parameters should be dereferenced to access the values of x and z.
> For example, if the actual parameter is &x and the formal parameter
> is ptr_x, the expression *ptr_x will translate to the value of x.

21. Predict the output from the following program by filling in values in
    the blanks below. Execute the program to verify your prediction.*

```
                PROGRAM:
/*                          la21.c                                    */
#include <stdio.h>

int    int1, int2, int3;

void p1(int*, int);

void main()
{
```

---

* Note the position of the declaration of int1, int2 and int3. When variables are declared before any
functions in a file, they can be accessed by all functions in the file. This is discussed in more detail in Chapter 8.

```
        int1 = 3;
        int2 = 7;
        int3 = 2;

        p1 (&int3, int1);
        printf ("Back in main, int1 is %d, int2 is %d, ", int1, int2);
        printf ("and int3 is %d.\n\n", int3);

        p1 ( &int3, int3);
        printf ("Back in main, int1 is %d, int2 is %d, ", int1, int2);
        printf ("and int3 is %d.\n", int3);
}

void p1 (int *i, int j)

{
        *i = *i  +  3;
        j  = 4 * j;
        int3 = int3 + j;
        printf ("In p1, *i is %d, j is %d, and int3 is %d.\n",
                                    *i, j, int3 );
}
```

   OUTPUT
```
        In p1, *i is _____, j is _____, and int3 is _____.
        Back in main, int1 is _____, int2 is _____, and int3 is _____.

        In p1, *i is _____, j is _____, and int3 is _____.
        Back in main, int1 is _____, int2 is _____, and int3 is _____.
```

Using Pointers and Parameters

The program exp.c in Example 4-7 calculates the value of e^x where x is input by a user. The calculation is done by expanding the Taylor series for e^x,

$$1 + x + x^2/2! + x^3/3! + . . . + x^n/n!$$

The expansion stops when the last term, $x^n/n!$, is less than some value epsilon which is between 0 and 1. The value of epsilon is also input by the user as an indication of the desired precision of the answer. The program is implemented with three functions. Values of variables declared in main() need to be changed by the other functions. The technique of passing the address of a variable as a parameter to a function is used.

Example 4-7: exp.c

```
/*                  exp.c
 *
 *    Synopsis  -  Inputs float values for x and epsilon and
 *                 calculates e to the x using the Taylor series.
 *                 The series is expanded to the point where
 *                 term is less than epsilon.
 *
 *    Objective -  Illustrates the use of pointers and the address
 *                 operator in simulating pass by reference.
 */

#include <stdio.h>

void main()
{
        double x, epsilon, val;                          /* Note 1 */
        void exp (double x, double eps, double *valptr);
        void getinput (double *xp, double *ep);

        printf ("This program will calculate the value of ");
        printf ("e raised to the power x.\nYou will be asked to ");
        printf ("enter a real number x,\nand a value epsilon that ");
        printf ("gives an indication of the desired accuracy.\n");

        getinput (&x, &epsilon);                         /* Note 2 */

        exp(x, epsilon, &val);                           /* Note 3 */
                                                         /* Note 4 */
        printf ("e raised to the power %.5lf is approximately %.5lf.\n",
                    x, val);
}
/***************************************** exp() **************/
/*    Uses the Taylor series expansion to calculate e to the x.  The
 *    series is terminated when the term is less than epsilon.  The
 *    value is passed back by the parameter valptr.
 */
void exp (double x, double eps, double *valptr)          /* Note 5 */
{
        double term;
        int count = 1;

        *valptr = 0;                                     /* Note 6 */
        term = 1;
        while ( term >= eps ) {
```

```
                        *valptr += term;                        /* Note 6 */
                        term *= x;
                        term /= count++;
                }
}
/********************************* getinput ()  ************/
/*      inputs two values of type double.   Values are  passed back by
 *      x_ptr and eps_ptr.
 */

void getinput (double *x_ptr, double *eps_ptr)                   /* Note 7 */
{
        printf ("\nEnter a value for x : ");
        scanf ("%lf", x_ptr);                                   /* Note 8 */
        printf ("Enter a value for precision that is less than one: ");
        scanf ("%lf", eps_ptr);                                 /* Note 8 */
}
```

The program consists of three functions, main(), exp() and getinput(). The function getinput() will input a value for x and a value for epsilon. The function exp() will calculate the value of e^x. The function main() calls the other functions and keeps track of the variables.

Note 1:   The variables x, epsilon, and val are declared with type double. The variable x will store the exponent; the variable epsilon suggests the precision; and val will hold the value of e^x.

Note 2:   The function getinput() will input values for x and epsilon. Because the values of those variables should be changed in main() after execution of getinput(), the address of each variable is passed to getinput().

Note 3:   The function exp() needs to be able to change the variable val so the address of val is passed to it. The variables x and epsilon will not be changed by exp() so their addresses are not passed in.

Note 4:   The call to printf() outputs the value of x that was input in getinput() and the value of val that was calculated by exp().

Note 5:   The formal parameters to exp() are declared. The parameters x and eps are declared to be type double. They will be passed by value. Any changes to the formal parameters will be made on a copy of the actual parameters. The parameter valptr is of type double *. The actual parameter should be the address of a double value. The function will be able to change the corresponding double value.

Note 6:   The dereference operator, *, is used with valptr. The value of the variable val in main() is being changed by these two assignment statements.

Note 7:   Both parameters to getinput() are pointer types. This will allow getinput() to input values that can be used in the main program.

Note 8: The addresses passed to scanf() are the addresses of the variables in main() that were passed in as actual parameters. Note that scanf() changes a variable in the calling function and therefore must be passed the address of that variable. The concept is the same as the one discussed in this section.

Learning Activities

22. Compile and execute this program. Test it with several different sets of input. Check the answers given with this program against the results given by a hand calculator.

23. Change the types of x, epsilon, val, and the parameters to the functions to have type float or float * instead of double or double *. Execute the program again with different inputs. Are the results different?

24. Modify the function exp() to calculate the numerator and denominator of each term separately. The numerator will be a power of x and the denominator will be n! (n factorial). Test the program again. Do the results differ?

25. Rewrite exp() so that the function itself returns the value of e^x instead of returning the value in valptr. Note that you will have to make some changes to main() also.

4.5   One-Dimensional Arrays

The concept of an array is common to most programming languages. In an array, multiple values of the same data type can be stored with one variable name.

When we declare variables to be arrays, we can use the name of the variable to access all the elements in the collection. Arrays are used to store collections of related data.

Suppose an array named test_scores will be used to store the scores on a test. This array might be visualized as follows:

```
test_scores
```

89	75	93	68	77	83	78	65	92	73
0	1	2	3	4	5	6	7	8	9

In this example, the variable name is test_scores. It is a collection of ten data objects, 89, 75, 93, 68, ..., 73. Each data object is said to occupy one cell of the array. The numbers, 0, 1, . . . , 9, that appear below the array cells are the indices into the array. The variable name together with an index are used to access the contents of the cells of the array. For example,

```
test_scores[2]
```

refers to the value 93 that is stored in the cell with the index 2.

To use arrays in a C program, we will need to know how to declare arrays, how the individual cells are addressed, and how to initialize arrays.

An array declaration contains the following information: the type of elements that will be stored in the array, the name of the array, and the number of cells in the array. For example, if all the test scores to be stored in the array test_scores are integers, the declaration of this variable would be

```
int test_scores[10];
```

The type of the array elements is int, the variable name is test_scores, and there will be ten cells in the array. The indices of the cells will be 0, 1, 2, 3, . . . , 9. In C, integers are the only choice for array indices; the first cell will always have index 0 and the last cell will always have index one less than the total number of cells.

When this array is declared, a contiguous* block of memory is allocated that is large enough to hold ten elements of type int. The elements will be stored in order of the indices.

The program scores.c in Example 4-8 illustrates declaring an array and initializing an array with user input. It might appear as a function in a teacher's grading program.

Example 4-8: scores.c

```
/*              scores.c
 *
 *   Synopsis  -  Inputs 10 integers from the keyboard into an
 *                array of ints.
 *
 *   Objective -  Illustrates basic array declaration and accessing
 *                of the elements.  Includes an example of specifying
 *                a minimum field width in a printf() call.
 */

#include <stdio.h>

void main()
```

---

* When we talk about a contiguous block of memory for an array, we mean that all the array cells are placed in adjacent memory locations. No holes or unused bytes are present within the memory block for the array.

```
{
        int test_scores[10];                            /* Note 1*/
        int i;

        printf ("Please enter the ten test scores now.\n");
        for (i = 0; i < 10; i++) {                      /* Note 2 */
                printf ("#%2d > ", i+1);                /* Note 3 */
                scanf ("%d", &test_scores[i]);          /* Note 4 */
        }
        printf ("Thank you.\n");
}
```

There is a single function, main(). Two variables are defined. The function body consists of a `for` loop surrounded by two printf() calls. The body of the `for` loop contains calls to printf() and scanf().

Note 1: The variable `test_scores` is declared as an array of 10 elements of type `int`. The indices will be the integers 0 through 9.

Note 2: In the `for` loop, the variable `i` will act as an index into the array. It will consecutively take on the values 0 through 9. The loop terminates when `i` is incremented to 10.

Note 3: The printf() call outputs a prompt for each of the test scores. For the user's convenience, the test scores are numbered 1 through 10 instead of the index values of 0 through 9.

Notice the 2 preceding the `d` in the conversion specification. This specifies a minimum field width of 2 spaces for the output of the decimal value. The decimal will be justified on the right. The effect is cosmetic. The single-digit numbers, 1 through 9, will be output in the same column as the 0 in the two-digit number 10 in the output.

Note 4: The expression `test_scores[i]` will reference the cell of the array `test_scores` with the index `i`. As `i` proceeds from 0 through 9 in the `for` loop, all cells of the array will be accessed. The `&` or address operator can be used with an array reference to inform scanf() where to store the input value. In the next section, a more efficient way of indicating this will be discussed.

Learning Activities

26. Modify scores.c by writing and calling a C function to calculate the average of the test scores and output that value.

27. To make sure that you understand the concept of the minimum field width in a conversion specification, delete or comment out the scanf() call in the `for` loop and:

    a. Change the `for` loop so that the loop control variable starts at 300 and terminates at 309. Change it again so that it starts at 991 and terminates at 1000. Execute the program each time and notice the spacing of that output.

    b. Modify the program to output the index `i` with a minimum field width of 10. Execute the program again and notice the output spacing.

    c. Give a general description of the effect of the minimum field width on the spacing of decimal output. Be as complete as possible.

The sizeof() an Array

The operations allowed on an array element are those allowed on any expression with the same underlying type. There is only one operator that can act on the array as a whole: the sizeof() operator. This operator indicates the total amount of memory used by the array. For purposes of the following example, assume that an `int` occupies two bytes. Consider the following declaration:

```
int example[4];
```

The value of the expression

```
sizeof (example)
```

would be 8 since four `int`s occupy $4 \times 2 = 8$ bytes.

4.6 Initialization of Arrays

When arrays are initialized at the time of declaration, the initial values are placed in a comma-separated list enclosed in braces. In this chapter the initial values are constant. Some examples of array initialization follow.[*]

```
char name[6] = { 'S', 'a', 'l', 'l', 'y', '\0' };
```

[*] Older (non-ANSI) compilers may not allow the initialization of all arrays at the time of declaration. For more information about this and non-constant initial values, see Chapter 8.

In this example, a variable named `name` is declared. It is an array of six elements of type `char`. The indices of the array range from 0 to 5. The values of the cells of the array at the start of the program execution are as follows:

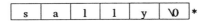

| s | a | l | l | y | \0 | *

Establishing the values in the array `names` could also be done with the following six assignment statements at the beginning of the program:

```
name[0] = 'S';   name[1] = 'a';   name[2] = 'l';
name[3] = 'l';   name[4] = 'y';   name[5] = '\0';
```

As a second example of initializing an array at the time of declaration, consider the following:

```
int numbers[8] = { 4, 0, 5, 6 };
```

A variable named `numbers` is declared to be an array of type `int`. There will be eight cells in the array; the indices will run from 0 through 7. In this example, the first four cells of the array have been initialized. The array will appear as follows:

| 4 | 0 | 5 | 6 | 0 | 0 | 0 | 0 |

Note that the number of initial values was less than the number of cells in the array. In this case the compiler assumes that the values are for the first cells of the array. Any cell that is not explicitly given an initial value is initialized to 0 by the compiler.

The third example of declaring and initializing elements of an array follows:

```
float dollars[] = { 1.37, 45.68, 3.45 };
```

In this example, a variable named `dollars` is declared to be an array of type `float`. Note that the declaration does not include the number of cells in the array `dollars`. In this case, this number is obtained from the number of initial values. The array `dollars` will have the following configuration at the start of program execution:

| 1.37 | 45.68 | 3.45 |

Because three initial values were given, the array will have three cells. Each cell will contain one of the initial values.

The program in Example 4-9 illustrates the sizeof() operator and the declaration and initialization of arrays in several ways.

---

* In C it is typical to terminate an array of characters with a null character so that it can be treated as a string. Further discussion about arrays and strings will be presented in Chapter 5.

Example 4-9: array1.c

```
/*                         array1.c
 *
 *    Synopsis  -  Three arrays are declared and initialized.  For
 *                 each array, the value in the storage cell with
 *                 index 3 is output.
 *
 *    Objective -  Illustrates declaration, initialization, and
 *                 accessing of elements in arrays.
 */

#include <stdio.h>
#define NUMCHARS   10
#define NUMFLOATS   8

char chararray[NUMCHARS];                              /* Note 1 */

void main()
{
        int intarray[] = {                            /* Note 2 */
              2, 1, 3, 5, 4, 8, 3, 7 };
        float floatarray[NUMFLOATS] = {               /* Note 3 */
              1.2, 3.4, -2.3, 1.4, 4.5 };
        void init_char_array();

        printf ("chararray occupies %d bytes.\n",     /* Note 4 */
                     sizeof(chararray));
        printf ("intarray occupies %d bytes.\n", sizeof (intarray));
        printf ("floatarray occupies %d bytes.\n", sizeof (floatarray));

        init_char_array();
                                                      /* Note 5 */
        printf ("The element in chararray with index 3 is '%c'.\n",
                        chararray[3]);
        printf ("The element in intarray with index 3 is %d.\n",
                        intarray[3]);
        printf ("The element in floatarray with index 3 is %5.2f.\n",
                        floatarray[3]);

}
```

```
/****************************         init_char_array()     *********/
/*    init_char_array()
 *    This function initializes the global character array chararray.
 */

void init_char_array()                                    /* Note 6 */
{
        int index;

        for (index = 0; index < NUMCHARS; index++)
                chararray[index] = 127 - index;
}
```

The functions main() and init_char_array() make up this program. Three arrays have been declared. After output of the sizeof() each array, the function main() calls init_char_array() and then makes three calls to printf() to output an element of each array. The function init_char_array() consists of a single `for` loop.

Note 1: An array of characters named `chararray` is declared. The number of storage cells is 10; the cells will be indexed from 0 through 9. During compilation, space will be allotted for 10 characters. No initialization is done on `chararray` at time of declaration. Because of the position of this declaration, this array can be accessed by init_char_array().

Note 2: This time an array of integers is declared. Its name is `intarray`. Since the number of storage cells is not given inside the brackets, the number of cells will be equal to the number of initial values in the list. In this case the number is 8. The indices will start at 0 and terminate with 7.

The array `intarray` is initialized by the numbers in the braces following the declaration. The first cell will contain 2, the second will contain 1, and so on.

Note 3: The identifier `floatarray` will refer to an array of elements of type `float`. The first value (with index 0) will be 1.2; the value with index 1 will be 3.4, etc. Note that the number of cells in the array has been declared to be 8, but that there are only five values between the braces for the array initialization. The five values will be put in the cells with indices 0 through 4.

Note 4: The sizeof() operator can be used with arrays. For example, the value of the expression `sizeof(intarray)` will be

((number of cells in the array) times (`sizeof(int)`))

The value is the total number of bytes used by the array. To demonstrate this, the sizeof() each array is output.

Note 5: In the following three printf() calls, individual storage cells are accessed by stating the name of the array followed by square brackets that contain the index of the storage cell desired.

Note 6: The function init_char_array() initializes the array `chararray`. For this reason `chararray` was declared outside the function main(). Later in this chapter the technique of passing an array as a parameter to a function will be developed so that this function could be rewritten as a useful tool.

A Word of Warning

There are only two times in C when an array can be declared without putting the number of cells inside the square brackets. The first is when the array is being initialized with its declaration. This is the case with the array `intarray` in the program array1.c. The second is when the array is being declared, but no memory is being allocated. This happens when an array is passed as an argument to a function. We will discuss this in Section 4.8. In all other cases, it is extremely important to indicate the number of cells in the array between the square brackets.

Learning Activities

28. a. Try to compile the program array1.c. Your compiler may not allow the initialization of the arrays `intarray` and `floatarray`. If it doesn't, add the word `static` in front of the type in both of those array declarations. The reasons for this will be discussed in Chapter 8.

b. Predict the output of array1.c and then execute it. Make sure the results are what you expect. Did you predict the correct values for the results of the sizeof() operator? Reconcile any differences between your predictions and the actual output.

29. Modify the program array1.c to output the contents of the cell with index 6 in `floatarray`. This cell was not initialized at the time of declaration. What value was in the cell?

30. Modify the program array1.c again to output `intarray[9]`. Note that `intarray[]` was declared with 8 initializers. Therefore, the indices should start at 0 and go through 7. Accessing `intarray[9]` is an error. How does your compiler and system handle this error?

31. Declare and initialize an array to hold the even integers between 0 and 20 inclusive in three different ways.

32. Write a declaration of an array of 24 characters. Initialize this array at declaration time with null characters in the first three spaces.

33. Consider the declaration

```
int intarray[] = {9, 5, 2, 3, 8, 7, 4};
```

a. How would the cell that contains the 7 be referenced?

b. What is the array index associated with the cell containing the 9?

c. Write the necessary declarations and statements to assign the sum of the contents of the third and the fifth cells in the array to a variable named `sum`.

d. How would the declaration above differ from the one below?

```
int intarray[7] = {9, 5, 2, 3, 8, 7, 4};
```

Which declaration is better in a stylistic sense? When might the first declaration be used instead of the second?

e. Predict what might happen during execution of the statement

```
intarray[7] = 24;
```

Put the declaration from part d. and the assignment statement in a program and test it to see if you were right. Try to generalize your findings.

34. Modify array1.c by rewriting the function init_char_array() so that it has a for loop with an empty statement body. That is, move the existing statement to bottom-of-the-loop processing.

Another Word of Warning

The program bounds.c in Example 4-10 has a bug in it. The programmer was not careful about the range of the indices into the array. In general, C compilers do not check the indices of an array during program execution to see that they are within the correct bounds. The omission of subscript range checking makes a program execute faster. Therefore, it is up to the programmer to insure that an index into an array is within the legal range.

Example 4-10: bounds.c

```
/*                  bounds.c
 *
 *    Synopsis  -  The program is supposed to increment each element
 *                 of an array and output the value of a unrelated
 *                 variable.  It has a bug in it.
 *
 *    Objective -  To illustrate a typical error and the fact that
 *                 the compiler does not check on array bounds.
 */

#include <stdio.h>

void main()
{
        int array[10];
        int nextvar = 5;
        int i;
```

```
        printf ("nextvar is %d.\n", nextvar);           /* Note 1 */
        for (i = 0; i <= 10; i++ )                       /* Note 2 */
                array[i]=i;
        printf ("nextvar is now %d.\n", nextvar);        /* Note 3 */
}
```

This program consists of a single function, main(). Inside main(), the value of the variable `nextvar` is output twice. A `for` loop initializes the contents of an array of type `int`.

Note 1: The value of `nextvar` is output.

Note 2: The variable `array` was declared to be an array of integers with 10 cells. Therefore, the legal indices go from 0 to 9 inclusive. In this `for` loop, the loop control variable `i` proceeds from 0 to 10, and each time the value of `array[i]` is incremented. The location accessed by `array[10]` is outside the array. Most compilers will not catch this error, either at compile time or at runtime.

Note 3: The value of `nextvar` is output again. In many implementations of C, the memory location of `nextvar` will be adjacent to that of the array. When the illegal value `array[10]` is incremented, this would actually increment the value of `nextvar` instead.

Learning Activities

35. Investigate the behavior of bounds.c on your system. Execute it to see if the value of `nextvar` was changed by the program. Add statements to output the addresses of the variables `array`, `nextvar`, and `i`. Is `nextvar` adjacent to the array? If your system does not change the value of `nextvar`, research the method utilized for memory allocation from the documentation supplied with the compiler.

36. Experiment to see if it is possible to change the value of `i` similarly. How far away is the memory location of `i` from that of `array`? Will your compiler allow you to go that far outside the bounds of the array?

37. Modify the program array1.c of the previous section to input the array index as an integer, and check its range before responding with the array elements.

4.7   An Array as a Pointer

In C, a very specific relationship exists between an array and a pointer. It is necessary to understand this relationship thoroughly.

In Section 4.1 we introduced the concept of a pointer. In review, a pointer variable holds an address of a memory location. The variable is said to point to that memory location.

A pointer variable declaration consists of a type followed by an asterisk followed by an expression list, terminated with a semicolon. In simple cases, each expression in the list is a variable name. For example,

```
int *intpointer;
```

declares a variable named `intpointer` with type pointer to `int` or `int *`. The only memory locations that `intpointer` can legally point to are those designated to hold a quantity of type `int`. Once the pointer variable `intpointer` has been declared and initialized, the contents of the memory address stored in `intpointer` are accessed by referring to `*intpointer` in the program.

Allowable operations with pointers include assignment (=), comparisons (==, !=, <=, <, >, >=), and arithmetic operations with the integers as illustrated in Example 4.3.

To illustrate the connection between an array and a pointer, consider the following declaration:

```
int intarray[10];
```

When the compiler processes this array declaration, it sets aside a region in memory large enough to store 10 quantities of type `int`. It also associates the address of the first cell in the array with the name `intarray` in the symbol table for the program. Anywhere in a C program that the identifier `intarray` is used without any accompanying brackets, the name evaluates to the address of the first cell in the array. The quantity `intarray + 1` is the address of the second cell in the array, and so on. The expressions `*intarray` and `intarray[0]` both refer to the contents of the first cell in the array. The expressions `*(intarray + 1)` and `intarray[1]` both refer to the contents of the second cell in the array, and so on. The name of an array can be used in a manner very similar to that of a pointer.

Arrays are similar to pointers, but there are differences in the two concepts. The name of an array evaluates to the address in memory of the first element in the array. Using the language of Chapter 2, it is an rvalue, but not an lvalue. It can be evaluated, but it cannot be changed. The location of the array is fixed in memory and cannot be moved during program execution. In contrast, a pointer variable can be both evaluated and changed. It can be used as both an rvalue and an lvalue.

Since the concepts of an array and a pointer are so closely linked, C allows the assignment of values between the two types. After the following declarations,

```
int intarray[10], *intpointer;
```

the identifier `intarray` refers to the address of the first element of the region set aside to hold 10 values of type `int`. The identifier `intpointer` remains uninitialized, but is designated to store the address of an `int`. The assignment

```
        intpointer = intarray;
```
assigns the address of the first cell in `intarray` to `intpointer` or makes `intpointer` "point" to the first cell in the array.*

Review of Pointer Arithmetic

Recall that in Section 4.2, we demonstrated that for a pointer variable named `ptr`, the meaning of `ptr + 1` is dependent on the type of quantity that `ptr` points to. Consider the following declarations:

```
        char    *   charptr;
        int     *   intptr;
        double  *   dblptr;
```

If `intptr` has been initialized to point to an integer, then `intptr + 1` is the address of the next integer. In a byte-addressable computer, it is `sizeof(int)` bigger than `intptr`. Similarly, `dblptr + 1` will be the address of the next memory location for a value of type `double`. It is `sizeof(double)` bigger than `dblptr` in numerical value. The value of `charptr + 1` is usually 1 more than the value of `charptr` because `sizeof(char)` is 1. The next program in Example 4-11 illustrates these concepts.

Example 4-11: arrayptr.c

```c
/*              arrayptr.c
 *
 *   Synopsis  -  Prints information about the address, the
 *                sizeof(), and the contents of an array, using both
 *                array and pointer notation.
 *
 *   Objective -  To illustrate the relationship between pointers
 *                and arrays and to demonstrate some of the
 *                different syntax that can be used.
 */

#include <stdio.h>

void main()
{
                                                   /* Note 1 */
        char    demoarray[5] = {'D', 'E', 'M', 'O', '!'};
        char    *demoptr = demoarray;
        int     i;
```

---

* This assignment could have been made as an initialization at the time of the declaration of `intpointer`, providing that `intarray` was the first of the variables declared.

```
                                                       /* Note 2 */
printf ("demoarray is %x.\n", demoarray);
printf ("sizeof(demoarray) is %d.\n", sizeof(demoarray) );
printf ("sizeof(demoarray[0]) is %d.\n",
                        sizeof(demoarray[0]) );

                                                       /* Note 3 */
printf ("\ndemoptr is %x.\n", demoptr);
printf ("sizeof(demoptr) is %d.\n", sizeof(demoptr) );
printf ("sizeof(*demoptr) is %d.\n", sizeof(*demoptr) );

printf ("\ni\tdemoarray[i]\t*(demoarray+i)\t*demoptr\n");
printf ("-\t------------\t--------------\t--------\n");

for ( i = 0; i < 5; i++, demoptr++)                    /* Note 4 */
        printf ("%d\t      %c      \t      %c      \t      %c\n",
             i, demoarray[i], *(demoarray + i), *demoptr);
                                                       /* Note 5 */

}
```

The body of the single function main() consists of calls to printf() followed by a `for` loop. The body of the `for` loop is another call to printf().

Note 1: The variables for this program are an initialized array of 5 elements of type `char` and a `char *` variable that is initialized to point to the array. The variable `i` will be used to control the `for` loop.

Note 2: The first three printf() calls give the address of the array, the sizeof() the array, and the sizeof() the first element in the array. The sizeof() the array is the total number of bytes in the whole array.

Note 3: The next three printf() calls give the address that is currently in the variable `demoptr`, the `sizeof(demoptr)` and the sizeof() the quantity pointed to by `demoptr`. Note that the address in `demoptr` should be identical to the address of `demoarray`. However, `sizeof(demoptr)` should give the number of bytes necessary to hold an address on the computer system. This illustrates one of the differences between pointers and arrays.

Note 4: The `for` loop will print out a table of the three named quantities. Notice the use of the comma operator. Both `i` and `demoptr` will be incremented during the bottom of the loop processing.

Note 5: Each of the parameters to be output by printf() references exactly the same quantity. The output from this loop should demonstrate the equivalences of the three different expressions. Notice that a pointer variable can be and was used to traverse the array.

Learning Activities

38. Predict the output of this program. Then compile and execute it to verify your predictions. Reconcile any differences between your prediction and the actual output.

39. Modify arrayptr.c by attempting to assign a value to demoarray after the `for` loop (or try to use the increment by 1 operator, ++, on demoarray). This is an error because the array cannot be moved in memory during execution (demoarray is a constant value). How does your system handle this error? Is it caught at compile time, at runtime, or not caught at all?

Toward Efficiency

The last example showed that both `* (demoarray + i)` and `demoarray[i]` refer to the same quantity. Most programmers are more comfortable with the notation `demoarray[i]` because this syntax is similar to that used to access array elements in many other languages. However, in C, for an array of `int`s, that syntax must be translated to the expression `* (demoarray + i)` in order to access the array element. This involves extra calculation. Therefore, it is more efficient to use the pointer notation.

4.8   Arrays as Parameters to Functions

Arrays can be passed as parameters to functions; however, in contrast to other variable types, it is not possible to pass a copy of an array as a parameter.* Instead, the address of the array serves as the parameter and the function can access the array elements through the address.

There are two ways of declaring an array as a parameter to a function. The first makes use of the relationship between pointers and arrays. As an example,

```
doit (int *intarray)
{
      /* function code */
}
```

---

* An exception to this statement occurs when an array is a component of another data structure and a copy of the other structure is passed as a parameter. In this case, a copy of the array is passed also.

would declare `intarray` as the parameter to doit(). The notation indicates that the address of the first element of the array is what the function sees.

In the second syntax the comparable part of the code would be

```
doit(int intarray[]) *
```

Note that the function will have no knowledge of the number of elements in the array from the declaration. It will only know the base address and the element type of the array. This makes programming tools using arrays much easier and more flexible.

Inside the code for the function body, either of the two notations (the subscripting notation with brackets, `[]`, or the pointer arithmetic notation with the indirection operator, `*`) can be used to access the array elements. Stylistically, it is better to be consistent with the notation chosen, at least throughout the code for any function.

The program in Example 4-12 gives an example of input and output of arrays. A function is invoked for both the input and the output of an array. The array is passed as a parameter to both functions.

 Example 4-12:   arraypar.c

```
/*                  arraypar.c
 *
 *    Synopsis  -  Inputs int values (an inventory) from standard
 *                 input into an array and outputs them to
 *                 standard output.
 *
 *    Objective -  To illustrate passing an array as a parameter to
 *                 a function.
 */

#include <stdio.h>
#define MAX      20

void main()
{
        int inventory[MAX];                             /* Note 1 */
        int num_items;
        void print_inventory(int inv[], int max);
        int input_inventory(int *inv, int max);         /* Note 2 */
```

---

* The corresponding declarations for older compilers would be
```
    doit (intarray)
    int *intarray;
```
and
```
    doit (intarray)
    int intarray[];
```

```
                printf ("Please enter the number of items in stock.");
                printf ("  Enter -1 when you are done.\n");
                num_items = input_inventory (inventory, MAX);   /* Note 3 */
                print_inventory (inventory, num_items);         /* Note 4 */
        }


/***************************   input_inventory()   **********/
/* input_inventory() - accepts input of MAX or less values
 * of type int and stores them in an array.  Returns the
 * number of items input. Checks for overflowing the end
 * of the array.
 */
int input_inventory (int *inventory, int maxnum)               /* Note 5 */
{
        int index;

        for (index = 0; index < maxnum; index++) {
                scanf ("%d", (inventory + index) );            /* Note 6 */
                if ( *(inventory + index) < 0)
                    break;                                     /* Note 7 */
        }
        if (index == maxnum)
                printf ("No room for more items.\n");
        return (index);
}
/*******************************   print_inventory()   *******/
/* outputs the values in an array of ints.  The parameter numitems
 * indicates the number of meaningful items in the array.
 */
void print_inventory(int inventory[], int numitems)           /* Note 8 */
{
        int index;

        for (index = 0; index < numitems; index++) {
                printf ("Item number %d:\t\t", index+1);
                printf ("Number on hand  %5d\n", inventory[index]);
        }
}
```

The program is made up of the functions main(), input_inventory(), and print_inventory(). The function main() is a driver; it outputs a message with printf(), calls input_inventory() to do some input, and calls print_inventory() to do some output. Both input_inventory() and print_inventory() are controlled by a `for` loop that traverses the array.

Note 1: The array `inventory` is declared to store twenty `int` values.

Note 2: The ANSI C prototype declaration of the function input_inventory() appears on this line. Since input_inventory() returns an `int`, it is not necessary to declare it here, but doing so gains the advantages of the ANSI C prototypes. These advantages are discussed in Chapter 8.

Note 3: The function input_inventory() takes two actual parameters: the address of the array `inventory`, and the total number of cells in the array. The value returned is the total number of cells that have data stored in them by the function input_inventory().

Note 4: The function print_inventory() also takes two actual parameters: the address of the array, and the number of cells that have data stored in them.

Note 5: When an array is passed as a parameter, its name and type must appear between the parentheses after the function name in the function declaration. Since the address of the array is passed to the function, the pointer notation can be used to declare the parameter. The pointer notation is used throughout the function body.

Note 6: A call to scanf() inputs a decimal integer. Recall that scanf() requires the address of the memory location where the input value is to be stored. The name `inventory` is the address of the base of the array. The expression

```
inventory + index
```

is the address of the cell with the proper offset.

Note 7: For each iteration of the `for` loop, values are read into successive cells of the array. There are two ways of exiting the `for` loop. If twenty values are entered, the loop will terminate normally, and the array will be full. If fewer than twenty values are entered, the user is directed to enter –1 as a sentinel value from the terminal. Note that –1 could not be the inventory of any item. When this `if` statement detects a negative value, it issues a `break` to terminate execution of the `for` loop.

Note 8: This parameter declaration demonstrates that the array notation can be used as well as the pointer notation. The array notation is used throughout this function. Stylistically, consistent notation should be used throughout a function.

Learning Activities

40. a. Rewrite input_inventory() using array notation throughout that function. Compile and execute the code with both functions written in array notation. If there is a facility for timing the execution of a program on your computer system, time the execution of the modified program and record the results.

    b. Rewrite the function print_inventory() using pointer notation instead of array notation. Using the original version of input_inventory() (in pointer notation also), compile and execute the modified program. If possible, time the execution of this version of the program and record the results.

    c. Compare the two versions of the program arraypar.c. Is there a difference in the size of the object code? Was there a difference in the execution time of the program? Draw any conclusions you can about the efficiency of each version.

41. Many beginning C programmers are tempted to put the number of elements in the array into the parameter declarations when an array is passed as an argument to a function. Starting with the version of arraypar.c that you modified in 1a above, change both parameter declarations of the array `inventory` to include the number of cells. Make both declarations read

    ```
    int inventory[20];
    ```

    Attempt to compile and run the program. What did you discover? If it runs correctly, compare the size of the executable versions of the code. Compare the contents of the two executable files. What conclusions, if any, can you draw?

42. If you do not have an ANSI C compiler, change both function definitions to conform to your compiler's requirements.

43. Write a function that will sum the elements in an array of `ints`. Have your function accept the array address and the number of elements as parameters and return the sum of the elements. Modify arraypar.c to have print_inventory() call this function and output the total to the inventory items after the output of the array contents.

44. If you chose to write your function in array notation, rewrite it in pointer notation. Otherwise, rewrite it in array notation.

Language Elements Introduced in This Chapter: A Review

** Arrays **

    Indices always start at 0.

    Accessing elements:
```
chararray[index]
```

    Initializing:
```
char chararray[10] = { '1', '2', '3' };
   /* only the first three cells are initialized */
char constarray[] = { '1', '2', '3' };
   /* the array will have only three cells   */
```

** Macro Definitions **

    NULL is defined as 0 in stdio.h and many other header files.

** Operators **

The address operator
    &   gives the address of a variable.
The dereferencing operator
    *   used with an address, gives the contents of that address.
The sizeof() operator with an array
        returns the number of bytes in that array.

** Parameters to Functions **

To simulate pass by reference,
    pass the address of a variable to the function, e.g.,

```
funct(x, y)
int x, *y;   /* funct() will be able to change
                 * whatever value y points at    */
```

To pass an array as a parameter to a function, pass in the address only, e.g.,

    function declaration:

```
funct (int *array)
```

    function call:

```
int array[50];
...
funct(array);
```

** Types **
    Pointer types
    One-dimensional arrays

** Variable Declarations **
    Pointers:

```
char * charptr;
int * intptr;
```

    Arrays:

```
char chararray[12];
float floatvals[20];
```

Things to Remember

1. A pointer holds a memory address.
2. Each pointer type, `char *`, `int *`, and so on, is a distinct type. The pointer arithmetic is defined differently for different pointer types.

3. Like all other variables, pointers must be initialized to point to something meaningful before either reading or writing their contents.
4. Setting a pointer to `NULL` indicates that it doesn't point anywhere.
5. The declaration `int *ptr;` indicates that `*ptr` is an `int` and that `ptr` is the address of an `int`.
6. Parameters to a function are passed by value. A function cannot change the value of a variable in the calling environment that is passed in as a parameter.
7. Remember to explicitly allocate space for an array either by placing the number of cells inside the brackets when declaring or by initializing all cells of the array.
8. Be careful: C may allow you to overrun the bounds of your array.
9. The name of an array without any brackets gives the address of the first cell of the array.
10. Pointers can be used to traverse arrays efficiently.
11. If the efficiency of a program is a major concern, array element access can be done more efficiently with pointer notation.
12. When an array is passed as a parameter to a function, only the address is passed in.

4.9 Exercises and Programming Problems

1. Consider the program you wrote for exercise 1 of Chapter 3. Make the following modifications to the program. For every variable in your program, add a declaration of a pointer variable of each type and initialize the pointer to point to the original variable. Modify the executable code in the program so that all data is accessed via pointer variables instead of the original variables.
2. a. Write a program that contains declarations of one variable of each of the basic types (`int`, `char`, `long`, `short`, `unsigned`, `float`, `double`) as well as declarations of one variable of each of the pointer types (pointer to `int`, pointer to `char`, pointer to `long`, etc.). Initialize each of the pointer variables to point to the corresponding variable of the base type. Initialize each of the nonpointer variables also. Have your program use the pointer notation to output the address of each of the nonpointer variables. Use the dereferencing `*` to output the value of each nonpointer variable. Use the address operator, `&`, to output the address of each of the pointer variables. Compile and execute your program.

   b. Use the values output from the execution of your program to draw a diagram of memory (a memory map) during your program's execution. Use the diagrams in Figure 4-2 as a model.

   c. Modify your program by changing the order of the variable declarations. Then execute it again and see if the memory map changes.
3. Write a program to input elements in an array of type `float` and to output those values in reverse order.

4. The following program is designed to input values for an array of three `ints` and then output the contents of the array. It does not work correctly. For example, try to enter the value 1 for each cell in the array. Because the problem has to do with memory management, the addresses of the variables are ouput before the array initialization begins. Find the bug in the program.

```
/*                      prob3.c
 *
 *      Synopsis   -    Designed to input values into an array of three
 *                      ints and then output the contents of that array.
 *                      Has a bug in it.
 *
 *      Objective  -    To provide practice debugging a program with a
 *                      common mistake.
 */

#include <stdio.h>

void main()
{
        int intarray[3], count;

        printf ("intarray %x,   &count   %x.\n", intarray, &count);
        for (count = 0; count <= 3; count++) {
                printf("Cell #%d : ", count);
                scanf("%d", intarray+count);
        }

        printf ("The contents of the array are: ");
        for ( count = 0; count <= 3; count++)
                printf ("%d\n", intarray[count]);
}
```

5. a. Write a function named addarray() that returns the sum of the elements of an array of `int` values. Your function should take two parameters, the array, and the number of elements in the array. Make your function work with the program below.

```
/*                  arraysum.c
 *
 *    Synopsis   -  Outputs the value returned by the function
 *                  addarray() with two different sets of parameters.
 *
 *    Objective  -  To provide a test program for the function
 *                  addarray() written for an exercise.  The answers
 *                  should be 55 and 0.
 */

#include <stdio.h>

void main()
{
        int array1[10] = {1, 2, 3, 4, 5, 6, 7, 8, 9, 10},
            array2[4]  = {0, 0, 0, 0};

        printf ("The sum of the elements in array1 is %d.\n",
                        addarray(array1, 10) );
        printf ("The sum of the elements in array2 is %d.\n",
                        addarray(array2, 4) );
}
```

b. If you used array subscript notation in your function addarray(), change it to pointer notation. If you used pointer notation initially, rewrite the function with array subscript notation. Test the new version of your function with the program in part a.

6. Write a menu-driven mini-statistics package. A user should be able to enter up to 200 items of `float` data. The program should calculate the number of items in the data, the mean, the standard deviation, the variance, the median and the mode of the data. A sample run follows. The symbol `<EOF>` in the sample run below should be replaced with `CTRL-Z` or `CTRL-D` or the end-of-file symbol on your system.

```
Mini-Stat Package
--------- -------
This program will perform the following:
1)  Enter data.
2)  Display the data and the following statistics:
    the number of data items, the high and low values
    in the data, the mean, median, mode, variance and
    standard deviation.
```

```
3)   Quit the program.
     -----------------------------------------------
Your choice? 1

Enter one data item after each prompt.  Press return
after each one.  Signal with <EOF> when you are done
with data input.
Item #1  :   25
Item #2  :   36
Item #3  :   27.5
Item #4  :   28
Item #5  :   32
Item #6  :   33.25
Item #7  :   <EOF>

This program will perform the following:
1)   Enter data.
2)   Display the data and the following statistics:
     the number of data items, the high and low values
     in the data, the mean, median, mode, variance and
     standard deviation.
3)   Quit the program.
     -----------------------------------------------
Your choice? 2

Data Items:
25       36       27.5      28       32       33.25
Number of data items : 6
Largest data item    : 36
Smallest data item   : 25
Mean                 : 30.292
Median               : 30
Mode                 : no mode
Variance             : 14.21
Standard Deviation   : 3.77

This program will perform the following:
1)   Enter data.
2)   Display the data and the following statistics:
     the number of data items, the high and low values
     in the data, the mean, median, mode, variance and
     standard deviation.
3)   Quit the program.
     -----------------------------------------------
Your choice? 1

Do you want to add new data to the existing sample?
(Y/N)   Y
Signal with <EOF> when you are done.
Item #7  :   29.7
Item #8  :   28.2
Item #9  :   35.3
Item #10 :   28
Item #11 :   <EOF>
```

```
This program will perform the following:
1)   Enter data.
2)   Display the data and the following statistics:
     the number of data items, the high and low values
     in the data, the mean, median, mode, variance and
     standard deviation.
3)   Quit the program.
----------------------------------------------------------
Your choice? 2

Data Items:
25      36      27.5      28      32      33.25      29.7      28.2
35.3    28
Number of data items : 10
Largest data item    : 36
Smallest data item   : 25
Mean                 : 30.295
Median               : 28.95
Mode                 : 28
Variance             : 12.03
Standard Deviation   : 3.469

This program will perform the following:
1)   Enter data.
2)   Display the data and the following statistics:
     the number of data items, the high and low values
     in the data, the mean, median, mode, variance and
     standard deviation.
3)   Quit the program.
----------------------------------------------------------
Your choice? 3

Thank you and goodbye!
```

7. Assume that an address and a variable of type `int` both occupy four bytes of
    memory. Predict the output of the following program.
    The answers for the first few are given.

```
/*              ptrex.c
 *
 *   Synopsis  -  Illustrates different ways of addressing
 *                pointers and arrays.  Outputs the values of
 *                expressions relevant to the arrays.
 *
 *   Objective -  To provide practice with  pointer and
 *                array expressions.
 */
```

```c
#include <stdio.h>

void main()
{
        static int intarray[5] = {
                32, -123, 4, 2, -24      };
        static char chararray[5] = {
                'e', 'f', 'g', 'h', 'i' };

        int *int_ptr = intarray;
        char *char_ptr = chararray,
             ch = 'a';

                                               /* ANSWERS */

        printf ("%d\n", int_ptr);        /* _8204_____ */

        printf ("%d\n", char_ptr);       /* _8224_____ */

        printf ("%d\n", &int_ptr);       /* _16756484_____ */

        printf ("%d\n", *int_ptr);       /* _____ */

        printf ("%d\n", intarray[4]);    /* _____ */

        printf ("%d\n", chararray[4]);   /* _____ */

        printf ("%d\n", intarray + 1);   /* _____ */

        printf ("%d\n", chararray + 1);  /* _____ */

        printf ("%d\n", int_ptr + 1);    /* _____ */

        printf ("%d\n", char_ptr + 1);   /* _____ */

        printf ("%d\n", *int_ptr + 1);   /* _____ */

        printf ("%d\n", *char_ptr + 1);  /* _____ */

        printf ("%d\n", *(int_ptr + 1)); /* _____ */

        printf ("%d\n", *(char_ptr + 1)); /* _____ */

        printf ("%d\n", &intarray[0]);   /* _____ */

        printf ("%d\n", ++*int_ptr);     /* _____ */
```

```
        printf ("%d\n", ++(*int_ptr));    /* _____ */

        printf ("%d\n", ++*intarray);     /* _____ */

        printf ("%d\n", *&ch);            /* _____ */

        printf ("%d\n", 3**int_ptr);      /* _____ */
}
```

8. Find and correct the bugs in the following program.

```
/*                  bug.c
 *
 *    Synopsis   -   Supposed to accept input values of 10 integer
 *                   values for the array, add 5 to each value, and
 *                   output the values in the array, but it doesn't work.
 *
 *    Objective  -   To provide practice in finding a common mistake.
 */

#include <stdio.h>
void init_array(int array[], int numelts);
void add_five (int array[], int numelts);
void print_array(int array[], int numelts);
void main()
{
        int intarray[10];

        init_array(intarray, 10);
        add_five(intarray, 10);
        print_array(intarray, 10);
}

void init_array(int array[], int numelts)
{
        int i;

        printf ("Please enter values for the array:\n");
        for ( i = 0; i < numelts; i++ ) {
                printf ("%d: ", i);
                scanf("%d", array+i );
        }
}
```

```
void add_five (int array[], int numelts)
{
        int i = -1;

        printf ("\nAdding five to each element of the array.\n");
        while (i++ < numelts - 1);
                array[i] += 5;
}

void print_array(int array[], int numelts)
{
        int i;

        printf ("\nThe values in the array are:\n");
        for (i = 0; i < numelts; i++)
                printf ("%d\t", *(array+i) );
        printf ("\n");
}
```

9. The following program contains a function named bubble_sort() and a function named swap(). Together they are supposed to implement the bubble sort algorithm to sort the elements in an array of integers. The function main() contains a call to bubble_sort() and a `for` loop to print the values in the array. The program has a bug in it.

```
/*              bubble.c
 *
 *   Synopsis  -  Attempts to implement a bubble sort of an array
 *                of integers.  It has a small bug in it.  Fix
 *                the bug.
 *
 *   Objective -  Gives practice in debugging.
 */

void main()
{
        void bubble_sort(int data[], int num_elts);
        int index, data[10] = {
                10, 3, 4, 8, 2, 5, 9, 7, 1, 6   };

        bubble_sort(data, 10);

        for (index=0; index < 10; index++)
                printf ("%d ", data[index]);
        printf ("\n");
}
```

```
void bubble_sort(int data[], int num_elts)
{
        void swap (int a, int b);
        int i, j;

        for (i = 0; i < num_elts; i++)
                for (j = num_elts-1; j > i; j--)
                        if ( data[j] < data[j-1])
                                swap (data[j], data[j-1]);
}

void swap (int a, int b)
{
        int temp;

        temp = a;
        a = b;
        b = temp;
}
```

a. Fix the bug in the program. The array should be sorted when it is output.

b. Rewrite the program so that a user may enter up to 100 values and the program will sort them.

10. Look up another sorting algorithm (quicksort, heap sort, insertion sort or merge_sort, for example). Implement that sort in C and test it. You may want to replace the call to bubble_sort() in your program from exercise 9b to implement the testing program.

11. The function sin(x) has the following infinite series expansion:

$$x - x^3/3! + x^5/5! - x^7/7! + \ldots + x^{2n+1}/(2n+1)! + \ldots$$

a. Write a program similar to exp.c in Example 4-7 that will calculate the sin(x) when the user enters x in radians. Make sure your functions are declared correctly and that you pass the parameters to the functions. Have the calculated value of sin(x) output in main().

b. After the program in part a is working, modify it so that the user can enter the angle in degrees instead of radians.

12. a Write a C function that will input values into an array of type `int`. Have the array and the number of elements in the array passed as parameters to your function. Use a local pointer variable to traverse the array.

b. Write a C function that will output the contents of an array of type `int`. Have the array and the number of elements in the array passed as parameters. Use a local pointer variable to traverse the array.

Strings

Chapter 5

5.1 Introduction to Strings

In computer science, a string is a sequence of characters from the underlying character set. Different methods for handling strings are implemented in different languages. A string in C is a sequence of characters terminated by a null character, '\0'.

String constants were first discussed in Chapter 1. A string constant was used as the first parameter in a call to printf(). Recall the statement from the program output.c of Example 1-3:

```
printf ("Testing 1, 2, 3\n");
```

The expression "Testing 1, 2, 3\n" is a string constant. A string constant appears in a C program inside a set of double quotes (").

When the compiler sees a sequence of characters enclosed in double quotes, it stores the sequence in a special place in the object code and appends a terminating '\0' to the end of the character sequence. For example,

T	e	s	t	i	n	g		1	,		2	,		3	\n	\0

It then associates the string constant with the address of the memory location of the first character in the string.

If the statement

```
printf ("Testing 1, 2, 3\n");
```

appeared in a program, the characters in the string would be stored in the executable code with a terminating null character (' \0') appended as shown. The address of the location of the ' T' would actually be the parameter to printf(). When that statement is executed, printf() will look at the address and start its output with the character found at that address. It stops output when it reaches the terminating null character.

The concept of a string is very closely related to that of a character array and to that of a pointer to a character. A string is very much like an array of characters in that the characters in the string are stored in contiguous memory locations. One difference is that a string must have a null character as the string terminator while a character array does not.

Because it is handled as an address, a string is like a pointer to char. In fact, since the compiler handles the string "Testing 1, 2, 3\n" as the address of the ' T', the string could be assigned to a char * variable. For example,

```
char *stringptr;
...
stringptr = "Testing 1, 2, 3\n";
```

Then the call to printf() could be rewritten as

```
printf (stringptr);
```

C allows the use of the array indexing syntax to access the individual elements of a string. For example, after the above sequence of code, the notation stringptr[0] would be the ' T', stringptr[6] would be the ' g', and stringptr[7] would be the first blank character. The assignment

```
stringptr[7] = '\0';
```

would shorten the string to "Testing" because the first ' \0' encountered would terminate the string.

Pointer arithmetic and dereferencing could also be used to access the individual characters in the string. For example, *stringptr would be the ' T', and * (stringptr + 6) would be the ' g'. The assignment

```
* (stringptr + 4) = '\0'
```

would change the string to "Test".

With printf(), the conversion specification %s signals the output of a string. When printf() sees %s in its control string, it expects the corresponding parameter to be the address of the first character in a string. It again starts output with the byte found at that address and proceeds outputting subsequent bytes until it encounters a null character. For example, the string "Testing 1, 2, 3\n" could be output with the following call to printf():

```
printf ("%s", stringptr);
```

Note that the %s conversion specification can be used with scanf() too. When %s appears in the control string for scanf(), the corresponding parameter should be the address of an array with enough space to handle the input. The string that scanf()

will put in the array will be the first sequence of nonwhitespace characters it finds. For example, if the input is

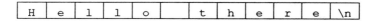

scanf() will place

in the array. The

will remain in the input stream.

The program string1.c in Example 5-1 illustrates some basics about using strings and about their compatibility with a char * variable.

Example 5-1: string1.c

```
/*              string1.c
 *
 *   Synopsis  -  Outputs some strings and addresses of strings.
 *
 *   Objective -  To illustrate how C compilers handle strings.
 */

#include <stdio.h>

void main ()
{
        char *stringptr;                            /* Note 1 */

        stringptr = "One two, buckle my shoe\n";    /* Note 2 */
        printf (stringptr);                         /* Note 3 */
        printf ("%s", stringptr);                   /* Note 4 */
        printf ("%x\n", stringptr);                 /* Note 5 */

        *(stringptr + 7) = '\n';                    /* Note 6 */
        stringptr[8] = '\0';
        printf (stringptr);

        printf ("%x,  %x\n", "Testing", "Testing"); /* Note 7 */
}
```

This program consists of the single function main(). The executable code consists simply of assignment statements and calls to printf().

Note 1: A variable of type char * is declared. It will be used to hold the address of the first character in a string.

Note 2: A string is assigned to the variable with type char *. The compiler stored the string in a special place in the executable code and in this statement, the address of the first character, 'O', is assigned to stringptr.

Note 3: The variable stringptr can be used as the first parameter to printf(). This emphasizes the fact that printf() looks for the address of the first character of its control string.

Note 4: This call to printf() illustrates another way of using stringptr as a parameter. The %s conversion specification indicates that a string is to be output. Then printf() expects the corresponding argument to hold the address of the first character in the string.

Note 5: The address of the first character in the string is output. This emphasizes the fact that stringptr really contains the address of a character, a numerical quantity. That quantity could be output in decimal or octal as well as hexadecimal.

Note that printf() can access the same argument in two different contexts, as a string and as a hexadecimal value. When it expects a string, it assumes that the value it finds is the address of the first character to be output. When it expects a numerical value, it does the conversion to hexadecimal and outputs it. The meaning comes from the context.

Note 6: The next two assignment statements change some of the characters in the string. Access of the individual characters in the string can be done in two ways: using pointer arithmetic and using array notation.

The first assignment statement, done with pointer arithmetic, places a newline, '\n', immediately after the word "two". The comma is overwritten. The second assignment statement, using array subscripting, places a '\0' after the newline to terminate the string at this point. The following call to printf() outputs the modified string. Output stops at the first null character.

Note that both array subscripting and pointer arithmetic can be utilized to access memory locations within the string. Recall that the name of an array evaluates to the address of the first element in the array.

Note 7: In this statement, printf() outputs the address of two identical strings. Notice that these addresses will be different. Every time a string appears in C source code, a copy of it is placed in the object code. No checking for identical strings is done. This would allow a program to change one copy and retain the original value of the other.

Learning Activities

1. Write a program like string1.c and have it output the poem

   ```
   One two, buckle my shoe.
   Three four, shut the door.
   ```

   on separate lines as shown, then manipulate those strings so that the program outputs

   ```
   One two three four!
   ```

   on one line.

2. Add output statements to string1.c to output the memory location of each of the original strings in the modified program. Are they stored next to each other in the object code? What happens when you add the statements

   ```
   *(stringptr + 27) = 'X';
   stringptr[28] = 'Y';
   ```

   after the last printf() call and output both strings in the modified program again? Are the 'X' and the 'Y' output? Explain what happened.

5.2 Variable Strings

As seen in the last example, a string can be assigned to a `char *` variable and any of the characters in the string can be changed by accessing the characters using the pointer variable. The access of individual characters can be done either in pointer arithmetic or array subscripting notation. However, an error occurs if an attempt is made to append new characters to the end of the string. This error may (or may not) cause a program to crash or corrupt the program's data. The problem arises because of the amount of memory allocated for the string. A programmer can only be sure that there is a byte allocated for each character in the string plus one for the terminating `'\0'`.

If a program needs to process strings of unknown or changing length, enough space must be allocated for a string of maximum length. This can be done with an array of characters. If the programmer wants to treat an array of characters as a string, it is necessary to write a terminating null into the array after the last meaningful character.

The program strngio1.c in Example 5-2 illustrates the creation of a string from an array of characters. It inputs a string from the keyboard and outputs it as a string with printf(). The function inputstring() in this program is a useful tool. It reads the characters from the system input buffer, stopping at the ' \n' , and stores them in a buffer that is internal to the program. It replaces the ' \n' with ' \0' so that input can be treated as a string. The only parameter to inputstring() is the address of the first character in the input buffer.

Example 5-2: strngio1.c

```
/*              strngio1.c
 *
 *   Synopsis  -  Accepts a line of text as input from the keyboard
 *                and echoes it to the terminal screen.
 *
 *   Objective -  To illustrate the use of an array to create a
 *                string and point out the connection among
 *                pointers, arrays, and strings.
 */

#include <stdio.h>

void main()
{
        char inputarray[512];                           /* Note 1 */
        char *inputptr = inputarray;
        void inputstring(char *ip);                     /* Note 3 */

        printf ("Enter a line of text.\n> ");
        inputstring(inputptr);                          /* Note 2 */
        printf (inputarray);

}
/******************************  inputstring()  ***********/

/*   inputstring() : accepts input of a line of
 *   text from the keyboard and stores it in
 *   the array pointed to by its argument.
 */

void inputstring (char *inputptr)
{
        while ( (*inputptr++ = getchar() ) != '\n')     /* Note 4 */
                ;
        *(--inputptr) = '\0';                           /* Note 5 */
}
```

Two functions, main() and inputstring(), make up this program. In main(), the executable code consists of two calls to printf() and a call to the function inputstring(). The function inputstring() consists of a `while` loop to do the input and an assignment statement.

Note 1: Space is allocated by declaring an array of 512 characters. This will serve as the internal buffer to hold the line of text entered from the keyboard. It is unlikely that a line entered from the keyboard will exceed this length. To be more precise, the maximum length of an input line should be researched in the operating system documentation. In the next declaration, a pointer to `char` variable is defined and initialized to point to the array.

Note 2: A call to the function inputstring() is made. The argument to this function is the address of the first character of the buffer where the input text is to be stored.

Note 3: The declaration of the parameter to the function inputstring() is made in the prototype syntax of ANSI C. (It must be changed on systems without an ANSI C compiler.) Note that the variable name is optional and does not have to be declared.

Note 4: In this `while` loop, the call to getchar() reads a single character and assigns it to the address pointed to by the parameter `inputptr`. Then `inputptr` is incremented to point to the next position in the array and the value is compared to a newline character. All of this is done in the expression of the `while` loop. The loop has an empty body.

Note 5: After the input of the line is done, a null character, `'\0'`, is placed in the position of the original newline character. The newline character had already been put in the buffer and `inputptr` incremented to point to the next position. Therefore, `inputptr` must be decremented before the assignment is made.

Learning Activities

To answer the following questions, it may be necessary to test the concept by modifying the program strngio1.c, compiling it, and executing it.

3. Could `inputptr` have been used as an argument to the second call to printf() in main()? Why or why not?

4. Could `inputarray` have been used as the actual parameter to inputstring()? Why or why not?

5. Are both variables in main() necessary? Why or why not? If not, which could be eliminated and why?

5.3   Initialization with Strings

A string constant can be used to initialize a pointer, as in

```
char * charptr = "testing"
```

Initialization is allowed for all variables with type `char *`. During initialization, the address of the `'t'` in the string `"testing"` is assigned to `charptr`.

A string constant can also be used to initialize an array of characters, as in

```
char chararray[] = "testing"
```

In this case, the characters `'t'`,`'e'`,`'s'`,`'t'`,`'i'`,`'n'`,`'g'`,`'\0'` are placed in the region set aside for `chararray`. The array `chararray` will have eight cells, one for each character in the word "testing" and one for the terminating null.

In the first example, a similar assignment statement might appear in the executable code of the program because the address of the first character of a string can be legitimately assigned to a `char *` variable. In contrast, the initialization of the array does not translate to a similar assignment statement in the executable code of the program. This syntax is only used when initializing an array at the time of declaration.

"The input and output of strings is often done in sea (C)." Based on *The Herring Net* by Winslow Homer, 1885.

5.4   Input and Output of Strings

The input and output of strings is done often in C programs. Consequently, standard library functions have been written to do string I/O. The library function gets() reads a string from standard input, and the library function puts() writes a string to standard output. Other library functions that can be used for string input and output will be discussed in Chapter 10.

The library function gets() acts very much like the function inputstring() from our last example. It takes a single parameter, which is the address of an array that has been declared in the program where the input is to be stored. It reads each character in the input stream and stores them in successive locations in the program buffer until it finds a newline character in input. The newline character is discarded and '\0' is placed in the buffer to terminate the string. One difference between gets() and inputstring() is that gets() returns a value of type char *. If the input was successful, gets() will return the address of the buffer where it put the input string. If an error occurs or the end-of-file was encountered in the input, a NULL pointer is returned. In either of these latter cases, there is no guarantee about the contents of the program buffer.

The function puts() outputs a string to standard output; it returns a value of type int. It also takes the address of an array declared in the program as a parameter. It expects to find a string stored there. It will output each successive byte at that location until the first '\0' is encountered. The '\0' is not output, but a newline is output in its place. If an error occurred during output, puts() signals the error by returning the value EOF. No special significance is attached to values other than EOF that are returned by puts().

Notice that it is possible to output a string with printf(). The statements

```
printf (string);
```

and

```
printf ("%s\n", string);
```

will both output the contents of the char * variable string. In the latter case a final newline character is output so that the printf() call has the same effect as the call

```
puts (string);
```

In terms of use, puts() is a single-purpose function; it outputs a string. In contrast, printf() is a multipurpose function; it can be used to output integers in any of three bases, characters, and strings. Furthermore, it can be used to produce formatted output and will pad with blanks, justify within a field, and so on. It is a much bigger piece of code and carries a great deal more overhead.

The program in Example 5-3 has the same functionality as strngio1.c. It accepts a line of text from standard input and echoes it to standard output. However, the function inputstring() from strngio1.c is replaced with the library function gets() and output is done with the library function puts(). Some error handling is included as well.

Example 5-3: strngio2.c

```
/*                    strngio2.c
 *
 *    Synopsis    -   Prompts for and accepts a line of text as input
```

```
*                   from standard input with the standard library
*                   function gets(). Echoes the line to standard
*                   output with puts().
*
*    Objective -  To illustrate gets() and puts().
*/

#include <stdio.h>                                   /* Note 1 */

void main()
{
        char inputarray[512];                        /* Note 2 */
        char *inputptr;

        printf ("Enter a line of text.\n> ");
        inputptr = gets(inputarray);                 /* Note 3 */
        if (inputptr != NULL)                        /* Note 4 */
                puts (inputptr);                     /* Note 5 */
        else
                puts ("error in input\n");           /* Note 6 */
}
```

The single function main() prompts for input and calls gets() to do the input. Then puts() is called to do the output. The value returned by gets() determines the output.

Note 1: Along with the declaration of a char * variable, inputptr, the function gets() must be declared as type char * since it does not return the default type, int. On most systems this declaration is in the file stdio.h.

Note 2: A buffer of size 512 bytes is declared to hold the input. The size of the buffer could be adjusted according to system requirements and knowledge about the nature of the input to the program.*

Note 3: This call to gets() does the input of a line of text from standard input. The actual parameter to gets() is the address of the buffer where the input is to be stored. The return value from gets() is assigned to the variable, inputptr.

Note 4: The return value of gets() is checked. Upon encountering either the end-of-file or an error, gets() will return a NULL pointer, a pointer whose value is NULL. Otherwise, gets() returns the address of the first character of the input buffer.

Note 5: The function puts() is called to output the string. The parameter is the address of the buffer where the string is stored.

---

* The size of the buffer is open to debate. Many programmers will go with an array of 80 cells since few users will type more than that. Others would go with the system limit on input lines. The main point is that the buffer must be sufficiently large to hold the line of input and the terminating null character because the library function gets() does not check on the bounds of the array. If the input contains more characters than the array has cells, gets() will place the extra characters in the next memory location and overrun the bounds of the array.

Note 6: In this puts() call, the parameter consists of the string enclosed in double quotes. During compilation, the string is stored with a terminating ' \0', and the address of the first character in the string becomes the effective parameter.

Learning Activities

6. Execute strngio2.c with several sets of input to make sure it works as you expect.
   a. What is output if the return key is pressed immediately after the prompt?
   b. What is output if end-of-file is signaled immediately after the prompt?
   c. Distinguish between the contents of `inputarray` and `inputptr` in the two cases mentioned in a and b. What are the different values returned by gets() and why?
7. Explain the difference between a NULL pointer, a null string, and a null character.
8. Can either `inputptr` or `inputarray` be eliminated from strngio2.c? Why or why not? Explain fully.
9. Modify strngio2.c by replacing the calls to puts() with calls to printf() and compile and execute the modified program. Compare the sizes of the executable code and, if possible, the execution times for the two versions of the program. What are your conclusions?
10. a. Write a short program that inputs a string using scanf() and the `%s` conversion specification. Have the string output with puts().
    b. Test the program with several different inputs until you understand what scanf() does with the `%s` conversion specification.
    c. Modify your program to read the character after the input string also. Test the program again with input like `"Hello there"`, `"Hello         there"`, `"Hello\tthere"`. Does the program behave as you expected?
    d. Explain scanf()'s behavior in your own words.

A Word of Warning

Allocation of memory for the characters in a string must be done during the compilation process. It is important to be aware of which declarations allocate what memory. Consider the following declarations:

```
char inputarray[512];
```

and

```
char *inputptr;
```

The declaration of inputarray causes 512 bytes of memory to be set aside for use during the program. The declaration of inputptr causes only enough memory for the address of a char to be allocated. This is normally only two or four bytes.

A common error could arise from misunderstanding the documentation for some of the C library functions. For example, most versions of the documentation for gets() indicate that the parameter must be of type char *, an address of a character buffer. What the documentation may not make clear is that the buffer space must be allocated by the program. The function gets() uses whatever address is passed to it. It does not provide the buffer.

The program in Example 5-4 illustrates this error. It attempts to input a string and output it. However, an error occurs because of the lack of memory allocated, a very common mistake by beginning C programmers. The misunderstanding is further compounded by the fact that the program may appear to run correctly on some computer systems. For example, on a microcomputer system, the user is allowed to write into any memory address. If a pointer happens to be pointing to an unused portion of memory, execution may proceed without noticeable error. The program is more likely to cause an error on a multiuser system where restrictions on memory use are more stringent. In any case, writing to unallocated space is an error whether the program crashes or not. Some of the newer compilers now give warning messages about this type of error.

 Example 5-4: strwarn.c

```
/*              strwarn.c
 *
 *    Synopsis  -  Attempts to enter a line of text with the library
 *                 function gets().  There is an error in the program
 *                 because space for the input line was not allocated.
 *
 *    Objective -  To point out a common error made by beginning C
 *                 programmers.
 */

#include <stdio.h>

void main()
{
        char *prompt = "Enter a line of text.\n> ";
        char *inputptr, *inputptr1;                    /* Note 1 */

        printf (prompt);
        inputptr1 = gets (inputptr);                   /* Note 2 */
        if (inputptr1 != NULL)
                puts (inputptr1);
        else
```

```
          puts ("Error in input\n");
}
```

The structure of this program is very much like that of strngio2.c. The function main() outputs a prompt for a line of text, calls gets() to do the input, and then calls puts() to do some output. The string output by puts() depends on the value returned by gets(). The major difference between strngio2.c and strwarn.c is the declaration of the variables.

Note 1: Two variables of type char * are declared. They are uninitialized. They may have garbage values left over from a previous use of that memory. The amount of memory allocated for each of these variables is only the amount necessary to hold the address of a character. No buffer space is allocated.

Note 2: The parameter to gets() is inputptr, one of the uninitialized pointers. The function gets() will attempt to store the input line at the memory location specified by inputptr. The error arises since inputptr does not point to a valid memory location. No buffer has been allocated.

Learning Activities

11. Execute strwarn.c on your system. Do you get a warning message when you compile it? Does it execute properly, or does it crash?

12. Modify strwarn.c so that it outputs the address of inputptr before the call to gets(). Find out as much as you can about that address. Is it part of the program address space? Is it part of the operating system address space?

An Example

The programs we have seen so far in this chapter process only one line of input. The program counter.c in Example 5-5, however, reads through multiple lines of input until end-of-file is signaled. The library function gets() is designed to return a NULL pointer when it sees end-of-file. The while loop is driven by comparing the value returned by gets() with NULL. When a NULL pointer is found, the while loop terminates. A while loop using gets() to read until end-of-file has the following form:

```
while ((inptr = gets(inarray)) != NULL)
              processing();
```

The program counter.c reads lines of text from standard input and counts the number of extra blanks in the text. The text needs one blank to separate words; if there are two blanks between words, one of the blanks is "extra." Only the extra blanks are counted. The program has another interesting feature. The function countem() has the job of counting the blanks and advancing a pointer into an array to the next nonblank character. Because the pointer to the current position of the array is declared local to main(), countem() needs to be passed an address of the pointer as a parameter to deal with the pass by value feature of C. Carefully inspect the declaration of the parameter, the function call, and the reference to the parameter inside the function to see the method.

 Example 5-5: counter.c

```
/*                counter.c
 *
 *    Synopsis  -  Reads standard input and keeps a count of the
 *                 number of extra blanks in the input.
 *
 *    Objective -  To illustrate a loop to read through many
 *                 lines of input and a method of having a function
 *                 change a pointer parameter.
 */

#include <stdio.h>

void main()
{
        char inarray[512], *inptr;                      /* Note 1 */
        int  count, white_count = 0;
        int countem (char **p);                         /* Note 4 */

        printf("Enter some text. Signal end of file when done.\n");
        printf("> ");
        while ((inptr = gets(inarray)) != NULL) {       /* Note 2 */
                while (*inptr != '\0') {
                        if (*inptr == ' ') {
                                count = countem (&inptr); /* Note 3 */
                                if (count >= 2)
                                        white_count += count - 1;
                        }
                        else
                           inptr++;
                }
                printf("> ");
        }
        printf("There were %d unnecessary spaces.\n", white_count);
}

/********************************   countem()   *********/
```

```
/*          countem() returns the number of blanks it finds and
 *          advances the pointer to the first nonblank character
 */

int countem (char **ptr)                                /* Note 4 */
{
        int counter = 0;

        while ( **ptr == ' ') {                         /* Note 5 */
                counter++;
                (*ptr)++;                               /* Note 6 */
        }
        return (counter);
}
```

The program consists of the functions main() and countem(). The code in main() consists of nested `while` loops. The outer `while` loop handles one line of input. The inner `while` loop looks at the input one character at a time and counts any blanks. The function countem() is called only when a blank character is found in the input array. It counts the number of blanks at that location and advances the pointer to the next nonblank character in the array.

Note 1: The array `inarray` will hold the input. The pointer `inptr` will serve as a pointer to the current position in the array.

Note 2: Input is done with the library function gets(). When it reads a line of input, it will return a pointer to the first character of `inarray`. That return value serves to initialize the value of `inptr`. If `inptr` is NULL, gets() encountered either an error or the end of the input. The `while` loop will terminate. If `inptr` is not NULL, the `while` loop is entered with `inptr` pointing to the first character of `inarray`.

Note 3: The actual parameter to countem() is the address of `inptr`. Because countem() needs to advance (change) `inptr`, the address of `inptr` must be passed as the parameter.

Note 4: The formal parameter `ptr` has type `char **` or the address of the address of a `char`. The function countem() will look at successive characters in the buffer until it finds a nonblank. It needs to advance the pointer into the buffer to the part that has not been processed. Therefore, it needs to change a pointer variable in main(). For this change to be effective after the function countem() terminates, the address of the pointer must be passed as the parameter.*

Note 5: The character in the array is accessed by dereferencing the parameter `ptr` twice. The first dereference accesses the value of `inptr` in main(). The second dereference accesses the contents of the address in `inptr`.

---

* This is a simplistic introduction to the important concept of a `char **` variable. The concept will be discussed in more detail in Chapter 9.

Note 6: The pointer in main() is accessed by dereferencing `ptr`. Because `ptr` contains the address of the pointer variable, `*ptr` is the value of the pointer.

Learning Activities

13. a. Compile and execute counter.c to see that it works. Test it with the following input:

H	O	W				N	O	W	'\n'				
B	R	O	W	N			C	O	W	'\n'			

There are five blanks in the input. Two are needed to separate the words. Therefore, this program should classify the other three as extra blanks. Does it?

   b. Test it with input of your choosing. Does it work for blanks at the beginning of an input line? At the end? A line consisting of nothing but blanks?

14. Look at the line with the statement `(*ptr)++;` Are the parentheses necessary? What is referenced if the parentheses are omitted?

15. The declaration of countem() starts with the line

```
int countem(char **ptr)
```

What does the `int` do? Is it necessary? Why or why not?

5.5   The Common String Library Functions

Strings are commonly used in C programs. Because of this, many utilities have been written that have been included in the standard C library. In the last section we investigated gets() and puts(), the standard C library functions designed to do string input and output from the terminal. More string input and output functions will be discussed in Chapter 10.

Utilities for other string manipulations are included in the library also. In this section we will discuss some of the more commonly used string-handling functions.

Library functions are available to find the length of the string, make a copy of a string, compare two strings, and concatenate one string to the end of another.

strlen()

The library function for calculating the length of a string is strlen(). It takes an address of a string as a parameter and returns an integer type.* The parameter to strlen() should point to the first character of the null-terminated string for which the length is to be calculated. Typical calls to strlen() would be

```
length = strlen("How now brown cow");
```

or

```
length = strlen (stringptr);
```

In both examples `length` would have been declared with the appropriate integer type. In the second example, `stringptr` would point to the string whose length is to be calculated. The quantity returned by strlen() is the number of characters in the string before the first null character; it does not count the terminating null character in determinating the length. For example, the value returned by strlen("How now brown cow") is 17.

strcpy()

The strcpy() library function makes a copy of a string. It takes two parameters of type `char *`. The first parameter must be the address of the buffer where the copy will be located. The space must be allocated in the program. The second parameter is the original string to be copied. It must be terminated with a null character. Typical calls to strcpy() would be

```
strcpy (copy, original);
```

or

```
strcpy (copy, "original string");
```

In both cases, the character buffer referred to by `copy` must have been allocated by the program. The function strcpy() does no memory allocation. The value returned by strcpy() is its first parameter, a pointer to the buffer where the copy was placed.

strcat()

The function strcat() does string concatenation, appending one string to the end of the other. It expects two parameters of type `char *`. Both must refer to null-terminated strings. In addition, there must be adequate unused space in the buffer pointed to by the first parameter to hold the string being appended there. If a `char *` variable named `result` points to the string `"one two button my shoe"` at the begining of a large buffer, the call

```
strcat (result, "three four");
```

would yield the null-terminated string, `"one two button my shoethree four"` in the location pointed to by `result`. (The lack of a blank character created `"shoethree."`) If adequate space was not available for the additional characters

---

* ANSI C has specified that the type returned by strlen() coincide with the type returned by the operator sizeof(). This type is `size_t`, which is defined in the standard header file <stddef.h>. In compilers that do not support the ANSI standard, the type returned by strlen() is usually `unsigned int`.

in the buffer `result`, strcat() would write over whatever was next in memory. The value returned to strcat() is its first parameter.

strcmp()

The standard library function strcmp() compares two strings by comparing the position of their characters in the underlying character set. It takes two parameters of type `char *`. Both must be null-terminated strings. The return value from strcmp() is of type `int` and has the following meanings: (1) If the two strings are identical, the return value is zero (0). (2) If the first string is lexicographically less than the second (the first differing character comes earlier in the underlying character set), the value returned is negative. (3) If the first string is lexicographically greater than the second, the value returned is positive. For example,

        strcmp ("now is the time", "She sells sea shells");

returns a positive value with the ASCII character set because `'S'` appears in the character set before `'n'`. The value returned by

        strcmp ("Bingo", "Parcheesi");

would be negative. The call can also be made with initialized `char *` variables or arrays of characters containing null-terminated strings. For example, if `phrase` is an initialized string and `attempt_to_match` is an array of type `char` that was initialized by input from the terminal, the call

        strcmp (phrase, attempt_to_match);

would return 0 if the strings were identical and some nonzero value if they differed.

The functions strlen(), strcat(), strcmp(), and strcpy() are only a few of the string-handling functions in the string library. The Programmer's Handbook gives an abstract of the functions commonly included with a C compiler.

The program in Example 5-6 illustrates some of the manipulations possible with these functions.

 Example 5-6: strnglib.c

```
/*              strnglib.c
 *
 *   Synopsis  -  Outputs information about two strings, including
 *                the length, and their lexical comparison. Then
 *                concatenates them into a character buffer and
 *                outputs the result.
 *
 *   Objective -  To illustrate basic use of the string library
 *                functions, strlen(), strcat(), strcpy(), and
 *                strcmp().
 */

#include <stdio.h>
```

```
#include <string.h>                                      /* Note 1 */

void main()
{
        char workstring[512];                            /* Note 2 */
        char *string1 = "I know an old lady";
        char *string2 = "who swallowed a fly";

        puts (string1);
        puts (string2);
        if (strcmp (string1, string2) > 0)               /* Note 3 */
                printf ("string1 is > string2.\n");
        else
                printf ("string1 is <= string2.\n");

                                                         /* Note 4 */
        printf ("The length of string1 is %d.\n", strlen(string1) );
        printf ("The length of string2 is %d.\n", strlen(string2) );

        strcpy (workstring, string1);                    /* Note 5 */
        if (!strcmp(string1, workstring))                /* Note 6 */
                printf("Copy completed successfully!\n");
        else
                printf ("Error found in copy.\n");

        strcat (workstring, " ");                        /* Note 7 */
        strcat(workstring, string2);
        printf ("The work string now contains \"%s\"\n", workstring);
        printf ("The length of the work string is now %d.\n",
                        strlen(workstring) );
}
```

There is one function named main() with three variables defined, two initialized char * variables, and an array of type char. Most of the statements perform output.

Note 1: The standard header file string.h has been included. This file contains the declarations of the functions in the string library. For example, the functions strcpy() and strcat() return a char * value instead of the default int type and therefore must be declared as such. The declarations are in string.h. If the file had not been included, the declarations of these functions must be.

Note 2: Buffer space is allocated for some string manipulation.

Note 3: The function strcmp() will compare the two strings, string1 and string2. The comparison is made character by character until either the end of a string is reached or a character in one of the strings appears earlier in the ASCII collating sequence than the corresponding character in the other string. The value returned by strcmp() is tested. If it is positive, the string with ">" is output. Otherwise the string with "<=" is output.

Note 4: In each of the next two calls to printf(), the second parameter is the value returned by a call to strlen(). That value will be output in decimal.

Note 5: This call to strcpy() copies the string pointed to by `string1` into the buffer. All of the characters, including the terminating `'\0'`, will be copied into `work-string`. From this point on, `workstring` can be treated as a string. In this call to strcpy(), the return value is ignored.

Note 6: The value returned by strcmp() is used to determine if `workstring` and `string1` point to identical strings. Note that strcmp() returns 0 if the two strings are identical; therefore, the negation of the value will test true when the strings are the same.

Note 7: The next two calls to strcat() illustrate the concatenation of strings to the string in `workstring`. In the first call, a string with a single blank, `" "`, is concatenated to the end of `workstring` to separate the words. It is important that sufficient space was allocated in `workstring` for these operations because strcat() does not check for space. The value returned by strcat() is ignored in both cases.

Learning Activities

16. a. Go over the description of the string library functions used in strnglib.c to make sure that you know what each does.

    b. Predict the output of strnglib.c and then execute it to verify your prediction.

17. a. Rewrite the program strnglib.c so that it will compare `string1` and `string2` and output "<", "=", or ">" (depending on which is correct).

    b. Rewrite the program so that a user can enter `string1` and `string2`. Test it to make sure everything works as it should.

A Word of Warning

The requirement that memory be allocated in the first parameters to both strcat() and strcpy() is an important one. The library functions assume that the memory exists, and the programmer really wants the function to do the concatenation or the copy. Example 5-7 shows what can happen when the memory needed has not been allocated.

Example 5-7: strngerr.c

```
/*              strngerr.c
 *
 *  Synopsis  -  Initializes, outputs the location of two strings.
 *               Outputs them again after concatenating the second
 *               string to the end of the first one.
 *
 *  Objective -  To demonstrate a common error in memory
 *               allocation when using the string library functions.
 */

#include <stdio.h>

void main()
{
        char *string1 = "I know an old lady who swallowed a ";
        char *string2 =
           "spider that wiggled and jiggled and tickled inside her";
        char *strcat();

        puts(string1);
        puts(string2);
                                                    /* Note 1 */
        printf ("\nstring1 begins at %x, and ends at %x.\n", string1,
                string1 + strlen(string1) );
        printf ("string2 begins at %x, and ends at %x.\n\n", string2,
                string2 + strlen(string2) );
                                                    /* Note 2 */
        strcat (string1, " horse.  She's dead of course.");
        puts(string1);
        puts(string2);
}
```

There is a single function main(). Two char * variables are defined and initialized. The executable code consists of output statements together with a single call to strcat().

Note 1: The address of the beginning and the end of both string1 and string2 are output with the next two printf() calls. In most systems, these strings will be located close to one another.

Note 2: The following call to strcat() will concatenate the second parameter onto the end of string1. No extra memory has been allocated for this concatenation. Therefore, strcat() will be writing over whatever is next to it in memory.

Learning Activities

18. Execute strngerr.c. Did the program crash? If not, did the content of string2 change during program execution?

19. If this program did not crash on your system, execute strngerr.c again and record the addresses of the beginning and end of string1 and string2 that are output by the first two calls to printf().

    a. Four addresses were output. What are the characters stored in those addresses? Do string1 and string2 originally point to adjacent locations? How many bytes lie between them?

    b. Diagram the part of memory where the strings are kept so that you can associate an address for each character in both string1 and string2.

    c. Hand execute the call to strcat() by replacing the characters in the proper place in your memory diagram.

    d. Does your diagram coincide with the strings that are output by the program?

    e. If string2 was not changed during execution of strngerr.c, would it be possible to change it by concatenating a longer string to string1? If it appears to be possible, try it.

5.6   Examples with strlen() and strchr()

The program chlincnt.c in Example 5-8 reads standard input and counts the number of characters and lines in its input. It is similar to utilities provided by many operating systems. The function gets() is used to input a line at a time and strlen() counts the number of characters in the line except for the characters at the end of the line.

Example 5-8: chlincnt.c

```
/*              chlincnt.c
 *
 *   Synopsis  -  Counts the number of characters and lines
 *                in standard input.
 *
 *   Objective -  Illustrates a use for strlen() in conjunction
 *                with gets().
 */
```

```
#include <stdio.h>
#include <string.h>

void main()
{
        char inarray[512];                              /* Note 1 */
        char *inptr;
        int line_count = 0,                             /* Note 2 */
            char_count = 0;

        printf ("Enter your text now\n");
        printf(">  ");
        while ((inptr = gets(inarray)) != NULL) {       /* Note 3 */
                line_count++;                           /* Note 4 */
                char_count += strlen(inptr) + 1;        /* Note 5 */
                printf(">  ");
        }
        printf ("%d lines, %d characters\n", line_count, char_count);

}
```

The program is simple in structure. The single function main() consists of a while loop using gets() to read through all of the terminal input.

Note 1: The array inarray will hold each line of input.

Note 2: The variables line_count and char_count will keep a running total of the number of lines and characters, respectively. They are both initialized to zero.

Note 3: The while loop is designed to read through multiple lines of input. Each time, the value returned by gets() is tested. When gets() sees the end of the input file, it returns a NULL pointer and the loop terminates.

Note 4: Since gets() attempts to read a line of input each time it is called, line_count is incremented each time the read is successful and gets() doesn't return a NULL pointer.

Note 5: The line of input is placed in inarray and the newline is replaced with a null character so that inarray contains a string. A call to strlen() returns the number of non-null characters in the string. Because the newline was input and discarded by gets(), the calculation of the character count must be adjusted by adding 1 for the newline. Note: If your system translates a carriage return pressed on the keyboard to a carriage return/line feed combination for a newline, you may need to add 2 instead of 1 to compensate.

Learning Activities

20. a. Test chlincnt.c with some simple input for which you know the correct answer. For example, test it with an immediate signal of end-of-file; test it with one line of input and four characters before the return; test it with an immediate carriage return for one line. Test it by typing some meaningless control characters. Does it count the control characters? Test it by pressing the tab key during your input. How many characters are counted for the tab key?

  b. Find out if your system has a utility that counts characters and lines in its input. If it does and will read from the terminal, compare the output from this program with the output from that utility. Is it the same? Do you need to adjust the character count at the end of a line?

  c. If your system will allow input redirection, redirect the input to come from a file. Does the program still behave correctly?

  d. Does chlincnt.c correctly count the end-of-line character(s)? If not, correct it.

21. Is `inptr` necessary in chlincnt.c? If not, modify the program to eliminate this variable.

22. Is this program a filter? Why or why not?

Many functions besides the ones just discussed have been written for the string library. The ones that are included with an ANSI C compiler are described in the Programmer's Handbook.

As an example of another string library function, the function strchr() is included with any ANSI C compiler. It takes two parameters. The first is of type `char *` and must point to a null-terminated string. The second parameter is of type `char`. The function strchr() searches the first parameter string for an occurrence of the character in the second parameter and returns a pointer to the first occurrence of that character in that string.

Example 5-9 uses strchr() to break an array of characters into "words." For this program, a word is considered to be a sequence of nonblank characters delimited with blanks. The array of characters is initialized by reading a line of text from standard input. Each word is output to standard output on a separate line.

Example 5-9: strchrex.c

```
/*              strchrex.c
 *
 *   Synopsis   -   Accepts a line of text as input from standard
```

```
*                      input and outputs each of the space-delimited
*                      words in the input on a separate line on
*                      standard output.
*
*    Objective  -   To illustrate the string library function
*                      strchr().
*/

#include <stdio.h>
#include <string.h>

void main()
{
        char instring[512];
        char *currentpos, *lastpos;                      /* Note 1 */

        printf("Enter a line of text.\n> ");
        gets(instring);                                  /* Note 2 */
        lastpos = instring;
                                                         /* Note 3 */
        while ( (currentpos = strchr(lastpos, ' ')) != NULL) {
                *currentpos++ = '\0';                    /* Note 4 */
                puts(lastpos);
                lastpos = currentpos;                    /* Note 5 */
        }
        puts(lastpos);
}
```

Again, the program consists just of the single function named main(). One array of type char and two char * variables are defined. After the input is done, a while loop is used to process the array that holds the input line. Each iteration of the while loop outputs one "word."

Note 1: The pointer lastpos will always point to the beginning of the word to be output; currentpos will point to the end of the word.

Note 2: The buffer instring is initialized by a call to gets().

Note 3: The call to strchr() begins its search for a blank character at the memory location pointed to by lastpos. It returns a pointer to the first blank character. If no blank is found before the terminating null character, strchr() returns a NULL pointer. In this program, the return of a NULL pointer by strchr() signifies that the whole input line has been processed.

Note 4: The blank character found by strchr() is replaced by '\0'. This creates a null-terminated string that consists of a single word. The pointer lastpos points to the beginning of the word. Note that currentpos is incremented after the assignment so that theoretically it points to the beginning of the next word.

Note 5: In preparation for another iteration of the `while` loop, `lastpos` is updated to point to the beginning of the next word.

Learning Activities

23. Test strchrex.c with several different input lines to see that it works as you expect it to.

24. Test strchrex.c with a line that does not contain any blank characters. Is the behavior what you would expect?

25. Test strchrex.c with input that contains two or more adjacent blanks. Describe what happens. Is this the behavior that a user would expect? If necessary, modify the program so that there are no blank lines in the output.

These last two sections are not a comprehensive treatment of the string library functions. They are meant to provide examples. A list of the string-manipulating functions in the standard C library appears in the Programmer's Handbook. That and the documentation with your compiler are strongly recommended as reading material.

5.7   Two Versions of strcat()

The string-handling functions in the standard C library are nothing more than ordinary C functions that have been written as tools to perform specific tasks. These functions are compiled and the object code is put into a library where it can be linked with a C program. The linker will search specified libraries to find the necessary code.

We will explore how one of the string-handling functions might have been written. You will be asked to write your own version of other string-handling functions in the exercises.

Two versions of the strcat() library function are presented in Examples 5-10 and 5-11. One is written with array notation and the other with the more efficient pointer notation.

Example 5-10: strcat1.c

```
/*                    strcat1.c
 *
```

```
 *      Synopsis  -   Concatenates its second argument onto its
 *                    first argument.  It uses array notation.
 *
 *      Objective -   To illustrate one version of the string library
 *                    function strcat().
 */
char *strcat(char oldpart[], char newpart[])
{
        int oldindex = 0,
            newindex = 0;

        while (oldpart[oldindex++] != '\0')          /* Note 1 */
            ;

        oldindex--;                                  /* Note 2 */
        while ( (oldpart[oldindex++] = newpart[newindex++]) != '\0')
            ;
        return (oldpart);
}
```

This code is a single function, not a program. It will not run without a function main().

Note 1: This `while` loop with null statement body finds the end of the first string, `oldpart`. It compares each character with the null character and increments `oldindex` after the comparison.

Note 2: The index is decremented since it referenced one cell beyond the `'\0'`. The `while` loop assigns successive characters to the end of `oldpart` and compares each character to `'\0'`. The first character of `newpart` overwrites the `'\0'`. The terminating `'\0'` from `newpart` is copied to `oldpart` to terminate the concatenated string.

The next version of strcat() does exactly the same thing using the pointer syntax to access the characters in the strings.

Example 5-11: strcat2.c

```
/*                    strcat2.c
 *
 *      Synopsis  -   Concatenates its second argument onto its
 *                    first argument.  It uses pointer notation.
 *
 *      Objective -   To illustrate one version of the string library
 *                    function strcat().
 */
```

```
char *strcat(char *oldpart, char *newpart)
{
        char *current = oldpart;

        while (*current++ != '\0')                      /* Note 1 */
        ;

        current--;                                       /* Note 2 */
        while (*current++ = *newpart++)
        ;
        return (oldpart);
}
```

Again, this file would need to be linked with a function main() that called it in order to be executed.

Note 1: The `while` loop looks for the end of the first string. Each character is compared to `'\0'`.

Note 2: The second `while` loop copies the second string to the end of the first string. The sequence of events is as follows. The character pointed to by `newpart` is copied to the space pointed to by `current`. The copied character is compared to `'\0'`, and then both `current` and `newpart` are incremented. The loop terminates when the `'\0'` is copied.

Learning Activities

26. Include the code for strcat() from strcat1.c in the program strnglib.c. Compile and execute it with each version to make sure that the behavior is the same.

27. Do the same for the code for strcat() from strcat2.c.

Language Elements Introduced in This Chapter: A Review

** Conversion Specifications **

%s   a string is to be output with printf()
%s   a whitespace-delimited string is to be input
      with scanf()

** Library Functions **

gets()	inputs a line of text from standard input
puts()	outputs a string to standard output
strlen()	calculates the length of a string
strcpy()	makes a copy of a string into an array of char
strcat()	concatenates one string to the end of another
strcmp()	compares two strings lexicographically
strchr()	searches for a character in a string

** Types **

char **	an address of an address of a char

Things to Remember

1. A string in C is a sequence of characters terminated by a null character, ' \0' .
2. The compiler handles a string as an address of the first character.
3. A string may be used as an initializer for either an array of char or a pointer to char.
4. gets() will return the address of the array where the input is stored or a NULL pointer in case of error or end-of-file.
5. Memory must be allocated in the program for gets() to use for the input.
6. A while loop to process many lines of terminal input with gets() would be written as

```
while ((inptr = gets(inarray)) != NULL)
                processing();
```

7. If a function is to change the value of a pointer in its calling environment, a pointer to the pointer should be passed in as a parameter. If the pointer is a pointer to char, the parameter type should be declared as char **.
8. Memory must be allocated for the use of strcat() and strcpy().
9. Individual characters within a string can be accessed with either array-indexing syntax or pointer arithmetic syntax. The pointer syntax is more efficient.
10. The standard header file contains declarations of the functions in the string library.

5.8 Exercises and Programming Problems

1. a. Write a program that reads standard input and counts all "words" in its input. For this program, a word will be delimited by blank spaces, tab characters, or newlines. Test your program thoroughly.

b. Package the word-counting part of your program as a function and write a new program that counts words (defined as in part a), characters, and lines in its input. You may want to borrow some of the code from chlincnt.c.

2. Write a program that will read standard input and echo each line to standard output with a line number and a tab preceding it. When you run this program and enter lines from the terminal, lines of input will be interspersed with lines of output, but if your system has output redirection and you redirect output to a file, the file will look like a line-numbered copy of the input. An example of a run with terminal input and output is below.The user's input is in **boldface**.

```
Enter your text:
This is line 1
1       This is line 1
This is line 2
2       This is line 2
This is the last line of input
3       This is the last line of input
```

3. Write your own version of puts(). Do not use printf(). Test your program by including it in one of the programs in the text that uses puts(), recompiling and executing it. If a version of puts() appears in the source file, the library version will not be linked into the object code.

4. Write a program that will read standard input and, where possible, replace each sequence of blank spaces with one or more tab characters and then echo the modified input to standard output. You may assume that tab stops occur at columns 1, 9, 17, 25, and so on.

The output from this program should appear identical to the input even though the characters might not be the same. In the sample run below, the user's input is in **boldface**. Blank characters have been denoted with ␣, and tabs have been denoted with ⌷tab⌷.

```
12345678901234567890
12345678901234567890
Name␣␣␣␣Numb.␣␣␣␣␣Id
Name⌷ tab ⌷Numb.⌷ tab ⌷␣␣Id
Bolt␣␣␣␣23␣␣␣␣␣␣␣␣al
Bolt⌷ tab ⌷23⌷ tab ⌷␣␣al
```

The first line was input in the example to establish the column count. It was echoed unchanged by the program. The second and third input lines had repeated spaces between the words. The program echoed these lines with some of the spaces replaced by tabs. On a terminal, the output should look identical to the input. (Hint: Before designing your program, decide how your program should handle backspace characters.)

This program would be used on a system that allowed input and output redirection. It would produce text that looked identical to the input text but contained fewer characters and therefore took up less memory or disk space.

Running the program at a terminal without redirection would alternate lines of input and output as shown.

5. Write a program that does the opposite of the program in exercise 4. Have it replace each tab in its input with an appropriate number of blank characters so that the output appears unchanged but in reality will contain no tab characters.

6. Write your own version of a function that meets the specifications for strchr() in the standard C library. Compile it with strchrex.c from Example 5-9 to test it. It should work the same as the original program.

7. a. Look up the specifications for the library function strstr() in the Programmer's Handbook. Predict the output of the following program.

```
/*              strtst.c
 *
 *    Synopsis  -  Calls strstr() twice to find substrings in
 *                 "how now brown cow".  One should be found, the
 *                 other is nonexistent.
 *
 *    Objective -  To provide a test program for personal version of
 *                 strstr().
 */

#include <stdio.h>
#include <string.h>

void main()
{
        char string[] = "How now brown cow";
        char *substring;

        substring = strstr(string, "own");
        if (substring == NULL)
                printf ("Not found.\n");
        else
                printf ("%s\n", substring);

        substring = strstr(string, "red");
        if (substring == NULL)
                printf ("Not found.\n");
        else
                printf ("%s\n", substring);
}
```

b. Write your own version of strstr(). Test your function with the program in part a.

8. a. Write a function in C that takes an array of `char` and a `char **` expression as parameters. The array of type `char` would contain a string that possibly starts with a sequence of decimal digits. Have the function convert the sequence of decimal digits it finds to type `int` and return the converted value. Have the function set the contents of its second parameter (a `char *` value) to point to the first character in the array that was not converted. For example, if the function was called convert() and the call to convert() was

```
intval = convert( array, &charptr);
```

where array contained the string

| 2 | 7 | 4 | | A | D | A | M | S | \0 |

then after the call, `intval` would contain the value 274, and `charptr` would point to the blank space in the string.

b. Test your function with the program below.

```
/*              testconv.c
 *
 *    Synopsis  -  Inputs lines with gets() and passes the string
 *                 to conv().  Outputs the value returned by conv()
 *                 and the remainder of the string.
 *
 *    Objective -  To provide a test program for the user-written
 *                 function to convert a string of digits to
 *                 type int.
 */

#include <stdio.h>
#include <string.h>

void main()
{
        int intval;
        char array[80], *remainder;
        int conv(char array[], char **rem);

        while (gets(array) != NULL) {
                intval = conv(array, &remainder);
                printf(" %d, %s\n", intval, remainder);
        }
}
```

9. a Write your own version of strcpy() using array notation.

   b. Write another version of strcpy using pointer notation.

10. a Test the program below with many different input strings. Try to figure out how the value returned by strcmp() is calculated.

```
/*                      strcmps.c
 *
 *    Synopsis   -  Outputs the values returned by library function
 *                  strcmp().
 *
 *    Objective  -  To investigate the return value from strcmp().
 */

#include <stdio.h>
#include <string.h>

void main()
{
        char string1[80];
        char string2[80];
        int result;

        printf("Enter the first string: ");
        gets(string1);
        printf("Enter the second string: ");
        gets(string2);

        if ((result = strcmp(string1, string2)) > 0)
                printf("string1 > string2\n");
        else if (result < 0)
                printf("string1 < string2\n");
        else
                printf("string1 = string2\n");

        printf("result is %d\n", result);
}
```

   b. Write your own version of strcmp() that returns the same value as the library version does. Test it with the program above.

Keeping Control

Chapter 6

6.1   Introduction

In Chapter 2, we discussed expressions and some of the C control statements. In this chapter, we present the remaining C control statements. These include the `do-while` loop and a multiway decision statement, the `switch` statement. Statements similar to these exist in many other languages.

C also contains statements that alter the flow of control. These give the language more flexibility and make a program more readable and easier to write. However, as with any statement that alters the established flow of control of a program in any language, these statements should be used with care so that the program remains structured.

The last topic of this chapter is recursion. When using recursion, a programmer must be aware of what is happening to the control of the program. Two examples are discussed in this chapter.

6.2 The `do-while` Statement

The `do-while` statement is the third loop in C. The `do-while` loop has the following syntax:

```
do
        statement;
while (expression);
```

The words `do` and `while` are the keywords. The expression can be any legal C expression, but it must appear in parentheses. The statement can be any legitimate statement in C. For example, it can be an assignment statement, any of the control statements, a function call, or a compound statement.

The execution of the `do-while` loop starts with the execution of the `state-ment`; the evaluation of the `expression` follows. If the `expression` is not 0, the `statement` is executed and the `expression` is evaluated again. This process is repeated until the `expression` evaluates to zero.

Note that the test for loop continuation appears after the `statement` in this loop construction. One consequence is that the statement in a `do-while` loop will always be executed at least once. In contrast, in a `while` loop the test for loop continuation is located before the `statement`, and the `statement` in a `while` loop may not be executed at all. Both loops are included in the C language to provide flexibility for the programmer.

The program do.c of Example 6-1 illustrates the use of the `do-while` loop. It also reminds us of the fact that parameters passed to C functions are passed by value.

Example 6-1: do.c

```
/*              do.c
 *
 *    Synopsis  -  A user is asked to enter an integer. The digits in
 *                 the number are output in reverse order and then in
 *                 the original order.
 *
 *    Objective -  Demonstrates the do-while statement and pass by
 *                 value for parameters.
 */

#include <stdio.h>
#define RADIX 10
```

```
void main()
{
        int number;
        void reverse(int number);

        printf ("Enter a decimal number: ");
        scanf ("%d", &number);

        printf("\nDigits reversed: ");
        reverse (number);
        printf ("Original number : %d\n", number);        /* Note 1 */
}

void reverse (int number)
{
        do {                                              /* Note 2 */
                printf ("%d", number % RADIX);
                number /= RADIX;
        }
        while (number != 0);                              /* Note 2 */

        printf ("\n");

}
```

The overview of this program reveals two functions, the mandatory function main() and a function named reverse(). A preprocessor constant RADIX is defined as 10. The function main() consists of some declarations, a call to printf() that outputs a prompt, and a scanf() call that inputs an integer. Another call to printf() precedes a call to the function reverse() and a final printf() call. The function reverse() consists of a do-while statement followed by a call to printf().

Note 1: This printf() call illustrates the fact that parameters in C are passed by value. The function actually works on a copy of the actual parameter and does not touch the variable in main(). The parameter number was changed in the function reverse(), but when accessed again in main(), number still has its original value.

Note 2: In this example of the do-while loop, the expression to be evaluated is the relational expression

$$(number != 0)$$

It must be in parentheses. The statement for this do-while loop is the compound statement consisting of a printf() call followed by a compound assignment statement. It is delimited by braces.

The do-while loop is always executed at least once. The expression is evaluated at the bottom of the loop. A nonzero (true) value causes the loop to be repeated while a zero (false) value causes the loop to terminate.

Learning Activities

1. Predict the output of the function reverse() for each of the following inputs. Write each output in boxes like those below. Write one character per box.

   a. 4235

   b. 19843

   c. 2200000000

   d. –234

2. a Run do.c and test it with the four inputs in activity 1.

   b. Did the program handle the minus sign in the input as you predicted? What would be a reasonable way for this program to handle negative integers as input? Modify the program so that it handles negative input in the way you think is most appropriate.

   c. Was the output for the input 2200000000 what you predicted? If it wasn't, try to explain what happened.

6.3 The `switch` Statement

The `switch` statement provides C programmers with a multiway decision statement. Depending on the results of a test on an expression, any number of alternative statements could be executed.

The usual syntax of the switch statement is illustrated below:

```
switch (expression1)   {
    case c1:
        statement;
    case c2:
        statement;
    .
    .
    .
    default:
        statement;
}
```

The keywords in the above construct are the words `switch`, `case`, and `default`. The expression `expression1`, which follows the keyword `switch`, is a control expression. Any legal C expression may be used here. The syntax demands that it be in parentheses.

The `switch` statement must be followed by a statement. In normal use, as shown above, the statement is a compound statement composed of two types of statements. The first type is of the form

```
case const_expr: statement;
```

Statements of this form are labeled statements with a `case` label. The colon is a mandatory part of the syntax. The `const_expr` in each `case` labeled statement must be a constant expression and must have one of the integer types. There can be multiple `case` labeled statements, but each `const_expr` must have a distinct value.

The second type of statement that may appear in the compound statement is another type of labeled statement. It carries a `default` label and has the form

```
default: statement;
```

The inclusion of the `default` labeled statement in a compound statement associated with a `switch` statement is optional. When included, it is usually the last statement in the compound statement.

When a `switch` statement is executed, the control expression, `expression1`, is evaluated and tested to see if the value matches one of the values `c1`, `c2`, and so on. When a match is found, control is passed to the `case` labeled statement with the matching value and *all* statements that appear from that point to the end of the `switch` statement are executed. This includes the statements associated with all of the following `case` labels as well as the statements associated with the `default`.[*] If a `default` labeled statement is included, it is executed when no match between the control expression and the constant expressions `c1`, `c2`, and so on is found. If no `default` labeled statement is present and no match is found, no action is taken.

The program switch.c in Example 6-2 illustrates the syntax and execution flow of the `switch` statement.

Example 6-2: switch.c

```
/*                switch.c
 *
 *   Synopsis   -  Outputs a triangle of numbers.
 *
 *   Objective  -  To illustrate the syntax and flow of control
 *                 of the switch statement.
 */
```

---

[*] In Section 6-4 we will see how to defeat this default behavior. This involves using the `switch` statement in conjunction with the `break` statement. The resulting construct is more complete and useful.

```
#include <stdio.h>

void main()
{
        int iochar;

        printf ("Enter a digit: ");
        iochar = getchar();
        switch (iochar) {                                       /* Note 1 */
                case '9':  printf ("9 9 9 9 9 9 9 9 9\n");
                case '8':  printf (" 8 8 8 8 8 8 8 8\n");       /* Note 2 */
                case '7':  printf ("  7 7 7 7 7 7 7\n");
                case '6':  printf ("   6 6 6 6 6 6\n");
                case '5':  printf ("    5 5 5 5 5\n");
                case '4':  printf ("     4 4 4 4\n");
                case '3':  printf ("      3 3 3\n");
                case '2':  printf ("       2 2\n");
                case '1':  printf ("        1\n");
                default :  printf ("----------------\n"); /* Note 3 */
        }
}
```

The program consists of the single function main(). It contains a call to printf(),
a call to getchar() to do input, and a `switch` statement. The `switch` statement
has printf() calls associated with all the cases.

Note 1: In this example, the program "switches" on the value of `iochar`. Its value is
compared to the constant expressions listed in the `case` labeled statements below.
The result of this comparison determines which statements are to be executed next.

Note 2: Notice that the values in the `case` labels are all constants. If the value of `iochar`
matches one of these values, execution starts with the corresponding statement.
The statements preceding the one with the matching value are not executed. The
statements after the one with the matching value are executed.

Note 3: If no match is found with the values after the `case` labels, the statement associated
with the `default` label is the only one executed.

Learning Activities

3. Run the program switch1.c with each of the following inputs: 9, 2, 4, 3, 0, 10, a. Are the results what you expected each time? If not, read the material again and reconcile the execution results with the discussion of the behavior of the switch statement.

4. *C by Discovery*   What happens when a variable is used as one of the values associated with a case label? Modify the program by declaring a variable of type char, initializing the variable to '2', and replacing the value '2' in the appropriate case labeled statement with your new variable. Then try to compile and execute the program again to test this concept.

6.4   Altering the Flow of Control

In this section we discuss the continue and break statements. Both statements are used in conjunction with the while loop, the for loop, and the do-while loop. They both alter the flow of control set up by those loops. The break statement is also used in conjunction with the switch statement.

The continue Statement

A continue statement is used inside a loop. When it is encountered during program execution, it causes control to pass to the point after the last statement in the loop body instead of executing the next statement as it would normally. The syntax of the continue statement is very simple; it consists of the keyword continue followed by a semicolon, as in

```
continue;
```

The action of the continue statement within a while loop can be diagrammed as follows:

```
while (expr) {
          .
          .
      continue;
          .
          .
}
```

In the above diagram, any statements after the continue statement would never be executed. After the continue statement executes, expr in the while loop would be evaluated and execution would continue from that point. The use of the continue statement is usually somewhat different than illustrated. The continue would be more likely to be a part of a conditional statement than to stand alone as shown.

With a do-while loop, execution would be as shown below:

```
do {
    . . .
    continue;
    . . .
}
while (expr);
```

After execution of the continue statement, expr would be evaluated and execution would continue from that point. The statements after the continue statement and before the evaluation of expr would be skipped. Again, the continue statement would be more likely to appear inside a conditional statement so that it would only be executed when certain conditions are met.

When a continue statement appears within a for loop, execution again passes to the point after the last statement in the body of the for loop.

```
for (init; test; bol) {
    . . .
    continue;
    . . .
}
```

The expression bol would be evaluated next, and execution would proceed from that point.

The program in Example 6-3 illustrates the use of the continue statement. The program will read a line of input from the keyboard and output it to the terminal. Every tab character in the input will be replaced by a backslash and a lowercase t. For example, the input

```
NAME<Tab>AGE
```

would be echoed as

```
NAME\tAGE.
```

Code similar to this could be used in writing an editor program where it might be desirable to display the difference between a tab and a sequence of spaces. The code that does the work has been packaged as a function in order to be used as a tool in several different programs.

Example 6-3: continue.c

```
/*              continue.c
 *
 *   Synopsis  -  Echoes its input to its output with each tab
 *                character replaced with '\t'.
 *
 *   Objective -  To illustrate the continue statement.
 */
```

```
#include <stdio.h>
void main()
{
        void showtabsinline();
        printf ("Enter a line with tab characters in it.\n\n");
        showtabsinline();
}
void showtabsinline()
{
        int iochar;

        while ( (iochar = getchar()) != '\n') {
            if (iochar == '\t') {
                    putchar ('\\');
                    putchar ('t');
                    continue;                           /* Note 1 */
            }
            putchar (iochar);                           /* Note 2 */
        }
}
```

This program consists of two functions. The function main() is very simple. It consists of a printf() call that asks for input and a call to the function showtabsinline(). It serves only to test the secondary function. When software tools are being developed, they can be tested with a driver program such as main(). The function can be tested with many different inputs, and then can be used with a high degree of confidence. The function showtabsinline() uses a `while` loop to read until a newline is read. Each character is processed separately.

Note 1: This `continue` statement is used in conjunction with a `while` loop. It appears inside an `if` statement and is only executed when the input character is a tab. In this case, the backslash (\) and the `'t'` are output before the `continue` statement causes execution to return to the top of the `while` loop, where another character is read.

Note 2: This putchar() statement is skipped whenever a tab character is read in the input, but is executed every time a character other than a tab is read. All other characters in the input will be echoed to the output. Only the tab characters will be replaced in the output.

Learning Activities

5. Execute continue.c with several different inputs to see how it works.
6. Modify continue.c so that it skips all characters in the input except tab characters, and outputs just the string "\t" for each tab character.

The break Statement

The break statement also alters the flow of control that has been set up by a for loop, a while loop, or a do-while loop. The break statement can be used in conjunction with the switch statement.

The syntax of the break statement is very simple. It consists of the keyword break followed by a semicolon, as in

```
break;
```

When a break statement is encountered during execution of a while, for, or do-while loop, it causes execution of the loop to terminate and control to pass to the point immediately after the loop. This execution flow is diagrammed below with each of the loops.

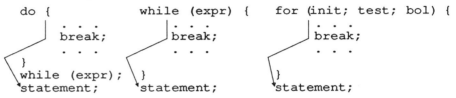

Any statements following the break in the above diagrams would never be executed. The expressions for continuing each loop would not be evaluated nor would the expression bol in the for loop. Again, this diagram is solely to indicate the flow of execution. Actual use would differ and is illustrated in the example below.

In the case of nested loops, a break statement would only break out of the closest loop. It does not break out of the whole nested formation.

The program break.c in Example 6-4 will read a line of input from the keyboard and echo that line to the terminal until the character '#' is read in the input. The input after the '#' is ignored. For example, the character '#' might signal the beginning of a comment or it might signal the beginning of a different type of information that would be handled by a different part of the program. This program illustrates the use of the break statement to terminate a loop early.

  Example 6-4: break.c

```
/*                  break.c
 *
 *   Synopsis   -   Outputs the part of a line before the
 *                  SENTINEL character.
 *
 *   Objective  -   To illustrate the break statement.
 */
```

```
#include <stdio.h>
#define EOLN '\n'
#define SENTINEL  '#'

void main()
{
        void readtosentinel();

        printf ("The sentinel character is %c.\n", SENTINEL);
        printf ("Enter a line with a sentinel character in it.\n\n");

        readtosentinel();

        printf ("\n\nThat was the first part of the line.\n");
}

void readtosentinel()
{
        int iochar;

        while ( (iochar = getchar()) != EOLN ) {
                if (iochar == SENTINEL) {
                        break;                          /* Note 1 */
                }
                putchar (iochar);
        }
}
```

This program has two functions. The function main() is a driver. Its purpose is to ask for input and to call the function readtosentinel(). The function readtosentinel() reads through a line of input and outputs the characters it read until the SENTINEL character is encountered. A function similar to this one might be used to position the pointer in the input stream so that another function could process the information that appears after the SENTINEL character.

Note 1:   The break statement is used in conjunction with a while loop. It appears inside an if statement and will only be executed when a SENTINEL appears in the input stream. When this happens, the while loop will terminate and control will be passed to the end of the function and back to main().

Learning Activities

7. Test the program break.c with several different inputs.
   a. How does it react when no SENTINEL character appears in the input? Is this acceptable behavior?
   b. How does it react when two SENTINEL characters appear in the input stream? Is this what a user might expect? How (or where) should a user be notified of this behavior?
8. Modify break.c so that it will just read (and not output) the data on a line of input until SENTINEL is encountered. After SENTINEL is read, the program should continue to read the input line and echo the input to the terminal.

The **break** Statement in Conjunction with the **switch** Statement

The program switch.c in Section 6.3 illustrates that when a switch statement is executed and a match is found between the control expressions and the constant expressions, all of the following statements are executed.

In some cases, we want only some statements to be executed when a match is found. For example, in the following code, suppose that if the runtime value of expr matches the value of expr2, statement2 is to be executed, but not statement3 or any of the following statements.

```
switch (expr) {
    case expr1: statement1;
    case expr2:
        statement2;
        break;
    case expr3: statement3;
        .
        .
        .
    default: statement_default;
}
next_statement;
```

The break statement is used to accomplish this. When a break statement is encountered in a switch statement body, it transfers control to the statement immediately following the switch statement. In this case next_statement would be executed after the break. As another example with the above illustration, if expr matches expr1, then statement1, statement2, and next_statement will be executed in that order.

The program in Example 6-5 shows a typical use of the break and switch statements together. The program outputs a menu and inputs the menu choice. The program then echoes the menu choice. This program could be extended to process the response in an appropriate way by writing a function to process each of the menu choices.

Example 6-5: switch2.c

```c
/*                   switch2.c
 *
 *    Synopsis  -  Outputs a menu and reads the response from
 *                 the user.
 *
 *    Objective -  Illustrates the switch and break statements
 *                 together.
 */

#include <stdio.h>

void main()
{
        char iochar = 0;
        void processresponse(char iochar);
        int menu();

        while ( (iochar = menu()) != '0') {               /* Note 1 */
                processresponse(iochar);
        }
}

/********************************** menu()    ***************/
/*     menu()  -  Outputs the menu choices and inputs the user's
 *     response.  The first character of the response is returned.
 */

menu()
{
        char response[40];

        printf  ("The following games are available:\n");
        printf  ("----------------------------------\n\n");
        printf  ("1. Guessit\n");
        printf  ("2. Nim\n");
        printf  ("----------\n");
        printf  ("Choose a game or type 0 to exit.\nYour choice? ");

        if (gets(response) == NULL)
                return('0');
```

```
        else
                return (response[0]);
}

/******************************* processresponse ()   **********/
/*    processresponse ()  -  Takes action depending on the value
 *    of its parameter.
 */

void processresponse (char iochar)
{
        switch (iochar) {                               /* Note 2 */
                case '0':  break;                       /* Note 3 */
                case '1':  printf ("You have chosen guessit.\n");
                           break;                       /* Note 4 */
                case '2':  printf ("You have chosen nim.\n");
                           break;                       /* Note 4 */
                default:   printf ("Illegal input.\n"); /* Note 5 */
                           printf ("Choose 0, 1, or 2: ");
        }
}
```

Three functions constitute this program. Function main() is a driver. It calls both of the other functions. A while loop is used to continue the program until the user decides to terminate it. The function menu() consists of printf() calls to output the menu and a call to gets() to do the input. The function processresponse() looks at its parameter and uses a switch statement to decide on the next action.

Note 1: The value returned by menu() is tested. If the value is '0', the program is terminated; otherwise, processresponse() is called to take appropriate action. Looking at the function menu(), we see that the user can terminate the program by typing '0' to the menu prompt or signaling end-of-file.

Note 2: The switch is done on the parameter iochar. Its value will be compared with the values in the case labeled statements below to determine the next program action.

Note 3: The break is used to terminate execution of the statements in the switch statement. If iochar has the value '0' control will pass to the point immediately following the switch statement. In this program, control would pass to the end of the function processresponse().

Note 4: For the next two case labeled statements in the switch statement body, the break is used in the same way. If iochar has either the value '1' or '2', the corresponding printf() call would be executed and control would pass to the point immediately after the switch statement.

Note 5: The printf() calls associated with the default label will be executed only in the case that iochar has a value other than '0', '1', or '2'. The use of break causes these statements to be skipped if `iochar` matches one of the values in the `case` labels.

A Closer Look

The function processresponse() is a "stub" function. It does not complete the action desired, but instead is used during program development to test another program part. In this case, it could be used to test the handling of the input and assure that meaningful characters are passed to processresponse() each time. Using function stubs during program development is a technique that can lead to more robust programs with fewer bugs.

Learning Activities

9. a Execute the program switch2.c. Test it with each of its requested inputs to make sure that it behaves as expected.

   b. Test the program by responding with more than one character to the menu. For example, what happens if you type "12" in response to the prompt "Your choice?" What happens if you type "quit"?

   c. Experiment by commenting out one or more of the `break` statements and executing the program again. Make sure you understand the functionality of the `break` statement in this context.

10. Note that the input character `'0'` is used both as the terminator for the `while` statement in main() and as a value for a `case` label in the `switch` statement. Are both of these necessary? What happens when the user enters `'0'`? If possible, modify the program so that this redundancy is removed.

6.5 Getting Out Gracefully

The two concepts discussed in this section are the `return` statement and the exit() library function. Both are used to alter the flow of control set up by other program elements.

The `return` Statement

The `return` statement is used to terminate execution of a function. When it is executed, it causes control to pass from the function back to the calling environment. It could be used to provide a point of exit from a function other than at the end of the source for that function.

The `return` statement can be used in two different ways. In the first, the syntax is simple. It consists of the keyword `return` followed by a semicolon, as in

```
return;
```

In the second syntax, the `return` statement is followed by an expression,

```
return expression;
```

where `expression` can be any legal C expression.

When a `return` statement with the first syntax is executed in a function other than main(), it causes the execution of the function to terminate. Execution resumes in the calling function at the statement following the function call. The following diagram indicates this.

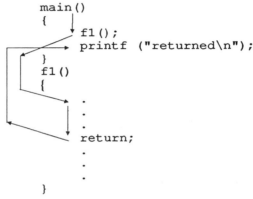

```
main()
{
    f1();
    printf ("returned\n");
}
f1()
{
    .
    .
    .
    return;
    .
    .
    .
}
```

When the `return` statement is used with an expression, control is passed to the point in the calling function immediately after the function call and the value of the expression becomes the value returned by the function. We saw examples of this use in Chapters 1 and 3.

The `return` statement can be used in main() also. When executed there, it will cause the program to cease execution. When the `return` statement is used with an expression, the value of that expression is returned to the program's calling environment. This is one way for C programs to communicate with a command interpreter.

Suppose we want to write a function to read to a position in an input line that is delimited by `'#'`. Example 6-6 implements this function with the `return` statement. The program is similar in concept to the one in Example 6-4 that illustrated the `break` statement, but this time we assume that the processing of the line will take place after our function has positioned the input pointer correctly.

Example 6-6: return1.c

```
/*                  return1.c
 *
 *    Synopsis  -  Positions input stream to either the character
 *                 after '#' or at the end of the input line.
 *
 *    Objective -  To illustrate the simplest form of the
 *                 return statement.
 */

#include <stdio.h>
#define END_OF_LINE   '\n'
#define DELIMITER     '#'


void main()
{
        void look_for_delimiter();
        printf ("Enter a line of text with a '#'.\n> ");   /* Note 1 */
        look_for_delimiter();
        printf ("Done looking!\n");                        /* Note 1 */
}

void look_for_delimiter()
{
        int iochar;
        while ( (iochar = getchar()) != END_OF_LINE) {
                if (iochar == DELIMITER)
                        return;                            /* Note 2 */
        }
        printf ("At end of line\n");                       /* Note 3 */
}
```

The program contains the functions main() and look_for_delimiter(). In main(), there is a request for input, a call to look_for_delimiter(), and a printf() call after look_for_delimiter() finishes executing. Again main() is a driver function; its purpose is to prepare for execution of look_for_delimiter() and to call it. In look_for_delimiter(), each passage through the while loop compares a character to the delimiter '#'. The while loop will terminate if a newline is seen or if '#' is found in the input stream.

Note 1:   These two printf() calls surround the call to the function look_for_delimiter(). The first asks the user for relevant input, and the second reports that the function has finished executing. The output serves as a trace through the execution of this program. If look_for_delimiter() were used as a tool in a larger program, statements like these might not appear in the final version. They could be included as an aid during the development phase of a program.

Note 2: This `return` statement will only be executed when ' #' is found in the line of input. In that case, control will immediately return to the function main() at the statement following the call to this function. Note that this provides a second point of exit from the `while` loop.

Note 3: This printf() call might be included during the development phase of a program to provide an additional trace through the program. Here, it will only be executed when there is no ' #' in the input stream. It serves to let the user know that fact and that exit from the function look_for_delimiter() took place at the end of the function's source. This printf() call would probably be removed after the function had been fully tested.

Learning Activity

11. Execute return1.c with several different input lines to make sure that it behaves as you expected.

In the second syntax, the `return` statement is followed by an expression. When this type of statement is executed, the expression is evaluated and that value becomes the return value of the function. In this case, the function result can be assigned to a variable. For example, if the function max() terminates by executing a `return` statement with an expression, then a call to the function might be combined with an assignment statement, as in

```
maxnum = max();
```

The value returned by max() is assigned to `maxnum` and can be referenced later in the program.

The next example is an extension of the previous example. There, the function look_for_delimiter() was to read input until the character ' #' was found in the input or until the end of the input line. The calling function would not know which case had occurred in the input stream. Using the `return` statement with an associated expression, the function can communicate which case it found. This modification is made in Example 6-7.

Example 6-7: return2.c

```
/*                      return2.c
 *
 *    Synopsis   -   Positions input stream to the character after
```

```
*                       '#' or after the end of the input line.
*
*     Objective  -   To illustrate a return statement with an
*                    expression.
*/

#include <stdio.h>
#define END_OF_LINE   '\n'
#define DELIMITER     '#'

void main()
{
      int found;

      printf ("Enter a line of text with a '#'.\n> ");
      found = look_for_delimiter();                          /* Note 1 */
      if (found)                                             /* Note 2 */
            printf ("found a %c.\n", DELIMITER);
      else
            printf ("read until end of line.\n");
}

int look_for_delimiter()
{
      int iochar;
      while ( (iochar = getchar()) != END_OF_LINE) {
            if (iochar == DELIMITER)
                  return 1;                                  /* Note 3 */
      }
      return 0;                                              /* Note 4 */
}
```

The structure of this program is very similar to that of the previous example program. It contains the function main() and a subfunction look_for_delimiter(). Again main() is a driver; it requests input for the subfunction to process, calls the subfunction, and reports the status at return from the subfunction. The subfunction look_for_delimiter() again uses a `while` loop to read a line of input and processes each input character separately.

Note 1: Since the `return` statement is used with an associated expression, the subfunction look_for_delimiter() returns a value. This assignment statement saves the value returned in the variable `found`.

Note 2: The value returned by the subfunction is checked by this `if` statement. If the value of the variable `found` is nonzero, the printf() call in the body of the `if` is executed; if `found` has a zero value, the printf() call in the body of the `else` is executed. In the current program, the findings are simply output. The printf() calls might be replaced in later development with calls to functions that further process the input in each case.

Note 3: This `return` statement is only executed when a ' # ' is found in the input. When that happens, execution of the subfunction will terminate and control will return to main(). The subfunction's return value is 1; the next source statement executed will be the assignment of that value to the variable `found`.

Note 4: This `return` statement will only execute when the input line does not contain a ' # '. Exit from the `while` loop resulted from a newline being read. This fact is communicated by the return value of zero. If this `return` statement is executed, control is passed back to main() and the next execution is that of assigning the value 0 to the variable `found`.

Learning Activities

12. Execute the program return2.c with several different input lines to make sure that you understand how it operates.
13. *C by Discovery* To see how your environment handles certain situations,
    a. Modify the program return1.c by changing the line

    ```
    look_for_delimiter();
    ```

    to

    ```
    found = look_for_delimiter();
    ```

    and try to compile and execute the program again. (You will also have to declare the variable `found`.) If the program compiles, modify it again to have it output the value of `found`. Generalize from this experience to understand what happens when such an assignment is made and the function does not return a value.

    b. Modify the program return2.c by changing the line

    ```
    found = look_for_delimiter();
    ```

    to

    ```
    look_for_delimiter();
    ```

    and try to compile and execute the program again. Did anything appear to be amiss with the function call? Try to explain the results of your test runs.

The exit() Library Function

The exit() function is available in the library on many implementations of C. This function provides a drastic means of altering the program's flow of control. When executed, exit() causes the program to terminate. Control is returned to the underlying operating system.

The exit function takes a single parameter of type `int`. Therefore, a call to exit() might have the form

```
exit(0);
exit(1);
```

or

```
exit(255);
```

This value is passed to the calling environment (the operating system) and could be used to indicate the reason why the program terminated. By convention, a parameter of 0 indicates normal termination. Different nonzero values can be chosen by the programmer to indicate different reasons for program termination.

When used in main() the statement

```
return expression;
```

is equivalent to the statement

```
exit (expression);
```

The exit() library function differs from the `return` statement when it appears in a function other than main(). The `return` statement causes control to pass back to the calling function. The exit() library function causes program termination from any function from which it is called.

Example 6-8 illustrates a use of the exit() library function to indicate an error in input. The function convert() expects a sequence of digits in its input. It converts the sequence to a value of type `int`. The sequence of digits should be terminated by a space or a newline in the input stream. A character other than a digit or a space appearing in the input stream is considered an error condition. One method of handling this type of error might be to output an error message and terminate the program. That is the approach taken in this example. Note, however, that the error handler is a separate function so that it can be changed if desired.

Example 6-8: exit.c

```
/*              exit.c
 *
 *   Synopsis  -  Reads a stream of digits for its input, converts
 *                the input to an integer value, and outputs it.
 *                Finding a nondigit in input is an error.
 *
 *   Objective -  To illustrate error handling with the exit()
 *                library function.
 */

#include <stdio.h>
#include <ctype.h>                          /* Note 1 */
#define BLANK          ' '
#define END_OF_LINE    '\n'
```

```
void main()
{
        printf ("Enter a positive integer > ");
                                                        /* Note 2 */
        printf ("The value entered was %d.\n", convert());
        exit(0);                                        /* Note 3 */
}


convert()
{
        int     ch,
                sum = 0;
        void error();

        while (( (ch = getchar() ) != BLANK) && (ch != END_OF_LINE)) {

                if (!isdigit(ch) )                      /* Note 1 */
                        error();
                sum = sum * 10 + (ch - '0');            /* Note 4 */
        }
        return (sum);
}

void error ()
{
        printf ("Nondigit found in input. Program terminated.\n");
        exit(1);                                        /* Note 5 */
}
```

Three functions make up this program. The function main() is a driver program and only serves to ask for input, call the function convert(), and report on the value returned. The function convert() uses a `while` loop to read until either an END_OF_LINE or a BLANK is read. The processing of the digits is done inside the `while` loop. The function error() does the error handling.

Note 1: The header file ctype.h is normally delivered with each implementation of C. It contains many definitions and macros that deal with character types. It is included in this example to allow a call to the macro isdigit() that appears in the second line referenced by `Note 1`. The macro isdigit() is defined in the file ctype.h. It looks at its parameter and returns a value of 1 if the parameter is one of the digits ′0′, ′1′, ′2′, . . . , ′9′; it returns a value of 0 if the parameter is not a digit.

Note 2:   The function call to convert() is made by this printf() call. The return value is output by printf().

Note 3:   This exit() call will be executed when no errors were found in the input and the program terminates normally. Traditionally, the argument of 0 to exit() will signify normal termination of the program to the calling environment. Nonzero values are used to signify error conditions.

Note 4:   Conversion from a string of characters to a value of type `int` takes place on this line. The variable sum was initialized to 0 and accumulation of the value is done here. The final value of sum is returned by convert().

Note that this algorithm will only work when the digits '0' through '9' are contiguous in the underlying character set. The code depends on C's automatic conversion from character to integer.

Note 5:   The exit() function will only be executed when the function error() was called from convert(). When executed, exit() causes the program to halt. The value of 1 is passed to the calling environment. By convention, 0 signifies normal termination, and a value of 1 would indicate an error.

"It is a convention of the exit() function that 0 signifies normal termination, and 1 signifies an error." Based on *Archangel Saint Michael* by Andrea della Robbia, c. 1475.

Learning Activities

14. a Find out if the file ctype.h is available on your system. If it is, inspect it. In particular, look for the definition of isdigit() and see if you understand the code.

    b. Without looking further in ctype.h, write a function named islower() that takes a single parameter. The function islower() should return 1 if its parameter is between 'a' and 'z', and 0 otherwise. Write a short driver program that will test your function.

    c. Look at the other definitions and macros provided in ctype.h so that you have a good idea of what facilities are available there.

15. Run the program exit.c.

    a. Test it with several strings of digits to make sure that the conversion is done correctly.

    b. Test it with a single string of input digits followed by a <Return> to make sure that the algorithm terminates correctly in this case.

    c. Test it with a string of digits separated from other input on the line with a blank character. Try a tab character as a separator. Modify the program, if necessary, so that it handles each of these cases correctly.

    d. Finally, test the program with some nondigit input to see that the exit() library function behaves as you thought it should.

6.6   The goto Statement and Labels

The goto statement in C allows transfer of control from one position in a function to another statement in the same function. The destination statement must be marked with a label.

A label in C is an identifier. It must be associated with a statement by using the following syntax:

```
label : statement;
```

The statement can be any legal statement in C.

The syntax of the goto statement follows:

```
goto identifier;
```

where identifier is a label associated with a statement in the same function as the goto.

The program in Example 6-9 illustrates a use of the goto statement. The program has the same functionality as exit.c in Example 6-8, but the error handling is done with a goto statement instead of a function call.

Example 6-9: goto.c

```
/*                  goto.c
 *
 *
 *   Synopsis   -   Expects a stream of digits in input.  The digits
 *                  are converted to an integer value and output.
 *
 *
 *   Objective  -   To illustrate error handling with the goto
 *                  statement.
 */

#include <stdio.h>
#include <ctype.h>
#define BLANK            ' '
#define END_OF_LINE     '\n'

void main()
{
        printf ("Enter a positive integer > ");
                                                        /* Note 1 */
        printf ("The value entered was %d.\n", convert ());
        exit(0);
}
convert()
{
        int     ch,
                sum = 0;

        while (((ch = getchar()) != BLANK) && (ch != END_OF_LINE)) {
                if (!isdigit(ch) )
                        goto error;                     /* Note 2 */
                sum = sum * 10 + (ch - '0');
        }
        return (sum);
                                                        /* Note 3 */
error:  printf ("Nondigit found in input. Program terminated.\n");
        exit(1);
}
```

The program contains the function main() and the function convert(). Again, main() is a driver. It only contains code necessary to initialize for, call, and report on the return of the function convert(). Like exit.c in Example 6-8, the function convert() uses a `while` loop to read in the string of digits. Each digit is processed separately. It uses the macro isdigit() defined in the header file ctype.h to check on errors in input. Only the error handling is different.

Note 1: The function main() asks for input and outputs the value returned by convert(). The call to convert() is in the second call to printf().

Note 2: The `goto` statement is only executed in case `isdigit (iochar)` returns 0. Control will transfer from this position in the program to the statement at the bottom of the function with the label `error`. The intervening statements will not be executed.

Note 3: When a nondigit is read in the input stream, control will transfer to this point in the program. The printf() call will give the error diagnostic and the program will terminate. Note that this code is only reached by means of the `goto` statement. If there is no error in input, the previous `return` statement will transfer control back to the function main().

Learning Activities

16. Test goto.c with many different inputs to verify that it behaves as you expected.

17. Modify the program goto.c by moving the printf() call labeled `error` and the subsequent exit() statement to the end of the function main(). Try to compile and execute the modified program. Try to explain what happens and why.

A Word of Warning

Much has been written about the use and misuse of the `goto` statement. Although opinions differ on the proper use of this statement, most authorities agree that indiscriminate use of the `goto` statement is one deterrent to structured programming.

In addition to the effect that `goto` has on the structure of a program, situations arise in the source code where the effects of using `goto` have some unexpected deleterious consequences. A major example of this is when the `goto` statement is used to jump into the middle of a block, as in the following code segment:

```
iochar = getchar();
if (isdigit(iochar))
      goto calculate;
      .
      .                             /* other code */
      .
```

```
        {                                    /* a block */
            int i = 0;                       /* local variable */
            while (isdigit(iochar)) {
                i = i + 1;
                                             /* labeled statement */
    calculate: for (j = 1; j < i ; j ++)
                    sum = 10 * (iochar - '0')
                iochar = getchar();
        }                                    /* end while */
        }                                    /* end block */
```

The local variable i in the block is not guaranteed to be initialized properly when the block is not entered from the top. If the block is entered by means of the goto statement above, the value of i could be garbage. The code would be unreliable.

6.7 Using Recursion

Recursion occurs when a function or subprogram calls itself. C allows recursion.

In mathematics, a recurrence relation is a formula in which the desired expression for a positive integer, n, is described in terms of corresponding values for integers less than n. Initial conditions or starting values (usually for n = 0, or n = 1) must also be given. The following formulas for powers of x and for factorials are simple examples of recurrence relations.

	Formula	*Initial Condition*
Power:	$x^n = x * x^{n-1}$	$x^0 = 1$
Factorial:	$n! = n * (n-1)!$	$0! = 1$

Using the initial condition, the formulas can be evaluated for any positive integer n. For example, 4! can be calculated using the recurrence relation in the following steps:

```
4!  =  4 * (3!)                   using      n! = n * (n-1)!
    =  4 * 3 * (2!)               using      (n-1)! = (n-1) * (n-2)!
    =  4 * 3 * 2 * (1!)                         .
    =  4 * 3 * 2 * 1 * (0!)                     .
    =  4 * 3 * 2 * 1 * 1    using      0! = 1
    =  24
```

One way of implementing a recurrence relation is to code a recursive function. As the initial condition allows the calculation of a recurrence relation to terminate, it also provides a way of terminating the sequence of recursive calls of a function. It is extremely important that every recursive function be given a termination condition that is sure to occur. Otherwise, the execution would be out of control.

A recursive function to calculate factorials is demonstrated in the program recurs.c in Example 6-10. The function main() serves only as a driver to call the recursive function and output the value returned by the function.

Example 6-10: recurs.c

```
/*                  recurs.c
 *
 *    Synopsis  -  Inputs a positive integer, calculates its factorial,
 *                 and outputs the result.
 *
 *    Objective -  A simple example of a recursive function.
 */

#include <stdio.h>
#include <ctype.h>                                        /* Note 1 */
#define BLANK          ' '
#define END_OF_LINE    '\n'

void main()
{
        int n;
        int factorial (int n);
        int convert();

        printf ("Program to Calculate Factorials.\n");
        printf ("------- -- --------- ----------\n");
        printf ("\n Enter a positive integer value : ");
        n = convert();                                    /* Note 2 */
        printf ("\n%d! is %d.\n", n, factorial(n) );
}

factorial (int n)
{
        if (n == 0)                                       /* Note 3 */
                return (1);
        else
                return ( n * factorial(n-1) );            /* Note 4 */
}
convert()
{
        int     ch,
                sum = 0;
        void    error();
```

```
        while (((ch = getchar()) != BLANK) && (ch != END_OF_LINE)) {

            if (!isdigit(ch) )
                    error();
            sum = sum * 10 + (ch - '0');
        }
        return (sum);
}

void error ()
{
        printf ("Nondigit found in input. Program terminated.\n");
        exit(1);
}
```

This program consists of four functions: main(), factorial(), convert(), and error(). Again, main() is not much more than a driver program. It requests input and calls the functions convert() and factorial() to do input conversion and factorial calculation.

Note 1: The header file ctype.h is included so that the macro isdigit() can be accessed.

Note 2: The function convert() from the program exit.c is used to input the integer. In this statement, the value returned by convert() is assigned to the variable n. The function convert() and the accompanying error handler embrace the concept of software tools. These tools can be moved to a different program without rewriting.

Note 3: The function factorial() is the recursive function. The first clause in the `if` statement implements the initialization condition for the factorial recurrence relation. This allows exit from the function without encountering a recursive call. Every recursive function must supply a method of exit from the recursion.

Note 4: This statement contains the recursive call to the function factorial(). When this occurs, control passes back to the beginning of the function. The earlier call to factorial() does not terminate but, instead, waits for the subsequent calls to terminate and return a value. If this program were used to calculate 4!, the hand calculation above indicates that there would be five calls to the function factorial() active at one time. The first call would be from the function main() with the parameter 4. Subsequent calls would be made by the function factorial() itself with the parameters 3, 2, 1, and 0, in that order. The initial value would be returned by the call with parameter 0, and that would allow the preceding calls to exit once they received the value for which they were waiting.

Learning Activities

18. a. Run the program and test it with the values 4, 6, 2, and 3 to make sure that it runs correctly.

    b. Modify recurs.c by including some printf() calls that will provide an execution trace. Make each message different and have the message indicate the position from which it is output. There should be a statement at the beginning and the end of the main program, and one for each time the function factorial() is entered and exited. The printf() messages from the function factorial() should mention the value of the parameter as well as whether it is entering or exiting the function. Both of the `return` statements in factorial() should have printf() calls. (You may have to restructure the `else` clause to get a true trace.) Once the trace is working properly, test the program again with the above input so that you can count how many calls to factorial() are active at one time.

    c. If you know how to use the debugger on your system, you may choose to trace through the execution of this program in the debugger.

19. Test the program with some larger numbers as input. There is no mechanism in the program to determine when the value returned by factorial() exceeds the value that can be handled by a variable of type `int`. On some systems this overflow error occurs for small values of n.

    a. Determine the largest value for which the function returns the correct value on your system.

    b. Modify the program so that the value is correct for larger values of n. This can usually be done by changing the type on some variables. What type will handle the largest result on your system?

20. a. Replace the call to our function convert() with a call to the C library function scanf(). Test the program now. In particular, what happens when there are errors in input? For example, what happens when the input consists of just an `' a '`, or the sequence of characters 2a3? Do you prefer the behavior of the program with scanf() or with convert()? Why?

    b. The function scanf() can return an indication of error. read your documentation on scanf() or the information in the Programmer's Handbook, and restructure the program to use scanf() for input and to output an error message for input errors.

A Closer Look

Recursive functions tend to use a lot of memory. In Chapter 3, we discussed activation records of functions along with parameter passing. The activation record of a function contains the local variables and parameters for a function (along with other information). The activation record is in existence only while the function is executing. Thus, the activation record for main() would be in existence during the full time of program execution, but the activation records for other functions were created when the function was called and destroyed when the function terminated.

When a recursive function calls itself, the original activation record is not destroyed, because that function is still active. Another activation record for the function is created with each recursive call. The activation records are "stacked up." None are destroyed until they complete execution. Below is the collection of activation records that are active at one time for the function factorial() in recurs.c. In each activation record, the only variable shown is the parameter n. The first activation record created was the one with n equal 4. Then the activation records to the right were created one at a time until finally the activation record with n equal to 0 was created.

n=4	n=3	n=2	n=1	n=0

Five calls were active at one time. The calls terminate in the order opposite to their creation. The call to factorial() with n equal 0 uses the initial condition and terminates instead of making another recursive call. That allows the call with n = 1 to calculate its return value and terminate. This pattern continues until the value of 4! has been calculated.

This was a simple example. If the example were more complicated or if the initial call to factorial() had a larger parameter, the memory usage would be much higher.

Another Example of Recursion

In spite of the large amount of memory it may use, recursion is a handy problem-solving tool. Some problems lend themselves naturally to recursive thinking.

For example, consider the problem of sorting an array. One approach might be to

1. Divide the array in half.
2. Sort the first half.
3. Sort the second half.
4. Merge the two halves together.

To sort the first half, this approach would be applied again: divide it in half, sort the first half, sort the second half, and merge the two halves together. This approach could be continued until half of one of the divided arrays was a single element and did not need sorting. Steps 2 and 3 would be implemented as recursive calls.

For example, consider the following array:

3	1	8	2

Sorting the array with this approach is diagrammed below. In each case letters indicate which recursive call is taking the action. A is the first call, B, the second, and so on. Each of the four steps in the algorithm above are executed in each recursive call to sort a portion of the array.

A. Divide the array in half.

3	1		8	2

A. Sort the first half.
    B. Divide the array in half.

3		1

    B. Sort the first half.

| 3 | Done
|---|

    B. Sort the second half.

| 1 | Done
|---|

    B. Merge the two halves together.

1	3

A. Sort the second half.
    C. Divide the array in half.

8		2

    C. Sort the first half.

| 8 | Done
|---|

    C. Sort the second half.

| 2 | Done
|---|

    C. Merge the two halves together.

2	8

A. Merge the two halves together.

1	2	3	8

The array has been sorted.

This approach has been documented in a well-known sorting algorithm, the merge sort algorithm. It is a recursive algorithm. An implementation in C appears in Example 6-11. Consider that code now.

Example 6-11: mergsort.alg

```
/*                      mergsort.alg
 *
 *    Synopsis   -   The merge sort algorithm package.  Not a complete
 *                   program.
 *
 *    Objective -  A second illustration of a recursive function.
 */

#include "mergsort.h"                                  /* Note 1 */

/************************************ merge_sort()  *********/
/*       merge_sort()-a recursive sorting algorithm.
 *       Upon entry, to_sort is the array with the elements to be
 *       sorted.  The elements will be contiguously placed in the array.
 *       first is the index of the first element and last is the
 *       index of the last.
 */

void merge_sort (int to_sort[], int first, int last)    /* Note 2 */
{
        if (first < last) {                            /* Note 3 */
                                                       /* Note 4 */
                merge_sort( to_sort, first, (first+last)/2 );
                                                       /* Note 5 */
                merge_sort( to_sort, (first+last)/2 + 1, last);
                                                       /* Note 6 */
                merge (to_sort, first, (first+last)/2,
                        (first+last)/2 + 1, last);
        }
}
```

```
/*************************************   merge ()   ***************/
/*      merge() - a utility function for merge sort, merges two lists.
 *      Both lists are in the array lists. The first list starts at
 *      index first1 and goes through index last1.  The second list
 *      starts at index first2 and goes through index last2.  The
 *      two lists are contiguous in the array.
 */
void merge (int lists[], int first1, int last1, int first2,
          int last2)
{
        int temp[MAX_ARRAY];
        int index, index1, index2;
        int num, num_in_1, num_in_2;


        index = 0;
        index1 = first1;
        index2 = first2;
        num = last1 - first1 + last2 - first2 + 2;

        /* while there are still elements in both lists,
         * put the smallest element in the temporary array.
         */
        while ( (index1 <= last1) && (index2 <= last2 ) ) {


                if (lists[index1] < lists[index2])
                        temp[index++] = lists[index1++];
                else
                        temp[index++] = lists[index2++];
        }

        /* after one list is empty, fill the temporary array
         * with the remaining elements in the other list
         */
        if (index1 > last1)            /* first list is empty */
              move (lists, index2, last2, temp, index);
        else                           /* second list is empty */
              move(lists, index1, last1, temp, index);

                        /* copy the list to original array */
        move (temp, 0, num-1, lists, first1);


}
```

```
/*********************************** move()  ****************/
/*      move() - a utility function for merge sort, copies the array
 *      list1 from positions with index first1 to last1 to the
 *      array list2 starting at the position with index first2.
 */

void move(int list1[], int first1, int last1,
          int list2[], int first2)
{
        while (first1 <= last1)
                list2[first2++] = list1[first1++];

}
```

This algorithm consists of three functions: merge_sort(), merge(), and move(). The function merge_sort() is recursive and the notes below refer to that code. Both merge() and move() are fairly straightforward. Nothing new is presented in that code.

Note 1: The header file mergsort.h has been created with the declarations necessary for using this sorting package. It contains a declaration of each of the functions as well as the definition of MAX_ARRAY. It reads as follows:

```
/*                mergsort.h
 *
 *      Contains declarations necessary for use of the
 *      merge_sort() package.
 */

#define MAX_ARRAY 512
void merge_sort(int ts[], int first, int last);
void merge(int l[], int f1, int l1, int f2, int l2);
void move(int list1[], int f1, int l1, int list2[], int f2);
```

Note 2: The first parameter to merge_sort() is an array. No size has been specified for that array; the parameters first and last indicate the portion of the array that is to be sorted. This function can be used for any array that has no more than MAX_ARRAY elements. If it is to be used for a larger array, only the declaration of MAX_ARRAY in mergsort.h needs to be changed.

Note 3: The test (first < last) provides the way out of the recursion. Each time the array is divided in half, the indices first and last are changed. When the portion of the array to be sorted has only one element, first is equal to last and this call to merge_sort() will terminate. This allows the algorithm to proceed to the merge phase for that portion of the array. Eventually, the algorithm will terminate with a sorted array.

Note 4: The first recursive call to merge_sort() will sort the first half of the array. The indices of that half are from first to (first+last)/2 inclusive.

Note 5: The second recursive call to merge_sort() sorts the remaining portion of the array.

Note 6: The call to merge() will merge the two halves back together. At each step the element in the final array will be the smaller of the next elements in each half of the array.

Learning Activities

21. Carefully go through the example with four elements to make sure that you understand how the recursion works.

22. Carefully read the code for merge() and move().

23. Hand execute the algorithm for the array to_sort[] that appears below:

```
        to_sort
      ┌───┬───┬───┬───┬───┬───┬───┐
      │ 5 │ 1 │ 4 │ 7 │ 2 │ 6 │ 3 │
      └───┴───┴───┴───┴───┴───┴───┘
```

Keep track of the activation records for mergsort(). Each activation record should contain a value of first, a value of last, and the array to_sort[]. You could model your hand execution after the example of sorting the array with four elements.

24. Does this algorithm require distinct elements in the array? To find out, hand execute an example with three elements where two are the same.

The program mergsort.c in Example 6-12 will test the merge sort algorithm. It allows the user to input any array of integers with up to 512 entries and will output the array in sorted order. The code for the merge sort was taken directly from the file mergsort.alg that was discussed previously. The other functions were added to allow input and output of the array.

 Example 6-12: mergsort.c

```
/*                mergsort.c
 *
 *    Synopsis  -  Allows a user to input elements into an array,
 *                 sorts the array, and outputs it in sorted order.
 *
 *    Objective -  To provide a program to test the merge sort
 *                 algorithm.
 */
```

```
#include "mergsort.h"                                /* Note 1 */
#include <stdio.h>
#include <ctype.h>
#define DONE 0                                       /* Note 2 */
#define MORE 1
#define ERROR -1

void main()
{
        int num;
        int array[MAX_ARRAY];
        void print_array(int array[], int first, int num);
        int fill_array (int empty[]);

        num = fill_array(array);
        merge_sort(array, 0, num-1);
        print_array(array, 0, num-1);
}

/******************************************  fill_array()   ******/
/*      fill_array() allows the user to input integers into an
 *      array of integers.  Returns the number of elements entered
 *      into the array.
 */

fill_array(int empty[])
{
        int count = -1,
            more = MORE;
        int get_int (int *intptr);

        printf("Enter your integers now. Enter 'Q' to quit\n");
        printf("%3d : ", ++count + 1);

        while  (count < MAX_ARRAY) {
            more = get_int ( empty + count );

            if (more == ERROR) {                      /* Note 3 */
                printf("Error in input - Try that one again\n");
                printf("%3d : ", count+1);
                continue;
            }

            if (!more)                                /* Note 4 */
                break;
            printf("%3d : ", ++count+1);
```

```
            }
            return (count);
    }


/********************************     print_array()     ***********/
/*      print_array() - outputs the elements of an array of ints
 *      from the position with index first to the position with
 *      index last, inclusive.
 */

void print_array (int array[], int first, int num)
{
        int index;

        for (index = first; index <= num; index++)
                printf ("%3d: %5d\n", index+1, array[index]);
}


/***********************************     get_int()     ************/
/*      get_int() - inputs an integer from standard input.
 *      Returns the integer in the location pointed to by intptr,
 *      and returns DONE if user signals quit, ERROR if a nondigit
 *      was seen, or MORE if neither of the above occurred.
 */

get_int (int *intptr)
{
        int  ch;
        char remainder[80];
        int  digit_count = 0;

        *intptr = 0;
        while (isdigit(ch = getchar() )) {
                *intptr = *intptr * 10 + (ch - '0');     /* Note 5 */
                digit_count++;
        }
        switch (ch) {                                    /* Note 6 */
                case 'Q':
                case 'q':
                        gets(remainder);                 /* Note 7 */
                        return (DONE);

                case ' ':
                        gets(remainder);
```

```
                        case '\n':
                                if (digit_count)
                                        return (MORE);
                                else
                                        return (ERROR);

                        default :
                                gets(remainder);
                                return (ERROR);
        }
}


/***********************************  merge_sort ()   **********/
/*      merge_sort() - a recursive sorting algorithm.
 *      Upon entry, to_sort is the array with the elements to be
 *      sorted.  The elements will be contiguously placed in the array.
 *      first is the index of the first element and last is the
 *      index of the last.
 */

void merge_sort (int to_sort[], int first, int last)
{
        if (first < last) {

                merge_sort( to_sort, first, (first+last)/2 );
                merge_sort( to_sort, (first+last)/2 + 1, last);
                merge (to_sort, first, (first+last)/2,
                        (first+last)/2 + 1, last);
        }
}


/***********************************   merge()    **************/
/*      merge() - a utility function for merge sort, merges two lists.
 *      Both lists are in the array lists. The first list starts at
 *      index first1 and goes through index last1.  The second list
 *      starts at index first2 and goes through index last2.   The
 *      two lists are contiguous in the array.
 */
void merge (int lists[], int first1, int last1, int first2, int last2)
{
        int temp[MAX_ARRAY];
        int index, index1, index2;
        int num, num_in_1, num_in_2;


        index = 0;
        index1 = first1;
```

```
        index2 = first2;
        num = last1 - first1 + last2 - first2 + 2;

        /* while there are still elements in both lists,
         * put the smallest element in the temporary array.
         */
        while ( (index1 <= last1) && (index2 <= last2 ) ) {

                if (lists[index1] < lists[index2])
                        temp[index++] = lists[index1++];
                else
                        temp[index++] = lists[index2++];
        }

        /* after one list is empty, fill the temporary array
         * with the remaining elements in the other list
         */
        if (index1 > last1)          /* first list is empty */
                move (lists, index2, last2, temp, index);
        else                         /* second list is empty */
                move (lists, index1, last1, temp, index);

                        /* copy the list to original array */
        move (temp, 0, num-1, lists, first1);

}


/********************************** move ()   ****************/
/*      move () - a utility function for merge sort, copies the array
 *      list1 from positions with index first1 to last1 to the
 *      array list2 starting at the position with index first2.
 */

void move(int list1[], int first1, int last1,
          int list2[], int first2)
{
        while (first1 <= last1)
                list2[first2++] = list1[first1++];
}
```

The program contains the functions main(), fill_array(), print_array(), and get_int() in addition to the functions necessary for the merge sort. Since the merge sort algorithm was discussed previously, the notes below concentrate on the rest of the program. The function main() is a driver. It calls fill_array() to input the array elements, merge_sort() to sort the array, and print_array() to output the array. The function fill_array() calls get_int() to input each integer; fill_array() prompts for the input, counts the number of integers input, and handles the values returned from get_int(). The function print_array() outputs the elements in the array. The function get_int() does the actual input of the integers; we have seen the algorithm used for conversion before in the function convert() in exit.c. This function is different in that it does a little bit of error handling.

Note 1: The file mergsort.h is included to provide the declarations needed for the merge sort algorithm.

Note 2: The values MORE (1), DONE (0), and ERROR (–1) are the values returned by get_int().

Note 3: The value ERROR is returned when get_int() finds an element other than a decimal digit in the input. When this happens, fill_array() gives the user another chance to input an integer without either keeping or counting the input that was in error. The continue statement effectively transfers control to the beginning of the while loop.

Note 4: If get_int() returned DONE, then !more will test true. Then the break statement will break out of the while loop without outputting an additional prompt or incrementing count.

Note 5: The algorithm for converting from the character input to an integer is the same as that from earlier programs. It depends on the contiguity of the digits in the ASCII collating sequence.

Note 6: On exit from the while loop, the variable ch contains something other than a digit. The switch statement allows action depending on the contents of ch. If ch contains 'q' or 'Q', the user has signaled that input is done; get_int() passes this information on by returning DONE. If ch contains a ' ' or a newline, then the input is correct and the user is not done; get_int() passes this information on by returning MORE. In any other case, an error has occurred and get_int() returns ERROR.

Note 7: If ch contains anything other than a newline, a call to gets() will flush the buffer.

Recursion has advantages and disadvantages. The major advantage is that some problems are easily solved with a recursive approach. More evidence of this appears in the study of data structures where tree traversal can easily be done recursively.

On the other hand, recursion can use a lot of memory. Every time the function is called, a new activation record is created. This activation record contains space for local variables, parameters, saved register values, and return addresses. If many calls to a recursive function are active at one time, a lot of memory is used.

Another disadvantage is that the recursion is often difficult to program and control. If a recursive function does not work the first time, it can be extremely difficult to find the problem.

Learning Activities

25. Compile and execute mergsort.c several times to make sure that it works with different sets of data.

26. a If you are still having trouble understanding the recursion, put in some printf() calls to output the values of `first` and `last` as merge_sort() is entered. If you want, the function print_array() can be used to output the portion of the array that is to be sorted. By running the program with this trace, you should be able to see the recursive calls with the different parameters.

   b. If you know how to work with the debugger on your system, you could execute the program with the debugger to watch the recursion. This method is preferred by many programmers.

27. a In the line

```
printf ("%3d: %5d\n", index+1, array[index]);
```
   what is the purpose of the 3 and the 5?

   b. Consider the `while` loop in fill_array(). What are the ways of exiting the `while` loop? Which do you think the programmer intended to be used more often?

28. Note that the function get_int() is a first attempt to write a robust input routine. There are still problems with get_int(). Can you think of some? For example, what if the number input is greater than the largest integer that your system can handle? How could that problem be fixed?

Language Elements Introduced in This Chapter: A Review

** Control Statements **

```
do
    statement;
while (expression);

switch (expression1) {
  case c1:
        statement;
```

```
    case c2:
        statement;
        .
        .
        .
    default:
        statement;
}

continue;
break;
return;
return expression;

label : statement;

goto label;
```

** Header Files **

    ctype.h   for character typing

** Library Functions **

    exit()   causes termination of its program

** Macros **

    isdigit()   returns 1 if its argument is a digit, 0 otherwise

Things to Remember

1. Every do-while loop will execute at least one time.
2. The values in the case labeled statements must be constant integral expressions.
3. When the switch statement finds a match in one of the case values, control is passed to that case labeled statement and execution continues from that point in the program.
4. Both the continue and the break statement work with the for, the do-while, and the while loop. The break statement is also used with the switch statement.
5. When a continue or break statement is used in a set of nested loops, it is only effective on the loop for which it is in the immediate statement body.

6. The `return` statement transfers execution control out of a function and back to the calling environment.

7. When the `return` statement is used with an expression, the expression determines both the value and the type of the function using it.

8. A `return` statement can be used to provide more than one point of exit from a function.

9. The parameter to exit() can be used to signal the reason for program termination. A value of 0 traditionally means normal termination. Other values can be chosen to represent various error conditions.

10. When used in main() the statement `return expression;` is equivalent to the statement `exit (expression);`

11. The `goto` statement is used to transfer control to some labeled statement in the same function. It cannot transfer control out of a function.

12. The `goto` statement is a deterrent to structured programming. Its use should be reserved for deeply nested code.

13. Recursion occurs when a function or subprogram calls itself.

14. Recursion can be used to implement recurrence relations.

15. Algorithms using recurrence tend to use more memory than iterative algorithms.

6.8   Exercises and Programming Problems

1. Rewrite the function convert() from Example 6-8 so that a negative integer can be input. Test your new function with the program exit.c from the same example. How does it handle the following inputs?
   a. `2378`   b. `-264`   c. `0238`   d. `5-47`
   Is the action of the program desirable? Fix any bug you might have encountered in your testing.

2. Modify the error handling in goto.c from Example 6-9 to allow the user to enter another line in case the first had a mistake in it.

3. Write a function that will input a real number from a string of digits, possibly a decimal point and possibly a minus. Test your function with a program similar to exit.c. Make sure that it appropriately handles input like
   a. 3.78   b. −45.893   c. 3.4.5 (an error)   d. −.25

4. Modify the programs continue.c and break.c from Section 6.4 so that the `continue` and `break` statements are not used in either program.

5. Write a program that will count the number of vowels, consonants, punctuation marks, and whitespace in its input. The input will be English text. For this program, the space, tab, and newline will be considered the whitespace characters. The punctuation marks consist of a period, a semicolon, a comma, a question mark, and an exclamation point. Vowels are `'a'`, `'e'`, `'i'`, `'o'`, and `'u'`. The rest of the alphabetic characters are the consonants. The output should report the number of characters in each category. Use the `switch` statement appropriately in your program. Test it thoroughly.

6. Write a program that writes a check. The user should enter the date, the check number, the payee, the amount and a memo. For example, consider the following run of the program (user input is in **boldface**):

```
Check Writing Program
----- -------- -------

Date: 11/29/91
Check Number:  351
Payee: Fears and Slowbuck
Amount: 350.13
Memo: Payment on Account 345-678-91


-------------------------------------------------------------
                                           Check 351

                          Date  11/29/91
Pay to the
Order of          Fears and Slowbuck           $ 350.13
Three Hundred Fifty Dollars and thirteen cents

Memo: Payment on Account 345-678-91      ------------------------
-------------------------------------------------------------
```

Assume that the largest check that can be written is for $9999.99. Your program should output values like 300.00, 50.14, 0.12 properly both in numbers and in words.

7. Write a program that plays a number guessing game with the user. A sample run of the game program would be as follows (user input is in **boldface**):

```
Welcome to the game of Guess It!

I will choose a number between 1 and 100.
You will try to guess that number. If you guess wrong, I
will tell you if you guessed too high or too low.

You have 6 tries to get the number.

OK, I am thinking of a number. Try to guess it.
Your guess? 50
Too high!
Your guess? 12
Too low!
Your guess? 112
Illegal guess.  Your guess must be between 1 and 100.
Try again.  Your guess? -20
Illegal guess.  Your guess must be between 1 and 100.
```

```
Try again.  Your guess? 23

***CORRECT*****

Want to play again? y

OK, I am thinking of a number.  Try to guess it.

Your guess? 85
Too high!
Your guess? 12
Too low!
Your guess? 57

***CORRECT*****

Want to play again ? n

Goodbye, it was fun.
Hope to play Guess It with you again soon.
```

Hint: Look up the library function rand() and use it to establish the number to be guessed.

8. Write a C program that outputs a bank statement. The user should be allowed to enter a beginning balance and the transactions one at a time. When the transaction is a deposit, the user precedes the transaction amount with ′D′; a withdrawal amount is preceded by ′W′; a check transaction is preceded by ′C′ and should include the check number. The program should output a full report of all transactions and a final balance. The checks should be ordered by check number. A suggested program run appears below. The user's input is in **boldface**.

```
XYZ Bank Statement Program
--- ---- --------- -------

Enter beginning balance: $1427.89

Enter transactions:
(W)ithdrawal, (D)eposit, (C)heck (Q)uit: D
Amount:  2478.36
(W)ithdrawal, (D)eposit, (C)heck (Q)uit: C
Check Number: 1035
Amount:  95.23
(W)ithdrawal, (D)eposit, (C)heck (Q)uit: W
Amount:  160
(W)ithdrawal, (D)eposit, (C)heck (Q)uit: C
Check Number: 1032
Amount:  46.41
```

```
(W)ithdrawal, (D)eposit, (C)heck (Q)uit: W
Amount:  45.50
(W)ithdrawal, (D)eposit, (C)heck (Q)uit: C
Check number: 1033
Amount:  25.72
(W)ithdrawal, (D)eposit, (C)heck (Q)uit: Q

Thank You!

                    B A N K    S T A T E M E N T
                    - - - -    - - - - - - - - -


                              Beginning Balance:        $1427.89

1 Deposit:
              $2478.36         Total deposits:          $2478.36
2 Withdrawals:
              $160.00
              $ 45.50          Total withdrawals:       $ 205.50
3 Checks:
         1033    $   25.72
         1035        95.23
         1032        46.41     Total checks:            $ 167.36
                                                        --------
                              Final Balance:            $3533.39
```

Note: the checks need not be in numerical order.

9. a. Write a program that reads English text as its input and echoes it to the output
        except that every time the characters .P are found in the input, a single blank
        line is output. For example, the following two inputs:

```
        text   followed by .P followed by text
```

   and

```
        text followed by
        .P
        followed by text
```

   should both give output in the form

```
        text followed by

        followed by text
```

   with a single blank line between the two text lines.

   b. Extend your program from part a to indent the text five spaces whenever the
       characters .I are encountered in the input. Indentation should always signify
       a new line of output. For example, the two inputs

```
        text .I more text
```

   and

```
text
.I
more text
```

should both give the output below.

```
text
        more text
```

10. Write a recursive function that implements the recurrence relation to calculate the nth power of a floating point value x. Both n and x should be parameters to the function. The return value of the function will be the value of x^n. To test your function, write a program to output the following table.

				Powers			
		1	2	3	4	5	6	7
	1 |	1	1	1	1	1	1	1
Bases	2 |	2	4	8	16	32	64	128
	3 |	3	9	27	81	243	729	2182

and so on to some reasonable number. Be careful of overflow errors.

11. Give the output of the following program for the given input.

```
/*                    epp11.c                    */
#include <stdio.h>
void stackit();

void main()
{
        stackit();
}

void stackit()
{
        int iochar;

        if ((iochar = getchar()) != '\n') {
                stackit();
                putchar(iochar);
        }
}
```

Input: `How now brown cow?`

12. The binomial coefficients can be defined recursively as

$$\binom{n}{r} = \binom{n-1}{r} + \binom{n-1}{r-1}$$

with the initial conditions that

$$\binom{1}{1} = 1 \quad \text{and} \quad \binom{1}{0} = 1$$

Write a program with a recursive function that will input n and r and calculate the corresponding binomial coefficient.

13. Modify the program do.c of Example 6-1 as necessary to obtain the answers to the following questions. Try to compile and execute it for each modification.

a. What happens when reverse is called without any parameters?

b. What happens when reverse is called with too many parameters?

c. Explain what you think is happening.

Structuring the Data

Chapter 7

7.1   Introduction to Structures

A structure in C is an aggregate type designed to hold multiple data values. In contrast to an array, which will hold many data values of the same type, a structure can concurrently hold data values of different types.

For example, if a program is being designed to keep track of an inventory of automobile parts, the information about each part includes the part identification, the price, and the number of items currently in stock. An array of eight characters might be appropriate for the part identification, whereas the price would be a floating point value, and the number of items in stock would be an integer. A structure could be declared to hold all three pieces of data. The declaration of the structure would be

```
struct auto_part {
    char  id[8];
    float price;
    int   cur_inv;
};
```

In the above declaration, the word `struct` is a keyword in C. It signals the declaration of a structure. The declaration of the members of the structure appears as a list between the mandatory set of matching braces. This structure has three members: `id`, `price`, and `cur_inv`. These members represent the identification, the price, and the number of items in inventory for an automobile part. Their types have been declared appropriately.

The identifier `auto_part` is an optional tag. When a tag is included, the pair of words

```
struct auto_part
```

can be used elsewhere in the program to identify structures with these members. When the tag is omitted, there is no way of referring to a structure of this type without redeclaring it. If it is redeclared, the compiler will not equate the two structure types.

There are very few restrictions on the types that the members of a structure may have. A member of a structure may not be a function, and it may not have type `void`. The only other restriction is that a structure may not nest a structure of its own type. For example, a `struct auto_part` may not have a member of type `struct auto_part`. It may have members that are structures of other types, and may have members that are pointers to a structure of the same type.*

The declaration above informs the compiler of the members of a structure. It does not declare any variables of type `struct auto_part` and does not cause the allocation of any memory. After the above declaration of the structure, variables named `part1` and `part2` can be declared in the following way:

```
struct auto_part part1, part2;
```

As an alternative, the declaration of the type `struct auto_part` can be combined with the declaration of the variables `part1` and `part2` of that type with the code

```
struct auto_part {
    char  id[8];
    float price;
    int   cur_inv;
} part1, part2;
```

Another variation on the declaration of these two variables might be to omit the tag, as in

```
struct {
    char  id[8];
    float price;
    int   cur_inv;
} part1, part2;
```

In this case the compiler would recognize `part1` and `part2` as structures having `id`, `price`, and `cur_inv` as members, but it would be more difficult to declare variables of this same type later in the program.

The individual fields of a structure can be accessed with the syntax

```
variable_name.member_name
```

---

* A pointer to a function may also be a member of a structure. Pointers to functions are discussed in Chapter 8.

For example, in a struct auto_part, the expression

        part1.id

is an array of 8 chars. The expression

        part1.price

is a quantity of type float while

        part1.cur_inv

is an int. The type of each member of a structure determines the operations that may be performed on that member. All the operations associated with an int can be performed on part1.cur_inv, but only array operations are allowed on part1.id. Note that the individual cells in part1.id can be accessed either through the subscript notation, as in

        part1.id[3]

or through the pointer dereferencing notation, as in

        *(part1.id+3)

In Example 7-1 the program defines a variable of type struct auto_part, initializes it from the keyboard, and outputs the contents to the terminal. It shows basic structure handling. The standard library function strncpy(), a relative of strcpy(), is used to copy a limited number of characters from one array to another.

Example 7-1: struct1.c

```
/*                      struct1.c
 *
 *      Synopsis  -   Inputs an auto_part from the keyboard and echoes
 *                    it back to the terminal.
 *
 *      Objective -   To illustrate declaring a structure and accessing
 *                    its members.
 */

#include <stdio.h>
#include <string.h>
#include <stdlib.h>

struct auto_part {                                          /* Note 1 */
        char id[8];
        float price;
        int cur_inv;
} part;                                                     /* Note 2 */

void main()
{
```

```
        void put_part(void), get_part(void);

        get_part();
        put_part();
}

/*************************************** get_part()  *********/
/*  inputs a struct auto_part from standard input              */
/*  inputs values into the global variable    part             */

void get_part(void)
{
        char instring[512];
        struct auto_part instruct;                         /* Note 3 */

        printf ("Enter the part number :");
        gets (instring);
        strncpy (instruct.id, instring, 7);                /* Note 4 */
        instruct.id[7] = '\0';                             /* Note 5 */

        printf ("Enter the price : ");
        instruct.price = atof( gets(instring) );           /* Note 5 */
        printf ("Enter the amount in inventory : ");
        instruct.cur_inv = atoi (gets(instring));          /* Note 5 */
        part = instruct;                                   /* Note 6 */
}

/*************************************** put_part()  *********/
/*   outputs contents of a struct auto_part to the terminal    */
/*   accesses the global variable    part                      */

void put_part(void)
{
        printf ("Part-id:  %8s\n", part.id);               /* Note 5 */
        printf ("Price :  $%8.2f\n", part.price);          /* Note 5 */
        printf ("Quantity: %8d\n", part.cur_inv);          /* Note 5 */
}
```

This program contains three functions: main(), get_part() and put_part(). The function main() is a driver. It calls the other functions. Both get_part() and put_part() access the global variable part. In Section 7.3 we discuss the technique of passing a structure as an argument to a function. With that technique we can avoid these side effects.

Note 1: Note the position of this declaration. It is above main() and can be accessed by any of the functions in the file. Declarations inside functions are local to those functions, and cannot be accessed outside their function block. Declarations that appear before any functions can be accessed by any of the functions in the file. In this declaration, the variable part is a global variable. Global variables will be discussed in more detail in Chapter 8.

Note 2: A struct auto_part is declared to have three members, an id member, a price member, and a cur_inv member. This declaration is combined with the declaration of the variable part.

Note 3: This line illustrates the declaration of a local variable of type struct auto_part. The earlier declaration of a struct auto_part declared the members of this structure. The inclusion of the tag auto_part in the earlier declaration allows the reference to that type in the declaration of this variable.

Note 4: The library function strncpy() copies exactly 7 characters from instring to the character array id. The notation part.id accesses the id member of the struct auto_part variable. If one of these characters is a null character (' \0'), the string will be terminated with the copied null. The copied string will not terminate properly if a null character does not occur within the first 7 characters. Therefore, the next statement copies a null into the last cell of the array to make sure that the string is terminated with a null character.

Note that instring is a large buffer. Having this much space allocated for input should help prevent errors.* The parameter 7 to strncpy() assures that the part identification will not overrun the array. If the input were read directly into part.id, the bounds of the array would be overrun when the input consisted of more than 7 characters.

Note 5: The members of the structure are accessed using the dot (.) notation in all of these statements.

Note 6: The assignment statement copies the contents of the local variable instruct bit by bit to the global variable part. Assignment is an operation that operates on a structure as a whole. Few operations have this property. The sizeof() operator is another example of an operation that can act on a whole structure.

Learning Activities

1. Compile and execute struct1.c to ensure that it works on your system.
2. *C by Discovery*
   a. Experiment by omitting the tag auto_part from the structure declaration and try to make the program work.

---

* When efficient memory usage is a priority, this buffer could be cut in size. However, when allocating space, remember that gets() will overrun the bounds of an array when there are too many characters on an input line.

b. Is it possible to make the modified program work with the declaration of a local variable like `instruct`?

c. List some advantages of including a tag. When might the tag be omitted?

3. Start with the original struct1.c again, and experiment by moving the declaration of the structure to different locations to test the scope (the positions where it can be accessed). Move it inside the function main() to see what additional modifications must be made to the program.

4. In the following code segment,

```
struct x {
     int x1;
     char x2;
     char * x3;
};

struct y {
     float y1, y2;
     char y3;
     int y4[5];
} structy1, structy2;
struct x   s1;
```

a. What are the tags in the structure declarations? What are the members of the structures?

b. Which lines allocate storage?

c. Which of the following expressions are illegal? State the types of the following expressions:

    i. `s1.x`   ii. `structy1.y4`   iii. `structy2.y4[3]`

    iv. `s1`   v. `*(s1.x3)`   vi. `&s1.x2`

5. Write a structure declaration that will hold the following information about a student: name, Social Security number, grade point average, total number of completed units, major code (a four-digit number).

6. *C by Discovery* Experiment to see if distinct identifiers must be used for structure tags, members, and variables. Similarly, experiment to see if members of different structure types need to have distinct member names. Summarize your findings and comment on the stylistic consequences.

7. *C by Discovery* Consider the following declarations:

```
struct a {
      char a1;
      int a2;
};
struct b {
      char a1;
      int a2;
};
```

The two structures declarations are very similar. Only the tag differs. Does your compiler recognize these similarities? Is it possible to assign a variable of type `struct a` to a variable of type `struct b` without a type cast and vice versa? Write a short program to answer these questions.

8. *C by Discovery* Consider the following two structure declarations:

```
struct x {                    struct y {
      int a;                        float c;
      float b;                      int d;
};                            };
```

Write a program that declares variables of type `struct x` and `struct y`, initializes one of the variables and attempts to assign the contents of the initialized structure variable to the other variables. Note that this creates an error condition since the two variables have different types. How is this error handled by your system? If there are compile-time errors, add a type cast to the left-hand side of the assignment statement and compile the program again. Once the program compiles, output the members of the structures. Try to generalize what you've learned from this exercise.

7.2 Operations on Structures

Initialization of Structures

Structures can be initialized at the time of declaration in a manner similar to initializing arrays. The member elements are enclosed in braces and separated by commas. For example, after the declaration of a `struct auto_part` that appeared in Example 7-1, the code

```
struct auto_part part3 = { "13J-B0", 13.95, 18 };
```

declares a variable named `part3` of type `struct auto_part` and initializes that variable so that the `id` member has value "13J-B0", the `price` is 13.95, and the `cur_inv` member has the value 18. The initialization values should be constants.*

It is possible to initialize only some of the members. In that case any members not given initial values are set to zero by default. For example,

---

* Older (non-ANSI) compilers may not allow the initialization of structures at the time of declaration. For more information about this see Chapter 8.

```
        struct auto_part part4 = {"23L-t7"};
```
would define the variable part4 and initialize only the id member.

Operations on Structures

Besides the operation of assignment that we saw in the last example, very few operations may operate on a structure as a whole. The operators that access a single member from the structure are always defined. The address operator, &, can be used in most instances. The sizeof() operator is usually defined for structures. The ANSI standards only specify these operators for use with structures. Therefore, the availability of other operators for structures may vary with different implementations of the language. For example, the comparison operators of == and ! = are generally not defined.

A Closer Look

When memory is allocated for a structure variable, space is allocated for each member. The members are stored in the same order as they appear in the member list in the structure declaration. However, there may be unused bytes or bits between structure members, since the computer system may require that certain quantities begin in certain positions in memory. One such common requirement is that an integer should begin on a word boundary in memory.

This is why comparison of two structures for equality is generally not supported. If unused bytes exist within the storage space for the structure, their contents cannot be determined. Therefore, any comparison that only compares bits will not be accurate. Since each different structure declaration may have different members, a single comparison operation for all structure types could not be easily implemented.

Example 7-2 demonstrates the storage of a structure in memory. It uses the sizeof() operator and the address operator on a variable of a structure type and outputs information about its structure variables.

 Example 7-2: stradd.c

```c
/*              stradd.c
 *
 *   Synopsis   -  Outputs the sizeof() a structure and the
 *                 addresses of two structure variables and their
 *                 members.
 *
 *   Objective  -  To demonstrate the layout of a structure in memory.
 */

#include <stdio.h>

struct empl {                                        /* Note 1 */
        char ssn[10];
        char initials[5];
```

```
                float rate;
                float hours;
        };
        void main ()
        {
                struct empl employee1, employee2;
                                                            /* Note 2 */
                printf ("sizeof(struct empl) is %d.\n",
                                        sizeof(struct empl) );
                printf ("employee1 is located at %x.\n", &employee1);
                printf ("employee2 is located at %x.\n", &employee2);

                printf ("\nIn employee1, \n");               /* Note 3 */
                printf ("\tssn is at %x.\n", &employee1.ssn);
                printf ("\tinitials is at %x.\n", &employee1.initials);
                printf ("\trate is at %x.\n", &employee1.rate);
                printf ("\thours is at %x.\n", &employee1.hours);

                printf ("\nIn employee2, \n");
                printf ("\tssn is at %x.\n", &employee2.ssn);
                printf ("\tinitials is at %x.\n", &employee2.initials);
                printf ("\trate is at %x.\n", &employee2.rate);
                printf ("\thours is at %x.\n", &employee2.hours);
        }
```

The program framework is simple. In the function main(), two variables of type `struct empl` are defined; the remainder of the code consists of printf() calls.

Note 1: Again, the declaration of the structure appears above any functions in this source file. Therefore any functions in the file would be able to access it. Often structure declarations like this one would be placed in a header file which would be included in the program source file with a `#include` preprocessor directive. In this program, no global variables are declared. All variables in this program are local to main().

Note 2: The sizeof() a `struct empl` is output. Then the memory location of each of the structure variables is output. This demonstrates that both the sizeof() and address operator can be used with structures.

Note 3: The address of each member of the structure variables is output. The `&` operator can be used with the members of a structure also.

Learning Activities

9. Find out if your system allows the use of the sizeof() and the address operators with structures in C. If it does, proceed with the next two problems.

10. a. Manually calculate the number of bytes in a `struct empl`. Then compile and execute stradd.c. Does the value output for `sizeof(struct empl)` match the value you calculated? If it doesn't, find out what was different and why.

    b. Calculate the difference between the addresses of `employee1` and `employee2`. Does it equal `sizeof(empl)`?

11. a. Draw the layout of the two structures in memory. If there are any unused bytes, mark them.

    b. Experiment by moving the two `float` members to the first members in the declaration of the structure and compile and execute the program again. Draw another memory map for the two variables in the modified program. Did the number or position of unused bytes differ?

7.3   Using Structures with Arrays and Pointers

In the previous section we discussed the fundamentals of using structures. We saw how to declare them and access the members. We also discussed the operations that can be done on a structure. In this section, we discuss arrays of structures, pointers to structures, and structures as parameters to functions. These concepts lay the groundwork for much of the use of structures.

Arrays of Structures

In the previous section we saw that a member of a structure could be an array. In this section we will explore arrays of structures. Consider the declaration

```
struct auto_part   inventory[20];
```

of an array of 20 elements where each element is of type `struct auto_part`. This definition has all properties of any array declaration. The only difference is that each cell is a structure. The expression

```
inventory
```

references the address of the first structure. The expression

```
inventory[2]
```

accesses the third structure (with index 2) in the array. The expression

```
inventory[2].cur_inv
```

accesses the `cur_inv` member of the structure in the third cell. The expression

```
inventory[2].id[3]
```

accesses the fourth character in the `id` member of the structure in the third cell.

Arrays of structures can be initialized by nesting the initial values for each structure as list elements in the braces enclosing the initial values for the array. For example,

```
struct auto_part inventory[20] = { { "3bJ-4F", 1.35, 20 },
                                    { "4tH-2J", .89, 45 },
                                    { "89J-3K", 2.78, 12 }
                                  };
```

will declare the array `inventory` and initialize the first three cells of the array. The remaining cells will be initialized with zeros.*

Pointers to Structures

As with other types in C, pointers to structures can be defined. The declaration

```
struct auto_part  *partptr;
```

declares a variable named `partptr` that is a pointer to a `struct auto_part`. Although a structure of the same type cannot be a member of a structure, a pointer to a structure is allowed. The following declaration should be rejected by the compiler:

Illegal

```
struct node {
    int data;
    struct node y;
};
```

However, the following two declarations are legal. The first is legal because it contains a pointer to a `struct node1` instead of a `struct node`. The second is legal because the structure it contains is not a structure of the type being declared.

Legal	*Legal*

`struct node1 {`
`    int data;`
`    struct node1 *next;`
`};`
	`struct node2 {`
	`    struct auto_part data;`
	`    struct node *next;`
	`};`

The concept of a pointer to structure is used so often in C that a special syntax was developed to reference the members of the target structure. If `partptr` is a variable of type `struct auto_part *` one notation using the `*` selection for referencing the `price` member of the structure pointed to by `partptr` is

```
(*partptr).price
```

The parentheses are necessary in the above syntax because the dot selector, `.`, has higher precedence than the dereferencing operator, `*`.

The following new syntax

---

* Compilers not supporting the ANSI C standards may require that the array of structures be declared outside any function or include the keyword `static`. See Chapter 8 for more information.

partptr->price

also references the `price` member. The syntax consists of the variable name, a hyphen (−), a greater than character (>), followed by the member name. Conventionally this −> notation is used more often with pointers to structures than the method of dereferencing a pointer with an asterisk.

One example of a pointer to a structure is a linked list. The following diagram depicts a linked list of auto parts. The definition for `struct node2` above is the basic structure declaration for this list.

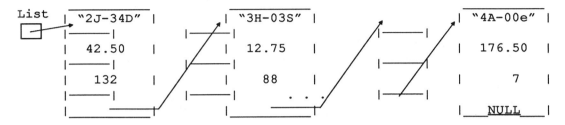

Some of the properties and code related to a linked list are presented in Chapter 11.

Passing Structures to and from Functions

Pointers to structures are also used to pass structures to functions.* When a pointer to a structure is passed to a function, the function can receive the information in the structure and can modify the information.

Example 7-3 declares an array of structures and passes structures to functions with and without a pointer. The latter method is shown for example only. Most programmers would choose to pass a pointer to a structure for efficiency. This program is an extension of program struct1.c from Example 7-1. It initializes an array of `struct auto_part`'s and prints out the inventory.

 Example 7-3: struct2.c

```
/*                      struct2.c
 *
 *   Synopsis   -    Initializes an array of structures from the terminal
 *                   and prints the total inventory to standard output.
 *
 *   Objective  -    To illustrate arrays of structures, pointers to
 *                   structures, and passing structures to functions.
 */
```

---

* Some of the older C compilers do not allow structures to be passed as parameters to functions, but a pointer to a structure can always be a parameter and is generally more efficient than passing the structure itself. Similarly, some but not all compilers allow a function to return a structure as its return value. All C compilers should allow a function to return a pointer to a structure.

```
#include <stdio.h>
#include <stdlib.h>
#include <string.h>
#define DONE      1                                  /* Note 1 */
#define NOTDONE   0
#define IDSIZE    8
#define MAXPARTS  4

struct auto_part {
        char id[IDSIZE];
        float price;
        int cur_inv;
};

void main()
{
        struct auto_part  parts[MAXPARTS];           /* Note 2 */
        int j, i = 0;
        int get_part(struct auto_part *partptr);     /* Note 4 */
        void put_part(struct auto_part part);        /* Note 6 */

        printf("Initializing Inventory\n");
        printf("------------ ---------\n\n");
        while  ( !get_part(parts+i) && ++i < MAXPARTS)  /* Note 3 */
        ;
        if (i == MAXPARTS) printf("Inventory full\n");

        printf("\n\nPrinting Inventory of Auto Parts\n");
        printf("-------- --------- -- ---- -----\n\n");
        for (j = 0; j < i; j++)
                put_part(*(parts+j));                /* Note 6 */
}
/****************************** get_part() ****************/
/*    Inputs information about an auto part from standard input.
 *    Returns value DONE if no information entered, returns
 *    NOTDONE otherwise.
 */
int get_part(struct auto_part *partptr)              /* Note 4 */
{
        char instring[512];

        printf ("Enter the part number (Return if done) : ");
        gets (instring);
        if (strlen(instring) == 0)
                return (DONE);
```

```
        strncpy (partptr->id, instring, IDSIZE-1);        /* Note 5 */
        printf ("Enter the price : ");
        partptr->price = atof(gets(instring));            /* Note 5 */

        printf ("Enter the amount in inventory : ");
        partptr->cur_inv = atoi (gets(instring));         /* Note 5 */
        return (NOTDONE);
}
/*********************************    put_part ()    ***********/
/*      Outputs the information in a struct auto_part.
 */
void put_part (struct auto_part part)                     /* Note 6 */
{
        printf ("Part-id:  %8s\n", part.id);
        printf ("Price :   $%8.2f\n", part.price);
        printf ("Quantity: %8d\n", part.cur_inv);
}
```

The program consists of three functions: main(), get_part() and put_part(). The function main() consists of a while loop and a for loop. The while loop calls get_part() repeatedly to input the inventory information about an auto part. The for loop calls put_part() each time to output the information for a single auto part.

Note 1: Four constants are defined to improve programming style. The constants DONE and NOTDONE relate to the values returned by get_part(). They indicate whether the user has signaled that the inventory input is completed. The constants MAXPARTS and IDSIZE are included to ease program modifiability. Usually there will be more than four different auto parts in the inventory. However, the program is more easily tested with a maximum of just four items. The size of the id member is also subject to change. The program currently allows for a maximum of eight characters. If either of these two values must be changed, it is a simple matter of changing the preprocessor constant.

Note 2: An array of structures is defined. Each cell of the array has enough memory to contain a complete struct auto_part. The array is local to main().

Note 3: The condition for the while statement consists of two tests combined with a logical and, &&. The first test looks at the value returned by get_part(). The value returned is 1 when the user has entered all the inventory information and 0 otherwise. The second test assures that the bounds of the array are not overrun. Note that the parameter to get_part() is the address of one of the elements in the array.

Note 4: The parameter to get_part() is a pointer to or address of a structure. On return from get_part() the referenced structure will have the inventory information that was input.

Note 5: The three statements indicated use the -> syntax to access the members of the structure.

Note 6: The parameter to the function put_part() is a structure.*

Learning Activities

12. a. Try to compile and execute struct2.c. Your compiler may not accept the form of the parameter to put_part().

    b. Modify the function put_part() and the function call to put_part() so that the structure parameter is replaced with a pointer to a structure.

    c. If your compiler accepts both the original and your modified version of the program, compare the size to the executable code to see if there is a difference.

13. Modify the program struct2.c by declaring a pointer to a structure in the function main(). Make all necessary changes so that the new pointer variable is used as an argument to get_part(). (Hint: The pointer variable should be initialized to point to the first cell of the array. Then the pointer variable should be incremented to traverse the array.)

14. a. Compile and execute the following program to verify that pointer arithmetic with structures works as you think it should.

```
/*                      la14.c
 *
 *     Synopsis   -   Outputs the sizeof() a structure and
 *                    the values of two pointer arithmetic
 *                    expressions.
 *
 *     Objective  -   To provide practice with pointer
 *                    arithmetic with pointers to structures.
 */

#include <stdio.h>
```

---

* Changes for efficiency or for older compilers that do not accept a structure as a parameter to a function would involve changing the type of the parameter to a `struct auto_part *` and accessing the members with the -> selection operator.

```
struct auto_part {
        char id[8];
        float price;
        int cur_inv;
} part;                                                        /* Note 1 */

void main()
{
        struct auto_part * partptr = &part;

        printf ("sizeof(part) %d\n", sizeof(part) );
        printf ("partptr %d, partptr+1 %d\n", partptr, partptr+1);

}
```

b. Predict the output of the following statement:

```
printf("%d\n", (partptr+1) - partptr);
```

Add the statement to the above program and verify your prediction. Explain the output and adjust any mistakes in your thinking.

15. *C by Discovery* Is it possible to have the field width spacing in the printf() calls in put_part() equal the contant IDSIZE? In other words, if IDSIZE replaces the field width 8 in the printf() control strings, will the preprocessor find it and substitute the value? Experiment to find out what happens. Explain every part of the output of these statements when the 8 is replaced by IDSIZE.

16. Write a function that returns a pointer to the first structure in an array of structures where the number of parts in the inventory is less than 5.

7.4   Bit Fields

C allows different members of a structure to be packed into one word of memory with a construct called a bit field. This construct allows the programmer to have direct access to the bits as well as having some control over the memory allocation in a program.

If a bit field is included in a structure definition, the number of bits that a bit field should occupy is specified. Theoretically, the compiler will pack as many bit field members as possible into a single word of memory. The following declaration

```
struct bits {
     unsigned  a : 4;
     unsigned  b : 2;
} bitvar;
```

declares a structure with two members. Both members are bit fields. The member a will occupy 4 bits; the member b will occupy 2 bits. Bit fields are declared by following the name of the member with a colon and the number of bits the member is to occupy.

The ANSI C standards require that a bit field must be either an int, unsigned int, or signed int.*

Often bit fields are used to try to match a hardware or software feature of a computer system exactly. For example, consider an assembly language that supports several addressing modes. The instruction (opcode), the operands, and the addressing modes for the instruction might be packed together into a single word of memory. If a word consists of sixteen bits, one way to pack this information for an assembly language instruction that takes two operands is as shown in Figure 7-1.

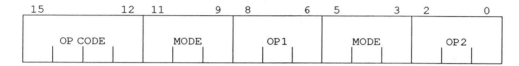

Figure 7-1

A structure defined to match that configuration exactly could be declared as follows:

```
struct two_ops {
       unsigned opcode      : 4;
       unsigned addr_mode1 : 3;
       unsigned operand1   : 3;
       unsigned addr_mode2 : 3;
       unsigned operand2   : 3;
} instruction;
```

In this structure, 4 bits would be allowed for the opcode and 3 bits would be allowed for each addressing mode and each operand. The structure could be packed into 16 bits. This configuration would allow for 2^4 or 16 different instructions and 2^3 or 8 different addressing modes and representation of operands. The identifier instruction is a variable of type struct two_ops. Code that tests the value of the member addr_mode1 in instruction is presented below. The action necessary to process addressing mode 3 is represented by a call to a function mode3().

```
if (instruction.addr_mode1 == 3)
    mode3(instruction);
```

Bit fields can also be used when memory is at a premium. For example, consider a system in which an integer occupies two bytes. Each variable of type struct bits that was defined above would occupy one byte of memory while a comparable structure with two members of type unsigned int that were not bit fields would occupy four bytes. The use of a variable of type struct bits would be even more space efficient on a system in which an integer occupies four bytes. The total amount of memory that is used might also depend on alignment requirements. These requirements might cause a variable's storage to begin on a word boundary and cut

---

* Older compilers may limit the type of a bit field member to unsigned int.

down the memory savings, but even so, bit fields offer the potential of using memory more efficiently.

A disadvantage of using bit fields lies in the lack of portability. The method with which bit fields are packed into words of memory can vary with the implementations of C. Therefore, programs that use bit fields may not port successfully to other implementations.

The program bitfld.c of Example 7-4 uses bit fields in an attempt to save memory. A structure that represents an employee is declared with two bit fields. The program demonstrates the assignment of values to a bit field and the accessing of those values.

Example 7-4: bitfld.c

```
/*                bitfld.c
 *
 *    Synopsis  -  Declares a structure with bit fields, outputs its
 *                 size in bytes, initializes the structure
 *                 and outputs it.
 *
 *    Objective -  Provides an example of a structure with bit fields.
 */

#include <stdio.h>
#include <string.h>

struct empl {
        char ssn[10];
        float rate;
        char initials[4];
        unsigned vested:1;                              /* Note 1 */
        unsigned years_of_service : 6;                  /* Note 2 */
};

void main()
{
        void put_empl(struct empl emp);
        struct empl empl;
                                                        /* Note 3 */
        printf ("sizeof(struct empl)  %d.\n", sizeof(struct empl) );

        strcpy (empl.ssn, "567624256");
        empl.rate = 7.50;
        strcpy (empl.initials, "WLF");
        empl.vested = 1;                                /* Note 4 */
        empl.years_of_service = 17;
```

```
            put_empl(emp1);
}


/********************************   put_empl()   **********/
/*   Outputs contents of a struct empl to the terminal         */

void put_empl(struct empl emp)
{
        printf ("SSN:    %12s\n", emp.ssn);
        printf ("Rate:   $%12.2f\n", emp.rate);
        printf ("Initials%12s\n", emp.initials );
        printf ("vested  %12d\n", emp.vested );                /* Note 5 */
        printf ("years of service %3d\n", emp.years_of_service);
}
```

The program consists of the functions main() and put_empl(). The function main() consists of a printf() call, calls to strcpy(), assignment statements to initialize the structure, and a call to put_empl(). The function put_empl() does output with calls to printf().

Note 1: The declaration of `struct empl` contains two bit field members and three members that are not bit fields. The member `vested` is a bit field that occupies one bit. The bit would be set to one to indicate that the employee is vested in the retirement plan and cleared to indicate lack of vesting.

Note 2: The field `years_of_service` consists of six bits. The allowable values are from 0 to 63 (2^6-1).

Note 3: The next call to printf() outputs the sizeof() a `struct empl`. Theoretically, the last two members of the structure should occupy only one byte.

Note 4: Assignments to the bit fields are done with unsigned expressions in ordinary assignment statements.

Note 5: The bit fields are output by the calls to printf(). Again, the access is the same as for other members of the structure. The `%d` conversion specification can be used, as could the `%o`, `%x`, and `%u`.

Learning Activities

17. Compile and execute bitfld.c to make sure that it works correctly on your system. Is the value output for
    sizeof(struct empl)
    consistent with the concept of packing the two bit fields into one byte?

18. Modify the function put_empl() so that the Social Security number is output in the form 567-62-4256.

19. Experiment to see if your system will allow types other than unsigned int for a bit field member of a structure. Explain your findings. What types are allowed?
20. Try to output the address of the bit field members of emp1. This should cause an error. Is it flagged as a compile-time error, a runtime error, or is it not flagged as an error at all?
21. Try to create an error condition by assigning values that take more memory than allocated in the bit fields to the members vested and years_of_service. Assign a value greater than 1 to vested and assign a value greater than 63 to the member years_of_service. Is this error caught at compile time? At runtime? Not at all?
22. Experiment by changing the size of the bit field years_of_service to see if your compiler imposes a maximum number on the bits in a bit field. Describe the results of your experiment.

Cautions with Bit Fields

We mentioned previously that programs using bit fields may not be portable. Bit fields must be stored sequentially in words of memory, but some computer systems store them from left to right while others store from right to left. This makes source code that accesses the bits by position, as with a bit mask, a potential portability problem.

The address operator, &, cannot be used with bit fields so that location of the fields in memory cannot be ascertained. Similarly, a pointer cannot be assigned to point to a bit field member of a structure. Both restrictions occur because a bit field is not required to start on a boundary of a byte or a word and therefore may not be able to be addressed. The method of storing the bit fields in memory should be documented in the compiler manual. Consult this manual before programming with bit fields.

Many implementations of C restrict the maximum number of bits that can be contained in a bit field. That maximum is usually the number of bits in a word of memory and can vary with different hardware systems.

Sometimes you may wish to access both the bits and the bytes in the same quantity. Program bitfld2.c in Example 7-5 illustrates one possibility for doing that. Two different structures containing bit fields are declared for the purpose of accessing the bits and the bytes in a word of memory. Structure pointers are initialized to point to a variable of type short int that contains the quantity in question. This allows both bit and byte access.

Example 7-5: bitfld2.c

```
/*              bitfld2.c
 *
 *   Synopsis  -  Outputs the values of the bits and the bytes in a
 *               short int.
 *
 *   Objective -  To illustrate the use of bit fields in accessing
 *               the bits and bytes of a quantity.
 */
#include <stdio.h>
void main()
{
        struct bits {                                     /* Note 1 */
                unsigned first:1;
                unsigned second:1;
                unsigned third:1;
                unsigned fourth:1;
                unsigned fifth:1;
                unsigned sixth:1;
                unsigned seventh:1;
                unsigned eighth:1;
                unsigned ninth:1;
                unsigned tenth:1;
                unsigned eleventh:1;
                unsigned twelfth:1;
                unsigned thirteenth:1;
                unsigned fourteenth:1;
                unsigned fifteenth:1;
                unsigned sixteenth:1;
        } *bit_access;

        struct bytes {                                    /* Note 2 */
                unsigned first:8;
                unsigned second :8;
        } *byte_access;

        unsigned short twobytes;                          /* Note 3 */

                                                          /* Note 4 */
        printf ("sizeof(struct bits)  %d.\n", sizeof(struct bits));
        printf ("sizeof(struct bytes) %d.\n", sizeof(struct bytes));
        printf ("sizeof(twobytes)     %d.\n\n", sizeof(twobytes) );

        twobytes = 0x1248;                                /* Note 5 */
        byte_access = (struct bytes *) &twobytes;         /* Note 6 */
```

```
bit_access  =  (struct bits *)   &twobytes;

                                                    /* Note 7 */
printf ("first byte %x, second byte %x.\n\n",
        byte_access->first, byte_access->second);
                                                    /* Note 8 */
printf ("Bits:\tfirst         %x,   second        %x,\n",
        bit_access->first, bit_access->second);
printf ("\tthird        %x,   fourth        %x,\n",
        bit_access->third, bit_access->fourth);
printf ("\tfifth        %x,   sixth         %x,\n",
        bit_access->fifth, bit_access->sixth);
printf ("\tseventh      %x,   eighth        %x,\n",
        bit_access->seventh, bit_access->eighth);
printf ("\tninth        %x,   tenth         %x,\n",
        bit_access->ninth, bit_access->tenth);
printf ("\televenth     %x,   twelfth       %x,\n",
        bit_access->eleventh, bit_access->twelfth);
printf ("\tthirteenth %x,   fourteenth %x,\n",
        bit_access->thirteenth, bit_access->fourteenth);
printf ("\tfifteenth    %x,   sixteenth   %x,\n",
        bit_access->fifteenth, bit_access->sixteenth);
}
```

The program consists of the single function main(). Besides the structure declarations, the code consists of three assignment statements and numerous calls to printf().

Note 1: A structure is declared that consists of sixteen bit fields. Each bit field contains one bit. The variable `bit_access` is a pointer to a quantity of type `struct bits`.

Note 2: A structure is declared that consists of two bit fields. Each bit field contains eight bits (one byte on most computer systems). The variable `byte_access` will point to a quantity of type `struct bytes`.

Note 3: A variable named `twobytes` of type `short int` is declared. The intent is that both structures take up the same number of bytes as this variable. If that is not true on your computer system, some adjustment may be needed for this program to work properly. The order in which your computer stores the bytes may also cause a problem with this program.

Note 4: The sizeof() each of the three quantities in question is output. If they do not agree with each other, adjust the declarations so that they do.

Note 5: A hexadecimal value is assigned to the variable `twobytes`. The value was written in hexadecimal for ease of checking the value of each bit and byte.

Note 6: Each of the pointer variables is assigned to point at `twobytes`. A type cast is used in each case to force the address of `twobytes` to be interpreted as the address of the relevant structure.

Note 7: The value of each byte is output.

Note 8: The value of each bit is output.

Learning Activities

23. a. Predict the output of bitfld2.c.

    b. Execute it to check your prediction. Resolve any differences between your prediction and the actual output.

    c. Is your concept of the first and second byte the same as the computer's?

    d. Notice the order in which your computer stores the bit fields in a word of memory. Is that what you expected?

24. Experiment by assigning different values to twobytes to make sure that the program works similarly with different values.

25. Experiment further with bitfld2.c by attempting some of the things mentioned under cautions. For example, try to output the address of a bit field and discover what type of error, if any, is reported. Try to port this program to a different computer system to see if the bit packing mechanism works the same.

Unnamed Bit Fields

Bit fields can be specified in a structure declaration without a name, as in this example:

```
struct unnamed {
    unsigned f1 : 5;
    unsigned    : 3;
    unsigned f3 : 7;
};
```

The second field does not have an identifier specified as the field name. The field serves as padding, and will force the third field to begin on the boundary of a byte. In this case, the second field cannot be accessed and its contents cannot be specified.

A special case of unnamed bit fields allows an unnamed bit field to be declared with zero bytes specified, as in

```
struct unnamed {
    unsigned f1 : 5;
    unsigned    : 0;
    unsigned f3 : 7;
};
```

This is a signal to the compiler that the programmer wants the field f3 to begin at the next "appropriate" spot in memory. That could be at a word or a byte boundary, depending on the underlying hardware and addressing modes.

7.5   Enumerated Types

Enumerated types are scalar types in C. They are presented in this chapter because they are often used in conjunction with structures and unions. Enumerated types are used to declare a set of integer constants in C. A declaration like

```
enum boolean {
     FALSE, TRUE
};
```

would be roughly equivalent to the two preprocessor directives

```
#define FALSE   0
#define TRUE    1
```

Without further specification in the `enum` declaration, `FALSE` would have the value 0 and `TRUE` would have the value 1. The word `enum` is a keyword. One of the differences between the two constructs is that after defining `enum boolean`, it is possible to define variables of that type. For example,

```
enum boolean   correct;
```

would define a variable named `correct` that is legally supposed to accept only the values `FALSE` and `TRUE`. Note that compilers are not required to check that an assigned value is in the declared list, and assignments such as

```
correct = 7;
```

may be accepted.*

A declaration of type `enum` has the following syntax: the keyword `enum`, an optional tag, an open brace, a comma-separated list of identifiers, and a close brace. In the declaration

```
enum trees {
     oak, maple, cherry, spruce, pine
};
```

the type `enum trees` and five constants have been declared. The identifier `trees` is the optional tag. The pair `enum trees` refers to this type declaration. No variables have been declared yet. A declaration

```
enum trees    tree1;
```

would define a variable named `tree1` that can legally assume any of the values in the identifier list. This variable declaration could have been combined with the type declaration as in the following:

```
enum trees {
     oak, maple, cherry, spruce, pine
} tree1;
```

The default values assigned to the identifiers are as follows: The first identifier, `oak` in this example, has the value 0, the second identifier, `maple`, has the value 1, and so on. By default, 0 is assigned to the first identifier in an `enum` definition,

---

* On a UNIX system, the program lint may catch errors of this type.

and each succeeding identifer is assigned successive integer values. The values assigned to these identifiers are constant. They cannot be changed.

The main reason for using enumerated types is to improve the readability and maintainability of C source code. Other advantages include the automatic assignment and accounting of values. Enumerated types may not be fully implemented on a compiler that does not meet the ANSI C standards. The program boolean.c in Example 7-6 demonstrates a simple use of an enumerated type variable to simulate Boolean variables.

 Example 7-6: boolean.c

```
/*                      boolean.c
 *
 *    Synopsis   -   Accepts input of a positive integer and displays
 *                   all its factors.
 *
 *    Objective  -   Illustrates the use of the enumerated type to
 *                   create a variable that takes values TRUE and
 *                   FALSE.
 */

#include <stdio.h>
#include <stdlib.h>

enum boolean { FALSE, TRUE };                            /* Note 1 */

void main()
{
        enum boolean prime;                              /* Note 2 */
        int num, divisor;
        char inarray[80];

        printf("Enter a positive integer to be tested: ");
        num = atoi(gets(inarray));

        if (num <= 0) {
                printf("Sorry, that number wasn't positive.\n");
                exit(1);
        }

        prime = TRUE;                                    /* Note 3 */
        printf("List of divisors: 1 ");

        for (divisor = 2; divisor < num; divisor++)
                if ( !( num % divisor )) {
```

```
                              printf(" %d ", divisor);
                              prime = FALSE;                    /* Note 4 */
                      }

              if (num != 1)
                      printf(" %d\n", num);
              else
                      prime = FALSE;                            /* Note 5 */

              if (prime)                                        /* Note 6 */
                      printf("%d is a prime number\n", num);
      }
```

The program consists of the single function main(). It does its input with gets() and converts the input to type int with atoi(). A for loop is used to test for and output all possible factors of num. The final factor is output for values of num that are greater than 1, with an added message when num is prime.

Note 1: The type enum boolean is declared. In this example, FALSE will have the value 0 and TRUE will have the value 1. These values agree with the usual interpretation of 0 and 1 by the C language. No variables have been declared yet, and no space has been allocated. The declaration appears above the function main() and therefore would be known by any functions in this source code file.

Note 2: A variable named prime of type enum boolean is declared. The only values that prime can take on are TRUE and FALSE.

Note 3: The variable prime is initialized to TRUE. It will only be assigned the value FALSE when a divisor of num is found.

Note 4: The variable prime is assigned the value FALSE. The expression num % divisor was zero, which indicated that divisor divided num evenly. Then divisor was output and prime set to FALSE. This suppresses the final message.

Note 5: The integer 1 is a special case. The factor 1 has already been output and should not be output again. Also, 1 is not a prime, but the previous for loop did not test that value. Here prime is set to FALSE if num is 1.

Note 6: The value of prime is tested to determine whether or not to output the final message.

Learning Activities

26. Compile and execute boolean.c and make sure that you understand how it works.
27. Modify boolean.c by adding a printf() call to output the value of prime as a decimal integer (%d conversion specification) at the end of the program. Test this modified program with both a prime and a nonprime integer as input. Are the values output the ones that you expected?
28. Modify boolean.c by declaring a variable named done of type enum boolean. Initialize done to FALSE and use it to drive a while loop that will allow a user to test many values without rerunning the program. Most of the existing program should be inside the while loop. You will also need to provide a way for the user to signal when there are no more integers to test. In this case, done should be set to TRUE and the while loop should terminate.
29. Write a program that inputs an integer and outputs a message indicating whether or not it is prime. You can use this program as a basis, but try to improve its efficiency. All your program needs to do is to determine whether or not its input is prime, so there is no need to test every factor.

A Closer Look

The default values of 0 for the first identifier in an enumerated type, 1 for the second, and so on can be overridden with specific assignment of values. In the declaration

```
enum trees {
    oak=5, maple=3, cherry, spruce=1, pine=1
};
```

oak is given the value 5, maple is given the value 3, spruce is given the value 1, and pine is given the value 1. Notice that two different identifiers can be assigned the same value. Also notice that cherry was not explicitly assigned a value. The compiler automatically assigns the value 4 to cherry, since it appears in the list immediately after maple, which was assigned the value 3.

Operations with the enum types are limited. The values represented by the identifier list are treated as constants of type int by the compiler and can appear anywhere in the syntax that any int constant can. After declaration of a variable of an enum type, values from the identifier list can be assigned to it, as in the following statement:

```
tree1 = oak;
```

Also, values can be tested for equality, as in

```
if (tree1 == spruce)
    dosomething();
```

Other than assignment and equality tests, no other operations must be supported by an ANSI C compiler. However, on many compilers, `enum` types are treated as `int`s and other comparisons and operations can be done. Code using these extended features may not be portable; therefore its use is discouraged.

The program enumindx.c in Example 7-7 makes use of the fact that the enumerated types are based on type `int`. It uses an enumerated type variable as an index into an array. This use depends on the first identifier in the type declaration having value 0, the second having value 1, and so on. These values match those used for array indices.

The enumerated type is used in this program for readability. Instead of the reader having to remember that `salesrecord[0]` is the number of jade items sold and that `salesrecord[1]` is the number of navy items sold, the program could refer to `salesrecord[jade]` and `salesrecord[navy]`. The routines get_sales() and print_sales() are utility functions that input and output the contents of the array `salesrecord`. These utility functions could be used in a program for a manufacturing or mail order firm that keeps sales and inventory records.

 Example 7-7: enumindx.c

```
/*              enumindx.c
 *
 *   Synopsis  -  Inputs the number sold of each color of an item
 *                into an array and outputs the contents of the array.
 *
 *   Objective -  Illustrates the use of enum types for indexing an
 *                array and the underlying connection between
 *                enum types and ints.
 */

#include <stdio.h>

enum color { jade, navy, white, coral, maize };         /* Note 1 */

void makestring(enum color icolor, char *s);            /* Note 2 */
void print_sales(int sales[]);
void get_sales(int *record);

void main()
{
        int salesrecord[5];

        get_sales (salesrecord);
        print_sales(salesrecord);

}
```

```
/*********************************    makestring()    **********/
/*      makestring() - Creates a string containing the color currently
 *      contained in item_color.  Used to aid output.
 */

void makestring (enum color item_color, char *string)    /* Note 3 */
{
        switch (item_color) {                            /* Note 4 */
                case jade:  strcpy (string, "jade");
                        break;
                case navy:  strcpy (string, "navy");
                        break;
                case white: strcpy (string, "white");
                        break;
                case coral: strcpy (string, "coral");
                        break;
                case maize: strcpy (string, "maize");
        }
}

/*******************************    print_sales()    ************/
/*      print_sales() - Will output the color and contents of each
 *      cell of sales[].  Uses the integer representation of the
 *      colors.
 */
void print_sales (int sales[])
{
        int i;
        char colorstr[6];

        printf("The sales record shows the following ");
        printf("sales by color.\n");

        for( i = 0; i < 5; i++) {
                makestring(i, colorstr);                 /* Note 5 */
                printf("%5s : %d\n", colorstr, sales[i]);
        }
}

/*******************************    get_sales()    ************/
/*      get_sales() - Inputs the sales record of each color item from
 *      standard input.  Uses the identifier form of the color.
 */
void get_sales(int *salesrecord)
{
        enum color dresscolor;
        char colorstr[6];
```

```
        printf ("Enter the number of each color sold:\n");
                                                    /* Note 6 */
        for (dresscolor = jade; dresscolor <= maize; dresscolor++) {
                makestring (dresscolor, colorstr);       /* Note 7 */
                printf ("%5s : ", colorstr );
                scanf ("%d", &salesrecord[dresscolor]); /* Note 8 */
        }
}
```

This program contains four functions: main(), makestring(), get_sales() and print_sales(). The function main() is a driver; it calls getsales() to input the sales record from the terminal and print_sales() to output the sales record. The function makestring() provides a connection between the identifiers used in the enumerated type and the corresponding string. For example, if the enumerated type value jade is passed in item_color, the string "jade" is passed back in string.

The functions get_sales() and print_sales() both call makestring(). Both functions use a different syntax. In get_sales(), a variable dresscolor of type enum color is declared and used as an index to the array of ints; this variable is passed as a parameter to makestring(). In print_sales() an int variable is used as the index to the array of ints and passed to makestring().

Note 1: The type enum color is declared. The value of jade will be 0, the value of navy will be 1, and so on.

Note 2: The functions makestring(), get_sales(), and print_sales() are declared with type void. Since this declaration is above all function blocks, it is valid until the end of this source file.

Note 3: The parameters to makestring() are declared in the syntax of ANSI C. If you do not have an ANSI C compiler, you will need to change the function declarations before running this program.

The first parameter is declared to be of type enum color. An integer in the range 0 through 4 could be passed as the actual parameter.

Note 4: The parameter is used as the expression in the switch statement. Because the identifiers jade, navy, white, coral, and maize are integer constants, they can be used in the case labeled statements.

Note 5: In this call to makestring() an integer in the range 0 to 4 is passed as the actual parameter. This same parameter is also used to index the array salesrecord[].

Note 6: The enumerated type variable dresscolor is used to drive this for loop. In the expression that is evaluated at the bottom of the loop, dresscolor is incremented as if it had type int. Note that the relational operator <= was used with the enumerated type. The operations of incrementing and using the relational operator with enumerated types may not be supported on all compilers.

Note 7: In this call to makestring(), the parameter has type enum color. This could be replaced with an int, as in the call referenced by Note 5.

Note 8: The variable `dresscolor` can be used to index the array `salesrecord[]`.

Learning Activities

30. Compile and execute enumindx.c. Test it with several different inputs.
31. Write a program that allows the user to request output of the number of items sold of any color. The program should first call get_sales() to initialize the array and then ask the user for a color. It should then output the contents of the corresponding element of the array.
32. Given the declaration

```
enum languages {
        french=12, english, russian, chinese=4,  C,
        swedish
};
```

what is the value of each of the following constants?

english	_____
russian	_____
C	_____
swedish	_____

33. Assume the following declaration:

```
enum languages  spoken;
```

Which of the expressions involve standard operations with the enumerated type `enum languages`? Which may cause portability problems?

Expression	*Legal or Illegal?*
spoken = C;	_____
french <= russian	_____
spoken++;	_____
french + english	_____
french + 15	_____
spoken == chinese	_____

7.6 Unions

A union is another aggregate data type that is designed to hold members of different types. It is like a structure in that a list of members is declared. However, it differs from a structure in that a union will only contain one of its members at any instant. When a union is declared, enough storage is allocated for the member requiring the greatest amount of memory. When a value is assigned to any member of a union, it will overwrite any data previously stored in the union.

"A union will only contain one of its members at any instant." From the painting
The Proposal **by William Powell Frith, 1877.**

The declaration of a union is like that of a structure. It has the general form

```
union tag { member list };
```

where union is a keyword and the tag is an optional identifier. The member list appears inside the matched braces and members are declared identically to the members in a structure declaration. For example,

```
union rate {
      float per_hour;
      int per_week;
};
```

declares a type that can later be referred to as union rate. It contains the two members, per_hour of type float and per_week of type int. Only one of those members can be occupied at any one time.

The rules for declaring unions are the same as those for declaring structures. The members of a union can be any type except void or a function type. A union may not contain a union of its own type as a member. Members of a union may be a pointer to a union of the same type or a pointer to a function.

As with structures, it is possible to have arrays of unions and pointers to unions. Also, arrays and pointers can be members of unions.

Again, like a structure, the members of a union can be accessed directly with the dot selector or through a pointer variable with the -> member selection method. For example, consider the following declarations:

```
union rate payrate,
         *ptr_rate = &payrate;
```

The variable payrate is a variable of type union rate. The variable ptr_rate is a pointer to a union rate; it has been initialized to point to payrate.

The assignment

```
payrate.per_hour = 10.85;
```

gives a value to the per_hour member of payrate. The statement

```
ptr_rate->per_hour += 1.50;
```

is a compound assignment that adds 1.50 to the per_hour member. The expression ptr_rate->per_hour refers to the per_hour member of the contents of ptr_rate. A subsequent assignment of

```
ptr_rate->per_week = 950;
```

initializes the per_week member of payrate (or *ptr_rate). At this point, the per_hour field no longer contains meaningful data. It has been overwritten.

There is no automatic mechanism to determine which member of a union is in use at any time. It is up to the programmer to keep track. Often an enumerated type is used with a union to establish which member is being used.

Unions are often included as part of a structure. The program unions.c in Example 7-8 includes a member of type union rate in a structure designed to hold information about an employee. A member of type enum paytype with the values hourly and salaried is also included to indicate which union member is in use.

 Example 7-8: unions.c

```
/*               unions.c
 *
 *    Synopsis  -  Inputs and outputs information for one employee.
 *
 *    Objective -  To demonstrate use of enum types to keep track
```

```
 *                    of the contents of a union.
 */

#include <stdio.h>
#include <stdlib.h>

enum paytype { hourly, salaried };                       /* Note 1 */

union rate {                                             /* Note 2 */
       float per_hour;
       int   per_week;
};

struct employee {
       char name[20];
       char ssn[12];
       enum paytype paytype;                            /* Note 3 */
       union rate payrate;
};

void reademp(struct employee *empp);
void printemp(struct employee emp);

void main()
{
       struct employee emp;

       reademp (&emp);
       printemp (emp);
}

/************************************   reademp()   ********/
/*  Inputs information from the keyboard into a struct employee  */

void reademp (struct employee *emptr)
{
       char instring[80];

       printf ("Enter the following information for the employee.\n");
       printf ("Name : ");
       gets(emptr->name);
       printf ("Social Security Number: ");
       gets (emptr->ssn);
       printf ("Hourly or salaried (h or s) : ");
       gets (instring);
```

```
                                                          /* Note 4 */
        if ( (*instring == 'h') || (*instring == 'H') )
                emptr->paytype = hourly;
        else if ( (*instring == 's') || (*instring == 'S') )
                emptr->paytype = salaried;
        else {
                printf ("Illegal paytype, program terminated.\n");
                exit(1);                                  /* Note 5 */
        }
        if (emptr->paytype == hourly) {                   /* Note 6 */
                printf ("Enter the hourly rate: ");
                emptr->payrate.per_hour = atof(gets(instring) );
        }
        else {
                printf ("Enter the weekly salary: ");
                emptr->payrate.per_week = atoi (gets(instring) );
        }
}


/************************************  printemp()  ********/
/*  Outputs the contents of the struct employee parameter      */

void printemp (struct employee emp)
{
        printf ("Name :    %s\n", emp.name);
        printf ("Social Sec. No. : %s\n", emp.ssn);
        if (emp.paytype == hourly)                        /* Note 7 */
                printf ("Hourly rate   : $%7.2f\n",
                                        emp.payrate.per_hour);
        else
                printf ("Weekly Salary : $%7d\n",
                                        emp.payrate.per_week);
}
```

The program consists of the functions main(), reademp(), and printemp(). A variable of type struct employee is declared in main(); main() then calls reademp() to input data into the variable and calls printemp() to output the data. The program might be a first step in developing a larger payroll program. Note that the ANSI C prototype has been used when declaring the functions reademp() and printemp(). You may need to modify this if you do not have an ANSI compiler.

Note 1: The type enum paytype is declared. It will be used to keep track of the active member of the union.

Note 2: The type union rate is declared. If the employee is paid by the hour, the pay rate is stored in type float. However, for an employee who is paid by the week, the pay rate is stored in an int.

Note 3: The type struct employee contains both a member of type enum paytype and a member of type union rate. Note that the identifier paytype can be used both as a tag in the declaration of the enum type and as the name of a member in the structure without conflict. Even though this double use of an identifier is discouraged, the compiler is able to distinguish the different contexts.

Note 4: To process the answer to the query "Hourly or salaried (h or s) : ", the following compound if-else statement inspects the first character of the input string. The appropriate value is assigned to the paytype member of the struct employee variable.

Note 5: The program is terminated in the case of incorrect input. This is a little extreme. Instead, the user could be given a chance to reenter the paytype.

Note 6: The value of the paytype member is checked before access to the payrate member. In this way the correct member of the union can be accessed.

Note 7: Again the value of the paytype member is tested before accessing the union member. One way to keep track of which member of the union rate is active is to set the paytype member every time the union member is set, and to evaluate the paytype member before every access to the member of type union rate.

Learning Activities

34. In the program unions.c, rewrite the error check on the paytype. Give the user another chance to enter the paytype correctly instead of terminating the program. If necessary, modify any other references to the paytype member so that a user can be sure that the paytype member has been set correctly at any time.

35. Note that no error check is done on the input of name or payrate.
    a. Can you think of any appropriate error check for the name input?

    b. What might be an appropriate error check for the input of payrate? Implement it.

36. Must the parameter to reademp() be a pointer? Why or why not?

37. What happens when one union member is active and the other is accessed in the program? Modify the program by having the function printemp() always output an hourly salary. Compile and execute the program and enter the data for a salaried employee. Does the program execute properly? Explain what you think happens.

A Second Example with a Union

The fact that the C language does not keep track of which member of a union is active can sometimes be used to advantage. Programmers can assign a value to one union member and access other union members to obtain or create different data. However, programs written using that technique may not be portable.

Program union2.c in Example 7-9 illustrates a second method of accessing both bits and bytes in a quantity. It is very similar to the program bitfld2.c except that it uses a union in conjunction with bit field members of structures. The same two structures are declared with the bit fields representing the bits and the bytes in a quantity of type `short`, which is assumed to contain 16 bits or two bytes. However, this time a union is defined with three members, one that references the whole quantity, one of type `struct bytes`, and one of type `struct bits`. These latter two members are used to access the bytes and the bits, respectively, of the quantity.

Example 7-9: union2.c

```
/*                 union2.c
 *
 *    Synopsis   -  Outputs the values of the bits and the bytes in a
 *                  short int.
 *
 *    Objective  -  To illustrate the use of bit fields and unions in
 *                  accessing the bits and bytes of a quantity.
 */
#include <stdio.h>

void main()
{
        struct bits {                                  /* Note 1 */
                unsigned first:1;
                unsigned second:1;
                unsigned third:1;
                unsigned fourth:1;
                unsigned fifth:1;
                unsigned sixth:1;
                unsigned seventh:1;
                unsigned eighth:1;
                unsigned ninth:1;
                unsigned tenth:1;
                unsigned eleventh:1;
                unsigned twelfth:1;
                unsigned thirteenth:1;
                unsigned fourteenth:1;
                unsigned fifteenth:1;
                unsigned sixteenth:1;
        } ;

        struct bytes {                                 /* Note 2 */
                unsigned first:8;
                unsigned second:8;
        } ;
```

```
union access {                                    /* Note 3 */
        short whole;
        struct bits bit_access;
        struct bytes byte_access;
} testvar;

                                                  /* Note 4 */
printf ("sizeof(struct bits)  %d.\n", sizeof(struct bits));
printf ("sizeof(struct bytes) %d.\n", sizeof(struct bytes));
printf ("sizeof(union access) %d.\n\n",
                                   sizeof(union access) );

testvar.whole = 0x1248;                           /* Note 5 */

                                                  /* Note 6 */
printf ("first byte %x, second byte %x.\n\n",
        testvar.byte_access.first, testvar.byte_access.second);
                                                  /* Note 7 */
printf ("Bits:\tfirst        %x,   second        %x,\n",
        testvar.bit_access.first, testvar.bit_access.second);
printf ("\tthird        %x,   fourth        %x,\n",
        testvar.bit_access.third, testvar.bit_access.fourth);
printf ("\tfifth        %x,   sixth        %x,\n",
        testvar.bit_access.fifth, testvar.bit_access.sixth);
printf ("\tseventh      %x,   eighth       %x,\n",
        testvar.bit_access.seventh, testvar.bit_access.eighth);
printf ("\tninth        %x,   tenth        %x,\n",
        testvar.bit_access.ninth, testvar.bit_access.tenth);
printf ("\televenth     %x,   twelfth      %x,\n",
        testvar.bit_access.eleventh,
        testvar.bit_access.twelfth);
printf ("\tthirteenth %x,   fourteenth   %x,\n",
        testvar.bit_access.thirteenth,
        testvar.bit_access.fourteenth);
printf ("\tfifteenth   %x,   sixteenth    %x,\n",
        testvar.bit_access.fifteenth,
        testvar.bit_access.sixteenth);
}
```

The program consists of the single function main(). The executable code consists of a single assignment statement and calls to printf().

Note 1: A structure is declared that consists of sixteen bit fields. Each bit field contains one bit.

Note 2: A structure is declared that consists of two bit fields. Each bit field contains eight bits or one byte on most computer systems.

Note 3: A union with three members is declared. If a short int occupies two bytes, all three members should occupy the same amount of space. The hope is that the member of type short int can be initialized and the structure members can be accessed. This should allow access to the bytes of the short int with the byte_access member and access to any specific bit with the bit_access member. A portability problem may occur since the bit fields may be packed in the 16 bits in either order, but the code should be workable for any one system. The method of packing the bit fields should be apparent from running this program.

Note 4: The sizeof() each of the three quantities in question is output. If they do not agree with each other, adjust the declarations so that they do before interpreting the results of the program.

Note 5: A hexadecimal value is assigned to the variable testvar. The value was written in hexadecimal for ease in checking the value of each bit and byte.

Note 6: The value of each byte is output.

Note 7: The value of each bit is output.

Learning Activities

38. a. Predict the output of union2.c. Execute it to check your prediction. Resolve any differences between your prediction and the actual output.

    b. Are the results consistent with the execution of the program bitfield2.c? Why or why not?

39. List any problems that you think might occur with this approach for accessing the bits and the bytes of a quantity.

40. Experiment with types other than short int.

41. If you have access to a C compiler on a significantly different computer system, try to execute this program on a second system. Do you get the same results? If something is different, try to find out why.

42. Describe the result of the sizeof() operator used on a union.

43. *C by Discovery*   Can a member of a union be a structure? A bit field? Experiment to find out.

A Closer Look

When a union is declared, only enough space for the largest member is allocated. Every member is stored at the beginning of the union. Subsequent assignments overwrite the existing members in the union. Any member of a union can be accessed at any time; however, the contents of a member may not be meaningful, if another member was most recently assigned.

The program union3.c in Example 7-10 is designed for experimenting with different types of members in a union and exploring the memory allocation. The experience gained with this experimentation should help you when writing other programs dealing with unions. Only one member of the union is assigned. The sizeof(), contents, and the address of the other members are output.

 Example 7-10: union3.c

```
/*                union3.c
 *
 *    Synopsis  -  Declares and initializes a union and outputs
 *                 information about the addresses and the contents.
 *
 *    Objective -  To illustrate the properties of memory allocation
 *                 with unions.
 */
main()
{
        union x {                                           /* Note 1 */
                int intmem;
                float floatmem;
                unsigned bitmem:4;
                char stringmem[20];
        } tryit;

        tryit.intmem = 0x1248;                              /* Note 2 */
                                                            /* Note 3 */
        printf ("Sizeof the union and its members.\n");
        printf ("--------------------------------\n");
        printf ("sizeof(union x)  %d\n", sizeof(union x) );
        printf ("sizeof(tryit.intmem) %d\n", sizeof(tryit.intmem) );
        printf ("sizeof(tryit.floatmem) %d\n", sizeof(tryit.floatmem) );
        printf ("sizeof(tryit.bitmem) %d\n", sizeof (tryit.bitmem) );
        printf ("sizeof(tryit.stringmem) %d\n\n",
                            sizeof(tryit.stringmem) );
                                                            /* Note 4 */
        printf ("Addresses of the union and the members.\n");
        printf ("---------------------------------------\n");
        printf ("&tryit  %x.\n", &tryit);
        printf ("&tryit.intmem  %x\n", &(tryit.intmem) );
        printf ("&tryit.floatmem %x\n", &(tryit.floatmem) );
        printf ("&tryit.bitmem %x\n", &tryit.bitmem );
        printf ("tryit.stringmem  %x.\n\n", tryit.stringmem);
                                                            /* Note 5 */
        printf ("Contents of members of the union.\n");
        printf ("---------------------------------\n");
        printf ("intmem = %x.\n", tryit.intmem);
        printf ("tryit.floatmem %5.2f\n", tryit.floatmem);
```

```
        printf ("tryit.bitmem %x\n", tryit.bitmem);
        printf ("tryit.stringmem[0] %x\n", tryit.stringmem[0]);
        printf ("tryit.stringmem[1] %x\n", tryit.stringmem[1]);
        printf ("tryit.stringmem[2] %x\n\n", tryit.stringmem[2]);
}
```

The executable code in the function main() consists of one assignment statement and many calls to printf(). Note that the value of the intmem member of the union x type variable is the only member assigned even though the program accesses all the members.

Note 1: A union named union x is declared. Its members include a bit field and an array for the purpose of experimentation.

Note 2: The member intmem is assigned a hexadecimal value so the calculation of the value of each bit is easy.

Note 3: The sizeof() operator is applied to the union itself as well as to its members.

Note 4: The address of each member is output. Note that the address of the array member is accessed with the array name. All members should start at the same location.

Note 5: The values of the members of the union are output. Note that only the member intmem was initialized. When another member is accessed, an attempt is made to interpret the contents as the appropriate type for that member.

Learning Activities

44. The program union3.c will not compile as is. Without help from the compiler, try to find the compile error. Take out the offending statements and explain why they are incorrect.

45. a. Predict the sizeof() each of the members.

    b. Given that the address of tryit is 0xce (hexadecimal), predict the addresses of each member of tryit.

    c. Predict the contents of each member. Use your experience from the other bit field problems to predict the output of the bit field member.

    d. Execute the program to check your prediction. Reconcile any difference in the execution output and your prediction. Try to explain what the compiler does when the different members are referenced.

46. Are the two expressions &(tryit.intmem) and &tryit.intmem the same or different? What is referenced by each syntax?

Language Elements Introduced in This Chapter: A Review

** Enumerated Types **

Declaration

```
enum boolean {
     FALSE, TRUE
};
```

** Functions **

Functions may return a pointer to a structure.
ANSI C functions may return a structure.
Functions may return unions or enumerated types.

** Library Functions **

strncpy()   Copies a specified number of characters from one string into an array of chars.

** Operators **

Operators allowed with structures and unions:
      assignment
      sizeof()
      address operator
Operators that can be used with ints can be used with
      enumerated types.

** Parameters to Functions **

Structures or pointers to structures can be parameters
      to functions in ANSI C.
Unions and pointers to unions can be parameters to
      functions.
Enumerated types and pointers to enumerated types can be
      parameters to functions.

** Structures **

Declaring a structure type:

```
struct tag {
     char namearray[20];
     int  intval;
     float floatval;
};
```

Declaring a structure variable:

```
struct tag structvar;
```

Accessing elements:

```
structvar.member
structptr->member
```

Initializing:

```
struct tag structvar = { "NAME", 5, 1.47 };
```

** Types **

bit fields
enumerated types
structure types
union types

** Unions **

Declarations:

```
union tag {
    char arrayfield[20];
    int  intfield;
    double doublefield;
};
```

Accessing elements:

```
unionvar.fieldname
unionptr->fieldname
```

** Variable Declarations **

An array of structures:

```
struct tag structarray[20];
```

A pointer to a structure:

```
struct tag *structptr;
```

A structure with bit fields:

```
struct a {
    unsigned a:4;
    unsigned b:2;
};
```

An enumerated variable:

```
enum boolean flag;
```

A union:

```
union tag unionvar;
```

A pointer to a union:

```
union tag *unionptr;
```

Things to Remember

1. A structure in C is an aggregate type that can hold multiple data values of different types at the same time.
2. Declarations inside functions are local to those functions, and cannot be accessed outside their function block.
3. Declarations that appear before any functions can be accessed by any of the functions in the file.
4. Including a tag with a structure declaration allows variables of that structure type to be declared later in the program by referencing a struct tag.
5. A structure cannot contain a member that is a structure of the same type.
6. Different members of a structure can be packed into one word of memory with a construct called a bit field.
7. In ANSI C, a bit field must have type int, unsigned int, or signed int. Older compilers may limit the type of a bit field member to unsigned int.
8. Bit fields could be used to match hardware configuration or to save memory.
9. A disadvantage of using bit fields lies in the lack of portability.
10. The address operator, &, cannot be used with bit fields.
11. Many implementations of C restrict the maximum number of bits that can be contained in a bit field.
12. Bit fields can be specified in a structure declaration without a name. Such a bit field cannot be accessed and its contents cannot be specified. It may be used to force data alignment.
13. An enumerated type consists of a set of integer constants.
14. A union is designed to hold members of different types. It will only contain one of its members at any instant.
15. There is no automatic mechanism to determine which member of a union is in use at any time. It is up to the programmer to keep track.
16. An enumerated type can be used with a union to establish which member is being used.

7.7   Exercises and Programming Problems

1. Write a program to figure the monthly salary for both hourly and salaried employees. Use the type `struct employee` that was illustrated in program unions.c of Example 7-8. Have the user enter the employee information with either the number of hours or the number of weeks worked, and have the program prepare a payroll report.

2. a. Write a structure (`struct card`) that will represent a card in a standard deck of playing cards. You will need to represent both the suit (clubs, diamonds, hearts or spades) as well as the rank (A, K, Q, J, 10, 9, 8, 7, 6, 5, 4, 3, 2) of each card. Note that a deck of playing cards can be represented as an array declared as

   ```
   struct card deck[52];
   ```

   b. Write a function that will perform a perfect shuffle on a deck of cards represented using the data structures from part a. In a perfect shuffle, the deck is broken exactly in half and rearranged so that the first card is followed by the 27th card, followed by the second card, followed by the 28th card, and so on.

   c. Write a program that tests how many perfect shuffles are necessary to return the deck to its original configuration.

3. a. The game of bridge is played with a 13-card hand. Write a data structure to represent a bridge hand.

   b. Write a function to rearrange a bridge hand with all cards of each suit together and with the cards of each suit arranged from high rank to low rank.

   c. Write a function to output a bridge hand in the following form.

   ```
   Clubs:          A, K, J
   Diamonds:       Q, 10, 8, 7, 6, 4, 2
   Hearts:         void
   Spades:         A, 10, 8
   ```

   The designation "`void`" means that the hand has no cards in that suit.

   d. Write a function to calculate the points in a bridge hand according to the following rules:

   4 points for each Ace in the hand

   3 points for each King in the hand

   2 points for each Queen in the hand

   1 point for each Jack in the hand

   3 points for each void suit in the hand

   2 points for each one-card suit in the hand

   1 point for each two-card suit in the hand

The points in the hand are calculated as the sum of the points above as they apply. For example, the hand represented in part c has 17 points: 2 Aces + 1 King + 1 Queen + 1 Jack + 1 void suit =

$$2 \times 4 \quad + \quad 3 \quad + \quad 2 \quad + \quad 1 \quad + \quad 3 \quad = 17$$

4. In mathematics, a rational number is defined as a quotient of two integers where the denominator is not equal to zero. For example, 1/2, 6/1, –5/4, 12/3, and 468/(–325) are all rational numbers as are all fractions where the numerator and denominator are integers and the denominator is not equal to zero.

   a. Declare a data structure that will contain a rational number.

   b. Write functions that will add, subtract, multiply and divide rational numbers. In all functions, pass in three parameters, each pointers to a data structure of the type you declared in part a. Use two of the parameters for the operands, and the third for the result.

   c. Write a function that takes a pointer to your data structure as a parameter and returns the greatest common divisor of the numerator and denominator.

   d. Use your function from part c to write a function that will reduce a fraction (rational number) to lowest terms. Pass in a pointer to the fraction and have the fraction modified by the function.

   e. Write input and output functions so that a user can enter a fraction in the form

   $$2/3, \quad -5/6, \quad 4/-5, \quad \text{or } -12/-33$$

   and the output is in the same form. Have your input function check for errors in the input and return a value of –1 in case an error was sensed. The error might consist of a zero denominator as in 3 / 0, or an error in form as in 4a / 5 or 4%5. Both the input function and the output function should take a single pointer to your data structure from part a as a parameter.

   f. Combine your functions from parts b through e to write a program that will perform rational number arithmetic for the user. The user should be allowed to enter any number of problems, and the program should output the answer in lowest terms. A sample dialogue is below. The user's input is in **bold-face**.

   ```
   FRACTION ARITHMETIC PROGRAM
   -------- ---------- -------
   Enter your problem:  2/3 + 1/5
   The answer is 13/15.    Another problem (y/n)? y
   Enter your problem:  4/2 - 5/0
   Illegal input!!         Another problem (y/n)? y
   Enter your problem:  2/9 * 3/4
   The answer is 1/6.      Another problem (y/n)? n
   Goodbye and thank you.
   ```

5. A state college charges state residents a flat fee of $300 for a semester's tuition. It charges nonresident students $85 per credit unit.

   a. Write a data structure using structures, unions, and enumerated types that will hold the following information about a student: name, Social Security number, resident/nonresident status, current semester units, and fee charged.

b. Write a function that takes a pointer to your data structure as an argument and assigns the correct fee to the appropriate member of the structure. Assume that the remainder of the members in the structure are properly initialized.

c. Write a function to input the name, Social Security number, resident status, and current semester units for a student. Have your input function call the function you wrote in part b to calculate the fee to be charged.

d. Write an output function to output the information about a student.

e. Incorporate parts a through d above into a program that inputs information about students and prepares a report with the student information and the total revenue from those students.

6. Expand the program struct2.c of Example 7-3 by adding a menu allowing a user to
    a. Insert an `auto_part` into the inventory.

    b. Delete an `auto_part` from the inventory.

    c. Find those parts whose current inventory are below a certain value.

    d. Change the inventory amount for an `auto_part` after a sale or receipt of an order.

    Write functions to implement each of the menu choices.

7. Use a bit field representation like that in program union2.c of Example 7-9 in a program that will input a value of type `char` and output its binary representation.

8. A string could be viewed as an array of characters with a specific length. This type of string could be implemented as a structure with a character array member and an `int` member for the length.
    a. Write a structure declaration (`struct string`) in C for a string implemented this way. The fields should be named `chars` and `length`.

    b. Write a version of the strlen() function for a string with this implementation. Call it mystrlen().

    c. Write a version of the strcat() function for a string with this implementation. Call it mystrcat().

    d. Write a function print_string() that takes a `struct string` as a parameter and outputs the meaningful characters to the terminal screen (a version of puts() for this implementation).

    e. Put your code for parts a, b, c and d in a file named mystring.h, and make sure your code will work with the following program:

```
/*          epp8.c                              */
#include <stdio.h>
#include "mystring.h"

main()
{
        struct string str1,
                      str2 = { "how now brown cow", 17 };

        str1.length = 0;
```

```
                    printf("Length of str1 - %d\n",
                                      mystrlen(str1));

            mystrcat(str1, str2);
            print_string(str1);
            printf ("\nLength of str1 - %d\n",
                                      mystrlen(str1));
    }
```

9. a. There are three major types of banking transactions for a personal checking account: a deposit, a withdrawal, and a check. Write a enumerated type declaration for the three types of banking transactions.

   b. Write a declaration in C for a data type that will hold a date (month, day and year).

   c. A bank transaction needs the following information: date, type of transaction, check number (when appropriate), payee for a check or memo for the other two types, and the amount. Write a C structure declaration to hold the information for a single banking transaction. Try to use a union within the declaration in an appropriate way.

   d. Write a function that allows a user to input a banking transaction from the keyboard. Your function should take the address of a transaction structure as a parameter.

   e. Write a function that outputs the contents of a transaction to the terminal. Your function should take a transaction structure as a parameter.

   f. Write a driver program that calls the input function and then the output function to test your functions.

10. The information kept about a student includes last name, first name, major code (four digits), year in school (freshman, sophomore, junior, senior or graduate), number of units completed, and grade point average.

    a. Write a C type declaration for a data structure that will hold the information about a student.

    b. Write a function that will input the information about a single student from the keyboard. Your function should take a pointer to the type you declared in part a as a parameter.

    c. Write a program that allows a user to enter student information for up to a maximum of 30 students from the keyboard. When the user is done, the program outputs a report about the students. The list of students should be in alphabetical order by last name, and the student information should be nicely formatted. Problems that should be addressed include the data structure necessary to hold all the students and the method of getting the students in alphabetical order by last name.

Intraprogram
Communication

Chapter 8

8.1 Introduction

When writing structured modular code in C, the programmer must set up effective communication between the different parts of the program. In this chapter we will consider topics that control this communication.

A structured program is composed of many separate subprograms. Different parts of the same program may reside in separate modules or files. Prewritten software tools like the C library functions, data structure implementations, or functions written by programmers to fill a specific need can be incorporated into the same program. For example, a software tool written to count the number of English words in an input string ideally should be able to work unchanged in many programs and not be dependent on the variable names used in the program for which it was originally written. To use tools and modules effectively, communication between the separate parts of a program must be understood.

The communication in C is accomplished through several mechanisms. We will discuss types, storage classes, scope of identifiers, function types, return values, and linkage in this chapter.

The scope of an identifier determines which program parts will know about the identifier and be able to use it. We saw an example of this in Section 2.2, where variables declared inside of blocks were unknown outside the blocks. The scope of these variables started at the point of declaration and went to the end of their block. These variables could only be accessed inside the block.

A variable's storage class indicates its life span. The storage class of an identifier determines whether it exists for the duration of program execution or only for part of the execution time. It indicates when the variable is available for use by different parts of the program. A related issue is when initialization is done: every time the variable is accessed or only once during program execution.

Other mechanisms for passing information deal with functions and their parameters. Functions that are written with parameters make better tools. They can be used in more programs without change.

Another way that a function can communicate with the surrounding code is through its type and returned value. The syntax of the `return` statement was discussed in Chapters 1 and 3. Some of the implications of the use of this statement in terms of communication between parts of a program will be discussed here.

Another mechanism we will consider is separating the source code into separate files, compiling each file separately, and linking the resulting object code files together to form an executable program. When this is done, the functions in one file may need to access some variables or functions in another file. We will study the linkage properties of the identifiers to determine how this can be used.

8.2 Automatic versus Static Variables

The keywords `auto` and `static` refer to two different storage classes in C. They specify the time that the variable is active. We will also consider the storage class `register` in this section. The other storage class specifiers include `extern`, which will be discussed in Section 8.4, and `typedef`, which will be discussed in Section 8.5.

Automatic Variables

Prior to this chapter we used the default storage class for all variables. If a variable is local to a function and its declaration does not specify otherwise, it has the default storage class automatic or `auto`. An automatic variable is created each time its function is called and destroyed when the execution of its function terminates. If an automatic variable is declared inside the function main(), it is created when the program starts executing and destroyed at the end of execution. The execution of the function main() does not terminate until the program finishes executing.

The declaration of an automatic variable can be done in two ways. The keyword `auto` can precede the declaration, as in

```
auto int counter;
```

However, since the storage class automatic is the default for local variables, the above declaration is equivalent to

```
int counter;
```

All variables that we saw prior to this section were automatic variables by default.

When an automatic variable is created, it is uninitialized. It may contain garbage values. When accompanied by an initializer, as in

```
int counter = 1;
```

the initialization is done each time the variable is created. The variable is reinitialized each time a function is called. Example 8-1 illustrates that concept.

 Example 8-1: automatc.c

```
/*                  automatc.c
 *
 *    Synopsis  -  Outputs two integer values.
 *
 *    Objective -  Illustrates automatic variables.
 */

#include <stdio.h>
int increment(void);

void main()
{
        printf("%d\n", increment() );                  /* Note 2 */
        printf("%d\n", increment() );
}

/*********************************  increment()   *********/
/*    increment() - Increments an automatic local variable and
 *                  returns its incremented value.
 */
int increment(void)
{
        int number = 0;                                /* Note 1 */

        return (++number);
}
```

Two functions make up this program. The function main() consists of two calls to printf(). Each time, the value returned by the function increment() is output. The function increment() contains the declaration of a variable named number, which is initialized to zero. The function increment() increments this variable and returns the incremented value.

Note 1: The declaration of number does not contain a storage class specifier. Since it is local to increment(), it has storage class automatic by default. This means that number is created and initialized each time increment() is called. The value of number will be dependably zero when increment() starts executing.

Note 2: These printf() calls print the value returned by the function increment(). Since the variable number is always zero at the start of execution of increment(), the value output will be the same in both printf() calls.

Static Variables

The concept of an automatic variable contrasts with that of a static variable. Whereas an automatic variable is in existence only when its function is executing, a static variable is in existence the whole time the program is executing. Its memory space has been allocated by the time the program starts executing and that memory space is not changed throughout the execution time. In consequence, a static variable retains its value from one use to the next.

To declare a static variable, begin with the keyword static. For example,

```
static int counter;
```

Without explicit initialization, a static variable would be given the default initial value of 0. However, an initializer can be added to the above declaration and would yield

```
static int counter = 1;
```

In this case the variable counter would be initialized once at the beginning of program execution.

Consider the situation in which the variable counter is local to a function. Suppose the function was called, the value of counter was changed during function execution, and then the function was called again. The value of counter on each entry to the function would be the same as when exiting the function the previous time.

Example 8-2 illustrates this concept. Note the similarity between this program, static.c, and the previous program, automatc.c. Note also the different output. Understanding this difference is the key to understanding the difference between automatic and static variables.

 Example 8-2: static.c

```
/*                  static.c
 *
 *    Synopsis  -  Outputs two integer values.
 *
 *    Objective -  Illustrates static variables.
 */

#include <stdio.h>
int increment(void);

void main()
```

```
{
        printf("%d\n", increment() );                    /* Note 2 */
        printf("%d\n", increment() );
}


/******************************** increment() *************/
/*   increment() - Increments a static local variable and returns
 *                 its incremented value.
 */
int increment(void)
{
        static int number = 0;                           /* Note 1 */

        return (++number);
}
```

This program is almost identical to the previous example program. It consists of two functions. The function main() consists of two printf() calls. Each time, the value returned by the function increment() is output. The function increment() contains a local variable named `number`, which is initialized to zero. The function increment() increments this variable and returns the incremented value.

Note 1: The variable `number` in this example has been declared with storage class `static`. It is in existence the whole time the program executes. It is only initialized once and holds its value between calls to increment().

Note 2: These printf() calls output the value returned by increment(). Since the value of `number` at the start of execution of increment() is not always the same, different values are output by each statement.

Learning Activities

1. a. Predict the values output by the program automatc.c.

   b. Predict the values output by the program static.c.

   c. Run both programs to verify your predictions. Correct any misconceptions you may have had.

2. a. Modify both automatc.c and static.c by adding the following call to printf() inside the function increment():

      ```
      printf("The address of number is %x.\n", &number);
      ```

   b. Compile and execute both programs again. Note the results. Was the address of `number` the same in both programs? If not, were the two addresses close in value, or were they significantly different? Many compilers store static and automatic variables in different sections of memory. Does that appear to be the case with your compiler?

Register Variables

The third storage class that we will discuss is register. The designation of a variable as a register variable is a request by the programmer that a variable be placed in a register. The declaration of a register variable is usually an indication that the variable will be used often, and might be done in an attempt to improve the speed and performance of a program. The specifications for the C language do not guarantee that a variable will be placed in a register when one is requested; however, the knowledge that a register was requested may allow the compiler to optimize the code for efficiency.

The keyword `register` begins the declaration of a register variable. For example,

```
register int counter;
```

declares a register variable with type `int` and name `counter`. Register variables have the same properties as automatic variables. They exist only while their function is executing. They are created and initialized every time the function is entered, and destroyed at termination of their function.

Variables that could be considered for the `register` storage class include array indices and loop counters. If a pointer variable is used to traverse an array, it could be given `register` storage class also. The number and type of register variables allowed in a program differs with different implementations of C.

Example 8-3 illustrates the properties of register variables. The program register.c is very similar to the previous programs in this section, but the register variable is used more heavily.

 Example 8-3: register.c

```
/*                  register.c
 *
 *    Synopsis  -  Outputs two integer values.
 *
 *    Objective -  Illustrates register variables.
 */

#include <stdio.h>
int increment_a_lot(void);

void main()
{
        printf ("%d\n", increment_a_lot() );
        printf ("%d\n", increment_a_lot() );
}
```

```
/***************************   increment_a_lot()   ***********/
/*   increment_a_lot() -   Increments a register local variable 1000
 *                         times and returns the incremented value.
 */
int increment_a_lot(void)
{
        register int number = 0;                        /* Note 1 */

        for ( ; number < 1000; number++)                /* Note 2 */
        ;
        return (number);
}
```

The similarities between this program and the previous example programs in this section should be noted. This program consists of two functions, main() and increment_a_lot(). The function main(), very similar to its counterpart in the previous examples, consists of two calls to printf(). Each printf() call outputs the value returned by the other function. The function increment_a_lot() has a local variable that is initialized to zero. The function returns the value of the variable after it has been incremented. The only difference is that the variable is incremented many times through use of a `for` loop.

Note 1: The declaration of `number` contains a storage class specifier of `register`. This is a request by the programmer that this variable be put in a register. The register variable is similar to an automatic variable in that it is created and initialized each time the function is called.

Note 2: The variable `number` is used to drive this `for` loop. Since the `for` loop is executed 1000 times, the variable is accessed 1000 times when the function is executed. Note that the initialization expression of the `for` loop can be omitted, because the variable `number` is dependably equal to zero at the start of the function execution.

Two final points about register variables should be considered before concluding this section. First, since the value of the variable might be stored in a register, it is illegal to use the address operator, `&`, with the name of a register variable. Second, different implementations of C might impose restrictions on the number and type of register variables allowed. In fact, in some implementations of C, the storage class indicator is simply ignored; in others, the restrictions are dependent on the underlying hardware for the implementation.

Learning Activities

3. Predict the output of register.c and execute it to verify your predictions.

4. a. Determine if it is possible to look at the assembly code generated by the compiler on your implementation of C. Find out how it is done.

   b. If it is possible, stop compilation of register.c at that phase and inspect the assembly code. Can you tell where the variable `number` is stored? Was it allocated a register?

   c. Omit the storage specifier `register` in the program and repeat the process described in part b. Look to see if this omission made a difference in the assembly code. If it didn't, try to find out how your implementation of C handles register variables.

   d. Change the storage class specifier to `static` and compile the code to assembly language again. What are the changes this time?

8.3   Global versus Local Variables

The distinction between local and global variables deals with the scope of variables. It deals with the part of the program in which variables can be referenced. A local variable is local to a function or a compound statement. It is declared inside a function or compound statement and can only be referenced inside its block. In contrast, a global or external variable is declared outside a function. It is possible to access a global variable in more than one function. We will discuss local variables first.

Local Variables

Up to this point in the text, most of the variables have been local variables. They were known only inside the function block or compound statement block in which they were defined.

A local variable is declared inside a pair of matching braces that delimits a compound statement or a function block. It can be legally referenced at any point from its declaration to the closing brace for that block or function.

As we saw in Section 8.2, the storage class specifiers `auto` and `static` can be used with local variables. The storage class specifier used with a local variable affects the life span of the variable and its initialization properties but does not change the scope of the variable.

Example 8-4 illustrates the fact that a variable declared inside a block will not be known outside the block. The program will not compile.

Example 8-4: error.c

```
/*              error.c
 *
 *   Synopsis -  This code will not execute because it contains
 *               compile time errors. Its intent is purposely vague.
 *
 *   Objective - To illustrate the compiler's understanding of
 *               local variables and their scope.
 */
#include <stdio.h>

void main()
{
        int counter;                                      /* Note 1 */
        int addit(void);

        for (counter = 1; counter < 5; counter++) {
                int i;                                    /* Note 2 */
                i = counter;                              /* Note 3 */
                i = i + 5;
                addit();
          }
                                                          /* Note 4 */
        printf ("i was %d; addit() returned %d.\n", i, addit() );

}

/******************************* addit ()  *****************/
/*   addit() -  Attempts to add sum to counter.  Has syntax errors.
 */

int addit(void)
{
        int sum = 0;                                      /* Note 5 */

        sum = sum + counter;                              /* Note 6 */
        return (sum);
}
```

The program consists of the function main() and a function addit(). In main(), the variable `counter` is declared and used to drive a `for` loop. The block that forms the body of the `for` loop contains the declaration of the variable `i`, two assignment statements, and a call to addit(). A final printf() call ends main(). The function addit() contains the declaration of sum, a single assignment statement, and a return statement.

Note 1: The variable counter is declared. Because it is declared inside the function block for main(), it is local to main(). It can be legally referenced only inside main().

Note 2: The variable i is declared inside the braces delimiting a compound statement. Its scope is limited to that compound statement.

Note 3: The variable counter can be referenced anywhere inside main(). The assignment to counter inside the block will not cause any compile errors.

Note 4: The printf() call lies just outside the compound statement and references the variable i. Since i is local to that compound statement and the printf() call is outside the scope of the variable i, this reference will cause a compilation error.

Note 5: The variable sum is local to the function addit(). It will be initialized to zero every time the function is called.

Note 6: This assignment statement references the variable counter. Since counter is local to main(), this reference is outside counter's scope. This causes another compile-time error in this program.

Learning Activity

5. Make the following changes to the program error.c.
    a. Remove the reference to the variable i in the printf() call. (For example, printf() could just report the value returned by addit() .)
    b. Make counter a parameter to the function addit(). You will need to change the call to addit() and the declaration of the function addit().
    c. Compile the program error.c. Make any necessary changes so that it will compile.
    d. Predict the output of your modified program. Then run the program to verify your prediction. Reconcile any differences between your prediction and the actual output for the program.

Global or External Variables

A global or external variable is a variable that can be referenced by more than one function. It is defined outside function or compound statement blocks.

If a variable is declared before all the functions in a source code file, it can be referenced by all the functions in that file. A reference to a variable consists of using its name in an expression. If a variable is declared between two functions in a file, it can be referenced from its point of declaration to the end of the file.

A global or external variable is in existence during the full execution time of the program. The keyword static has a special meaning with global variables. This will be discussed in Section 8.4. A global variable is initialized to zero by default. An initializer can be included in the declaration to defeat the default.

The program global.c in Example 8-5 illustrates the difference between local
and global variables.

 Example 8-5: global.c

```
/*                  global.c
 *
 *    Synopsis  -  Assigns values to some variables and outputs those
 *                 values.
 *
 *    Objective -  Illustrates the difference between global and
 *                 local variables.
 */
#include <stdio.h>
int globalvar;                                          /* Note 1   */
int same_name = 3;                                      /* Note 1   */

void main()
{
        int localvar;                                   /* Note 2   */
        void sub_fcn(void);

        globalvar = 2;                                  /* Note 3   */
        localvar = 3;                                   /* Note 4   */
        printf ("Starting in main, ");
        printf ("globalvar is %d, localvar is %d.\n",
                                        globalvar, localvar);

        sub_fcn();

        printf ("\nAfter returning to main, ");
                                                        /* Note 9   */
        printf ("globalvar is %d, localvar is %d,\n",
                                        globalvar, localvar);
        printf ("and same_name has value %d.\n", same_name);
}
/********************************* sub_fcn()   *************/
/*   sub_fcn()  -  Assigns values to local and global variables and
 *                 outputs the values.
 */

void sub_fcn(void)
{
        int localvar;                                   /* Note 5   */
        int same_name;                                  /* Note 6   */
```

```
        globalvar = 4;                                      /* Note 7  */
        localvar = 5;                                       /* Note 8  */
        same_name = 127;
        printf ("\nIn sub_fcn, ");
        printf ("globalvar is %d, localvar is %d,\n",
                                          globalvar, localvar);
        printf ("and same_name has value %d.\n", same_name);
}
```

This program consists of two functions, main() and sub_fcn(). Two variables, `globalvar` and `same_name`, are declared before the beginning of main(). The function main() consists of assignment statements, calls to printf(), and a call to sub_fcn(). The function sub_fcn() consists of assignment statements and printf() calls. The variables and their values are of specific interest.

Note 1: The variables `globalvar` and `same_name` are global variables. They can be accessed by any function in this source file. Global variables are declared before the declaration of any functions in the file. The variable `globalvar` will have the default initial value of 0; `same_name` will be initialized to 3 before execution of main() begins.

Note 2: The variable `localvar` is local to the function main(). Local variables are declared inside function blocks.

Note 3: A value is assigned to `globalvar`. This variable can be referenced by any function in this source code file. The function need only mention the variable's name.

Note 4: A value is assigned to `localvar`.

Note 5: A local variable named `localvar` is declared. This variable has no connection with the variable in the function main(); this variable is local to sub_fcn() and can only be referenced there.

Note 6: A local variable named `same_name` is declared. Note that the name of this variable conflicts with the name of a global variable previously defined. This is legal in C, but any reference to `same_name` inside sub_fcn() will always access the local variable with that name. It is impossible for sub_fcn() to reference the global `same_name` directly.

Note 7: A value is assigned to `globalvar`. The variable will retain this new value even after sub_fcn() has terminated. The action of changing the value of a global variable by a function is called a side effect. Side effects should be kept to a minimum for ease of reading, debugging, and maintaining a program.

Note 8: Assignment statements change the values of `localvar` and `same_name`. In both cases, the value of the local copy of the variable is changed. The value of `localvar` in main() is not changed. The value of the global variable `same_name` remains unchanged also. The following printf() call reflects the results of these assignment statements.

Note 9: After sub_fcn() executes, the values of `globalvar`, `localvar`, and `same_name` are output. Note that sub_fcn() made assignments to three variables with those names; however, not all of the values have been changed. The value of `globalvar` was changed by sub_fcn() since both functions could access the same global variable. The values of `localvar` and `same_name` were not changed. This `localvar` is local to main() and cannot be accessed outside main(). The reason that `same_name` was not changed is that sub_fcn() had its own variable named `same_name` and therefore could not access the global variable with that name.

"Execute the program to verify your prediction. Correct any errors in your thinking." Based on *The Bull Hunt* **by** *Antoine-Louis Barye, 1834.*

Learning Activities

6. a. Predict the values of the variables in the output of global.c. Fill in the values in the following output.

```
Starting in main, globalvar is ____, localvar is ____.
In sub_fcn, globalvar is ____, localvar is ____,
and same_name has value ____.
After returning to main, globalvar is ____, localvar is ____,
and same_name has value ____.
```

   b. Execute the program to verify your prediction. Correct any errors in your thinking.

7. a. Modify the program global.c by having the program output the address of each variable in each function. Compile and execute the program again. Inspect the output addresses. Do you see a similarity between the addresses of the local variables? Are they close to each other in memory or distant? What about the global variables? Are they close to the local variables or are they distant?

   b. Add a parameter to sub_fcn() and have the address of the formal parameter output also. Use `localvar` as the actual parameter to sub_fcn(). Compile and execute the program. Note the results.

   c. Modify the program once more to use `globalvar` as the actual parameter to sub_fcn(). Compile and execute the program again. Are the results the same?

        d. Explain your results. Can you conclude anything about the location in memory of global and local variables? What about parameters to functions? Do they seem to be handled more like global variables or local variables?

8. Global variables cannot be referenced in functions that are declared before their point of declaration. Convince yourself of that fact by moving the declaration of `globalvar` to a spot between main() and sub_fcn() and try to execute it again. Do you get a compilation error, a runtime error, or no error at all?

9. Consider the following program.

```c
/*                      la9.c                    */
#include <stdio.h>
int a, b, c;
void f1 (void);
void f2 (void);

void main ()
{
        int a;
        a = 5;
        b = 3;
        c = 7;
        printf ("%d, %d, %d\n", a, b, c);
        f1 ();
        printf ("%d, %d, %d\n", a, b, c);

}

int d = 4;

void f1 (void)
{
        char c = 'A';

        a = 3;
        b++;
        printf ("%d, %d, %d, %d\n", a, b, c, d);
        f2 ();
        printf ("%d, %d, %d, %d\n", a, b, c, d);
}

void f2 (void)
{
        int d = 45;

        a += 4;
        b = 7;
        c = d + a;
        printf ("%d, %d, %d, %d\n", a, b, c, d);

}
```

a. List the variables that can be referenced by the function main().

b. List the variables that can be referenced by the function f1().

c. Predict the output from this program and then execute it to verify your prediction. Correct any mistakes in your thinking.

10. We mentioned that global variables act like static variables in the sense that they are in existence for the full execution time of the program.

   a. Would it be theoretically possible to have an automatic global variable? What would this mean? When would it exist? When would it be initialized? Which functions would be able to access it?

   b. Experiment with the program above to see if automatic global variables are allowed. What happens? Did everything work as you expected?

A Word about Style

Global or external variables should be used with discretion. A structured program should effect most of its communication through the use of function parameters and return values rather than by accessing global variables.

When a program's variables all are global, all functions may access them and change their values. This change of value of a global variable by a function is referred to as a "side effect." Side effects cause problems in debugging because if the value of a global variable is incorrect, a detailed search through all the functions in the program for access to the variable must be made. This often involves a painstaking execution trace to find the instance where the offending value was assigned.

The same problem occurs with program maintenance. If a proposed change involves a global variable, a trace must be made to see what effect the change will have on the whole program. However, if the variable is local to a function, only that function needs to be examined.

8.4 Modules and External Variables

A source module might consist of the source code for all functions performing related tasks. In a C program, each module could be placed in a separate file. For example, all functions dealing with input and output might comprise one module while all arithmetic processing would be in a separate module. A third module might contain a driver, a function that does nothing more than call the other modules.

Each source module can be compiled separately. This would produce a corresponding object code module. Before executing the program, the object modules must be linked together. The ability to compile and link the code from source in different files is a feature of most C compilers.

The advantages of using separate source files include ease of editing and compiling shorter files. This organization also allows for teamwork in programming projects. Different members of the team could work on different modules.

It is often necessary for the functions in different modules to access the same variables. This can be accomplished in the following way. The variable could be declared in one module as a global or external variable. In the other modules, it would be referenced with a declaration using the keyword `extern`.

To discuss the concept of external variables and the use of the keyword `extern`, we need to make a distinction between declarations and definitions. The declaration of a variable states the type of the variable. The definition of a variable states its type and causes memory to be allocated for that variable. A definition is a declaration, but not vice versa.

When a global or external variable is defined, it is known from its point of declaration to the end of the source file. Another property of global variables is that they have external linkage; they can also be referenced in other source code files or in functions below their point of definition. Functions in other source code files can declare (not define) the variable and give it the storage class `extern`. For example, if a source code file, containing the function main(), defined an external variable, it might have the following structure:

```
int globalvar;
main()
{
    ...
}
```

In this example, the code

```
int globalvar;
```

would usually be taken as the definition of the variable `globalvar`; storage would be allocated. If functions f1() and f2() in another source code file needed to access the variable `globalvar`, they could include an `extern` declaration at the top of the source file.

```
extern int globalvar;

f1()
{
    ...
}

f2()
{
    ...
}
```

The keyword `extern` is used with declarations, but not with definitions of variables. It indicates that the variable is defined elsewhere; references to this variable should be resolved during the link phase of compilation.* Note that an external definition of a variable and an `extern` declaration are different.

Since global variables can be linked to other source files, there may be additional restrictions on the identifiers used. The allowed maximum length of the identifier

---

* On some compilers, the keyword `extern` is not necessary. The linker takes the first declaration as the definition. The method illustrated in this text should work with most compilers.

could be shorter if it has external linkage, and distinction between uppercase and lowercase may not be made. This is not specified by the ANSI standards, so it needs to be researched for each compiler.

As a very simple example of a program with its source split between different files, suppose that a program is to (1) output the value of a variable, (2) increment that variable, and (3) output the value of that variable again. To illustrate modular programming, this simple program will be broken down into three separate modules: one to output the variable, one to increment the variable, and one, the driver module, to call the other two modules. The variable will have the name x.

The output module will be named output.c and will contain a single function named output() that outputs the current value of x. The increment module will be named incr.c and will contain a single function named incr() that increments the value of x. The driver module will be named driver.c and will contain the single function main(). Execution of the program will start at the beginning of the function main(). The function main() will call output(), incr(), and output() in that order.

The variable x needs to be known to incr() and to output(), but not necessarily to main(). However, by stylistic convention, most global variables for a program are declared either in an include file or in the module containing main(). Therefore, for stylistic reasons, the variable x will be declared in driver.c.

Example 8-6 shows the driver module in the file driver.c.

Example 8-6: driver.c

```
/*                driver.c
 *
 *    Synopsis  -  Outputs the value of a variable, increments it, and
 *                 outputs it again.
 *
 *    Objective -  To demonstrate a very simple modular program with
 *                 a variable declared externally.
 */

int      x = 5;                                    /* Note 1 */
extern void output(void);                          /* Note 2 */
extern void incr(void);

void main()
{
        output();                                  /* Note 3 */
        incr();
        output();

}
```

This file contains a single function named main(). When the program is executed, execution begins with the function main(). A single global variable named x is declared. The code for main() consists of three function calls.

Note 1: The variable x is declared as a global variable in this file. It will be accessed by the functions in the other files. The initialization takes place before the program begins execution. The variable x is not accessed in this file, and could have been defined in one of the other modules just as well.

Note 2: The functions that do not appear in this source code file are declared here. Just as with variables, the keyword extern indicates that the functions are defined in another file and will be linked to the executable file. This declaration is not necessary with all compilers.

Note 3: The code in main() consists of calls to functions that are not in this file. When the program is compiled for execution, the code for these functions must be found in other files. This is usually done in the last phase of compilation which is known as linking. The names of all the source files must be supplied to the linker.

The contents of the file output.c are shown in Example 8-7.

Example 8-7: output.c

```
/*                  output.c
 *
 *    Synopsis  -   The function output() outputs the value of the
 *                  variable  x.
 *
 *    Objective -   Part of a very simple modular program
 *                  illustrating variables that are externally declared.
 */

#include <stdio.h>                                         /* Note 1 */

extern int      x;                                         /* Note 2 */

void output(void)
{
        printf ("The value of x is %d.\n", x);
}
```

This file consists of the single function output(). The function main() is in a different module. The code in output() consists of a single printf() call.

Note 1: The file stdio.h is included here by a preprocessor directive. Since the call for output is in this file, it is the only one with use for the information in stdio.h. No preprocessor statements are necessary in the other files.

Note 2: This line contains a reference to the variable x. The keyword `extern` indicates that this variable is declared in a different file. All references to x in this module will refer to that externally declared variable. The address of x is resolved in the link phase of compilation.

The module incr.c is shown in Example 8-8.

 Example 8-8: incr.c

```
/*              incr.c
 *
 *   Synopsis  -  The function incr() increments the variable x.
 *
 *   Objective -  Part of a very simple modular program illustrating
 *                variables declared externally.
 */

extern int     x;                                    /* Note 1 */

void incr(void)
{
        x++;
}
```

This file contains the single function incr(). The code for incr() increments the variable x.

Note 1: The variable x is referenced in this file also. Again, the keyword `extern` indicates that x has been declared in a different file but will be referenced here. The external reference will be resolved at link time.

Learning Activities

11. Find out if separate compilation of source files is possible with your implementation of C. If it is,

    a. Compile, link, and execute the program consisting of the files driver.c, output.c, and incr.c.

    b. *C by Discovery*   Experiment with the placement of the declaration and external declaration of the variable x. Determine the answers to the following questions.

        i. Can the declaration for x be omitted from driver.c?

        ii. Can the external reference to x in output.c be moved from the top of the file to a position inside the function? Can it be moved to the bottom of the file? Try these modifications to get the answer.

        iii. What happens if the word extern is omitted from the file output.c? Try it.

    c. Explain the general concept illustrated by each of the above experiments.

12. In the above program, the variable x is initialized in the file driver.c. Modify the program so that a user can input initial value rather than having it initialized in the source code. Modify it by creating a fourth source file named input.c that will access the variable x correctly and do the input. You will also need to modify the function main().

The Static Storage Class with External Variables

Earlier in this section, we saw that global variables can be linked with variables declared externally in other modules. It is possible to have a situation in which a variable needs to be accessed by many functions in one module but should not be available to any other modules. The information it contains may need to be hidden from the other modules. That is, we want the variable to be global but not to have external linkage.

We have seen that by default, a variable that is defined outside any function in a source code file has external linkage. This default can be defeated by declaring the variable to have storage class static. It can then be accessed by any function below its point of declaration in its source code file, but it will be unknown in other source code files. This static declaration affords a measure of privacy when needed.

Learning Activity

13. Consider again the modular example presented in this section. The variable x was defined as a global variable in the file driver.c. It was declared externally in both of the other files, output.c and incr.c. Modify the module driver.c by changing the line

```
int x = 5;
```

to

```
static int x = 5;
```

Now try to compile the files again and link the three object files together. Did you get an error? If so, try to determine which phase of the compile-link phase reported the error.

A Word about Style

Note that the previous example had the sole purpose of demonstrating a modular program. It was extremely simple so that the elements of communication between the modules would be evident. However, it was not a model for a well-designed program. A program that simple would not need to be modularized. Also, the side effect caused when incr() changes the global variable x could easily be avoided by writing incr() to accept x as a parameter. If this was done, incr() would be more like a software tool. It would work in any program and would not depend on the program having a variable named x.

8.5 Typedefs

The typedef storage class is used to associate an identifier with a type. Unlike other storage classes, a typedef declaration does not cause any storage to be allocated. The word typedef is a key word in C; it appears in declarations. For example,

```
typedef long big_int;
```

will associate the identifier big_int with the type long.

A typedef can be viewed as similar to a #define preprocessor directive with the following differences. A typedef is processed by the compiler and is limited to data types; a #define directive is processed by the preprocessor and can be used to define constants, macros, and other entities as well as data types.

The syntax of using a typedef is:

```
typedef old_type   new_type;
```

where new_type is the identifier being declared and old_type is a type declaration.

After a `typedef`, the new identifier can be used to declare variables of that type. For example,

```
typedef struct {
     float radius;
     float x_center;
     float y_center;
} CIRCLE;
```

might be declared to provide a data structure to hold information about a circle. This statement does not allocate any storage, it just associates the identifier CIRCLE with that particular structure. Later in the program, variables c1 and c1 can be defined with a declaration like

```
CIRCLE c1, c2;
```

where the identifer CIRCLE serves as the data type in the declaration. Since a CIRCLE is declared as a structure, the `radius` member of c1 can be referenced with the syntax

```
c1.radius
```

Portability Considerations

`Typedef` declarations are often put in header files. They are used for readability and for portability. For example, suppose a program must be ported to many different computer systems on which word sizes vary. If a program needs the size of a certain type to be two bytes, a new type named `twobytes` might be defined with a `typedef`. The main program source code might make reference to the type `twobytes`. When this program is distributed, several header files might be supplied with the source. In one header, the definition might be

```
typedef int twobytes;
```

In another, the definition might be

```
typedef short twobytes
```

When the program is configured for a certain system, the appropriate header file with the definitions that match the hardware and implementation of C would be included with a preprocessor directive and the program would be configured properly.

One specific example of this type of configuration is in the ANSI additions to the C compiler. In earlier compilers, the return value of many of the library functions was of type `int`. For example, consider the library function strlen() that calculates the length of a string. Since the number of bytes in an `int` varied on different computer systems, any program that depended on the return value from strlen() having a certain number of bytes posed a portability problem. With ANSI C, the return value of strlen() is defined to be of type `size_t`. The identifier `size_t` is declared in one of the standard header files supplied with an ANSI C compiler. It is generally one of the unsigned integer types. When any program declaring strlen() to be of type `size_t` is ported to a different ANSI C compiler, the type of the strlen() function will be automatically adjusted. In contrast, if strlen() is declared to return type `int` and the program is ported from a computer in which an `int` occupies two bytes to one in which an `int` occupies four bytes, a potential portability problem exists.

An Example of typedefs and Data Types

A `typedef` declaration can be used in the implementation of a data type. A data type would be declared with a `typedef`, and the specific operations for the data type would be implemented as C functions. After the declaration, a programmer would be able to use the data type without depending on the specifics of the implementation. The implementation could be changed to better match the specific application without causing the main program to be modified.

As an example, a stack is a data type that is defined as a list where all additions and insertions take place at the same end of the list. It is often called a LIFO (last in, first out); one familiar model is that of a stack of cafeteria trays. Trays are taken off the top, and additions to the stack of trays are added to the top.

The basic operations are to push (or add) a value to the top of the stack or to pop (or remove) a value from the top of the stack. A stack could be implemented as an array or a linked list. The basic operations would be implemented as functions in C. The functions push() and pop() would be written to access the underlying data type, but their functionality would remain the same in either case.

Examples 8-9, 8-10, and 8-11 illustrate an array implementation of a stack, using many of the concepts in this chapter and the previous one. The example consists of three files. The function main() appears in the file stackex.c; it is a driver and has the single purpose of testing the other code. The file stack.h is a header file; it contains the `typedef` declaration of a `STACK` and the ANSI prototype declarations of the stack utility functions.

The file stack.c is the stack utility module that contains the C source code for the functions push() and pop() that perform the major operations on the `STACK`. Three other functions have been included also. The function is_empty() checks to see if there is valid data in the stack; it returns a value of 1 if the `STACK` is empty and 0 otherwise. The function is_full() returns 1 if there is no room for additional data in the `STACK` and 0 otherwise. The function init_stack() initializes a `STACK` to the state where is_empty() tests true.

Before looking at the source code, we need to understand how these functions will work. The `STACK` is implemented as a structure with two members. The actual data is kept in the array member with the name `elts`, which has MAX elements. This `STACK` will contain elements of type `char`. The type could be modified for other use. The second member is an `int` named `top`. It will serve as an index into the array that indicates the element on the top of the stack.

After initialization by a call to init_stack(), a stack would have the configuration shown in Figure 8-1.

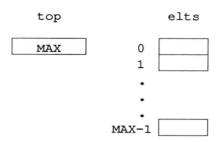

Figure 8-1

The index top would be set to one position beyond the bottom of the array to indicate that there is no meaningful data in the STACK.

A call to push() will put an element on the STACK. The element is put in the last available position in the array and the index top is adjusted to point to the element at the top of the array. The function push() takes two parameters, a pointer, S, indicating which STACK to access and the element to be pushed on the STACK. After the following three calls to push(),

```
push ('a', S);
push ('b', S);
push ('c', S);
```

the stack pointed to by S has the contents shown in Figure 8-2. The member top contains the index of the last element pushed on the stack.

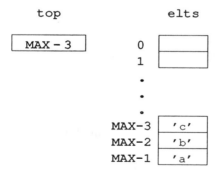

Figure 8-2

The function pop() takes a single parameter, a pointer to the STACK to be popped. After the call

```
pop(S)
```

the STACK pointed to by S has the contents shown in Figure 8-3. Note that the element was not actually removed from the stack. The index top was adjusted instead. The function pop() returns the value that was at the top of the stack, the 'c' in this case.

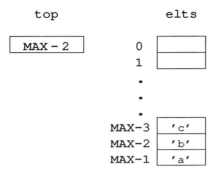

Figure 8-3

We start by examining the header file stack.h in Example 8-9. Note that ANSI C function prototypes are declared, which may need to be changed for older compilers.

Example 8-9: stack.h

```
/*                stack.h
 *
 *    Contains the declaration of the data type STACK and the
 *    declarations of the stack utility functions. This header
 *    file should be included in every C source file that references
 *    a STACK or any of its utility functions.
 */

#define MAX     8                                  /* Note 1 */
typedef  struct {
        char   elts[MAX];
        int    top;
} STACK;                                            /* Note 2 */

int push(char item, STACK *s_ptr);                  /* Note 3 */
int pop(STACK *s_ptr);
void init_stack(STACK *s_ptr);
int  is_empty( STACK s);
int  is_full ( STACK s);
```

This file contains the typedef declaration of a STACK and the declarations of the associated utility functions. The file should be included with the #include preprocessor directive in every source code file that needs to declare a STACK.

Note 1: Currently, the constant MAX is set to 8. This is the maximum number of items that are allowed in a STACK. The choice of 8 makes it easy to test for things like overflow and underflow, but in a practical application, the number would probably be increased.

Note 2: The data type STACK has been declared with a typedef. In the program source code reference can be made to a STACK instead of having to specify the contents of this structure. The stack contains an array, elts, that will hold the elements on the stack, and an integer top that acts as an index into that array and keeps track of the top of the stack.

Note 3: The next five lines of source code contain declarations of the five STACK utility functions. When this header file is included in a program, a programmer will not have to make additional declarations about the function types.

The second file to be discussed, stack.c, is listed in Example 8-10. It contains the declarations of the stack utility functions.

Example 8-10: stack.c

```
/*                  stack.c
 *
 *    Synopsis  -  Not a full program!  This file contains the
 *                 stack utility functions push(), pop(),
 *                 init_stack(), is_empty(), and is_full().
 *
 *    Objective -  To illustrate use of typedef to create
 *                 a data structure.
 */

#include "stack.h"                                  /* Note 1 */

/******************************** init_stack() **************
 *    Initializes a stack to an empty state by setting
 *    top beyond the end of the array.                       */

void init_stack(STACK *s_ptr)                        /* Note 2 */
{
        s_ptr->top = MAX;                            /* Note 3 */
}


/******************************** is_empty() **************
 *    Returns 1 if the STACK is empty and 0 if not.          */

int  is_empty( STACK s)
{
        if (s.top >= MAX)                            /* Note 4 */
```

```
                        return (1);
        else
                        return (0);
}

/******************************   is_full()   ****************
 *    Returns 1 if the STACK is full, and 0 if not.                    */

int  is_full ( STACK s)
{
        if (s.top <= 0)                                  /* Note 5 */
                return(1);
        else
                return (0);
}

/********************************   push()   *****************
 *    Puts a new item on the stack and adjusts top.                    */

int push(char item, STACK *s_ptr)
{
        if (is_full(*s_ptr))                             /* Note 6 */
                return(-1);
        else {
                s_ptr->top--;                            /* Note 7 */
                s_ptr->elts[ s_ptr->top ] = item;
                return (0);
        }
}

/***********************************   pop()   ***************
 *    Removes an item from the top of the stack, adjusts top,
 *    and returns the removed item, or -1 if the stack was
 *    empty.                                                           */

int pop(STACK *s_ptr)
{
        if (is_empty(*s_ptr) )                           /* Note 8 */
                return (-1);
        else {
                return (s_ptr->elts[ s_ptr->top++]);     /* Note 9 */
        }
}
```

This module contains the five utility functions for a STACK. It needs to be linked with a function main() in order to execute.

Note 1: The header file stack.h is included here so that the declaration of STACK is known to all functions in this file.

Note 2: The identifier STACK is used in this declaration because it now represents a type. The parameter s_ptr is a pointer to a STACK. The function init_stack() will change the contents of the STACK pointed to by s_ptr. Even though the formal parameter is declared as type STACK *, the actual use in the function indicates that a more accurate description of the parameter type is "address of a STACK." In use, a STACK should be declared in the calling function and the address of that variable should be passed to init_stack().

Note 3: To establish an empty STACK, the index, top, is set to the bottom of the array of elements.

Note 4: The function is_empty() checks the index top to determine if the STACK is empty or not. A value of MAX indicates an empty STACK.

Note 5: Similarly, the function is_full() checks the index top to determine if there is still space in the STACK. A value of 0 for top indicates that the STACK is full.

Note 6: The function push() checks for overflow before pushing a new element on the STACK. If it is full, a value of −1 is returned to indicate that the attempt to push the element on the STACK was not successful.

Note 7: If space is still available in the elts array, the value of top is adjusted and the element is placed in the array. The return value of 0 indicates success. Note that the actual parameter to push() should be the address of a STACK instead of an uninitialized STACK * variable.

Note 8: The function pop() checks for underflow before popping an element from the STACK. The value −1 is returned if the STACK is empty. Because STACK has been implemented as an array of type char and the popped value is returned by pop(), a value that could not possibly be part of the array must be returned in case of failure to pop a value. Since the value −1 is not a char value, it was chosen as the return value in case of error.

Again the parameter to pop() should be the address of an existing STACK. The fact that pop() changes the contents of its parameter indicates this.

Note 9: All that is necessary to pop a value from the STACK is to increment the index top. The return statement returns the value at the cell in the elts array that is indexed by the old value of top and increments top.

The last module, stackex.c in Example 8-11, is the one containing the test program. It will simply read one line of input from the terminal and echo it back to the terminal with the characters reversed.

Example 8-11: stackex.c

```
/*                  stackex.c
 *
 *    Synopsis   -  A driver program to test the stack utilities. This
 *                  program accepts a line of input from standard
 *                  input and outputs the characters in reverse
 *                  order to standard output.
 *
 *    Objective  -  To demonstrate and test the stack utilities.
 */
#include <stdio.h>
#include "stack.h"                                      /* Note 1 */

void main()
{
        char inbuff[80];
        int index;
        STACK st;                                       /* Note 2 */

        printf ("Enter a line of characters : ");
        gets(inbuff);

        init_stack (&st);                               /* Note 3 */
        for (index = 0; inbuff[index] != '\0'; index++) {
                push (inbuff[index], &st);
        }

        while ( !is_empty (st)) {
                putchar ( pop(&st) );
        }
        putchar ('\n');
}
```

The function main() is in this source file. It is designed as a driver function to test the STACK utility functions. Note that no reference is made to the specifics of the implementation of a STACK. The constant MAX, the elts array, and the index top are not mentioned. The program is written using the identifier STACK and the STACK utility functions.

Note 1: The header file stack.h must be included to provide the declaration of a STACK.

Note 2: The identifier STACK is used as the type name in this declaration of a variable of type STACK.

Note 3: The address of the variable st is passed to those STACK utility functions that need a parameter of type STACK *. Since the functions change the contents of a STACK, it is not enough to pass in a pointer to a STACK; the address of a STACK declared in the program should be the actual parameter.

Learning Activities

14. If your compiler supports linking code from separate source files, compile and link the files stackex.c and stack.c. Execute the program with several different lines of input to ensure that it works properly.

15. If your compiler does not support separate source modules, you can make this program work by combining the files stackex.c and stack.c into one source code file. The second occurrence of the line

```
#include "stack.h"
```

should be omitted from your file before compiling it. Test the program with several different lines of input.

16. a. What happens if more characters are put into the stack than there is room in the buffer? Do the stack utility functions allow you to overwrite the end of the array? Why or why not?

b. Modify main() to output a diagnostic message when an attempt is made to overrun the array. The modification should not reference the constant MAX, the array elts, or the index top, since those are part of the specifics of the STACK implementation. Instead, the values returned by the STACK utility functions should be examined to provide the needed information.

17. Test stackex.c by entering a carriage return immediately after the prompt. Does this cause any problems? Trace the execution of the program by hand for this case.

18. *C by Discovery*   With the following declarations,

```
typedef int INTEGER;
int x;
INTEGER y;
```

will x and y be recognized as the same type? Write a short program to test this. Your program will not need to do any more than declare and initialize the variables and try to test them for equality, or to assign one variable to the other to see if the compiler will allow the mixing of these types.

8.6 Function Definitions

As with variables, there is a distinction between function definitions and function declarations. We will discuss function definitions here. Declarations will be discussed in Section 8.7. Many examples of functions have appeared earlier in the text.

The information communicated by the function definition includes the function type, the function name (an identifier), the names, types and number of formal parameters, and the executable statements for the function. The syntax for defining the functions and the formal parameters will be reviewed here.

Formal Parameters

The parameters as they appear in the definition of the function are called formal parameters. The parameters that appear in function calls are known as actual parameters. The names of the formal parameters must appear inside the parentheses that follow the name of the function in the definition. The formal parameter list consists of the parameter names separated by commas. They appear in the order that is expected in the function call.

For older compilers, the declarations of the parameter types appear together with the names between the first line of the function definition and the opening brace for the function block. The information given in these two places is the number of parameters, the type of the parameters, and the names by which they will be referred in the function code. An example of the declaration of the parameters for a function in the older style appears below.

```
type function_name ( param1, param2, param3)
int param1, param3;
char *param2;
{

        /* function code goes here */

}
```

The function in the example takes three parameters named `param1`, `param2`, `param3`. Both `param1` and `param3` are of type `int`, while `param2` is a pointer to a `char`. The function code will reference these parameters by their names.

Defining Functions in ANSI C

A new feature that has been introduced in the ANSI Standards for C is the method of defining functions. Current compilers meeting the ANSI standards will accept and understand the syntax above, but also allow a new syntax for parameters to functions. This new syntax consists of including the type of each formal parameter with its name inside the parentheses following the function name. Again, the order of the formal parameters should match the order of the parameters in the function call. The ANSI C definition for the example above is given here.

```
type function_name (int param1, char *param2, int param3)
{

        /* function code goes here */

}
```

The first line in this example takes the place of the first three lines of the previous example. Again, there are three parameters named `param1`, `param2`, and `param3`. Again, `param1` and `param3` are of type `int`, while `param2` is a pointer to a `char`.

If a function does not take any parameters, the formal parameter list should consist of the single keyword `void`, as in the following example.

```
type funct_name(void)
{

    /* function code */

}
```

Function Types

Another way that functions communicate with other parts of the program is through their return value and its type. When a function is defined, the function type appears first in the definition. The default type for a C function is type `int`. Any other type must be explicitly defined. Other possible function types include any of the integer or floating point types, pointers, structures, and unions. A function may not return an array or another function. The type of a function matches the type of the expression associated with its `return` statement.

If a function does not return a value, type `void` should be indicated in its definition. There are two ways in which a function will not return a value. First, a function may not contain a `return` statement. In this case, the function would terminate execution at the closing braces for the function block. Second, the `return` statement may be used without an accompanying expression.

If an expression accompanies the `return` statement, the value of the expression becomes the value of the function and the type of the expression becomes the function's type. In C, the function value can be assigned to a variable, as in the statement

```
total = sum(n1, n2, n3);
```

This assignment is optional. If the function does tasks other than simply returning a value, it could be called without assigning the return value.

For example, a function could be written to find the end of a sentence in input. If it is known that every sentence in the input ends with either a period, a question mark, or an exclamation point, the code might be written as shown in Example 8-12.

 Example 8-12: endofsen.c

```
/*              endofsen.c
 *
 *    Synopsis  -  A function that finds the end of a sentence if it
 *                 ends in '.', '?', '!'.  Returns 1 for success, 0
 *                 for end-of-file.
 *
 *    Objective -  To illustrate a use for the return statement.
 */
```

```
#include <stdio.h>

int endofsen(int * punctptr)                            /* Note 1 */
{
        int iochar;
        while ( (iochar = getchar()) != EOF)
                if ((iochar == '.') || (iochar == '?')
                                    || ( iochar == '!')) {
                        *punctptr = iochar;             /* Note 2 */
                        return 1;                       /* Note 3 */
                }
        return 0;                                       /* Note 4 */
}
```

This is a single function, not a whole program. The input is read character by character in a while loop with getchar(). Each input character is tested against the given punctuation. The function will terminate its execution if it reads one of the given punctuation marks or if end of input is sensed.

Note 1: The parameter to endofsen() is punctptr. The punctuation mark that terminates the current input sentence will be passed back to the calling function in the parameter. Since a value of a variable in the calling function is to be changed, a pointer to that variable is passed into endofsen().

Note 2: If one of the punctuation marks is read, its value is assigned to the contents of the address in punctptr.

Note 3: If one of the given sentence terminators is read, the function returns the value 1.

Note 4: This line will only be executed when end of input is sensed before one of the stated punctuation marks. The return value is zero to indicate this situation.

This function might be used in a program to analyze English sentences and classify them as questions, statements, or exclamations. In this case it would be necessary to check value of the parameter upon return from the function. However, if the program reads to the end of input without encountering one of the specified punctuation marks, that fact should be checked by the program too. A program to do that is shown in Example 8-13.

Example 8-13: classify.c

```
/*              classify.c
 *
 *   Synopsis  -  Reads through English sentence input and counts
 *                each sentence that ends with '.', '?', or '!'
 *                as a statement, a question, or an exclamation.
 *
```

```
*     Objective -   To illustrate checking the return value of a
*                   function as well as the value of of a parameter.
*/

#include <stdio.h>
extern int endofsen (int *pp);

void main()
{
        int punct;
        int statementcounter = 0,
            questioncounter  = 0,
            exclaimcounter   = 0;

        printf ("Enter English sentences as input.  ");
        printf ("Terminate input with an End of File mark.\n");

        while ( endofsen (&punct)) {                     /* Note 1 */
                if (punct == '.')                        /* Note 2 */
                        statementcounter++;
                else if (punct == '?')
                        questioncounter++;
                else if (punct == '!')
                        exclaimcounter++;
        }
        printf ("%d statements, %d questions, and %d exclamations.\n",
                statementcounter, questioncounter, exclaimcounter);
}
```

This program will need to be linked with the object code from the function endofsen.c. The linker will take care of the unresolved reference to the function endofsen() that appears in the `while` loop expression. Other than variable declarations, initializations, and printf() statements, the code consists of a compound `if-else` statement nested inside a `while` loop.

Note 1: The `while` loop tests the value returned by endofsen(). If it is 1 (true), the loop will be entered because the end of a sentence was found. If it is 0 (false), the `while` loop will terminate because end of input was sensed.

Note 2: The value of `punct` is checked in the compound `if-else` statement. This statement is only executed when the end of a sentence is found, and in that case, `punct` contains the sentence-terminating punctuation mark. The classification of the sentence depends on this value.

Learning Activity

19. Test classify.c with several different input streams.

   a. Does it work correctly with input consisting of English sentences that end in the characters ' . ', ' ? ', ' ! '? (Does it work for the input for which it was designed?)

   b. If the input stream consists of the characters in the boxes below,

   what is the output of the program? How many times would the function endofsen() be called?

   c. Does the program handle end-of-file correctly? Test it with empty input. Test it with the end of the last sentence coinciding with the end of the input stream. Test it with the input stream ending in mid-sentence without any punctuation.

   d. Obviously this program would not behave correctly if there were real numbers (containing decimal points) in the input stream. List several other types of input that would cause the program to misbehave.

Another use of the function endofsen() might be to simply position the input pointer after the current sentence so that other input processing could take place. As long as the other input processing would be doing its own checking on the end of input, neither the parameter nor the return value of the function need be checked. The program in Example 8-14 implements this situation. The function that does the other input processing is written as a stub.

Example 8-14: position.c

```
/*              position.c
 *
 *   Synopsis  -  Program calls endofsen() to read input up to the
 *                first occurrence of '.', '?', or '!' and then
 *                calls a stub function that needs to be completed to
 *                process the remaining input.
 *
 *   Objective -  To illustrate calling of a function for the tasks
 *                it performs and not for its return value or its
 *                parameter value.
 */
```

```
#include <stdio.h>
extern int endofsen (int *pp);

void main ()
{
        void processinput (void);
        int dummy;

        printf ("Enter your input now.  Terminate by ");
        printf ("signaling end of file.\n");

        endofsen (&dummy);                                  /* Note 1 */

        processinput ();
}

/*********************************** processinput ()  ********/
/*   processinput () -  A stub function.  It reads to end of input.
 */

void processinput (void)
{
        int iochar;

        while ((iochar = getchar ()) != EOF ) {             /* Note 2 */
                /* code for processing would go here */
        }
}
```

Two functions, main() and processinput(), make up this file. Again, the object code from this module would be linked with the object code from endofsen() before execution. The function main() simply prompts for input and calls the other two functions. The function processinput() is a stub. It announces its entry and exit. A `while` loop reads through input to end of file.

Note 1: This call to endofsen() is different from the call in the last program. The return value is not assigned to any variable or checked in any way. The parameter is simply a place holder. Its value upon return from the function is not checked either.

Note 2: Because the return value from endofsen() was not checked, it is imperative that processinput() check for end of input. Depending on the processing to be done and what is known about the form of input, the way that the check is done may change.

8.7   Function Declarations and Calls

A function may be called by another function. When this happens, an execution environment is created for the function and control passes to its code. The execution environment contains memory for the parameters to the function and the local variables. When the function terminates execution, the memory space occupied by the execution environment is returned for other use. The space occupied by the local variables and parameters is not guaranteed to retain their contents.

A function call consists of the function name and a pair of left and right parentheses enclosing a list of the actual parameters. The actual parameters or arguments to a function are those expressions that appear in a call to that function. The program communicates with the function through the actual parameters in the function calls.

If a parameter is passed by value, as it is in C, the current values of the actual parameters are copied to a special place in memory (usually a stack) where the function will access them. This occurs every time the function is called. Changes to the parameters are made to these copies. The values of the actual parameters are not touched. Diagrams indicating the execution environment for the program param.c appeared in Section 4.4.

Declarations of Functions

As we stated earlier, the default type for a function's return value is type `int`. In older compilers, if a function returned an `int` it did not need any further declaration. If it returned a value with type other than `int`, a declaration that could be seen by the calling function was necessary so that the program would set up correctly for the return value. The information contained in that declaration consisted of the function's type and its name. For example, the function strcpy() returns a `char *` value. An old-style declaration of strcpy() would be

```
char *strcpy();
```

The declaration should appear in an external position (outside a function) above the position where strcpy() was called, in an included header file, or in the function block where the call to strcpy() appears. If this declaration was missing, the compiler would assume that strcpy() returned an `int` and would probably complain about any attempt to assign the value returned by strcpy() to a variable of any other type.

Prototyping in ANSI C

A new feature that has been introduced in the ANSI Standards for C is that of function prototyping. Current compilers meeting the ANSI standards will accept and understand the syntax above, but also allow a new syntax for declaring functions. This new syntax, known as prototyping, consists of including the type of each formal parameter inside the parentheses following the function name in a declaration. The parameters in the prototype declaration should match the parameters in the function definition and in the function call. The prototype declaration for the function strcpy() is given here.

```
char *strcpy(char *copy, const char *original);*
```

The information communicated by this declaration includes the number and the type of the parameters as well as the type returned by the function. Function prototype declarations allow the C compiler to check the type and number of parameters. This was not a possibility in earlier C compilers.

ANSI compilers will accept the old-style function declarations for a transition period. For this reason, the syntax

```
char *strcpy();
```

is taken to mean that the compiler can make no assumptions about parameters to strcpy(). It turns off type checking; it does *not* mean that strcpy() does not take any parameters. If a function does not take any parameters, its prototype declaration would contain the keyword `void` between the parentheses. For example,

```
char *f1(void);
```

declares f1() as a function that does not take parameters and returns a `char *` value.

Currently, the old-style declarations are more portable because not every system has an ANSI C compiler. If you do have an ANSI compiler, you should use the new prototype declarations. The ability of the compiler to do parameter checking is very desirable.

A Closer Look

In the old style of function parameter declaration, the automatic conversion features of C come into play. For example, if an actual parameter is declared to be of type `char`, the compiler will automatically widen it to a value of type `int`. The same is true for the other automatic conversions in C. These conversions make type checking of actual parameters against formal parameters very difficult.

Another difficulty with type checking arose from the fact that different source files were compiled separately. There was no mechanism for communicating the type and number of parameters to a C function across the different files. The verification of the number and type of the parameters to a function was left to the

---

* The keyword `const` is new in ANSI C. It is a type qualifier and indicates that `original` will not be changed. It is added in ANSI C for additional optimization possibilities.

programmer. Now the ANSI prototype declarations allow external declarations of functions that include the function type and the number and type of the formal parameters.

With ANSI C prototyping, the declared type of a parameter is explicit; the compiler will expect the declared type. An actual parameter may still be converted by the usual conversion rules in C, but the converted value must match the formal parameter in type. It is still possible to pass an actual parameter that does not match the declared parameter type in the function; however, it is now necessary to explicitly cast the actual parameter to the declared type.

Scope of Function Declarations

Since the function name in a function definition is outside a function block, functions will have external linkage by default. This default can be defeated by defining the function with the `static` storage class. As with `static` variables defined externally to a function block, a `static` function will not be known outside its source file.

When a function is called whose code does not appear in the source file, the function is assumed by the compiler to have external linkage. An attempt to resolve the reference will occur during the link phase of the compilation. The linker will search other specified object files as well as the standard or specifically named libraries for the function definition. An error is reported only if the function is not found.

An Example

The program avg.c in Example 8-15 illustrates the syntax for declaring and defining functions that return values other than `int`. The ANSI C prototype is used. The program calculates the mean or average of a collection of integers.

Example 8-15: avg.c

```
/*                  avg.c
 *
 *    Synopsis  -  Computes and outputs the average of
 *                 a set of up to 100 integers.
 *
 *    Objective -  To illustrate the syntax of a function returning
 *                 a noninteger value.  Also illustrates the use of
 *                 the value returned by scanf().
 */

#include <stdio.h>
#define MAX 100

void main()
{
```

```
        int count;
        int values[MAX];
        float average(int array[], int c);              /* Note 1 */
        int getinputvalues(int array[]);

        printf ("Enter your data now.  Enter one integer per line.\n");
        printf ("Enter 'Q' when you want to quit.\n");

        count = getinputvalues(values);                 /* Note 2 */
                                                        /* Note 3 */
        printf ("The average is %5.2f.\n", average(values, count));
}

/***************************  getinputvalues()  *************/
/*   getinputvalues() - Reads integers from the keyboard until a non-
 *                      integer is found.  Puts input into an array.
 *                      Returns the number of integers read.
 */

int getinputvalues (int *valarray)                      /* Note 4 */
{
        int i = 0;

        printf (">  ");
                                                        /* Note 5 */
        while (i < MAX && scanf("%d", valarray + i) ) {
                i++;
                printf (">  ");
        }
        return (i);
}


/*******************************  average()  *************/
/*   average() -  Calculates and returns the average of the
 *               integers in the array intarray.
 */

float average (int *intarray, int count)                /* Note 6 */
{
        int i, sum = 0;

        if (count != 0) {
                for (i = 0; i < count; i++)
                        sum = sum + intarray[i];
                return ((float) sum / count);           /* Note 7 */
        }
        else
```

```
              return (0.0);                          /* Note 8 */
}
```

The program consists of three functions, main(), getinputvalues(), and average(). The function main() makes its declarations, prompts for input, and calls the other functions. The function getinputvalues() reads the integers that are input. It uses a `while` loop and puts the input into an array. It also keeps track of how many integers are input. The function average() calculates the sum and returns the average.

Note 1: The function average() returns a noninteger value. It must be declared. The ANSI C prototype also gives the type and the number of parameters to average(). Note that the names given to the parameters in the prototype do not have to match either the names of the formal parameters in the definition of average() or the names of the actual parameters in any call. In fact, these names can be omitted entirely.

The prototype declaration of getinputvalues() appears on the next line. Since this function returns a value of type `int`, it was not absolutely necessary to declare it. However, without this declaration, the parameter checking would not be done.

Note 2: In this call to getinputvalues(), the actual parameter is the array `values`. The function getinputvalues() is to fill up the array, so the array must be declared in the program to allocate the space properly. The address of the first cell in the array is passed to the function. The function will return the number of cells into which it placed a value.

Note 3: The function average() returns a value of type `float`. This is converted by the printf() function to the `%f` format. It will use a minimum field width of five spaces with two decimal places.

Note that printf() is an example of a function whose code does not appear in this source code file. The compiler assumes that printf() has external linkage and the reference is resolved by the linker.

Note 4: The new style of function definition is used for getinputvalues(). This function returns an `int` so that the type does not need to be declared. The parameter is declared to have type `int *`. This type is compatible with the type in the prototype declaration in main(). Note that it is important to know what this function does with its parameter. An unknowledgeable programmer might call this function by passing it an uninitialized `int *` variable instead of the address of an array. If the space for the array has not been allocated properly, the program may have unexpected results.

Note 5: Two conditions determine the fate of this `while` loop. First the index into the array is checked to insure that the array bounds are not overrun. Then the value returned by scanf() is checked.

In this case, scanf() reads the sequence of digits on the input line, converts them to a value of type `int`, and stores this result in the array. If this is done successfully, scanf() returns the number of successful conversions. In this case, 1 would be returned if a conversion was made and 0 would be returned if noninteger characters were encountered before any conversion took place.

A sequence of input digits would cause a successful conversion and the `while` loop would be entered. When an alphabetic character such as `'Q'` is entered, scanf() would return 0 and the `while` loop would terminate.

Note that scanf() is another example of a function in which external linkage is assumed. The code for scanf() will be found by the linker when the C library is searched. A declaration for scanf() is usually in the file stdio.h.

Note 6: The fact that average() returns a `float` must be declared with the function. The parameters are declared in the new-style definition.

Note 7: The return value is `(sum / count)`. Since both `sum` and `count` are variables of type `int`, the result of this operation would be of type `int` also. The cast to type `float` is necessary to preserve the fractional part of this quotient.

Note 8: The function average() returns a value of 0.0 when the number of elements entered was 0. Since the average of the input integers could be 0.0, a different return value could be chosen.

Learning Activities

23. Execute avg.c to make sure it runs as you expected.
24. Modify avg.c in the following ways. After each modification, recompile the program, and if that is successful, test the program by entering the integers 1, 2, 3, 4. The result should be 2.50.
    a. Move the declaration of average() from inside main() to a position above main(). What happens when you test it?

    b. Remove the declaration of average() from the new position above main(). What happens when you test it this time?

    c. Remove the keyword `float` from the first line of the function definition. At this point the type of the function should not be mentioned in your modified version of the program. What happens when you test the program this time?

    d. Now add both declarations of average() as type `float` to their original positions. Remove the cast, `(float)`, from the `return` statement in average(). What happens when you test the program?

    e. Try to generalize from these experiences about the types of functions, their declarations, and their return values.

25. Experiment with scanf(). Try entering different input to see what the action is. What happens when you signal end of input? What happens for the other control characters? The alphabetics? The punctuation marks? If you have access to the documentation for scanf(), read about its return value. Did scanf() behave as the documentation specified?

8.8   Pointers to Functions

When a C program is compiled and loaded into memory, the executable code is organized in such a way that an address is associated with every identifier with either external linkage or `static` storage class. This is true of identifiers that represent variables, as well as identifiers that name functions.

When the name of a function is mentioned in C source code, it is interpreted as the address of the code for that function in memory. This is analogous to the use of an array name to mean the address of the first cell of the array.

In C it is possible to declare a variable that is a pointer to a function returning any legitimate type. The values that can be assigned to such a variable are the addresses of functions in the source code.

In the older style of declaration, a pointer to a function returning an `int` would have the following form:

```
int (*fnptr)();
```

In our usual way of decoding a C declaration, we note first that anything of the form `(*fnptr)()` is an `int`. Also we note that the parentheses around `*fnptr` serve to hold the `*` closer to the identifier `fnptr` than the `()`. Removing the `()`, we see that `(*fnptr)` is a function returning an `int`. The final step removes the dereferencing operator, `*`, and tells us that `fnptr` is a pointer to a function returning an `int`.

This notation is further complicated in an ANSI C prototype declaration because the type and number of the parameters must be specified also. For example,

```
int (*fnptr)( char *s, int i);
```

declares a pointer to a function that returns an `int` and takes two parameters, a `char *` value and an `int`. In the declaration

```
float (*fn (int y, float z)) (char *x);
```

`fn` is a function that takes two parameters: `y` of type `int` and `z` of type `float`. The value returned by fn() is a pointer to a function that returns a `float` and takes a single parameter of type `char *`. This declaration can be decoded in the same way as other C declarations. Each set of tokens can be removed and the type of the resulting expression can be determined. It will take some practice.

To illustrate this concept, we will use the signal() library function. In certain instances, when a software error occurs, a signal can be sent from the operating system to a running program. For example, a user who wants to abort a running program might press a sequence of keys to request the operating system to abort that program. The operating system then sends a special signal to the program to cause it to terminate. Other cases when a signal might be sent are when a program encounters a floating point error, an overflow condition, or an illegal memory reference. Each of these conditions might cause the operating system to "signal" the program to terminate.

In contrast, the user might notice that the same sequence of keys pressed to abort a running program has a totally different effect when in an editor program. This is due to the signal-handling properties of the editor program. When the interrupt sequence of keys is pressed, the operating system will still send the signal to the editor program, but the editor program handles the signal differently. This signal handling is done with the signal() library function. It is a part of the standard C library that is delivered with ANSI C compilers.

The purpose of the signal() library function is to specify how a particular signal is to be handled. It takes two parameters, the signal number that is to be handled and the address of the function that should be executed when a signal occurs. The second parameter has type pointer to function.

An ANSI C implementation should provide a header file, signal.h, that contains the relevant signal numbers for each system. Each signal has a specific meaning and a specific default action set by the system. When the signal() library function is called, the default action can be changed.

The function signal() also returns a pointer to a function. Its value could be the address of the previous signal-handling routine, a representative of the default, or a system-provided signal-handling routine. The program signal.c in Example 8-16 illustrates signal handling and the use of a pointer to a function.

The example is very simple in concept. An infinite loop is started. The only way out of this program would be to press the keys on the keyboard to signal an interrupt. Usually, when those keys are pressed, the program would terminate quietly. Any messages would be output by the operating system. With this new signal handling, the program would output the message "You got me!" before terminating.

Example 8-16: signal.c

```
/*              signal.c
 *
 *    Synopsis  -  Changes the interrupt signal handling to output
 *                 a message before terminating the program.
 *
 *    Objective -  To illustrate a use for a pointer to a function.
 */

#include <stdio.h>
#include <signal.h>                              /* Note 1 */

void main()
{
        void printit(void);

        signal (SIGINT, printit);                /* Note 2 */
        while (1)
                printf("Still looping.\n");
}
/********************************* printit () ***********/
/*      printit() - Outputs a message and exits the program.
 */
```

```
void printit(void)
{
        printf("You got me!\n");
        exit(0);
}
```

The program consists of the function main() and printit(). The code for main() consists of a call to signal() and an infinite loop. The code for printit() consists of a call to printf() and a call to exit().

Note 1: The file signal.h is included. It is necessary for the list of signal numbers and the proper declaration of the signal() library function. As an example, the ANSI C declaration of signal() should have the following form:

```
void (*signal(int sig, void (*sighandler)(int)))(int);
```

This gives the following information about signal():

a. It returns a pointer to a function that does not return any value and takes a single parameter of type int.

b. The parameters to signal are a value of type int, and a pointer to a function that does not return any value and takes a single parameter of type int. The return value from signal is the address of the previous signal handler, and the second parameter is the address of the new signal handler.

Note 2: In this call to signal(), the signal being handled is SIGINT, the interrupt signal. The function to be executed when an interrupt occurs is printit(). The return value from signal() is ignored.

Learning Activities

26. a. If the signal-handling functions are available on your system, run the program signal.c to see how it works.

b. Modify signal.c by removing the call to exit() in printit(), and run the program again. Explain what you think happened this time.

27. Decode the following declarations. When one of the identifiers is a function or a pointer to a function, state the return type of the function and the type of the parameters.

a. In the declaration

```
int (*compare)(void * val; void * datum);
```

state the types of compare, val, and datum.

b. In the declaration

```
float (*what ( char *x, int (*y)(char *z))) (int w);
```

state the types of what, w, x, y, and z.

Be aware that in this section, the example of signal handling was used to show a use for pointers to functions. This section did not provide a complete discussion of signal handling. Much of the signal handling is dependent on the specific operating system and hardware. This discussion is beyond the scope of this text.

Language Elements Introduced in This Chapter: A Review

** ANSI Function Definitions **

```
type function_name (int param1, char *param2,
                         int param3)
{
      /* function code goes here */
}
```

** ANSI Function Prototype Declarations **

```
type function_name (int param1, char *param2,
                         int param3);
char f1(void);                 /* No parameters */
```

** Storage Class Specifiers **

```
auto
static
register
extern
typedef
```

** Types **

```
typedef old_type  new_type;
```

** Variable Declarations **

```
auto int counter;
static int counter;
register int counter;
extern int x;
int (*fnptr)();       /* pointer to a function - old
                         style */
int (*fnptr)( char *s, int i);       /* new style
*/
```

Things to Remember

1. `Auto` and `register` variables are created each time their function is called.
2. External and `static` variables are in existence for the full program execution.
3. It is illegal to use the address operator, `&`, with the name of a `register` variable.
4. Different implementations of C might impose restrictions on the number and type of `register` variables allowed.
5. Local variables are declared inside a function or block. They can only be accessed in that function or block and are unknown outside it.
6. Global or external variables are declared outside function blocks and can be referenced by any function in the file that occurs after the declaration of the variable.
7. If a local variable in a function has the same name as a global variable, all references to that name will access the local variable.
8. A side effect is produced when a function modifies the value of a global variable. Side effects should be kept to a minimum and clearly documented with comments.
9. A source module consists of source code related to a single task. In C each source module can be put in a separate file and compiled separately. The corresponding object modules must be linked together before the program can be executed.
10. By default, external variables have external linkage. This default is overridden by declaring an external variable with `static` storage class.
11. `Typedefs` associate an identifier with a type.
12. `Typedefs` are used for readability and portability. They are often put in header files.
13. A stack is a data type defined as a list in which all additions and insertions take place at the same end of the list. The basic operations are to push (or add) a value to the top of the stack or to pop (or remove) a value from the top of the stack.
14. The parameters as they appear in the definition of the function are called formal parameters. The parameters that appear in function calls are known as actual parameters.
15. ANSI compilers will accept the old-style function declarations for a transition period.
16. In ANSI C, the syntax `char *f_name();` is taken to mean that the compiler can make no assumptions about parameters to f_name().
17. The ANSI C prototype declarations allow the compiler to check the type and number of the parameters in a function call. This was not possible with older compilers.
18. Functions have external linkage by default. This default can be defeated by defining the function with the `static` storage class.
19. When the name of a function is mentioned in C source code, it is interpreted as the address of the code for that function in memory.

8.9 Exercises and Programming Problems

1. Write two versions of a program that outputs the following table:

    ```
         X                X cubed

    -----------          ---------

         1                    1
         2                    8
         3                   27
         4                   64

                    .
                    .
                    .
    ```

    Have the table continue until X is 20.

    a. For the first version, write a function to do the cube calculation that takes a single parameter. If the parameter is 2 on entry to the function, the parameter should have the value 8 on exit from the function. That is, implement a "pass by reference" on the function's parameter and have the cubed value passed back in the parameter.

    b. For the second version, write a function that does the cubing, but, have the cubed value passed back to the main program as the return value of the function.

2. Write a function that interchanges two values of type int. Write a driver program to test your function.

3. Write a program that inputs the date in the form

    ```
    10/14/89
    ```

    and outputs it in the form

    ```
    October 14, 1989
    ```

    Write the program in a structured style, and plan the communication between parts of the program before you start coding.

4. Write a program that reads its input and outputs the number of characters, words, and lines that it reads. For this problem, a word will be defined as a sequence of characters delimited by whitespace, a blank, ' ', a tab, '\t', or a newline, '\n'. Use the communication concepts in this chapter.

5. Predict the output of the following program by filling in the blanks below.

```
/*                              epp5.c                              */
#include <stdio.h>

int   W, X, Y, I;
void demonstrate (int *y, int v);

main()
{
      W = 3;
```

```
        X = 2;
        Y = 1;
        I = 2;

        demonstrate (&W, Y);
        printf ("%d, %d, %d, %d\n", W, X, Y, I);

        demonstrate (&I, X);
        printf ("%d, %d, %d, %d\n", W, X, Y, I);

}

void demonstrate (int* Y, int V)
{

        int    W, X;

        X = (*Y) * V;
        W = X / 2;
        *Y = W - V;
        I++;
        printf ("%d, %d, %d, %d\n",   V, W, X, *Y);
}
```

Output: ____, ____ , ____, ____
             ____, ____ , ____, ____
             ____, ____ , ____, ____
             ____, ____ , ____, ____

6.   Predict the output of the following program by filling in the blanks below.

```
/*                              epp6.c                         */

#include <stdio.h>
int int1 = 7,
    int2 = 8,
    int3 = 9;

void main()
{
        void p1 (int *x, int y);
        int int3, int4, int5;

        int1 = 1;
        int2 = 2;
        int3 = 3;
        int4 = 4;
        int5 = 5;
```

```
        p1 (&int3, int4);
        printf ("int1 %d, int2 %d, int3 %d, int4 %d, int5 %d\n",
                        int1, int2, int3, int4, int5);

        p1 (&int2, int5);
        printf ("int1 %d, int2 %d, int3 %d, int4 %d, int5 %d\n",
                        int1, int2, int3, int4, int5);
}

void p1 (int *x, int y)
{
        static int int2 = 5;
              int int1 = 2;

        *x = *x + 3;
        y = y - 4;
        int1* = 2;
        int2+ = 5;
        int3- = 1;

        printf ("int1 %d, int2 %d, int3 %d, *x %d, y %d\n",
                        int1, int2, int3, *x, y);
}
```

Output: int1 ____ , int2 ____ , int3 ____ , *x ____ , y ____

int1 ____ , int2 ____ , int3 ____ , int4 ____ , int5 ____

int1 ____ , int2 ____ , int3 ____ , *x ____ , y ____

int1 ____ , int2 ____ , int3 ____ , int4 ____ , int5 ____

7. Write a program to do fraction arithmetic. A sample run follows:

```
Welcome to the Fraction Arithmetic program.
--------------------------------------------

Your problems with fractions can be solved here.

Enter a fraction arithmetic problem ( Example 2/5 - 4/7)
1/2 + 1/4
The answer is 6/8.
```

Your program should handle the operations of addition, subtraction, multiplication and division. The answer does not have to be in lowest terms for this version of the program.

Plan your program so that it is modular. Have the input done in one module, the output done in a second module, and the calculation done in a third. Put each module in a separate source code file. The function main() should reside in its own module and be a driver program. If possible, try to write the program without using of any global variables.

8. Write a program that will simulate a soft drink machine that dispenses four types of soft drinks. The program will accept character input only. The symbols `'C'`, `'O'`, `'L'`, and `'S'` will stand for the drinks (Cola, Orange, Lemon, and Spritzer). The symbols `'N'`, `'D'`, and `'Q'` will stand for the coins (nickel, dime, and quarter). No other coins will be accepted. The character `'R'` when read as input will stand for the coin return. Any time that an `'R'` is input, all money should be returned to the user.

The program will output messages that simulate the output from the soft drink machine. For example, `"Cola dispensed,"` `"30 cents returned,"` `"Sorry, out of Spritzer,"` or `"Your change is 10 cents."`

In addition to inputting the money and drink selections, and outputting the messages to the user, the program will internally keep track of the amount of change, and the inventory of each drink. A sample run follows.

```
Enter 65 cents for a drink > Q
25 cents received        > D
35 cents received        > D
45 cents received        > Q
70 cents received
Make your drink selection now  > O
Orange drink dispensed
5 cents in change given

Enter 65 cents for a drink > Q
25 cents received        > Q
50 cents received        > C
Sorry, insufficient funds entered
Please enter additional 15 cents > R
50 cents returned

Enter 65 cents for a drink >
```

Write your program in a modular structured style with the different modules in separate source files. Plan the communication between the different parts of the program. Minimize your use of global variables.

9. The data structure stack was discussed in Section 8-5. A queue is another specialized list in which insertions are done at one end (the rear) of the list and deletions are done at the other (the front of the list). For example, a supermarket checkout line operates on the queue principle. Like a stack, a queue can also be implemented with an array. In addition to the array to hold the elements, two additional values must be stored, the index of the front of the list and the index of the rear of the list. Note that a queue can start and end at any position of the array. For example, if the array contains 8 cells, consider the configuration after 8 additions to the queue and 3 deletions, as shown in Figure 8-4.

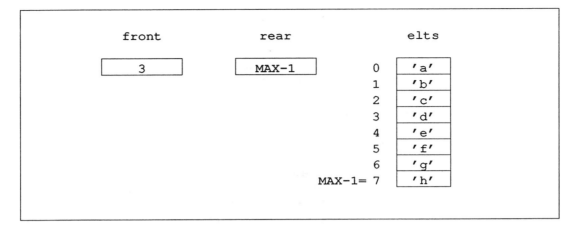

Figure 8-4 **After Inserting a, b, c, d, e, f, g, h and Deleting a, b, c**

The next addition to the queue would not fit at that end of the array but could be stored in the cell with index 0 in a wraparound or circular fashion. The resulting configuration is shown in Figure 8-5.

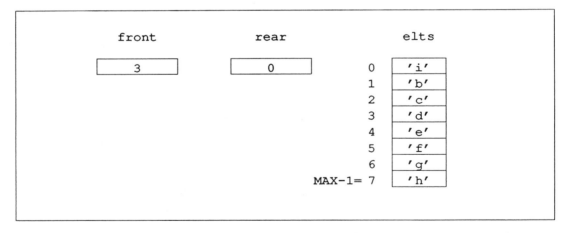

Figure 8-5 **After Inserting i**

a. Write a declaration of a data structure to store a queue where the elements are of type `char`.

b. To add an element to the rear of a queue is to enqueue the element. Write a function enqueue() that takes the following parameters: an element of type `char` that is to be enqueued, and a pointer to the queue that will receive the addition. Have the function return 1 for success and 0 for failure in case the queue is already full.

c. To delete an element from the queue is to dequeue an element. Implement the function dequeue(). Have it take a single parameter, the queue, and have it return the value dequeued or −1 in case of error (the queue was empty).

d. Write the utility functions is_full(), is_empty(), and init_queue() to complete your queue implementation.

10. Consider the following `typedef` declaration of a different implementation of a string. This should be similar to your declaration for problem 8 of Chapter 7.

```
typedef struct {
        char word[80];
        short length;
} STRING;
```

a. Write a conversion function with the ANSI C prototype

```
STRING *strconv(STRING *newform, char * oldform)
```

that will take C's usual representation of a string and convert it to a value of type `STRING` which is stored in the contents of newform. Have your function report an error by returning a `NULL` pointer if the string `oldform` does not fit correctly in `newform->word`. What should be the value returned in the member `newform->word` in case of buffer overflow?

b. Write a version of the string copy function that will copy one element of type `STRING` to another.

c. Modity your version of the string concatenation function. It should have ANSI C prototype

```
STRING *strconcat (STRING *s1, STRING *s2)
```

and should concatenate `s2` onto the end of `s1`. Have your function report an error by returning a `NULL` pointer if the concatenated string would overflow the buffer.

11. The package for the data type stack was written with an array implementation. Rewrite this package using a linked list implementation.

a. Use a `typedef` to declare a `node` that has space for a data element and a pointer to the next `node`. Your stack will be represented by a pointer to a node. After the elements `'a'`, `'b'`, and `'c'` are pushed on, in that order, a stack `s` would have the following representation:

After a pop() operation, the stack `s` would have the following configuration:

b. Write C functions for the operations push(), pop(), is_full(), is_empty() and init_stack(). These functions should take the same parameters and return the same values and types as the functions in the text.

c. Put the `typedef` declarations and the function declarations in a header file stack.h and the function definitions in a file stack.c. (You may want to save your other versions of stack.h and stack.c first.) Test your package with the program stackex.c. It should run properly without any changes to stackex.c.

Multidimensional Arrays and Double Indirection

Chapter 9

9.1   Two-Dimensional Arrays

A two-dimensional array can be thought of as a matrix or rectangle of elements. For example,

	col 0	col 1	col 2	col 3
row 0	3.1	7.6	9.4	2.2
row 1	5.3	8.2	1.4	2.7
row 2	6.0	4.2	7.8	5.1

This depicts a two-dimensional array with base type `float`. It has three rows and four columns. Indices are used to access the elements in each cell of the array. In this array, the row indices would start at 0 and terminate at 2 and the column indices would start at 0 and terminate at 3. For example, 4.2 is in the position with row index 2 and column index 1. This could be referred to as the [2][1] position.

A two-dimensional array is declared by stating the type of the element, the variable name, and both dimensions in brackets ([]). The following line of code declares a two-dimensional array of `float` elements. The name of the array is `two_d` and it will have 3 rows and 4 columns. It would serve to declare the array depicted above.

```
float two_d[3][4];
```

The expression `two_d[2][3]` would reference the element in the [2][3] position, with row index 2 and column index 3.

The program determ.c in Example 9-1 gives an illustration of declaring and accessing the elements in a two-dimensional array. A 2 x 2 array of type `float` is declared, and its determinant is calculated.

 Example 9-1: determ.c

```
/*              determ.c
 *
 *   Synopsis  -   Inputs a 2 x 2 matrix and calculates its
 *                 determinant.
 *
 *   Objective -   To show the basics of two-dimensional arrays.
 */

#include <stdio.h>

void main(void)
{
        int i, j;
        float m[2][2], determinant;                      /* Note 1 */

        printf("Calculate the determinant of a 2x2 matrix.\n");
        printf("--------- --- ----------- -- - --- -------\n");

        printf("\nEnter the matrix now.\n");
                                                         /* Note 2 */
        for ( i = 0; i <=1; i++)
                for (j = 0; j <= 1; j++) {
                        printf("\tPosition %d,%d: ", i+1, j+1);
                        scanf("%f", &m[i][j]);           /* Note 3 */
                }
                                                         /* Note 4 */
```

```
        determinant = m[0][0] * m[1][1] - m[0][1] * m[1][0];

        printf(" The determinant is %8.2f\n", determinant);
}
```

The program consists of the single function main().[*] Calls to printf() are used to prompt the user for input and give the result. A call to scanf() inside a nested for loop does the input. Calculation of the determinant is done with a single assignment statement.

Note 1: The variable m is a two-dimensional array of float values. It has two rows and two columns. Both the row and column indices will go from 0 to 1.

Note 2: The following nested for loop is used to access each element in the two-dimensional array. The outer for loop works through the rows of the array. The inner for loop works through each element in a row. Each row will be indexed by the variable i and each column by j.

Note 3: Accessing an element of the array m requires two subscripts. The expression m[i][j] is the element in the i*th* row and j*th* column. Since scanf() requires an address, the address operator, &, is used also; &m[i][j] is the address of the cell in the i*th* row and j*th* column.

Note 4: The determinant is calculated by multiplying the elements in the 1,1 and 2,2 positions and subtracting the product of the elements in the 1,2 and 2,1 positions. The array name with two indices is used to access the elements.

Learning Activities

1. Declare a two-dimensional array of type int with 3 rows and 3 columns.
2. Write a program to calculate the determinant of a 3x3 matrix of integers. If the matrix is given by

$$\begin{pmatrix} a_{11} & a_{12} & a_{13} \\ a_{21} & a_{22} & a_{23} \\ a_{31} & a_{32} & a_{33} \end{pmatrix}$$

the determinant can be calculated using the formula:
```
        a11*a22*a33 + a12*a23*a31 + a21*a32*a13
        - a12*a33*a21 - a11*a23*a32 - a13*a22*a31
```

---

[*] Prior to this chapter we have omitted any mention of parameters to main() in an attempt to keep the code simple. However, main() is a function and can take parameters. This will be discussed in Section 9.7. Consequently, in this chapter, we have started putting the designation void inside the parameters to main() when it does not take any parameters.

9.2   Storage Class and Scope of Multidimensional Arrays

Multidimensional arrays share the same storage class, scope, and initialization properties as one-dimensional arrays and variables of other types.

If `two_d` had been declared inside a function, it would have had the default storage class of `auto`, would have been in existence only during execution of the function, would be known only inside its block, and would have had no initialization done. Inserting the word `static` at the beginning of the declaration, as in

```
static float two_d[3][4];
```

would have changed the storage class and initialization properties. In this case, `two_d` would be in existence during the full execution time of the program, and would have been initialized with zero values for every cell.

Had `two_d` been declared outside of all functions, it would be known from point of declaration to the end of the file, would be able to be accessed by other source modules, would be in existence during program execution, and would be initialized with all zero values.

Static or external arrays can be initialized at the time of declaration. To give `two_d` the values in the array pictured above, the declaration would have been either

```
static float two_d[3][4] = { {3.1, 7.6, 9.4, 2.2},
                             {5.3, 8.2, 1.4, 2.7},
                             {6.0, 4.2, 7.8, 5.1}
                           };
```

or the same expression with the first dimension omitted as in

```
static float two_d[][4] = { {3.1, 7.6, 9.4, 2.2},
                            {5.3, 8.2, 1.4, 2.7},
                            {6.0, 4.2, 7.8, 5.1}
                          };
```

Each of the element lists in the inner sets of braces is used to initialize one row of the array. The reason that the first dimension can be omitted and the second dimension must be included will be discussed later.

As an example, an investor is following six stocks. He wants a program that will compare the prices of his six stocks with their buying price. He wants to have the buying prices stored in the program and he will input the prices he wants to compare.

We could use a two-dimensional array for the stock prices. The array might have 2 rows and 6 columns. The first row (index 0) would be initialized with the buying prices of the six stocks. The second row would be input at time of execution. Each column in the array would store the prices of one of the stocks.

In Example 9-2, the program has been blocked out and the input function has been written. The functions process() and output_results() have been left as stubs and will appear as exercises. Another library function, atof(), is used to aid in the input. Its basic functioning is explained in the notes, but the Programmer's Handbook should be consulted for error handling and other details.

Example 9-2: stocks.c

```
/*                 stocks.c
 *
 *    Synopsis  -  Inputs six stock prices into a two-dimensional array.
 *
 *    Objective -  Illustrates the declaration, initialization, and
 *                 accessing of elements of two-dimensional arrays.
 */

#include <stdio.h>
#include <string.h>
                                                    /* Note 1 */
float stock_prices[2][6] = { {  12.5, 76.125, 34.875,
                                112,  43.25,  88 } };

void main(void)
{
        void input_prices(void);
        void process (void);
        void output_results (void);

        printf ("STOCK INFORMATION PROGRAM\n");
        printf ("------------------------\n");
        printf ("This program will give information about the ");
        printf ("prices of \nsix specific stocks.  You are to enter ");
        printf ("the current prices of \nthe stocks.  A comparison ");
        printf ("will be made with the buying prices \n");
        printf ("of the stocks.\n\n");

        input_prices();
        process();
        output_results();
}

/************************************** input_prices()  ******/
/* Function input_prices() accepts input of 6 quantities of type
 * float to be stored in the second "row" of the array.  The
 * combination of library functions gets() and atof() is used to
 * input the float value.
 */

void input_prices(void)
{
        int i;
        double atof(const char *s);                    /* Note 2 */
```

```
        char instring[20];

        printf ("Please enter the current stock prices now.\n");
        printf ("Stock\tBuying price\tCurrent price\n");
        printf ("-----\t------------\t-------------\n");
        for (i = 0; i < 6; i++) {
                                                    /* Note 3 */
                printf ("#%d: \t%6.2f   \t   ",
                            i+1, stock_prices[0][i]);
                                                    /* Note 4 */
                stock_prices[1][i] = atof( gets(instring) );
        }
        printf ("Thank you!\n");
}

/****************************************** process ()    *********/
/* Function process () - a stub
 */

void process(void)
{
        printf ("process() stub entered.\n");
}

/************************************** output_results () *********/
/* Function output_results () - a stub
 */

void output_results(void)
{
        printf ("output_results() stub entered.\n");
}
```

The program stocks.c consists of four functions, main(), input_prices(), process(), and output_results(). The two functions process() and output_results() are simply stubs. They will be completed in the exercises. The function main() is a driver program. It outputs some messages and then calls the other functions. The meaningful code is in the function input_prices(), which consists of a `for` loop. Notice that the array was declared to be global since the passing of multidimensional arrays as parameters will not be discussed until the next example program. This program could be modified at that time.

Note 1: This illustrates the declaration of a two-dimensional array. This array will be in existence during the total execution time of the program and can be accessed by any of the functions in the program. The array is partially initialized at the time of declaration. The outer braces define the two-dimensional array. The inner set of braces delimit the values for the first row of the array. The second row has been left uninitialized and will therefore be given values of 0.0 for each cell.

Note 2: The standard library function atof() is used as part of the input routine. The name atof() stands for *ascii to float*. It takes a single parameter of type char *, which should point to a null terminated string that contains the ASCII representation of a value of type float. The function atof() returns the corresponding float value. For example, if instring contains the characters

'1'	'2'	'.'	'5'	'\0'

then atof() will return the float value 12.5.

The standard header file stdlib.h contains the declaration of this function. If that file had been included, this line could be omitted.

Note 3: The elements in the array are accessed using the subscript notation. An element in the first row (first index 0) of the array is output in this call to printf(). As with one-dimensional arrays, the pointer notation can be used with more efficiency. The pointer notation for the cell stock_prices[0][i] would be

```
*(*(stock_prices + 0) + i)
```

The rationale for this is presented later.

Note 4: The library function gets() will input a string of characters into instring. The address of instring is returned and passed to atof(); then atof() converts the ASCII characters in the string to a float value. That value is assigned to a cell in the second row (first index 1) of the array.

Learning Activities

3. Extend the stub for output_results() so that it outputs the contents of both rows of the array. Depending on your implementation you may need to change the declarations. For the input

```
15 <CR> 75.5 <CR> 36.25 <CR> 98.5 <CR> 55 <CR> 87.5
```

the output should be

```
Buying price :    12.50  76.12  34.87 112.00  43.25  88.00
Current price:    15.00  75.50  36.25  98.50  55.00  87.50
```

Problem 1 at the end of the chapter gives specifications for the function process() and the completion of this program.

4. a. Execute stocks.c and convince yourself that it works. Experiment with erroneous input and see how the combination of atof() and gets() handles the errors.

   b. Look up atof() in the Programmer's Handbook. Are the errors in input handled by your system as stated in the handbook?

5. The program stocks.c used subscript notation to access the elements of the two-dimensional array. Change this notation to the equivalent pointer notation as described in **Note 3** and test it to make sure that it works.

9.3 Multidimensional Arrays as Parameters to Functions

In the previous example, the array `stock_prices` was declared externally to any function so that it could be accessed by all functions. It would be better programming style to pass the array into the functions as a parameter. When a multidimensional array is passed as an argument to a function, every dimension except the first must be known to the function. As with one-dimensional arrays, the address of the array is actually passed in, but the dimensions must be declared so that the function can properly locate elements in specific locations. For example, if the array were to be passed as a parameter to input_prices() in the last example, the ANSI C definition of the function would have either of the following two forms:

```
void input_prices(float pricearray[][6])
{
        /* function code */
}
```
or
```
void input_prices(float (*pricearray)[6])
{
        /* function code */
}
```

The second form makes use of the fact that a copy of the address of the array is actually passed in and can be treated as a pointer.[*]

Example 9-3 prints a multiplication table for the nonnegative integers through the product 3*4 The products are stored in a two-dimensional array. The ? : construction is used in the output routine.

Example 9-3: multi.c

```
/*                  multi.c
 *
 *    Synopsis  -  Outputs a multiplication table for positive
 *                 integer products between 0*0 and 3*4.
```

---

[*] For older compilers the first line of the function definition would be replaced by either
```
void input_prices (pricearray)
float pricearray [][6];
```
or
```
void input_prices (pricearray)
float (*pricearray) [6];
```

```
 *
 *    Objective  -  Demonstrates multidimensional arrays and
 *                  the ?: construct.
 */

#include <stdio.h>

void main(void)
{
        int multiarray[4][5],                          /* Note 1 */
            row, column;
        void printab (int rows, int columns, int array[][5]);/* Note 2 */

        for (row = 0; row < 4; row++)                  /* Note 3 */
                for (column = 0; column < 5; column++)
                        multiarray[row][column] = row * column;

        printab ( 4, 5, multiarray);
}

void printab (int rows, int columns, int array[][5])       /* Note 2 */
{
        int i = 0, j = 0;

        while (i < rows) {
                printf ("%d%c", array[i][j],
                    (j == columns-1) ? '\n' : '\t');        /* Note 4 */

                (j == columns - 1) ? i++,j=0 : j++;         /* Note 4 */
        }
}
```

Two functions, main() and printab(), make up this program. Variables are declared inside main(). The code consists of a nested `for` loop and a call to printab(). The function printab() uses a `while` loop to output the contents of the array in tabular form.

Note 1: The two-dimensional array is declared. No initialization is done.

Note 2: Three parameters are passed to printab(). `rows` and `columns` inform the function of the shape of the array. The array itself is also passed in as the address of the first element. The declaration must include the second dimension of this array; this value must be a constant.

Note 3: A nested `for` loop is used to assign values to each cell of the array. Individual cells are accessed with the subscript notation.

Note 4: The two ? : expressions are used to aid in the output format. The first tests the value of j to see if the last element in a column is being output. If so, a newline is output instead of a tab character. The second ? : expression makes the same test and uses the result to determine when to update i and j for a new row.

Learning Activities

6. a. Execute multi.c.

   b. Modify multi.c so that the row and column of zeros in the table are eliminated and the products go from 1*1 to 4*5. Do this without changing the size of the array.

   c. Modify multi.c again so that the output looks like this:

   ```
   *  | 1        2        3        4        5
   ------------------------------------------
   1  | 1        2        3        4        5
   2  | 2        4        6        8        10
   3  | 3        6        9        12       15
   4  | 4        8        12       16       20
   ```

   Use a hyphen (-) for the horizontal line and the vertical bar (|) for the vertical line. Make the spacing as even as possible.

7. Modify multi.c so that it requests the upper limits on the multiplication table as input from a user and outputs a table containing the products from 1*1 to upper*upper where upper is the value input by the user. For practical purposes, do not allow the user to input a value greater than 10.

8. Modify the program stocks.c from the last example so that the array is passed as a parameter to all three functions.

9.4 Arrays with More Than Two Dimensions

The extension to more than two dimensions is straightforward. For example,

```
double three_d[2][3][4];
```

declares a three-dimensional array with base type double. The element in the position with first index 1, second index 2, and third index 0 is accessed with the expression

```
three_d[1][2][0]
```

These arrays have the same concepts of storage class, scope, and initialization properties.

Initializing three_d at the time of declaration would be done as follows:

```
double three_d[2][3][4] = {
                            { {0.0, 0.1, 0.2, 0.3},
                              {1.0, 1.1, 1.2, 1.3},
                              {2.0, 2.1, 2.2, 2.3}     },
                            { {10.0, 10.1, 10.2, 10.3},
                              {11.0, 11.1, 11.2, 11.3},
                              {12.0, 12.1, 12.2, 12.3}   }
                          };
```

Arrays of four, five, or even more dimensions can be declared and initialized in a similar fashion. Accessing the elements is also done in an analogous fashion.

A three-dimensional array could be visualized as a rectangular solid of values,

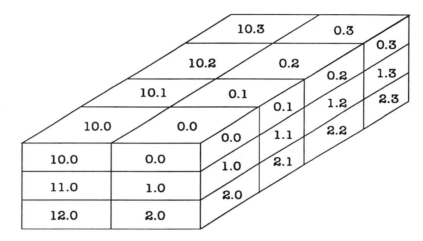

but is more often thought of as multiple two-dimensional arrays. The program threedim.c in Example 9-4 outputs the elements of `three_d` as two 3 x 4 arrays.

Example 9-4: threedim.c

```
/*                    threedim.c
 *
 *    Synopsis   -   Outputs the contents of a three-dimensional array
 *                   as a pair of two-dimensional arrays.
 *
 *    Objective  -   Illustrates declaration, initialization, and
 *                   accessing of elements in a three-dimensional array.
 */

#include <stdio.h>
```

```
void main (void)
{                                                          /* Note 1 */
        double three_d[2][3][4] = {                        /* Note 2 */
                                { {0.0, 0.1, 0.2, 0.3},
                                  {1.0, 1.1, 1.2, 1.3},
                                  {2.0, 2.1, 2.2, 2.3}
                                },
                                { {10.0, 10.1, 10.2, 10.3},
                                  {11.0, 11.1, 11.2, 11.3},
                                  {12.0, 12.1, 12.2, 12.3}
                                }
                            };
        int i, j, k;


        for (i = 0; i < 2; i++) {
                for (j = 0; j < 3; j++) {
                        for (k = 0; k < 4; k++) {          /* Note 3 */
                                printf ("%5.1f\t", three_d[i][j][k]);
                        }
                        printf ("\n");
                }
                printf ("\n\n");
        }
}
```

The program consists of the single function named main(). The array is declared and initialized. The executable code consists of nested for loops.

Note 1: The declaration of a three-dimensional array. The type is specified and followed by the array name and the three dimensions in brackets.

Note 2: The initialization of the array follows. The contents of each array must be in a comma-separated list enclosed in braces. Since this is actually an array of arrays of arrays, this initialization consists of three nested comma-separated lists enclosed in braces.

Note 3: The elements of the array are accessed through the subscript notation.

Learning Activities

9. Execute threedim.c to understand how it works.

10. *C by Discovery*   With the declaration of one-dimensional arrays, the dimension could be omitted from between the braces when the array was initialized. Experiment with the declaration of the variable three_d to see if that is true with three-dimensional arrays. Which if any of the dimensions can be omitted?

11. In threedim.c rewrite the statement with the call to printf() using pointer notation instead of subscript notation to access the elements.

12. Modify threedim.c so that the current values of i, j, and k are output with the two arrays. That is, make the output match the following:

```
                    k   =   0     1     2     3
   i = 0
           j = 0        0.0   0.1   0.2   0.3
           j = 1        1.0   1.1   1.2   1.3
           j = 2        2.0   2.1   2.2   2.3


   i = 1
           j = 0       10.0  10.1  10.2  10.3
           j = 1       11.0  11.1  11.2  11.3
           j = 2       12.0  12.1  12.2  12.3
```

"A closer look at the discovery of C." From the Naval Museum in Pegli. The reference reads "Amerigo Vespucci, after whom the American continents are named." Artist unknown, date unknown.

A Closer Look

Recall that in C, an array of almost any type can be declared. The concept of multidimensional arrays is built on this fact. A two-dimensional array is an array of one-dimensional arrays. A three-dimensional array is an array of two-dimensional arrays, and so on.

The syntax for declaring a two-dimensional array is that of declaring an array of arrays. The declaration

```
int two_d[3][4];
```

can be viewed as

```
int (two_d[3])[4];
```

Analyzing the above declaration, we see that the expression `two_d[3]` is an array of 4 `int`s. The expression `two_d` is an array of 3 elements. Each element is an array of 4 `int`s. The fact that a two-dimensional array is really an array of arrays has several consequences. The first is the meaning of the expressions involving the array name `two_d`.

The value of the expression `two_d` itself is the address of the first of its three elements or the address of the first array of 4 `int`s.

The expression `*two_d` is an array of 4 `int`s. The expression `*two_d` evaluates to the address of the first element in that array.

The following list gives the meanings of other expressions

`two_d[0]`	The same as `*two_d`.
`**two_d`	The first element in the array. Actually, it is the first `int` in the first array of four `int`s.
`two_d[0][0]`	The same as `**two_d`.
`two_d + 1`	The address of the second element in `two_d` or the address of the second array of four `int`s.
`*(two_d + 1)`	The second array of four `int`s. Its value is the address of that array.
`(two_d + 1)[0]`	The same as `*(two_d + 1)`.
`**(two_d + 1)`	The first element in the second array of four `int`s. It is synonymous with `two_d[1][0]`.

The following diagram indicates the three levels of expressions in the list above.

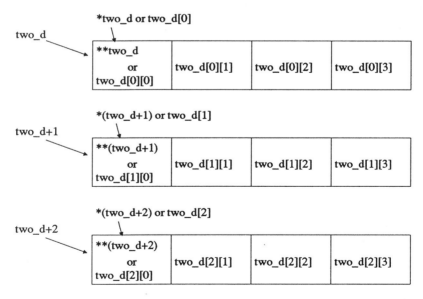

Notice that the address of the first array of 4 `int`s is the same as the address of the first element in that array. Numerically, the values of `two_d` and `*two_d` are identical. However, the two expressions have different types. This can be seen by inspecting the value of the sizeof() operator applied to the two expressions. The expression `sizeof(two_d)` is the total number of bytes in the whole array while `sizeof(*two_d)` is the number of bytes in the first of the three arrays of four `int`s.

Second, the concept of a multidimensional array as an array of arrays leads to the fact that the elements of multidimensional arrays are stored contiguously and in row major form. For example, for the array two_d declared previously, the elements actually are stored in memory in the following pattern:

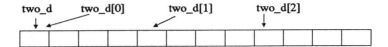

The program in Example 9-5 illustrates the meaning of expressions related to a two-dimensional array by outputting their values. It also outputs the result of the sizeof() operator applied to several of the expressions to illustrate that the types are different even when the values are the same. Third, it outputs the addresses of elements in the array to illustrate the contiguous storage.

 Example 9-5: md.c

```
/*                 md.c
 *
 *    Synopsis  -  Outputs information about the 2 x 3 array of
 *                 characters.
 *
 *    Objective -  To illustrate the relationship between different
 *                 expressions relevant to an array.
 */

#include <stdio.h>

void main(void)
{

        static char t[2][3] = { {'a', 'b', 'c'}, {'d', 'e', 'f'} };

        printf ("sizeof(char)    %d\n", sizeof (char) );

        printf ("   2 X 3 array\n");
        printf ("---------------------\n");
        printf ("t                %x\n", t);          /* Note 1 */
        printf ("sizeof(t)        %d\n\n", sizeof (t)); /* Note 2 */

        printf ("  First 1X3 array\n");
        printf ("---------------------\n");
        printf ("*t               %x\n", *t);         /* Note 1 */
        printf ("sizeof(*t)       %d\n\n", sizeof (*t));/* Note 2 */
```

```
        printf ("First element in array\n");
        printf ("---------------------\n");
        printf ("&t[0][0]             %x\n", &t[0][0]);        /* Note 1 */
        printf ("sizeof(&t[0][0])     %d\n",
                                      sizeof(&t[0][0]) );      /* Note 2 */
        printf ("t[0][0]              %c\n", t[0][0]);         /* Note 3 */
        printf ("sizeof (t[0][0])     %d\n", sizeof (t[0][0]) );
        printf ("**t                  %c\n\n", **t);           /* Note 3 */

        printf (" Second 1X3 array\n");
        printf ("-------------------\n");
        printf ("t+1                  %x\n", t+1);             /* Note 4 */
        printf ("sizeof(t+1)          %d\n", sizeof(t+1) );
        printf ("*(t+1)               %x\n", *(t+1));          /* Note 4 */
        printf ("sizeof (*(t+1))      %d\n", sizeof (*(t+1)));
        printf ("*(t+1) +2            %x\n", *(t+1) + 2);      /* Note 5 */
        printf ("*(*(t+1) +2)         %c\n", *(*(t+1) + 2));  /* Note 5 */
}
```

The program consists of a single function, main(). A 2 x 3 array of characters is declared and initialized. The remainder of the code consists of calls to printf() to output the information about the array. Before this program is discussed, it should be compiled and executed. Have a copy of the output available for examination as we go through the notes. In this program, **Note 1** is associated with more than one statement. The discussion will refer to all of the statements.

Note 1: This note refers to the printf() calls where values of t, *t, and &t[0][0] are output. Check these values in the output. The values should all be identical.

Note 2: This note refers to the printf() calls where the values of sizeof(t), sizeof(*t), and sizeof(&t[0][0]) are output. These values should be different from one another since the three quantities that had the same value in the **Note 1** statements all have different types. The expression t refers to a 2 x 3 array of characters or two 1 x 3 arrays; its size should be that of a buffer that will store 6 characters. The expression *t refers to the first of the 1 x 3 arrays. Its size reflects that of a buffer to hold 3 chars. The expression &t[0][0] is the address of the first character in the array. It should have the "sizeof" an address on your system.

Note 3: This note refers to printf() calls where t[0][0] and **t are output. Both expressions are synonyms for the first character in the array.

The expression **t uses double indirection to access an element of the array. Recall that * is the dereferencing operator. When used with an address, it refers to the contents of the address. In this example, t is the address of the 2 x 3 array of chars, *t is the first array of three chars or the address of the first char, and **t is the first char value. It is equivalent to t[0][0].

Note 4: The next four statements extend the relationship between t and *t. The expression t + 1 evaluates to the address of the second 1 x 3 array. It is an address and should have the "sizeof" an address. The value of the expression * (t + 1) should be identical, but its "sizeof" is different since it has a different type. (Determine its type.)

Note 5: The next two statements refer to the last element in the array. The expression * (t + 1) + 2 refers to the address of the last element. It should be 2 * sizeof (char) beyond the address t + 1. The expression * (* (t+1) +2) refers to the last element in the array. It should be an ' f'.

Learning Activities

13. As you read the above discussion, questions about other expressions may have occurred to you. If so, modify md.c to output the values of those expressions. Try to reconcile the results of the execution with your understanding of the concepts.

14. a. What would be output by the call

```
printf ("%x\n", &t[1][0]);
```

   b. What does the expression

```
*(*t+2)
```

   reference?

   c. What does the expression

```
**(t+1)
```

   reference?

15. Predict the output from the program md.c if it were modified by making the following changes.

   a. Change the declaration to read

```
static double t = { {1.0, 2.0, 3.0},
                     {4.0, 5.0, 6.0} };
```

   b. Change every %c output specification to %f.

   You may have to determine sizeof (double) before you can answer accurately. You will not be able to predict the address of the first element in the array.

16. In the expression ** (two_d + 1) convince yourself that the parentheses are necessary. Consult the precedence chart in the Programmer's Handbook to find the relative precedence of * and +.

9.5   Arrays of Pointers

The following type of declaration is very useful and often seen in C code:

```
char *ptrarray[4];
```

Analyzing this declaration, we see that `*ptrarray[4]` is a `char`. Since the `[]` have higher precedence than the indirection operator, `*`, the next step in the analysis indicates that the type of any expression of the form `ptrarray[x]` is `char *`, and that `ptrarray` is an array of four elements of that type. In other words, `ptrarray` is an array of four pointers to elements of type `char`. When the identifier `ptrarray` appears in a program, it refers to the address of the first element of that array. This data structure can be pictured as shown below.

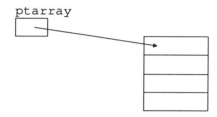

To see the concept of an array of pointers in use, consider the code in Example 9-6, which might be part of a text processing program. Assume again that a word is defined as a sequence of nonblank characters delimited by blanks. A line of text consisting of a sequence of these words is input from the terminal and kept in a one-dimensional array.

The program ptrarray.c uses an array of type `char *` to keep track of the beginning of each word. It counts the words and outputs them to the terminal in reverse order.

 Example 9-6: ptrarray.c

```
/*                ptrarray.c
 *
 *    Synopsis   -   Accepts a line of text as input from the terminal.
 *                   Parses the input text to find individual words,
 *                   counts them, outputs the count, and outputs the
 *                   words in reverse order.
 *
 *    Objective  -   Illustrates use of an array of pointers to char.
 */
#include <stdio.h>
#include <string.h>
```

```
void main(void)
{
        char instring[512];
        char *words[50],                               /* Note 1 */
             *current;
        int  i = 1;

        printf ("Enter text with words delimited by blanks:\n");
        gets(instring);

        words[0]=current=instring;                     /* Note 2 */
                                                       /* Note 3 */
        while ( (current = strchr(current, ' ')) != NULL) {
                *current++ = '\0';
                words[i++] = current;                  /* Note 4 */
        }

        printf ("There were %d words in that line.\n", i);
        printf ("In reverse order they are :\n");
        for (--i; i >= 0; i--)
                printf ("%s\n", words[i]);             /* Note 5 */
}
```

There is one function, main(). Input is done by a call to gets(). A `while` loop is used to work through the line of input to find the beginning of each word. A `for` loop outputs the words in reverse order.

Note 1: An array of 50 pointers to `char` is defined. No initialization is done.

Note 2: The first element in the array is initialized to point to the beginning of the input line. The auxiliary variable `current` is assigned to point there also.

Note 3: In each pass through the following `while` loop, strchr() looks for a blank that delimits the end of a word. The blank is then replaced by a `'\0'` and `current` is incremented to point to the beginning of the next word. If a blank is not found, strchr() returns `NULL` and the loop terminates.

Note 4: The next element in the array is assigned to point to the beginning of the next word, and the index into the array is incremented. Assume that the input line is `"Frick and Frack"`. After the `while` loop has terminated, the memory configuration would be represented as follows:

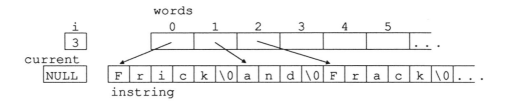

Note 5: The individual words are output on separate lines. The index `i` goes from the number of words back to zero so that the words are output in reverse order.

Learning Activities

17. Compile and execute ptrarray.c. Test it with several different input strings to see how it behaves. What happens when there are no blanks in the input? What happens when there are two blanks between one word and the next? If either of these behaviors is not acceptable, modify the program accordingly.
18. When a single carriage return is entered in response to the prompt, the word count is reported to be one. Fix this bug in the program so that it counts zero words correctly.
19. When more than fifty words are entered, an error condition occurs. Fix this bug by having the program check on the number of words and not process more than fifty words even if more exist on the input line.
20. Modify ptrarray.c so that it outputs the words in the same order that they were input.

A Closer Look

An array of pointers shares properties with other arrays. In particular, an expression consisting of the array name itself is evaluated as the address of the first element of the array. Therefore, since it is an address, the pointer notation can be used for it.

If an array of strings was created as in the last program, then the data structure could be thought of as having two dimensions, as in the following diagram for the input `"Frick and Frack"`.

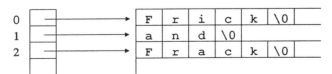

This data structure is similar to a two-dimensional array of characters, but each row of the structure can have a different number of elements. However, the array subscript notation can be used to reference elements in arrays of pointers also.

In each of the following examples, the expressions are equivalent:

        words[0]

and

        *words

both refer to the first word in the input string, `"Frick"`.

        *words[0]

and

```
**words
```

and

```
words[0][0]
```

all refer to the first letter in that string, `'F'`.

```
*(words[0]+3)
```

and

```
*(*words + 3)
```

and

```
words[0][3]
```

all refer to the fourth letter in that string, `'c'`.

```
*(words[2]+1)
```

and

```
*(*(words+2)+1)
```

and

```
words[2][1]
```

all refer to the second letter in the third string, `'r'`.

9.6   Double Indirection

Since any type in C can have a pointer to it, we can declare a pointer to a pointer. For example, we can declare a pointer to a pointer to an int. The declaration would be

```
int **ptr;
```

Reading the declaration, the expression `**ptr` is of type `int`. Therefore, `*ptr` is the address of or pointer to an `int`, and `ptr` itself is the address of a pointer to a pointer to an `int`.

Consider the following declarations:

```
int r = 3,
    *q = &r,
    **p = &q;
```

The variable `r` has type `int` and has been initialized to 3. The variable `q` has type pointer to `int` and has been initialized to point to `r`. That means that it contains the address of `r`. The variable `p` has type pointer to pointer to `int`. It has been initialized to point to `q`. That means that the following relationships hold:

> `p` contains the address of `q` or is said to point to `q`.
> `*p` is equivalent to `q` or points to `r`.
> `**p` is equivalent to either `*q` or `r` and has the value 3.

C does not put a limit on the number of levels of indirection. It is possible to declare

```
float ***f;
```

which is a pointer to a pointer to a pointer to a `float`, or even

```
char ****w;
```

where w would be a pointer to a pointer to a pointer to a pointer to a `char`. Typically, the level of indirection is kept low for ease of understanding the code.

The program ptrptr.c in Example 9-7 explores the relationship between an array of pointers and a pointer to a pointer.* It also shows techniques for accessing strings and individual characters using either an array of pointers to `char` or a variable of type `char **`. The variable with type `char **` is used to traverse the array of type `char *`. This is a major use of `char **` variables in C.

Example 9-7: ptrptr.c

```
/*                 ptrptr.c
 *
 *   Synopsis  -  Outputs information, strings, and individual
 *                characters in an array of pointers to characters.
 *
 *   Objective -  To illustrate double indirection and use the
 *                pointer to a pointer to traverse an array of
 *                pointers.
 */

#include <stdio.h>

void main (void)
{
        char *ptrarray[] = {"George",
                            "Elliot's",
                            "Oldest",
                            "Girl",
                            "Rode",
                            "A",
                            "Pig",
                            "Home",
                            "Yesterday",
                            ""                          /* Note 1 */
                           };
        char **ptrptr = ptrarray;                       /* Note 2 */

                                                        /* Note 3 */
        printf ("sizeof(ptrarray)  %d,\tsizeof(ptrptr)  %d\n",
                    sizeof(ptrarray), sizeof(ptrptr) );
        printf ("ptrarray          %x,\tptrptr          %x\n",
```

---

* The phrase in this program is the one my father-in-law used to remember the spelling of "geography."

```
                              ptrarray, ptrptr);
            printf ("ptrarray[0]        %x,\t*ptrptr           %x\n\n",
                              ptrarray[0], *ptrptr);

                                                              /* Note 4 */
            printf ("ptrarray[0]   %s,\t*ptrptr         %s\n",
                              ptrarray[0], *ptrptr);
            printf ("ptrarray[1]   %s, *(ptrptr+1)   %s\n\n",
                              ptrarray[1], *(ptrptr+1) );

                                                              /* Note 5 */
            printf ("*ptrarray[0]        %c,\t**ptrarray        %c\n",
                              *ptrarray[0], **ptrarray);
            printf ("ptrarray[0][4]      %c,\t*(*ptrarray + 4) %c\n\n",
                              ptrarray[0][4], *(*ptrarray+4) );

                                                              /* Note 6 */
            for ( ;strcmp (*ptrptr, ""); ptrptr++)
                  printf ("%s ", *ptrptr);
            printf ("\n");
                                                              /* Note 7 */
            for (ptrptr = ptrarray ;strcmp (*ptrptr, ""); ptrptr++)
                  printf ("%c", **ptrptr);
            printf ("\n");
}
```

In the one function, main(), the executable code consists primarily of calls to printf(). Two `for` loops are used to output the strings and the first character of each string.

Note 1: An array of pointers is declared and initialized. The initial values for the array are the addresses of the given strings. They must be in a comma-separated list enclosed in braces. A null string is placed as the array terminator. The picture is as follows:

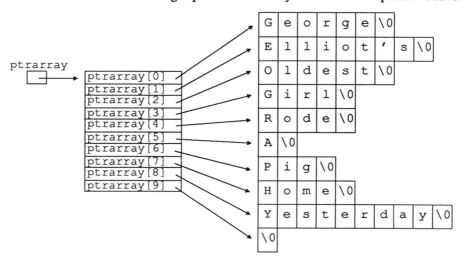

Note 2: A pointer to a pointer to a `char` variable is declared and initialized to point to the first element in the array of pointers.

Note 3: Information about the values of expressions involving `ptrptr` and `ptrarray` is output in the next three printf() calls. The first printf() call outputs the sizeof() both `ptrptr` and `ptrarray` to point out the fact that these two expressions have different types. The expression `sizeof(ptrarray)` gives the total number of bytes in the array while the expression `sizeof(ptrptr)` should be that of a pointer to (address of) a `char`. In the next two printf() calls, each expression involving `ptrptr` should have a value identical to the one involving `ptrarray`. The expressions `ptrptr` and `ptrarray` both refer to the address of the first of the pointers, and the expressions `ptrarray[0]` and `*ptrptr` both refer to the contents of the first element in the array of pointers or the address of the first string.

Note 4: The next two calls to printf() illustrate how to access the strings in the array. They can be accessed either through the array subscript notation or through the pointer notation. Notice that the first of these printf() calls has exactly the same arguments as the previous call to printf(). This emphasizes the fact that the expressions `ptrarray` and `ptrptr` evaluate to addresses. They can be accessed either numerically with the `%x` conversion specification or as a string with the `%s` conversion specification.

Note 5: The technique of accessing individual characters is demonstrated by the next two calls to printf(). The first printf() call contains two expressions that access the `'G'` in `"George"`. Note that either subscript notation, pointer notation, or a combination of the two can be used. The second call to printf() illustrates two ways of accessing the `'g'` in `"George"`.

Note 6: This `for` loop will output all the strings in the array of pointers. The variable `ptrptr` of type `char **` is used to traverse the array. In particular, notice the test for continuing the `for` loop. The loop will continue until the strcmp() function returns a zero or until `ptrptr` points to the null string.

Note 7: This `for` loop will output the first character in each of the strings. The variable `ptrptr` needed to be reassigned to point to the array since it was changed in the last `for` loop. The test for continuing or terminating the `for` loop is the same as in the last loop.

Learning Activities

21. Predict the output of ptrptr.c. You should be able to correctly predict the output of all the printf() calls except the ones with the %x conversion specifications that refer to addresses. Execute the program and correct any misconceptions in your thinking.
22. Modify the first `for` loop in ptrptr.c so that the strings are output in reverse order.
23. Modify ptrptr.c so that the last character in each of the strings is output by the second `for` loop.
24. After the assignment `ptrptr = ptrarray`, state the meaning of each of the following expressions from the last program. Two have been done for you.

   a.   `ptrptr` == address of the first element in the array of pointers.

   b.   `*ptrptr`

   c.   `**ptrptr`

   d.   `ptrptr+1`

   e.   `*(ptrptr+1)`

   f.   `**(ptrptr+1)` == `'E'`

   g.   `*(*(ptrptr+1)+2)`

   h.   `**ptrptr + 1`

   i.   `*ptrptr + 1`

   j.   `*ptrptr[1]`

   k.   `*(*ptrptr + 2)`

Reading C Declarations

Before proceeding, we will review some of the symbols used in C declarations and see how they can be combined. The symbols we will discuss are the brackets, [ ], the parentheses, ( ), and the asterisk, *. The precedence of these operators is important.

The parentheses have the highest precedence when they are used to group elements of an expression. They can also be used in a declaration to declare a function. The brackets are next in precedence and the asterisk has the lowest precedence of the three symbols.

To read a C declaration, we remove the operator with lowest precedence from the declared expression and determine what the remaining expression must represent. This process continues until we reach the identifier alone.

We will start with an example for which we know the answer to illustrate the process. Consider the declaration

```
int   *x[8];
```

The expression `*x[8]` must represent an `int`. Since `*` has lower precedence than `[]`, the declaration could be written equivalently as

```
int   *(x[8]);
```

This implies that the expression `x[8]` or any expression of the form `x[i]` has type `int *`. Therefore, `x` is an array of 8 elements of type `int *`, or `x` is an array of 8 pointers to `int`.

In contrast, the declaration

```
int   (*y)[8];
```

indicates that the expression `*y` is an array of 8 `int`s or that `y` is the address of a pointer to an array of 8 `int`s.

Consider the following declaration as another example:

```
int   (*z[5])();
```

The expression `(*z[5])()` is an `int`; therefore, `*z[5]` is a function returning an `int`. Again `*` has lower precedence than `[]` so that the `*` is removed first to get the expression `z[5]`, which is the address of or a pointer to a function returning an `int`. Finally, `z` is an array of 5 pointers to functions returning `int`s.

Learning Activity

25. Determine the legality or illegality of each of the following declarations. If the declaration is legal, state the type of the variable `what`.

    a. `float    (what[3])();`   b. `float    what[3]();`
    c. `char     (*what)();`   d. `char     *what();`
    e. `double   (*what())[3];`   f. `double   *(what()[3]);`
    g. `int      **what[3];`   h. `int      **what();`
    i. `int      (**what)[3];`   j. `int      *(*what)[3];`

9.7   Command Line Parameters

Most computer systems have the facility of passing information to a C program at execution time. This information takes the form of a sequence of strings that are known as command line parameters. They appear as strings on the command line after the name of the program when it is executed. These strings are separated by blanks, tabs, or other allowed whitespace. The command line parameters are available throughout the time that the program is executing.

A C program can be structured to access the command line parameters by declaring arguments to main() in the form of an ANSI C prototype.*

```
main (int argc, char *argv[])
```

The parameter names, argc and argv, are traditionally used by C programmers, but like parameter names in other functions, they are not specified by the language.

The parameter argc contains the count or the number of parameters on the command line. The name of the program being executed is the first command line parameter counted so that argc is always at least one. Examples appear below.

The parameter argv is the vector of the actual command line parameters. It is an array of pointers to chars. In this case the pointers point to the strings that appeared on the command line. The array is indexed by the integers from 0 to argc-1 and terminated with a NULL pointer.

Suppose that the operating system prompt is "# " and consider a program named sample. When sample is executed, its name would appear on the command line as

```
# sample
```

With this program invocation, argc would be 1 and argv would have the following configuration:

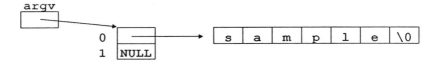

With the invocation

```
# sample  p1  p2  p3
```

argc would be 4 and argv would look like this:

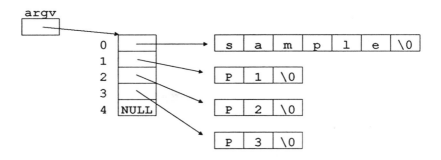

---

* For older compilers, this line would be replaced with the three lines
```
main(argc, argv)
int argc;
char *argv[];
```

The program cmdline.c in Example 9-8 declares the parameters `argc` and `argv` to the function main() so that the command line parameters can be accessed. It simply outputs the value of `argc` and demonstrates techniques for accessing the strings in `argv`.

Example 9-8: cmdline.c

```
/*                  cmdline.c
 *
 *    Synopsis  -  Prints the value of argc and the command
 *                 line arguments.
 *
 *    Objective -  To illustrate how command line arguments work
 *                 and to demonstrate two techniques for accessing
 *                 the arguments.
 */

#include <stdio.h>

void main (int argc, char *argv[])                      /* Note 1 */
{
        int index ;

        printf ("There were %d arguments on the command line.\n", argc);
        printf ("They are :\n");

        for (index = 0; index < argc; index++)          /* Note 2 */
                printf ("\t%x \t%s\n", argv[index], argv[index]);
        printf ("\n\n");
                                                        /* Note 3 */
        printf ("Terminating char * value in argv, %x\n", argv[argc]);
        printf ("\n");

        while (argc-- > 0)                              /* Note 4 */
                printf ("   %s ", *argv++);
        printf ("\n\n");
}
```

The function main() consists of two printf() calls, a `for` loop that outputs the command line parameters, two more printf() calls, and a `while` loop that again outputs the command line parameters but uses a different syntax to reference them. One auxiliary variable `index` was declared.

Note 1: The parameters `argc` and `argv` are declared inside the parentheses for main(). The types are declared; `argc` is of type `int` and `argv` is an array of type `char *`. The address of the array of pointers is passed into main(). Each value in the array is the address of one of the parameter strings on the command line.

Note 2: Each time through the `for` loop, one of the command line parameter strings is printed. The string can be accessed with the subscript notation used with `argv`. The value in one cell of the array is the address of the first character in the string. It can be accessed as a numerical quantity with the `%x` conversion specification or as a string with the `%s` conversion specification.

Note 3: The strings on the command line occupy the first `argc` cells in the array with indices 0 through `argc-1`. The next cell contains a terminating `NULL` pointer. This call to printf() outputs the `NULL` as a hexadecimal value.

Note 4: The `while` loop uses a different technique to output the strings on the command line. Note that `argc` is decremented each time the condition for continuing the `while` loop is evaluated. The strings can be accessed using the `*` to reference the contents of address `argv`. After the one parameter string is output, `argv` is incremented to point to the next address of a parameter string. Note that after the `while` loop terminates, both the count and location of the command line arguments have been destroyed. This program would not be able to access these arguments again.

Learning Activities

26. Find out if you are able to use command line arguments with a C program on your system and what, if anything, needs to be done to use them.

27. If you can use command line arguments, compile and execute cmdline.c with several different sets of command line arguments.[*]

    a. Test the program with no command line arguments other than the program name. What happens?

    b. Test to see if you can find a reasonable limit for the number of command line arguments. Test the program with a large number of short command line arguments. Do not press the Return key until you have entered all the parameters.

    c. Test to see if you can find a reasonable limit for the length of a command line argument. Test the program with the program name and one very long argument string.

---

[*] If you do not have an ANSI C compiler, you will need to replace the declaration of the parameters with the old-style declaration.

Command line parameters can be used in many ways. For example, many operating system utilities need this facility. An editor might take the name of the file to edit as a command line parameter. A program that makes a copy of a file might take the name of the existing file and the name of the future copy as command line parameters. A debugger might take identification of a running process as a command line parameter. The possibilities are endless.

The program count.c in Example 9-9 gives a simple use of command line parameters. It takes three command line parameters after the program name. Assume that the executable version of the program is in a file named "count". If the invocation to count is

        count   3   20   5

the program will count from 3 to 20 by fives. The output would be

        3   8   13   18

This program also introduces the standard library function atoi(), which stands for **a**scii **to i**nteger. It is a close relative to atof() (**a**scii **to f**loat), which we saw in a previous section. It takes a string of digits as an argument and converts the string to the corresponding integer. For example, the string

1	2	3	\0

would be converted to the integer 123. The function declaration is in the file stdlib.h.

Example 9-9: count.c

```
/*              count.c
 *
 *    Synopsis  -  Takes values of initial, final, and step from the
 *                 command line arguments.  Counts from the low
 *                 value of initial to the high value of
 *                 final with increments of step.
 *
 *    Objective -  To illustrate a use of command line arguments.
 *                 Also uses the library function atoi().
 */

#include <stdio.h>
#include <stdlib.h>

void main(int argc, char *argv[])
{
        int result, initial, final, step;
```

```
        if (argc != 4) {                                        /* Note 1 */
                printf ("Usage: count initialvalue finalvalue step\n");
                exit(1);
        }


                                                                /* Note 2 */
        printf ("Counting from %s to %s by %s's.\n",
                        *(argv+1), *(argv+2), *(argv+3) );
        initial = atoi (argv[1]);                               /* Note 3 */
        final   = atoi (argv[2]);
        step    = atoi (argv[3]);

        for (result = initial; result <= final; result += step)
                printf ("%d\t", result);
        printf ("\n");
}
```

The program code consists of an `if` statement, several assignment statements, and a `for` loop. The auxiliary variable `result` is used to drive the `for` loop and its current value is output in each iteration of the `for` loop.

Note 1: The value of `argc` is checked to see that the program was invoked correctly. If it was not invoked with the correct number of command line arguments, execution terminates after an error message is output.

Note 2: The call to printf() accesses the command line arguments as strings using pointer arithmetic to obtain the address of each separate argument.

Note 3: The command line arguments are passed in as strings of digits. The digits must be converted to type `int` for counting. The standard library function atoi() is used. Each command line parameter is used as an argument to atoi(). The equivalent integer value is returned.

Learning Activities

28. a. If your system implements command line arguments, execute the program with several different inputs. Does the check on the number of parameters seem to work?

    b. What happens when nondigits are used as command line arguments, as in

        count two twentyseven three.

    What do you think happened?

29. Read about the library function atoi() in your documentation. Does this shed any light on the happenings in your question 1b experiment? Explain what happened in view of this.

30. Add an error check to count.c to ensure that each command line argument consists of digits only. Have the program terminate execution if a nondigit is found. (Hint: Look up the function isdigit() in your compiler documentation or the Programmer's Handbook. It might be handy for this problem.)

31. Modify count.c so that the format of the output is changed to 8 columns of numbers per line. For example, with the invocation

```
count    4  49  5
```

the output should be

```
4       9   14   19   24   29   34   39
44      49
```

A Closer Look

Since the address of the array of strings is what is passed to main(), `argv` is a pointer to a pointer to a `char`. It could be declared as

```
char **argv;
```

In most implementations of C, the command line arguments are put on a stack and the address of each argument is recorded. The list of addresses is terminated with a `NULL`. The address of the list of addresses is the initial value of `argv`. For example, assume that the invocation of the program `count` above is

```
count   5    84   7
```

Then, assuming it takes 2 bytes to represent an address, a hypothetical configuration of memory might be as follows.

Name	Hexadecimal Address	Contents
argv	2000	2060
	.	.
	.	.
	.	.
	2060	3000
	2964	3006
	2068	3008
	206c	300b
	2070	0
	.	.
	.	.
	.	.
	3000	count\0
	3006	5\0
	3008	84\0
	300b	7\0
	300d	????

Language Elements Introduced in This Chapter: A Review

** Library Functions **

atoi()   converts a string of digits into the corresponding integer

** Multidimensional Arrays **

Accessing elements

```
two_d[2][3]
three_d[1][2][0]
```

Initializing

```
static float two_d[3][4] = { {3.1, 7.6, 9.4, 2.2},
                             {5.3, 8.2, 1.4, 2.7},
                             {6.0, 4.2, 7.8, 5.1}
                           };
static float two_d[][4] = { {3.1, 7.6, 9.4, 2.2},
                            {5.3, 8.2, 1.4, 2.7},
                            {6.0, 4.2, 7.8, 5.1}
                          };
double three_d[2][3][4] = {
                  { {0.0, 0.1, 0.2, 0.3},
                    {1.0, 1.1, 1.2, 1.3},
                    {2.0, 2.1, 2.2, 2.3}        },
                  { {10.0, 10.1, 10.2, 10.3},
                    {11.0, 11.1, 11.2, 11.3},
                    {12.0, 12.1, 12.2, 12.3}  }
                };
```

** Parameters to Functions **

To pass an array as a parameter to a function,
pass address and second dimension,
e.g., function declaration

```
funct (float two_d[][4])
```

or

```
funct (float *two_d[4])
```

or pass in as a pointer to a pointer

```
funct (float **two_d)
```

e.g., function call

```
float array[4][5];
...
funct (array);
```

Parameters to main()—command line parameters

```
main (int argc, char *argv[])
```

** Variable Declarations **

Multidimensional arrays

```
float two_d[3][4];
double three_d[2][3][4];
```

Arrays of pointers

```
char *ptrarray[4];
```

Pointers to pointers

```
int **ptr;
```

Things to Remember

1. Multidimensional arrays share the same storage class, scope, and initialization properties as one-dimensional arrays and variables of other types.
2. A three-dimensional array is more often thought of as multiple two-dimensional arrays.
3. A two-dimensional array is an array of one-dimensional arrays.
4. A three-dimensional array is an array of two-dimensional arrays, and so on.
5. Given the declaration int two_d[3][4];
    a. the value of the expression two_d is the address of the first array of 4 ints.

    b. the expression *two_d evaluates to the address of the first element in the first array of 4 ints.

6. The elements of multidimensional arrays are stored contiguously and in row major form.
7. With the declaration

```
static char t[2][3];
```

the expressions t, *t, and t[0] all have the same numerical value but are of different types.
8. There is no limit on the number of levels of indirection.
9. To decode a C declaration, look at the types of the elements of a sequence of expressions. Start with the declaration and continually peel off the operator with the lowest precedence until you can determine the type of the identifier alone.
10. Pointers to pointers can be used to traverse an array of strings and to access individual strings and characters.
11. Command line parameters appear as strings on the command line after the name of the program when it is executed.
12. The parameter argc contains the count of the parameters on the command line. The parameter argv is the vector of the actual command line parameters.
13. The command line parameter argv can be used with either the array subscript or the pointer * notation.

9.8   Exercises and Programming Problems

1. Complete the function process() from the program stocks.c of Example 9-2 so that it calculates and stores the net change in price for each stock. Modify output_prices() so that it outputs the buying price, the current price, and the net change in price for each stock.

2. Write a program that will write a report about the activity of stocks traded on the New York Stock Exchange for a week's time. The program should ask for and accept input of the name of the stock and its closing price for each day of the week. The report should include the name of each stock, the high and low prices, and the net change for the week. A sample run appears below. The user's response is in **boldface**.

```
                STOCK INFORMATION PROGRAM
                ----- ----------- -------
      This program will create a report on the weekly
      activity of any stocks that you wish. You need only
      enter the stock name and the closing prices for
      Monday through Friday. Press Return at the stock
      name prompt when you are through.

      Ending date of the week of this report: 11/30/90

      Stock name (Press Return when done):  AT&T
      Monday's close:    40.5
      Tuesday's close:   41
      Wednesday's close: 40.875
      Thursday's close:  41.125
      Friday's close:    41

      Stock name (Press Return when done):  IBM
      Monday's close:    116.25
      Tuesday's close:   114
      Wednesday's close: 117.875
      Thursday's close:  116.25
      Friday's close:    115.875

      Stock name (Press Return when done): <Ret>

                   STOCK ACTIVITY REPORT
                Week Ending Friday 11/30/90

      ---------------------------------------------------
      Stock    |   High   |  Low  |  Final   |  Net Change
      ---------------------------------------------------

      AT&T     |  41.125  | 40.5  |  41      |   0.5
      IBM      | 117.875  | 114   | 115.875  |  -0.375

                     END OF REPORT
```

3. Write a program that will help a teacher keep track of a class of students. The teacher wants to create a report with the initials, the grades on three tests, the total of the three test scores and the final letter grade for each student. A sample run follows. Again, the user's response is in **boldface**.

```
              SEMESTER GRADE REPORT
              -------- ----- ------
You will need the class identification, the initials of and
the three test scores for each student, and the low cutoff
score for a grade of  'A', 'B', 'C', and 'D'.

When you have entered the scores for the last student, press
Return at the initials prompt.

Press Return when you are ready to proceed:

Fall or Spring semester?  (F or S):  F
Year: 1991
Which class:  Math 101
Low score for an 'A' (out of 300) : 270
Low score for a  'B' (out of 300) : 230
Low score for a  'C' (out of 300) : 190
Low score for a  'D' (out of 300) : 160

Student's initials: MHN
Scores:
      Test #1: 78
      Test #2: 85
      Test #3: 87

Student's initials: ATR
Scores:
      Test #1: 88
      Test #2: 65
      Test #3: 58

Student's initials:  GJW
Scores:
      Test #1: 63
      Test #2: 68
      Test #3: 92

Student's initials: WLF
Scores:
      Test #1: 95
      Test #2: 93
      Test #3: 89

Student's initials: <Ret>
```

```
              SEMESTER GRADE REPORT
              -------- ----- ------
              Semester:  Fall, 1991
                 Class: Math 101
       Number of students completing course: 4

        -------------------------------------------------
        STUDENT | TEST 1 | TEST 2 | TEST 3 | TOTAL | GRADE
        -------------------------------------------------
        MHN     |   78   |   85   |   87   |  250  |  B
        ATR     |   88   |   65   |   58   |  211  |  C
        GJW     |   63   |   68   |   92   |  223  |  C
        WLF     |   95   |   93   |   89   |  277  |  A
```

4. The following program is a modification of the program stocks.c from Example 9-2. Again, the buying price for six stocks is stored in the program. The user inputs the current price. The program is intended to output the percentage change of the current price from the buying price.

   a. The program has a syntax error. Find and correct it so that the program runs correctly.

   b. Draw diagrams like those in the text that represent the variables stock_prices from main() and new and old from output_change(). Include the contents of the arrays.

```c
/*              epp4.c
 *
 *   Synopsis  -  Inputs 6 stock prices into a two-dimensional array
 *                and should output the percent change from the old
 *                prices.  Has a syntax error.
 *
 *   Objective -  To provide practice with the C syntax and the
 *                relationship between different expressions.
 */

#include <stdio.h>
#include <stdlib.h>

double stock_prices[2][6] = { {  12, 80, 30,
                                100, 40, 50 } };

void main(void)
{
        void output_change(double *new, double *old);
        void input_prices(void);

        printf ("STOCK INFORMATION PROGRAM\n");
        printf ("-------------------------\n");
```

```
        printf ("This program will give information about the ");
        printf ("prices of \nsix specific stocks.  You are to enter ");
        printf ("the current prices of \nthe stocks.  The percent of ");
        printf ("change from the buying prices\n");
        printf ("will be output.\n\n");

        input_prices();
        output_change(*stock_prices, *(stock_prices+1));
}


/*********************************    input_prices()    *******/
/*  Function input_prices() accepts input of 6 quantities of type
 *  float to be stored in the second "row" of the array.  The
 *  combination of library functions gets() and atof() is used to
 *  input the float value.
 */

void input_prices(void)
{
        int i;
        char instring[20];

        printf ("Please enter the current stock prices now.\n");
        printf ("Stock\tBuying price\tCurrent price\n");
        printf ("-----\t------------\t-------------\n");
        for (i = 0; i < 6; i++) {

                printf ("#%d: \t%6.2f   \t  ",
                                    i+1, stock_prices[0][i]);
                stock_prices[1][i] = atof( gets(instring) );
        }
        printf ("Thank you!\n");
}


/*********************************    output_change() *********/
/*  Function output_change() outputs the percentage change of
 *  the new prices in comparison with the old.
 */

void output_change(double *old, double *new)
{
        double change;
        int i;

        printf ("\nPercent change of each stock:\n");
        for (i = 0; i < 6; i++) {
            printf ("Stock #%d: ", i );
```

```
                    change = (*new++ / *old++ - 1) * 100;   /* percent change */
                    printf ("Percent change is %5.0f%%.\n", change);
            }
    }
```

5. El Cilantro Tacos has stores in three locations. They sell burritos, tacos, tostadas and taquitos. The owner wants a program that will keep track of sales and calculate the profit for each item, for each store, and the total profit. He expects to enter each store's number, the profit margin for each item, and the quantity of each item sold at each store. He would like the program to output a full report summarizing each store's activity and profits. An example of a report is below.

```
                        El Cilantro Tacos
                        -- -------- -----


                Burritos    Tacos   Tostadas  Taquitos    Store Totals
                --------    -----   --------   --------   ------------
Store #1    |     134       345        87        240          806
Store #2    |     578       623       400        397         1998
Store #3    |     436       421       258        376         1491
                --------    -----   --------   --------   ------------
Item totals      1148      1389       745       1013         4295

Profit
Margin            .74        .38       .53        .26
                                                         Total Profit
Item Profit     849.52    527.82    394.85     263.38        2035.57
```

6. Write a statistical program that uses command line parameters to input the data. The program will sort the data and output the sorted data and its maximum, minimum, mean, and variance. For example, if the executable version of the program is in a file named "stats" and the call to the program is

```
            stats 12 3 6 5
```

the output would be

```
            Data:    3   5   6 12
            Maximum:  12
            Minimum:  3
            Mean:     6.5
            Variance: 11.25
```

7. Write a program that will output the graph of $y = 1/(x^2 + 1)$. To do this, declare a two-dimensional array of type `char` whose dimensions match the number of character positions on the monitor. For example, many monitors will hold 23 rows of 80 characters each. For this graph, let each pixel in the vertical direction represent 1/20 of a unit, and let each pixel in the horizontal direction represent 1/10 of a unit. The elements of your array that lie on the graph could contain the asterisk, ' * '. The horizontal axis could be represented by the hyphen, ' - ',

and the vertical axis could be the vertical bar, ' | ' . The rest of the array could be filled with blank characters. You will need to decide the placement of your graph for the best viewing and calculate and fill in each element in the array. Then the graph could be displayed by simply printing the contents of the array.

8. Write a program that will search its input for and count the number of occurrences of a given character. The character should be given as a command line argument. Suppose that the executable version of the program is in the file count. A sample run of a similar program is below. The user's input is in **boldface**.

```
# count s
Counting s's. Enter your input now. Press return to finish.
> She sells sea shells down by the sea shore.
There were 8 s's in that text.
```

9. Write a function in C that takes three parameters: the address of a two-dimensional array of type int, the number of rows in the array, and the number of columns in the array. Have the function calculate the sum of the squares of the elements. For example, for the array nums that is pictured below,

```
23   12   14    3
31   25   41   17
```

the call to the function might be

```
sumsquares (nums, 2, 4);
```

and the value returned would be 4434. Write a short program to test your function.

Input and Output

Chapter 10

10.1   Review of Input and Output

Up to this point in the text, we have worked with terminal input and output only. In this chapter, we will study it more closely and also explore file handling in C.

Input and output are not included as part of the C language. They are accomplished by the use of the library functions, which in turn make system calls to interact with each specific operating system. A set of standard specifications for these functions is included in ANSI C so that programs using them will be portable to other implementations of ANSI C. Most of the functions discussed in this chapter are available in non-ANSI compilers also and, in addition, some compilers may have functions that are not defined in ANSI C. A full list of the ANSI C input and output functions appears in the Programmer's Handbook.

A variety of different library functions exists for different input and output situations. We have seen the use of printf() to perform formatted output, scanf() to perform formatted input, getchar() to read a single character at a time from the keyboard, putchar() to output a single character at a time to the terminal, gets() to input a string from the keyboard, and puts() to output a string to the terminal.

With many compilers, the above functions do buffered input and output. That is, if input is performed in a C program, the input characters are usually kept in a buffer until the user presses Return. Then the input buffer can be processed by the C program. Similarly, output characters are kept in an output buffer. Usually, both standard input and standard output are "line buffered" since each holds a line of text at a time. An output buffer is flushed in case of five separate events: when a newline character is output, when the buffer becomes full, when the system must prepare to do input, when the program terminates, or when fflush() is called with `stdout` as its argument. An input buffer is flushed when the program terminates, and when all the input has been read and the program needs to do more input. (As we have seen before, the identifiers `stdin` and `stdout` usually refer to terminal input and output.)

In many situations a programmer needs to be aware of the buffering of standard output. For example, if output statements are used to trace execution of a program, they must be concluded with a newline character if the programmer wants the output to appear when the output statement is executed. Otherwise, the output either may appear considerably after the statement was executed, or may not appear at all in case of a program crash.

In the following sections we will look at the C library functions that do file handling, and study the above functions and their counterparts for files.

10.2   An Introduction to Files in C

A file is a stream of bytes to a C program. Any structure put on a file is put there by the programmer.

When a C program is executed, three files are automatically opened:

1. Standard input, which is usually input from the terminal.

2. Standard output, which is usually output to the terminal.

3. Standard error, which is also usually associated with terminal output.[*]

These three files are referenced with the identifiers `stdin`, `stdout`, and `stderr`, respectively. The identifers have FILE * type. The identifer FILE is declared in the file stdio.h with a `typedef` declaration. A FILE is a structure in which C keeps information about a file. The FILE structure is discussed in more detail in Section 10.8.

When an additional file is to be opened for use in the program, the programmer must declare a new variable of type FILE *. Therefore, the header file stdio.h must be included in programs using external files. For example, the declaration below declares two variables of type FILE *:

```
FILE *infile, *outfile;
```

---

[*] On many computer systems the programmer can manipulate these three files so that they are not associated with the terminal. This is done with operating system calls. However, the association with the terminal is the default.

After this declaration, `infile` and `outfile` need to be initialized. This is done by using the C library routine fopen() to open the files. The function fopen() makes the file available for use by the program. A typical call to fopen() is

```
infile = fopen("fname", "r");
```

The value returned by fopen() is of type `FILE *`. It is assigned to `infile`, and the program can then use the identifier `infile` to refer to the file. There are two parameters to fopen(), the pathname of the file to be opened and the mode for the file. Both are strings. The mode of a file determines whether the file is opened for reading, writing, or a combination of the two. The mode "r" indicates that the file is opened for reading only. Other possible modes are

`"w"`	open a new file for writing only
`"a"`	open a file for appending or writing at the end
`"r+"`	open an existing file for update (reading and writing)
`"w+"`	open (create) a new file for update
`"a+"`	open a (new or existing) file for reading and appending (writing at the end of the file)

The file can be closed with the C library function, fclose(). The call to fclose() to close `infile` would be as follows:

```
fclose (infile);
```

The parameter to fclose() is the `FILE *` variable that references the file to be closed. The function fclose() returns an integer.

The program fopen1.c in Example 10-1 simply opens a file named `"info"` and then closes it. It illustrates the simplest use of the C library functions fopen() and fclose().

Example 10-1: fopen1.c

```
/*                  fopen1.c
 *
 *    Synopsis  -  Opens a file for reading and then closes it.
 *
 *    Objective -  To present the most basic file handling.
 */

#include <stdio.h>                                        /* Note 1 */

void main (void)
{
        FILE *fp;                                         /* Note 2 */

        fp = fopen("info", "r");                          /* Note 3 */
```

```
/* Other code to process the file might
 * be placed here.
 */

    fclose(fp);                                          /* Note 4 */
}
```

This program is very simple. It opens a file and then closes it. Before any expansion to process the file is added, the program consists of two lines of executable code.

Note 1: The file stdio.h must be included since the `typedef` declaration of a `FILE` is in that file. Since fopen() returns a `FILE *` instead of an `int`, it must be declared also. Most systems include that declaration in stdio.h.

Note 2: In preparation for opening a file, a variable `fp` of type `FILE *` is declared.

Note 3: The standard library function fopen() will attempt to open a file. The name of the file is the first parameter to fopen() and the mode of opening is the second. In this example, the function fopen() attempts to open a file named "`info`" for reading ("`r`"). If the file is opened successfully, fopen() will return a pointer to the `FILE` structure that will contain the current information about the file. A `NULL` pointer is returned in case of error.

Note 4: The standard library function fclose() will attempt to close the file. The parameter to fclose() is the `FILE *` value that was returned to fopen() when the file was opened.

Learning Activities

1. Create a file named "`info`" and then compile and run this program.
2. Now delete or rename "`info`" and execute the program again. Since the program was trying to open "`info`" and there was no file by that name, an error condition was created. Was there any notification by the compiler or the system of the error?
3. Get a copy of the header file stdio.h from your system. Look at it briefly to get a feeling for its contents. In particular, look at the declaration of a `FILE` in stdio.h. See if fopen() and fclose() were declared.

Error Handling with fopen() and fclose()

In the last Learning Activities, an error condition was created. Most systems would not have reported the error condition. In a longer, more complicated program, the error would probably cause either a program crash or, at least, unreliable output at some other point in the program. The library function fopen() has facilities for reporting the error when it occurs. It is up to the programmer to access the facilities.

In case no error occurs, the C library function fopen() returns a pointer to the FILE * structure that is created by the system when the file is opened. In case an error occurs while opening the file, a NULL pointer is returned instead. The value of the pointer returned by fopen() should be checked for the indication of an error.

Similarly, the return value from fclose() will signal an error condition. If the function fclose() is successful in closing a file, the value 0 is returned. Otherwise EOF is returned to signal the error.

The program fopen2.c in Example 10-2 is a slight modification of fopen1.c from the previous example. The program still attempts to open the file "info" and to close it, but now the program also reports on error conditions and terminates the program if the file cannot be opened.

Example 10-2: fopen2.c

```
/*                  fopen2.c
 *
 *    Synopsis  -  Opens a file named info and closes it.
 *
 *    Objective -  Demonstrates elementary error handling with
 *                 fopen() and fclose().
 */

#include <stdio.h>

void main(void)
{
        FILE *fp;

        if ( (fp = fopen("info", "r") ) == NULL ) {      /* Note 1 */
                printf ("Input file could not be opened\n");
                exit(1);
        }

        /* Other code to process the file might
         * be placed here.
         */

        if (fclose(fp) == EOF)                           /* Note 2 */
                printf ("File couldn't be closed\n");
}
```

This program has essentially the same functionality as fopen1.c; however, now some error handling has been added. Since the program attempts to open and close a file, the file stdio.h has been included and the declaration of fp has been made. The calls to fopen() and fclose() are now embedded in if statements. The return value from each function is checked for indication of error.

Note 1: In the expression for this if statement, a call to fopen() is made to open the file "info" for reading ("r"). The value returned by fopen() is tested. If that value is NULL, an error occurred while opening the file. In that case, an error message is output and the program is terminated.

Note 2: The program will only reach this if statement if the file was opened successfully. The function fclose() is called to close the file. The value returned by fclose() is tested to see if an error occurred. If the value is zero, no error occurred; the value EOF signifies an error. Not many errors occur when attempting to close a file. Therefore, in C programming, testing the return value of fclose() is not done as often as testing the return value of fopen().

Learning Activities

4. Test fopen2.c in the three following situations:
   a. The file "info" exists and contains information.
   b. The file "info" does not exist.
   c. The file "info" exists and is empty.

   Explain what happens in each case.

5. a. Modify the call to fopen() to open the file "info" for writing.
   b. Execute the program without an available file named "info". Does this cause an error? Check on the status of "info" after running the program. Does it exist now? What are its contents?
   c. Execute the modified program when the file "info" exists and has some unimportant contents. Check on the contents of "info" after executing the program. Did the contents change?
   d. Give a general explanation of the effect of the fopen() call on the status of a file when fopen() is called to open a file for writing.

6. Check the documentation that was supplied with your compiler to see what conditions might cause a call to fopen() to fail. Test those conditions on your system and report on the results of your experiment. Do the same for fclose(). Try to create a situation where fclose() fails.

7. The action to be taken when an error occurs in a program should be carefully considered. Program termination may not always be appropriate. What other actions might be appropriate when a file cannot be successfully opened or closed?

"Action to be taken when an error occurs in a program should be carefully considered."
Based on an illustration in *Harpers Weekly*, 1884 (artist unkown).

10.3   Character Input and Output

The utility getchar() is used to read a single character from standard input; the utility putchar() is used to write a single character to standard output. Both getchar() and putchar() are specialized versions of other utilities. The utility getchar() is implemented as a macro; it is defined in the file stdio.h. A discussion of macros appears in Section 11.7.

The utility getc(), a generalized version of getchar(), takes a parameter of type FILE *. When used correctly, the parameter would be initialized by a call to fopen() and would point to a FILE that has been opened for reading. A typical call to getc() is

```
getc(fp);
```

where fp is the parameter of type FILE *. The value returned by getc() is the next byte in the input buffer. It is returned as a value of type int. When the end of the input file is sensed, getc() returns EOF, a preprocessor-defined value in stdio.h. The facility getc() is also implemented as a macro in stdio.h. In fact getchar(), the macro that reads a byte from standard input, is usually defined in stdio.h by the preprocessor directive

```
#define getchar()    getc(stdin)
```

Similarly, putc() is the generalized version of putchar(); putc() will output a single byte to a file. The parameters to putc() are a value of type int that holds the byte to be output, and the FILE * value indicating the file that will receive the output. A typical call to putc() is

```
putc(charval, fp);
```

where charval is of type int and fp is a pointer to a FILE that was returned by fopen(). The corresponding file must have been opened for writing. Similarly, putc() is usually implemented as a macro in the header file stdio.h, and putchar(x) is defined as putc(x, stdout).

The program file2.c in Example 10-3 makes a copy of a file. Both the input and the output file are opened with calls to fopen(). The contents of the input file are read with getc(); output is done with calls to putc(). The names of the original file and the new copy are passed to the program with command line arguments. Note that the command line arguments are declared with ANSI C prototypes. If you do not have an ANSI C compiler, these declarations may have to be changed.

Example 10-3: file2.c

```
/*                  file2.c
 *
 *    Synopsis  -  Makes a copy of a file. The names for the original
 *                 file and the copy are on the command line.
 *
 *    Objective -  To illustrate file handling.
 */

#include <stdio.h>                                     /* Note 1 */

void main(int argc, char *argv[])
{
        FILE *fpin, *fpout;                            /* Note 2 */
        int iochar;

        if (argc != 3) {
                printf ("Usage: cp oldfile newfile\n");
                exit(1);                               /* Note 3 */
        }
```

```
        if ( (fpin = fopen (argv[1], "r")) == NULL) {
                printf("Can't open input file.\n");        /* Note 4 */
                exit(1);
        }
        if ( (fpout = fopen (argv[2], "w")) == NULL ) {
                printf ("Can't open output file.\n");       /* Note 5 */
                exit (1);
        }

        while ( (iochar = getc(fpin)) != EOF)                /* Note 6 */
                putc (iochar, fpout);
}
```

This program consists of the single function named main(). The executable code consists of three `if` statements and a `while` loop.

Note 1: The header file stdio.h must be included in this program for the declaration of the `FILE` structure and the macros getc() and putc().

Note 2: Two variables of type `FILE *` are declared. The variable `fpin` will denote the input file and the variable `fpout` will denote the output file.

Note 3: The program is designed to be invoked with the command

```
cp oldfile newfile
```

The executable version of this program is expected to be in a file named `cp`. The number of arguments on the command line is checked as an indication of the correct invocation of the program. If the program was invoked with the wrong number of command line arguments, a message as to the correct usage of the program is output and the program is terminated.

Note 4: If the number of arguments is correct, a file with the name that appears as the second command line argument (`argv[1]`) is opened with a call to fopen(). The return value of fopen() is examined to detect an error. If one is found, an error message is output and the program is terminated.

Note 5: If no error is encountered in opening the input file, an attempt is made to open a file with the name that appears as the third command line argument. Again, if an error is encountered, a message to that fact is output and the program is terminated.

Note 6: If all the files have been successfully opened, the contents of the input file are copied to the output file with this `while` loop. The macro getc() is used to read a byte at a time from the input file, and putc() is used to write a byte at a time to the output file. There is no error handling available with getc() and putc().

Learning Activities

8. Test file2.c for the following situations.
   a. A nonexistent input file.

   b. An empty input file and an existent nonprotected output file.

   c. An existent input file and an existent protected output file.

   d. An existent input file and a nonexistent output file.

   Generalize the findings from your tests.

9. Would it be appropriate to open the output file with the mode "a", "a+", or "w+"? Why or why not?

10. If you can look at the source code after it has been preprocessed, do so for this program. Find the macro expansions for getc(), putc(), and EOF. Try to interpret them and explain how they work. (They are C expressions or statements.)

A Word of Warning

The macros getc() and getchar() return a value of type `int`; the `int` represents a single byte of input. A typical mistake for beginning C programmers is to declare a variable of type `char` to hold the value input by one of these utilities. This will work correctly for most of the input, but in case the default `char` type on your implementation of C is that of `unsigned char`, the usual test for end-of-file will not work correctly. For example, the program filerr.c in Example 10-4 is a modification of file2.c of Example 10-3. It attempts to make a copy of a file named on the command line. Be advised that it may hang your system if you are using a microcomputer.

 Example 10-4: filerr.c

```
/*              filerr.c
 *
 *    Synopsis  -  Attempts to make a copy of a file.  Designed to be
 *                 invoked with the file names on the command line.
 *
 *    Objective -  To illustrate the need for storing the return value
 *                 from getchar() in a variable of type int.
 */

#include <stdio.h>
```

```
void main(int argc, char *argv[])
{
        FILE *fpin, *fpout;
        unsigned char iochar;

        if (argc != 3) {
                printf ("Usage: cp oldfile newfile\n");
                exit(1);
        }

        if ( (fpin = fopen (argv[1], "r")) == NULL) {
                printf("Can't open input file.\n");
                exit(1);
        }
        if ( (fpout = fopen (argv[2], "w")) == NULL ) {
                printf ("Can't open output file.\n");
                exit (1);
        }

        while ( (iochar = getc(fpin)) != EOF)          /* Note 1 */
                putc (iochar, fpout);
}
```

This program is almost identical to file2.c of Example 10-3. The only change in the code is in the declaration of the variable iochar. It was of type int in file2.c. Here it is of type unsigned char.

Note 1:   The program will execute almost identically to file2.c. The only exception is in the test for end-of-file in the while loop. Here the return from getc() is stored in a variable of type unsigned char. When end-of-file is sensed getc() will return EOF, which is usually defined to be –1 in stdio.h. This value was chosen to represent EOF because it is impossible to type from the keyboard as a single char. It is outside the range for an ASCII character. Normally, when EOF is returned by getc() and stored in type int, a loop like this one would terminate. However, in this case, the –1 (EOF) is stored in type unsigned char. When this value is tested against the EOF in the while loop expression, the type unsigned char is promoted to integer by C's automatic conversion feature. When this promotion takes place, the extra bits are set to zero so that the promoted value will not test equal to –1. This causes an infinite loop.

Learning Activities

11. Run filerr.c as it is with an existent input file. Does it terminate normally? (Be sure to use the proper command line parameters.)
12. Change the declaration of `iochar` to type `signed char` and execute filerr.c again. Does it behave better this time?
13. Omit the keywords `signed` and `unsigned` from filerr.c and execute it again. Can you tell if the default `char` type on your system is `unsigned` or `signed`? Explain your conclusion.

The Utility ungetc()

The C library provides a facility, ungetc(), for putting a single character back in an input stream. The character will be the first character read in the next input statement. This can be done because input is buffered in C. The parameters to ungetc() are the character to be returned to the input buffer and the `FILE` pointer associated with the file. The first parameter is of type `int`.

Certain restrictions exist for the use of ungetc(). Only one character can be returned to each `FILE` and `EOF` cannot be returned.

The program ungetc.c in Example 10-5 illustrates the use of the ungetc() facility. The program seeks out all strings of alphabetic characters and strings of digits. This is done with `while` loops where the input value is tested by character processing facilities that are defined in the standard header file ctype.h. The facility isalpha() returns a nonzero value if its argument is an alphabetic character and zero otherwise. Similarly isdigit() returns nonzero if its argument is a decimal digit and zero otherwise. Both isalpha() and isdigit() are usually implemented as macros. (See Section 11.4.)

The standard function feof() is also introduced in this program. It takes a single argument of type `FILE *`, and returns a nonzero value if the current file position is at the end of the file. A zero is returned when the current position in the file is not at the end.

The ungetc() facility is used since exit from each preceding `while` loop that finds a string of alphabetic characters happens when the character read is not alphabetic. It may be a digit to be included as part of the test for a string of digits. A separate test could be written for that character, or it could be returned to the input buffer with ungetc() as it is here. Similar reasoning applies to the other calls to ungetc().

Example 10.5: ungetc.c

```
/*                    ungetc.c
 *
 *    Synopsis   -   Picks out all strings of alphabetic characters
 *                   and all strings of digits from "text" and prints
 *                   each on a separate line of terminal output.
 *
 *    Objective  -   Illustrates the use of the file facilities ungetc(),
 *                   feof() and the character typing facilities
 *                   isalpha() and isdigit().
 */

#include <stdio.h>
#include <ctype.h>                                    /* Note 1 */

void main(void)
{
        FILE *fp;
        int iochar;

        if ( (fp = fopen ("text", "r")) == NULL) {
                printf ("text couldn't be opened\n");
                exit(1);
        }

        while (!feof(fp)) {                            /* Note 2 */
                while (isalpha(iochar = getc(fp)) )    /* Note 3 */
                        putchar(iochar);
                putchar('\n');
                ungetc (iochar, fp);                   /* Note 4 */
                while (isdigit(iochar = getc(fp))  )   /* Note 5 */
                        putchar (iochar);
                putchar('\n');
                ungetc(iochar, fp);                    /* Note 6 */
                while ( !isalpha(iochar = getc(fp) ) && /* Note 7 */
                        ( !isdigit(iochar) ) &&
                        (!feof(fp)) )
                        ;
                ungetc(iochar, fp);                    /* Note 8 */
        }
}
```

Handwritten annotations: gets(input); "C:\\CBOOK\\Test.dat"; single

The program consists of the single function main(). A file named "text" is opened with the appropriate error handling. Nested while loops direct the reading of the contents of "text". After each while loop, the program uses ungetc() to set up to the next while loop.

Note 1: The macros isdigit() and isalpha() are defined in ctype.h.

Note 2: The function feof() will return a zero while there is more input to be processed. Its declaraton is in stdio.h. When the end-of-file associated with fp is reached, feof() will return 1 and the expression ! feof (fp) will test false and terminate the outer while loop.

Note 3: Input is done with a call to getc() and the return value is tested by isalpha(). If either an uppercase or lowercase alphabetic character was read, isdigit() will return a nonzero value. A zero value indicates a nonalphabetic character and terminates the while loop.

Note 4: Since the character just read may have been a digit, it is put back into the input buffer so that it will be read and tested in the next while loop.

Note 5: Again input is done by getc() and the input character is tested. If the character input is a digit, isdigit() returns a nonzero value and the next character is read. A nondigit will terminate the while loop.

Note 6: The nondigit character may have been an alphabetic so it is put back in the input buffer to be read and tested again.

Note 7: This while loop will skip over all nondigits and nonalphabetics. It terminates if either a digit or an alphabetic character is read or if end-of-file is reached.

Note 8: Again, since the read that terminated the previous while loop may have been a digit or alphabetic character, it is put back in the input buffer to be read and tested again. Note that if end-of-file is reached, the ungetc() call will not push anything back. In that case, the program is terminated in the feof() call at the top of the outer while loop.

Learning Activities

14. a. Create a file named "text" with good test material for ungetc.c. For example, input like

        NOW123is 456   789the time .

    has several combinations of data: alphabetic strings delimited by both strings of digits and strings of nondigits. Incorporate as many test situations for this program as you can into "text".

    b. Test ungetc.c with your file "text". Write up any bugs that you find and try to fix them.

    c. The program ungetc.c tests for end-of-file twice. Is this neccessary? Write up your conclusion.

15. a. Modify ungetc.c to get the name of the file to be processed from the command line so that the program becomes more of a tool.

    b. Will your modified program find strings of alphabetic characters in object code? Test it with the object code from the program ptrptr.c of Section 9.6.

10.4 String Input and Output

In Chapter 5, we discussed the use of the function gets() to input a line of text from standard input and store it as a string. We also discussed the use of puts() to output a string to standard output as a line of text. These functions work with standard input and output only. In this section we will consider the C library functions fgets(), which was designed to input a line of text from a file, and fputs(), which was designed to output a string to a file.

The function fgets() takes three parameters, the address of a buffer where the input text will be stored, the maximum number of characters to be read, and a FILE * value that references the file that contains the input. For example, the call

```
fgets(buffer, 80, fp);
```

instructs fgets() to read characters from the file associated with fp and store them in buffer. Note that buffer should be the address of an array declared in the program. The read will continue until a newline character is read, 80 characters have been read, or the end-of-file is encountered. The input text is stored in the array addressed by buffer and is terminated by a null character (' \0'). The newline character, if read, is stored in buffer also. If the input proceeded without error, fgets() returns buffer or the address of the first character it stored. If either an error occurred or end-of-file was encountered before any characters, a NULL pointer is returned and buffer may contain invalid data.

The function fputs() takes two parameters, the address of the string to be output and the FILE * value associated with the output file. For example, the call

```
            fputs(buffer, fp)
```

will output the data in `buffer`, starting with the first character and stopping with the first null (`'\0'`) character, to the file associated with `fp`. An error is indicated by the return of EOF by fputs().

The program in Example 10-6 gives a use of fgets() and fputs(). The program is a simplified version of the UNIX utility `nl`. It reads a file named on the command line and outputs each line of the file preceded by a line number. To make the error message meaningful, the executable version of this program should be in a file named `nl`.

 Example 10-6: fgets.c

```c
/*              fgets.c
 *
 *   Synopsis   -  Opens a text file and copies the lines of the file
 *                 to standard output preceded by a line number.
 *
 *   Objective  -  To illustrate the use of fgets() for input and
 *                 fputs() for output.
 */

#include <stdio.h>
#define NUMCHARS 512

void main(int argc, char *argv[])
{
        char inarray[NUMCHARS+1];                      /* Note 1 */
        int linecount = 1;
        void exit(int);
        FILE *fp;

        if (argc < 2) {
                printf ("Usage:  nl  filename\n");
                exit(1);
        }
        else if ( (fp = fopen(argv[1], "r")) == NULL ) {
                printf ("Unable to open file %s.\n", argv[1]);
                exit(1);
        }

        while (fgets(inarray, NUMCHARS, fp) != NULL) {  /* Note 2 */
                printf ("%d\t", linecount++);
                fputs(inarray, stdout);                 /* Note 3 */
        }
}
```

The program consists of the single function main(). The executable code begins with an `if-else` statement that checks for the correct number of command line parameters and attempts to open the file named as the second command line parameter. An error message is output and the program is terminated if an error is found in either case. The `while` loop will read and process the lines in the text file.

Note 1: The array `inarray` is declared to have one more cell than the maximum number of characters that will be read by fgets(). This will allow room in the array for the terminating `'\0'`.

Note 2: The standard library function fgets() is used to do the input. It will return a NULL pointer in the case of either an error or the end of the input file; it returns a pointer to the input buffer, `inarray`, if no error is encountered. The parameters to fgets() are the address of the input buffer, the maximum number of characters to put in the buffer and the FILE pointer for the input file. fgets() will stop reading either when it reads a newline character or when it has read the number of characters mentioned in the second parameter.

Note 3: A call to fputs() outputs each line. It takes two parameters, the address of the buffer to be output and the FILE pointer for the output file.

Learning Activities

16. Compile and run fgets.c to ensure that it works on your system. Test the program with several different sets of input.

17. a. This program inputs a line of text into an array of 512 characters. If the file is a text file, it would be unusual for a line of text to contain more characters than the space allocated in the array, but, depending on the system and the input file, it still might be possible. Note that fgets() ensures that the bounds of the array will not be overrun. To see how the program behaves if the input lines contain more characters than the buffer, change NUMCHARS to 8, compile and run the program, and use a file with lines longer than 8 characters as input. Describe how fgets() works.

    b. What would be one reason for declaring `inarray` to have one more cell than NUMCHARS?

18. If fgets.c misbehaves with a buffer shorter than the length of the lines in the file, change the program so that it behaves as follows:
    a. Lines with 70 characters or less are displayed in their entirety.

    b. The first 70 characters of longer lines are displayed.

    c. The end of long lines (more than 70 characters) will be truncated.

d. The program only assigns one line number to a line.

How many cells were declared in your array? Why did you make that choice?

19. Modify fgets.c to output the numbered lines to either a file or standard output. If the output is to go to a file, that file will be named as the third command line parameter. If there is no third command line parameter, the output should go to standard output.

10.5 Reading Blocks of Data at a Time

The C library provides the functions fread() and fwrite() to read and write blocks of data at a time. The function fread() takes four parameters:

```
fread (buffer, size, number, fp);
```

The first parameter, `buffer`, is the address of an array or area of memory where the input data will be stored. The memory must be allocated in the program. The second parameter, `size`, indicates the size of the elements to be read; its type coincides with the type returned by sizeof(), `size_t` in ANSI C, and one of the integer types, usually `unsigned int`, in earlier versions of C. The third parameter to fread() is the `number` of elements to read; its type will be either `size_t` (in ANSI C) or an integer type. The product of the values passed in the second and third parameters gives the total number of bytes to be read. The final parameter is of type `FILE *`; it represents the file from which the input data is to come. The parameters to the library function fwrite() are analogous to those of fread().

Both of these functions will return the number of elements actually read or written. If no error occurs, the number returned should agree with the third parameter in the function call. If the value returned is less than the third parameter, then an error has occurred or end-of-file was encountered by the call to fread().

These functions do not expect any particular type of data nor do they do any conversions. They simply attempt to input or output the requested number of bytes. For the following examples, consider the declarations below:

```
char ch, chararray[10];
int intgr;
struct emp {
    char name[30];
    float salary;
} staff[30];
```

The call

```
fread(&ch, sizeof(ch), 1, stdin);
```

would get a value for ch. It reads a single byte from standard input. The expression &ch is used as the address of a one-byte "buffer" in memory.

The call

```
fwrite (&intgr, sizeof(int), 1, fp);
```

writes a value of type `int` that is stored in `intgr` to the file associated with `fp`. The function fwrite() will output binary data. Conversion to ASCII digits is not done by this output function.

The call

```
fread(staff, sizeof(struct emp), 30, fp);
```

would read a block big enough to contain thirty structures of type `struct emp` from the file associated with `fp`. The structures would fill up the array `staff`. Recall that the name `staff` is the address of the array buffer in memory. Again, binary data is expected for the `salary` member of this structure.

The program fwrite.c in Example 10-7 is a first step in a program to manage a checking account. It inputs information about checking account transactions from the keyboard and stores it in a file. A structure is used to hold the transaction information. The first member of the structure, `t_type`, indicates the type of the transaction. It will hold the value `'W'` when the transaction is a withdrawal, `'D'` when the transaction is a deposit, or the check number for a check. The second member, `payee_memo`, will hold the name of the person to whom a check is written or a memo describing a transaction. The third and fourth members are bit fields. The `tax_deduct` member will be 1 when the entry is tax deductible and zero otherwise. Similarly, the `cleared` member will be set to 1 when an entry has cleared the bank; it will be zero otherwise.

 Example 10-7: fwrite.c

```
/*                  fwrite.c
 *
 *   Synopsis  -   Inputs information about banking transactions and
 *                 stores the information in a file.
 *
 *   Objective -   To illustrate the use of fwrite() to do block
 *                 output of a structure.
 */

#include <stdio.h>
#include <ctype.h>
#include <stdlib.h>
#define TRUE     1
#define FALSE    0
#define BUFFSIZE  50
```

```
struct trans {                                              /* Note 1 */
        int t_type;
        char payee_memo[BUFFSIZE];
        float amount;
        unsigned tax_deduct:1;
        unsigned cleared:1;
};

void main(void)
{
        struct trans transact;
        FILE *fp;
        int get_type(void);
        void get_trans(struct trans *tp),
            put_trans(struct trans *tp, FILE *fp);
                                                            /* Note 2 */
        if ( (fp = fopen("transact", "a+") ) == NULL) {
                printf ("Transaction file couldn't be opened.\n");
                exit(1);
        }

        /*  The following while loop will continue until the
         *  user types a 'Q' for the transaction type.  Each
         *  time the loop is executed, one transaction is input
         *  and stored in the file.
         */
        while ( (transact.t_type = get_type() ) != 'Q') {
                get_trans(&transact);
                put_trans(&transact, fp);
        }
        fclose (fp);
}
/********************************************  gettype() *********/
/*  Requests and inputs the transaction type from the keyboard.
 *  Any letter entered is converted to uppercase before returning,
 *  and a string of digits is converted to type int.  Ensures that
 *  a correct transaction type is returned.
 */
int get_type(void)
{
        char buffer[80];
        int correct = FALSE, t_type;

        while (!correct) {
                printf ("D=deposit, W=withdrawal, or Check Number\n");
                printf ("Enter transaction type or 'Q' to quit: ");
                gets(buffer);
```

```
                    if (isdigit(*buffer) ) {
                            /* convert string of digits to
                             * type int
                             */
                            correct = TRUE;
                            t_type = atoi(buffer);
                    }
                    else {
                            /* Translate any alphabetic character
                             * to uppercase for testing and storage.
                             */
                            t_type = toupper( (int) *buffer );
                            if ( (t_type !='D' ) && (t_type !='W')
                                                && (t_type != 'Q') )
                                    printf("Incorrect, try again\n");
                            else
                                    correct = TRUE;
                    }
            }
            return (t_type);
}
/************************************* get_trans() **********/
/*  Inputs a single transaction from the terminal.
 */
void get_trans(struct trans *trans_ptr)
{
        char inbuf[80];

        printf("Amount: $");
        trans_ptr->amount = atof(gets(inbuf));

        switch(trans_ptr->t_type) {
                case 'W':
                case 'D': printf ("Memo: ");
                        fgets(trans_ptr->payee_memo, BUFFSIZE,
                                stdin);
                        break;
                default: printf ("Payee: ");
                        fgets (trans_ptr->payee_memo, BUFFSIZE,
                                stdin);
        }

        printf ("Tax_deductible? (y/n) : ");
        gets(inbuf);
        if ( (*inbuf == 'y') || (*inbuf == 'Y') )
                trans_ptr->tax_deduct = 1;
        else
```

```
                trans_ptr->tax_deduct = 0;

        printf ("Cleared? (y/n) : ");
        gets(inbuf);
        if ( (*inbuf == 'y') || (*inbuf == 'Y') )
                trans_ptr->cleared = 1;
        else
                trans_ptr->cleared = 0;
}
/*****************************************  put_trans()  ********/
/*  Outputs the structure pointed to by trans_ptr to the file
 *  associated with fp.
 */
void put_trans(struct trans *trans_ptr, FILE *fp)
{
                                                    /* Note 3 */
        fwrite (trans_ptr, sizeof(struct trans), 1, fp);

}
```

The program consists of the functions main(), get_type(), get_trans(), and put_trans(). The function main() opens the file and handles file-opening errors. A while loop calls the other functions to get the information about the transactions and store the transaction information in a file. The function get_type() will always return a valid transaction type or a 'Q' to stop execution of the program. The functions get_trans() and put_trans(), respectively, input a single transaction from the keyboard and output it to the file.

Note 1: The structure for a bank transaction is declared. The sizeof() this structure will be important for the call to fwrite() when the information is output to a file.

Note 2: The call to fopen() opens the file with the mode "a+". This would allow both reading the file and writing at the end of the file (appending). In this program, we will just be writing to the file, but these routines might well be used in a program that would both read and write to a file.

Note 3: This call to fwrite() will output the information about a single transaction to the file. The first parameter to fwrite() is the address of the buffer where the information to be output resides. In this case, the buffer is the structure itself, and the address is passed to fwrite() by the pointer trans_ptr. The next two fields combine (multiply) to give the total number of bytes to be written. In this case, one structure is being written so that the number of bytes is given by sizeof(struct trans) * 1. The final parameter indicates the file where the output is to be stored.

> ### *Learning Activities*
>
> 20. a. Compile and run fwrite.c. Make up three or four transactions to enter.
>
>   b. After you have completed part a, you should have a file named "transact" in your directory. This file will contain both binary and ASCII data. Inspect the contents of the file with a dump program if your system has one.
>
> 21. The function fwrite() returns the number of items actually written. If this number is less than the third argument to fwrite(), an error has occurred. The program fwrite.c does not currently check on the value returned by fwrite(). Modify fwrite.c to check on this return value and to handle any errors that may occur.
>
> 22. Give a single call to fwrite() that would write an array of type struct trans to a file. Assume that the array has five entries.

The program fread.c in Example 10-8 is a companion program to fwrite.c. It reads a file created by fwrite.c and outputs each transaction structure to standard output.

Example 10-8: fread.c

```
/*                 fread.c
 *
 *   Synopsis  -  Reads transactions (elements of type struct trans)
 *                from a file and outputs them to standard output.
 *
 *   Objective -  To illustrate the use of fread() with structures.
 */

#include <stdio.h>
#include <stdlib.h>
#define BUFFSIZE   50

struct trans {
        int t_type;
        char payee_memo[BUFFSIZE];
        float amount;
        unsigned tax_deduct:1;
        unsigned cleared:1;
};
```

```
void main(void)
{
        struct trans transact;
        FILE *fp;
        void print_trans(struct trans *tp);
        int read_trans (struct trans *tp, FILE *fp);

        if ( (fp = fopen("transact", "r") ) == NULL) {
                printf ("Transaction file couldn't be opened.\n");
                exit(1);
        }

        while ( read_trans (&transact, fp) )                /* Note 1 */
                print_trans(&transact);
        fclose (fp);
}
/****************************************  read_trans() **********/
/*  Reads a single transaction from the file associated with fp.
 */
int read_trans(struct trans *trans_ptr, FILE *fp)
{
        int retval;
                                                            /* Note 2 */
        retval = fread (trans_ptr, sizeof(*trans_ptr), 1, fp);
        return (retval);
}


/***************************************** print_trans() ********/
/*  Outputs the structure outtrans to standard output.  Each field
 *  is separated with a vertical bar character.
 */
void print_trans(struct trans *outtrans)
{
        /* Cleared field */
        if (outtrans->cleared)
                printf ("C | ");
        else
                printf ("  | ");

        /* Transaction type */
        if ( (outtrans->t_type =='D') || (outtrans->t_type == 'W')
                                      || (outtrans->t_type == 'I'))
                printf ("%4c | ", outtrans->t_type);
        else
                printf ("%4d | ", outtrans->t_type);
```

```
            /* tax_deduct field */
            if (outtrans->tax_deduct)
                    printf (" T | ");
            else
                    printf ("   | ");

            printf ("%10.2f  | ", outtrans->amount);
            printf ("%s", outtrans->payee_memo);
}
```

The program consists of the functions main(), read_trans() and print_trans(). The declaration of a `struct trans` is made globally. This declaration is exactly the same as the one in the program fwrite.c of Example 10-7. In the function main(), a file is opened and a `while` loop is executed. The functions read_trans() and print_trans() are called within the `while` loop. The function print_trans() outputs the members of its parameter. The members are separated with a ' | ' character.

Note 1: In evaluating the expression for the `while` loop, a call is made to the function read_trans(). The value returned by read_trans() is 1 if a transaction has been read successfully and 0 if either the end-of-file was encountered or if an error occurred.

Note 2: A call to fread() reads a block of data to fill a variable of type `struct trans`. The address of a `struct trans`, `trans_ptr`, is passed in as the first parameter to fread(). It serves as a buffer to be filled by fread(). The next two parameters indicate the total number of bytes to read. The final parameter is the `FILE *` variable associated with the input file. The value returned by fread() is the number of objects actually read. This value is passed back to the calling function. When the value is zero, no elements have been read and the `while` loop in main() terminates.

Learning Activities

23. Execute fread.c with the file created by fwrite.c to ensure that it displays the correct data.
24. Modify the program by having the value returned by fread() output before it is returned by read_trans(). Is the number of characters read on successful calls to fread() a constant value?
25. The function read_trans() can be shortened. Rewrite read_trans() as a single statement that combines the `return` with the call to fread().
26. Modify the program once again by rewriting the `if-else` statements in print_trans() as `? :` expressions.

10.6 Formatted Input and Output

The functions printf() and scanf() do formatted input and output to and from the terminal (standard output and input). The C library contains counterparts, fprintf() and fscanf(), that perform the same type of output and input to and from a file. Similar functions, sprintf() and sscanf(), do their output and input to and from a string.

The first parameter to fscanf() and fprintf() is an expression of type FILE * that is associated with the file for the input or output. The second parameter is the control string, and the remainder of the parameters have the same meaning as for scanf() and printf(). Typical calls to these functions would be

```
fscanf(fp1, "%d", &intvar);
```

to read a decimal value from the file associated with fp1 and store it in the variable intvar. Also,

```
fprintf(fp2, "That value was %d.\n", intvar);
```

will output the control string with the %d replaced by the decimal value of intvar to the file associated with the FILE * value fp.

The functions sscanf() and sprintf() have the address of a memory buffer as their first parameter. Otherwise, their parameters are the same as their companion functions printf() and scanf(). In the case of sscanf(), the contents of the buffer are scanned for characters that match the conversion specifications contained in the control string. In the case of sprintf(), the control string with the indicated conversions performed is written to the buffer. Take care to ensure that the memory buffer is large enough to hold the whole output string.

The program in Example 10-9 illustrates some of these functions. It reads a text file that is composed of student information. Each line of the file contains the information about one student: a first name, a last name, and the grade point average. The names are made up of alphabetic characters and possibly a single quote; the grade point average is a float value. The first and last names are separated with spaces. The grade point average is separated from the names with some spaces also. The program will create two new files; one file will contain only the student names, written with the last name first; the second file will contain only the grade point averages. For example, if the input file contains the information

```
Albert Einstein 3.47
Alfred Neuman 2.29
Donald Knuth  3.79
```

after running the program, the file names will contain

```
Einstein, Albert
Neuman, Alfred
Knuth, Donald
```

and the file gpas will contain

```
3.47
2.29
3.79
```

The program uses fgets() to input a line from the file into an array inbuff. The function sscanf() scans inbuff to find the first name, the last name and the grade point average of each student. Then the function fprintf() is used to output the information to the files names and gpas.

Example 10-9: prntscan.c

```
/*              prntscan.c
 *
 *    Synopsis  -  Opens a file of student names and grade point
 *                 averages, reads the file, and puts the names in
 *                 one file and the grade point averages in another.
 *
 *    Objective -  To demonstrate some of the printf(), scanf() family
 *                 of functions, sscanf() and fprintf() in particular.
 */
#include <stdio.h>
#include <stdlib.h>

void main(void)
{
        FILE *fp, *name_fp, *gpa_fp;
        char first[15], last[15], inbuff[80];
        double gpa;

        if ( (fp = fopen("studinfo", "r") ) == NULL) {
                printf("Unable to open input file.\n");
                exit(1);
        }

        /* Open output files and report any errors.  */
        if ( (name_fp = fopen("names", "w") ) == NULL) {
                printf ("Unable to open names file.\n");
                exit(2);
        }

        if ( (gpa_fp = fopen("gpas", "w") ) == NULL) {
                printf ("Unable to open gpa file.\n");
                exit(3);
        }

        while  (fgets(inbuff, 80, fp) != NULL) {
                                                     /* Note 1 */
                sscanf (inbuff, "%s %s %f%*c", first, last, &gpa);
```

```
                                                             /* Note 2 */
            fprintf (name_fp, "%s, %s\n", last, first);
            fprintf (gpa_fp, "%4.2f\n", gpa);
     }
}
```

This program consists of a single function, main(). The three `if` statements open the input file, `studinfo`, and the two output files, `names` and `gpas`. If an error occurs while opening any of the files, an error message is output and the program terminates. The `while` loop processes the contents of the input file. Each iteration of the loop processes one line of the file, the information about one student. The input is done with fgets(), which reads a line of the file at a time.

Note 1: The array `inbuff` contains one line of the file and is terminated with a null character (`'\0'`). The function sscanf() will look for two strings delimited by whitespace (blanks, tabs, and so on), and a string of digits with a possible decimal point that will be converted to a `float` value.* The addresses of the memory locations where the strings and the `float` value will be stored are given as additional parameters.

Note the fourth conversion specification, `%*c`, in the control string for sscanf(); it demonstrates the use of the conversion suppression flag, `*`. This tells sscanf() to read an extra character, but not to convert or store it. With this syntax in the control string, sscanf() will read past the newline character.

Note 2: The library function fprintf() is used to output both the student name to the `names` file and the grade point average to the `gpas` file. The `FILE *` variable that is associated with each of the output files is used as the first parameter. The remainder of the parameter list could be used with a printf() statement. Note that the student name is output with the last name first, followed by a comma and the first name.

Learning Activities

27. a. Create an input file named "studinfo" with data in the form

     LAST<space>FIRST<space>GPA

   on each line.

   b. Compile and run prntscan.c with this input file to see how it executes.

   c. Experiment by putting a variable number of spaces and/or tab characters between the names and the grade point average. Run the program again. Does the new format change the result? Why or why not?

---

* The function sscanf() has been used here without properly checking on its return value. You will be asked to modify this program to provide this check in the Learning Activities after the next example program.

28. In the sscanf() statement, the `*` before the `c` in the control string tells sscanf() that there will be an additional character, the newline character, `'\n'`, and that it should not be converted and stored. Is this conversion specification necessary? Experiment with the following cases.

    a. Omit the `*` from the `%*c` and attempt to run the program again. If the results are not correct, explain why.

    b. Omit the whole conversion specification, `%*c`, and run the program again. Explain what happens.

    c. Run the program in its original form, but change the input file by adding some blank characters at the end of each line. Does this cause an error? Explain what you think happens.

    d. Modify the input file again by placing some alphabetic characters at the end of each line. Run the program with this modified input file and explain what happens.

29. In prntscan.c, the input from the terminal was done with fgets() and then sscanf() was called to scan the input string. Could fscanf() have been used directly on the input file instead of using fgets() on the file and sscanf() on the resulting string? Experiment and find out.

Error Detection with the printf() and scanf() Families

We have mentioned before that printf() and scanf() are powerful, flexible functions. The same is true for fprintf(), fscanf(), sprintf(), and sscanf().

The input functions, in particular, may give unexpected results when the actual input is not formatted the way that the control string parameter to the function specifies. When this happens, the function does not terminate the program as might happen with general-purpose input routines in other programming languages. The program continues with possibly invalid data in the input variables. Therefore, if the conversion values are not validated by the program, erroneous results may occur.

Values are returned by printf(), scanf(), and the related functions. The printf() family will return an `int` value indicating the total number of characters output by each particular call. The scanf() family also returns a value of type `int`; it returns the number of conversions that were made matching the conversion specifications in its control string. If the number of actual conversions made is less than the number requested, an error in input has occurred.

The program in Example 10-10 examines the values returned by printf() and scanf(). It is designed to be used solely as a learning aid. It should be tested with different forms of input, and the resultant values should be studied with the goal of fully understanding when and what conversions are made by scanf() with different input values.

Example 10-10: retval.c

```
/*                  retval.c
 *
 *   Synopsis   -   Requests and accepts input of a string, an int, a
 *                  char, and a float.  Echoes those quantities and
 *                  outputs the values returned by printf() and scanf().
 *
 *   Objective  -   To allow the student to experiment with input to
 *                  scanf() to get a feel for when and how conversions
 *                  are made and what feedback is provided by scanf().
 */

#include <stdio.h>

void main(void)
{
        char charvar, buff[80];
        int intvar, printret, scanret;
        float floatvar;

        printf ("Enter a string, an int, a character, and a float: ");
                                                    /* Note 1 */
        scanret = scanf("%s%d%c%f", buff, &intvar,
                                &charvar, &floatvar);
                                                    /* Note 2 */
        printret = printf("Values : %s, %d, |%c|, %5.3f\n",
                                buff, intvar, charvar, floatvar);
        printf ("printret %d, scanret %d\n", printret, scanret);
}
```

The executable code consists of three printf() calls and a call to scanf(). The return values from the scanf() call and one of the calls to printf() are stored and output.

Note 1: When scanf() finishes executing, it returns the number of successful conversions it made; it will read until it completes the required number of conversions or it encounters a character that cannot be converted.

Note 2: The value returned by printf() is the number of characters it output. It will vary with the data, but if successful output has occurred this value will be greater than a calculated minimum.

Learning Activities

30. Predict the output of retval.c with each of the following sets of input.
    a. `hi 7r4.5`

    b. `hi 7 r 4.5`

    c. `hi 7r 4.5`

    d. `hi`
       `7`
       `r`
       `4.5`

    e. `hi`
       `7r`
       `4.5`

    f. `hi there`

    Explain what you think happens with each set of input values.

31. Compile and execute retval.c to test your predictions. Correct any mistakes in your thinking. Execute the program with several additional sets of input to test any concept questions that may have occurred to you. Continue to experiment until you are sure you understand the way that scanf() operates.

32. Answer the following questions.
    a. Why does scanf() sometimes read past carriage returns and sometimes appear to terminate when the carriage return is pressed?

    b. What significance does a space make

       i. between the `hi` and the `7` in 1a and 1b?
       ii. between the `7` and the `r` in 1b?
       iii. between the `r` and the `4.5` in 1c?

33. If the value returned by scanf() is less than 4, an error has occurred since 4 conversions were requested. Modify the program to output an error message and terminate the program in that case.

34. In retval.c, what is the minimum value that can be returned by printf() without the occurrence of an error in output? Allow the possibility that errors were encountered by scanf(). Determine a set of input that will produce that minimum return value.

35. a. Read your documentation to discover the meaning of the value returned by sscanf().

    b. Modify the program prntscan.c of Example 10-9 to check the value returned by sscanf() and take appropriate action.

10.7 Random versus Sequential Access in Files

So far, we have discussed sequential access to files. When a file is opened, reading (or writing) starts at the beginning of the file and proceeds through the file in a sequential manner. The current position in the file is recorded in something we will loosely refer to as the file pointer. Whenever a read is done, the file pointer then moves to point to the next element in the file to be read.

Consider the file "transact" created by fwrite.c of Example 10-7. The file was written sequentially; the first write took place at the beginning of the file and subsequent writes appended information to the end of the file. The program fread.c of Example 10-8 reads the records in sequential order from the first record in the file to the last. In sequential access, reading the nth record requires first reading the n − 1 previous records.

In contrast to sequential access, random access allows the reading of the records in any order. For example, the third record could be read, then the fifteenth record, and then the first record. Two library functions in the standard C library help with random access of files. These functions are fseek() and ftell().

The function fseek() moves the file pointer to any byte position in the file. It takes three parameters. A typical call to fseek() might be

```
fseek(fp, offset, start);
```

where `fp` is the FILE * variable associated with the file whose pointer is to be moved. The parameter `offset` is a `long` variable that represents the byte offset or number of bytes that the pointer is to be moved. The parameter `start` indicates the beginning position for the file pointer. The legal values for `start` are 0, 1, and 2. A value of 0 requests fseek() to move the file pointer `offset` bytes from the beginning of the file; a value of 1 requests that the movement (or seek) start from the current position in the file; and a value of 2 requests a seek from the end of the file. (In ANSI C the constant values SEEK_SET for 0, SEEK_CUR for 1 and SEEK_END for 2 have been defined in stdio.h for use with the fseek() function. They may be used to make the code more readable.)

The function ftell() returns the current byte offset from the beginning of the file. It takes a FILE * parameter that indicates the relevant file. For example, the code

```
fseek(fp, (long) 0, 0);
```

positions the file pointer at the beginning of the file. The code

```
fseek (fp, (long) 0, 2);
length = ftell(fp);
```

first positions the file pointer at the end of the file; `ftell(fp)` then returns the byte offset from the beginning of the file and stores it in `length`. The value of `length` will be the number of bytes in the file. The call

```
fseek(fp, 2*sizeof(struct trans), 0);
```

should position the file pointer at the beginning of the third record of type `struct trans` in the file.

The program fseek.c in Example 10-11 allows a user to view any record in the file "transact" that was created by fwrite.c of Example 10-7. The user enters record numbers corresponding to the position of the record in the file, 0 for the first record, 1 for the second, and so on, and the program displays the requested records on the screen.

 Example 10-11: fseek.c

```c
/*                  fseek.c
 *
 *    Synopsis  -  Opens a file and displays records at a user's
 *                 request.
 *
 *    Objective -  To introduce the standard library functions
 *                 fseek() and ftell().
 */

#include <stdio.h>
#include <stdlib.h>
#define BUFFSIZE  50

struct trans {
        int t_type;
        char payee_memo[BUFFSIZE];
        float amount;
        unsigned tax_deduct:1;
        unsigned cleared:1;
};

void main(void)
{
        FILE *fp;
        void print_trans(struct trans *tp), browse(FILE *fp, int nrecs);
        int recnum, totalrec;
        int read_trans (struct trans *tp, FILE *fp);
        int getnumrecs (FILE *fp);
                                                    /* Note 1 */
        if ( (fp = fopen("transact", "r+") ) == NULL) {
                printf ("Transaction file couldn't be opened.\n");
                exit(1);
        }
        totalrec = getnumrecs(fp);

        printf ("Transaction Browser\n");
        printf("Enter the record number you want to see ");
        printf ("or 'Q' to quit.\n");
        browse (fp, totalrec);
}
```

```
/***************************************  read_trans() **********/
/*  Reads a single transaction from the file associated with fp.
 */
int read_trans(struct trans *trans_ptr, FILE *fp)          /* Note 2 */
{
        int retval;

        retval = fread (trans_ptr, sizeof(*trans_ptr), 1, fp);
        return (retval);
}
/*****************************************  print_trans() ********/
/*  Outputs the structure outtrans to standard output.  Each field
 *  is separated with a vertical bar character.
 */
void print_trans(struct *outtrans)                          /* Note 3 */
{
        /* Cleared field */
        if (outtrans->cleared)
                printf ("C | ");
        else
                printf ("  | ");

        /* Transaction type */
        if ( (outtrans->t_type =='D') || (outtrans->t_type == 'W')
                                      || (outtrans->t_type == 'I'))
                printf ("%4c | ", outtrans->t_type);
        else
                printf ("%4d | ", outtrans->t_type);

        /* tax_deduct field */
        if (outtrans->tax_deduct)
                printf (" T | ");
        else
                printf ("   | ");

        printf ("%10.2f  | ", outtrans->amount);
        printf ("%s", outtrans->payee_memo);
}

/*******************************  browse() *****************/
/*     Inputs record numbers, finds and outputs the records
 *     until the user signals quit with a 'Q'.
 */
void browse (FILE *fp, int numrecs)
{
        int recnum;
```

```
        struct trans transact;

        printf ("Transaction number: ");
        while (scanf("%d", &recnum)) {                    /* Note 4 */
                if (recnum >= numrecs)
                        printf("Enter a number between 0 and %d\n",
                                numrecs-1);
                else {
                                                           /* Note 5 */
                        fseek(fp, (long) recnum*sizeof(transact),0);
                        if (read_trans(&transact ,fp))
                                print_trans(&transact);
                        else
                                printf("Transaction %d not found.\n",
                                        recnum);
                }
                printf ("Next transaction Number: ");
        }
}
/******************************   getnumrecs()   ************/
/*     Calculates the number of records in the file by getting
 *     the total length of the file and dividing by the number
 *     of bytes in a record.
 */
int getnumrecs(FILE *fp)
{
        int numbytes;

        fseek(fp, (long) 0, 2);                           /* Note 6 */
        numbytes = ftell(fp);                             /* Note 7 */
        if (numbytes != -1)
                return (numbytes/sizeof(struct trans));
}
```

This program consists of the functions main(), read_trans(), print_trans(), browse(), and getnumrecs(). The function main() opens the file "t r a n s a c t", calls getnumrecs() to calculate the number of records in the file, outputs some messages to the user and calls the function browse() to browse through the file.[*]

---

[*] In order to have the set of programs fwrite.c, fread.c, and fseek.c work with some of the micro-computer implementations of C, it may be necessary to open the file with modes "ab+", "rb", and "rb+" respectively. The 'b' indicates a binary file.

Note 1: In this call to fopen(), the file "transact" is opened with mode "r+"; this allows both reading and writing to the file. The file contents are left intact when the file is opened. The modes "w+" and "a+" also allow both reading and writing; with "w+", any existing file contents are destroyed when the file is opened, and with "a+", writes to the file are only done at the end of the file.

Note 2: The function read_trans() is exactly the same as the one that appeared in the program fread.c of Example 10.8.

Note 3: The function print_trans() is also taken from fread.c. Both of these functions could be kept in a separate utilities file and linked in during the link step of the compilation process.

Note 4: The expression in this while loop exploits the behavior of scanf(). When a 'Q' is entered, scanf() will not be able to make a conversion to type int and will therefore return 0. The value of 0 will stop the execution of the while loop.

Note 5: The function fseek() is called to position the file pointer at the beginning of the correct record. The offset value is the total number of bytes from the beginning of the file that must be skipped to position the file pointer at the beginning of the recnumth record. This assumes that the user knows that record numbering begins with 0.

Note 6: This call to fseek() will position the file pointer at the end of the file.

Note 7: The function ftell() returns the byte offset from the beginning of the file. This number is stored in numbytes, and used to calculate the number of records in the file.

Learning Activities

36. Run fseek.c using the file created by fwrite.c of Example 10-7 as input.[*] If it does not work correctly, modify the program fread.c to output the offset of each record before it reads it. Check to see if the records are evenly spaced within the file. If so, modify fseek.c to seek the correct distance to find each record and run the program again. If the records are not evenly spaced within the file, it may not be possible to make this program work without major modifications.

37. Modify fseek.c to allow a user to start counting records with 1. That is, 1 should refer to the first record in the file, and the number returned by getnumrecs() should refer to the last record.

---

[*] This program does not work properly with some of the earlier versions of C compilers for an MS-DOS system. The problem is in the way fwrite() executes on those systems. The number of bytes written to the file is not constant. This Learning Activity addresses this problem.

10.8   A Closer Look at stdio.h

The file stdio.h contains facilities for input and output. This file differs on different implementations of C because most of the input and output library functions are redesigned for each computer system. Here we will examine the contents of a typical stdio.h file.

Preprocessor-defined constants are defined with a #define in stdio.h. We have used the constants EOF and NULL. Another constant typically defined in stdio.h is BUFSIZ. Input and output from files are generally buffered, and BUFSIZ is the size of the default buffer.

As mentioned earlier in this chapter, a typedef declaration of the identifier FILE also appears in stdio.h. A FILE is declared to be a C structure that is used by the library functions and the operating system to keep information about a file. Typically, a FILE contains at least three members, a member that counts the number of characters still to be processed before the buffer needs to be refreshed, the address of the buffer, and the pointer into the current position in the buffer. One example of the declaration of a FILE is below.

```
typedef   struct {
            short count;    /* number of unprocessed characters
                             * (cells) in the buffer */
            char *bufaddr;  /* the address of the buffer */
            char *curptr;   /* pointer to the current position
                             * of the buffer */
            .
            .
            .

        } FILE;
```

Different compilers may implement the FILE structure with different members or different names for these members, but the three members mentioned above are typical. Additional members might include flags that indicate whether the file is opened for reading, writing, or a combination; an indication if end-of-file has been encountered; an error indicator; and a member by which the operating system keeps track of the file.

One FILE structure is kept up to date for every open file in the program. The operating system updates the current information in the FILE every time the status changes.

The program stdio.c in Example 10-12 outputs the values of the members in the FILE structure for stdin and stdout as changes occur. Input and output are done by calls to getchar() and putchar(). The program is a modification of inout2.c from Example 2-13. The names of the FILE members are those used in Borland's Turbo C compiler. If you are not using this compiler, this program will have to be modified to run correctly on your system. It will require the examination of the declaration of a FILE in stdio.h and the adjustment of at least the names of the members of the FILE structure in the program to match those in your stdio.h file.

Example 10-12: stdio.c

```
/*               stdio.c
 *
 *    Synopsis  -  Echoes its input to its output and outputs
 *                 information about contents of stdin and stdout.
 *
 *    Objective -  To provide a vehicle for studying the changes
 *                 in the FILE structure.
 */


#include <stdio.h>

void main(void)
{
        int iochar;
        void FILEinfo (FILE *fp, char *fn);

        printf("Enter text - signal EOF to quit.\n");
        while ((iochar = getchar()) != EOF) {
                FILEinfo(stdin, "stdin");               /* Note 1 */
                putchar (iochar);
                FILEinfo(stdout, "stdout");             /* Note 2 */
        }
}
/********************************* FILEinfo()  **************/
/*     Outputs the current information from a FILE structure.
 *     Names taken from Borland Turbo C stdio.h.  May need
 *     to be changed for other compilers.
 */
void FILEinfo(FILE *fp, char *FILEname)
{                                                       /* Note 3 */
        fprintf (stderr,"%s : level %d, buffer %x, ",
                FILEname, fp->level, fp->buffer);
        fprintf (stderr,"curp %x, *curp %x, previous %x.\n",
                fp->curp, *(fp->curp), *(fp->curp-1) );
}
```

The program consists of the function main() and a subfunction FILEinfo(). The function main() consists of a while loop that reads from standard input and writes to standard output until the end of the input file. After each input and output call, a call to FILEinfo() outputs the information in the FILE structures.

Note 1: The call to FILEinfo() contains the `FILE` pointer from which the information is to be output and the name of the `FILE` pointer as a string so that it can be identified in the output.

Note 2: The information output from this call to FILEinfo() may not change as the program is executing. This could be because both `stdout` and `stderr` refer by default to terminal output and the terminal output may be flushed with every output statement.

Note 3: The information output is the name of the `FILE *` variable being referenced; the value of `level` (which is a reference to the number of processed or unprocessed characters in the buffer); the value of `buffer` (the address of the buffer); the value of `curp` (the address of the current position in the buffer), and the contents of `curp` (the actual character). Note that all values except the name of the `FILE *` variable being referenced are all output in numeric quantities to avoid unprintable characters messing up the terminal screen.

Learning Activities

38. Obtain a copy of stdio.h from your system. Modify the names of the `FILE` structure members throughout stdio.c to match those in the definition of the `FILE` in your stdio.h.

39. Compile and execute stdio.c. Feed it very short lines of input. Try a line with 0 characters before the newline (`'\n'`), with one character before the newline, with two characters before the newline, etc.

40. Describe what happens to the members of the `FILE` structure pointed to by `stdin`, and what happens to the corresponding members of the `FILE` structure pointed to by `stdout`. How do these changes differ? How are they the same?

41. If the values output for `stdout` do not change, try removing the `'\n'` character in the fprintf() call in FILEinfo(). Since this will make reading the output difficult, it should only be done as a last resort. However, it may show some of the changes in `stdout`.

Language Elements Introduced in This Chapter: A Review

** File Opening Modes

        `"r"`   open a file for reading

        `"w"`   open a new file for writing only

        `"a"`   open a file for appending (writing at the end)

        `"r+"`   open a file for update (reading and writing)

"w+"   open a new file for update

"a+"   open a file for reading and appending

** Header Files **

stdio.h

** Library Functions **

fopen()	opens a file
fclose()	closes a file
fgets()	reads a line of text from a file and stores it as a string
fputs()	outputs a string to a file
fread()	reads a block of bytes from a file
fwrite()	writes a block of bytes to a file
fprintf()	does formatted output to a file
fscanf()	does formatted input from a file
fseek()	moves the file pointer to an indicated position in the file
ftell()	returns the byte offset of the current position from the beginning of a file
sprintf()	does formatted printing to a string
sscanf()	scans a formatted string and converts embedded values

** Macros **

getc()	inputs a single character from a file
putc()	outputs a single character to a file
ungetc()	pushes a single character back onto an input stream

** Types **

FILE

FILE *

** Variable Declarations **

FILE *infile, *outfile;

Things to Remember

1. Input and output may be either buffered or line buffered.
2. A file is a stream of bytes to a C program. Any structure put on a file is put there by the programmer.
3. When a C program is executed, three files are automatically opened: standard input, standard output, and standard error.
4. The return value from a call to a library function usually indicates when an error has occurred.
5. The macros getc() and getchar() return a value of type `int`. Using type `char` will, at best, produce nonportable code.
6. Some compilers do not write a precise number of characters with fwrite() and, therefore, random access is not easily accomplished.
7. A `FILE` is a structure that C uses to keep track of the current position in a file. One `FILE` structure is kept up to date for every open file in the program.

10.9   Exercises and Programming Problems

1. The program file2.c makes a copy of a file. It uses getc() and putc() to do the input and output. Write four new versions of a file copy program. Each of the programs should have the same functionality as file2.c.

   a. In the first version, use fgetc() to do the input and fputc() to do the output.

   b. In the second version, use fgets() to do the input and fputs() to do the output.

   c. In the third version, use fread() to do the input and fwrite() to do the output.

   d. In the fourth version, use fscanf() to do the input and fprintf() to do the output.

   e. Compare the sizes of the object code from all five versions of the file copy programs. If facilities for testing execution efficiency are available on your system, test the efficiency of each version. Report on your findings.

2. Write a program that will open a file and report on the number of lines, characters, and words in a file. Have the name of the file to be opened appear as a command line argument. You will need to find out what characters your computer system uses to mark the end of lines. For this program, assume that words are sequences of printable characters that are delimited by either whitespace or unprintable characters.

3. Write a program that searches for every occurrence of a string in a text file and outputs every line in which it finds the string. Have the string appear as the first command line parameter after the executable program name, and the filename appear as the second command line parameter.

4. a. Write a program that will create an inventory file for a `struct auto_part` (from Section 7.1). Have the inventory information for each auto part entered

from the terminal and stored in a file. Use fwrite() to write the structure to the file.

b. Write a program that will read a file like the one created by the program in part a and write the inventory information about each of the auto parts in the file to the terminal screen.

c. Write a program that will read a file like the one created by the program in part a and report the part identification for each automobile part for which there are less than 5 items in the inventory.

5. Write a C program that will change every occurrence of one string in a text file to another. If the program is named change, the invocation

```
change Smith Johnson namefile
```

should open the file namefile and change every occurrence of the string "Smith" to the string "Johnson".

6. Write a C program that reads a file and outputs it on the terminal with a header for each page. Have the name of the file and the number of lines in a page entered as command line parameters. The header should consist of a blank line, a line with the file name and the page number, and another blank line. For example, if the program is named prfile, the invocation

```
prfile 6 filename
```

should produce a header like this:

```
File : filename                          Page Number 1
```

and three lines of text on each page.

7. Write a C program that compares two files and outputs the message

```
filename1 and filename2 are identical
```

when the files are the same or the message

```
filename1 and filename2 :   first difference in byte
                            number _____.
```

when they are different. The names of the two files should appear as command line parameters.

8. Write a C program that will copy the contents of a text file to the terminal screen and pause for instructions after each screen of text has been displayed. After a pause, the user may press different keys to signify different actions to the program:

a. Pressing <Return> will be the signal to display the next page.

b. Pressing a 'q' and then <Return> will be the signal to quit displaying the file and terminate the program.

c. Pressing a 'd' followed by a <Return> will be the signal to display 11 more lines.

9. Write a C program designed to open and read a binary file and display all null-terminated strings of ASCII characters in the file that consist of alphabetic, numeric, whitespace or punctuation characters and have length greater than 1.

Display the hexadecimal representation of the byte offset of the string within the file and the string itself on a single line of output. Sample output might be:

```
Byte Offset         String
-----------         ---------
30a2                Flat as a flounder
3182                Not a patch on you
452e                Running at rovers
534c                In my mind's eye
```

if those strings were in the file. Again, the file name should be given as a command line argument. To test your program, write a simple C program that calls printf() to output the four strings above. Compile the program and use the compiled version to test your program. Your program should get the four strings above. Your program will probably output many other meaningless strings.

C Library and
Preprocessor Facilities

Chapter 11

11.1   Introduction to the C Library

A library is a collection of functions that can be easily used in different programs. A function may be placed in a library because it provides a standard method for accessing parts of the hardware in a computer; such functions usually interface with an operating system. The input and output functions and file handling functions are examples of functions put in a library for that reason. Functions may also be put in a library because they do standard things that are often used in a program. The string library functions are examples of these types of functions.

A C library is usually provided with a C compiler. The selection of functions included in a library evolves with the different uses of the C language, and changes from installation to installation. Functions may be added that have proved useful for a specific operating system. For example, the C library developed for the UNIX operating system is especially rich and varied. However, a common core of functions are usually included. The specification of the C language by ANSI also includes specifications for the functions that must be included with an ANSI C compiler.

The standard library includes functions on the following topics: file handling, formatted input and output, character input and output, block input and output, error handling and diagnostic functions, character testing, string handling, mathematical functions, general utility functions, and date and time functions.

Earlier in this text we have seen uses of library functions dealing with files, input and output, and string handling as well as some of the general utility functions like atof() and atoi() to convert ASCII strings to numeric quantities. This chapter will introduce some of the other library functions like those to dynamically allocate and deallocate memory, do mathematical calculations, and manipulate characters. A more complete list of the library functions included in the ANSI Standards for C is in the Programmer's Handbook.

A second topic that is introduced in this chapter is the preprocessor facilities of conditional compilation and macros. In C source code a macro may appear to be a function, but it is handled by the preprocessor and expanded in place before being translated into assembly or object code. Examples of using macros appear in Section 11.7 and examples of conditional compilation are done in Section 11.8.

The Time and Date Functions

We will look at some of the functions that allow a program to know the current time and date. The functions that we will consider are time(), ctime(), and localtime(). These functions are specified in ANSI C. They are very similar to functions and systems calls that are available on a UNIX system. For a list of the other ANSI C library functions that deal with the time and date, see the Programmer's Handbook.

The function time() returns a measure of the current time. It is defined to return a value of type `time_t`, which is declared in the standard header file time.h. The parameter to time() is a pointer to a quantity of type `time_t`. If the variable t has been declared as type `time_t`, typical calls to time() might be

```
time (&t);
```
or
```
t = time ( (time_t *) 0);
```

In the former call, the current time is put in the variable t and the value returned by time is ignored. In the latter call, the return value is stored in the variable t on return from time(). Passing a zero value as the parameter to time() suppresses the return of the current time in the parameter.

The function ctime() accepts the value returned by time() as its parameter; it returns a `char *` value that references a string with the date in a readable form. For example, the return value from ctime() might point to the string

```
Sun Oct 23  17:35:54  1990\n
```

If `timestr` is declared to be of type `char *`, a typical call to ctime() might be

```
timestr = ctime (&t);
```

where t was returned by time(). Note that `timestr` should not point to a buffer.

The function localtime() gives the programmer another method of working with the time and date. The parameter to localtime() is again the value returned by time(); however, the value returned by localtime() is a pointer to a `struct tm` structure that is declared in time.h. A `struct tm` structure contains the following fields:

```
struct    tm    {
          int   tm_sec;      /* 0 - 59 */
          int   tm_min;      /* 0 - 59 */
          int   tm_hour;     /* 0 - 23 */
          int   tm_mday;     /* 1-31, the month-day */
          int   tm_mon;      /* 0 - 11 */
          int   tm_year;     /* since 1900 */
          int   tm_wday;     /* 0(Sunday) - 6*/
          int   tm_yday;     /* 0(Jan 1) - 365 */
          int   tm_isdst;    /* 1 if Daylight Savings
                                Time, 0 if not */
     };
```

This structure allows the programmer to access any of the members separately and allows manipulation of the structure or output in different forms.

The program timex.c in Example 11-1 shows the use of these three functions to output some dates. It also calls the function clock() which is included in the ANSI C library. A measure of the processor time used by the program since the beginning of execution is returned by clock(); it does not take a parameter.

Example 11-1: timex.c

```
/*                timex.c
 *
 *    Synopsis  -  Outputs today's time and date, the date tomorrow,
 *                 and the processor time used by the program.
 *
 *    Objective -  To introduce the time and date library functions.
 */

#include <time.h>                                    /* Note 1 */
#include <stdio.h>

void main(void)
{
        time_t t1;                                   /* Note 2 */
        struct tm *tptr;
        clock_t ticks;
        char *s, timestr[80];

        if ( (t1 = time((time_t *) 0)) != -1) {      /* Note 3 */
                s = ctime (&t1);                     /* Note 4 */
                printf ("currentdate is %s", s);
```

```
                        tptr = localtime(&t1);                      /* Note 5 */
                        printf ("Tomorrow is %d/%d/19%d.\n",        /* Note 6 */
                                 tptr->tm_mon+1, tptr->tm_mday+1,
                                 tptr->tm_year);
             }
             if ((ticks = clock()) != -1)                           /* Note 7 */
                        printf ("%5.2f seconds used by the processor.\n",
                                      ticks/CLK_TCK);                /* Note 8 */
}
```

The program consists of the single function main(). The executable code consists of two `if` statements: one to output the dates, and one to output the processor time.

Note 1: The file time.h must be included. It contains type declarations, constant declarations, and function prototypes for the time and date functions. In particular, the declarations of the types `time_t`, `clock_t`, and `struct tm` are included.

Note 2: The variable `t1` must be declared of type `time_t` since it will hold the value returned by time(). The variable `ticks` is declared to be type `clock_t` to agree with the value returned by clock(). The variable `tptr` will point to the value returned by localtime().

Note 3: The function time() is called with 0 as the actual parameter. This value has been cast to type `time_t *` to match the parameter type required by time(). When time() is called with a value of 0 as its parameter, the calendar time is returned by the function. If a legal pointer value is passed to time(), the function will put a copy of the calendar time in the location pointed to by the parameter as well as return the value. The return value is tested against –1 to ensure that the call is completed successfully.

Note 4: The function ctime() takes the value returned by time() as its parameter and converts it to a string that contains the local time in a format suitable for output. It returns a pointer to the first character in the string. That string is output by the next printf() call.

Note 5: This call to localtime() also converts the value returned by time() to local time. However, the value returned is a pointer to a quantity of type `struct tm`. The individual members of the `struct tm` quantity have been populated with the correct values representing the local time. This structure is used to output tomorrow's date in a different format. The return of a pointer to a `struct tm` gives the localtime() library function much flexibility in use.

Note 6: The printf() function call outputs tomorrow's date in the form 1/31/91. The individual members of the `struct tm` populated by localtime() give the month, day, and year.

Note 7: The function clock() returns a measure of the processor time used by this program's execution. It returns –1 if an error occurs.

Note 8: The constant CLK_TCK is defined in time.h. The expression `ticks/CLK_TCK` represents the number of seconds of processor time.

Learning Activities

1. If you have an ANSI C compiler, compile and run timex.c to make sure that it works correctly on your system. If your compiler is not yet fully ANSI C compatible, you may have to comment out some of the function calls. If you are working on a UNIX system, much of this program may work by accessing the UNIX system calls instead of library functions.
2. The actual implementation of the time() function and what is meant by calendar time will differ with different operating systems. One popular method is to have time() return the total number of seconds since some predetermined date. Look at the include file, time.h, and your compiler documentation to try to determine how time is recorded by your compiler. Have the value returned by time() output and try to do the conversion yourself to verify the results of your research.
3. Modify timex.c so that it outputs the time in a different time zone. For example, if you live in New York, have the program output the time in Hawaii.

11.2   Error Handling with the ANSI C Library

Many of the C library functions indicate that an error has occurred with their return value. For example, we have seen that fopen() returns a NULL pointer when an error occurs in opening a file; many of the string functions do also. The function fseek() returns any nonzero value when it discovers an error; ftell() returns –1 as a long value on error.

ANSI C specifies an additional error handling device. An external variable errno is provided that indicates more precisely which error has occurred. When an error occurs, errno is given a value that corresponds to the error and an implementation-dependent error message. A C program may access that value after any error. The variable errno is declared in the standard header file errno.h along with a list of different errors.

Some error handling functions are also provided in the ANSI C library. The functions ferror() and clearerr() deal with errors that occur when reading or writing with a file. Both take a FILE * parameter that is associated with the file for which errors are being checked. The call

```
ferror(fp);
```

checks to see if an error has occurred on the file associated with fp. If it has, ferror() returns a nonzero value. Otherwise, it returns zero. The call

```
clearerr(fp)
```

explicitly clears the error condition for the file associated with `fp`. Without this call, any subsequent call to ferror() would always return an error.

The function perror() checks on and reports more general errors. The parameter to perror() is a `char *` value that holds the address of the first character in a string to be output. The call

```
perror(s);
```

will output the string s followed by a colon, a space, and a description of the error message associated with the current value of `errno`.

As an example of these three functions in action, consider the program perror.c in Example 11-2. The program attempts to open a file and read through the file. It uses perror() to report on any errors it encounters. The functions ferror() and clearerr() are used to detect errors associated with reading from the file. The values returned by fopen() and by fread() are inspected for error indications also.

 Example 11-2: perror.c

```
/*                  perror.c
 *
 *   Synopsis  -   Checks for the correct number of command line
 *                 parameters, opens the file in argv[1], reads
 *                 through the file and reports on any errors found.
 *
 *   Objective -   To demonstrate the use of some of the error
 *                 handling functions.
 */

#include <stdio.h>                               /* Note 1 */

void main(int argc, char *argv[])
{
        void processit(void);

        FILE *fp;
        char buf[100];
        int numread;

        if (argc < 2) {
                printf ("Usage: perror file\n");
                exit(1);
        }

        if ((fp = fopen(argv[1], "r")) == NULL) {
                perror ("fopen error");           /* Note 2 */
        }
```

```
        while (fread(buf, sizeof(char), 100, fp) > 0) {
                processit();
        }
        if (ferror(fp)) {                                /* Note 3 */
                perror (argv[0]);                        /* Note 4 */
                clearerr(fp);                            /* Note 5 */
        }

        /* Processing may continue */
}
void processit(void)
{
        printf ("File processing stub.\n");
}
```

The program consists of two functions, main() and processit(). The function processit() is a stub. It symbolizes processing that might be done on each line of text. The function main() uses `if` statements to check for the correct number of command line arguments, open the file, and check for errors. A `while` loop reads through the contents of the file.

Note 1: The functions perror() and clearerr() are of type `void` and should be declared as such. In ANSI C, these functions and ferror() are declared in the header file stdio.h.

Note 2: The function perror() is called in case an error occurs while opening the file. The function will output the string "fopen error" followed by the reason for the error. These reasons are implementation dependent. They could be different on different computers.

Note 3: When the previous `while` loop terminated, the return value from fread() was either 0 or negative. This call to ferror() determines whether or not an error occurred while reading from the file. The function ferror() returns a nonzero value when it senses an error.

Note 4: This call to perror() passes in the name of the executing program to be output with the error message. This technique is used in many UNIX utility programs for reporting errors.

Note 5: The function clearerr() is called to explicitly clear the error condition so that processing can continue and ferror() can be used again to check on errors. Without this call, the error condition would not be cleared and once an error occurred, ferror() would always report an error.

Learning Activities

4. If you have an ANSI C compiler or work on a UNIX system, compile and run perror.c. (You may need to change the function prototypes if you don't have an ANSI C compiler.)

   a. Test it without command line parameters.

   b. Test it with `argv[1]` naming a file that does not exist.

   c. Test it with the name of a relatively short file in `argv[1]`.

   d. Is reading at the end-of-file considered an error?

5. In the documentation for your compiler, look up other error conditions. Try to devise tests to see how this program handles these errors. If necessary, rewrite the program to test for the other error conditions.

11.3 Using Mathematical Functions

Many mathematical functions are included with the C library: the major trigonometric functions, inverse trigonometric functions, hyperbolic functions, exponents, logs, powers, and square roots, among others. A complete listing of the functions specified in the ANSI standards appears in the Programmer's Handbook.

Most of the mathematical functions return a value of type `double`. When such a function is used, either the function must be declared to return type `double`, or the header file math.h must be included in the program with `#include`. This file contains macros, type declarations, and constants used by the mathematical functions in addition to the declarations of the functions themselves.

On some systems, UNIX for example, the mathematical functions are kept in a separate library which must be explicitly searched at link time. This usually involves a modification of the compiler call so that the linker will know to search the different library. In some other systems, all of the library functions are automatically searched at link time.

The use of the mathematical functions in the C library is illustrated in the program polar.c of Example 11-3. This program converts Cartesian coordinates of a point to polar coordinates. The Cartesian coordinates and the polar coordinates of a point are illustrated in Figure 11-1.

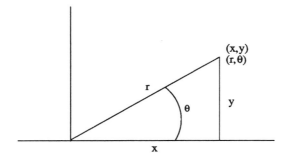

Figure 11-1

The Pythagorean theorem gives the conversion formula for obtaining the radius, r, of the polar coordinates from the Cartesian coordinates x, y. It is illustrated in Figure 11-2.

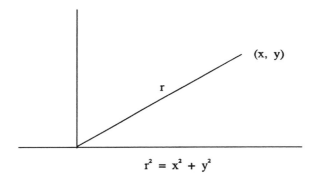

Figure 11-2

The angle is obtained by applying the arctangent to the expression y / x. This is illustrated in Figure 11-3.

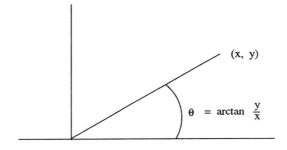

Figure 11-3

The Cartesian coordinates and the polar coordinates of a point are stored in C structures. They are declared before the function main() so that the declaration will be available throughout the program. Both structures are composed of two members of type double, but the names of the members reflect the different coordinates.

The mathematical functions from the C library used in this program are sqrt(), pow(), and atan2(). The sqrt() function takes a parameter of type double and returns the square root of its argument. The return value is of type double also. The sqrt() function is not defined for negative arguments.

The pow() function takes two arguments of type double and returns a value of type double. For example, the call

```
pow(x, y);
```

will return the value x^y. Errors will occur with the pow() function when either

x is zero and y is negative

or

x is negative and y is not an integer

The function atan2() takes two arguments of type double and returns an angle between -PI and PI. For example, the call

```
atan2(y, x);
```

will return the angle between the positive x axis and the line from the origin through the point (x, y) in Cartesian coordinates. This function was chosen over the library function atan(), which takes a single argument and returns a value between -PI/2 and PI/2, since the latter function would require the program to adjust for the angle in different quadrants. The function atan2() has this functionality built in.

A final utility function, strtod(), is used in this program. It will convert a string of ASCII characters that represent a floating point value to a numeric value of type double. The name strtod() stands for *string* to *double*. It takes two parameters. The first is a pointer to the first character in the string. The second is a pointer to a pointer to a character. The function will convert as many elements in the string as possible to type double, return that value, and set the contents of its second parameter to point to the unconverted remainder of the string. For example, if the call to strtod() was

```
strtod("123.4abc", remainder);
```

the value 123.4 would be returned as type double and *remainder would point to the 'a'. In this program, we will not need to look at the remainder of the string after conversion so we can suppress this part of the functionality by passing in a NULL value.

 Example 11-3: polar.c

```
/*                    polar.c
 *
 *     Synopsis    -    Converts sets of points in Cartesian coordinates to
 *                      polar coordinates.
```

```
 *
 *    Objective -   Illustrates the use of some of the mathematics
 *                  in the ANSI C library.
 */

#include <stdio.h>
#include <math.h>                                      /* Note 1 */
#include <stdlib.h>

struct cartesian {
        double x;
        double y;
};

struct polar {
        double radius;
        double angle;
};

void main(void)
{
        struct cartesian cpoint;
        struct polar     *ppoint, *to_polar(struct cartesian *cart);
        double           get_c_coord(char *s);
        char             buff[80];
        int              more = 1;

        printf ("Conversion: Cartesian to polar coordinates.\n");
        while (more) {
                cpoint.x = get_c_coord("x");
                cpoint.y = get_c_coord("y");
                ppoint = to_polar(&cpoint);
                printf ("Polar coordinates: ");
                printf ("radius %5.2lf, angle %5.2lf\n",
                                ppoint->radius, ppoint->angle );
                printf ("Another one? (y/n) ");
                gets (buff);
                if (buff[0] != 'y')
                        more = 0;
        }
}
/******************************** get_c_coord()   ***********/
/* Inputs a string from standard input and converts the string to
 * type double.
 */
double get_c_coord(char *s)
{
```

```
        char buffer[80];

        printf ("Enter the %s value: ", s);
        gets(buffer);
        return (strtod(buffer, (char **)NULL) );          /* Note 2 */
}
/********************************* to_polar()  *************/
/*  Converts a point from Cartesian coordinates to polar coordinates.
 */
struct polar *to_polar(struct cartesian *cart)
{
        static struct polar p;
        double temp;

        temp = pow(cart->x, 2) + pow(cart->y,2);          /* Note 3 */
        p.radius = sqrt(temp);                            /* Note 4 */
        p.angle = atan2(cart->y, cart->x);                /* Note 5 */
        return (&p);
}
```

The program consists of the three functions main(), get_c_coord(), and to_polar(). The function get_c_coord() takes care of input. A value is input as a string of characters, and as much as fits is converted to type `double` and returned. The function to_polar() takes a pointer to a `struct cartesian` and returns a pointer to the polar equivalent of the point. The function main() calls get_c_coord() to input the cartesian point, calls to_polar() to convert it to polar coordinates, and outputs the result in every pass through its `while` loop.

Note 1: The header file math.h should be included whenever functions from the mathematics portion of the C library are used. The declarations of the functions and declarations of relevant constant values and types are in that file.

Note 2: The function strtod() is called to convert the input string to a value of type `double`. The first parameter points to the first character in the string. In this case, the second parameter is NULL since the unconverted part of the string is not of interest in this program. The function strtod() was declared of type `double` in stdlib.h.

Note 3: The function call `pow(val, 2)` will compute the square (power 2) of val. The sum of the squares of the x and y coordinates is calculated in this statement.

Note 4: The C library function sqrt() is called to compute the square root of the sum of the squares of the x and y coordinates or the distance of the point from the radius. This call completes the computation of the radius coordinate.

Note 5: The function atan2() was chosen to calculate the angle, given the x and y coordinates of the point. This function was chosen over atan() since it will give values from $-PI$ to PI instead of the smaller interval from $-PI/2$ to $PI/2$. The latter interval refers only to the first and fourth quadrants of the plane. Note that a zero value for the x coordinate is not an error in this expression.

Learning Activities

6. Compile polar.c. If error messages indicate that the functions sqrt(), pow(), and atan2() are not found, you may have to use a different compiler call to tell the linker to search the mathematics library to resolve those references. If that is the case, find out how to link the mathematics library functions and compile the program again.
7. Run polar.c with different inputs. Hand calculate the expected answers to verify that the program is correct.
8. Many people expect the angles to be given in degrees instead of radians. Modify polar.c to output the angle in degrees.

Error Handling with the Mathematical Functions

The external variable `errno` is set to indicate the specific error when one occurs in a mathematical function. The errors are primarily of two types. An error can occur when the parameter passed to a mathematical function is not in the domain of that function. For example, such an error would occur when a negative number was passed to the function sqrt() that calculates square roots. The constant value `EDOM`, defined in errno.h, signifies that error.

A second type of error occurs when the calculated value is too large for the computer to handle. For example, the pow() function calculates powers. The call

```
pow(x,n)
```

calculates x^n. If both x and n were very large, the value x^n might cause an overflow error. In this case, the function pow() would return `HUGE_VAL`, and the value of `errno` would be `ERANGE` to indicate the error. Both `HUGE_VAL` and `ERANGE` are constants defined in errno.h.

The program math.c in Example 11-4 is designed to allow you to experiment to find out how errors are handled with the mathematical functions.

Example 11-4: math.c

```
/*                math.c
 *
 *    Synopsis   -  Inputs values for x and n and outputs the calculated
 *                  values from the pow(), sqrt() and tan() functions.
 *
 *    Objective  -  To illustrate error handling with the mathematical
 *                  functions in the ANSI C library.
 */

#include <math.h>
```

```
#include <stdio.h>
#include <errno.h>                                        /* Note 1 */
#include <stdlib.h>

void main(void)
{
        void error(char *s);
        double n, x, y;
        char buff[50];

        printf ("Enter a value for n: ");
        n = strtod ( gets(buff), NULL);
        printf ("Enter value for x: ");
        x = strtod ( gets(buff), NULL);
        printf ("x is %5.2f.\n", x);
        printf ("n is %5.2f.\n", n);
        y = sqrt(x);                                      /* Note 2 */
        error("sqrt");
        printf ("sqrt(%4.2f) is %5.2f\n",x, y);           /* Note 3 */
        y = tan(x);                                       /* Note 4 */
        error("tan");
        printf ("tan(%4.2f) is %5.2f.\n", x, y);
        y = pow(x, n);                                    /* Note 5 */
        error ("pow");
        printf ("pow(%4.2f, %4.2f) is %5.2f.\n", x, n, y);
}
void error(char *s)
{
        if (errno)                                        /* Note 6 */
                perror(s);
}
```

The program consists of two functions, main() and error(). The expression strtod(gets(buff), NULL) is used to input two double values from standard input. Then the mathematical functions sqrt(), tan(), and pow() are called with the input values as parameters. The function error() outputs error messages by calling perror() when an error has occurred.

Note 1: The header file errno.h contains the declaration of the external variable errno and the codes for the different error messages.

Note 2: Domain errors could occur with the sqrt() function. For example, a negative number is not in the domain of the sqrt() function. When you run this program, you may notice that the mathematical functions output their own version of the error messages.

Note 3: The value of y is output even when an error occurred. This should demonstrate that the value is meaningless in case of error. This output is done in this program for the other three functions also. Learning Activity 2 addresses this action.

Note 4: The tan() function excludes the value PI/2 from its domain. The function value is undefined when x is PI/2 or -PI/2.

Note 5: Errors occur with the pow() function when either x is 0 and n is negative or when x is negative and n is not an integer.

Note 6: The value of errno is checked before calling perror(). In most implementations, no error has occurred in cases where errno is zero.

Learning Activities

9. If you have an ANSI C compiler or are working on a UNIX system, compile math.c and test it with different sets of input. Specifically, try
   a. a negative number for x and an int value for n.
   b. a huge number for both x and n.
   c. a negative number for x and a fractional value for n.
   d. the numerical value of PI/2 for x.

   Each of the above should give at least one error. Try to find more combinations that give errors.
10. Note that the functional value output is invalid if an error has occurred. Modify the function error() to return 1 if an error occurred and 0 otherwise and have the functional value output only in the case that no error occurred.

11.4 Character Manipulation

Facilities are present in C to test the properties of the character set. The facilities may be implemented as either functions or macros. They are declared in the standard header file ctype.h, which should be included in any program using these facilities.

The facilities are of two basic types: facilities to test the properties of a character, and facilities to perform conversions on a character. All the functions or macros take a single argument of type int.

Facilities to test the properties of characters all return a nonzero value if the character tested has the desired property and zero otherwise. They include

isalpha()	which tests to see if its argument is an alphabetic character
isdigit()	which tests to see if its argument is a digit
isspace()	which tests to see if its argument is a whitespace character
isupper()	which tests to see if its argument is an uppercase alphabetic character

ispunct()   which tests to see if its argument is a punctuation character

A complete list appears in the Programmer's Handbook. Facilities to perform conversions on characters include

toupper()   which converts any lowercase alphabetics to uppercase and leaves all other characters unchanged

tolower()   which converts uppercase alphabetics to lowercase and leaves other characters unchanged

Other conversion routines may be provided with individual installations, but the two above are the ones specified in the ANSI C standards.

The program ctype.c in Example 11-5 provides an example of the use of many of the facilities that test for a specific property of a character. The program reads from a text file or from standard input and counts the number of alphabetics (uppercase and lowercase), digits, whitespace characters, punctuation, and control characters.

 Example 11-5: ctype.c

```
/*                  ctype.c
 *
 *   Synopsis  -   Counts the number of alphabetics, digits,
 *                 whitespace, punctuation and control characters
 *                 in its input. The input can come from a file
 *                 or the keyboard.
 *
 *   Objective -   To illustrate the use of the functions defined in
 *                 ctype.h.
 */

#include <stdio.h>
#include <ctype.h>                                          /* Note 1 */

void main(int argc, char *argv[])
{
        FILE *fp;
        int ch;
        int numlower = 0, numupper = 0, numdigit = 0, numspace = 0,
            numcntrl = 0, numalpha = 0, numpunct = 0;

        if (argc < 2)
                fp = stdin;                                 /* Note 2 */
        else if ( (fp = fopen(argv[1], "r")) == NULL) {
                printf("Can't open file %s.\n", argv[1]);
                exit(1);
        }
```

```
while (( ch = getc(fp)) != EOF) {
        if (isalpha(ch) )   {                       /* Note 3 */
                numalpha++;
                if (islower(ch))                    /* Note 4 */
                        numlower++;
                else
                        numupper++;                 /* Note 5 */
        }
        else if (isdigit(ch))                       /* Note 6 */
                numdigit++;
        else if (isspace(ch))                       /* Note 7 */
                numspace++;
        else if (ispunct(ch))                       /* Note 8 */
                numpunct++;
        else if (iscntrl(ch))                       /* Note 9 */
                numcntrl++;
}
printf("That data contained %d alphabetic characters ",
                        numalpha);
printf("of which %d were uppercase \n", numupper);
printf("and %d were lowercase.  It also contained ",
                        numlower);
printf("%d digits, %d whitespace", numdigit, numspace);
printf("characters,\n%d control characters, ", numcntrl);
printf("and %d punctuation characters.\n", numpunct);
}
```

This program consists of the single function named main(). The number of command line parameters determines whether the input will come from standard input or whether a file is to be opened. A while loop processes the input; it consists of a compound if-else statement. A sequence of printf() calls outputs the results.

Note 1: The file ctype.h contains declarations of all the character typing facilities. Some of them may be macros defined in this file, and some may be implemented as functions.

Note 2: If no file is specified, the input will come from stdin. The variable fp will reference standard input here.

Note 3: The function isalpha() will return a nonzero value if its parameter is 'a', 'b', 'c', 'd',... 'z', 'A', 'B', 'C',..., or 'Z' and zero otherwise.

Note 4: The function islower() will return nonzero if its parameter is 'a', 'b', 'c',..., or 'z' and zero otherwise.

Note 5: Instead of calling the function isupper(), it is more efficient to simply increment the counter numupper since at this point, it has been determined that the character is an alphabetic character and is not lowercase. The only other possibility is for it to be uppercase.

Note 6: If the character being tested is one of the digits, ′0′ to ′9′, isdigit() returns a nonzero value. It returns 0 otherwise.

Note 7: The function isspace() tests for spaces, formfeeds, newlines, carriage returns, tabs, and vertical tabs and returns a nonzero value if it finds one of the whitespace characters.

Note 8: The function ispunct() tests for the punctuation characters. This includes exclamation points, quotes, periods, commas, parentheses, braces, brackets, slashes, and so on.

Note 9: Finally, the function iscntrl() tests for the presence of a control character and returns a nonzero value when one is found. The control characters are those at the beginning or at the very end of the ASCII sequence. Their decimal equivalents are 0 through 31 and 127.

Learning Activities

11. Execute ctype.c with very simple input for which you can easily hand calculate the expected result. Verify that it works correctly on your system.

12. Modify ctype.c by removing all the else keywords except the first from the program. Execute it with the same input to see if the output is the same or if some of the characters are counted twice.

    a. For example, how is a tab counted? Is it a control character, a space, punctuation, or all three?

    b. What about ^M?

    c. Which characters, if any, are counted in two categories?

13. If your system has facilities to test the efficiency of execution of a program, test the version with the else keywords included against the version with them omitted. Which would you expect to be more efficient? Is there any noticeable difference with this short program?

Often the facilities that test a character for a specific property are used to validate the input to a particular routine. For example, the program convert.c in Example 11-6 converts a string of digits to an integer value. It provides much the same functionality as the library function atoi() and, if packaged as a function with a return value and some error handling added, might be used as a substitute for that library function. The facility isdigit() is used to validate the input to the conversion routine.

Example 11-6: convert.c

```
/*              convert.c
 *
 *   Synopsis  -  Accepts the input of a string of digits and
```

```
 *                      converts those digits to a decimal integer.
 *
 *    Objective -   To show the use of the facility isdigit() in
 *                  validating input.
 */

#include <stdio.h>
#include <ctype.h>                                      /* Note 1 */

void main(void)
{
        int ch, index = 0, num = 0;
        char inbuff[80];

        printf("Enter a string of decimal digits: ");
        gets(inbuff);

        while ( isdigit(inbuff[index]) )                /* Note 2 */
                num = 10*num + inbuff[index++] - '0';    /* Note 3 */

        printf ("That number is %d.\n", num);
}
```

The program consists of a single function, main(). A call to gets() accomplishes the input of the string of digits. A while loop converts the digits to type int, and a printf() call outputs the result.

Note 1: The file ctype.h must be included. If isdigit() is implemented as a macro, that implementation will be in ctype.h. If it is implemented as a function, the function will be declared there.

Note 2: Each character in inbuff is passed to isdigit(). If the character is a digit, the return value will be nonzero and another iteration of the while loop will be executed. When the value returned by isdigit() is zero, the while loop is terminated since the character referenced is not a digit.

Note 3: This algorithm to convert from character to integer depends on the contiguity of the digits in the ASCII character set. The difference between any digit and '0' is the numerical value of that digit. For example, '3' corresponds to the integer 51 in the ASCII collating sequence, and '0' corresponds to the integer 48. The expression '3' − '0' translates to 51 − 48, which evaluates to the integer 3, thus accomplishing the conversion of the character. The accumulation of the integer value is kept in the variable num.

Learning Activities

14. Hand execute convert.c for

| 1 | 4 | w | \n | and | 2 | 5 | 8 | \n | as input to make sure

that you understand the conversion algorithm.

15. a. Execute convert.c to verify your prediction.

b. Predict the output for each of the following inputs and explain what happens.

    i. A single carriage return is pressed.

    ii. Two spaces are typed before the string of digits is input.

    iii. The word "one" is entered and the carriage return is pressed.

    iv. The string "938492838747567345" is entered and the carriage return is pressed.

c. Explain the differences between the action of convert.c and the action of the following program for different input strings.

```
/*                      la15.c                      */
#include <stdio.h>
void main(void)
{
    int num;
    printf("Enter a string of decimal digits: ");
    scanf("%d", &num);
    printf ("That number is %d.\n", num);
}
```

11.5 Dynamic Allocation and Deallocation of Memory

The C library provides functions for dynamic allocation and deallocation of memory. The functions malloc() and calloc() allocate memory, and the function free() deallocates memory.

The declarations for the dynamic allocation functions are provided in a header file. In ANSI C, the declarations will be in the file stdlib.h while earlier compilers might keep these declarations in alloc.h or malloc.h. The documentation provided with the compiler should give this information.

The function malloc() takes one parameter. In ANSI C, the parameter's type is size_t which is defined with a typedef in several header files. With older C compilers, the parameter's type will probably be one of the integer types. The parameter tells malloc() the number of bytes to allocate. The return value from malloc() is the address of the first byte in the newly allocated buffer. In ANSI C, the address is typed as void *. In older compilers, the type of the return value from malloc() is usually char *. When the address of the space is returned, a type cast is used to convert it to the correct type. Examples of calls to malloc() with the appropriate variable declarations might be

```
char *string, buffer[50];
string = (char *) malloc( strlen(buffer) + 1);
```

The length of the string in buffer is tested with strlen() and one is added to allot space for the terminating ' \0'. When the space is allocated, the return value is cast to type char * before assigning it to the variable string.

"Another look at testing the length of the string." From the painting *Childhood of Blondin,* **Joseph Cornell, 1943.**

Another example:

```
struct trans *transaction;
transaction = (struct trans *)malloc( sizeof(struct
trans) );
```

In this example, malloc() will allocate the number of bytes necessary to store a value of type struct trans. The return value is cast to type struct trans * before being assigned to the variable transaction.

The function free() will deallocate space that was allocated by either malloc() or calloc(). Its parameter is a pointer to the space to be freed. It will have type void * on ANSI C compilers and most likely type char * on other compilers. If that pointer was cast to a different type on allocation, it must be recast on return. For example, the call

```
free ((void *) transaction);
```

would deallocate the space that was obtained on the second call to malloc() above.

The program malloc.c in Example 11-7 gives an example of the use of malloc(). The program inputs a line of text from standard input into a buffer. It copies each word to a dynamically allocated buffer that will exactly fit the word, and prints the word on standard output.

 Example 11-7: malloc.c

```
/*              malloc.c
 *
 *   Synopsis   -   Inputs a line of text, separates each of the
 *                  blank-separated words in the line, and outputs
 *                  each word.
 *
 *   Objective  -   To illustrate use of the malloc() function.
 */

#include <stdio.h>
#include <stdlib.h>                                    /* Note 1 */
#include <string.h>

void main(void)
{
        char instring[512], *currentpl, *endword, *word;


        printf ("Enter a line of text ");
        printf ("with words separated with blanks:\n");
        gets (instring);
        currentpl = instring;
                                                        /* Note 2 */
        while ( (endword = strchr(currentpl, ' ')) != NULL) {
                *endword = '\0';                        /* Note 3 */
                                                        /* Note 4 */
                word = (char *) malloc(strlen(currentpl)+1);
                strcpy (word, currentpl);
                printf ("I read that as\n\t %s.\n", word);
                currentpl = endword+1;                  /* Note 5 */
```

```
                free ( (void *) word);              /* Note 6 */
        }
                                                    /* Note 7 */
        word = (char *) malloc(strlen(currentpl)+1);
        strcpy (word, currentpl);
        printf ("I read that as\n\t %s.\n", word);
        free ( (void *) word);
}
```

The program consists of the single function main(). The variable instring is used to hold a line of input from standard input. The pointers currentpl and endword are used as pointers into instring to mark the beginning and the end of the individual words. The variable word will point to a separate buffer in memory where the individual words are to be copied. Input is done with a call to gets(). The while loop works through the line of input, picking out the end of each word with a call to strchr(). The last word in the buffer instring is handled outside the while loop.

Note 1: In ANSI C, the memory allocation functions are declared in the file stdlib.h. In earlier versions of C this filename may have to be changed. For example, on older UNIX systems, the memory allocation functions are declared in a file named malloc.h or alloc.h.

Note 2: The string library function strchr() was first discussed in Section 5.6. This call to strchr() will return a pointer to the first blank character that it finds in the part of the buffer pointed to by currentpl. It returns a NULL pointer if no blank is found.

Note 3: The blank character in the buffer is replaced with a '\0' to form a string referenced by currentpl. This allows the "word" to be accessed as a string by the string library function.

Note 4: The library function malloc() is called to dynamically allocate the correct amount of space for the string. The number of bytes is measured by the strlen() of the string plus one byte for the terminating null character ('\0'). In ANSI C, malloc() returns a void * value which must be cast to the correct type in order to be used properly. In this case the correct type is char *. With older C compilers, malloc() returns a value of type char * and the cast would not be necessary, but it would not cause an error and would allow the program to be ported with less work.

Note 5: The pointer currentpl is advanced to the position in the buffer immediately after the blank that terminated the previous word. This will set up the pointers for the next iteration of the while loop.

Note 6: The space pointed to by word is no longer needed and is therefore returned for possible reuse. It is a good idea to return dynamically allocated space that is no longer needed. Be aware that some implementations of C ignore this request.

Note 7: The last word in the input buffer was not handled by the while loop, and must now be handled.

The library function calloc() is also used to allocate memory during a program's execution. One difference is that the memory allocated by calloc() is initialized to

Learning Activities

16. Compile and execute malloc.c. Test it with several sets of input.
17. What happens when multiple contiguous blanks exist in the input? If necessary, fix malloc.c so that this situation is handled correctly.
18. Note that the only delimiting characters allowed by malloc.c are blanks while in reality, in English text, words are delimited by blanks, tabs, and punctuation characters. The standard C library function strtok(), when called repeatedly, will find all "words" delimited by a user-defined set of characters.

    a. Read the information on strtok() in the Programmer's Handbook and in the documentation for your C compiler.

    b. Modify the program so that it finds "words" delimited by blanks, tabs, periods, and commas. If strtok() is available on your system, replace strchr() with an appropriate use of strtok() to make this modification.

    c. If strtok() is not available on your system, write your own version of strtok() to use for this purpose.

zero while the memory allocated by malloc() is uninitialized. Another difference is that calloc() takes two parameters. The first gives a number of items; the second gives the size of each item. The number of bytes of memory allocated is the product of the two parameters. Memory for arrays can be allocated with calloc(). For example, the call

```
trans_array = (struct trans *)calloc(20, sizeof(struct trans) );
```

will allocate enough space for twenty structures of type `struct trans`. Since array names signify the address of the buffer in memory, `trans_array` can be treated as an array in most situations. For example, `trans_array[0]` will access the first structure in the buffer, `trans_array[1]` will access the second structure, and so on.

The program calloc.c in Example 11-8 gives an example of calloc() in use. It will read the file that was created by the program fwrite.c of Example 10.7 where information for a `struct trans` value was entered from standard input and fwrite() was called to write the information to a file. In this program, the number of records in the file is calculated and calloc() allocates memory for all of the file contents. A single fread() will read the contents of the file and place it in the allocated buffer. The contents of that buffer is output one record at a time.

Example 11-8: calloc.c

```
/*                 calloc.c
 *
 *    Synopsis  -  Reads transactions (elements of type struct trans)
 *                 from a file into a dynamically allocated array
 *                 and outputs them to standard output.
 *
 *    Objective -  To illustrate the use of calloc() in allocating
 *                 space for an array of structures.
 */

#include <stdio.h>
#include <stdlib.h>                                  /* Note 1 */
#define BUFFSIZE  50

struct trans {
        int       t_type;
        char      payee_memo[BUFFSIZE];
        float     amount;
        unsigned tax_deduct:1;
        unsigned cleared:1;
};

void main(void)
{
        struct trans *t_array;
        FILE          *fp;
        void          print_trans(struct trans *outtrans);
        int           i, numbytes, nrecs;

        if ( (fp = fopen("transactions", "r") ) == NULL) {
                printf ("Transaction file couldn't be opened.\n");
                exit(1);
        }

        fseek(fp, 0L, 2);                            /* Note 2 */
        numbytes = ftell(fp);
        nrecs = numbytes / sizeof(struct trans);

                                                     /* Note 3 */
        if ((t_array = (struct trans *) calloc(nrecs,
                       sizeof(struct trans)) ) == NULL) {
                printf ("Unable to get the space.\n");
                exit (1);
        }
```

```
        fseek (fp, 0L, 0);                                   /* Note 4 */

                                                             /* Note 5 */
        if (!(fread (t_array, sizeof(*t_array), nrecs, fp))) {
                printf ("Error in reading the file\n");
                exit(2);
        }

        for ( i = 0; i < nrecs; i++)
                print_trans(&t_array[i]);

        fclose (fp);
}
/****************************************** print_trans() *********/
/*  Outputs the structure outtrans to standard output.   Each field
 *  is separated with a vertical bar character.
 */
void print_trans(struct trans *outtrans)
{
        /* Cleared field */
        if (outtrans->cleared)
                printf ("C | ");
        else
                printf ("  | ");

        /* Transaction type */
        if ( (outtrans->t_type =='D') || (outtrans->t_type == 'W')
                                      || (outtrans->t_type == 'I'))
                printf ("%4c | ", outtrans->t_type);
        else
                printf ("%4d | ", outtrans->t_type);

        /* tax_deduct field */
        if (outtrans->tax_deduct)
                printf (" T | ");
        else
                printf ("   | ");
        printf ("%10.2f | ", outtrans->amount);
        printf ("%s", outtrans->payee_memo);
}
```

The functions main() and print_trans() make up this program. The function print_trans() is used unchanged from the program fread.c of Example 10-8. A call to fopen() opens the file "transactions" for reading; the program is terminated if the file cannot be opened. Then the number of records in the file is calculated, space is allocated, the file is read into memory, and each `struct trans` entry is output.

Note 1: The file stdlib.h is included since the declaration of the function calloc() is included there. ANSI C specifies stdlib.h as one of the standard header files. In older versions of the compiler, the declaration of calloc() may appear in another file instead. For example, on UNIX systems, it might be included in the header file malloc.h. The declaration

```
void    *calloc (size_t nitems, size_t size);
```

for ANSI C compilers or the declaration char *calloc() for older compilers would take the place of the include file in this program.

Note 2: To calculate the number of records in the file, fseek() is called to seek to the end of the file, ftell() is called to return the number of bytes in the file, and then that number is divided by the sizeof() a struct trans to give the total number of records.

Note 3: Enough space to hold all the records in the file is allocated by the call to calloc(). The parameter nrec indicates the number of items for which memory is to be allocated, and the second parameter, sizeof(struct trans), indicates the size of each item. The total number of bytes allocated would be

```
nrecs * sizeof(struct trans)
```

An equivalent call to malloc() would be

```
malloc( nrecs * sizeof(struct trans) );
```

The value returned by calloc() has type void * in an ANSI C compiler (or char * in an older compiler). It needs to be cast to the correct type for this application. In this case, it is cast to type struct trans * before assigning to the variable t_array.

Note 4: The file pointer is set back to the beginning of the file in preparation for the input of the file.

Note 5: The entire contents of the file are input with one call to fread(). The contents are placed in the memory allocated earlier and pointed to by t_array. From this point on, t_array can be treated almost as if it were an array of struct trans items.

Learning Activities

19. Compile and run calloc.c with the sample file you created when you tested the program fwrite.c of Example 10-7.
20. Does calloc.c work correctly if the file exists but is empty? What happens? What do you think should happen? Modify the program to work correctly if necessary.

11.6   A Linked List —The Theory and an Example

One of the uses of pointers and dynamic allocation is to create linked lists. The concept of a linked list is common in creating data structures to organize data. Many data structures can have either array or linked list implementations. In Section 8.5, we saw a simple implementation of a stack (a LIFO) with an array. A stack can also be implemented as a linked list.

To create a linked list we first need to declare the type of the items in the list. This can be anything from a `char` value to a more complicated structure. It would need to be changed for different applications, and is usually done with a `typedef`. For example,

```
typedef _____ element;
```

where the blank would be filled in with the appropriate type. Each `element` in the list would be embedded in a node, which is declared as a structure as

```
struct node {
    element data;
    struct node *next;
};
```

Each node has two members, the `data` member, which will hold a value of type `element`, and the `next` member, which points to the next node in the list. A node with a `NULL` pointer in the `next` member will signify the end of the list. The linked list itself is declared as a pointer to a node. For example,

```
struct node *list;
```

When the list is set up properly, it has the configuration depicted in Figure 11-4.

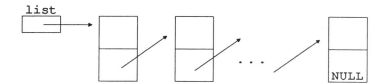

Figure 11-4   A Completed Linked List

One of the advantages of using a linked list is that unlike in an array, the number of items in the list does not have to be accurately approximated at compile time. Another advantage is that insertions and deletions in a linked list can be done by adjusting two pointers, while insertions and deletions in an array involve shifting data up or down to preserve the ordering. The steps necessary to insert a node in a linked list are shown in Figure 11-5.

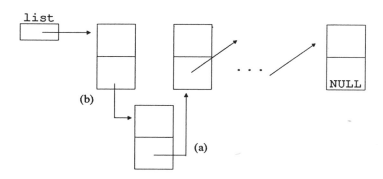

Figure 11-5   Inserting a Node in a Linked List

(a) Adjust the `next` member of the new node to point to its successor in the list.

(b) Adjust the `next` member of the previous node to point to the new node.

The program linklist.c in Examples 11-9 through 11-14 gives an example of a linked list. It essentially echoes its input to its output, but internally, each line of input is stored in a node of a linked list. Each node of the linked list contains two pointers as members. The first member is a `char *` value named `word` that will point to a dynamically allocated array of characters holding the input line as a string. The second member is the `next` field; it points to the next node in the list. For example, if the input to the program is

```
To bed
To bed
said
Sleepy Head
```

the internal linked list is shown in Figure 11-6.

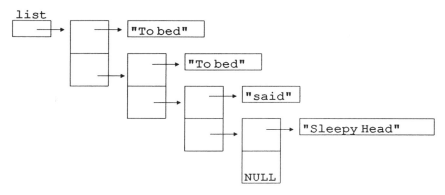

Figure 11-6

We will discuss each subfunction from the program linklist.c separately to see what each one does before putting them together in the program. To compile this program, all functions could be placed in the same file. If separate source files are desired, it will be necessary to include some header files.

Example 11-9: linklist.c: function get_node_space()

```
/****************************   get_node_space()   *********/
/*      Allocates the space for a single node and returns the
 *      pointer to the first byte of the space.
 */

struct node *get_node_space(void)
{
        struct node *temp_ptr;
                                                        /* Note 1 */
        temp_ptr = (struct node *) malloc ( sizeof(struct node) );
        if (temp_ptr == NULL) {
                printf ("out of memory for nodes\n");
                exit(1);
        }
        return (temp_ptr);
}
```

The purpose of this function is to allocate the space for a node in the linked list. It calls malloc() to get the space and checks its return value to make sure that the space allocation was successful. The program is terminated if the space was not obtained. The pointer to the first byte of space is returned to the calling function.

Note 1: The parameter in the call to malloc() specifies that enough memory to store a struct node is requested. The cast to a struct node * must be used to force that address to be the address of a struct node.

Example 11-10: function hook_it_up

```
/*******************************   hook_it_up   *************/
/*      Attaches new_node to the end of a list.  The parameter
 *      old_list must point to the last node in the list.
 */
void hook_it_up (struct node *old_list, struct node *new_node)
{
        new_node->next = NULL;
        old_list->next = new_node;
}
```

The purpose of this function is to put the new node on the end of the linked list. The parameters are both pointers to nodes. The first parameter, old_list, will point to the last node in the list. The second parameter, new_node, points to the node to be added to the list. The configuration is illustrated in Figure 11-7.

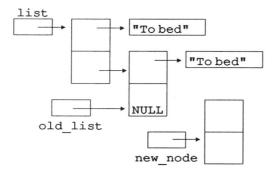

Figure 11-7

The code for the function consists of adjusting two pointers. The next member of new_node is set to NULL to signify the end of the list, and the next member of old_list points to new_node. The final configuration is shown in Figure 11-8.

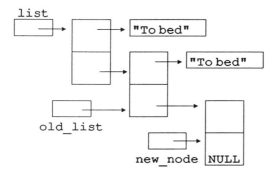

Figure 11-8

Example 11-11: function get_word_space()

```
/********************************  get_word_space()  *******/
/*      Allocates space for the string contained in its
 *      first parameter.  Returns a pointer to the first byte.
 */
char *get_word_space(char *string)
{
        char *temp;

        temp = (char *) calloc (strlen(string)+1, 1);
        if (temp == NULL) {
                printf ("Out of memory for text.\n");
                exit(2);
        }
        return (temp);
}
```

This function dynamically allocates the memory needed for the string in its parameter st ring. The library function calloc() is used to obtain space for an array of strlen (string) +1 elements of size one byte. The value returned by calloc() is checked to make sure that the memory allocation is successful. If it was not, the program is terminated with an error message. If it was successful, the address of the first byte of the buffer is returned.

Example 11-12: function release()

```
/********************************  release()  **************/
/*      Systematically deallocates the memory used by the list.
 *      Works from the front of the list to the back.
 */
void release (struct node **listptr)                    /* Note 1 */
{
        struct node *temp1, *temp2;

        temp1 = *listptr;
        while (temp1->next != NULL) {
                temp2 = temp1->next;
                free ((void *)temp1->word);             /* Note 2 */
                free ((void *)temp1);
                temp1 = temp2;
        }
        free ((void *)temp1->word);
```

```
            free ((void *)temp1);
            *listptr = NULL;
}
```

This function does the job of memory deallocation. It moves through the list with the local variables, `temp1` and `temp2`. At each `node`, it first adjusts `temp2` to point to the next `node` in the list and then calls free() to release the space occupied by the `node` at which `temp1` points (see Figure 11-9). It first releases the space occupied by the string (Figure 11-10) and then the space occupied by the `node` itself (see Figure 11-11).

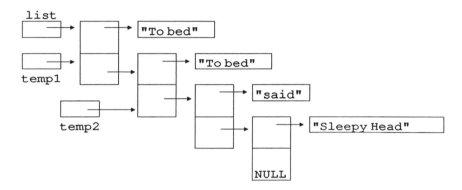

Figure 11-9

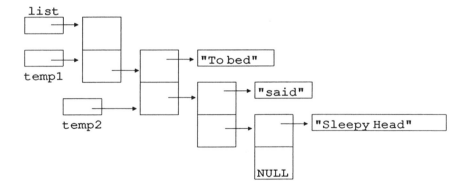

Figure 11-10

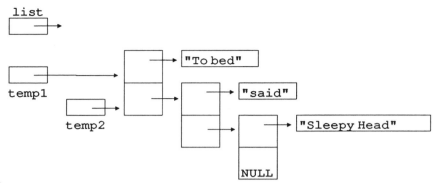

Figure 11-11

The while loop is exited when temp1 points to the last node in the list. The space it occupies still has to be deallocated. Finally, the contents of listptr are set to NULL. Note that the order of these steps is important. If things are done in a different order, some of the memory pointers might be lost and the attached memory could not be deallocated.

Note 1: The purpose of the function is to change the value of the pointer to the list. On entry a list of nodes exists; it will be represented by a pointer to the first node. On exit the list should be empty and the pointer should have been set to NULL. Since release() needs to change the list, a pointer to the struct node * value that represents the list must be passed in. In the body of the function, the parameter, listptr, is dereferenced so that the contents of the struct node * value representing the list are actually changed.

Note 2: When the space was obtained by calloc() or malloc(), the return value from those functions had type void *. That pointer was cast to the appropriate type for each specific use. Now that the space is to be released, the pointer should be recast to void * when it is passed to free().

Example 11-13: function print()

```
/******************************   print ()   ****************/
/*      Outputs the contents of the word member of nodes in the list.
 */
void print (struct node *ptr)
{
        while (ptr->next != NULL) {
                printf("%s\n", ptr->word);
                ptr = ptr->next;
        }
        printf("%s\n", ptr->word);
}
```

A while loop moves through the list and outputs the string stored in each node. Note that auxiliary pointers are not necessary. The parameter ptr is used to move through the list. Since the parameter is passed by value, the changes to ptr in this function will not affect the value of the actual parameter in the rest of the program.

Now that we know what the utility functions do, we will study the driver function main() to see how it all works together (see Example 11-14).

 Example 11-14: function main()

```
/*                  linklist.c
 *
 *    Synopsis  -  Echoes its input to its output, but keeps the
 *                 input in a linked list.
 *
 *    Objective  - Illustrates building a linked list of words with
 *                 dynamic allocation of memory.
 */

#include <stdio.h>
#include <stdlib.h>

struct node {                                        /* Note 1 */
        char *word;
        struct node *next;
};

void main(void)
{
        char            *get_word_space(char *s);
        char            inputbuffer[512];
        struct node     *list, *lead_ptr,
                        *follow_ptr, *get_node_space(void);
        void            release (struct node **listptr),
                        print(struct node *listptr),
                        hook_it_up(struct node *old, struct node *new);


        printf ("Enter some text for the linked list.\n");
        printf ("Terminate the input by signaling end of file.\n");
        if (gets(inputbuffer) != NULL) {             /* Note 2 */
                list = get_node_space();             /* Note 3 */
                list->next = NULL;                   /* Note 4 */
                follow_ptr = list;
                                                     /* Note 5 */
```

```
                      list->word = get_word_space(inputbuffer);
                      strcpy (list->word, inputbuffer);        /* Note 6 */
              }

              while (gets(inputbuffer) != NULL) {
                      lead_ptr = get_node_space();              /* Note 7 */
                      hook_it_up(follow_ptr, lead_ptr);         /* Note 8 */
                      follow_ptr = lead_ptr;                    /* Note 9 */
                                                                /* Note 10 */
                      lead_ptr->word = get_word_space(inputbuffer);
                      strcpy (lead_ptr->word, inputbuffer);  /* Note 11 */
              }

              print (list);
              release(&list);                                  /* Note 12 */
      }
```

An `if` statement inputs the first line of input and a `while` loop handles the remainder of the input. Finally, calls to print() and release() output the contents of the list and deallocate the space. The notes below and accompanying figures will trace through the execution of the program with the two lines

```
          Tweedledee
          Tweedledum
```

as sample input.

Note 1: A `struct node` is declared. It consists of two pointer values, and has the configuration shown in Figure 11-12.

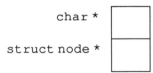

Figure 11-12

Note 2: The input to the program is done with calls to gets(). A NULL pointer returned by gets() signifies that either an error has occurred or end-of-file was sensed.

Note 3: The function get_node_space() is called to obtain the space for a `node`. The configuration is pictured in Figure 11-13.

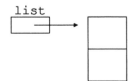

Figure 11-13

Note 4: Two pointers are adjusted. The `next` member of the `node` is set to `NULL` to signify the end of the list, and `follow_ptr` is set to point to the `node` in preparation for the next input. The configuration is shown in Figure 11-14.

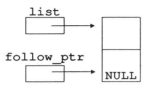

Figure 11-14

Note 5: The function get_word_space() will allocate the correct amount of space for the first line of input, "Tweedledee". On return, the configuration is like that in Figure 11-15.

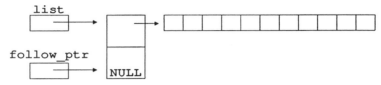

Figure 11-15

Note 6: The input is copied from `inputbuffer` to the `node`. The first line of input has been processed and the configuration is shown in Figure 11-16.

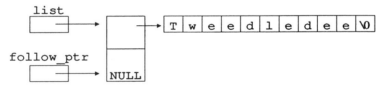

Figure 11-16

Note 7: After the second line of input, get_node_space() is called to allocate space for a new `node`. See Figure 11-17.

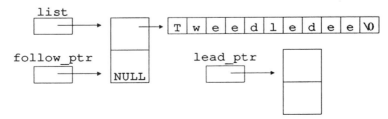

Figure 11-17

Note 8: The new `node` is hooked into the list by hook_it_up(). See Figure 11-18.

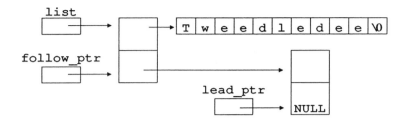

Figure 11-18

Note 9: The pointers are adjusted for the next input, if any. See Figure 11-19.

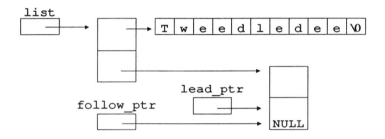

Figure 11-19

Note 10: Space is allocated for the string in `inputbuffer`. See Figure 11-20.

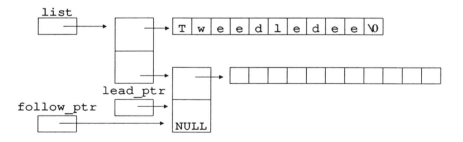

Figure 11-20

Note 11: The string in `inputbuffer` is copied into the new `node`, thus completing the construction of the linked list for these two lines of input (see Figure 11-21). The `while` loop will be exited when end-of-file is signaled on the next input attempt.

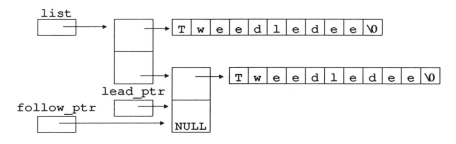

Figure 11-21

Note 12: After the list is output, release() is called to deallocate the memory used by the list. Because the program ends here, this step was not really necessary, but since a routine like this could be part of a larger program, deallocating memory would be necessary in that situation. See Figure 11-22 for the final configuration.

```
       list
      ┌──────┐
      │ NULL │
      └──────┘
```

Figure 11-22

Learning Activities

21. Execute the program with several sets of input to make sure that it works. Try it with long lines and short lines, many lines and few lines. If you ran out of memory, did that seem reasonable for the amount of input you entered?
22. What happens when end-of-file is signaled immediately after the prompt? Does the program terminate properly? If it doesn't, what happens? Modify it so that it works correctly, if necessary.

11.7 Defining Macros

A macro consists of source code. A macro is like a function in that the macro code is defined and associated with an identifier. Calling a macro is much like calling a function; it consists of placing the name of the macro in the source code accompanied with the actual parameters in a comma-separated list enclosed in parentheses.

A macro differs from a function in that when a program has been translated to object code, the code for the macro is expanded in every place where the macro was called, while the code for a function remains in a separate location in memory.

Executing a function requires transferring control to a separate part of the object code in memory and transferring control back after execution is finished. There is other overhead in setting up and removing the execution environment for the function. In contrast, the code for the macro is expanded at the position of the call, and thus avoids the transfer of control and the overhead. In general, macros execute faster than functions, but take up more memory if they are called often.

In C, macros are handled in the preprocess phase of compilation. They are defined with the `#define` directive. For example, the directive

```
#define printit            printf("it");
```

at the top of a source code file would cause every occurrence of the identifier `printit` in the source code to be replaced with the statement

```
printf("it");
```

Note that the expression

```
printit;
```

would be replaced with

```
printf("it");;
```

since the semicolon is included in the macro expansion.

Macros can be declared with parameters, and the preprocessor will substitute the actual parameters for the formal parameters when it expands the macro. For example, the macro

```
#define print(s) printf("current value is %d.\n", s);
```

would cause the expression

```
print(counter);
```

to be replaced with

```
printf("current value is %d.\n", counter);;
```

The preprocessor expects to find macro definitions contained on one line of source code. If it is necessary to continue the definition onto a second line, the character `'\'` may be placed at the end of a line to indicate that the definition continues on the next line. For example,

```
#define pr(s)        printf("The value is %d\n",\
                                   s);
```

is equivalent to

```
#define pr(s)        printf("The value is %d\n",s);
```

Some of the facilities available in the standard header files are macros. For example, getc(), getchar(), putc() and putchar() are implemented with macros. Many of the character handling functions like isalpha(), isprint(), and so on are implemented as macros.

The program macros.c in Example 11-15 uses the standard macros getchar() and isdigit() in its input/conversion routine getint(). A user-defined macro MAX() is called to calculate the maximum of the input values.

Example 11-15: macros.c

```
/*                macros.c
 *
 *    Synopsis  -  Inputs two integers from the keyboard and outputs
 *                 the maximum of the two values.
 *
 *    Objective -  Will illustrate the expansion of macros by the
 *                 preprocessor.
 */

#include <stdio.h>                                       /* Note 1 */
#include <ctype.h>                                       /* Note 2 */

#define MAX(a, b)  (a > b) ? a : b                       /* Note 3 */

void main(void)
{
        int x, y;
        int getint(int *val);

        printf("Ready to calculate the maximum of two numbers.\n");
        printf("Please enter the first nonnegative number : ");
        getint (&x);
        printf("Please enter the second nonnegative number : ");
        getint (&y);
        printf("The maximum of %d and %d is %d.\n",
                x, y, MAX(x,y) );                        /* Note 4 */

}
/*************************************   getint ()   ************/
/*      Reads a line of input and converts input digits to a value
 *      of type int and stores the result in its parameter. Returns a 0
 *      for success and a 1 if any nondigit is found. In the
 *      latter case, the contents of val are set to 0.
 */
int getint(int *val)
{
        int iochar, num;

        num = 0;
        while ( ( iochar = getchar()) != '\n') {         /* Note 5 */
                if (isdigit(iochar) )                    /* Note 6 */
                        num = 10*num + iochar - '0';
                else {
                        printf ("Illegal input found %c\n", iochar);
```

```
                        fflush(stdin);
                        *val = 0;
                        return (1);
                }
        }
        *val = num;
        return (0);
}
```

The functions main() and getint() comprise this program. Calls to printf() for output and calls to getint() to process the input make up main(). The function getint() uses a `while` loop driven by calls to getchar() to do the input. If digits are found, conversion to type `int` takes place. In case of a nondigit input error, an error message is output, the input buffer is flushed, the contents of `val` are set to 0, and 1 is returned to indicate the error. If the `while` loop terminates normally, `val` gets the value of the converted integer and 0 is returned to indicate success.

Note 1: The macros getchar() and getc() are defined in stdio.h.

Note 2: The macro isdigit() is defined in ctype.h.

Note 3: This line has the definition of the macro MAX(). It is defined with a ? : conditional expression. First the expression a > b is evaluated. If it is true, the value returned by the macro is a; otherwise, the return value is b.

Note 4: The call to the macro MAX() appears as a parameter to this printf() call. The preprocessor will replace this call by the defining sequence above and substitute the actual parameters for the formal ones.

Note 5: The macro getchar() is called on this line. During preprocessing, this line will be modified by the macro expansion capability.

Note 6: The macro isdigit() on this line will also be expanded during the preprocess phase of compilation.

Learning Activities

23. a. Compile and run macros.c to make sure that it works correctly on your system.

    b. Test it several times with both positive, negative, equal and unequal input values.

    c. What happens with negative values? Modify getint() so that it works for negative values also.

    d. What happens if either of the values entered is larger than the maximum `int` that can be handled by your system? How might you improve this performance? Does any change have to be made to the macro MAX()?

24. Look at the files stdio.h and ctype.h. Pick out the definition of the macros getchar() and getc() in stdio.h and isdigit() in ctype.h.

25. a. Compile macros.c again, but, if possible, stop the compilation after the preprocess phase and look at the preprocessed file.

   b. Locate the macro substitutions for getchar(), isdigit(), and MAX().

   c. Compare this code with the code in the header files and the definition of the source files.

   d. Explain the substitutions made by the preprocessor in macro expansion.

26. Write your own version of the macro isdigit(). Test it by removing the line

```
#include <ctype.h>
```

from the source in macros.c, and replace it with your macro definition.

27. The function getint() returns 1 in case an error in conversion has occurred and 0 otherwise. Currently, the function main() ignores the return value. Therefore, if there is an error in the input, the output will be in error also. Modify the program to correct this deficiency. Have main() check the return value from getint() and repeatedly ask for input until the user gets the input correct.

A Word of Caution

The substitution for parameters in macros is exact. If the argument is a++ or a+1, that is what is substituted for the parameter in the macro. Many times this causes unexpected problems. Some of them are illustrated in the program squares.c of Example 11-16. In this program, a function and two macros are defined to perform the squaring operation on a value. The results of different calls to the functions and macros are output to illustrate some of the unexpected results.

Example 11-16: squares.c

```
/*              squares.c
 *
 *   Synopsis  -  Outputs results from the macros SQUARE(x), SQR(x),
 *                and the function square(x).
 *
 *   Objective -  To illustrate some of the differences between
 *                macros and functions: how substitutions take
 *                place and how macros are expanded.
```

```
    */

#include <stdio.h>

#define SQUARE(x)       x * x                                /* Note 1 */
#define SQR(x)          ( (x) * (x) )                        /* Note 2 */
int SQR2_x;
#define SQR2(x)         (SQR2_x=(x), SQR2_x * SQR2_x)   /* Note 3 */

void main(void)
{
        int a;
        int square (int x);

        a = 3;                                              /* Note 4 */
        printf ("square(a) is %d.\n", square(a) );
        printf ("SQUARE(a) is %d.\n", SQUARE(a) );
        printf ("SQR(a) is %d.\n", SQR(a));
        printf ("SQR2(a) is %d.\n", SQR2(a) );

                                                            /* Note 5 */
        printf ("\nsquare(a+1) is %d\n", square(a+1) );
        printf ("SQUARE(a+1) is %d.\n", SQUARE(a+1));
        printf ("SQR(a+1) is %d.\n", SQR(a+1) );
        printf ("SQR2(a+1) is %d.\n", SQR2(a+1));

                                                            /* Note 6 */
        printf ("\nsquare(a++) is %d, and ", square(a++) );
        printf ("a is %d\n", a);

        a = 3;
        printf ("SQUARE(a++) is %d, and ", SQUARE(a++) );
        printf ("a is %d\n", a);

        a = 3;
        printf ("SQR2(a++) is %d, and ", SQR2(a++) );
        printf ("a is %d\n", a);

        a = 3;
        printf ("SQR(a++) is %d, and ", SQR(a++) );
        printf ("a is %d\n", a);
}
/********************************   square()   ***************/
/*      Returns the square of its argument.
 */
```

```
int square(int x)                                              /* Note 7 */
{
        return (x * x);
}
```

This program is very simple. Three macros, SQUARE(x), SQR(x), and SQR2(), and a function, square(x), all have the purpose of squaring their arguments. The function main() outputs the results of different calls to the macros and the function. Before reading the notes, look over the program and predict the output. That is, do Learning Activity 1 before reading the notes.

Note 1: The simplest way of squaring a value is defined by the macro SQUARE (). When the expression SQUARE (parm) is found in the source code, it will be replaced by parm * parm. As will be seen later in this program, this macro has some problems.

Note 2: A second form of a macro to square a value contains three sets of parentheses. Although SQR () works better than SQUARE (), it is not trouble free.

Note 3: The macro SQR2() uses the comma operator in its definition. The assignment of x to SQR2_x is done first and then SQR2_x is squared. The value of the expression is the square of SQR2_x. Notice that the variable SQR2_x must be declared in order to use this macro.

Note 4: The variable a is initialized to 3, and the values of the macros and the function are output with a as the actual parameter. All four results are correct.

Note 5: This sequence of printf() calls outputs the values of both macros and the function when the actual parameter is a+1. The function square() and the macros SQR() and SQR2() return the correct value, but the macro SQUARE() does not. When a+1 is substituted for x in the macro definition, the macro expansion has the form

```
a+1 * a+1
```

Since multiplication has precedence over addition, the expression groups as

```
a+(1 * a) + 1
```

Since the value of a is 3, this evaluates to

```
3+(1 * 3)+1   or 7.
```

This is probably not the desired result.

Note 6: In the next sequence of statements, the value of the macros and the function is output with the argument a++. The value of a is reinitialized to 3 before each call. The value returned by the function is 9, or 3 squared, and the value of a has been incremented to 4. However, in two of the macros, the value returned is 12 and a has been incremented to 5. In SQUARE() the replacement of the formal parameter x with the actual parameter a++ results in the expression

```
a++ * a++
```

In SQR(), it results in

```
( (a++) * (a++) )
```

Both expressions evaluate to 12 since a gets incremented after the first factor is evaluated. Since it also gets incremented after the second factor is evaluated, the final value of a is 5.

Note that the macro SQR2_x() gave the correct value in both of these last two cases. Performing the assignment of x to SQR2_x in a separate step removed the problems in the other two macros.

Note 7: The function square() will always return the square of its parameter. The mechanism of passing parameters to functions is not sensitive to the ++ operator.

Learning Activities

28. Predict the output from squares.c, then compile and run the program to verify your prediction. Resolve any differences between your prediction and the actual output.
29. Look at the code produced by the preprocessor to verify the claims in **Note 5** and **Note 6**.
30. Try to write another macro that will return the square of its parameter correctly in all three cases in the program. Were you able to create one? Summarize your findings.

11.8   Conditional Compilation

Conditional compilation is a facility provided by the C preprocessor. The directives used are:*

#define	used to define symbols to the compiler
#ifdef	tests whether a symbol is defined to the compiler
#else	provides an alternative to #ifdef
#elif	used to build compound conditional directives
#endif	signals the end of the body of an if directive
#ifndef	tests whether a symbol is not defined
#if	tests values of constant expressions
defined	used in conjunction with #if to replace #ifdef

In Section 11-7 and earlier, we have seen the use of the #define directive to define macros, which are then expanded during the preprocess phase of compilation. A second use is to make a symbol known to the compiler. A directive such as

```
#define  XYZ
```

* The directives #elif and defined may not be available with some older compilers.

makes the symbol XYZ known to the compiler, but does not require much macro expansion. (In this example, any occurrence of XYZ in the source code essentially would be removed by macro expansion.)

Other ways of defining symbols to the compiler may be available with a particular implementation of C. For example, in the UNIX system, the -D command line option for the compiler can be used to define symbols for a particular compilation without modifying the source code.

The directives

```
            #ifdef XYZ          or          #if defined XYZ
```

can be used to test whether the symbol XYZ has been defined to the compiler. If it has, the lines following the directive until the occurrence of either #else, #elif, or #endif in the source code file will be included for compilation. If the symbol XYZ has not been defined to the compiler, the lines are omitted.

The directives #else and #elif work similarly to else or else if in a conditional statement. With them it is possible to choose which source lines to include.

As an example, suppose a company is writing a software package to do billing for several commercial firms. One of the programs in the package is to input a customer name, account number, and the transactions for that month, and write the information to a file for further processing by another program. Most of the firms that will use this program have a 16-digit account number for their customers and an integer transaction code. However, ACME Electric has an 8-digit account number and a 4-character transaction code. It is possible to handle both situations with a single program by using conditional compilation and compiling a different version for ACME. With conditional compilation, the structure holding the monthly transactions of a customer can be modified for ACME without doing any more than recompiling.

The program ccomp.c of Example 11-17 is a start on a program to input the customer's name, account number, and monthly transactions from standard input, and store them in a file.

Example 11-17: ccomp.c

```
/*              ccomp.c
 *
 *    Synopsis  -  Inputs information about customer transactions from
 *                 standard input, and stores the information in a file
 *                 named "transactions".
 *
 *    Objective -  To illustrate conditional compilation.
 */

#include <stdio.h>
```

```
struct statement {
        char name[30];
#ifdef ACME                                                    /* Note 1 */
        char account[9];
#else
        char account[17];
#endif
        float balance;
        struct {
#ifdef ACME                                                    /* Note 2 */
                char t_code[5];
#else
                int t_code;
#endif
                int quantity;
                float price;
        } transactions[50];
};

void main(void)
{
        struct statement customer;
        FILE *fp;
        int get_customer (struct statement *cust);

        if ( (fp = fopen("statements", "w")) == NULL) {
                perror("File Opening Error");
                exit(1);
        }

        printf("Enter your customer transactions now.\n");
        printf("Signal EOF when you are done.\n");

        while (get_customer(&customer) )
                fwrite (&customer, sizeof(customer), 1, fp);

        printf("Thank you, the statements will be prepared.\n");
}
/*********************************  get_customer()   *********/
/*      Inputs transactions for a single customer.
 */
```

```
int get_customer(struct statement *cust)
{
        printf("Enter customer name: ");
        if (fgets(cust->name, 30, stdin) == NULL)
                return (0);

        printf("Enter customer account number: ");
#ifdef ACME                                              /* Note 3 */
        fgets(cust->account, 8, stdin);
#else
        fgets(cust->account, 16, stdin);
#endif

        /* code to enter the transactions goes here */
        return (1);
}
```

The program consists of main() and get_customer(). The function main() opens the output file and handles any resulting errors. It then enters a while loop to input and store the customer information. The function get_customer() will return a value of 1 when it has valid customer information and a value of 0 when it reached the end of input. The code for get_customer() consists of printf() calls to prompt to input, and calls to fgets() and fflush() to handle the information in the input buffer.

Note 1: If the symbol ACME has been defined for a particular compilation, the size of the character array will be 9 (for the 8-character account number and a terminating null character). If ACME is not defined, the account array will hold a 16-digit account number plus a terminating null character.

Note 2: For ACME, the t_code member will be able to store 4 characters plus a terminating null character. For other companies, it is declared to hold a value of type int.

Note 3: Since the account array has fewer cells when ACME is defined, a separate fgets() call could be used to input the account number for ACME.

Learning Activities

31. a. Find out how to define a value for a specific compilation with your C compiler.

b. Compile the program but stop the compilation process after the preprocess phase and inspect the file to see which lines of source code have been included. Compile the program down to object code and execute it.

c. Compile the program with the identifier ACME defined. Again, stop the compilation process and inspect the file after the preprocess phase. Compile this version to object code and test it also.

32. a. List two or more ways to verify that the compiler actually made the requested changes at compilation time.

b. Implement at least two of these methods and test the two different compilations of the code.

c. Summarize your findings from the tests.

Conditional Compilation in Program Development and Debugging

A popular use for conditional compilation is to provide a trace through a program and possibly output the values of some important variables. This use would occur as the program is being developed or possibly when modifications might be made in the program maintenance phase of the programming cycle.

The program debug.c in Example 11-18 illustrates this use. The program linklist.c of Examples 11-9 through 14 has been modified by adding conditional compilation directives and source code to provide a trace of execution.

 Example 11-18: debug.c

```
/*              debug.c
 *
 *   Synopsis   -  Echoes its input to its output, but keeps the
 *                 input in a linked list.
 *
 *   Objective  -  Illustrates the use of conditional compilation
 *                 during program development and debugging.
 */

#include <stdio.h>
#include <stdlib.h>
```

```
#ifdef DEBUG                                            /* Note 1 */
int     nesting = 0;                                    /* Note 2 */
                                                        /* Note 3 */
#define ENTER(fn)  printf("%*s{ ENTER %s\n", ++nesting * 4, "", fn)
#define EXIT(fn)   printf("%*s} EXIT  %s\n", nesting-- * 4, "", fn)
#else
#define ENTER(fn)                                       /* Note 4 */
#define EXIT(fn)
#endif


struct node {
        char *word;
        struct node *next;
};

void main(void)
{
        char            *get_word_space(char *s);
        char            inputbuffer[512];
        struct node     *list, *lead_ptr,
                        *follow_ptr, *get_node_space(void);
        void            release (struct node **listptr),
                        print(struct node *listptr),
                        hook_it_up(struct node *old, struct node *new);

        ENTER("main");                                  /* Note 5 */
        printf ("Enter some text for the linked list.\n");
        printf ("Terminate the input by signalling end of file.\n");
        if (gets(inputbuffer) != NULL) {
#ifdef DEBUG                                             /* Note 6 */
                printf ("%s: %d\n", inputbuffer, strlen(inputbuffer));
#endif
                list = get_node_space();
                list->next = NULL;
                follow_ptr = list;
                list->word = get_word_space(inputbuffer);
                strcpy (list->word, inputbuffer);
#ifdef DEBUG                                             /* Note 7 */
                printf ("added %s\n", list->word);
#endif
        }

        while (gets(inputbuffer) != NULL) {
#ifdef DEBUG                                             /* Note 6 */
                printf ("%s: %d\n", inputbuffer, strlen(inputbuffer));
```

```
#endif
                lead_ptr = get_node_space();
                hook_it_up(follow_ptr, lead_ptr);
                follow_ptr = lead_ptr;
                lead_ptr->word = get_word_space(inputbuffer);
                strcpy (lead_ptr->word, inputbuffer);
#ifdef DEBUG                                               /* Note 7 */
                printf ("added %s\n", lead_ptr->word);
#endif
        }

        print (list);
        release(&list);
        EXIT("main");                                     /* Note 8 */
}
/********************************  get_node_space()   **********/
/*      Allocates the space for a single node and returns the
 *      pointer to the first byte of the space.
 */

struct node *get_node_space(void)
{
        struct node *temp_ptr;

        ENTER("get_node_space");                          /* Note 5 */
        temp_ptr = (struct node *) malloc ( sizeof(struct node) );
        if (temp_ptr == NULL) {
                printf ("out of memory for nodes\n");
                exit(1);
        }
        EXIT("get_node_space");                           /* Note 8 */
        return (temp_ptr);
}
/********************************   hook_it_up()   *************/
/*      Attaches new_node to the end of a list.  The parameter
 *      old_list must point to the last node in the list.
 */
void hook_it_up (struct node *old_list, struct node *new_node)
{
        ENTER("hook_it_up");                              /* Note 5 */
        new_node->next = NULL;
        old_list->next = new_node;
        EXIT("hook_it_up");                               /* Note 8 */
}
```

```
/********************************    get_word_space()    *******/
/*      Allocates space for the string contained in its
 *      first parameters.  Returns a pointer to the first byte.
 */
char *get_word_space(char *string)
{
        char *temp;

        ENTER("get_word_space");                        /* Note 5 */
#ifdef DEBUG                                             /* Note 9 */
        printf("g_w_s received %s: %d\n", string, strlen(string));
#endif
        temp = (char *) calloc (strlen(string)+1, 1);
        if (temp == NULL) {
                printf ("Out of memory for text.\n");
                exit(2);
        }
        EXIT("get_word_space");                          /* Note 8 */
        return (temp);
}
/********************************    release()    **************/
/*      Systematically deallocates the memory used by the list.
 *      Works from the front of the list to the back.
 */
void release (struct node **listptr)
{
        struct node *temp1, *temp2;

        ENTER("release");                                /* Note 5 */
        temp1 = *listptr;
        while (temp1->next != NULL) {
                temp2 = temp1->next;
#ifdef DEBUG                                             /* Note 10 */
                printf ("releasing %s\n", temp1->word);
#endif
                free ((void *)temp1->word);
                free ((void *)temp1);
                temp1 = temp2;
        }
#ifdef DEBUG                                             /* Note 10 */
        printf ("releasing %s\n", temp1->word);
#endif
        free ((void *)temp1->word);
        free ((void *)temp1);
        *listptr = NULL;
        EXIT("release");                                 /* Note 8 */
}
```

```
/******************************** print() ***************/
/*      Outputs the contents of the word member of nodes in the list.
 */
void print (struct node *ptr)
{
        ENTER("print");                                   /* Note 5 */
        while (ptr->next != NULL) {
                printf("%s\n", ptr->word);
                ptr = ptr->next;
        }
        printf("%s\n", ptr->word);
        EXIT("print");                                    /* Note 8 */
}
```

The basic program is identical to linklist.c of Examples 11-9 through 11-14. The only things that have been added are some preprocessor directives that control conditional compilation and some printf() calls that will be conditionally included in the object code.

Note 1: The symbol to be defined is DEBUG. It can be defined at the time of compilation by using the facilities of the compiler or it can be defined with the preprocessor directive

```
#define DEBUG
```

which should appear above the #ifdef directives.

Note 2: The variable nesting will be declared when the symbol DEBUG is defined to the compiler. It will indicate the level of nesting of a particular function or the number of functions that are active at any instant during execution of the program.

Note 3: ENTER() and EXIT() are preprocessor macros. When the symbol DEBUG is defined, they will expand to a call to printf(). The macro ENTER() will be called each time a function starts executing. The macro EXIT() will be called each time a function terminates.

Consider the first conversion specification, %*s. The asterisk, *, is in the position of the field width specifier, and indicates that the field width is variable. When the asterisk is present in this position, printf() evaluates its next argument, which should be of type int, to give the field width. In this case, the incremented value of nesting multiplied by 4 provides the minimum number of spaces for this field. The string to be output is the empty string so that this expression will cause the remainder of the output to be indented.

Note 4: When the symbol DEBUG is not defined to the compiler, the macros ENTER() and EXIT() will be replaced by a blank line. This way, the calls to ENTER() and EXIT() can remain in the finished source code without affecting execution. Then if the code needs to be modified or debugged, they can be reactivated by compiling the program again with DEBUG defined.

Note 5: The macro ENTER() is called as the first line of executable code for each function in the program. The parameter to ENTER() will be a string containing the name of the function. When the macro is the printf() call, this macro will announce that the function is being entered and give an indication of the level of nesting. The code will have no effect on program execution in a version where DEBUG has not been defined at compile time.

Note 6: In the DEBUG version, the input is checked with a call to printf() to output both the output string and its length. This is done after each call to gets().

Note 7: After the new node has been added to the list and the word field initialized, the string in the new node is output to verify that the list is correct.

Note 8: The macro EXIT() is called every time a function terminates. The parameter is a string consisting of the function name. In a version where DEBUG has been defined to the compiler, the macro announces that the function is being exited and gives the level of nesting. The nesting level should match that at the start of execution of the function. The macro EXIT() has no effect on program execution in a version where DEBUG is not defined to the compiler. The macros ENTER() and EXIT() will provide a trace of the execution of the program when they are activated.

Note 9: The printf() call in this conditionally compiled statement checks on the parameter string. These values should match those output by the conditionally included printf() call associated with Note 6.

Note 10: The conditionally included printf() calls here provide a trace through the list as the space is being deallocated.

Learning Activities

33. Compile debug.c without defining DEBUG and test it to make sure that it executes like linklist.c of Examples 11-9 through 11-14. If there are file comparison facilities on your system that work with object code, use them to check on any differences in the executable code produced from debug.c and linklist.c. What differences did you find?

34. Compile both debug.c and linklist.c again, but stop the compilation process after the preprocess phase. Use the file comparison facilities to discover the differences in the preprocessed code from debug.c and from linklist.c.

35. Define the symbol DEBUG to the compiler, and compile debug.c again.
    a. Stop the process after the preprocess phase to see if the conditional code was included.
    b. Compile down to executable code with DEBUG defined to the compiler. Execute the program several times with different inputs. Make sure you see how the conditionally compiled statements provide a trace through the program. In particular, make sure you understand the purpose of the variable nesting and how the variable field width specification works.

Language Elements Introduced in This Chapter: A Review

** Header Files **

```
time.h
math.h
ctype.h
stdlib.h
malloc.h      non-ANSI compilers
```

** Library functions **

time()	returns a measure of the current time
ctime()	works with time() to provide a character string representation of time and date
localtime()	works with time(); returns the information about the time and date in a `struct tm`
clock()	returns a measure of time used by the processor
ferror()	reports on errors associated with a file
clearerr()	clears an error condition associated with a file
perror()	reports on general errors
sqrt()	returns the square root of its argument
pow()	raises a number to an integral power
atan2()	returns the angle between $-PI$ and PI whose tangent is the quotient of the arguments to the function
strtod()	converts as many characters in its parameter string as possible to a double value
isalpha()	tests to see if its argument is an alphabetic character
isdigit()	tests to see if its argument is a digit
isspace()	tests to see if its argument is a whitespace character
isupper()	tests to see if its argument is an uppercase alphabetic character
ispunct()	tests to see if its argument is a punctuation character
toupper()	converts any lowercase alphabetics to uppercase and leaves all other characters unchanged
tolower()	converts uppercase alphabetics to lowercase and leaves other characters unchanged
malloc()	dynamically allocates memory
calloc()	dynamically allocates memory and initializes it to bytes of NULL
free()	releases dynamically allocated memory

** Preprocessor Directives **

`#define`	used to define symbols to the compiler
`#ifdef`	tests whether a symbol is defined to the compiler
`#else`	provides an alternative to `#ifdef`
`#elif`	used to build compound conditional directives
`#endif`	signals the end of body of an if directive
`#ifndef`	tests whether a symbol is not defined
`#if`	tests values of constant expressions
`defined`	used in conjunction with `#if` to replace `#ifdef`

** Types **

`time_t`	declared in time.h
`struct tm`	declared in time.h
`size_t`	declared in stdlib.h and other header files.

Things to Remember

1. Many of the standard library functions have built-in error reporting facilities with their return value.
2. Some libraries will not be searched by default. The compiler may have a switch that will allow the programmer to indicate which libraries other than the default to search.
3. Errors to the mathematical functions could occur if a parameter to a function is not in the domain of that function or when a calculated value is too large for the computer to handle.
4. The character manipulation facilities are implemented as functions or as macros.
5. The values returned from malloc() and calloc() need to be cast to appropriate types when they are assigned. The pointer arithmetic counts on the cast value.
6. When using free(), remember to cast the parameter to type `void *`.
7. A structure declaration such as

```
struct node {
    element data;
    struct node *next;
};
```

   can be used for the nodes of a linked list.
8. A macro is a code segment that is expanded in the code at compilation time. It looks like a function, but is declared using the `#define` preprocessor directive.
9. The substitution for parameters in macros is exact. If the argument is a++ or a+1, then that is what is substituted for the parameter in the macro.
10. Conditional compilation can be used to help customize software for a specific application or to help in the software development phase.

11.9 Exercises and Programming Problems

1. In the program linklist.c, the new nodes are always placed at the end of the linked list. Modify this program so that the new nodes are always placed at the beginning of the list. When your program is correct, the print() function will output the input lines in reverse order.

2. The data type stack was discussed in Section 8.5. It was implemented with an array there. For this problem, implement a stack as a linked list. Write a data structure for a STACK element and define a STACK as a pointer to the data structure. Note that the data structure should have a pointer field to link to the next element in the stack. Write the stack utility functions with the declarations below.

   ```
   int push(char item, STACK *s_ptr);
   int pop(STACK *s_ptr);
   void init_stack(STACK *s_ptr);
   int  is_empty( STACK s);
   int  is_full ( STACK s);
   ```

   Put the STACK declaration and declarations of the functions in a header file named stack1.h, put the function definitions in a separate module named stack1.c, and insert a line #include "stack1.h" at the beginning of stack1.c. To test your package, modify the program stackex.c of Example 8.9 by changing the line

   ```
   #include "stack.h"
   ```

   to

   ```
   #include "stack1.h"
   ```

   Now you should be able to compile the modules stackex.c and stack1.c and link them together. The results should be the same as those for stackex.c compiled with the array implementation of a stack that appears in the files stack.h and stack.c.

3. A queue was discussed in problem 10 of Section 8.9. In that problem you were asked to write an array implementation of a queue. Now write a linked list implementation of a queue. You will need to write a declaration of a node to hold a queue element (a pointer to another node should be a member). A data structure for the queue itself should contain a pointer to the first node and a pointer to the last. Write the functions enqueue(), dequeue(), is_full(), is_empty() and init_queue() with declarations identical to those in problem 10 of Section 8.9.

4. a. Look up the functions rand() and srand() in the Programmer's Handbook. The function rand() will output a "random" number between 0 and some implementation-defined maximum. The function srand() seeds the random number generator.

   b. Use the data type you developed in problem 3 of Chapter 7 and write a function to deal bridge hands (13 cards of a standard deck) to four people.

    c. Test your function by writing a program that incorporates your functions from parts b and c of problem 3 of Chapter 7 to output the bridge hands. Run your program several times. If the random number generator rand() has been seeded properly with srand(), you should almost certainly get different results each time.

5. Finish the function get_customer() in the program ccomp.c. Have the transaction code, quantity, and price input for each transaction. Have the user input 0 for the transaction code to signal the end of the transactions. If the transaction code "REFD" for ACME and 11 for other companies signals a refund, have your function calculate the ending balance from the input transactions.

6. ACME wants the program to write a monthly balance report with each customer listed in the form

    Account No.   Name   Balance

while the other companies want their monthly balance report with each entry written in the form

    Name   Account No.   Balance

Write a single program to read the file "statements" and write a transaction report. Use conditional compilation to make sure that ACME's and the other companies' files are read correctly and that their transaction report has the desired form.

7. Modify your program written for exercise 6 by having the program print the date and time that the report was created as the first line of the report.

8. Write a program that outputs a list in tabular form of each of the ASCII characters in the following categories: alphabetic, alphanumeric, control, decimal digit, hexadecimal digit, graphical, printable, punctuation, and whitespace. Use the macros defined in the standard header file ctype.h.

9. a. Write a function toint() that takes a single character as a parameter and returns its decimal value. For example, `toint('9')` should return 9 and so on.

    b. Rewrite the function in part a as a macro.

    c. Use the code that you wrote in parts a and b to write a function myatoi() that takes a string of digits as a parameter and returns the decimal value of the ASCII string. For example, if the input string is `'1','2','3','\0'`, the function myatoi() should return the `int` value 123. Have your function handle strings with characters other than digits the same way that the library function atoi() does.

    d. Test your function in a simple program that inputs a string of digits and outputs the `int` value. Test it with both the function and macro version of toint() that you wrote in parts a and b of this problem. Test to see which version is more efficient.

10. Modify your program in problem 9 so that it assumes that the input string is a hexadecimal digit, and outputs the conversion of the input hexadecimal string to a decimal integer. You will have to modify both versions of toint() as well as the function myatoi().

11. Write a program that inputs an array of `int`s and outputs them in sorted order. Use the standard library function qsort() to do the sorting. Look it up in the Programmer's Handbook and in the documentation for your compiler.

Programmer's Handbook

A

Identifiers in ANSI C

ANSI C identifies two types of identifiers, those whose scope does not go beyond the end of the source module in which they are defined (or those with internal linkage) and those that are available to be linked with other modules (those with external linkage). The rules for the two types of identifiers may differ, but both consist of alphabetic characters, digits, and underscores, and must begin with a letter or an underscore.

Identifiers with internal linkage can be any length. At least the first 31 characters will be significant. Uppercase and lowercase letters will be distinguished. Identifiers with internal linkage include local variables, function parameters, static global variables, and preprocessor-defined macro names.

The rules for identifiers with external linkage are implementation dependent and may be considerably more restrictive. They may be limited to as few as 6 characters, and uppercase and lowercase alphabetic characters may not be distinguished.

B

Keywords in C

auto	a storage class
break	control statement—breaks out of loops and switches
case	case labels used with switch statement
char	a data type
const*	a type qualifier—value will not be changed
continue	control statement—continue at top of loop
default	marks default case in switch statement
do	do-while loop control statement
double	a data type
else	if-else control statement
enum	enumerated data type
extern	a storage class
float	a data type
for	for loop control statement
goto	control statement
if	if control statement
int	a data type
long	long int and long double data types
register	a storage class
return	return control statement

short	short int data type
signed*	signed, signed short, signed long, signed char data type
sizeof	sizeof operator
static	a storage class
struct	structure data type definitions and declarations
switch	switch control statement
typedef	typedef declarations
union	union data type definitions and declarations
unsigned	unsigned, unsigned char, short or long data types
void	void data type
volatile*	type qualifier—suppress optimization
while	while loop and do-while loop control statements

---

*These keywords are new with the ANSI standards.

C

Declarations in C

Each declaration of a single identifier in C has the following form. The brackets []
indicate that the enclosed item is optional.

```
[storage class] [qualifier] type  identifier [= initializer];
```

Declaration of multiple identifiers can be made with the same declaration in the form

```
[storage class] [qualifier] type  identifier-list;
```

where the identifier-list is a comma-separated list of entries of the form

```
identifer [= initializer];
```

Storage Class Specifiers

These were discussed in Chapter 8. The possible storage class specifiers are given
in the list below.

```
auto
extern
register
static
typedef
```

Type Qualifiers

These are new with ANSI C. They include the keywords

`const`	indicates that the value will not be changed
`volatile`	announces that the normal optimization should not be applied to this object
`noalias`	may or may not be included in ANSI C

Compilers may choose to ignore these qualifiers with the exception of flagging attempts to change a `const` identifier as an error. Note that an identifier declared with the type qualifier `const` differs from a preprocessor constant in that a memory location is allocated, and it is handled in the compiler phase rather than the preprocess phase.

Type Specifications

The scalar types (with the exception of enum) were discussed in Chapter 3, the void type was discussed in Chapter 4, and the structured types (struct and union) were discussed in Chapter 7. The possible type specifiers are listed below.

```
void
char
short
int
long
float
double
signed
unsigned
structure type specifiers
enum type specifiers
union type specifiers
```

Initializers

When initializing a variable at the time of declaration, the variable's identifier is followed by an equal sign, =, and an initializer. For scalar types, this initializer is an expression having the same type as the variable. For aggregate types (arrays and structures), the initial values are placed in a comma-separated list in a pair of matching braces.

For an array, each initial value goes in one cell of the array. Uninitialized cells will be set to zero. For older compilers, only static and external arrays can be initialized. In ANSI C, automatic arrays can be initialized with constant values.

For a structure, each initial value in the comma-separated list will be stored in the corresponding member of the structures. Uninitialized members will be set to 0 bytes.

Reading C Declarations

The technique for interpreting C declarations was discussed in Chapter 8. It will be reviewed here. The technique involves peeling off operators in inverse order of precedence and building up the type of the resulting expressions. A precedence table should be within reach during this process. For example, consider the declaration

```
float (*ident())[];
```

We will successively peel off the operators and determine the resulting type until we can conclude the type of the identifier `ident`.

	Expression	*Type*
Step 1:	`(*ident())[]`	`float`
Step 2:	`(*ident())`	array of `floats`
Step 3:	`ident()`	pointer to an array of `floats`
Step 4:	`ident`	function returning a pointer to an array of `floats`

For a second example, see Section 8.8.

D

Operators and Expressions

In the chart below, the U/B column states whether the operator is unary or binary. The result type for numeric operands is affected by the automatic conversion that takes place in C.

Name	U/B	Symbol	Operand Type	Result Type
Arithmetic Operators				
Unary minus	U	–	numeric	same as operand
Addition	B	+	numeric and enum	same as operands
Subtraction	B	–	numeric	same as operands
Multiplication	B	*	numeric	same as operands
Division	B	/	numeric	same as operands, e.g., truncating division with `int`s
Remainder	B	%	`int`	`int`
Increment	U	++	scalar	same as operand
Decrement	U	– –	scalar	same as operand
Logical Operators				
negation	U	!	scalar	`int` (1 if operand is zero 0 if operand not zero)
or	B	||	scalar	`int` (0 or 1)
and	B	&&	scalar	`int` (0 or 1)

Name	U/B	Symbol	Operand Type	Result Type
Bitwise Operators				
negation	U	–	integral	integral
and	B	&	integral	integral
or	B	|	integral	integral
xor	B	^	integral	integral
shift right	B	>>	integral	integral
shift left	B	<<	integral	integral
Assignment Operators				
assignment	B	=	arithmetic, pointer, enum structure, union (also pointer = 0)	type of the left operand
compound assignment	B	+=, –=,	arith. or (ptr += int)	left operand
		*=, /=,	arithmetic	left operand type
		%=,	integral	integral
		^=, |=, &=,	integral	integral
		<<=, >>=	integral	integral
Relational Operators				
equality	B	==	arithmetic, pointer, enum, pointer == 0	int (0 or 1)
not equal	B	!=	"	int (0 or 1)
less than	B	<	arithmetic, pointer, or enum	int (0 or 1)
less than or equal to	B	<=	"	int (0 or 1)
greater than	B	>	"	int (0 or 1)
greater than or equal to	B	>=	"	int (0 or 1)

Name	U/B	Symbol	Operand Type	Result Type
Miscellaneous Operators				
sizeof	U	sizeof()	expression any type	unsigned integral (`size_t` in ANSI)
address	U	&	lvalue or function not bitfield or register variable	pointer to operand type
indirection	U	$\star$	pointer to object	type of object
sequential	B	,	any expressions	type of right operand
-> selection	B	->	structptr->member	type of member
cast	U	()	(type)expression	same as type

Operator Precedence Chart

A PRECEDENCE CHART FOR OPERATORS IN C

In the following chart, all operators on the same line have the same priority. The grouping order is indicated with each group.

HIGHEST

primary	()	[]	.	->	group left to right
unary	++	--	sizeof	(type name)	group right to left
			~ ! - & *		
binary	$\star$	/	%		all group left to right
	+	-			
	>>	<<			
	<	>	<=	>=	
	==	!=			
	&				
	^				
	|				
	&&				
	||				
	?:				
assignment	= += -= *= /= %= >>=				group right to left
	<<= &= ^= |=				
	,				groups left to right

LOWEST

E

Control Statements in C

The `break` Statement

SYNTAX

```
break;
```

FUNCTIONALITY

Used to break out of a `switch` statement, a `while` loop, a `do-while` loop or a `for` loop. Causes control to be passed to the statement immediately following.

See examples on pages 264, 267, and 291.

The Compound Statement or Block

SYNTAX

```
{
        declarations;
        statements;
}
```

FUNCTIONALITY

Allows several statements to be grouped together and treated as one statement, and allows variables inside block to be hidden from the outside block. Executed by sequentially processing declarations and executing statements.

See examples on pages 49 and 53.

The `continue` Statement

SYNTAX

```
continue;
```

FUNCTIONALITY

Used in conjunction with the `while` loop, the `for` loop and the `do-while` loop. Causes control to pass to the end of the loop body to prepare and test for another iteration.

See example on page 262.

The `do-while` Statement

SYNTAX

```
do
            statement;
while ( expression );
```

FUNCTIONALITY

A test at the bottom loop. The statement is repeatedly executed and the expression evaluated. Loop terminates when the expression evaluates to zero.

See example on page 256.

The Expression Statement

SYNTAX

```
expression;
```

FUNCTIONALITY

Causes the expression to be evaluated.

See examples on pages 47, 64, and 72.

The `for` Statement

SYNTAX

```
for ( expr1; expr2; expr3)
        statement;
```

FUNCTIONALITY

An iterative statement. Upon entering, `expr1` is evaluated. For each iteration, `expr2` is first evaluated; if it evaluates to zero, the loop terminates; otherwise it continues. The statement is executed and then `expr3` is evaluated to complete one iteration.

See examples on page 82.

The `goto` Statement

SYNTAX

```
goto label;
```

FUNCTIONALITY

Causes execution to jump to the designated labeled statement in the program.

See example on page 279.

The `if` and `if-else` Statements

SYNTAX

```
if (expression)
    statement;

if (expression)
     statement1;
else
     statement2;
```

FUNCTIONALITY

In the first syntax, the expression is evaluated. If it is nonzero, the `statement` is executed; otherwise, no action is taken.

In the second syntax, the expression is evaluated. If it is nonzero, `statement1` is executed; otherwise, `statement2` is executed.

See examples on pages 53, 55, 59, 61, and 453.

The Labeled Statements

SYNTAX

Named or identifier labels

```
identifier : statement;
```

Case labels

```
case const-expr : statement ;
```

where const-expr is a constant and one of the integer types

Default labels

```
default : statement;
```

FUNCTIONALITY

The statement executes as it would without the label. The named or identifier label is used in conjunction with the `goto` statement. The case and default labels are used in conjunction with the `switch` statement. Notice that the expression in a case label must be a constant.

See examples on pages 260, 267, and 279.

The Null Statement

SYNTAX

```
;
```

FUNCTIONALITY

The statement does nothing, but serves to syntactically complete other statements.

See example on page 82.

The `return` Statement

SYNTAX

```
return;
```

or

```
return expression;
```

FUNCTIONALITY

Used in a function to cause execution to return to the calling environment to the point immediately after the function call. In the syntax where return is followed by an expression, the expression is evaluated and passed back to the calling environment as the return value of the function.

See examples on pages 38, 271, 272, and 385.

The `switch` Statement

SYNTAX

```
switch (expression) statement;
```

Typical use:

```
switch (expression) {
    case label1 : statement1;
    case label2 : statement2;
    ...
    case labeln : statementn;
    default : statement;          /* optional */
}
```

where the expression must be one of the integer types and the case labels must be constant integral types

FUNCTIONALITY

In the typical use, the expression is evaluated and compared with the labels. If a match is found, execution resumes at the statement associated with that label. All statements following that label are executed unless a `break` statement is encountered. If no match is found, the statement associated with the `default` is executed. If there is no `default`, no execution is done.

See examples on pages 259 and 267.

The `while` Statement

SYNTAX

```
while (expression)
    statement;
```

FUNCTIONALITY

An iterative statement. Upon entering the expression is evaluated. If it is nonzero, the statement is executed and the expression is evaluated again. The loop will terminate whenever the expression evaluates to zero.

See examples on pages 68, 72, 234, 245, 461, 464, 499 and 511.

F

The ANSI C Library

The ANSI Standards for C have specified the functions that are to be included in a standard library. Many of these useful functions are listed here with information about the functionality, the parameters, the return value, and possibly an example or a reference to an example in the text where it was illustrated. The list is not complete.

Input and Output Functions

Declarations of the input/output functions and associated types appear in the header file stdio.h.

Many examples of these functions appear throughout the text. References will be made to the program and section in which some of the examples appear.

File Handling

The definition of a FILE appears in stdio.h, which must be included in programs using a file. Files are buffered by default; terminal input and output are line buffered by default.

`fopen(filename, mode)`   makes a file available for use by the program.

    Parameters: `filename`, a null-terminated string containing the name of the file to be opened. `mode`, a null-terminated string with the mode of opening. (See Section 10.2.)

Return value:	a value of type `FILE *` by which the file can be referenced within the program.
Example:	See fopen2.c (Section 10.2).
`fflush(fp)`	with a file opened for output, causes the contents of the buffer to be written to the file.
Parameters:	fp, the `FILE *` variable associated with the open file.
Return value:	0 for success, `EOF` (−1) for error.
`fclose(fp)`	closes the file. Flushes the associated buffer and releases it.
Parameters:	fp, the `FILE *` variable indicating the file to be closed.
Return value:	0 for success, `EOF` (−1) for error.
Example:	See fopen2.c (Section 10.2).
`setbuf(fp, buf)`	uses `buf` for buffering on the file associated with fp, instead of the default buffer. If `buf` is `NULL`, buffering is turned off.
Parameters:	fp, the `FILE *` variable associated with the file. `buf`, the address of the memory buffer to be used instead of the default buffering. A `NULL` value indicates that buffering is to be turned off.
Return value:	0 for success, nonzero for error.
Example:	`setbuf(stdout, (char *)NULL);` defeats buffering for `stdout`.
`fseek(fp, offset, start)`	changes the current position in the file associated with `fp`.
Parameters:	fp, the `FILE *` value associated with the open file. `offset`, a long value indicating the number of bytes the new position should be from the start position. `start`, an `int` indicating the start position: 0 indicates the start position is at the beginning of the file, 1 indicates the current position in the file, and 2 indicates the end of the file.
Return value:	0 for success, nonzero for error.
Example:	`fseek(fp, 0L, 0)` seeks to the file beginning.
	See also fseek.c (Section 10.7).
`ftell(fp)`	gives the current position in the file associated with fp in bytes.
Parameters:	fp, the `FILE *` value associated with the file.
Return value:	a `long` value—the current byte offset from the beginning of the file.
Example:	See fseek.c (Section 10.7).

`feof(fp)`	indicates if the end of the file associated with `fp` has been reached.
Parameters:	`fp`, the `FILE *` value associated with the open file.
Return value:	nonzero if end-of-file has been reached, 0 if not.
Example:	See ungetc.c (Section 10.3).
`ferror(fp)`	indicates if an error has occurred on `fp`.
Parameters:	`fp`, the `FILE *` value associated with the open file.
Return value:	nonzero if an error has occurred; 0 if not.
Example:	See perror.c (Section 11.2).
`clearerr(fp)`	resets the error flag on the file associated with `fp`.
Parameters:	`fp`, the `FILE *` value associated with the open file.
Return value:	None. Function type is `void`.
Example:	See perror.c (Section 11.2).
`ungetc(iochar, fp)`	pushes `iochar` back into the input stream for the input file associated with `fp`.
Parameters:	`iochar`, an `int` value, the value to be pushed onto the input file associated with the `FILE *` value `fp`. Note `iochar` will be the next value read from the file.
Return value:	`iochar`, or `EOF` for error.
Example:	See ungetc.c (Section 11.3).

Input Functions

Terminal Input Functions:

`getchar()`	gets a single character from standard input (the keyboard). A macro.
Parameters:	none.
Return value:	the value input as a value of type `int`, or `EOF` when end-of-file is reached.
Example:	See inout.c (Section 2.3).
`gets(inbuff)`	inputs a string from standard input
Parameters:	`inbuff`, the address of a buffer that will hold the input.
Return value:	a `char *` value, the address of `inbuff` or `NULL` in case of error or end-of-file.
Example:	See strnglib.c (Section 5.5) and struct2.c (Section 7.3).

File Input Functions:

NOTE: The following functions do file input. When a parameter `fp` is mentioned, it should refer to a file that has been opened for input with a call to fopen() or an equivalent function.

`getc(fp)` — gets a single character from the file associated with `fp`. Usually implemented as a macro.

Parameters: `fp`, of type `FILE *`, indicates the file for input.

Return value: the value input as type `int`, or `EOF` when end-of-file is reached.

Example: See file2.c (Section 10.3).

`fgetc(fp)` — gets a single character from the file associated with `fp`. The functional version of getc().

Parameters: `fp`, of type `FILE *`, indicates the file for input.

Return value: the value input as type int, or `EOF` when end-of-file is reached.

`fgets(inbuff, n, fp)` — inputs a string of maximum length n from one line of the file `fp`.

Parameters: `inbuff`, the address of the buffer that will hold the string; n, an `int` representing the maximum length of the string; `fp`, a `FILE *` representing the open file from which the input is to come.

Return value: A `char *` value, the address of `inbuff` or `NULL` in case of error or end-of-file.

Example: See the discussion in Section 10.4 and programs fgets.c (Section 10.4) and fwrite.c (Section 10.5).

`fread(buffer, size, num, fp)` — reads a block of data from `fp`.

Parameters: `buffer`, the address of a memory buffer big enough to hold the input. `size`, the size of the items being read, of type `size_t`; num, the maximum number of items being read, of type `size_t`; fp, the `FILE *` value associated with the input file.

Return value: the number of items read.

Example: See fread.c (Section 10.5) and calloc.c (Section 11.5).

Formatted Input Functions:

The following functions will input characters according to a format specified in the parameter `control_string`. The `control_string` contains conversion specifications much like those for the printf() family of functions. Each conversion specification has the following form where the items in square brackets ([]) are optional.

```
% [*] [field-width][width] conversion
```

where

*	indicates suppression of conversion and storage of this input item.
field_width	an unsigned decimal integer.
width	one of the characters `'h'`, `'l'`, and `'L'`. An `'h'` indicates a conversion to `short`; an `'l'` to `long` or `double` depending on the conversion character, and `'L'` indicates a conversion to `long double`.
conversion	a single character indicating which conversion to make. The list of character meanings is below.
d	a decimal integer. Corresponding argument: the address of a memory location for an `int`.
i	an integer. Argument: address of an `int`.
o	an octal integer. Argument: address of an `int`.
u	unsigned integer. Argument: address of `unsigned`.
x	hexadecimal integer. Argument: address of `int`.
c	a character. Argument: address of a `char`.
s	a string delimited by whitespace. Argument: the address of a memory buffer.
p	a pointer value. Argument: a pointer to `void`.
n	No input is read. No conversion is made. Instead, the number of characters read by this point in the call is stored in the corresponding argument.
%	a single percent sign. No argument.
e	a floating point number. Argument: address of a `float, double,` or `long double`.
f	a floating point number. Argument: address of a `float, double,` or `long double`.
g	a floating point number. Argument: address of a `float, double,` or `long double`.

`scanf(control_string, args, ...)` scans input for characters in the control string. For each conversion specification in the `control_string`, attempts to convert the input value and store in the corresponding argument.

Parameters:	`control_string`, the address of a null-terminated string that specifies the format as described earlier; `args`, one additional argument appears for each conversion specification in the control string. Each argument should be the *address* of the memory location where the input is to be stored.
Return value:	The number of conversions made for specifications in the control string or `EOF` for end-of-file or an error.
Example:	See input1.c (Section 1.5) and retval.c (Section 10.6).

`fscanf(fp, control_string, args, ...)`   same as scanf() except that the input is to come from the file associated with `fp`.

Parameters: `fp`, of type `FILE *`. Associated with the open file from which the input is to come. The other parameters are the same as for scanf().

Return value: The number of conversions made for specifications in the control string or `EOF` for end-of-file or an error.

Example: `fscanf(fp, "%c", &charvar);` reads a single character from `fp` and stores it in `charvar`.

`sscanf(buffer, control_string, args, ...)`   same as scanf() except that `buffer` is scanned for the values to convert instead of standard input.

Parameters: `buffer` is a memory buffer which is to be scanned for items in the `control_string`. The other parameters are the same as for scanf().

Return value: The number of conversions made for specifications in the control string, or `EOF` in case of end-of-file or error.

Example: See prntscan.c (Section 10.6).

Output Functions

Terminal Output Functions:

`putchar(iochar)`   outputs a single character to standard output (the terminal). A macro.

Parameters: `iochar`, the character to be output, as an `int` value.

Return value: the value output, or `EOF` when end-of-file is reached.

Example: See inout.c (Section 2.3).

`puts(outbuff)`   outputs a string to standard output.

Parameters: `outbuff`, the address of a buffer that will be output.

Return value: `EOF` in case of error, nonnegative otherwise.

Example: See strngio2.c (Section 5.4).

File Output Functions:

NOTE: The following functions do file output. When a parameter `fp` is mentioned, it should refer to a file that has been opened for output with a call to fopen() or an equivalent function.

`putc(iochar, fp)`   outputs a single character to the file associated with fp. Usually implemented as a macro.

Parameters: `iochar`, an `int` with the character to be output stored; `fp`, of type `FILE *`, indicates the file for output.

Return value:	the value output as a value of type int, or EOF for error.
Example:	See file2.c (Section 10.3).

fputc(iochar, fp)   outputs iochar to the file associated with fp. The functional version of putc().

Parameters:	iochar, the value to be output, stored as an int; fp, of type FILE *, indicates the file for output.
Return value:	the value output or EOF for error.

fputs(outbuff, fp)   outputs a string to the file fp.

Parameters:	outbuff, the address of the buffer that holds the string; fp, a FILE * representing the open file to which the output is to go.
Return value:	EOF for error; a nonnegative value otherwise.
Example:	See fgets.c (Section 10.4).

fwrite (buffer, size, num, fp)   writes a block of data to fp.

Parameters:	buffer, the address of memory buffer holding the data. size, the size of each item to be written, of type size_t; num, the number of items to be written, of type size_t; fp, a FILE * value associated with the output file.
Return value:	The number of items written.
Example:	See fwrite.c (Section 10.5).

Formatted Output Functions:

The following functions will output characters according to a format specified in the parameter control_string. The control_string contains conversion specifications much like those for the scanf() family of functions. Each conversion specification has the following form; the items in square brackets ([]) are optional.

```
% [flag] [field width] [.precision] [size] conversion
```

flags: (optional)

−	left justify
0	pad with zeros instead of spaces
+	always print the sign (+ or −)
space	print either a space or a − (minus sign)
#	use a variant of the usual conversion (see the documentation with your compiler)

field width: (optional) a decimal integer constant specifying the minimal field width.

precision specification: (optional) a period followed by a decimal integer specifying the number of digits to be printed in a conversion of a floating point value after the decimal point.

size: `'h'` for a `short` or `unsigned short` argument, `'l'` for a `long` or `unsigned long` argument, `'L'` for `long double`.

conversion: a single character indicating which conversion to make. The list of character meanings is below.

d	signed decimal conversion (types `int`, `char`, `short`, or `long`)
i	signed decimal conversion
u	unsigned decimal conversion (unsigned types)
o	unsigned octal conversion (integer types)
x	unsigned hexadecimal conversion using `0123456789abcdef` (integer types)
X	unsigned hexadecimal conversion using `0123456789ABCDEF` (integer types)
c	the argument will be printed as a character whenever it is a character or integer type and its value is a valid character code
s	the argument to be printed is a string
f	for floating point or `double`—print in decimal form.
e, E	for floating point or `double`—print in exponential form.
g, G	for floating point or `double`—print in whichever format (f or e,E) that requires the least amount of space
p	a pointer value (implementation dependent)
n	no output is done, no conversion is made; the number of characters output by this point in the call is stored in the corresponding argument, which must be of type `int *`
%	print a single percent sign

`printf(control_string, args, ...)` outputs the control string with conversion specifications replaced with requested conversions of the arguments.

Parameters:	`control_string`, the address of a null-terminated string that specifies the format as described earlier; `args`, one additional argument appears for each conversion specification in the control string. Each argument should be an expression representing the value to be converted and output.
Return value:	The number of characters output or a negative value in case of error.
Example:	Almost every program in the text.

`fprintf(fp, control_string, args, ...)` same as printf() but outputs to the file associated with `fp`.

Parameters: `fp` , of type `FILE *`, associated with the open file to which the output is to go. The other parameters are the same as for printf().

Return value: Same as for printf().

Example: See prntscan.c (Section 10.6).

`sprintf(buffer, control_string, args, ...)`   same as printf() except that characters are written into the array `buffer`.

Parameters: `buffer` is a memory buffer which is large enough to hold the string and all the conversions. The other parameters are the same as for printf().

Return value: Same as for printf(). The number of conversions made.

Mathematics Floating Point Library Functions

Declarations of these functions and related types and constants are contained in the header file math.h.

TYPES: Unless otherwise noted, all of these functions return a value of type `double` . Any additional information about the return values is given with the function description.

PARAMETERS: Unless otherwise noted, all parameters are of type `double`. Any additional restrictions are given with the function description.

Trigonometric Functions

`sin(x)`   the sine of the angle `x`
`cos(x)`   the cosine of the angle `x`
`tan(x)`   the tangent of the angle `x`

Arguments: The argument `x` is a `double` value that represents the angle in radians. Note: `x` cannot be a multiple of `PI/2` for `tan(x)`.

Examples:
```
#define PI 3.14159
double x, y = PI/3;

x = sin(PI/2)
x = tan(y)

double sec(double x)
{
        return ( 1/cos(x) );
}
```

See also math.c (Section 11.3).

Inverse Trigonometric Functions

asin(x)   the inverse sine (or arcsine) of x. x must be between −1 and 1. The result is between −PI/2 and PI/2.

acos(x)   the inverse cosine of x. Domain: −1 to 1. Result: between 0 and PI.

atan(x)   the arctangent of x. Result: between −PI/2 and PI/2.

atan2(x,y)   the angle made by the positive x axis and the ray through the origin and the point (x,y). The result is between −PI and PI.

Examples:
```
double x, y;

x = asin( (double) 1/3);
y = acos(0.5);
y = atan(1);
x = atan2(2, -3);
```
See also polar.c (Section 11.3).

Hyperbolic Functions

sinh(x)   the hyperbolic sine of the angle x: $(e^x - e^x)/2$

cosh(x)   hyperbolic cosine of x: $(e^x + e^x)/2$

tanh(x)   hyperbolic tangent of x: sinh(x) / cosh(x)

Examples:
```
double x, y;

x = cosh(1);
y = -1/sinh(x);     /* csch(x) */
```

Exponential and Logarithmic Functions

exp(x)   exponential function (e^x) with base e (=2.718).

log(x)   natural logarithm function with base e. x > 0.

log10(x) base 10 logarithms. x > 0.

Examples:
```
double x, y;

x = log(2.718);
y = exp(x);
```

Some Other Mathematical Functions

pow(x,y) x^y. See math.c (Section 11.3) for restrictions on the parameters.

sqrt(x)   the square root of x. (x > 0)

ceil(x)   the smallest integer >= x (returned as a double)

floor(x) the greatest integer <= x (returned as a double)

fabs(x)   the absolute value of x

Examples:
```
double x, y;

y = ceil(4.72934);  /* 5 */
y = floor(4.72934); /* 4 */
```
See also math.c, polar.c (Section 11.3).

String Library Functions

The string library provides functions that manipulate strings. In the following discussions, a string is considered to be a sequence of ASCII characters terminated with a null character, `'\0'`. A buffer refers to a memory buffer that has been allocated in the program. Both a string and a buffer are referenced in the string library functions by the address of the first cell. The declarations of the string library functions are contained in the standard header file string.h. The type `size_t` is also declared in string.h and represents one of the unsigned integer types.

`strlen(string)`   calculates the length of `string`.

Parameters:	`string`, a null-terminated string.
Return value:	the length of `string` not including the terminating `'\0'`, of type `size_t`.
Example:	See strnglib.c (Section 5.5) and malloc.c (Section 11.5).

`strcpy(buffer, string)`   copies `string` into `buffer`.

Parameters:	`buffer` is the address of a memory buffer in the program; `string`, a null-terminated string.
Return value:	the address of `buffer`, a `char *`.
Example:	see strnglib.c (Section 5.5) and linklist.c (Section 11.6).

`strcat(buffer, string)`   concatenates `string` onto the end of the current string in `buffer`.

Parameters:	`buffer`, the address of a memory buffer in the program; `string`, a null-terminated string.
Return value:	the address of `buffer`, a `char *`.
Example:	See strnglib.c (Section 5.5).

`strcmp(string1, string2)`   compares the contents of `string1` with that of `string2`.

Parameters:	`string1` and `string2` are both null-terminated strings.
Return value:	a value of type `int`: 0, if the strings are identical; positive if string2 would occur before string1 in the ordering given by the ASCII character set, and negative if string1 would occur before string2.
Example:	See strnglib.c (Section 5.5) and ptrptr.c (Section 9.6).

`strncpy(buffer, string, n)`   copies n characters from `string` to `buffer`, pads with null characters if `string` doesn't have n characters. Doesn't copy a terminating null character unless one occurs within first n characters of `string`.

Parameters:	`buffer`, a memory buffer allocated in the program; `string`, a null-terminated string; n, an `int` value indicating the number of characters to copy.

Return value: the address of `buffer`, a `char *` value.

Example: See struct2.c (Section 7.3).

`strncat (buffer, string, n)`   concatenates at most n characters from `string` to the end of the current string in `buffer`. The new string in `buffer` is terminated with a null character.

Parameters: `buffer`, a memory buffer allocated in the program; `string`, a null-terminated string; n, an `int`, the number of characters to concatenate.

Return value: the address of `buffer`, a `char *` value.

Example: `strncat (buffer, "the time", 4);` If `buffer` is at least 11 bytes long and contains the string `"NOW IS"` before the call to strncat(), then after the call it will contain the string `"NOW ISthe "`.

`strncmp (string1, string2, n)`   compares the first n characters of `string1` to the first n characters of `string2`.

Parameters: `string1`, and `string2` are null-terminated strings; n is an `int` indicating the number of characters to compare.

Return value: Same return value as strcmp().

Examples: `strncmp ("Daisy", "Daffy", 2);` returns a zero while `strncmp ("Daisy", "Daffy", 3)` returns a negative value.

`strchr (string, ch)`   looks for the first occurrence of ch in `string`.

Parameters: `string`, a null-terminated string; ch, a character.

Return value: a pointer to the first occurrence of ch in `string`. A `char *` value.

Example: See strchrex.c (Section 5.6).

`strrchr (string, ch)`   same as strchr(), but looks at the string in reverse order.

Parameters: Same parameters as strchr().

Return value: A pointer to the last occurrence of ch in `string`. A `char *` value.

`strspn (string1, string2)`   count the number of characters at the beginning of `string1` that are contained in `string2`.

Parameters: `string1` and `string2` are both null-terminated strings.

Return value: A value of type `size_t` giving the length of the longest substring at the beginning of `string1` that is composed entirely of characters of `string2`.

Example: `strspn ("??? why", "?\t !")` would return 4.

`strcspn(string1, string2)`   the "complement" of strspn(), the number of characters at the beginning of `string1` that are not contained in `string2`.

Parameters: `string1` and `string2` are both null-terminated strings.

Return value: a value of type `size_t` indicating the length of the longest substring at the beginning of `string1` that contains no characters from `string2`.

Example: `strcspn("abc 456","0123456789");` would return 4.

`strstr(string1, string2)`   find the first occurrence of `string2` as a substring of `string1`.

Parameters: `string1` and `string2` are both null-terminated strings.

Return value: a pointer to the first character of the first occurrence of `string2` in `string1`. A `char *` value.

Example: `strstr("Mississippi", "is");` would return the address of the `'i'` immediately after the `'M'`.

Memory Manipulation Functions

The functions that manipulate memory have much the same functionality as those manipulating strings. The addresses mentioned in the parameter descriptions refer to memory buffers allocated within the program. The declarations of these functions are also in string.h.

`memcpy(buff1, buff2, n)`   copies n bytes from `buff2` to `buff1`.

Parameters: `buff1` and `buff2` are both memory buffers allocated in the current program. They should not overlap. n, a value of type `size_t` indicating the number of bytes to copy.

Return value: the address of `buff1`.

Example: with the declarations
`char array1[5], array2[8];`
`memcpy(array1, array2, 5);`   will copy 5 bytes from `array2` to `array1`

`memcmp(buff1, buff2, n)`   compares the first n characters of `buff1` and `buff2`.

Parameters: `buff1` and `buff2` are memory buffers allocated in the program; n is a value of type `size_t` that indicates the number of bytes to compare.

Return value: the same return value as strcmp().

`memchr(buff1, ch, n)`   finds the first occurrence of the character `ch` in the first n bytes of `buff1`.

Parameters: `buff1` is a memory buffer in the program; `ch` is the character to be located; n, of type `size_t`, is the maximum number of characters to search.

Return value: the address of the first occurrence of `ch` in `buff1` or NULL if `ch` does not occur. A `char *` value.

Example: `memchr("fizz", 'z', 2);` returns NULL.

`memchr("fizz", 'z', 3);` returns the address of the first `'z'`.

`memset(buff1, ch, n)`   initializes the first n bytes of `buff1` to hold the character `ch`.

Parameters: `buff1` is a memory buffer in the program; `ch` is the character.

Return value: the address of `buff1`, a `char *` value.

Example: With the declaration,
`char array[10];`
`memset(array, '\0', 10);`   initializes the `array` to bytes of `'\0'`.

Character Testing

All the facilities for character testing are similar. Most of them are implemented as macros, and are defined in the standard header file ctype.h. The following information is valid for all of the functions listed here.

Parameters: `ch` is of type `int`, and either represents a character or EOF for end-of-file.

Return value: A value of type `int`: nonzero if the parameter passes the test; 0, if not.

Example: See ctype.c (Section 11.4) for an example of several of these macros.

`islower(ch)`   tests whether `ch` is a lowercase alphabetic character, `'a'` to `'z'`.

`isupper(ch)`   tests whether `ch` is an uppercase alphabetic character, `'A'` to `'Z'`.

`isalpha(ch)`   tests whether `ch` is an alphabetic character, either uppercase or lowercase.

`isalnum(ch)`   tests to see if `ch` is either an alphabetic character or a decimal digit.

isdigit(ch)   tests whether ch is a decimal digit.

isxdigit(ch)   tests whether ch is a hexadecimal digit.

iscntrl(ch)   tests whether ch is a control character (a character in the ASCII character set corresponding to one of the integers in the range 0 through 31 or 127).

isprint(ch)   tests whether ch is a printing character (a character in the ASCII character set corresponding to one of the integers in the range 32 to 126).

isgraph(ch)   tests whether ch is a graphical character (all printing characters except space , ' ' , make up the graphical characters).

ispunct(ch)   tests whether ch is a punctuation character (a graphical character that is not an alphabetic character or a digit).

isspace(ch)   tests whether ch is a whitespace character (a space, a tab, a newline, a formfeed, a carriage return, or a vertical tab).

Utility Library Functions

A large number of functions in the standard library do tasks like converting from a string of ASCII digits to one of the integer types, allocating and deallocating memory, providing execution control of a program and so on. Some of them are discussed here. The declarations of the functions in this section are in the standard header file stdlib.h. The necessary types and constants, like size_t and RAND_MAX, are also declared in that header file.

Functions That Do Conversions

atof(buffer)   converts a string of digits with a possible decimal point in buffer to type double.

Parameters: buffer, a null-terminated string of digits possibly containing a decimal point.

Return value: a double value represented by the contents of buffer.

Example: See struct2.c (Section 7.3).

atoi(buffer)   converts a string of digits in buffer to the represented int.

Parameters: buffer, a null-terminated string of digits.

Return value: an int value represented by the contents of buffer.

Example: See unions.c (Section 7.6).

`atol(buffer)` converts a string of digits in `buffer` to the corresponding `long` value.

Parameters: `buffer`, a null-terminated string of decimal digits.

Return value: the long value represented by the contents of `buffer`.

`strtod(buffer, remainderptr)` converts the string of digits with a possible decimal point to type `double`, and puts the address of the first character that could not be converted in the contents of `remainderptr`.

Parameters: `buffer`, a null-terminated string of digits possibly with an imbedded decimal point and extra nonnumeric characters at the end. `remainderptr`, the address of a `char *` variable that will hold the address of the first non-converted character in `buffer`.

Return value: a `double` value represented by the first part of the string in `buffer`.

Example: See polar.c and the discussion in Section 11.3.

Functions That Manage Memory Allocation

`calloc(num, size)` allocates a block of memory large enough to hold `num` objects of size `size`.

Parameters: `num` is the number of items for which to allocate memory; `size` is the size of each item. Both parameters have type `size_t`.

Return value: the address of the allocated memory block of `num * size` bytes or a `NULL` pointer if memory cannot be allocated. Note that the return type is `void *` and C expects a cast of the return value to point to the type of the item so that the pointer arithmetic will behave correctly.

Example: See calloc.c (Section 11.5) and linklist.c (Section 11.6).

`malloc(size)` allocates a block of memory with `size` bytes.

Parameters: `size`, the number of bytes to be allocated; `size` has type `size_t`.

Return value: the address of the allocated block of memory or a `NULL` pointer if a block cannot be allocated. Note that the return type is `void *` and C expects a cast of the return value to point to an appropriate type so that the pointer arithmetic will behave correctly.

Example: See malloc.c (Section 11.5) and linklist.c (Section 11.6).

`free(ptr)`	deallocates the block of memory pointed to by `ptr`.
Parameters:	`ptr` is the `void *` pointer value that was returned by a previous call to calloc() or malloc(). Note that `ptr` must be recast to type `void *`.
Return value:	none, free() is declared to return type void.
Example:	See malloc.c, calloc.c (Section 11.5) and linklist.c (Section 11.6).

Other Utility Functions

`rand()`	a random number generator that returns a random number between 0 and `RAND_MAX`, an implementation-defined constant.
Parameters:	none.
Return value:	a nonnegative value of type `int`.
Example:	See discussion of srand() below.
`srand(seed)`	seeds the random number generator rand(). The random number generator would always return the same sequence of random numbers unless seeded by a call to srand() with a different value of `seed`.
Parameters:	`seed` can be any unsigned `int` value, but is usually a value associated with the current time or some other value that will change from one execution of a program to another.
Return value:	none—srand() returns type `void`.

Example:	`srand((unsigned) time( (time_t * )NULL));`
	`rand();`
	Note that the seeding in the example is done with a call to the time() library function. The parameters have been cast to match the types in the function definitions.

`exit(status)`	causes orderly program termination by closing all files, and so on.
Parameters:	`status`, a value of type `int` that indicates the reason for program termination. The value of `status` is defined by the programmer, but a `status` of zero will always indicate normal termination.
Return value:	none. exit() is declared to return type `void`.
Example:	See file2.c (Section 10.3).
`abs(n)`	returns the absolute value of n.
Parameters:	n, a value of type `int`.
Return value:	a value of type `int`.
Example:	`x = abs(y);` where both x and y were declared of type `int`.

Miscellaneous Library Functions

The following list of library functions do not fit into one category, but represent a selection of other facilities that are available in the ANSI library.

perror(string)

outputs an error message beginning with string and concluded with an implementation-defined reason for the error. Program should include the line #include <errno.h>

Parameters:

string, a null-terminated string containing the first part of the error message to be output.

Return value:

none. perror() is declared to return type void.

Example:

See perror.c (Section 11.2) and math.c (Section 11.3).

clock()

gives the processor time used by the calling program or −1 if not available. Program should include the line #include <time.h>

Parameters:

none.

Return value:

the number of clock ticks used by the program up to this point. A constant, CLK_TCK is declared in time.h so that the expression clock()/CLK_TCK is the time in seconds.

Example:

See time.c (Section 11.1).

time (tp)

returns a value indicating the current time, day, month, and year or −1 if the time is not available. Include the line #include <time.h>

Parameters:

tp, an address of variable of type time_t (defined in time.h). The current calendar time is returned in *tp, in addition to being the return value of the function. time() can also be called with a NULL pointer and time() will not duplicate its return value in the parameter.

Return value:

a value of type time_t that represents the current time.

Example:

See time.c (Section 11.1.

For other time functions, see time.c (Section 11.1).

G

The C preprocessor

Traditionally, the preprocess phase is the first phase of compilation. In many implementations, a UNIX C compiler for example, the preprocess phase is a separate phase of compilation and the preprocessed source code can be inspected. Even in implementations where the preprocess phase is not separate from the compiler, a facility for executing just the preprocessor may exist.

The tasks done by the preprocessor include stripping comments and processing the preprocessor directives. The directives include facilities for defining macros, including other source code files usually referred to as header files, and facilitating conditional compilation.

The syntax of the preprocessor directives is independent of the rest of the C language. Each directive must start with the character ′#′. Each directive is expected to lie entirely on one source code line, but the appearance of the "escape" character ′\′ immediately before the end of the line will escape the usual meaning of the end of the line (to terminate the directive) and allow the directive to continue onto the next line. Some compilers require that the ′#′ appear in the first column of each line, and some do not allow any whitespace to appear between the ′#′ and the name of the directive . Both of those restrictions have been relaxed in the ANSI C standards.

List of Preprocessor Directives

Defining Macros:

    Directive: `#define`
    Examples:

```
#define MAX     100
#define MIN((a,b)        ( a < b ? a : b )
```

Including Source Code Files:

    Directive: `#include`

    Example:

        `#include <stdio.h>`

Conditional Compilation:

Directive:	`#if constant_expression`
	In case `constant_expression` is not zero, the preprocessor includes the following lines of source code until the occurrence of `#else`, `#elif` or `#endif`. If `constant_expression` is zero, the lines are not included.
Directive:	`#ifdef identifier`
	If `identifier` has been defined either through a `#define` directive or through a compiler option, then the following section of source code (until the occurrence of either `#else`, `#elif`, or `#endif`) are included. If the identifier has not been defined, the code is not included.
Directive:	`#if defined identifier`
	Equivalent to `#ifdef`.
Directive:	`#ifndef identifier`
	If `identifier` has not been defined, the following code (until the occurrence of `#else`, `#endif`, or `#elif`) will be included. If `identifier` has been defined, the code will not be included.
Directive:	`#endif`
	Signals the end of conditionally included source code lines.
Directive:	`#else`
	Must be paired with a preceding `#if`, `#ifdef`, or `#ifndef`. In case the requirement for the preceding if directive is not met, include the following code (until the occurrence of `#endif`). If the requirement of the preceding if directive is met, the code is not included.
Directive:	`#elif constant_expression`
	Must be used in conjunction with a preceding `#if` or another `#elif` directive. If the requirements for the preceding directives are not met, then `constant_expression` is tested. If its value is nonzero, then the following code (until the occurrence of `#endif`, `#else`, or `#elif`) is included. If the value of `constant_ex-`

pression is zero, the code is not included. Note that the #elif directive is relatively new and may not be supported on all compilers.

Directive: `#undef identifier`

Causes identifier to be undefined. It is not an error to use #undef with an identifier that has not previously been defined.

Examples: (Conditional Compilation. See Section 11.8)

1.
```
#define  DEBUG

#ifdef DEBUG
printf("i is %d, string is %s.\n", i, string);
#endif
```

2.
```
#if  FLAG >> 3        /* FLAG shifted right 3 bits  */
    /* code dependent on FLAG's value goes here   */
#elif FLAG >> 2
    /* code dependent on FLAG's value goes here   */
#elif FLAG >> 1
    /* code dependent on FLAG's value goes here   */
#else
    /* code dependent on FLAG's value goes here   */
#endif
```

Miscellaneous Directives:

The directives #line, #error, #pragma, and # (the null directive) are not as commonly used and will not be taken up here.

ANSI C Additions to the C Preprocessor

Directives: #error, #pragma, and #.
Trigraph Sequences:

Three-character sequences can now be used for certain characters that are found in the ASCII character set but not in other character sets, like the ISO 646-1983 Invariant Code Set.

Trigraph Sequence	Char	Trigraph Sequence	Char
??<	{	??(	[
??>	}	??)	]
??=	#	??-	~
??/	\	??!	|
??'	^		

Operators with Macro Expansion:

\#

The operator # is used with a parameter in the macro definition. When it appears immediately before the parameter, it causes the parameter to be enclosed in double quotes.

Example:

```
#define print(s)    printf(#s)
```

When called

```
print(error)   expands to printf("error");
```

The operator ## causes concatenation of the parameters on either side of it. Any whitespace is discarded.

Example:

```
#define concat(s1,s2)   s1 ## s2
```

When called

```
concat ("Humpty ,Dumpty")   expands to
"HumptyDumpty"
```

Several Predefined Macros:

__DATE__	date of compilation as a string
__FILE__	name of the file as a string
__LINE__	current line number in the source file
__TIME__	time of compilation as a string
__STDC__	1 if the implementation is ANSI Standard C

These macros cannot be undefined with the #undef directive.

H

Linking C Object Code with Object Code from Other Languages

Many times it may be desirable to link object code from a C compiler with object code from another compiler. In some cases this can be done relatively easily while in other cases it may require additional or different software. Several requirements must be met by the software on the computer. For simplicity, let us assume that we will be linking code from just two different language compilers, C and some other language.

First there must be a common format for executable object code from the two compilers. That is, once a program has been compiled and linked, the executable code should be independent of the compiler that was used. For example, on a UNIX system, every compiler must produce a code that meets the a.out format. On an MS-DOS system, there are two executable code formats: the .com format and the .exe format. In the case of more than one format for the executable code, the compilers for the languages involved should both target the same executable file format.

Second, facilities should exist with the compilers for both languages to suppress the link phase of the compilation and leave the code in an object file. This is commonly available if the compiler supports separate compilation of source modules.

Third, there must exist a linker that will take the relocatable (unlinked) object code from both compilers and link them together into the executable code format. This usually implies that the relocatable object code from both compilers must be compatible. On a UNIX system, the link editor, *ld,* is just such a linker. On MS-DOS systems, a linker, *link.exe,* is supplied with the macro assembler (and in some cases the operating system). It links object code files that have the .OBJ format.

If all of the above requirements are met, then it is realistic to start researching the properties of the individual compilers to see if the source code from two different languages could possibly be linked together into one executable file. The remaining discussion centers on the passing of information to and from the functions in C and the subroutines in the other language.

Three issues that must be explored are the passing of parameters between different subprograms, the values returned by subprograms, and compatible data types in the two languages. The documentation for the compilers will probably have to be consulted often.

First it must be determined where each compiler stores the values returned by functions. Although it is not specified, many C compilers will place the return values from functions on the stack. Another common practice is to place return values in registers. If the two languages implement return values differently, it may be difficult to make them communicate.

A similar situation arises with parameters to subprograms. Some compilers may place the parameters on a stack while others may pass the values in registers or designate a different location and method of communication between functions. If the two compilers do not use the same method, communication between the different subprograms will be limited at best. If the two compilers are both produced by the same software company, the method of passing information between program parts is more likely to be compatible, and many of these issues will be resolved.

It must also be determined which data types in C are equivalent to the data types in the other language. For example, if the other language has an `integer` data type, is it the same as a `short`, an `int`, or a `long` in C? Similarly, if the other language has a `real` data type, is it equivalent to `float`, `double`, or `long double`? What about character types? In designing programs to link with C code, only compatible data types should be used. The compiler documentation should contain the answers to many of these questions.

If linking the code from the two different languages still looks feasible, then the specific properties of parameter passing in the languages themselves must be considered.

For example, in C, parameters are always passed by value to a C function. That means that a location is set aside for the execution environment for the function and a copy of the current value of the parameters is put into that environment. The function acts only on a copy of the variables and not on the actual parameters themselves. If it is desired that a C function change the value of a variable to be passed in as a parameter, then the address of (or pointer to) the variable to be changed should be passed in as a parameter.

In contrast, parameters to FORTRAN subroutines and functions are always passed in by reference. This means that the address of the parameter is passed into the subprogram and when a change is made to a parameter, the change is being made in the memory location whose address was passed in. The variables in the calling environment are changed when a FORTRAN subprogram changes one of its parameters.

If FORTRAN routines are to be linked with C routines, these differences must be taken into account. If a FORTRAN program calls a C function, the C function must be written with parameters that are pointers, since FORTRAN will be passing in an address. The code for the C program would need to dereference its parameters if it needs to change a value passed in by FORTRAN. Similarly, if a C program calls a FORTRAN function or subroutine, the C program must pass in the address of the parameters since the FORTRAN subprogram expects an address.

Another example can be seen with the language Pascal. Standard Pascal does not support separate compilation of source modules, but many implementations of Pascal do provide this feature. The concepts discussed can be applied to other languages. As with the FORTRAN/C pairing, it is necessary to check on the methods used by the different language compilers for passing parameters and returning values from functions. Second, equivalent data types should be identified. Finally, since Pascal is very strict about identifiers being declared before use, the Pascal compiler must provide a way to declare the C functions used. If all this is accomplished, it is feasible to talk about the specifics of passing parameters. Pascal accepts two types of parameters to its functions and procedures, var (or pass by reference parameters) and value (or pass by value parameters). For a var parameter, the address of the parameter is passed into the subprogram and any changes to the parameter are reflected in the calling environment. A copy is made of a value parameter and changes to a value parameter are not known in the calling environment. If a Pascal program calls a C function, it should declare a var parameter for any parameter to the C function that is either a pointer type or an array. It should declare a value parameter for any other parameter to the C function.

Another way of combining code from a different language with code from C that is easier to use is sometimes available with a C compiler. A C compiler may allow code from another language, notably FORTRAN or assembly, to be placed inline in a C source code program. This is usually done by adding words like `fortran` and `asm` to the list of keywords in C. For example, when the keyword `asm` appears in the C code, a segment of assembly code can follow it. A similar situation exists with the keyword `fortran`. The implementation of the `asm` keyword would involve having the compiler bypass the `asm` section until the assembly phase. The implementation of the `fortran` keyword would be more complicated.

In summary, there are many details to consider in trying to link source code from two different languages. If all the software requirements are met by the system software and the compilers, then it is up to the programmer to ensure that the two modules communicate properly through their data types, parameter passing, and handling of return values. If the code is linked successfully on one system, it would only port to another system if all the requirements are met.

I

The ASCII Collating Sequence

DEC	HEX	CHAR	DEC	HEX	CHAR	DEC	HEX	CHAR	DEC	HEX	CHAR
0	00	^@ NUL	32	20	SPC	64	40	@	96	60	'
1	01	^A SOH	33	21	!	65	41	A	97	61	a
2	02	^B STX	34	22	"	66	42	B	98	62	b
3	03	^C ETX	35	23	#	67	43	C	99	63	c
4	04	^D EOT	36	24	$	68	44	D	100	64	d
5	05	^E ENQ	37	25	%	69	45	E	101	65	e
6	06	^F ACK	38	26	&	70	46	F	102	66	f
7	07	^G BEL	39	27	'	71	47	G	103	67	g
8	08	^H BS	40	28	(	72	48	H	104	68	h
9	09	^I HT	41	29	)	73	49	I	105	69	i
10	0A	^J LF	42	2A	*	74	4A	J	106	6A	j
11	0B	^K VT	43	2B	+	75	4B	K	107	6B	k
12	0C	^L FF	44	2C	, 76	4C	L	108	6C	l	
13	0D	^M CR	45	2D	–	77	4D	M	109	6D	m
14	0E	^N SO	46	2E	.	78	4E	N	110	6E	n
15	0F	^O SI	47	2F	/	79	4F	O	111	6F	o
16	10	^P DLE	48	30	0	80	50	P	112	70	p
17	11	^Q DC1	49	31	1	81	51	Q	113	71	q
18	12	^R DC2	50	32	2	82	52	R	114	72	r
19	13	^S DC3	51	33	3	83	53	S	115	73	s
20	14	^T DC4	52	34	4	84	54	T	116	74	t
21	15	^U NAK	53	35	5	85	55	U	117	75	u
22	16	^V SYN	54	36	6	86	56	V	118	76	v
23	17	^W ETB	55	37	7	87	57	W	119	77	w
24	18	^X CAN	56	38	8	88	58	X	120	78	x
25	19	^Y EM	57	39	9	89	59	Y	121	79	y
26	1A	^Z SUB	58	3A	:	90	5A	Z	122	7A	z
27	1B	^[ESC	59	3B	;	91	5B	[	123	7B	{
28	1C	^\ FS	60	3C	<	92	5C	\	124	7C		
29	1D	^] GS	61	3D	=	93	5D	]	125	7D	}
30	1E	^^ RS	62	3E	>	94	5E		126	7E	
31	1F	^_ US	63	3F	?	95	5F	_	127	7F	DEL

Note: ^A means Control-A, etc.

ASCII chart copyright 1984 Borland International, Inc. Used by permission.

Selected Answers to Learning Activities

1. `Which#` has the illegal character #.
   `Who's_on_first` has the illegal character '.
   `struct` is a keyword
   `3meninatub` doesn't start with a letter or underscore
   The rest are legal identifiers.

2. The list of tokens follows. A token is listed once even though it may appear more than once in the program. The tokens are: each of the two comments at the beginning of the program, `main`, `(`, `)`, `{`, `sub_funct`, `;`, `}`, /* **Notes 1 and 2** */, /* **Note 3** */

5.
   ```
   main()
   {
           printf("\07");
   }
   ```

7. either   or
       `"whew`   `"whewps`
    `"`   `"`

   depending on whether the backspace key erases the characters beneath.

8. `"` starts the control string; `\` escapes the meaning of the `n` to indicate a newline; the comma `,` separates parameters; the period `.` ends the sentence that is output.

10. 1 line of output

12.
```
main ()
{
     int first = 1,
         second = 2,
         third = 3,
         fourth = 4;

     printf ("First %d, second %d, third %d, fourth %d.\n",
                      first, second, third, fourth);
}
```

15. In general, scanf() stops converting the input to decimal when it encounters a character other than a decimal digit.

23. With the modified statement
```
     celsius = 5/9 * (fahrenheit - 32);
```
the quotient 5/9 is calculated first. The quotient of this truncating integer division is 0 and therefore, the right hand side of the assignment statement will always have value 0.

25. 40

30.
ANSI C	non-ANSI C
`cube (int x)`	`cube (x)`
`{`	`int x;`
`      return (x*x*x);`	`{`
`}`	`      return (x*x*x);`
	`}`

34. The only change that is necessary is
```
     #define BASE 7
```

35. If we change BASE to 12 and each 10 in todecimal() to 16, the program will convert base 12 numbers (using a for 10 and b for 12) to decimal.

Chapter 2

5. a. The conditional statement is
```
          if (sum < 20)
                    printf("The number is small.\n");
```
b. The control expression is
```
                    (sum  < 20)
```

11. 17

12. The number of lines output will be 4 since the first, the second and the last printf() statement will always be executed plus exactly one line for the compound if-else statement.

13. d.

20. a. 7   b. 8

26. the digit ' 9 '
    the tab key
    the character ' @ '
    error — ' 6 4 ' is not a character. If this program compiles, it will produce an infinite
    loop when executed.

29. ```
    int i;

    for ( i = 1; i < 513; i *= 2)
        printf("%d     ", i);
    ```

31. ```
    int i, col;

    for (i = 1, col = 1; i <= 10; i++, col++) {
            printf("\t%d", i);
            if (col == 5) {
                    col = 0;
                    printf("\n");
            }
    }
    ```

Chapter 3

2. For example, if there are 4 bytes to an int and 8 bits to a byte, then x is 4 and y is 8.
   The value of 2^{x*y-1} is $2^{32}-1$ or 2147483648. The maximum value that could be represented as an int would be 2147483647.

4. a. 0001000000000000, 1111111111111111, 000110101011, 00101110
   b. 4096,   65535,   427,   46

6. a)

Decimal	Octal	Binary
0	0	000
1	1	001
2	2	010
3	3	011
4	4	100
5	5	101
6	6	110
7	7	111

   b)   001111011101   011110001   001100011001101

   c)   326,   431,   32

7.

Input	Bit Pattern	Hexadecimal	Octal
29	11101	1d	35
3	11	3	3
256	100000000	100	400
251	11111011	fb	373

12. `char charvar = 'c';`

14. a. For example, if a short occupies 16 bits, an int occupies 32 bits, and a long
    occupies 32 bits, then the range for each of the types is as follows:

short	-32768	to	32767

```
            int        -2147483648      to     2147483647
            long       -2147483648      to     2147483647
```

15. If an `int` occupies 16 bits, the maximum `unsigned` value will be 65535. If an `int` occupies 32 bits, the maximum unsigned value will be 4294967295.

22.
```c
#include <stdio.h>
main()
{
        unsigned number, factor;
        int first = 1;
        printf ("This program will print the prime factors ");
        printf ("of an integer that is greater than 2.\n\n");

        /* Prompt for and input the integer. */
        printf ("Enter an integer that is greater than 2 : ");
        scanf ("%u", &number);

        printf ("%d = ", number);
        for (factor = 2; factor <= number; factor++)

                /* if factor divides number evenly */
                if ( ! (number % factor) ) {

                /* output factor */
                if (first) {
                        printf("%d " , factor);
                        first = 0;
                }
                else printf("* %d", factor);

                /* take the factor out of number */
                number /= factor;

                /* decrement factor so that it can test
                 * for a repeated factor.
                 */
                factor--;
        }
        printf("\n");

}
```

25. a. w1 <<= 3;
    b. w3 <<= 6; will multiply w3 by 64 unless either (1) overflow occurs or (2) w3 is negative.

30. a. 01111100
    b. ?111111?? 0??????00

35.
```c
#include <stdio.h>
main()
{
        float x1, y1, x2, y2;           /* The points */
        float slope, y_int;

        /*  Input the coordinates of the points */
        printf("Enter the first point.\n");
        printf("x: ");
```

```
          scanf("%f", &x1);
          printf("y: ");
          scanf("%f", &y1);
          printf("Enter the second point.\n");
          printf("x: ");
          scanf("%f", &x2);
          printf("y: ");
          scanf("%f", &y2);

          /*  Check for a horizontal line */
          if (y1 == y2)          /* slope is 0 */
                    printf("The equation is y = %5.2f\n", y1);
          else if (x1 != x2) {   /* not a vertical line */
                  slope = (y2 - y1) / (x2 - x1);
                  y_int = y1 - slope*x1;
                  printf("The equation is y = %5.2fx + %5.2f\n",
                                          slope, y_int);
      }
   else                     /* vertical line */
          printf ("The equation is x = %5.2f\n", x1);

}
```

40. c1 + 3 is an int, (us + f) * i is a float, (ul % c1) / i is an unsigned
    long, us + c1 is an int, d + f + ul is a double, u + l is either type long or
    type unsigned long, 3 * us is an int, and c1 + c2 is an int.

Chapter 4

1. 1 line of output.

5. &ptr_to_intvar is the address of the location of the variable
   ptr_to_intvar.

9. The statement "The value of (intptr + 1) is sizeof(int) more than that of
   int_ptr." is the only true statement.

11. The following program has examples for type double.
```c
#include <stdio.h>

main()
{
        double dble, *dble_ptr1 = &dble, *dble_ptr2;

        printf("%x %x\n", dble_ptr1, dble_ptr2);

        dble_ptr2 = dble_ptr1 + 1;

        printf("%x\n", dble_ptr2);
        printf("%x\n", dble_ptr1 - 1);
        printf("%x\n", dble_ptr2 + 2);
        printf("%x\n", ++dble_ptr2);
        printf("%x\n", dble_ptr2 - dble_ptr1);
}
```

14. `*char_ptr is 'H'`
    `*char_ptr + 1 is 'I'`
    `*(char_ptr + 1) is 'e'`
    `(*char_ptr) + 1 is 'I'`
    `*char_ptr + 3 is 'K'`
    `*&char_ptr is 108`
    `&char_ptr is 100`
    `&char_ptr + 2 is 102`

16.

```
#include <stdio.h>
void main ()
{
        int intgr,
            *ptr_int = &intgr;

        *ptr_int = 7;

        printf ("The value of intgr is %d.\n", intgr);
        printf ("ptr_int points to %d.\n", *ptr_int);

        *ptr_int += 5;

        printf ("The value of intgr is now %d.\n", intgr);
        printf ("ptr_int now points to %d.\n", *ptr_int);
}
```

17. The variables `input_ptr` and `c` have been declared as types `int *` and `int` respectively because they are used to store the values returned by getchar() which returns an `int` value. Even though variables of type `char *` and `char` may work correctly some of the time, they may also create error conditions and should not be used with getchar().

20. Just the code changes are given here.

    CHANGES TO main():
    ```
    void switchxz (int *, int *);      /* fill in declaration */

    switchxz (int_pointer , &z);      /*  fill in the call */
    ```
    SWITCHXZ():
    ```
    void switchxz (int *int1, int *int2)
    {
            int temp;

            temp = *int1;
            *int1 = *int2;
            *int2 = temp;
    }
    ```

21. `In p1, *i is 17, j is 12, and int3 is 17.`
    `Back in main, int1 is 3, int2 is 7, and int3 is 17.`

    `In p1, *i is 88, j is 68, and int3 is 88.`
    `Back in main, int1 is 3, int2 is 7, and int3 is 88.`

25. CHANGES TO main():

```
double exp (double x, double eps); /* function declaration */

val = exp (x, epsilon);              /* function call */
```

FUNCTION exp()

```
double exp (double x, double eps)
{
        double term;
        int count = 1;
        double value;

        value = 0;
        term = 1;
        while ( term >= eps ) {
                value += term;
                term *= x;
                term /= count++;
        }
        return (value);
}
```

26.
```
double avg ()
{
        double sum = 0.0;
        int i;

        for (i = 0; i < 10; i++)
                sum += test_scores[i];

        return (sum / 10);
}
```

31.
```
int arr1[] = {0, 2, 4, 6, 8, 10, 12, 14, 16, 18, 20};
int arr2[11] = {0, 2, 4, 6, 8, 10, 12, 14, 16, 18, 20};
int arr3[11];
int i;

for (i = 0; i < 11; i++)
        arr3[i] = 2 * i;
```

33. a. `intarray[5];`
    b. 0
    c. `int sum;`
       `sum = intarray[2] + intarray[4];`
    d. The two declarations have the same effect. The second has more information for the reader of the program. The first form might be used when there are many initializers; the compiler is less likely to count incorrectly than a programmer.

40. a.

```
int input_inventory (int inventory[], int maxnum)
{
        int index;

        for (index = 0; index < maxnum; index++) {
```

```
                        scanf ("%d", &inventory[index] );
                        if ( inventory[index] < 0)
                                break;
                }
                if (index == maxnum)
                        printf ("No room for more items.\n");
                return (index);
        }
```

b.

```
void print_inventory(int *inventory, int numitems)
{
        int index;

        for (index = 0; index < numitems; index++) {
                printf ("Item number %d:\t\t", index+1);
                printf ("Number on hand  %5d\n",
                                        *(inventory + index));
        }
}
```

43. LINE ADDED TO BOTTOM OF print_inventory():

```
    printf ("The total number of items:  %d\n",
                        sum(inventory, numitems));
```

FUNCTION sum():

```
int sum(int inventory[], int num)
{
        int i, tempsum = 0;

        for (i = 0; i < num; i++)
                tempsum += inventory[i];
        return (tempsum);
}
```

Chapter 5

1. ```
   #include <stsdio.h>

   void main ()
   {
           char *str1, *str2;

           str1 = "One two, buckle my shoe.\n";
           printf (str1);
           str2 = "Three four, shut the door.\n";
           printf (str2);

           *(str1 + 7) = ' ';
           *(str1 + 8) = '\0';
           printf (str1);
   ```
   ```

```
        *str2   =   't';
        *(str2 + 10) = '!';
        *(str2 + 11) = '\n';
        *(str2 + 12) = '\0';
        printf(str2);
}
```

3. Yes, `inputptr` and `inputarray` both evaluate to the address of the first character in the array.

5. The variable `inputptr` could be eliminated. The variable `inputarray` is necessary since its declaration causes the necessary space to be allocated.

7. When the value NULL (0) is assigned to a pointer variable, we refer to a NULL pointer. A null character is the character ' \0' or the first ASCII character. A null string is a string where the only character stored is a null character. For example, " " designates a null string. As with other strings, this is handled as the address of the first character in the string. The first character in a null string is the terminating null character.

8. No, to take full advantage of the value returned by gets(), both variables are necessary. The variable `inputarray` contains the space for the input characters. The variable `inputptr` will store the value returned by gets() which may be either equal to `inputarray` or NULL.

15. The type of the function countem() is type `int`. Since `int` is the default return type for functions, the word `int` is not necessary in the declaration, but it could help the reader.

17. Parts a. and b. are incorporated in the following program. No error checking on the input is done.

```c
#include <stdio.h>
#include <string.h>

void main()
{
        char work1[80], work2[80], workstring[512];
        char *string1, *string2;
        int comparison;

        printf("Enter two strings.\nString1 ");
        string1 = gets(work1);
        printf("String2 ");
        string2 = gets(work2);

        if ((comparison = strcmp (string1, string2)) > 0)
                printf ("string1 is > string2.\n");
        else if (comparison < 0)
                printf ("string1 is < string2.\n");
        else
                printf("string1 = string2.\n");

        printf ("The length of string1 is %d.\n",
                                        strlen(string1) );
        printf ("The length of string2 is %d.\n",
                                        strlen(string2) );
```

```
            strcpy (workstring, string1);
            if (!strcmp(string1, workstring))
                    printf("Copy completed successfully!\n");
            else
                    printf ("Error found in copy.\n");
            strcat (workstring, " ");
            strcat(workstring, string2);
            printf ("The work string now contains \"%s\"\n",
                                        workstring);
            printf ("The length of the work string: %d.\n",
                                        strlen(workstring) );
    }
21. #include <stdio.h>
    #include <string.h>

    void main()
    {
            char inarray[512];
            int line_count = 0,
                char_count = 0;

            printf ("Enter your text now\n");
            printf (" > ");
            while (gets(inarray) != NULL) {
                    line_count++;
                    char_count += strlen(inarray) + 1;
                    printf("> ");
            }
            printf ("%d lines, %d characters\n",
                                line_count, char_count);

    }
```

22. It reads standard input and writes to standard output. Therefore, it is a filter.

```
25. #include <stdio.h>

    void main()
    {
            char instring[512];
            char *strchr(), *currentpos, *lastpos;

            printf("Enter a line of text.\n >");
            gets(instring);
            lastpos = instring;

            while ( (currentpos = strchr(lastpos, ' '))
                                != NULL) {
                    *currentpos++ = '\0';
                    puts(lastpos);
                    lastpos = currentpos;
                    while (*lastpos == ' ')
                            lastpos++;
            }
            puts(lastpos);
    }
```

Chapter 6

1. b. 34891   d. –4–3–2

6. Only the function showtabsinline() needed to be changed. The use of the continue statement is no longer necessary.
```
void showtabsinline()
{
        int iochar;

        while ( (iochar = getchar()) != '\n')
                if (iochar == '\t')
                        printf("\\t");
}
```

8. There are many ways to accomplish this. One is presented here. The only change to main() was to change the string in the third call to printf().
```
        printf ("\n\nThat was the second part of the line.\n");
```

The function readtosentinel() could be changed as follows:
```
void readtosentinel()
{
        int iochar;

        while ( (iochar = getchar()) != EOLN )
                if (iochar == SENTINEL)
                        break;
        if (iochar != EOLN)
                while ( (iochar = getchar()) != EOLN )
                        putchar(iochar);
}
```

10. The case '0' in the switch statement can be eliminated. The new version of processresponse() is below. The rest of the program remains unchanged.

```
void processresponse (char iochar)
{
        switch (iochar) {
                case '1': printf ("You have chosen guessit.\n");
                        break;
                case '2': printf ("You have chosen nim.\n");
                        break;

                default:  printf ("Illegal input.\n");
                        printf ("Choose 0, 1, or 2: ");
        }
}
```

13. a. To get the program to compile it is necessary to change both declarations of look_for_delimiter() to declare the function as type int as well as make the changes suggested in the learning activity. The program should compile and execute in most C environments. Any change in execution will not be apparent to a person running the program.

Generalization: The program sets up a location to hold the return value from a function; after execution the value in that location is returned and assigned. The error would only become apparent when the program needed to access the return value (the value assigned to found in this program).

    b. The program will compile and run. An runtime error may occur when the value in found is accessed since it has not been initialized properly, the contents of its memory location are unpredictable.

14. b.

```
#include <stdio.h>
main()
{
        int iochar;

        while ((iochar = getchar()) != EOF)
                if (islower(iochar))
                        printf("lowercase ");
                else
                        printf("notlowercase ");
}
islower(io)
int io;
{
        if ('a' <= io && io <= 'z')
                return 1;
        else
                return 0;
}
```

17. This change should cause compile-time errors since the labelled statement is not in the same function as the goto.

20. b. The value returned by scanf() gives the number of conversions made. The program will run correctly with the following changes:

    1. Declare a variable to store the value returned by scanf(). For example:

```
        int scanned;
```

    2. Replace the last two lines in main() with the following lines:

```
        scanned = scanf("%d", &n);
        if (scanned)
                printf("\n%d! is %d.\n", n, factorial(n));
```

27. a. The 3 and the 5 are field width specifiers. The integer index+1 will be right justified in a field of at least 3 spaces; array[index] will be right justified in a field of at least 5 spaces.

    b. Two ways to exit the while loop: when count = MAX_ARRAY and when get_int() returns DONE. The second method of exit would probably be used more often. If the first is used very often, the constant MAX_ARRAY should be increased.

Chapter 7

4. a.   tag `x` members `x1, x2, x3`
         tag `y` members `y1, y2, y3, y4`

   b.   Storage is allocated by the lines
```
            } structy1, structy2;
```
   and
```
            struct x s1;
```

   c.   i. illegal   ii. array of 5 `ints`   iii. `int`
        iv. `struct x`   v. `char`   iv. address of a `char`

5.
```
struct student {
            char    name[30];
            char    ssn[11];
            double  gpa;
            int     totalunits;
            int     majorcode[4];
};
```

13. Only three things need to be changed: In the function main(),

    1. Declare the pointer:
```
            struct auto_part *partptr;
```
    2. Initialize the pointer:
```
            partptr = parts;
```
    3. Pass the pointer to get_part():
```
                while  ( !get_part(partptr++) && ++i < MAXPARTS)
```

16. The function:
```
struct auto_part *low_inv( struct auto_part *pp, int numparts)
{
            int i = 0;
            while ((pp->cur_inv >= 5) && (i++ < numparts))
                    pp++;
            if (i < numparts)
                    return (pp);
            else
                    return NULL;
}
```

    Declaration of the function:
```
        struct auto_part *low_inv(struct auto_part *, int);
```

    Code to call the function and process the result:
```
        partptr = low_inv(parts, i);
        if (partptr != NULL)
                printf("Less than 5 in stock: part %s\n",
                                partptr->id);
        else printf("Adequate inventory of all parts in stock.\n");
```

18. One method would be to include the following seven lines at the beginning of the function:

```
char ssnout[12];
strncpy (ssnout,emp.ssn,3);
* (ssnout + 3) = '-';
strncpy( ssnout + 4, emp.ssn + 3,2);
* (ssnout + 6) = '-';
strncpy (ssnout + 7, emp.ssn + 5, 5);
        printf ("SSN:    %12s\n", ssnout);
```

28.

```
#include <stdio.h>
#include <stdlib.h>
enum boolean { FALSE, TRUE };

void main()
{
        enum boolean prime, done
        int num, divisor;
        char inarray[80];

        done = FALSE;
        while (!done) {
                printf("Enter a positive integer to be tested: ");
                num = atoi(gets(inarray));

                if (num <= 0) {
                        printf("That number wasn't positive.\n");
                }
                else {
                        prime = TRUE;
                        printf("List of divisors: 1 ");

                        for (divisor = 2; divisor < num; divisor++)
                                if ( !( num % divisor )) {
                                        printf(" %d ", divisor);
                                        prime = FALSE;
                                }

                        if (num != 1)
                                printf(" %d\n", num);
                        else
                                prime = FALSE;

                        if (prime)
                                printf("%d is a prime number\n", num);
                }
                printf("Another number (Y/N)? ");
                gets(inarray);
                if ( (inarray[0] == 'N') || (inarray[0] == 'n'))
                        done = TRUE;
        }
}
```

29.
```c
#include <stdio.h>
#include <stdlib.h>
enum boolean { FALSE, TRUE };

void main()
{
        enum boolean prime;
        int num, divisor;
        char inarray[80];

        printf("Enter a positive integer to be tested: ");
        num = atoi(gets(inarray));

        if (num <= 0) {
                printf("Sorry, that number wasn't positive.\n");
                exit(1);
        }

        prime = TRUE;
        if (num ==1)
                prime = FALSE;
        else {
                for (divisor = 2; divisor < num; divisor++)
                        if ( !( num % divisor )) {
                                prime = FALSE;
                                break;
                        }
        }

        if (prime)
                printf("%d is a prime number\n", num);
        else
                printf("%d is not prime.\n", num);
}
```

32. english 13
    russian 14
    C   5
    swedish 6

33. legal, illegal, illegal, illegal, illegal, legal

34. Declaration of a variable:
```c
int correct;
```

Modification of the error check on the input of the paytype:
```c
correct = 0;
while (!correct)
        if ( (*instring == 'h') || (*instring == 'H') ) {
                correct = 1;
                emptr->paytype = hourly;
        }
        else if ( (*instring == 's') || (*instring == 'S') ) {
                correct = 1;
                emptr->paytype = salaried;
        }
        else {
```

```
                    printf ("Enter 'h' or 's': ");
                    gets(instring);
              }
```

36. Yes, the parameter to reademp() must be a pointer since reademp() needs to change the contents of the variable referenced by the parameter.

42. The sizeof() operator applied to a union returns the number of bytes occupied by the widest of the union members.

46. They are the same thing. Both syntaxes reference the address of the intmem member of the union which is the same as the address of the union.

Chapter 8

7. d. On most systems, the automatic local variables and parameters will be in the same section of memory, and static and global variables will be located close to each other.

9. a. main() can reference global variables b, and c and the local variable a.
   b. f1() can access the global variables a, b, and d, and the local variable c.

16. When the function push() is called, it calls isfull() to determine if there is room on the stack. This protects the bounds of the array from being overwritten.

21. The program position.c would not understand any input with a non-standard use of the characters '.', '?', or '!'. For example, position.c would have a hard time with a program written in C.

27. b. what is a function that takes two parameters, a char * parameter, and a pointer to a function that takes a single parameter of type char * and returns an int. The function what() returns a pointer to a function that returns a float.
   x is a pointer to a char.
   y is a pointer to function that returns an int and takes a single parameter of type char *
   z has type char *.
   w has type int.

Chapter 9

1. `int two_d[3][3];`

3. The solution below uses an array of strings (array of pointers to type char) to hold the labels for each line. Arrays of pointers to char are discussed later in this chapter. Another method of labelling each line would be equally effective.

```
void output_results(void)
{
        int i,j;
        char *label[2] = { "Buying Price: ",
                           "Current Price: "};
```

```
            for ( i = 0; i < 2;i++) {
                printf("%s", label[i]);
                for ( j = 0; j < 6; j++)
                    printf("%8.2f", stock_prices[i][j]);
                printf("\n");
            }
    }
```

5. For example, the reference `stock_prices[0][i]` would be rewritten as `*(*(stock_prices + 0) + i)`. The + 0 can be omitted in this special case.

8. These changes entail

    1. A change in the declaration of the functions:

        ```
        void input_prices(float sp[][]);
        void process(float sp[][]);
        void output_results(float sp[][]);
        ```

    2. A change in the calls to the functions:
        ```
        input_prices(stock_prices);
        process(stock_prices);
        output_results(stock_prices);
        ```

    3. A change in the first line of the function definitions: (Note that if a different name had been chosen for the parameter to input_prices(), additional changes to the function code would have been necessary.

    ```
    void input_prices(float stock_prices[][6])

    void process(float sp[][6])

    void output_results(float sp[][6])
    ```

10. The first dimension can be omitted from the declaration of a three-dimensional array as long as the array is initialized with the correct number of initializers.

11. `printf ("%5.1f\t", *(*(*(three_d + i) + j) + k));`

14. `&t[1][0]` is the address of the `'d'`
    `*(*t+2)` is the `'c'`
    `**(t+1)` is the `'d'`

18. and 20. Solutions to both learning activities are in the program below.

    ```
    #include <stdio.h>

    void main(void)
    {
            char instring[512];
            char  *words[50],
                  *current, *strchr();
            int   j, i = 1;

            printf ("Enter text with words delimited by blanks:\n");
            gets(instring);

            if (instring[0] == '\0')
                    i = 0;
            else {
                    words[0]=current=instring;
    ```

```
                while ( (current = strchr(current, ' ')) != NULL) {
                        *current++ = '\0';
                        words[i++] = current;
                }
        }

        printf ("There were %d words in that line.\n", i);
        if (i > 0) {
                printf ("They are :\n");
                for (j = 0; j < i; j++)
                        printf ("%s\n", words[j]);
        }
}
```

22. Replace the first `for` loop with the following code:

```
for ( ;strcmp (*ptrptr, ""); ptrptr++)
        ;                /* position the pointer at the last word */

for (;ptrptr >= ptrarray ;ptrptr--)
        printf ("%s ", *ptrptr);
printf ("\n");
```

24. c.   `**ptrptr` is the character   `'G'`

   e.   `*(ptrptr + 1)` is the string   `"Elliot's"`

   g.   `*(*(ptrptr + 1) + 2)` is the character `'l'`

   i.   `*ptrptr+1` is the string   `"eorge"`

   k.   `*(*ptrptr +2)` is the character   `'o'`

25. a.   `what` is an array of three functions returning type `float`.

   c.   `what` is a pointer to a function returning type `char`.

   g.   `what` is an array of three pointers to pointers to type `int`.

   i.   `what` is a pointer to a pointer to an array of three `int`s.

30. The changes consist of

   1. Including a header file:
       ```
       #include     <ctype.h>
       ```

   2. Declaring some variables
       ```
       int i, j;
       ```

   3. Adding the following code

       ```
       for (i = 1; i < argc; i++)
               for ( j = 0; j < strlen(argv[i]); j++)
                       if (!isdigit(argv[i][j])) {
                               printf("Non-digit found\n");
                               exit(2);
                       }
       ```

Chapter 10

5. a.
```
if ( (fp = fopen ("info", "w") ) == NULL ) {
        printf ("Input file could not be opened\n");
        exit (1);
}
```
b. After running the program a file named info is in the directory. It is empty.

c. After running the program, the file info is empty. The contents were destroyed.

d. When fopen() opens a file for writing, it creates it if it did not previously exist and truncates it if it did previously exist.

7. One other action might be to allow the user to enter a different file name.

9. The modes "a", "a+", and "w+" would allow the program to write to the file so that the program will work with these modes. Modes "a", and "a+" would cause the program to write at the end of the file which may not be desired. Modes "a+" and "w+" would also allow the program to read from the file; if the program is not going to read from the file, these modes might cause a point of confusion to a person reading the source code.

15. a. Changes:

1. Declare the command line parameters:
```
void main(int argc, char *argv[])
```
2. Add code to check on the correct number of command line parameters.
```
if (argc != 2) {
        printf("Usage: ungetc filename\n");
        exit(1);
}
```
3. Change the code to open the file named on the command line.
```
if ( (fp = fopen (argv[1], "r")) == NULL) {
        printf ("%s couldn't be opened\n", argv[1]);
        exit(1);
}
```

17. b. To allocate room for the terminating null character.

19. Changes:

1. Declare a FILE * variable for the output file.
```
FILE *fp, *fpout;
```
2. Add code to open the file when argc is 3 and substute stdout when it's not.
```
if (argc == 3) {
        if ( (fpout = fopen(argv[2], "w")) == NULL) {
                printf("Unable to open %s\n", argv[2]);
                exit(1);
        }
}
else
        fpout = stdout;
```
3. Change the output statements to access fpout instead of stdout.
```
while (fgets(inarray, NUMCHARS, fp) != NULL) {
        fprintf (fpout, "%d\t", linecount++);
        fputs(inarray, fpout);
```

```
        }
```
22. `fwrite(array, sizeof(struct trans), 5, fp);`
    or
    `fwrite (array, sizeof(array), 1, fp);`

25.
```
    read_trans(struct trans *trans_ptr, FILE *fp)
    {
            return(fread(trans_ptr, sizeof(*trans_ptr), 1, fp));
    }
```

29. Yes, the only change necessary to the prntscan.c is in the final loop:
```
    while (fscanf (fp, "%s %s %f%*c", first, last, &gpa) == 3){
            fprintf (name_fp, "%s, %s\n", last, first);
            fprintf (gpa_fp, "%4.2f\n", gpa);
    }
```

32. b. i.   The space between `hi` and 7 terminates the string.

    ii.   The space is the character converted in the `%c` conversion specification. Since the `'r'` cannot be part of a floating point number, the scanning stops at that point and `scanret` is 3. No values willl be stored in `floatvar`.

    iii. The space separates the character `'r'` from the floating point number 4.5. Whitespace is skipped by scanf() when it looks for the floating point number.

34. The minimum value is 26. There are 18 characters specified in the control string plus at least 1 character for the string, 1 character for the decimal, 1 character for the input character, and 5 characters for the floating point number.

37. The only changes are to the function browse() and only deal with the adjusting the user values.

    1. Change the error check on the number of records and adjust the number of bytes in the parameter to fseek().
```
        if (recnum > numrecs)
            printf("Enter a number between 1 and %d\n",
                        numrecs);
        else {
            fseek(fp, (long) (recnum-1)*sizeof(transact),0);
            if (read_trans(&transact ,fp))
                    print_trans(&transact);
            else
                    printf("Transaction %d not found.\n",
                                        recnum);
        }
```

40. The change in values for `stdin` should reflect the progression through the input buffer. The value for `level` decreases, the position in the buffer increases, the contents of the buffer position reflects the next character to be read. The values for `stdout` may not appear to change because the output buffer is emptied after each output and may not be filled until after the conversions are made.

Chapter 11

3. For example, a program in California might include the following lines to output the time on the east coast since there is a 3 hour time difference between the two coasts. Note the conversion specifications `%02d` which will right justify the output in a field of two spaces and pad on the left with zeros. Also note the expression `(tptr->tm_hour + 3) % 24` which will calculate the correct time when the value of `tm_hour + 3` exceeds 24.

```
            tptr = localtime(&t1);
            printf ("On the east coast it is %d:%02d:%02d.\n",
                    (tptr->tm_hour + 3) % 24,
                    tptr->tm_min, tptr->tm_sec);
```

8. One method consists of

    1. A preprocessor definition:
    ```
    #define PI 3.14159
    ```

    2. Declaration of a new variable:
    ```
        int degrees;
    ```

    3. The declaration of a new function to_degrees():
    ```
    int to_degrees (double angle)
    {
            return ( (int) (angle *360 / (2*PI) ));
    }
    ```

    4. In main(), a call to to_degrees() and a modification to the printf() call.
    ```
            degrees = to_degrees(ppoint->angle);
            printf ("Polar coordinates: ");
            printf ("radius %5.2lf, angle %d degrees\n",
                    ppoint->radius, degrees );
    ```

10. The function error() might be modified as follows:
    ```
    error(char *s)
    {
            if (errno) {
                    perror(s);
                    return 1;
            }
            return 0;
    }
    ```

    Each call to error() might be made in a conditional statement. For example, the call
    ```
        error("sqrt");
    ```
    might be replaced with
    ```
        if (!error("sqrt"))
                printf ("sqrt(%4.2f) is %5.2f\n",x, y);
    ```

12. When the experiment was run using the Borland Turbo C compiler, both the tab character and ^M were counted both as whitespace and control characters. So was ^L. The character ^J was not counted in any category.

13. It would be expected that the version with the `else` keywords would run faster since it would bypass several of the tests in the case of alphabetic input. Note that the test should be made with a file as input instead of the keyboard so that the user's response time would not affect the timing.

15. c.   In convert.c, the variable `num` is initialized to zero and the conversion is accumulated in `num`. In la15.c, scanf() only stores a value in `num` after a conversion is made. Another difference is that convert.c will only read a single line from standard input while the scanf() call in la15.c will skip over newlines, and other whitespace to find the start of the string of decimal digits.

18. b. The program modification follows:
```
#include <stdio.h>
#include <stdlib.h>
#include <string.h>

void main (void)
{
        char instring[512], *place, *neword, *word;

        printf ("Enter a line of text ");
        printf ("with words separated with blanks:\n");
        gets (instring);
        place = instring;
        while ((neword = strtok(place, " \t.,")) != NULL) {
                place = NULL;
                word = (char *) malloc(strlen(neword)+1);
                strcpy (word, neword);
                printf ("I read that as\n\t %s.\n", word);
                free ( (void *) word);
        }
}
```

20. When this experiment is run on Borland's Turbo C compiler, the error message "Unable to get the space" is output. Apparently, when calloc() is requested to allocate zero bytes, it returns a NULL pointer. This could be corrected by only calling calloc() when there is space to allocate. For example,
```
if (nrecs > 0) {
        if ((t_array = (struct trans *) calloc(nrecs,
                        sizeof(struct trans)) ) == NULL) {
                printf ("Unable to get the space.\n");
                exit (1);
        }
        .
        .
        .
```

22. The program linklist.c does not work properly as it is. It attempts to get another line of input and outputs garbage since the list is non-existant. It can be corrected by extending the compound statement that is associated with the line
```
        if (gets(inputbuffer) != NULL) {        /* Note 2 */
```
to encompass the rest of the code in main().

26. One version that will work in simple cases is
```
#define isdigit(a) (a >='0' && a <='9')?1:0
```
See the discussion in the "Word of Warning" for cautions.

Index

1